PROGRESSIVE EDUCATION ASSOCIATION PUBLICATIONS

COMMITTEE ON WORKSHOPS

WHEN PEOPLES MEET

A Study in Race and Culture Contacts

WHEN PEOPLES MEET

A Study in Race and Culture Contacts

EDITED BY

ALAIN LOCKE

Professor of Philosophy, Howard University

AND

BERNHARD J. STERN

Lecturer in Sociology, Columbia University
Lecturer in Anthropology, New School for Social Research

COMMITTEE ON WORKSHOPS

PROGRESSIVE EDUCATION ASSOCIATION

New York

PRINTED IN THE UNITED STATES OF AMERICA
BY THE HADDON CRAFTSMEN, INC., SCRANTON, PA.

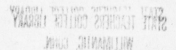

CONTENTS

PART II—VARIETIES OF CULTURE CONFLICT

PART III—THE WAYS OF DOMINANT PEOPLES:
DEVICES OF POWER

PART IV—THE WAYS OF SUBMERGED PEOPLES: TACTICS OF
SURVIVAL AND COUNTER-ASSERTION

CONTENTS

FOREWORD AND ACKNOWLEDGMENTS

There is growing interest and concern over the issues and problems of human relations. Tensions that arise in society over the divisive influences of racial, national, credal and cultural group loyalties seem to make imperative scholarly inquiry which will place these problems in scientific perspective. Educational authorities are becoming increasingly aware of the need for vitalizing the social studies through the incorporation of an analysis and discussion of these important problems in the school curriculum. This is felt to be necessary in order that students may grapple more realistically with the critical issues of contemporary life.

The primary objective of this study is to co-ordinate the specialized and authoritative literature of the various pertinent social science disciplines through a generalized and synthetic frame of reference, in order to illuminate the effects of the contacts of peoples and cultures and to clarify situations growing out of the interrelationships between dominant and minority groups. The work was undertaken under the auspices of the Progressive Education Association through a grant from the General Education Board.

The project was initially conceived by Alain Locke, who prepared the original outline. As the work proceeded, both editors revised the plan considerably on the basis of the source materials as selected, edited and documented by Bernhard J. Stern. The present form of the book is the joint work of both editors. Alain Locke is primarily responsible for the text commentary.

Thanks are due to executive officers of the Progressive Education Association for their helpful co-operation in the promotion and execution of the project, particularly to W. Carson Ryan, Frederick L. Redefer, and Alice V. Keliher of the Commission on Human Relations; also to the members of the Committee on Intercultural Education, of which Professor Ruth Benedict is Chairman. The Editors also acknowledge the helpful results of fruitful discussion with members, both staff and students, of the Summer Workshops held under the auspices of the Progressive Education Association at Sarah Lawrence College, and at Chicago, Northwestern and Syracuse Universities.

The Progressive Education Association and the Editors wish also to express here their gratitude to the various publishers who have generously consented to the use of the source materials included in this book. Credit for the materials used appears in footnotes throughout the book. We wish here to add to that acknowledgment of our indebtedness, our thanks for such splendid co-operation.

Alain Locke acknowledges his indebtedness to the co-editor, Bernhard J. Stern, not only for his sustained and arduous co-operation during the whole period of collaboration, but for his critical reading of the text commentary and helpful suggestions; also for considerable helpful consultation with his colleague, Professor W. O. Brown. Stimulating reactions and criticisms in consultation are acknowledged from Professor Melville J. Herkovits, Dean Ralph Tyler, and Professors Earl Johnson, Paul Witty, Donald Young, and Drs. Harold S. Cummings, Donald Pierson, Stewart Cole, Miss Gene Weltfish and Miss Annette Smith.

Bernhard J. Stern expresses his appreciation to his wife Charlotte Stern for her indispensable help in the task of gleaning the kernel from the chaff in the vast and uneven literature in the fields covered by this book and for her significantly constructive suggestions in all stages of the preparation of the source materials.

ALAIN LOCKE
BERNHARD J. STERN

Part I

CULTURE CONTACT AND THE GROWTH
OF CIVILIZATION

1

IN THE SETTING OF WORLD CULTURE

THE INCREASED and increasing knowledge about human cultures which has come to us in modern times has unfortunately not led to any very general improvement in the common understanding of the nature of civilization, or the nature of culture itself. With the broadened scientific perspective on human social history that has been achieved one might logically expect enlightened social understanding and intercultural appreciation and tolerance. But this has not been so. People still read and write history from chronic attitudes of cultural pride and prejudice, and sometimes deliberately, sometimes subconsciously, impose interpretations upon civilization that are steeped in cultural bias and partiality. The social sciences even, which are usually relatively objective on matters of detail, in their large-scale interpretations of social history revert frequently to the traditional cultural provincialisms.

Popular thinking is even more deeply enmeshed in cultural chauvinism and bigotry. Issues of practical conflict and historic rivalry cloud over the broader and clearer panorama which the scientific study of culture is ready to give, and as a result traditional misconceptions of culture and civilization not only persist but flourish. The contemporary welter of group rivalries with the confusion of their clashing factionalisms makes imperative a search for new clues and basic insights on the complex problems of human group relations. These are not new problems, but their aggravated contemporary manifestations urgently focus renewed attention upon them. In response to these increasing tensions, there is increased resort to theorizing about the nature of culture and civilization, but far too much of it is mere rationalization of the claims and counterclaims of various national and racial groups seeking

3

partisan vindication and glory. Special interests and asserted superiorities are thereby reinforced with justifications bearing the outward stamp of scientific objectivity and impartiality. But in reality, as these traditional national and racial partisanships debate their conflicting claims, they further augment cultural intolerance, and irrationality in social thinking grows apace.

In this situation of cultural confusion is one doomed to the dubious choice between obvious and subtly concealed cultural propaganda? Or, in this modern Babel, must one trust solely to the haphazard corrective of expecting one bias to off-set another? At least one other alternative seems possible, and that is to search beneath the complex historical events of human group contacts and relations for more basic and objective common denominators. These should show what characteristically happens when peoples meet, and what interests, attitudes and policies condition their subsequent relations. This source book attempts to offer just such information by means of authoritative descriptions and expert first-hand analyses of some of the more typical situations and instances of cultural contact, cultural conflict, cultural interaction.

Tracing social history in terms of the broad outlines of culture contacts is one of the important modern approaches in the social science field. In addition to the advantage of panoramic perspective, it offers a more objective basis of appraisal for the relative achievements and the relative influence both of the peoples and of the cultures involved. Various cultural biases, all too prevalent in the more conventional historical and sociological viewpoints, are thus avoided and insights into the more basic and universal processes involved in human group relations are achieved. Such is the task and main objective of this book.

To be properly understood, civilization should be studied in the setting of world culture. Many of the current misconceptions in regard to culture and civilization become apparent only after a consistent application of objective viewpoints resulting from the broadest possible comparison of all types of human culture. Contemporary anthropology has made available a considerable amount of fresh and illuminating material, in the light of which many doctrines that have the superficial appearance of scholarship turn out to be sophisticated versions of the fallacies and assumptions more obviously involved in popular and propagandist thinking. Clearly, much of this contemporary doctrine is not consciously biased or avowedly partisan. But a limited viewpoint, even with innocent motivation, induces the same errors of overemphasis and distortion which characterize deliberate partisanship. Naïve and subconscious projections of cultural bias are in fact more insidious and harmful than set prejudice, because less obvious.

Many current views of culture, however, are based on attitudes and interests more sinister than naïve bias and innocent misconception. They are the deliberate coinage of propaganda and rationalization, and circulate dangerously and deceptively in the general currency of ideas and opinion. They turn up repeatedly in the context of much honest-intentioned social thought. The "racial myth," as it has been aptly called, is a noteworthy case in point. This Trojan horse of our national wars and racial quarrels crops up in its most typical form when masking its career of rationalized partisanship and propaganda under the innocent guise of a science of mankind or a philosophy of history. So insidious can this become that it finally introduces self-deception into our understanding of ourselves. Racialism, indeed, has had its worst effects and has bred its most sinister distortions as a source of general misconception about the nature of civilization and culture.

It is insufficient, however, merely to expose the theoretical fallacies of racialism, which carry the blight of pseudo-science into history and social theory. The practical role of such fallacious doctrines must also be traced, since their deepest significance and explanation lies in their practical objectives and consequences. For through subtly misinterpreting the clash of culture groups as the inevitable clash of their cultures, racialism is used as an effective mechanism of group rivalry. Its doctrines are in reality by-products of historic conflict and rivalry and are rationalizations of such conflict. Their main reason for being is to provide auxiliary weapons in the struggle for group power and dominance, and it is of the greatest importance to see and understand them in this light. Carefully analyzed, their major objectives are seen to be the justification of conflict and exploitation through the disparagement of other group cultures and the promotion of prestige and group morale through self-glorification and claims of superiority. Any careful tracing of racialist theories will reveal this political tactic, as the doctrine is observed to follow the changing alignments of the successive issues of political opposition and struggle. The history of racist theory in Europe for the last century alone presents a contradictory cavalcade of superiority claims and shifting "superior" races;— in turn it has been Latin, Aryan (Old Style), Teutonic, Anglo-Saxon, "Nordic," European, Caucasian ("white") and Aryan (New Style),— all competing in obvious theoretical inconsistency and practical self-contradiction.

Racism is only one of the fictions involved in current false perspectives of human history, all of which need to be examined and corrected in a sound and balanced view of human civilization. The prevailing notion of separate, distinctive and ethnically characteristic cultures is another example, and it, too, is shown by broad historical analysis to be contrary to fact. Culture is not related functionally to definite ethnic groups or races, but varies independently. Races change their culture on many historic occasions and various culture advances are made independently by different racial stocks. Each culture, also, upon examination is discovered to be dynamic and constantly changing, with an increasing tendency, on the whole, to become more and more composite, in the sense of incorporating aspects of other cultures with which it comes in contact. Thus, even as the tradition of a characteristic group culture develops, the less true it is apt to be to actual fact, since the older a culture, the more composite it usually is. So it is evident that our theories of culture must be scrutinized carefully, since there are so many possible sources of error. Some have the fault of parochialism, and need the corrective of enlarged historical perspective. Others are pseudo-scientific and need to be squared by wide-scale comparison with the fullest known facts. Still others, most difficult of all, must be submitted to a critical examination of their ulterior motives and the stark exposure of their partisan objectives. Thoroughgoing analysis on such a scale may sustain but few of our contemporary beliefs and theories about culture, but only on the foundation of what remains can any sound view of human civilization be constructed.

One of the first results of this approach to social history is a realization of the close connection between culture contacts and the growth of civilization itself. Cultures may develop complexity through certain internal development and variation, but by far the main source of cultural growth and development seems always to have been through the forces of external contact. Even in relatively early historic periods culture was already composite in many areas, due largely to group contact and cultural interchange. Many internal spurts of cultural development have also been the result of the stimulating "cross-fertilizing" effects of cultural contact. Civilization is largely the accumulative product and residue of this ever-widening process of culture contact, interchange and fusion.

In modern times and under modern conditions, as mechanisms of intercommunication are multiplied and group contacts inevitably increase, cultures tend to become increasingly hybrid and composite. As a result, cultural complexity and variability become the rule rather than the exception. Added to the normal forces of cultural interaction is that particularly active and militant movement of "Europeanization." European expansion, more extensive in scope than any of its predecessor imperialisms, but less tolerant of cultural diversity, has augmented and speeded up these trends of intercultural contact and interchange to an unprecedented degree. Over great colonial areas, forced or pressure acculturation has become the order of the day, with much rapid and disruptive displacement of other cultures. However, even in this more or less one-sided process, a certain amount of reciprocal influence and interchange has persisted. Modern imperialism has bred, in addition to its half-castes, its hybrid and border-line cultures. A number of complex cultural reactions have resulted, according to the variations in modern colonial contacts and the divergent degrees of cultural level and resistance encountered. But, despite its historical uniquenesses, Europeanization and its moving force of economic imperialism are best understood as an interesting and complex variant of the process which has basically underlain all historic culture contacts; a process which has been the primary cause of the growth of what we know as "civilization." More significant, then, than its unique features are the factors modern culture contact has in common with the movements of cultural interchange that it has succeeded. Indeed, as will be seen later, a good part of the supposed uniqueness of the modern cultural scene is an illusion and conceit of our present-day cultural pride and egotism.

It is this traditional European view which is responsible for the most basic modern misconception of culture—the false identification of civilization with one particular type of culture. Ruth Benedict's discussion clearly points this out. What she aptly calls "our assumed monopoly of civilization" explains why our current cultural perspectives are so defective. In this the Western mind has become the victim of its own cultural success. Its type of civilization has experienced unparalleled expansion, attended by the rapid engulfment of other divergent cultures. On the fringes of that expansion, other cultures have been invaded or driven back, to be incorporated or ignored as the case may be. Attitudes of cultural condescension and disparagement are typically involved in either event. Since within the extensive boundaries of this superficially uniform civilization there is poverty of obvious cultural contrast, the sense of the real significance of cultural difference has almost completely lapsed. Such is the culture predicament of the Western world.

Franz Boas, in the next selection, analyzes modern views and theories of culture and civilization from another important critical angle. Again we encounter widely accepted and popular doctrine involving misconceptions of culture fundamentally misleading and unscientific. Though twofold, the doctrine, as Boas points out, has a single deep root in the ethnocentric view of culture. First, it falsely identifies varieties of race with varieties of culture, and in the second place, erroneously deduces racial superiority from cultural superiority, or even from mere cultural complexity or political dominance. Whether advocated in terms of Nordic, Latin, Germanic, Anglo-Saxon or Aryan culture, or the still more generalized concepts of Caucasian, European or "white" civilization—the specific claims make little difference in the substance of the argument, these doctrines of race superiority rest basically upon the false identification of race and culture. To the list should be added that progenitor of modern European superiority claims, the cultural sectarianism of "Christian civilization" as opposed to the non-Christian and "pagan." The obsession reaches its climax in the identification of the nation with "culture and civilization," as present-day ethnic nationalism makes only too obvious. But in the latter instance the political character of the concept is completely revealed.

Boas traces the historical factors which have fostered this contemporary creed, with its double-edged assumption of the innate superiority of the race and culture of those who possess more complex and advanced forms of civilization, and of the inferiority of those who do not. The doctrine, he thinks, is particularly a product of the modern colonial era, and thus of Occidental origin, at least in its extreme and characteristic form. Particularly in its aspect of associated color prejudice, it seems peculiarly and intimately associated with modern European colonial expansion. On that basis it furnishes the standard ideology and stock rationalization of economic imperialism. Both the race culture and the race superiority aspects of the doctrine are examined and criticized by Boas, and completely invalidated so far as the case rests on grounds of scientific warrant or historical truthfulness.

It is by now apparent how a combination of particular circumstances, viz., European industrial and colonial expansion, has combined with the age-old tendency to cultural chauvinism to produce these serious modern misconceptions about culture. They, in turn, have led to chronic disparagement and underestimation of racial and culture groups particularly different from our own. Under such circumstances, most cultural divergence is interpreted as cultural inferiority, and the appreciation of cultural interaction and indebtedness becomes almost completely obscured. This merges into one grand over-all misconception, the fallacy of cultural separatism—the belief that in being distinctive cultures are separate and water-tight units of civilization. Historical evidence shows this view to be unfounded; for, much to the contrary, all cultures are composite and most culture elements interchangeable.

No group has proprietary hold on the culture that it originates, and at any moment of its history, most of its own culture will be found to be a composite of culture elements from all the centuries and from the rest of the world. Waterman and Linton, in their selections, document how unsuspectedly composite our own contemporary culture actually is. Their analysis is all the more dramatic because they trace primarily our technological indebtedness to the past and to other cultures—in the very field of what is considered our most characteristic supremacy. Had they chosen to document our institutional concepts or our heritage of ideas the result would have been equally revealing. So many peoples and races have made their contribution to civilization that the ethnocentrist's view becomes scientifically ridiculous.

The composite character of present-day civilization, however, is exceptional in only a few respects. Other and earlier cultures have been just as definitely composite. Our distinctiveness lies almost solely in the rapidity with which new elements permeate the general practice and in our having so many channels of formalized cultural export and import. As for permanent cultural absorption, we have probably no greater capacity than many earlier periods and types of civilization, many of which were deliberately cosmopolitan. The frequently cited instance of the wholesale adoption of Greek culture by the Romans is really not exceptional. Time after time, through transfusions of conquest, cultural exchanges of all sorts—artistic, literary, technological and institutional—have occurred.

It should also be noted that cultural exchange passes in reciprocal streams from the conquerors to the conquered and from the conquered to the dominant groups. It is not always the dominant stock or the upper classes who are the carriers or importers of culture. Societies have just as frequently received infiltrations of alien culture from the bottom through the absorption of conquered and subject groups. In other cases, the outside influences enter through the elite, who usually have greater access to outside cultures, and are often themselves of foreign derivation. Cultural variation, initiated at any point, radiates considerably and often spreads to general acceptance.

Progress, indeed, in many instances seems proportional to the degree to which a society has a many-sided cultural exposure. Provided it can integrate them, a variety of culture contacts is a favorable situation for any culture. Groups do, of course, differ widely in their susceptibility to cultural change, but none are so conservative as to be completely resistant. Progressive societies, on the other hand, maintain and extend their formal agencies of contact, and thereby both share and contribute to the sum total of civilization.

The realization of the composite character of civilization, however, does not gainsay the fact of the distinctive character of individual cultures. It is a misapplication of this truth to regard it as sanctioning a uniformitarian theory or criterion of culture. Not only is it important to recognize the wide variety in the patterns and types of culture, but also to realize how vital variety and variability are in the growth and development of culture itself. Variation is at the root of cultural change, and cultural diversity is conducive to it. The processes of cultural interchange have fed on cultural diversity, and in milleniums of operation do not seem to have obliterated it. The several types of culture, then, are significant as variant adaptations, each functional in its own setting. Actually or potentially each has a role to play in cultural contact. In the perspective of culture history, a culture that is dormant now may have been crucially active and influential at another historical period, just as one that is creative and dominant now may at some other time have been dormant and uncreative, or in the future, may become so. In the setting of world culture, all peoples and nations have contributed importantly, though often without due credit, to the sum of human civilization, which itself, most broadly viewed, is the product of an extensive collaboration of cultural forces and an age-old interchange of cultures.

PATTERNS OF CULTURE

*The white man knows little of any ways of life but his own.
World-wide cultural diffusion has protected him as man has never
been protected before from having to take seriously the civilizations
of other peoples; it has given to our culture a massive universality
that we have long ceased to account for historically, and which we
read off rather as necessary and inevitable.*

WESTERN CIVILIZATION has spread itself more widely than any other local group that has so far been known. It has standardized itself over most of the globe, and we have been led, therefore, to accept a belief in the uniformity of human behavior that under other circumstances would not have arisen. Even very primitive peoples are sometimes far more conscious of the role of cultural traits than we are, and for good reason. They have had intimate experience of different cultures. They have seen their religion, their economic system, their marriage prohibitions, go down before the white man's. They have laid down the one and accepted the other, often uncomprehendingly enough, but they are quite clear that there are variant arrangements of human life. They will sometimes attribute dominant characteristics of the white man to his commercial competition, or to his institution of warfare, very much in the fashion of the anthropologist.

The white man has had a different experience. He has never seen an outsider, perhaps, unless the outsider has been already Europeanized. If he has traveled, he has very likely been around the world without ever staying outside a cosmopolitan hotel. He knows little of any ways of life but his own. The uniformity of custom, of outlook, that he sees spread about him seems convincing enough. He accepts without more ado the equivalence of human nature and his own cultural standards.

Yet the great spread of white civilization is not an isolated historical

Excerpt from Ruth Benedict, *Patterns of Culture*, (Boston, Houghton Mifflin Company, 1934), pp. 5-16.

circumstance. The Polynesian group, in comparatively recent times, has spread itself from Ontong, Java, to Easter Island, from Hawaii to New Zealand, and the Bantu-speaking tribes spread from the Sahara to southern Africa. But in neither case do we regard these peoples as more than an overgrown local variation of the human species. Western civilization has had all its inventions in transportation and all its far-flung commercial arrangements to back up its great dispersion, and it is easy to understand historically how this came about.

The psychological consequences of this spread of white culture have been out of all proportion to the materialistic. This world-wide cultural diffusion has protected us as man had never been protected before from having to take seriously the civilizations of other peoples; it has given to our culture a massive universality that we have long ceased to account for historically, and which we read off rather as necessary and inevitable. We interpret our dependence, in our civilization, upon economic competition, as proof that this is the prime motivation that human nature can rely upon, or we read off the behavior of small children as it is molded in our civilization and recorded in child clinics, as child psychology or the way in which the young human animal is bound to behave. It is the same whether it is a question of our ethics or of our family organization. It is the inevitability of each familiar motivation that we defend, attempting always to identify our own local ways of behaving with Behavior, or our own socialized habits with Human Nature.

Now modern man has made this thesis one of the living issues in his thought and in his practical behavior, but the sources of it go far back into what appears to be, from its universal distribution among primitive peoples, one of the earliest of human distinctions, the difference in kind between "my own" closed group and the outsider. All primitive tribes agree in recognizing this category of the outsiders, those who are not only outside the provisions of the moral code which holds within the limits of one's own people, but who are summarily denied a place anywhere in the human scheme. A great number of the tribal names in common use, Zuñi, Déné, Kiowa, and the rest, are names by which primitive peoples know themselves, and are only their native terms for "the human beings," that is, themselves. Outside of the closed group there are no human beings. And this is in

spite of the fact that from an objective point of view each tribe is surrounded by peoples sharing in its arts and material inventions, in
elaborate practices that have grown up by a mutual give-and-take of
behavior from one people to another.

Primitive man never looked out over the world and saw "mankind"
as a group and felt his common cause with his species. From the
beginning he was a provincial who raised the barriers high. Whether
it was a question of choosing a wife or of taking a head, the first and
important distinction was between his own human group and those
beyond the pale. His own group, and all its ways of behaving, was
unique.

So modern man, differentiating into Chosen People and dangerous
aliens, groups within his own civilization genetically and culturally
related to one another as any tribes in the Australian bush are among
themselves, has the justification of a vast historical continuity behind
his attitude. The Pygmies have made the same claims. We are not
likely to clear ourselves easily of so fundamental a human trait, but
we can at least learn to recognize its history and its hydra manifestations.

One of these manifestations, and one which is often spoken of as
primary and motivated rather by religious emotions than by this more
generalized provincialism, is the attitude that has universally held in
Western civilizations so long as religion remained a living issue among
them. The distinction between any closed group and outside peoples,
becomes in terms of religion that between the true believers and the
heathen. Between these two categories for thousands of years there
were no common meeting-points. No ideas or institutions that held in
the one were valid in the other. Rather all institutions were seen in
opposing terms according as they belonged to one or the other of the
very often slightly differentiated religions; on the one side it was a
question of Divine Truth and the true believer, of revelation and of
God; on the other it was a matter of mortal error, of fables, of the
damned and of devils. There could be no question of equating the
attitudes of the opposed groups and hence no question of understanding from objectively studied data the nature of this important human
trait, religion.

We feel a justified superiority when we read a description such as
this of the standard religious attitude. At least we have thrown off

that particular absurdity, and we have accepted the study of comparative religion. But considering the scope, a similar attitude has had in our civilization in the form of race prejudices, for example, we are justified in a little scepticism as to whether our sophistication in the matter of religion is due to the fact that we have outgrown naïve childishness, or simply to the fact that religion is no longer the area of life in which the important modern battles are staged. In the really live issues of our civilization we seem to be far from having gained the detachment that we have so largely achieved in the field of religion. . . .

The study of different cultures has another important bearing upon present-day thought and behavior. Modern existence has thrown many civilizations into close contact, and at the moment the overwhelming response to this situation is nationalism and racial snobbery. There has never been a time when civilization stood more in need of individuals who are genuinely culture-conscious, who can see objectively the socially conditioned behavior of other peoples without fear and recrimination.

Contempt for the alien is not the only possible solution of our present contact of races and nationalities. It is not even a scientifically founded solution. Traditional Anglo-Saxon intolerance is a local and temporal culture-trait like any other. Even people as nearly of the same blood and culture as the Spanish have not had it, and race prejudice in the Spanish-settled countries is a thoroughly different thing from that in countries dominated by England and the United States. In this country it is obviously not an intolerance directed against the mixture of blood of biologically far-separated races, for upon occasion excitement mounts as high against the Irish Catholic in Boston, or the Italian in New England mill towns, as against the Oriental in California. It is the old distinction of the in-group and the out-group, and if we carry on the primitive tradition in this matter, we have far less excuse than savage tribes. We have traveled; we pride ourselves on our sophistication. But we have failed to understand the relativity of cultural habits, and we remain debarred from much profit and enjoyment in our human relations with peoples of different standards, and untrustworthy in our dealings with them.

The recognition of the cultural basis of race prejudice is a desperate need in present Western civilization. We have come to the point where we entertain race prejudice against our blood brothers the Irish, and where Norway and Sweden speak of their enmity as if they too represented different blood. The so-called race line, during a war in which France and Germany fight on opposite sides, is held to divide the people of Baden from those of Alsace, though in bodily form they alike belong to the Alpine sub-race. In a day of footloose movements of people and of mixed marriages in the ancestry of the most desirable elements of the community, we preach unabashed the gospel of the pure race.

To this anthropology makes two answers. The first is as to the nature of culture and the second is as to the nature of inheritance. The answer as to the nature of culture takes us back to prehuman societies. There are societies where Nature perpetuates the slightest mode of behavior by biological mechanisms, but these are societies not of men but of the social insects. The queen ant, removed to a solitary nest, will reproduce each trait of sex behavior, each detail of the nest. The social insects represent Nature in a mood when she was taking no chances. The pattern of the entire social structure she committed to the ant's instinctive behavior. There is no greater chance that the social classes of an ant society, or its patterns of agriculture, will be lost by an ant's isolation from its group than that the ant will fail to reproduce the shape of its antennae or the structure of its abdomen.

For better or for worse, man's solution lies at the opposite pole. Not one item of his tribal social organization, of his language, of his local religion, is carried in his germ-cell.

An Oriental child adopted by an Occidental family learns English, shows toward its foster parents the attitudes current among the children he plays with, and grows up to the same professions that they elect. He learns the entire set of the cultural traits of the adopted society, and the set of his real parents' group plays no part. The same process happens on a grand scale when entire peoples in a couple of generations shake off their traditional culture and put on the customs of an alien group. The culture of the American Negro in northern cities has come to approximate in detail that of the whites in the same cities. . . .

All over the world, since the beginning of human history, it can be shown that peoples have been able to adopt the culture of peoples of another blood. There is nothing in the biological structure of man that makes it even difficult. Man is not committed in detail by his biological constitution to any particular variety of behavior. The great diversity of social solutions that man has worked out in different cultures in regard to mating, for example, or trade, are all equally possible on the basis of his original endowment. Culture is not a biologically transmitted complex.

What is lost in Nature's guaranty of safety is made up in the advantage of greater plasticity. The human animal does not, like the bear, grow himself a polar coat in order to adapt himself, after many generations, to the Arctic. He learns to sew himself a coat and put up a snow house. From all we can learn of the history of intelligence in pre-human as well as human societies, this plasticity has been the soil in which human progress began and in which it has maintained itself.

The corollary in modern politics is that there is no basis for the argument that we can trust our spiritual and cultural achievements to any selected hereditary germ-plasms. In our Western civilization, leadership has passed successively in different periods to the Semitic-speaking peoples, to the Hamitic, to the Mediterranean sub-group of the white race, and lately to the Nordic. There is no doubt about the cultural continuity of the civilization, no matter who its carriers were at the moment. We must accept all the implications of our human inheritance, one of the most important of which is the small scope of biologically transmitted behavior, and the enormous rôle of the cultural process of the transmission of tradition.

The second answer anthropology makes to the argument of the racial purist concerns the nature of heredity. The racial purist is the victim of a mythology. For what is "racial inheritance"? We know roughly what heredity is from father to son. Within a family line the importance of heredity is tremendous. But heredity is an affair of family lines. Beyond that it is mythology. In small and static communities like an isolated Eskimo village, "racial" heredity and the heredity of child and parent are practically equivalent, and racial heredity therefore has meaning. But as a concept applied to groups distributed over a wide area, let us say, to Nordics, it has no basis in reality. In the first place, in all Nordic nations there are family lines which are represented also in Alpine or Mediterranean communities. Any analysis of the physical make-up of a European population shows overlapping: the dark-eyed, dark-haired Swede represents family lines that are more concentrated farther south, but he is to be understood in relation to what we know of these latter groups. His heredity, so far as it has any physical reality, is a matter of his family line, which is not confined to Sweden. We do not know how far physical types may vary without intermixture. We know that inbreeding brings about a local type. But this is a situation that in our cosmopolitan white civilization hardly exists, and when "racial heredity" is invoked, as it usually is, to rally a group of persons of about the same economic status, graduating from much the same schools, and reading the same weeklies, such a category is merely another version of the in- and the out-group and does not refer to the actual biological homogeneity of the group.

What really binds men together is their culture—the ideas and the standards they have in common. If instead of selecting a symbol like common blood heredity and making a slogan of it, the nation turned its attention rather to the culture that unites its people, emphasizing its major merits and recognizing the different values which may develop in a different culture, it would substitute realistic thinking for a kind of symbolism which is dangerous because it is misleading.

RACE AND HISTORY

As time passes, the bloom of civilization bursts forth now here, now there. A people that at one time represented the highest type of culture sinks back into obscurity, while others take its place. At the dawn of history the ancestors of the races that are today among the most highly civilized were in no way superior to primitive man as we find him now. No civilization was the product of the genius of a single people.

A SURVEY of our globe shows the continents inhabited by a great diversity of peoples different in appearance, different in language and in cultural life. The Europeans and their descendents on

Excerpt from Franz Boas, *The Mind of Primitive Man*, (New York, The Macmillan Company, 1938), pp. 3-10, 15-17.

other continents are united by similarity of bodily build, and their civilization sets them off sharply against all the people of different appearance. The Chinese, the native New Zealander, the African Negro, the American Indian present not only distinctive bodily features, but each possesses also his own peculiar mode of life. Each human type seems to have its own inventions, its own customs and beliefs, and it is very generally assumed that race and culture must be intimately associated, that racial descent determines cultural life . . .

We are accustomed to speak both of primitive races and primitive cultures as though the two were necessarily related. We believe not only in a close association between race and culture; we are also ready to claim superiority of our own race over all others. The sources of this attitude spring from our everyday experiences. Bodily form has an aesthetic value. The dark color, the flat and wide nose, the thick lips and prominent mouth of the Negro; the slanting eye and prominent cheekbones of the East Asiatic do not conform to those ideals of human beauty to which we of West European traditions are accustomed. Furthermore such strange types as are members of our society occupy, very generally, inferior positions and do not mingle to any great extent with members of our own race. In their native land their cultural life is not as rich in intellectual achievement as our own. Hence the inference that strangeness of type and low intelligence go hand in hand. In this way our attitude becomes intelligible, but we also recognize that it is not based on scientific insight but on simple emotional reactions and social conditions. Our aversions and judgments are not, by any means, primarily rational in character.

Nevertheless, we like to support our emotional attitude toward the so-called inferior races by reasoning. The superiority of our inventions, the extent of our scientific knowledge, the complexity of our social institutions, our attempts to promote the welfare of all members of the social body, create the impression that we, the civilized people, have advanced far beyond the stages on which other groups linger, and the assumption has arisen of an innate superiority of the European nations and of their descendants. The basis of our reasoning is obvious: the higher a civilization, the higher must be the aptitude for civilization; and as aptitude presumably depends upon the perfection of the mechanism of body and mind, we infer that the White race represents the highest type. The tacit assumption is made that achievement depends solely, or at least primarily, upon innate racial ability. Since the intellectual development of the White race is the highest, it is assumed that its intellectuality is supreme and that its mind has the most subtle organization.

The conviction that European nations possess the highest aptitude supports our impressions regarding the significance of differences in type between the European race and those of other continents, or even of differences between various European types. Unwittingly we pursue a line of thought like this: since the aptitude of the European is the highest, his physical and mental type is also highest, and every deviation from the White type necessarily represents a lower feature.

This unproved assumption underlies our judgments of races, for other conditions being equal, a race is commonly described as the lower, the more fundamentally it differs from our own. We interpret as proof of a lower mentality anatomical peculiarities found in primitive man which resemble traits occurring in lower forms of the zoological series; and we are troubled by the observation that some of the "lower" traits do not occur in primitive man, but are rather found in the European race.

The subject and form of all such discussions show that the idea is rooted in the minds of investigators that we should expect to find in the White race the highest type of man.

Social conditions are often treated from the same point of view. We value our individual freedom, our code of ethics, our free art so highly that they seem to mark an advancement to which no other race can lay claim.

The judgment of the mental status of a people is generally guided by the difference between its social status and our own, and the greater the difference between their intellectual, emotional and moral processes and those which are found in our civilization, the harsher our judgment. It is only when a Tacitus deploring the degeneration of his time finds the virtues of his ancestors among foreign tribes that their example is held up to the gaze of his fellow-citizens; but the people of imperial Rome probably had only a pitying smile for the dreamer who clung to the antiquated ideals of the past.

In order to understand clearly the relations between race and civilization, the two unproved assumptions to which I have referred must be subjected to a searching analysis. We must investigate how far we are justified in assuming achievement to be primarily due to exceptional aptitude, and how far we are justified in assuming the European type—or, taking the notion in its extreme form, the North-west European type—to represent the highest development of mankind. It will be advantageous to consider these popular beliefs before making the attempt to clear up the relations between culture and race and to describe the form and growth of culture.

It might be said, that, although achievement is not necessarily a measure of aptitude, it seems admissible to judge the one by the other. Have not most races had the same chances for development? Why, then, did the White race alone develop a civilization which is sweeping the whole world, and compared with which all other civilizations appear as feeble beginnings cut short in early childhood, or arrested and petrified at an early stage of development? Is it not, to say the least, probable that the race which attained the highest stage of civilization was the most gifted one, and that those races which have remained at the bottom of the scale were not capable of rising to higher levels?

A brief consideration of the general outlines of the history of civilization will give us an answer to these questions. Let our minds go back a few thousand years until we reach the time when the civilizations of eastern and western Asia were in their infancy. The first great advances appear. The art of writing is invented. As time passes, the bloom of civilization bursts forth now here, now there. A people that at one time represented the highest type of culture sinks back into obscurity, while others take its place. At the dawn of history we see civilization cling to certain districts, taken up now by one people, now by another. Often, in the numerous conflicts of these times the more civilized people are vanquished. The conqueror learns the arts of life from the conquered and carries on their work. Thus the centers of civilization are shifting to and fro over a limited area, and progress is slow and halting. At this period the ancestors of the races that are today among the most highly civilized were in no way superior to primitive man as we find him now in regions that have not come into contact with modern civilization.

Was the civilization attained by these ancient people of such a character as to allow us to claim for them a genius superior to that of any other race?

First of all, we must bear in mind that none of these civilizations was the product of the genius of a single people. Ideas and inventions were carried from one to the other; and, although intercommunication was slow, each people which participated in the ancient development contributed its share to the general progress. Proofs without number have been forthcoming which show that ideas have been disseminated as long as people have come into contact with one another. Neither race nor language limit their diffusion. Hostility and timid exclusiveness against neighbors are unable to hinder their flow from tribe to tribe and they filter through distances that are measured by thousands of miles. Since many races have worked together in the development of the ancient civilizations, we must bow to the genius of all, whatever group of mankind they may represent, North African, West Asiatic, European, East Indian or East Asiatic.

We may now ask, did no other races develop a culture of equal value? It would seem that the civilizations of ancient Peru and of Central America may well be compared with the ancient civilizations of the Old World. In both we find a high stage of political organization, division of labor and an elaborate ecclesiastical hierarchy. Great architectural works were undertaken, requiring the cooperation of many individuals. Plants were cultivated and animals domesticated; the art of writing had been invented. The inventions and knowledge of the peoples of the Old World seem to have been somewhat more numerous and extended than those of the races of the New World, but there can be no doubt that the general status of their civilization measured by their inventions and knowledge was nearly equally high. This will suffice for our consideration.

What, then, is the difference between the civilization of the Old World and that of the New World? It is essentially a difference in time. The one reached a certain stage three thousand or four thousand years sooner than the other.

Although much stress has been laid upon the greater rapidity of development of the races of the Old World, it is not by any means conclusive proof of exceptional ability. . . . The difference of a few thousand years is insignificant as compared to the age of the human race. The time required to develop the existing races is a matter of conjecture, but we may be sure that it is long. We also know that man existed in the Eastern Hemisphere at a time that can be measured by geological standards only, and that he reached America not later than the beginning of the present geological period, perhaps a little earlier. The age of the human race must be measured by a span of time exceeding considerably one hundred thousand years. As the initial point of cultural development we must assume the remotest times in which we find traces of man. What does it mean, then, if one group of mankind reached a certain stage of cultural development at the age of one hundred thousand years and another at the age of one hundred and four thousand years? Would not the life history of the people, and the vicissitudes of their history, be fully sufficient to explain a delay of this character, without necessitating the assumption of a difference in their aptitude to social development? Such retardation would be significant only if it could be shown that it occurs regularly and at all times in one race, while in other races greater rapidity of development is the rule.

If the achievements of a people were a measure of their aptitude, this method of estimating innate ability would hold good not only for our time but would be applicable under all conditions. The Egyptians of 2000 or 3000 B.C. might have applied the argument in their judgment of the people of northwestern Europe who lived in the Stone Age, had no architecture and a very primitive agriculture. They were "backward" people like many so-called primitive people of our time. These were our ancestors, and the judgment of the ancient Egyptians would now have to be reversed. Precisely in the same way must the customary estimate of the Japanese of one hundred years ago be reversed on account of their adoption of the economic, industrial and scientific methods of the western world. The claim that achievement and aptitude go hand in hand is not convincing. . . .

Several races have developed a civilization of a type similar to the one from which our own has sprung, and a number of favorable conditions have facilitated its rapid spread in Europe. Among these, similar physical appearance, contiguity of habitat and moderate difference in modes of manufacture were the most potent. When, later on, Europeans began to spread over other continents, the races with which they came into contact were not equally favorably situated.

Striking differences of racial types, the preceding isolation which caused devastating epidemics in the newly discovered countries, and the greater advance in technical processes made assimilation much more difficult. The rapid dissemination of Europeans over the whole world destroyed all promising beginnings which had arisen in various regions. Thus no race except that of eastern Asia was given a chance to develop independently. The spread of the European race cut short the growth of the existing germs without regard to the mental aptitude of the people among whom it was developing.

In how far are we justified in considering those anatomical traits in regard to which foreign races differ from the White race as marks of inferiority? We have recognized that achievement alone is no satisfactory proof of an unusual mental ability of the White race. It follows from this, that anatomical differences between the White race and others can be interpreted as meaning superiority of the former, inferiority of the latter, only if a relation between anatomical form and mentality can be proved to exist.

Too many investigations relating to mental characteristics of races are based on the logical fallacy of first assuming that the European represents the highest racial type and then interpreting every deviation from the European type as a sign of lower mentality. When the formation of the jaws of the Negroes is thus interpreted without proof of a biological connection between the forms of the jaw and the functioning of the nervous system an error is committed that might be paralleled by a Chinaman who would describe Europeans as hairy monsters whose hirsute body is a proof of a lower status. This is emotional, not scientific reasoning.

The question that must be answered is: In how far do anatomical traits determine mental activities? By analogy we associate lower mental traits with theromorphic, brutelike features. In our naïve, everyday parlance, brutish features and brutality are closely connected. We must distinguish here, however, between the anatomical characteristics of which we have been speaking and the muscular development of the face, trunk and limbs due to habits of life. The hand, which is never employed in activities requiring those refined adjustments which are characteristic of psychologically complex actions, will lack the modeling brought about by the development of each muscle.

The face, the muscles of which have not responded to the innervations accompanying deep thought and refined sentiment will lack in individuality and expressiveness. The neck that has supported heavy loads, and has not responded to the varied requirements of delicate changes of position of head and body, will appear massive and clumsy. These physiognomic differences must not mislead us in our interpretations. We are also inclined to draw inferences in regard to mentality from a receding forehead, a heavy jaw, large and heavy teeth, perhaps even from an inordinate length of arms or an unusual development of hairiness. A careful consideration of the relation of such traits to mental activities will be required, before we can assume as proven their significance.

It appears that neither cultural achievement nor outer appearance is a safe basis on which to judge the mental aptitude of races. Added to this is the one-sided evaluation of our own racial type and of our modern civilization without any close inquiry into the mental processes of primitive races and cultures which may easily lead to erroneous conclusions.

ALL PEOPLES HAVE CONTRIBUTED TO CULTURE

Civilization, as we know it, has come to us from various sources. The American Indians and the Chinese have apparently made important contributions to human culture. The American Indian has, in fact, made more numerous original contributions than the classical Greeks made.

THE FOLLOWING is a tabulation showing the first historical appearance of certain inventions:

Men of Lower Palaeolithic Europe: Fire, stone tools.

Men of Upper Palaeolithic Europe: The bow and arrow, clothing, the earliest art, first traces of religion, houses.

Excerpt from T. T. Waterman, "The Great World Theatre," in *Essays in Anthropology Presented to A. L. Kroeber* (Berkeley, California: University of California Press, 1936), p. 421.

Egyptians: Copper, bronze, wheat, the plow, donkeys, paper, ink, the alphabet, glass, barley, millet, bricks, playing-cards, checkers, chess.

Sumerians: Wheels, a scale of weights, steeples, the spread-eagle design.

Babylonians: Codified law, coined money, the arch.

Hittites: Horses as draft animals, iron.

Assyrians: Cotton, banks, postal system.

Chaldeans: Astronomy, the Zodiac, the week, degrees of the circle, names of the days in the week.

Persians: Monotheism, Satan, chickens (the barnyard fowl), trousers, moustaches.

Arabs: Camels, the use of milk, calculus, algebra, the Arabic numerals, zero, coffee.

Greeks: Euclidian geometry, the screw, the perfected column in architecture.

Chinese: Tea, porcelain, gunpowder, silk, rice, parasols and umbrellas, spectacles (eyeglasses), pepper, the printing press, the mariner's compass, asbestos, paper money, watertight compartments in ships, the fingerprint system of identification, kites.

American Indians: Maize, tobacco, potato, sweet potato, hammocks, quinine, casava, toboggans, snowshoes, the tipi (original of the Sibley tent), the "cocaine" plant, zero (independently discovered before its discovery by the Arabs), cocaine, the Scuppernong grape, vanilla, chocolate, cochineal, guinea pigs, peanuts.

This tabulation indicates that "civilization," as we know it, came to us from various sources. The American Indians and the Chinese, two people that we rarely think of as civilized at all, have apparently made a full contribution to human culture. The American Indian has, in fact, made more numerous *original* contributions than the classical Greeks made.

OUR DEBT TO OTHER CIVILIZATIONS

There can be no question about the average American's American-
ism or his desire to preserve this precious heritage at all costs. Never-
theless, some foreign ideas have already wormed their way into his
civilization without his realizing what was going on.

THERE CAN be no question about the average American's
Americanism or his desire to preserve this precious heritage at
all costs. Nevertheless, some insidious foreign ideas have already
wormed their way into his civilization without his realizing what was
going on. Thus dawn finds the unsuspecting patriot garbed in
pajamas, a garment of East Indian origin; and lying in a bed built
on a pattern which originated in either Persia or Asia Minor. He
is muffled to the ears in un-American materials: cotton, first domesticated in India; linen, domesticated in the Near East; wool from
an animal native to Asia Minor; or silk whose uses were first discovered by the Chinese. All these substances have been transformed
into cloth by methods invented in Southwestern Asia. If the weather
is cold enough he may even be sleeping under an eiderdown quilt
invented in Scandinavia.

On awakening he glances at the clock, a medieval European invention, uses one potent Latin word in abbreviated form, rises in haste,
and goes to the bathroom. Here, if he stops to think about it, he must
feel himself in the presence of a great American institution: he will
have heard stories of both the quality and frequency of foreign
plumbing and will know that in no other country does the average
man perform his ablutions in the midst of such splendor. But the
insidious foreign influence pursues him even here. Glass was invented
by the ancient Egyptians, the use of glazed tiles for floors and walls
in the Near East, porcelain in China, and the art of enameling on
metal by Mediterranean artisans of the Bronze Age. Even his bath-

Excerpt from Ralph Linton, "One Hundred Per Cent American," *The*
American Mercury, Vol. 40 (April 1937), pp. 427-429.

tub and toilet are but slightly modified copies of Roman originals. The only purely American contribution to the ensemble is the steam radiator.

In this bathroom the American washes with soap invented by the ancient Gauls. Next he cleans his teeth, a subversive European practice which did not invade America until the latter part of the eighteenth century. He then shaves, a masochistic rite first developed by the heathen priests of ancient Egypt and Sumer. The process is made less of a penance by the fact that his razor is of steel, an iron-carbon alloy discovered in either India or Turkestan. Lastly, he dries himself on a Turkish towel.

Returning to the bedroom, the unconscious victim of un-American practices removes his clothes from a chair, invented in the Near East, and proceeds to dress. He puts on close-fitting tailored garments whose form derives from the skin clothing of the ancient nomads of the Asiatic steppes and fastens them with buttons whose prototypes appeared in Europe at the close of the Stone Age. This costume is appropriate enough for outdoor exercise in a cold climate, but is quite unsuited to American summers, steam-heated houses, and Pullmans. Nevertheless, foreign ideas and habits hold the unfortunate man in thrall even when common sense tells him that the authentically American costume of gee string and moccasins would be far more comfortable. He puts on his feet stiff coverings made from hide prepared by a process invented in ancient Egypt and cut to a pattern which can be traced back to ancient Greece, and makes sure they are properly polished, also a Greek idea. Lastly, he ties about his neck a strip of bright-colored cloth which is a vestigial survival of the shoulder shawls worn by seventeenth-century Croats. He gives himself a final appraisal in the mirror, an old Mediterranean invention, and goes downstairs to breakfast.

Here a whole new series of foreign things confronts him. His food and drink are placed before him in pottery vessels, the popular name of which—china—is sufficient evidence of their origin. His fork is a medieval Italian invention and his spoon a copy of a Roman original. He will usually begin the meal with coffee, an Abyssinian plant first discovered by the Arabs. The American is quite likely to need it to dispel the morning-after effects of over-indulgence in fermented drinks, invented in the Near East; or distilled ones, invented by the alchemists of medieval Europe. Whereas the Arabs took their coffee straight, he will probably sweeten it with sugar, discovered in India; and dilute it with cream, both the domestication of cattle and the technique of milking having originated in Asia Minor.

If our patriot is old-fashioned enough to adhere to the so-called American breakfast, his coffee will be accompanied by an orange, domesticated in the Mediterranean region, a cantaloupe domesticated in Persia, or grapes, domesticated in Asia Minor. He will follow this with a bowl of cereal made from grain domesticated in the Near East and prepared by methods also invented there. From this he will go on to waffles, a Scandinavian invention, with plenty of butter, originally a Near-Eastern cosmetic. As a side dish he may have the egg of a bird domesticated in Southeastern Asia or strips of the flesh of an animal domesticated in the same region, which have been salted and smoked by a process invented in Northern Europe.

Breakfast over, he places upon his head a molded piece of felt, invented by the nomads of Eastern Asia, and, if it looks like rain, puts on outer shoes of rubber, discovered by the ancient Mexicans, and takes an umbrella, invented in India. He then sprints for his train— the train, not the sprinting, being an English invention. At the station he pauses for a moment to buy a newspaper, paying for it with coins invented in ancient Lydia. Once on board he settles back to inhale the fumes of a cigarette invented in Mexico, or a cigar invented in Brazil. Meanwhile, he reads the news of the day, imprinted in characters invented by the ancient Semites by a process invented in Germany upon a material invented in China. As he scans the latest editorial pointing out the dire results to our institutions of accepting foreign ideas, he will not fail to thank a Hebrew God in an Indo-European language that he is a one hundred per cent (decimal system invented by the Greeks) American (from Americus Vespucci, Italian geographer).

2

THE UNIVERSALITY OF CULTURAL INTERCHANGE

THE WHOLE HISTORY of civilization takes on new aspects from the viewpoint of a scientific tracing of culture and culture history. Not only does an entirely different type of fact stand out as the truly important set of historical events, but there is also a radical reversal of values through which discoveries and inventions become more important than disasters and battles, peoples and varieties of living more interesting than heroes and dynastic successions, and cultural contacts and interchanges more significant than treaties and annexations. A principle of continuity and accumulative development looms up as the link principle of significant history. The cultural pedigree of the newspaper, for example, "imprinted," as Linton characterizes it, "in characters invented by the early Semites by a process invented in medieval Germany upon a material invented in China," has many parallels in culture history, any one of which can bring more understanding into our social thinking through its widening of the cultural perspective than pages of orthodox history. The accurately reconstructed story of corn or silk or of iron or porcelain, or, for that matter, of the alphabet or the idea of monotheism contains, along with significant evidence of cultural interaction and indebtedness, deep insights into the nature of civilization.

Much of this culturally important information is unfamiliar and much has yet to be documented, so recent is our appreciation of its value. Particularly unacknowledged are the instances of cultural advance outside the boundaries of European history and civilization. Yet the American Indians, the ancient Chinese, the ancient Africans have all made notable contributions to human culture, some of them in the opinion of anthropologists more original and influential than later historical and much more lauded contributions. Ironically enough in many cases, these much-lauded accomplishments are themselves based on the forgotten and unacknowledged contributions. Still deeper irony ensues when specious claims of cultural superiority are made to rest on cultural developments which, like a good deal of Western technology, involves these bases. The hand-loom, for instance, stands in an ancestral relation to the power-loom which hardly justifies the cultural arrogance of the peoples of the power-loom stage of culture, as they foist the products of their machine age upon cultures still in the hand-loom stage. The civilizing process was at one time flowing in the other direction. This reciprocity, even if separated by centuries, cannot be overlooked or ignored; indeed it is vital to the complete understanding of both the past and the present stages of culture.

The source materials aim to illustrate the vast, and to many, unsuspected scope of the process of intercultural exchange. They also show the basic character of these influences in the making of civilization. It will be a revelation to many readers to learn how far-flung were the trade routes of the ancient world, how deliberate and elaborate the exchanges of culture products were then, and how much the development of our civilization has depended upon the technological and institutional influences of cultures now decadent or vanished. Rostovtzeff shows in the excerpt from *Caravan Cities* how crucial for succeeding civilizations the early Asiatic civilizations were, and how through the ancient caravan routes, they had developed contacts over distances spanning half the globe.

From fragments of ancient record, Rostovtzeff pieces out an illuminating mosaic of the culture contacts of this very ancient world. The foundations of our composite civilization were really laid by the ancient empires, most of them Oriental. They, too, in their day had their great expansions of far-flung political and economic interests. Nor were they so radically different from modern European expansion as not to have significant analogies. Through the wide-scale contacts of these empires, in the course of the long exchange between the civilizations of the East and those of the West, many of the primary bases of civilization came into the orbit of European culture, such as pottery, the smelting of metals, weaving, brick making, china, paper, agriculture, the alphabet—a list too long to be briefly documented. This is the European cultural debt to the Orient, until recently so unacknowledged, and only now being slowly retrieved by the newer, more scientific historical scholarship.

The processes of exchange between Europe and China passed through elaborate caravan relays of interconnecting civilizations: to trace them in detail one must track down the forgotten empires of Cappadocia, Sumer, Ur, Babylon, Syria, Palmyra and the Arab Kingdoms of the 8th Century B.C. In addition on the Mediterranean side there were the better-known culture shuttles of Egypt, Crete, the Phoenician colonies, the Macedonian Empire and Rome. These relays of culture contact were world movements in their day, much more impressive on their economic and cultural side than in their military exploits and political combinations. Throughout the rise and fall of dynasties and military leaders, these constructive processes went on, extending in geographical scope from farthest China to beyond Italy on both shores of the Mediterranean. The time span, too, is impressive, for it runs back at least to the fourth millennium, B.C.

Neither the grand scale nor the antiquity of these interchanges is as significant, however, as the resultant character of the civilizations. For many of these earlier civilizations are now known to have been composite and cosmopolitan to a degree not previously suspected, especially during their peak periods when, in the height of their power, they had ramifying contacts throughout the world of their day. The archeological evidence of exchange and cross-influence is so great that some interpretations credit their brilliance and creativeness to the direct results of cultural cross-fertilization and fusion. Converging streams of culture, often of very diverse and distant varieties, are part of the historical record of many of the more significant of these civilizations; the Cretan, which was Egypto-Grecian, the Hebrew-Canaanite, the Perso-Egyptian, the Athenian, the Punic-Phoenician, the Etrusco-Roman, the Graeco-Roman, the Alexandrine, to mention only the more outstanding. In most of these instances, there was something considerably more than routine contact and cultural borrowing, there was a definite merger of cultures. The hyphenate cultural character of the Moorish-Hispanic civilization, as well as of the Revival of Learning, the Italian Renaissance and the Enlightenment is generally known, but somehow this has not served to drive home the full realization of the probable connection between culture contact and significant and creative cultural advance.

Teggart shows conclusively that at the time of the barbarian migrations what happened in the Roman Empire and Western Europe can only be fully explained historically in connection with what was contemporaneously happening in China. On another frontier of culture contact, Dopsch examines the record of the economic and social relations of the Romans with the Germanic tribes. He finds, among other interesting new interpretations, that there was considerable peaceful penetration of the Germans into the Roman economy, not only as mercenaries but in agricultural settlements about the Roman towns. There was sufficient absorption of Roman civilization to account for the successful taking over by the "barbarians" of the Roman institutions and tradition, and eventually their assumption of the political administration of the empire. Here, again, political and military history has failed to give us the true picture through overlooking the cultural exchanges and the economic and technological apprenticeship of the Germans, which, once recognized, account for their assimilation of Roman culture. Even the term "barbarian," Dopsch discovers, had little or no invidious meaning for the Romans, according to the context of well-documented descriptions and references to the Germans in contemporary Roman writings. The tradition to the contrary seems to have been an added and erroneous interpolation by later historians, projecting the Christian attitude toward the "heathen" into the distinctions of the Romans.

Hudson in *Europe and China* traces the cultural intercourse between the Far East and Europe over a period of many centuries succeeding the earliest contacts. As he points out, the sustaining contact was the all important silk-trade, which, until the introduction of silk-culture in Europe, was an almost unbroken bond between the two continents. Chinese civilization during much of that long period was flourishing and richly creative, and furnished Europe not only with basic materials, but time and again with technological skills, scientific inventions, and occasionally even institutional ideas and models. Periodically in the art and literature of medieval and Renaissance Europe, interest in China makes its appearance, reflecting these

cultural relations. Such interchange continued as late as the eighteenth century, when there was also a sustained Chinese cultural
vogue, affecting influentially the art, literature and philosophy of that
period. A little known phase of that comparatively recent influence
is called to attention in the Maverick account of *The Chinese Influence Upon the Physiocrats*. Although affecting primarily a small
group of intellectuals, this was by no means a negligible cross-influence,
because it became the base of the classical economic theory as well as
stimulating much of the rationalistic and Utopian political thought
of the same period. Some authorities credit the Chinese influence with
having been the dominant inspiration of the physiocrats.

The excerpt from Singer on *The Jewish Factor in Medieval
Thought* brings forward another significant example of constructive
and influential cultural interchange. Between the Dispersion and the
early thirteenth century, Jewish scholarship had experienced prolonged contact with the Arab and the Byzantine cultures. At the time
when the Jews became important culture-carriers for Europe, their
own culture had blossomed out in a definite cultural synthesis which
was an eclectic fusion of culture strains from the Arabic, Hellenic,
Byzantine, Roman and Judaic traditions. They brought into the somewhat sterile culture of medieval Europe more direct contact with
repressed aspects of the Graeco-Roman tradition, from which both
the Aristotelian period of Scholasticism and the classical elements of
the Revival of Learning were derived.

Turning in another direction, Westerman traces other little known
European cultural contacts—those with Africa. Particularly illuminating is his comparison between the Islamic and the Christian contacts
with the African pagan societies, although the contrast between the
older and the modern European contacts is also analyzed. The diversity
of its native cultures, the number of cultural invasions it has sustained, and the sharp divergence of many of these cultures with the
native ones make Africa, in historical review, a laboratory of culture
contacts. Since the days of ancient Egypt, successive waves of cultural
invasion have swept over this continent. Those from Arabia and
Mesopotamia penetrated deeply into the Nile valley for centuries,
the Phoenician and Graeco-Roman penetration also reached deeply
into the continent from the Mediterranean littoral, and a prolonged

infiltration of the Moslem civilization and religion spread into interior Africa in the early medieval period through the trans-Saharan trade routes. Additionally, in the Southeast, from yet undetermined dates, waves of Malay and Melanesian contact came over and established settlements of which the mixed culture of Zanzibar is only a particularly stubborn remnant. All this occurred considerably before the Portuguese voyages of the fifteenth century, which began the European slave trade and was to culminate in the final phases of colonial imperialism partitioning Africa almost completely among the European colonial powers.

Throughout all this, Westerman notes that African cultures have "always manifested an extraordinary stability and power of assimilation," a fact far from general belief. "Neither the migrations of the Hamites," he says, "and the political upheavals caused by them, nor the settlements of the Arabs and their devastating slave raids, neither the Indian and Persian immigrants on the east coast, nor even the slave and alcohol trade of Europe have been able fundamentally to change the face of Africa. The Negro has remained and his civilizations have remained; the foreign elements which they have adopted have been so completely absorbed and adapted that today they appear indigenous." This presents us with the rather unorthodox but significant view of African cultures as highly adaptive and composite prior to the colonial era, and still somewhat so in instances, as we shall later see.

For the correct perspective of its cultural history, then, the present-day chapter of decadent African tribal cultures and enfeebled colonial subjection must be supplemented by these almost forgotten chapters of vigorous cultural assimilation, marked by flourishing civilizations such as the mixed Moslem-pagan empires of the Melle, Songhay and Timbuctu during the thirteenth to the sixteenth centuries, and as well, by the pagan West African kingdoms of Ife, Benin, Dahomey. All of these were historically associated with contacts in which the native cultures had favorable conditions of reciprocal interaction and fusion, contrasting sharply with the one-sided and smothering later contacts of European colonial imperialism. Even today Westerman finds cultural reciprocity the main reason for the more successful competition of the Islamic culture and religion in Africa as compared with the Christian-European wave of civilization. The Moslem penetration, with a tradition of greater cultural tolerance, of legalized intermarriage, and of trade policies not disruptive of the native economy, has resulted in the successful Mohammedanization of half the African continent, with considerable cultural influence even beyond this extensive area of direct proselytization. "Islam," as Westerman says, "forged closer links between itself and the African peoples." Whereas, European contacts in Africa, with belligerent emphasis on the differences in cultural levels, a passion, until very recently at least, for the wholesale reconstruction of native cultures both on the part of governmental and missionary policy, and trade and labor policies directly disruptive of the native economy, have resulted on the one hand in superficial and precariously unstable Christianization and in economic and cultural disintegration on the other. The history of African culture contacts thus seems to indicate that cultural contact on a more or less equilateral basis is productive of results far more stable and constructive than those produced by the characteristically unilateral contacts and policies of European imperialism. Where Islam practiced such a one-sided policy, as it did in the African slave trade, beyond the boundaries of its converts, it, too, had similar blighting effects upon the native tribes and their way of life.

Herskovits continues this narrative of the complex cultural associations of the African with other continental cultures, and concludes that in the light of its long cultural history, Africa must be considered as "an integral part of the Old World cultural province," mutually conditioning and being conditioned by European and Asiatic cultures till its prostration under the Western colonial system. From the time the ancient Egyptians were in contact with Africa's indigenous inland cultures, intermittent contacts are traceable between Africa and Asia Minor and between Africa and Southern Europe, particularly Spain. This resulted not only in the well-known presence of the blacks in these comparatively distant centers, but in traceable but scarcely recognized cultural Africanisms. Herskovits thinks these are particularly clear in folklore, but are discernible along several other institutional lines.

He then turns to the evidence of more extensive African cultural influence in the New World through the transplanted African in

North America, the West Indies and South America. Here incontestable data is available of a sustained and important influence, particularly in musical idioms, folklore and superstition, speech, dance and a few fragmentary institutional customs. These all stem so directly from the parent West African civilization as to give clear evidence of their origin. In this case also, these Africanisms, though everywhere rather distinctive, have exerted their fullest and most creative influence in areas of cultural lenience and reciprocity. Slavery shattered the native institutional inheritance of the American Negro, so that only elements like music and folklore had any chance of survival. These, however, did survive notably, but as is not generally recognized, survived in their purest intensity not in the United States, where there was cultural suppression, but in countries like Brazil, several of the Central American countries, in some of the provinces of Mexico and in the French and Spanish West Indies, where, even though there was slavery, there was more cultural tolerance. Apart from the question of culture survivals, Herskovits finds that even under the onus and stigma of slavery, a reciprocal interchange of tradition has taken place between black and white in the New World, and that though the heavier stream has been the assimilation by the Negroes of the white man's civilization, counter-influences of some importance and value have flowed from the Negro side into the composite American culture.

As a final example of the universality of cultural interchange, comes the Wissler article on *The Influence of the Aboriginal Indian Culture on American Life*. Here apparently on the colonial frontier there was enacted one of the most significant yet rarely recognized instances of the inevitable give-and-take of all sustained contacts between peoples. In this case the absorption of elements of Indian culture by the white settler-colonists was so complete as to have been entirely forgotten in the course of a generation or so. Indeed many do not know that the North American Indian culture has been so crucially influential, and that some of the elements of American culture boasted of as distinctively American are due to cultural exchange with the Indian. Wissler points out how the Indian was a link in the commercial exploitation of the natural resources and natural wealth of the American continent, an economic process without which the early colonial economy could never have taken root, later to flourish. "The Indian," says Wissler, "taught the American colonist to survive in what for him was a 'wilderness,' gave to the woodsman and the pioneering frontiersman a number of strategic skills and tools, traditional and useful yet, but crucial at that period." In addition to this important apparatus of frontier skill and technology, the "American farmer took over the whole maize culture of the Indian with the exception of its ceremonial and social elements." So that not just merely a temporary technique of subsistence but also the agricultural base of the extensive mid-West economy was derived from Indian sources and contact. Contrasted with the typical and biased history text-book account of early colonial contacts with the Indian, one can see vividly the enlightening significance of the more objective and scientific account of these race and culture group relations.

So from the new scientific evidences of culture contacts, between all varieties and levels of culture, and from every quarter of the globe, comes convincing testimony of the universality and constructive role of cultural interchange.

CARAVAN CITIES

*Even at an early date the oldest city-states of Sumer in Meso-
potamia were linked to far distant lands by caravans: to Egypt in
the west, to Asia Minor in the north, to Turkestan, Seistan, and
India in the east and southeast.*

AS SOON as the earliest civilizations known to us were born in
the deltas of the Tigris, the Euphrates, and the Nile, and began
to prosper and to develop, caravans from all parts began to journey
toward Babylonia and Egypt. First came the nearest neighbors: the
Arabs of the desert and the dwellers in the Iranian hills. Strings of
camels followed in their tracks, shaggy two-humped dromedaries of
Arabia, bringing goods from the mountains of Iran. From the north,
from northern Syria and Asia Minor, trains of donkeys, heavily laden,
moved down the Euphrates and Tigris valleys. At the same time the
first ships began to traverse the sea, putting out from Egypt, and
from the shores of the Persian Gulf, from southern Arabia, and from
the sea-coast of India.

These ships and caravans were laden with the goods which Babylonia and Egypt lacked, goods which were daily becoming more of a
necessity and less of a luxury to civilized man. They carried stone
and wood for the erection of temples, palaces, and cities; copper for
the manufacture of arms and of agricultural and industrial implements; gold and silver, ivory, rare woods, precious stones, pearls, and
incense for the delectation of gods and men; scents and cosmetics ever
dear to the Oriental, or spices for use in cookery. In Syria and Cappadocia, on the Iranian plateau and in India, in southern and central
Africa such wares abounded and in exchange for them civilized
society sent her various new products: specimens of metal-work, especially weapons of the chase and war, elaborate colored fabrics, glass
beads, wine, dates, oil and fine bread were exported, the foodstuffs
being especially acceptable to the half-starved Bedouin of the desert.

Excerpt from M. Rostovtzeff, *Caravan Cities* (Oxford: The Clarendon Press,
1932), pp. 6-8; 10-12; 14-22; 23-25; 29; 34-35.

Soon a similar intercourse arose between civilized countries, for it was impossible for them to avoid an exchange of their most recent products. Thus Babylonia would send her latest novelties to Egypt and Egypt hers to Babylonia; India would export her products to Babylonia and Babylonia hers to India.

Recent excavations in Babylonia and Egypt have penetrated to the very lowest levels of inhabited sites and they have brought to light objects from temples and palaces, houses and tombs, which date back to the earliest stages of civilization. Amongst them are some of the earliest written texts in existence. Both the objects and the texts tell us that even at this early date the oldest city-states of Sumer in Meso-potamia were linked to far distant lands by caravans: to Egypt in the west, to Asia Minor in the north, to Turkestan, Seistan, and India in the east and southeast. The discovery of similar seals in India at Harappa and Mohenjo Daro and in Babylonia at Ur, the presence of archaic gold objects of Sumerian type at Astrabad on the Caspian Sea, the similarity in type of the copper arms and utensils of Egypt, Baby-lonia, Syria, and Iran are further proof of this fact. A number of resemblances, not only in objects of daily use but also in the decorative motifs of Egypt and Babylonia, show the close connection between these two lands. Even more conclusive evidence of early foreign trade is discoverable from the analysis of finds in the predynastic tombs of Ur and Kish. Beautiful objects of gold, silver, copper, and of different kinds of wood embellished with rare stones have been found here in amazing profusion, and the materials of none of them are indigenous. They were imported from a great distance, and the lion's share in this import business fell to caravan trade.

With the advance of the centuries civilization spread over wider and still wider fields. Sargon and Naramsin, kings of Akkad in Baby-lonia in the third millennium B.C., were largely responsible for this by their creation of the first extensive empire known to mankind. They formed it by uniting western Asia into a single state. This enabled them not only to strengthen the already existing lines of intercourse between various regions within the empire, but also to establish fresh connections with their neighbors to the north, south, east, and west. The most important result of this policy was, however, the appearance of numerous trading towns in the valleys and fields of the "fertile crescent" and the development of the maritime settlements of Palestine, Phoenicia, and Syria into important centers of commerce. Cities appeared in Asia Minor also, and a trade was begun with the European coast of the Mediterranean Sea, where a demand upon similar commercial lines was nascent. The use of Indian, Arabian, and African goods steadily increased and commercial relations with Arabia and through Arabia with India and Africa on the one hand and with the Iranian plateau on the other gradually became more binding and led by degrees to a more efficient organization. . . .

The Cappadocian documents [c. 3000 B.C.] have brought to light numerous facts of interest regarding the organization and development of caravan trade. Important trading and banking houses equipped and financed the large caravans, generally composed of donkeys, which traveled south and southwest. The tablets tell us of the complicated business enterprises of the period and of the fully developed legal and civil procedure of the time. As we read, it becomes evident that these documents must have had behind them hundreds of years of organized barter, and that the law which governed it must also have developed through hundreds of years. Babylonia laid the first foundations of this evolution, but as early as the third millennium B.C. we find Asia Minor introducing much which was new and original.

One of the greatest achievements of the Sumero-Babylonian culture in the realm of trade took place at the later part of the third millennium B.C. This was the introduction of a metal unit of exchange which was partly created by, and partly responsible for, an amazing development in the standard of individual life and an ever-growing complexity in the life of civilized humanity. This metal unit was the direct predecessor of coined currency, which made its first appearance two thousand years later, in the seventh century B.C., in Asia Minor and in Greece.

All the events of the time led to a more extensive development and to a more complex organization of caravan trade. The Bedouins of the desert and the highlanders of the Upper Euphrates or the Tigris, the inhabitants of the Iranian plateau and of Asia Minor, all of whom used to be shepherds or highwaymen, now became merchants and business men. The caravan became a definite body, it assumed the character of a complicated and carefully regulated world of its own, and it still remains the same today, for railways and motor-cars have not yet put an end to its strangely independent existence.

While the Babylonian kingdom was still powerful and alive, while it still ruled firmly at the mouth of the Tigris and Euphrates, and while its greatest rival, Egypt, far in the west, became ever more strong politically and created an amazingly high civilization, Indian and Arabian goods found an excellent market both in Mesopotamia and the countries which depended on it, and in Egypt. . . .

Centuries passed, Hammurabi's Babylonian empire fell and the so-called "balance of power" was established in the Near East. The culture and trade of Babylonia passed into the hands of the larger and smaller cities and states of the Near East, her successors being the Indo-European Mitanni, the alternately powerful and powerless Assyria, the Aryan Hittite empire, the large trading cities of northern Syria, more especially Aleppo and Damascus, and the towns of the Phoenician coast. Egypt, too, experienced changes and after a temporary subjection she created, in the middle of the second millennium B.C., the Egypto-Asiatic empire of the great eighteenth dynasty, which survived just long enough to leave a deep mark upon the future development of cultured and commercial life.

For the first time in the history of civilized man the west was now united with the east in a single kingdom and the Babylonian manner of life was definitely linked up with the Egyptian. For the first time in history commerce flowed in increasing volume between regions lying within the boundaries of a single great empire, the power of which extended not only over the Near East but also over Cyprus and Crete. Thus it is not surprising that caravan trade developed at this time with amazing vigor, and that the different states which upheld the "balance of power" in the second millennium struggled in an endeavor to surpass one another in the splendor of their life, in the beauty and magnificence of their buildings, and in the high standard of their military equipment. A study of the diplomatic correspondence of the time is a convincing proof of this. It is evident, for example, that Thothmes III, who speaks with such pleasure of the Assyrian tribute of Persian lapis lazuli and its Babylonian equivalent, considered the cultured world of the period as a single, complex organism, closely bound together by commercial ties.

At the beginning of the first millennium the Sumero-Babylonian, the Egyptian, and the short-lived Hittite empires were succeeded by a single empire, that of Assyria, and Assyria, after a short revival of Babylonia, was superseded in its turn by the mighty empire of Persia. Throughout this period trade, and more especially caravan trade, was in process of constant development and was gradually becoming better organized. It was this caravan trade that brought riches and splendor to Aleppo and later to Damascus, the most flourishing cities of the Near East, and it was this caravan trade that put the Phoenician cities of Tyre, Byblos, and Aradus in a position which enabled them to acquire outstanding importance in the development of commerce. . . .

Organized caravan trade was not limited to the confines of the Assyrian empire. Royal inscriptions dating from the time of Tiglath-pileser III and of Sargon and of inscriptions and bas-reliefs of Ashurbanipal (from Nineveh) show that a series of campaigns into northern Arabia had enabled the Assyrians to compel the Minaeans and the Sabaeans to obey their dictates. Although these kingdoms never became the vassals of Assyria they did conform to her wishes, and from time to time they would send gifts—an unofficial tribute—to the Assyrian kings.

These gifts were, no doubt, a mere trifle in comparison with the profits which the southern Arabs drew from a safely organized trade with Assyria. From this time we may probably date the dawn of their prosperity which is testified by the ruins of their cities, especially by those of Mariba, the Sabaean capital. In the light of what has become known through excavations we find that the Bible stories of the fabulous wealth of the Sabaeans and of their mighty queen is correct enough, and that the events there recorded were even somewhat prosaic. Thus the Biblical description of the Ismaelite caravan laden with perfumes which traveled from Gilead across the desert to Egypt no longer seems miraculous or incredible, while the account in the Book of Kings of the sumptuous gift of one hundred and twenty golden talents, of perfumes, and of precious stones sent to Solomon by the Sabaean queen does not seem at all improbable. . . .

The mantle of the Assyrian and Neo-Babylonian empire fell on the Persians, and this union of all the cultured states of the East into one powerful and splendidly organized state gave enormous impetus to Persian trade. Persia possessed excellent roads which intersected it from east to west and from north to south and had a firm and stable currency, her "golden daricus" which penetrated to every corner of the Mediterranean world. Literary references tell of constant commercial intercourse between Persia and the Farther East, India and China, and this is corroborated by the great influence exercised by Persian art on the development of architecture and carving in India and on monumental sculpture in China. . . .

Even more extensive was Persia's trade with the west, her intercourse with the city-states of the Greek mainland, with the Black Sea coast, with Italy and Sicily, and with the Phoenician colonies in northern Africa, and through these channels with the tribes of southwestern and northern Europe. It was chiefly the products of caravan trade that were exported to these countries, notably the various kinds of incense essential for religious observances, a number of luxuries such as perfumes, cosmetics, ornaments of ivory, precious woods, or stuffs dyed in purple and embroidered with gold. The Phoenician cities of the Mediterranean coast and the Greek cities of Asia Minor, especially Miletus, all of them under Persian control, flourished and prospered on account of this trade; the riches of Phrygia, and later of Lydia in Asia Minor during the early period of the Persian monarchy, were the result of the role which these states played as the middlemen between the east and the west; and last, but not least, we must mention the enormous commerce carried on by Greek Naucratis, the predecessor of Alexandria. This city had been founded by Greek traders on the coast of northern Egypt to serve as entrepôt between Egypt and the west. Moreover, the Greek cities of the northern coast of the Black Sea, though they owed much of their prosperity in the sixth and fifth centuries B.C. to their trade with their kinsmen of the Mediterranean, no doubt also profited considerably by a lively commerce with the Persian empire, both by way of the Caucasus and the Black Sea, and by the ancient caravan route across the steppes of southeastern Russia from Turkestan to the Don and to Panticapaeum. The influence of Persian art in the sixth and fifth centuries B.C. on the Graeco-eastern art of southern Russia has not yet received due recognition in the works of Russian scholars.

But the Persian empire fell before the advance of Alexander the Great, and under his followers the center of affairs gradually shifted from east to west. A similar change occurred in caravan trade, especially in Arabia and Syria. In the organization of his Graeco-eastern power Alexander generally acted in accordance with Persian custom and tradition, but both as an innovator and also as a follower of Darius he wished to go farther than the Persians had gone. . . .

After Alexander's death his empire was broken up and the east was divided into a number of states, some of them Greek, some semi-Greek, some purely local. The Iranian plateau withdrew from Greek influence and became the sea of the Parthian kings, who followed Persian traditions; semi-Greek Bactria (Afghanistan) grew and developed independently; India, which had first been a province of Persia and then of Alexander's empire, returned to independence. A powerful, though temporary, empire was even created there, later separated into a number of independent states. From Egypt Hellenistic influence penetrated in a varying degree both to the northern and southern kingdoms of Arabia.

The growth and development of civilization remained unaffected by this dismemberment of a once mighty empire, and the demand for Indian, Arabian, and African goods became increasingly great. But the route which eastern trade should follow became a sore question in the politics of the Hellenistic world. Pompey placed the government of Syria, Palestine, and Phoenicia in Roman hands. This marked the dawn of a new era in the history of caravan trade, for its market could now become the entire *orbis Romanus*. The whole of the Mediterranean and all the countries adjoining it were now open to it. During the long period of internal and external peace which ensued, the empire's prosperity steadily increased from the time of Augustus and with it the demand for foreign goods continually developed. . . .

Trajan and his successors stabilized Roman policy in the caravan trade and the caravan cities for a considerable time. Petra's turn had come and gone: now it was that of Palmyra and, nominally at least, she in her turn became a city of the Roman empire. This new policy had a favorable effect on the development of caravan cities, and the second and third centuries A.D. mark their greatest prosperity.

ROME AND CHINA

Necessity has arisen for an examination of all the historical data in regard to the activities and relations of barbarian peoples for a period of some length, without geographical restriction to Europe, and without predilection in favor of European history. Between 58 B.C. and A.D. 107 there were no barbarian uprisings in Europe which were not preceded by respective disturbances in the Near or Far East, and there were no wars in the Roman East or the T'ien Shans which were not followed by the respective outbreaks in Europe.

THE CLASSICAL sources offer two contrasting reasons for the movements of barbarian peoples; one, of unknown authorship, lays emphasis upon overpopulation and the need of land; the other sets forth the factual details of historical happenings. Notwithstanding the character of the first of these categories, it has been accorded a wide currency, and has even been taken as the point of departure for extended speculation. Thus investigators have elaborated theories to show how the stipulated overpopulation could have been brought about, and to demonstrate how the presumed need of land could have arisen. It has been argued, for example, that overpopulation would be a natural consequence of a change from pastoral life to agricultural pursuits; similarly, it has been maintained that the need of land would follow from the exhaustion of the soil brought about by a rudimentary system of agriculture. Since, however, the literary tradition cannot be regarded as an acceptable ground for the investigation of the problem, there will be no reason to discuss these secondary elaborations.

When, for any reason, historians have been led to reject the overpopulation theory, they have usually adopted another suggestion from the Roman literary tradition and discovered the origin of migrations in the psychological traits of barbarian peoples. William Robertson, for example, thought that the impulse came from "the martial spirit" of

---

Excerpts from Frederick J. Teggart, *Rome and China* (Berkeley, Cal.: University of California Press, 1939), pp. 229-235; 236; 240-242; 244-245.

the Germans, and expressed the opinion that "their first inroads into the empire proceeded from the love of plunder, rather than from the desire of new settlements." In this opinion he has had many followers, though, more recently, the militaristic motive has been transmuted into "the desire for change," "the longing for adventure," "the attraction of the unknown," and even "the hope of enjoying some of the advantages of their civilized neighbors."

The views which have been put forward in modern times to account for the movements of Asiatic tribes have their point of departure, about the middle of the eighteenth century, in the publication of the *Histoire générale des Huns, des Turcs, des Mogols, et des autres Tartares occidentaux*, by Joseph de Guignes. The importance of this work lies in the fact that it connected the irruption of Asiatic peoples into Europe with events in Central Asia, and thus, as Gibbon remarked, "laid open new and important scenes in the history of mankind." Gibbon himself sought to reach an understanding of these movements through inquiry into the conditions of life of nomadic tribes, and came to the conclusion that "the thirst of rapine, the fear or the resentment of injury, the impatience of servitude, have, in every age, been sufficient causes to urge the tribes of Scythia boldly to advance into some unknown countries, where they might hope to find a more plentiful subsistence or a less formidable enemy." Following de Guignes, he directed attention to the fact that, about the end of the first century of our era, the Huns had been overthrown by the "Sienpi" and had moved westward; but he gave his own interpretation of the later events in saying that "the most warlike and powerful of the Huns . . . resolved, under the conduct of their hereditary chieftains, to discover and subdue some remote country, which was still inaccessible to the arms of the Sienpi and to the laws of China."

Since the eighteenth century, speculation has ranged widely in the endeavor to discover a general theory explanatory of the migrations from Mongolia. It has been suggested that the movements were due to the domestication of the horse; that they were occasioned by the building of the Chinese Wall; that they followed from the rise, from time to time, of military leaders; that they were the outcome of struggles for the possession of pastures—struggles in which "the relatively weakest horde" was forced out of the steppe and driven to conquer a new home. Concurrently, a strong predilection has manifested itself to establish some hypothesis which would link these Asiatic migrations with changes in the physical environment of the nomadic peoples. The idea was put forward that the nomads had been "rendered waterless, and thus driven into a forced emigration" by reason of topographical changes, due to the slow upward movement of the earth's crust, which converted the Gobi from the bed of a sea to its present condition as a great sandy desert. The suggestion met with favor and, as modified in the course of transmission, is represented in current literature by the theory that the Asiatic migrations were brought about by "change of climate" in the form of "progressive desiccation," "climatic cycles," or merely a succession of dry seasons. It may be that "the geographer who believes in pulsatory changes of climate can scarcely avoid the conclusion that great movements of peoples have been induced by such causes," but it is evident from the literature that there are many investigators who have not been convinced that the effects in question have followed from pulsatory or other changes of climate; it may also be added that no instance has been adduced in which the postulated impulse was followed demonstrably by the corresponding exodus.

The survey which has been made shows that the theories advanced to account for "migrations," Asiatic as well as Germanic, are inconclusive, and indicates the reason for the inadequacy of the explanations in regard to the barbarian invasions. The reason is, in short, that theories once suggested have been retained and repeated with endless variations and elaborations, but without critical examination. Since, then, the older views are unsatisfactory, the necessity has arisen for an examination of all the historical data in regard to the activities and relations of barbarian peoples for a period of some length, without geographical restriction to Europe, and without predilection in favor of European history . . .

In the present investigation it has been taken for granted that inquiry into a historical problem must necessarily begin with the collection of data having reference to a given class of events, and proceed by making comparison of the different happenings in a consecutive series of occurrences. In practice, this procedure has led to unexpected and hitherto unnoticed results. Thus it has been found that between 58 B.C. and A.D. 107 barbarian uprisings in Europe were preceded invariably by the outbreak of war on the eastern frontiers of the Roman Empire or in the "Western Regions" of the Chinese. Also it has been found that the invasions which followed disturbances in the Roman East occurred both on the lower Danube and on the Rhine, whereas the uprisings which followed disturbances in the T'ien Shan affected only the upper Danube. Further, there were no uprisings in Europe which were not preceded by the respective disturbances in the Near or Far East, and there were no wars in the Roman East or the T'ien Shan which were not followed by the respective outbreaks in Europe . . .

It may therefore be said without qualification that the barbarian outbreaks were consequent upon wars in the T'ien Shan or the Roman East. Now, wars at all times break in upon the established routine of orderly existence and interfere with the everyday activities of the peoples in conflict, and more especially they put a stop to usual forms of intercourse between the inhabitants of the opposing countries. Hence, when China initiated war in Mongolia or against the kingdoms of the Tarim basin, and when Rome invaded Parthia or Armenia, the inception of hostilities automatically interrupted communications, however well established, across the border. It follows, therefore, that the problem of the relationship between wars in the Far or the Near East and barbarian uprisings in Europe calls for the identification of some usual activity of men which would be subject to immediate interruption in the event of war, and which also might be resumed promptly on the return of peace. The activity which at once suggests itself as complying with these requirements or conditions is that of trade or commerce.

In detail, it is well known that the Chinese carried on trade with the kingdoms in the Tarim basin and, through these and other intermediaries, with Syria. Also it has been shown in the course of this investigation that, when war occurred on the routes in the Tarim basin, disturbances broke out in Parthia and either in Armenia or on the borders of Syria. Evidently, then, war in the Tarim occasioned an interruption of traffic on the silk route, and this interruption aroused hostilities at points along the route as far west as the Euphrates. It seems highly probable, for example, that the invasions of Armenia by the Parthians, while Armenia was controlled by Rome, were inspired by the suspicion that the Romans had succeeded in diverting the movement of commodities from Central Asia to some route which avoided Parthian territory. But these secondary or derivative wars, that is, the conflicts between Parthia and Rome for control of Armenia, brought about new interruptions of trade, and thus led to new wars in more and more distant areas. So interruptions of traffic on the Black Sea stirred up peoples north of the (lower) Danube, and the long train of disturbances ended finally in the collisions of the barbarians with the Roman legions on the Rhine. Consequently it is to be seen that peoples in no way concerned with the silk route might yet be connected with the interruptions of trade on that route through the hostilities which the interruptions precipitated between Parthia and Rome. North of the Caspian, though the operations of the fur trade differed widely from the traffic in silk, similar results ensued when the Chinese made war on the Hsiung-nu, and the disturbances extended into Central Europe, and into Media and Armenia.

Wars which were undertaken by the governments of China and Rome in pursuit of what were conceived to be important national aims led inevitably to conflicts among the peoples of northern Europe and to invasions of the Roman empire. It is of some importance to note that the statesmen who were responsible for or advocated the resort to war, on each of forty occasions, were entirely unaware of the consequences which this policy entailed. The wars of the Chinese, indeed, were initiated only after lengthy discussions at the imperial court by ministers who were well versed in Chinese history, and who reasoned from historical experience no less than from moral principles and from expediency. But the Chinese emperors and their advisors were unconscious of the fact that their decisions were the prelude to conflicts and devastations in regions of which they had never heard. The Romans were equally in the dark with respect to the consequences of their wars in Bosporus, Armenia, and Syria, but here the fact is striking, for the reason that their wars in the East were followed invariably by outbreaks in Europe. Even though, time after time, disturbances in the East and attacks by the northern barbarians are mentioned in the same context by poets (including Virgil) and historians, there is no intimation in the sources that the conjunction ever provoked comment or inspired reflection. So Augustus persisted in his attempts to dominate Armenia, though the actual results on the Danube and the Rhine might have been unerringly predicted . . .

It may be argued that, although in the ancient world causes were followed uniformly by effects, such correlations in historical events are not to be expected in modern times. It is true that at the beginning of the modern period Western Europe turned from the continental land routes to the outer seaways and skirted the coasts of Africa and Asia; it is true that the seamen of the fifteenth and sixteenth centuries changed the pattern of events, which up to their time had been set by the policies and interests of the Far East. So it may be imagined that the new situation in the world is altogether distinct from the old. Yet the activities of the merchant adventurers were of the same kind and were directed to the same ends as those of their Chinese, Persian, and Arabian predecessors. The actual character of the changes wrought by the seamen of Western Europe can be determined by comparing the new situation with the old, or, more specifically, by comparing the correlations in events characteristic of different periods of time both before and after the West embarked upon the exploitation of the world. And since, unfortunately, it is obvious that even the data necessary for the discovery of these correlations have not been assembled, it must be admitted that the essential consequences of Europe's bid for mastery remain hidden at the moment when the Far East offers to resume its former position as the protagonist in the drama of civilization. . . .

There is no reason to doubt that both historians and their public are content with that form of literature which has for its object the appreciative description of the successes of some particular national state. Nevertheless no enthusiasm for the greater moments and more distinctive characters in the history of one's country, no interpretation of the course of world events in terms of some philosophy of history, no insight of practical statesmanship can make available for the guidance of men the resources of human experience. The study of the past can become effective only when it is fully realized that all peoples have histories, that these histories run concurrently and in the same world, and that the act of comparing is the beginning of knowledge. Thus, only by facing an undertaking of new scope and of significant difficulty can history fulfill its obligation of making inquiry, not merely into what has happened, but into the way things actually work in the affairs of men.

ROME AND THE BARBARIANS

The Germans were political opponents of Rome but not enemies of her civilization. The Romans did not use barbarian in the modern sense of destroyers of civilization. Barbarian meant nothing more than "devoid of Roman culture" or later "devoid of Christianity." The so-called age migrations involved no great interruption of civilization, no complete demolition and devastation of late Roman life.

THE LATEST archaeological research has unrolled before us a new picture of the connection between Roman and German life. Its results make it impossible to hold the opinion that the [German] migrations completely destroyed the Roman settlements, and caused widespread desolation in town and country. Although there may have been much pillage and destruction, yet the old settlements were not permanently deserted, the towns were soon restored and the damage, to some extent at any rate, made good. In the most important centers of the older civilization, settlement continued throughout the period of the wars between the Germans and Romans. . . . It was easily possible for the Germans to come into close contact with the Romans and to acquire their culture. Long before the collapse of Roman rule the provincials had settled on Roman territory and had entered Roman service as *coloni,* or soldiers, and had then been employed in administration including even the execution of menial household tasks. Now, after the conquest of the Roman border provinces, they remained everywhere in considerable numbers. The fact that those who remained must have been the poorer part of the population, had important consequences so far as the transference of

Excerpts from Alfons Dopsch, *The Economic and Social Foundations of European Civilization* (London: Kegan Paul, Trench, Trubner & Co., Ltd., 1937), pp. 88-92.

culture was concerned; for they were the people who had tilled their own land in the countryside, or had cultivated little holdings as tenants of the great landed proprietors, and therefore knew Roman agricultural methods well from their own experience. They could therefore hand them on, just as the small tradesman, merchant, or artisan in the town could hand on the technique of manual labor in its various branches.

The peaceful penetration of Germans into the Roman state, which had already made so much progress during the Empire, found its counterpart in the new German forms of government which arose on Roman soil after the collapse of the Roman power. A considerable number of the provincial population, although in a dependent position, became the teachers and instructors of their new masters in the cultural, and above all in the economic, sphere. For Germans and provincials soon began a peaceful common existence in which they worked beside and with but never against each other. The earlier view that there had been an actual war of extermination between the two peoples, a fight to the death which ended at last in the ruin of Roman civilization, arose from two causes. The first is that historical research, concerned itself chiefly with the external destinies of states and with military events, paying less attention to the internal development of civilization, and least of all to economic life. The natural result of the exaggerated importance thus attached to the political attributes of the state was that the same fate was ascribed to its material culture, i.e., destruction and ruin, a complete change of the old order. But economic life, and indeed the whole evolution of culture, often follow paths quite different from those of political development. Above all, those responsible for the latter are not always the guides of the former, and the politically subject part of the population is, in fact, often culturally the richer and more productive. . . . The return to peaceful occupations brought with it also to a great extent an economic adjustment and reconciliation. The Germans valued Roman culture and tried to acquire it. They were political opponents of Rome but not enemies of her civilization. . . .

The wrong meaning of the word barbarian, given in general to the Germans was first naturalized by the Italian Humanists, and by their disciples, the French cultural historians. We know today that the Romans did not use barbarian in the modern sense of enemies or destroyers of civilization. "It is first of all an expression for what is strange in speech and national characteristics"; and then [later] the idea of paganism, of hostility to Christianity becomes connected with it. It meant nothing more or less than "devoid of Roman culture" or "devoid of Christianity"; the barbarians were thus strangers to Roman civilization, not its assailants or destroyers. Gregory of Tours uses the term *barbari* of the Franks and others, even in passages where no evil meaning can possibly be attached to it, as when monks seek their protection and ask for their goodwill. At that time it can have had no disgraceful connotation. Moreover, the Germans speak of themselves as *barbari* in the accounts of contemporary writers. . . . What is indicated is a contrast to Roman ways, a difference in mode of life, with less education and culture, and harder and ruder customs.

The same expression, "barbarian," has been used of other peoples and at other times, both earlier and later, in order to express similar differences of culture and education, and especially of religion. In old Indian literature wheat was called "barbarian food" because it was little eaten there compared with rice, but was known as the usual bread-stuff of the non-Indians in the West and North-West. . . .

Finally, the word also indicates a contrast in nationality. Several sources belonging to the so-called age of the migrations use the phrase *natione barbarus*. . . . In the same period *barbarus* also took on the meaning of "soldier," or "mercenary," which probably arose from the employment of numerous Germans and other foreigners in this capacity.

The Romans saw the Germans as captives of war, as *coloni* (i.e. peasants), then as soldiers, and finally and increasingly, as house-servants; and all these were occupations which were certain to give the cultured and well-to-do Romans in the towns the impression of a lower social grade among these foreigners. Moreover, they were heathens or Aryans, a fact which must not be under-estimated in an age of sharp religious contrasts. . . .

There is no reason to assume from the expression *barbari* that the Germans lacked culture. Such a view is definitely contradicted by the well-known description of the decay of Roman conditions given by Salvianus of Marseilles, who continually compares them with those of the German *barbari*. He describes the latter not only as purer and more chaste in their mode of life, but as more just to their dependents and tenants and even to the Romans who live among them, and asserts that the latter actually fled to their enemies, in order to escape the injustice of their own authorities. The sharp antithesis which he draws in this connection is significant: "Let men seek Roman humanity among the barbarians, for the barbarous inhumanity among the Romans can no longer be borne." He says that all the bad qualities ascribed to the barbarians, such as injustice, avarice, faithlessness, shamelessness, are found just as much or even more among the Romans; and therefore it is wrong to look down on the barbarians, for their circumstances and conditions of life are much better than those of Rome. . . . In the sixth century Agathias said of the Franks that they seemed to him uncommonly polished and able, for a barbarian people. "The only ways in which they differ from us," he says, "are in their barbarian clothes and their peculiar speech."

The agreement of our authors about the relations between Germans and Romans does not hold good only of the Visigoths in Southern France and Spain. The same story is told also of Italy. In 537 when the Ostrogoths were besieging Rome, they sent ambassadors who boasted that since the conquest of Italy they had strictly conserved Roman arrangements; that not only had they guarded and fostered Roman laws and state institutions as carefully as any Emperor had done, but that the religious interests of the Romans had been observed with the greatest care, so that no one had had to change his faith; and that the Romans had kept all public offices, none having ever been held by a Goth. Here the maintenance of the *status quo* is actually stated to be the political program of the conquering Germans. . . .

The accounts of the great destruction caused by the barbarians are explicable if we realize the peculiar psychological effect upon the Romans of the political developments of the time. We cannot expect an objective description of actual events from them. Must not these enthusiastic adherents of Roman power naturally have been prone to exaggerate the unavoidable consequences of a war which overcame that power, and finally caused its collapse? Their despair about its future caused their descriptions to become more pessimistic, as before their eyes the world turned more and more to the new rule of foreign "barbarians," and the latter not only gained political success, but found support among the Roman population. . . . The greater the dislike of cultured Romans for this change, the sharper would be the contrast with the "barbarians," and the blacker the descriptions of the fate of conquered Rome. . . .

The proofs of early Germanic settlement which have been found [by archaeological research] on the most important Roman sites, are unmistakable evidence against the catastrophic theory, and reliable testimony to a friendly attitude toward culture on the part of the Germans who entered the declining Roman world. The so-called age of the migrations involved no great interruption of civilization, no complete demolition and devastation of late Roman life, the pulse of which continued to beat. . . .

EAST MEETS WEST

An indirect trade gradually developed through Western Asia linking China with Europe by the end of the second century B.C. But it did nothing to open a road to China which remained separate, secluded, utterly unknown as if it had been on another planet. It was largely travel to China in the 13th and 14th centuries which captured the imagination and altered the mental perspective of Latin Europe.

BY THE end of the second century B.C. . . . Chinese arms had penetrated triumphantly west of the Pamir divide, and regular intercourse with Western Asia had been established. And now through Western Asia an indirect trade gradually developed, linking China with Europe. During the early years of the first century the use of silk, which at the Parthian court probably dated from the coming of the first Chinese embassy, spread from Parthia to the Mediterranean.

Excerpts from G. F. Hudson, *Europe and China. A Survey of Their Relations from the Earliest Times to 1800* (London: E. Arnold, 1931), pp. 66-67; 77; 82; 90-93; 104-105; 120-122; 161-164. By permission of Longmans, Green & Co., Inc.

The taste won its way to Europe at a time when the unification by Rome of the whole Mediterranean world had given unprecedented stimulus to industry and commerce and had created an enormously rich ruling class with an appetite for every kind of exotic luxury. By the Augustan Age silk is familiar merchandise in Italy, and its Chinese name finds its way into the poetry of Propertius, Horace and Virgil. . . .

The great march of Alexander from the Hellespont to the Pamirs and the Punjab spread Greek settlements over Western Asia and brought Mesopotamia, Iran and India into one world of inter-communication with the lands of the Mediterranean. But it did nothing to open a road to China, which remained separate, secluded, utterly unknown, as it had been on another planet. . . . The bridging of "the most appalling desert on the face of the earth" was accomplished not from the west but from the east, not by the Persians or by the Greeks but by the Chinese themselves. It was the Chinese who, first by an exploring diplomacy and then by force of arms, broke through to the land which alike for Achaemenid and Macedonian had been nothing but a cul-de-sac. . . .

Silk was probably introduced into Western Asia by the Parthians when they had been made familiar with it by the presents of Chinese embassies; after a while the Parthians bought it not only for their own consumption but also to sell further west. Silk thus first reached the Mediterranean by an overland route, via Seleucia (on the Tigris) and Antioch, and this continued to be the main channel of the trade. But with the great expansion of direct commerce in the Indian Ocean Roman shipping from the Red Sea tapped the silk trade, not merely by the all-sea route from Egypt to Tongking which was discovered late and was never decisive in its effects, but also at ports in Burma, in Bengal, in North-West India and in the Persian Gulf. By the competition of these various routes the trade was developed until at Rome in about 380, in the words of Ammianus Marcellinus, "the use of silk which was once confined to the nobility has now spread to all classes without distinction, even to the lowest." . . . We do not know for certain that any Roman subject ever reached China or any Chinese ever reached the borders of Rome by overland travel. . . .

The attainment of Chinese ports by Roman merchants toward the end of the second century seemed to promise a new era of economic expansion; with the Mediterranean a Roman lake and Roman direct commerce extending from the Red Sea to the Pacific it might have been expected that the third and fourth centuries would show a prosperity in the Roman world surpassing that of the first and second. In the event it was of course quite otherwise. Rome's story in the third century is one not of advance but of decline. Prolonged political and economic troubles diminished her purchasing power and a debased coinage upset her foreign trade, while at the same time she was unable to prevent the interception of the Red Sea route by Nubians, Abyssinians and Arabs. A few Roman merchants slipped or bribed their way through the cordon thus drawn, and among these were the visitors to China in 226 and 284. But even the voyage to India soon became exceptional. From the early years of the third century to the middle of the sixth, when the Chinese silkworm was introduced into the Roman empire, the silk traffic was in the hands of middlemen, and during most of the time the supply for Rome was an almost absolute monopoly of Persia. . . . At the zenith of its prosperity in the age of the Antonines silken fabrics are well nigh as familiar in Londinium as in Lo-yang.

Though we may reckon that silk constituted at least 90 percent of China's export to Rome, there were also two or three other items on the Chinese side of the commerce. Pliny represents the Seres as sending to Rome, besides their silks, very valuable skins and the most highly prized kind of iron. Pliny was quite right in attributing a trade in furs to the Chinese, and the balance of probability is in favor of his having been right about the iron also; as there was a large and highly skilled iron industry in North China in Han times, and Yule suggests that Pliny's iron was "that fine cast-iron, otherwise unknown to the ancients, which is still one of the distinguishing manufactures of China."

More important probably in the volume and value of its trade than either furs or iron, though the Romans did not know that it came from China, was the cinnamon bark which held a high place among Roman luxuries. . . .

In the history of world commerce the third century is as decisive as in the domestic history of Europe. Rome's oriental trade which had grown to such vast dimensions reflected the decline of the empire; the great event was the interception of the Red Sea commerce by Abyssinians and Arabs. It was an event the decision of which was not reversed for more than a millennium. The revival of Roman power under Diocletian and his successors did not avail to reopen the all-important sea corridor; Egypt and the Isthmus of Suez were held until the Arab conquest in 641 [A.D.] but there was virtually no unimpeded, direct communication between a European nation and the "Indies" from the time of Caracalla to the voyage of Vasco da Gama to Calicut in 1498. . . .

The silk trade became a Persian monopoly, a situation intolerable for buyers to whom the material had become almost a necessity of life. An acute crisis was reached when in 540 Justinian attempted to fix a maximum price to be paid for imported silk, and the Persian traders refused to sell at all. But, faced with the dreadful prospect of a silkless city, the Byzantine genius rose to the occasion, and a formidable economic problem was solved by the smuggling of silk-moth eggs from Kashgaria and the introduction of sericulture into Europe. . . .

The event whereby the Roman empire and thus ultimately Europe as a whole were rendered independent of China for the supply of raw silk took place just over ten years after the establishment of the state silk manufacture monopoly in 542. Whoever he was and whether he came from Khotan or from Chryse, someone guilefully brought to Europe in a hollow stick, just as Prometheus stole fire from Heaven, the power of making silk. As for *Bombyx mori*, introduced after its long journey into a new world of mulberry leaves, it did not pine for the home of its ancestors, but obeyed the order to increase and multiply, and labored dutifully in its humble way to create wealth for mankind, to embody the visions of artists, to serve the glory of the Church and the vanity of princes. Byzantine sericulture was first developed in Syria, where textile manufactures had so long been concentrated, and by the end of the sixth century appears to have been meeting the demand for the raw material. Then Syria and its industries fell into the hands of the Saracens, and the Byzantines made a new center of silk production in the central part of Greece; it brought there a prosperity unknown since the second century B.C. Meanwhile from Syria silk cultivation and manufacture were carried by the Arabs to Sicily and Spain. But as the silk industry of Syria had passed by conquest in the seventh century from the Romans to the Arabs, so that of Sicily passed by conquest in the eleventh from the Arabs to the Normans. The Normans added to the textile inheritance of Sicily by carrying off Greek silk operatives from Thebes and Corinth as spoil of their wars in the Balkans. From Sicily the arts of silk spread northward through Italy in the time of the Crusades, and contributed in no small measure to that great economic development of the Italian cities which was the condition of the Renaissance. . . .

The accounts of China given by the European travelers in the time of the Mongol empire had a profound psychological effect in shifting the point of balance in the Latin Christian conception of *Weltpolitik.* In this respect the fourteenth century marks an advance not only over the early Middle Age but also over the Classical Age. It is usual to make the voyage of Columbus to America the point of division between the "Mediterranean" and "Oceanic" areas. But the mental transition from the outlook that accounted all other seas as secondary to the Mediterranean to a point of view already "oceanic" began two centuries before Columbus, and it was the outcome of the discovery . . . of the vast extent, population and wealth of the Asiatic lands beyond Syria and of the range and volume of maritime traffic in the Indian and Pacific Oceans. . . . In the twelfth century European knowledge of Asia and Africa beyond the Mediterranean littoral was meager in the extreme, and most maps arranged the three continents with Jerusalem at the center and the Mediterranean stretching halfway through the land-mass from east to west. But after the Mongol conquests Asia was explored from end to end and made known in shape and condition with a high degree of accuracy; the result was a decisive breach in the Mediterranean-centered attitude of the Latin mind and a new sense of being cooped up in a corner of the world, in the margin instead of in the middle of human affairs. Travel had revealed in Further Asia an empire not only equaling but exceeding the measure of Europe in population, wealth, luxury and the greatness of its cities.

It was the travel to China more than that to any other part of Asia which captured the imagination and altered the mental perspective of Latin Europe. Most of the Latin travelers of the period visited Persia and India as well as China, but it is for China that they reserve their superlatives of description. The earliest accounts of China, indeed, aroused nothing but incredulity, so contrary were they to European preconceptions and so like fairy tales. A tradition relates that when Marco Polo was dying some of his friends implored him to save his reputation for veracity by cutting out from his book whatever went beyond the facts, to which he replied that he had not told half of what he had really seen. . . . In Manzi or South China, called by Marco Polo the "richest country in the world," Odoric declares there were 2,000 cities "so large that neither Treviso nor Vicenza could be named with any one of them"; Canton, he says, was three times as large as Venice, and Zayton twice as big as Bologna. But these places were small compared with Hangchow, the old Sung capital, the *Quinsai* of Marco Polo, *Cansaia* of Odoric and *Campsay* of Marignolli, the greatest city at that time in China and, almost certainly, in the whole world. Marignolli calls it "the most marvellous city that now exists or perhaps ever did exist"; Marco Polo says that it had a circuit of 100 miles and 12,000 stone bridges over its network of canals, and Odoric adds that each of the great suburbs outside its twelve gates was larger than Venice or Padua. The size of Hangchow was only less remarkable than its abounding wealth and delicate luxury. All travelers in the Far East in this period tell of the "great ships of Zayton," the huge ocean-going junks with which the Chinese traded to Java, Malaya and India. . . .

The Polos, indeed, before Columbus, may be said to have discovered a New World for medieval Europe. The discovery had a profound effect on European habits of thought. The revolution in geographical conceptions coincides with the appearance of the first scientific maps for practical use, the Italian and Catalan *portolani*; the new knowledge is assimilated to an intellectual system worked out in terms of the mariners' chart. All that is known is clearly defined, and all the interrelations of place shown at once to the eye with a firm precision and certainty that urge on by the very quality of the lines to the conquest of the unknown. The thoughts of the new age extend beyond Europe and the Mediterranean lands. In 1428 Prince Pedro, a brother of Henry the Navigator, brought back to Portugal from a visit to Venice a copy of Marco Polo's book and a map "with all the parts of the earth described, whereby Prince Henry was much furthered." Within a hundred years of this one of the ships of Magellan will have circumnavigated the globe.

One other sequel to the contact between China and Europe promoted by the Mongol empire demands attention. About a decade after Prince Pedro brought his Marco Polo to Portugal printing with movable type began in Europe, and there is good reason to believe that this innovation owes something to the report of a similar process used on a large scale for some time previously in the Far East.

CHINESE INFLUENCES ON THE WEST

Western economists who study the economic and social thought of the Chinese may well regard it not as something alien and irrelevant to Western civilization, but as having contributed directly to the development of Western thought.

THE GREAT geographical discoveries of the fifteenth and sixteenth centuries made many lands accessible to the Europeans. Chinese, Indian, Aztec, and Inca civilizations were studied for the first time, and the Mohammedan culture, formerly regarded as inimical since it was anti-Christian, now received sympathetic study. Even primitive and savage societies aroused the interest of the Europeans. Trade with the new lands had far-reaching effects upon the European economy and economic thinking. The economists who dominated European thought in the period before the physiocrats—namely, the mercantilists—found their chief interest in the new trade. Artists were charmed with the beautiful Chinese and Japanese painting on silk, porcelain and lacquer; designers of gardens turned from formal geometrical patterns to a free imitation of nature on the Chinese model; architects imitated Chinese roofs and other features; Chippendale and others imitated Chinese furniture; porcelain manufactories were set up at Sèvres, Delfft and Meissen, and by Wedgewood in

Excerpt from L. A. Maverick, "Chinese Influences Upon the Physiocrats," in *Economic History (Supplement)*, February 1938, pp. 55-61, 65-66.

England. The manufacture of silk was introduced, influenced not only by China, but also by the Near East, which had earlier imported this industry from China. The building of canals, roads and dikes had already begun in Europe, but was greatly stimulated by the Chinese example. The common people used chinaware, drank tea, and enjoyed fireworks; they decorated their mantels with Oriental objects of art. The Courts adopted Eastern luxuries, silks, perfumes, sedan-chairs, and new fashions of dress and ceremony. Statesmen interested in taxation, public education, civil service, and prison reform, found that China was worth studying.

The intellectual movement in Europe, which arose partly, of course, from European causes, but which was influenced certainly by the stream of exotic goods and thought, is known as the European Enlightenment. This movement reached its height in France in the eighteenth century. Not only economics but many other fields of thought and action felt the new influence. In philosophy Roger Bacon had been greatly impressed with the accounts of journeys to the Mongol Court, and Leibniz and Voltaire were enthusiastic about China. The new intellectual ferment also had influence upon the great religious movements in Europe, both within and without the Roman Catholic Church.

A series of events of particular interest to this study occurred within the Roman Catholic Church. China and Europe were theaters in which a struggle was waged among the missionary orders and societies for a century from about 1650. Books were published and memorials and deputations sent to the Pope by the partisans. One of the parties was composed chiefly of the Society of Jesus, which dominated the China mission until 1773. The Jesuit missionaries employed the current Chinese word for God, a word too impersonal in its significance to please their opponents; they dressed and comported themselves as Chinese scholars, a procedure which offended the mendicant orders; they permitted their convents to continue to participate in services honoring their ancestors and Confucius (Kung Fu tzu), and their opponents branded these services as idolatrous and superstitious. On the other hand, the Jesuits advanced in their defence that their opponents had done great harm to the China mission. Their opposition to the ceremonies for the ancestors and for Confucius (which the Jesuits said were merely civil and respectful, not religious) was regarded by the Emperor as seditious. This attitude of the non-Jesuit missionaries alienated those Chinese who might have become Christians. The Jesuits also showed a record of significant accomplishment. Before the year 1600 they had converted Paul Hsi, one of the important scholars of China, a member of the distinguished Han Lin Academy. About the year 1640 they converted several members of the Ming imperial family, which at that time was being overthrown and replaced by the Manchu dynasty. Under the emperors of both these dynasties the Jesuits were trusted advisers at Court, employed in the bureaus which dealt with astronomy, map-making and mathematics, and used as interpreters and advisers when European embassies called at Peking. Examples of European embassies which found Jesuit fathers advising the Emperor are the seventeenth-century Dutch embassy and the eighteenth-century Russian embassy. . . .

The Jesuits have been everywhere marked as students of the languages and customs of the peoples among whom they have labored. To China, where the civilization was of a particularly high order, the Society sent missionaries of great intellectual attainments, and, as a result, their scholarly accomplishment was signally great. Moreover, their scientific and linguistic labors in China, and those of their eminent opponents as well, were probably multiplied as a result of the long quarrel which hung over the China mission. The reports about China from the two groups of missionaries, and the translation from Chinese authors, were seized upon by a wide and eager circle of readers in both the Catholic and Protestant countries of Europe. There came to be a widely disseminated knowledge (faulty, of course, since adequate criticism was not yet available) of Chinese government, economy, philosophy, morals, religion, and ancient chronology.

There were, of course, other travelers than the missionaries whose reports upon China exerted an influence upon Europe. Explorers, conquerors, traders and ambassadors wrote about China; they seldom accomplished, however, an understanding portrayal of Chinese religion, philosophy, ethics or government. Besides the books of genuine travels, there appeared also books of pretended or imaginary travels, a remarkable literature. These writings began as soon as Columbus had returned from his voyage to America. St. Thomas More's *Utopia* is among the first of these works. Marco Polo's report was long thought to belong to this class. The names of Psalmanazaar, Mendez Pinto, Daniel De Foe and Oliver Goldsmith are associated with this type of literature. These fanciful works are mentioned here because they definitely shaped the impression of the remote lands that was being formed in the minds of Europeans.

Among the important European thinkers who were interested in China, Leibniz occupies a position of particular interest for this study. Leibniz was in Paris for several years about 1675, ten years before the departure of the French mission to China. He praised Colbert for having promoted voyages of discovery, and Pinot writes that from this year Leibniz was informed in detail about the plan for sending a French mission to China, if he was not actually the one who suggested it. Leibniz hoped devoutly for the reunion of the great religions, for the dissemination of the Christian religion in the East, and of Eastern learning, morality and governmental techniques in the West. A letter from Father Fontaney tells of the formation in France of the Jesuit mission and of the scientific instructions given to the missionaries. The group left France in 1685 bearing certificates as "Royal Mathematicians." Another great scholar interested in China was Voltaire.

The soil was prepared for an actual borrowing of ideas from the Orient by French thinkers, and in particular by the physiocrats. Some looked to earlier French writers such as Sully, and others searched abroad for ideas regarding the proper organization of a stable nation. One line of inquiry led to England. In the seventeenth century France and England had jointly defeated the naval and commercial power of Holland. Under Louis XIV France had been the greatest nation in Europe. Why had England prospered more than France? In searching for the answer, Voltaire visited England, Gournay, Turgot and others translated the works of English writers, the French intellectuals read Hobbes, Locke and Hume. It was in this time of despair that the accumulated fund of information about China had its greatest effect on French thought.

Quesnay and his associates concluded from the reports that in China agriculture was held in great esteem and was given governmental assistance; that the natural order prevailed in simple perfection with a minimum of interference by man-made statutes; and that the intellectual mandarins were given such power that it might be said that China exemplified the dream of Plato as the country where philosophers were kings. Reichwein, in discussing Quesnay, says that he was influenced by Chinese models from an early period, but that he kept his models secret and pretended that he was inventing the schemes he proposed. Subsequently, though, when Quesnay prepared to publish his hundred-page work, *Le Despotisme de la Chine*, his interest in the Orient became evident, and Baudeau, his editor, wrote of him as the great law-giver, the Confucius of Europe.

It need not concern us that Goldsmith had previously referred to himself as the Confucius of Europe, in a letter written in 1758, when he was preparing for the publication of his *Chinese Letters*. In 1767, the same year that saw the publication of Quesnay's *Le Despotisme de la Chine*, there appeared another physiocratic work by Mercier de la Rivière. Quesnay actively participated in the preparation of this work of his friend and disciple. In it the concept of the natural order was given a more thorough exposition than in Quesnay's own work.

The significant economic and political works on China were available to Quesnay and his associates, and may have been used by them in preparing their proposals regarding the proper economic and political organization of Europe. . . . [Especially important were the works of] Fernandez Navarrete, a Dominican missionary from Spain to the Philippines and to China, and later Archbishop of Santo Domingo, of Le Comte, a Jesuit missionary and "Royal Mathematician" from France to China, of Du Halde, a Jesuit editor in Paris, and of le Poivre, who had been a missionary under the Foreign Mission Society and an officer of the Company of the Indies, and who was subsequently made a colonial official in Mauritius. These relate to the esteem in which agriculture and agriculturists are held in China, the support given by the Government to agriculture, the Chinese attitude toward domestic and foreign trade, the system of taxes, and the natural order. . . .

The physiocrats occupy a basic position in the history of economic thought. It seems clear that they were definitely influenced by the Chinese. Very likely, furthermore, our twentieth-century heritage from them has retained deposits from the Orient. Western economists who study the economic and social thought of the Chinese may well regard it not as something alien and irrelevant to Western civilization, but as having contributed directly to the development of Western thought.

JEWISH INFLUENCES ON MODERN THOUGHT

Such influence on thought other than religious thought, as can be called specifically Jewish was exercised mainly in the period that preceded the great classical Renaissance. The Jewish carriers represent perhaps the most continuously civilized element in Europe. European Jewish thinkers in numbers were consciously developing Hellenic philosophy and discussing Plato and Aristotle, the Stoics and Plotinus, while the rest of Europe was, as yet, in its barbaric incoherent childhood. In a cultural sense the Jews were the first Europeans. The scholastic system came to the Latins largely from Islam, and from Islam it was largely brought by Jews.

IT WOULD be easy to draw up a list of individuals of Hebrew origin who have made important contributions to our science, our art, our literature, our philosophy. But we cannot thus discern any Jewish legacy of true cultural distinctness, for it might justly be said that these men owed their eminence to the great European civilization in which they had been nurtured, and not to a narrower and less significant Jewish training. There is, however, a deeper sense in which our European science, art, literature, and philosophy owe a debt to Israel. . . . If we search the foundations of the modern way of thinking, even external to the department of religion, we shall discover a real Jewish factor. This factor is, however, particularly intricate and far more difficult of presentation than are the Greek and Roman elements.

Such influence on thought, other than religious thought, as can be called specifically Jewish was exercised mainly in the period that preceded the great classical Renaissance. It is in the earlier "Revival of Learning," that of the thirteenth century, that this influence may be

Excerpts from Charles and Dorothea Waley Singer, "The Jewish Factor in Medieval Thought," in *The Legacy of Israel*, edited by E. R. Bevan (Oxford: The Clarendon Press, 1927), pp. 173-182.

most clearly discerned. Without Jewish aid this earlier Renaissance would have been long delayed and would have assumed a different form. Without the earlier Renaissance the more familiar classical and humanist revival of the fifteenth and sixteenth centuries would have been retarded. The one movement was historically, intellectually, and spiritually the preparation for the other. . . .

Arabic thought, like Latin thought, Arabic culture, like Latin culture, comes from Greece. The Eastern culture with which we have to do in these pages differs from the Western culture mainly in this, that it is derived more directly and at an earlier date from the Hellenic fountain head. Greek thought, as we shall find, was in the charge of men of Arabic speech, for centuries before it reached the Latins, and the first effective contact of the medieval West with Greek thought was in translations from the Arabic. These translations were conveyed largely through Hebrew channels.

The Jewish carriers represent perhaps the most continuously civilized element in Europe. European Jewish thinkers in numbers were consciously developing Hellenic philosophy and discussing Plato and Aristotle, the Stoics and Plotinus, while the rest of Europe was, as yet, in its barbaric incoherent childhood. A reasonable claim may be made for the Jewish communities of Southern France, the Iberian Peninsula, and the Rhineland, as having had the longest and most ancient continuous civilized history in Europe outside the classical zone. In a cultural sense the Jews were the first Europeans. . . .

From the first impact of the Arabic hordes on the Byzantine Empire in the seventh century till the Turks were rolled back from the gates of Vienna a thousand years later, the dominion of the Crescent ever waxed. During the five centuries of Abbasid rule at Bagdad (749-1258) the Islamic world developed its great intellectual system. The language, the law, the religion of the Kuran came to reach from the frontiers of China to the Atlantic. Although Islam was only for a short time even nominally under the suzerainty of a single Caliph, yet the Arabic-speaking world acquired an intellectual homogeneity which was in some ways even greater than that of the Latin West. The Latin and Arabic cultures competed for universal domain, while Greek civilization was as between the upper and nether millstone.

The main intellectual basis of this imposing Eastern civilization was the brilliant revival of learning that spread from Bagdad in the ninth and tenth centuries. In that great Renaissance, the wisdom of ancient Greece played a part comparable to that which it served in the better known Western Renaissance of the fifteenth and sixteenth centuries. Greek writings and Greek ideas gradually found their way into Arabic. In this cultural development the leading part was played not by Arabs, but by Syrians, Persians, Jews and others who were neither of Arab race nor domiciled in Arabia. Many were not Muslim by faith. A multitude of the works in Arabic produced by this culture was ultimately rendered into Latin. This literature is described as *Arabian*. It is the Arabian literature, product of this culture, rather than merely literature in Arabic, that specially concerns us here.

The Eastern Renaissance, spreading from Bagdad, though comparable in many ways to the later Western Renaissance of the fifteenth and sixteenth centuries, differed from it greatly in the character of the material selected for transmission. In the West the revival of classical learning was mainly in the hands of men of letters. It was essentially "humanist," and the poets, historians, orators, and writers of *belles lettres* of antiquity were especially studied. The Renaissance in Europe, surrounded by the models of classical architecture and sculpture, reacted profoundly also in the arts. The direction assumed by the Eastern revival of learning under the Abbasids was very different.

In estimating this difference we must recall certain differences of environment. All graphic art was forbidden to the Muslim as to the Jew. Eastern architecture developed without any direct dependence on "classical" models. The form of literature in Arabic, as in Hebrew, was affected hardly, if at all, by Greek literary methods and style. It was on philosophy and the positive sciences that the Arabic writers and their Jewish exponents chose to concentrate. Aristotle was even more fervently followed than in our own scholastic ages. Platonic and Neoplatonic writings were also studied to some extent, while the sciences of mathematics, astronomy, astrology, geography and medicine, of which the Latin West as yet knew naught, were eagerly pursued at Bagdad and were rapidly diffused throughout the Muslim world. Once this material became available among the Arabic-speaking peoples it was developed along characteristic lines which may be regarded as the *Arabic version of Hellenism*. These lines were, in effect, *Scholasticism*. The scholastic system came to the Latins largely from Islam, and from Islam it was largely brought by Jews.

ISLAM IN AFRICA

It is inaccurate to say that Africa had lived in complete isolation before its modern contact with Europe. The spread of Islam took the form of a gradual transference of culture which included religion. It was an internal affair of Africa alone, not the proselytizing enterprise of strangers.

ALREADY in very early times merchants from the north and east came to Africa, and trade routes existed to the interior. Gold, ivory, slaves, and spices have for thousands of years been bartered for the wares of the foreigner. Strangers settled on the coasts; in the north, Phoenicians, Greeks, and Romans; in the east, Arabs, Persians, and Indians. It is probable that for many centuries prehistoric cultural influences came from the Pacific, from India and the Near East.

It is therefore inaccurate to say that Africa had lived in complete isolation before its modern contact with Europe. Certainly it was cut off from the outer world on the Atlantic coast, but traces of contact with the north and the east are evident in many parts of the continent. The strangers not only brought their wares, but settled in Africa, taught the Africans their arts, introduced new cultivated plants and domestic animals, and familiarized them with new social and political institutions. With the exception of the ass, Africa received all its domestic animals from Asia, and many of its cultivated plants from Asia and America. Such accomplishments as the founding and working of iron and other metals, the art of weaving, the introduction of new food plants such as dura, rice, and the banana, and the raising of cattle must have led to a complete upheaval in life and in social and political institutions. The high cultural development in the empires of Monomotapa on the Zambesi, of Loango, Congo, Lunda,

Excerpt from Diedrich Westermann, *The African To-Day* (London: Oxford University Press, 1934), pp. 266-276.

Luba, Benin, and the civilizations of the Mandingo, Hausa, Kanuri, and Swahili, are clear proof to what an extent external influences have been accepted and have taken root in Africa. All these stimuli from abroad, however, reached the interior of the continent in thin streams and with many interruptions, so that in the interim sufficient time was left for the natives to assimilate what they had received as far as was congenial to them, and to reject the rest or merely let it die out. Thus the New, at any rate in the centers of its diffusion, meant an enriching and fresh stimulation of organic growth but no break with the Old, and even where this did locally occur it had time to close up.

African cultures have always manifested an extraordinary stability and power of assimilation. Neither the migrations of the Hamites and the political upheavals caused by them; nor the settlements of the Arabs and their devastating slave-raids; neither the Indian and Persian immigrants on the east coast; not even the slave and alcohol trade of Europe have been able fundamentally to change the face of Africa. The Negro has remained and his civilizations have remained; the foreign elements which they adopted have been so completely absorbed and adapted that today they appear indigenous. . . .

Portuguese settlements, which early arose on both the east and west coast, show a transition from older to modern times. These Portuguese colonists have assimilated much of the indigenous mode of life and reveal a remarkable capacity for adapting themselves to African conditions. In some coastal centers their descendants live as half-castes and belong to the better-class natives. The assertion that those born of unions between black and white are sterile, or that they unite in themselves the less valuable qualities of both races, is not true. If bad elements have been produced by them, it is because they have an ill-defined position socially, and their education has been neglected. . . .

Among the pre-European foreign invasions of Africa that of Islam is the one which in recent times has brought about the most visible changes in the social and political as well as in the religious life of a large part of the continent. After North Africa had been conquered by the Arabs in the seventh century, Mohammedan influence soon began to be felt in the countries farther south. It may be assumed that from the tenth or eleventh centuries onward Mohammedan groups or single traders penetrated into the Sudan by the trade routes from the Mediterranean. As early as the eleventh century a Mohammedan dynasty ruled in Kanem. In the fourteenth century, following the fall of the Christian Nubian kingdom, Kordofan, Darfur, Wadai, and Bornu were invaded by mixed Arab tribes who came from Upper Egypt, and many of these gained ruling positions in the new lands. Even earlier, between the eighth and eleventh centuries, Arab merchants from Morocco and Algiers had reached the Western Sudan, which had for a long time previously been in commercial relation with North Africa. Finally, in the eleventh century, tribes of nomad Arabs left Egypt and wandered westward along North Africa, part of them reaching the Sudan and forcing the already Islamized Berbers farther south. Owing to these movements the groups of people known today as Hausa were probably forced into their present area. At that time they were still pagan, but from the second half of the fourteenth century they adopted Islam. By about 1400 the new religion had spread so far that the countries east of Lake Chad, and to some extent those west of it, were covered by a thin but influential layer of Mohammedan culture. These conditions remained almost stationary, until in the beginning of the nineteenth century religious propaganda, influenced by political ambition, was started by the Fulani in northern Nigeria and the neighboring lands, and Hausa, Kanuri, and Mandingo, thanks to the opening up of Africa by the Europeans were able to carry Islam into unknown regions. This resulted in the rise of an important Islamic diaspora in most of the larger places of West and Central Africa as far as the southern Cameroons. . . .

Islam owes its progress in modern times mainly to European colonization. The Mohammedans, as traders and craftsmen, reaped the first benefit of the *pax Europaea* and the economic progress following in its train. In consequence they came into the foreground, so much so that in [European] colonial and missionary circles a "Moslem peril" was apprehended.

The bearers of Islam were mostly either political conquerors or merchants. It was to the advantage of the new religion that its first contacts were with Hamitic peoples. Most of the Hamites—Berber, Moor, and Tuareg, Fulani, Hausa, and Somali—are today Islamized. Islam came to the Negroes as the religion and civilization of aristocratic peoples who as political masters or as traveled, wealthy merchants and scholars, richly dressed, and with the claim of owning the one true religion, must have appeared superior to the Negroes in many ways. At the same time they were sufficiently akin to them in their habits to live a common social life with them and to become connected with them by blood. The representatives of Islam were people of a higher standard of life, but this was not so different from that of the Negroes as to prevent a new unit arising out of a combination of the two. The new religion and its civilization were assimilated and became African. The process was facilitated by the fact that Islam recognized no race discrimination. The converted Negro was willingly admitted into Islamic society, and to him the Moslem was a brother not only in name but throughout the sphere of social life. It soon became the ambition of the Negroes, primarily of the chiefs and the higher classes, to attain the socially higher status of the Moslem. This meant the adoption of the new religion and this was made easier by the fact that Islam adapted itself in large measure to indigenous customs and views, and that its moral demands were not exacting. This rising into the higher social class has been an essential factor in the advance of Islam. There was also in some cases a desire to escape in this way the oppression and slave raids of Mohammedan rulers, to which they were exposed as long as they remained Unbelievers. . . .

The spread of Islam took place not through what we call "Missions." It took the form of a gradual, almost imperceptible transference of culture which included religion. It was distributed in the same way as Christianity in its early beginnings, in a way which may be regarded as the ideal one. Its adherents who traveled to foreign lands were by word and deed confessors of their religion and so won for it new followers. This natural way of spreading was possible for Mohammedanism, because practically all its followers acknowledged their faith daily in their prayers and in other religious observances, and these could not fail to make a deep impression on the African. Missionary activity on a larger scale was never practiced; when missionaries were sent from Egypt or other centers, they devoted themselves to lax Mohammedans, not to pagans. The conversion of Africa to Islam thus took place without the employment of a costly apparatus. It was an internal affair of Africa alone, not a proselytizing enterprise of strangers. After the new religion had once taken hold of Africa, its propagators were people who lived in Africa and were or had become Africans. Wherever a congregation, however small, was founded, a Mosque was built and a school which had its teacher. No one ever thought that the money for the erection or the maintenance of such buildings or the payment of the teacher should come from a central institution for the propagation of the Faith. It was from the first moment an understood thing for each congregation that this was its own affair. Islam forged the closest links between itself and the African people. It became a part of this people, and for that reason took such a firm hold that many African tribes can be counted among its most faithful adherents. . . .

Islam has had a far-reaching civilizing influence in Africa. It has given the African a greater self-possession and sense of security in his outlook. The membership of a world-wide religious community, the connection with North Africa, Egypt, and Arabia, the participation in the Moslem brotherhoods, widened the horizon, created new trade connections, and enriched the indigenous culture in many ways. Trade and industry were not unknown in the Sudan before the arrival of Islam, but under the bond of animistic beliefs and the narrowness of clan life they would have needed, without the many stimuli caused by Mohammedan life, much longer time to attain the high status which distinguishes these countries today.

AFRICA LIVES ON

> *Africa is not separate and unique but an integral portion of the Old World culture province. Negroes brought to the New World the high cultures of Africa which have exhibited great tenacity. Moreover, the extent to which New World white populations have received aspects of their present cultural behavior from Negroes is not generally recognized.*

THE SPREAD of Mohammedanism is the result only of the most recent of those numerous contacts between Africa and the remainder of the Old World which have been going on for untold

Excerpt from Melville J. Herskovits, "Social History of the Negro" in *A Handbook of Social Psychology*, edited by Carl Murchison (Worcester, Mass.: Clark University Press, 1935), pp. 211-212, 213, 255-256, 258-259, 260-262.

centuries. The contacts between Egypt, southern Europe, and Asia Minor are well established and the influence of Egypt, which was exerted to the south and southwest, could not have been other than significant. It must be stressed, however, that contacts between two cultures inevitably leave their mark on both of the cultures involved; hence the influence of the Negro cultures of Africa on Egypt, something rarely taken into account in the study of Egyptian civilization, is also to be reckoned with when the mutual interaction between the cultures of all the Old World is considered. Culture was carried in both directions across the Red Sea, and the same was undoubtedly true of the entire littoral of the Mediterranean. The numerous caravan routes across the Sahara, which have existed from the earliest times, indicate how northern Africa, whose cultural orientation for centuries has been essentially toward Europe, was in contact with the regions south of the desert. Africa has undoubtedly been influenced by Carthage, and through Carthage by Rome; in return, the influence of the African Moors on Spanish culture, and, in earlier times, of Africans who were in contact with Greece, Rome, and Babylon must be given full cognizance.

This would seem to indicated that a realistic view of the origin, development, and present affiliations of the civilizations of Africa must hold them to be not something separate and unique, but an integral portion of the Old World cultural province. As the history of man goes, it is not so long ago since what is now the Mediterranean Sea was a series of great inland lakes, with several passages from Africa to Europe which allowed communication by land. The Isthmus of Suez facilitated contacts between Africa and Asia Minor, while the Strait of Bab-El-Mandeb at the mouth of the Red Sea is not of sufficient width to have hindered intercourse. Furthermore, the fact that large enough numbers of Indonesian folk were able to make their way by out-rigger canoe either across the Indian Ocean or along the coasts of Asia and Africa to populate Madagascar shows that contacts between the Far East and Africa have also taken place; conversely, the demonstration that the giraffe, an African animal, was exhibited in China as early as the fifth century indicates that the flow of culture assumed an eastward as well as a westerly direction.

Evidence drawn from the distribution of certain aspects of culture go far in supporting this theory of an Old World culture province of which Africa is but a part. The Uncle Remus folktales told by American Negroes, which can be matched by stories from all sections of Africa, are not greatly different from the stories contained in the collection of Aesop's Fables, or which constitute the medieval cycle of Reynard the Fox, or the Indian Panchatantra tales, or the sacred Jataka tales of China. The institution of trial by ordeal which marked medieval Europe and is still found in portions of Asia is a fundamental aspect of African jurisprudence. The mythological organization of the gods in relationship groupings, the widespread use of mechanical means of divination or of the inspection of the entrails of freshly killed animals to foretell the future, the importance of the ancestral cult, and many other cultural traits characterize the whole of this area. . . .

The presence of adequate historical documentation . . . makes it possible to discover the civilizations from which the Negro slaves who were brought to the New World derived, and thus gives the student a cultural base line against which the behavior of contemporary New World Negroes can be projected. The regions of the New World to which the Negroes were taken are well known, and the history of these New World regions is similarly documented, so that the peoples and the customs which the Africans encountered in the Western Hemisphere can likewise be studied. These non-Negroid peoples with whom the slaves of the Western Hemisphere came into contact are more numerous and exhibit greater differences than might be thought on first glance to be the case. There were, first of all, the aboriginal Indian tribes, who differed among themselves in culture and physical type and who mixed both physically and culturally to an appreciable degree with the Negro slaves. Of Europeans, there were British, French and Dutch, Spanish, Portuguese and Danish. Thus in North America, in the islands of the Caribbean Sea and in South America, the Negroes came into contact with Europeans who among themselves spoke different languages and had differing customs. Furthermore, within each of the regions of the New World where slavery obtained, the contact of the Negroes with the cultures of their European masters varied in intensity; on the same island, house-servants and field-hands had anything but equal opportunities to know the customs of their masters. Finally, . . . in all parts of the New World the contact, particularly between the younger members of the master class and their personal slave servants, was usually sufficiently intimate to cause the results to be manifested in both directions and on all concerned. . . .

It is (generally) assumed that the African who was imported into the New World came as a "naked savage," with a cultural background which had neither sufficient depth nor enough vitality to stand against the impact of the experiences of slavery. It is further assumed, as a corollary to the preceding concept, that even though these "naked savages" might conceivably have had a strong cultural heritage the practice of separating slaves belonging to the same tribe, coupled with the fact of the diversity of African languages and their lack of mutual intelligibility, would in any case have made it impossible for these slaves to preserve what they might have brought with them in the way of cultural endowment. . . . It has been taken for granted by most students, both Negro and white, that the behavior of New World Negroes is essentially European behavior—though, to be sure, of a more or less infantile order. Moreover, the point that African culture could be sufficiently tenacious so that not only might Africanisms have been retained by Negroes in the New World but that African influences might have infiltrated into certain elements in the behavior of the white population has been regarded as so improbable as to require no verification by students.

Yet . . . by a combination of historical and ethnographic methods, it is quite possible to trace New World Negroes to specific points of origin despite the fact that scholarly tradition has had it that these regions from which Negroes were derived might not be recovered except in the most general way. Similarly it has been seen how the Negroes who were brought to the New World, far from being "naked savages," were the carriers of the high cultures of Africa, cultures that, as one student puts its, display "on the average, a more complex development of government, art, industry, and material culture than the non-literate inhabitants of any other great continental area." Not only that, but the individuals sold into slavery represented at the least an adequate cross-section of the population, with possibly a weighting to include more than its proportion of the upper strata, while, finally, Africanisms have been pointed out again and again in discussing the life of the various New World Negro groups. . . . If one regards the history of slaving in the New World objectively, a number of reasons why Africanisms should have been carried over become apparent. The plantation system which was universal in the New World and the conditions of life of the Negro workers were such that large numbers of them were constantly thrown together. Though supervised in their labor, what they did during the evenings was of no concern to their masters as long as it did not affect their efficiency and their acquiescence to control. The Negroes on the plantations must, therefore, have led an inner life of their own, as would seem to be indicated by the fact that among the first specimens deposited in the British Museum was a Gold Coast type of drum, collected in Virginia during the late eighteenth century. It must also be understood that slave children were not ordinarily separated from their mothers, for such cases were sufficiently unusual to give rise to comment. Even when a child was sold away from his mother, he remained in contact with other Negroes whose behavior was not greatly dissimilar from that of his parents. Since the mechanism by means of which tradition is handed down from one generation to the next is the contact of a child with his elders, slave-children thus absorbed and perpetuated the behavior patterns of their parents and associates rather than those of their masters.

Again, the cultural unity of West Africa is much greater than is commonly conceived. This unity, of course, does not mean that dissimilarities are not present, for they are often sufficiently great to bewilder the student. Yet, for example, though descent may be on the father's side in one tribe, and on the mother's side in another, unilateral descent is the rule. In economic life, in fundamental religious beliefs and practices, and in manifestations of the aesthetic, this underlying unity is also apparent. Granting that the slaves could not at first understand each other, this difficulty must have been surmounted when they learned the tongue of their masters sufficiently well to speak the pidgin dialects that arose, and once pidgin was created, it was natural for the unity of West African cultures to become a significant factor in the maintenance and perpetuation of aboriginal patterns.

A third reason for the retention of Africanisms in the New World was the leadership that Africans of the ruling, warrior, and priestly classes continued to exert in their new home. This leadership was principally evident in the numerous revolts which occurred wherever slavery obtained. In the Caribbean and Guianas, in Brazil and in the United States—even on the slave-ships—these revolts went on intermittently, as recounted in contemporary records, and indicated by the increasing severity of the penalties for rebellion that, as time went on, were authorized by the New World makers of law. . . . It must be evident that in the New World these African patterns of behavior have exhibited a vitality and a tenaciousness that far transcends the concept ordinarily held concerning their living quality. It must not be held that contact with Europeans in the New World has not enormously modified the African behavior of the Negroes brought here. The point that cannot be emphasized too greatly is that cultural contact is a matter of give and take, and that although Africanisms have persisted in the New World they are to be seen only as a result of extended analysis, while in Africa European expansion and conquest have left their mark on the indigenous civilizations. Similarly, both in Africa and the New World, the degree of interaction between European and African cultures varies with geographical regions and according to the aspect of culture under consideration. Europeanization of South and East Africa is occurring much faster and to a greater degree than in West Africa or the Congo, whereas the Africanisms of the Guianas and Haiti have persisted more strongly than elsewhere in the New World, the amount of Europeanization of New World Negroes increasing as Jamaica, Brazil, and Cuba are reached, being more intensive in other West Indian islands and the southern portions of the United States, and becoming almost complete when the culture of the urban northern Negroes is considered.

In the light of the description of New World Negro cultures that has been given, it is apparent that the survival rate of cultural patterns lying within different fields of culture has shown wide variation. Thus, in the realm of material culture, little if anything African has been preserved except in the Guiana bush and possibly in the interior of

Haiti. In dress and in occupation, Negroes are like other citizens of New World nations of European descent; in the implements they use, or in the kinds of houses they occupy, they are very generally no different than their white neighbors. In the graphic and plastic arts almost everything that is distinctly African has been lost, while in the field of social organization even the relatively little that can be found is difficult to discover except by inference. It is in music and folklore, in religious beliefs and ceremonialism that Africanisms are most readily seen. Yet even here, certainly in the United States, direct comparisons between New World Negroes and those of Africa cannot be made. . . .

Thus it would seem that both geographically and from the point of view of the various inner elements of culture a scale of cultural tenacity for Negro cultures can be set up which may perhaps point to similar scales for the cultures of other folk. In the instance of the peoples being considered here, these propositions may at least be set forth: Where there has been the greatest opportunity for isolation, the most Africanisms have been retained; while in all cases it is the tangible aspects of culture that have been the first to be sacrificed, the intangible ones which have persisted most strongly and longest.

However, the principle that has been laid down concerning the fact that cultural contact involves a give and take must not be neglected. The extent to which New World white populations have derived aspects of their present cultural behavior from Negroes is not generally recognized. The English dialect spoken in the South of the United States, though unquestionably based on the speech of old England of the eighteenth century, is vastly different from the English dialect spoken in New England, where the speech is also based on British pronunciation of the same words at the same period. The difference is the element of African phonetics, which was transmitted to the Southern whites by their Negro nurses. The distinctive dishes which mark the cuisine of the Southern states and the West Indies derive to an unrecognized extent from the African cooking traditions introduced by the slaves into the kitchens of their masters. The religious hysteria that marks the manner of worship by certain white groups in the United States is so different from the kind of evangelical excitation found in Europe that it can be referred only to influences—

in some cases, indeed, two or three times removed—which emanated from Negro religious gatherings. On the other hand, the things which the white man brought to Africa, like the tobacco and maize which came from America, or the guns and gunpowder and machines introduced from Europe, have deeply influenced many of the aboriginal cultures of the Continent. Thus on all sides a process of mutual give and take is to be noted, a process the importance of which is not to be held the less because in Africa European influences are relatively slight and in America the African patterns have not changed the behavior configurations of the whites to any major extent.

OUR CULTURE DEBT TO THE INDIANS

The colonists learned much from the Indians. The first American farmers found themselves projected into the midst of a new culture, where it was much easier to adopt trait complexes than to invent them.

THE CULTURE, or civilization, of the United States is usually looked upon as transplanted from Europe, but the cultures of the aboriginal inhabitants of the New World have had their influences upon the present culture of the United States.

While the occupation of what is now the United States by England and France did not at once increase the gold and silver supply of these nations, it did enrich them in other ways. For example, the native Indian tribes residing in that territory offered a virgin field for trade. As a market for trade goods the situation was unique. The Indian was ready to exchange furs, maple sugar, maize, etc., for cutlery, firearms, cloth, beads and numerous other articles. The opening up of such a ready market was not only an asset but a stimulus to the industry of the time. Nor was it merely a material advantage that accrued; but the religious, educational and humanitarian impulses of England and

Excerpt from Clark Wissler, "The Influence of Aboriginal Indian Culture on American Life, with References to Traces of Oriental Origins," in *Some Oriental Influences on Western Culture* (New York: American Council of the Institute of Pacific Relations, 1929), pp. 16-23.

France were challenged. Many new tribes of pagans were discovered, concerning which information was desired and whose welfare needed to be taken into account. We are not unmindful of the wars between Indians and colonists and the ultimate suppression of the native tribes; but on the other hand there was more often peaceful intercourse than not. The mere volume of trade, the number of missions and schools, all testify to this; and throughout it all, as we shall see, the colonists learned much from the Indians.

It is generally believed that the Indian population of the Americas came from eastern Asia and had occupied this new land for several thousand years before the time of Columbus. During that period the Indian had learned to live in America, developing many varieties of a culture peculiarly his own. The first English and French settlers learned from the Indian the art of living in America, and much of what they learned is deeply rooted in the life of the contemporary United States.

It is obvious that the first task confronting the white colonists in the United States was to learn how to live in this new country. The first settlements were in the forests of the Atlantic seaboard. The Indian had lived there a long time and had acquired a technique for the purpose which is now spoken of as woodcraft. The details of this woodcraft were taught the first colonists by Indians; and while it is true that the colonists made some changes in them, the woodcraft of the present as practiced by Boy Scout and other organizations is fundamentally that of the Indian. Many Indian inventions were acquired with little change—as moccasins, snowshoes, birch bark canoes, toboggans, wigwams, tipis, etc. The game of lacrosse was borrowed from the Indians. Along with these material contributions to the culture of the United States went certain concepts—as trail, warpath, war paint, scalping, counting coup, peace pipe, burying the hatchet, council fire, scouting, totem, etc., all of which have enriched our language and literature. In the matter of geographical names the contribution of the Indian is conspicuous. At least twenty of the states comprised in the United States bear Indian names, while for rivers, lakes and towns the list of Indian names is in almost equal proportion. In a less direct sense, modern art has been enriched by the Indian, a large number of contemporary painters and sculptors working exclusively with Indian themes. Also the literature and folklore of the United States owes much to the Indian; he is the most unique and most fascinating character in fiction and border romance. In general, to eliminate the Indian from the present culture of the United States would leave a great gap, would remove most of the non-European elements from contemporary American culture. . . .

The Indian had developed the plant food resources of America to an unusual degree. Before 1492 the natives of North and South America had under cultivation some forty plants, many of which are now known to the civilized world; for example, alligator pear, lima bean, cacao, manioc, maize, peanut, potato, tobacco, tomato. . . .

It may be contended that, since these plants were native to the Americas and so once flourished in a wild state, the white colonists would have utilized them at once. It is possible that in time most of them would have been discovered; but it is important to note that the Indian had spent centuries in developing these plants and in learning how best to cultivate them. Maize, for example, as found in the hands of the Indian, is so far removed from its wild ancestor that its origin is still in dispute. Yet, even granting the possibility of all these food plants being discovered eventually, the contributions of the Indian are none the less real, because they were immediately available to the settlers. The annals of the Plymouth colony in Massachusetts tell us how an Indian instructed the settlers to heap up little mounds of earth, put a fish in the bottom of each, and then plant a few grains of maize. This incident is illuminating, for it was not only cultivation of maize that was learned in this way, but numerous other arts as well.

Turning now to tobacco, every schoolboy learns that Columbus saw Indians smoking rolls of tobacco, or cigars. Every form of using tobacco—pipes, cigarettes, cigars, snuff, chewing—was known to Indian tribes in the Americas. The settlers who came later originated no important new uses, so the case for tobacco is about what it was when handed over by the Indian. . . .

Farmers in the United States formerly planted, and often yet plant, maize in hills; this was the universal Indian mode, four to five grains being dropped in one place at regular intervals of about three feet, quite like a maize field of today. In cultivation, the Indian hoed the earth up around the growing stalks, which is still the principle of the mechanical cultivator. For husking, white farmers use a husking pin which, while now of iron, was not so very long ago of bone and wood, precisely like those still in use among our surviving eastern Indians. Ears of maize, to be dried or preserved for seed, often have their pendent husks braided together; this is typically Indian. The maize crib was used by the Indians and elevated on posts to keep the contents dry and to protect it from rodents. The type of crib to be seen everywhere today, which is larger at the top than at the bottom, was also in use by the southern Indians.

The Indian planted beans and squashes among the maize. This has always been a favorite custom among American farmers. He also understood the art of testing his seed and of preparatory germination in warm water; this is also the practice of the white farmer.

The methods of cooking maize are not only the same in white America as they were in Indian days, but many of the Indian names are retained, as hominy and succotash. The famous roasting-ear in all its forms was known to the Indian. Then we must not forget the favorite "mush" of America, which is stirred with a wooden ladle strikingly like those used by the Algonkin tribes. Some years ago American country people still made "lye hominy" with wood ashes, just as described by some early observers of the Indian.

One may still see in American country homes floor mats woven of maize husks, and the method of weaving is the same as observed in Indian mats of the same material.

It is true that white farmers have added something to the maize complex they borrowed from the Indians. Thus one important innovation was the substitution of the mill for the mortar. Later, of course, came various kinds of machinery for the cultivation and gathering of maize, but all such machines are but mechanical appliances to perform more expeditiously the same old processes. It is clear that in pioneer days the white farmer took over the whole maize culture complex entire, except its ceremonial and social elements. Even here we find some curious similarities. The husking-bee, which was one of the great social events of colonial times, is strikingly paralleled by an old Indian custom. No doubt if we knew more of the homely history of the American colonists we should find some surprising intrusions of ceremonials and superstitious practices to propitiate the growth of their crop.

If we reduce these data to a generalization, it appears that the white colonist took over the entire material complex of maize culture. He did not simply borrow the maize seed and then, in conformity with his already established agricultural methods, or on original lines, develop a maize culture of his own. In fact, he has no basis for any claims to originality except in the development of mechanical appliances and the somewhat recent rationalization of agriculture by scientific investigation.

In this connection the maize culture of the Old World is particularly suggestive. At the discovery of America, samples of maize were carried home, seed was planted, and in a surprisingly short time its cultivation spread even so far as China; but the maize complex of the Old World has scarcely anything in common with that of the Indian and the American farmer. The reason is plain—it was the isolated plant that came into European culture, necessitating original experimentations with the new seed or, at least, the adaptation of its culture to the methods, or "patterns," for the raising of other plants. The first American farmers, on the other hand, found themselves projected into the midst of a new culture, where it was much easier to adapt trait complexes than to invent them.

In general, then, it appears that the whole maize culture complex of the United States was the contribution of an aboriginal race. The same can be said for tobacco, cacao, maple sugar and, to a less degree, a large number of other culture traits. No doubt, all the great civilizations of today contain culture complexes borrowed from others and not infrequently from primitive tribes. That the contemporary culture of the United States illustrates this tendency so well is due to the fact that the history of the case is completely known.

EUROPE AIMS AT DOMINANCE

THE FIFTEENTH century "voyages of discovery," so-called, were in some respects voyages of self-discovery. They mark the beginning of the dominant expansion of the European type of culture as contrasted with the more reciprocal cultural contact and interchange that, even as late as the Crusades, characterized previous periods. This change in the general character and trend of culture contacts really marks more clearly than any other single feature the great divide between modernity and the historic past. Since this time, Western civilization has extended its influence more widely than any previous culture and has sought to spread that culture over the whole globe. As Hudson points out, this movement is the product of sea power, though it has also gained much of its almost irresistible momentum from the accruing might of Western technological skill and organized science. Behind it also is the push of the machine and mass production, requiring the capture of ever-enlarging markets. Thus in a movement crowned for a long while with apparently overwhelming success, Europe ventured, along with unprecedented political and economic expansion, cultural dominance.

The pressures and objectives of this Europeanization movement are new, at least in their combination, which accounts in large part for its particular momentum. Characteristic of it above all, however, is a highly organized, self-confident and aggressive ideology. A panoramic survey of Europeanization is vital to the story of culture contacts in modern times. Europeanization is described by George Young as follows: "The term Europeanization is intended to express the effects on Asiatic, American and African cultures and civilizations of permeation by the peculiar social system set up in modern Europe as a consequence of the classical Renaissance, the Protestant Reformation and the industrial revolution. It may be expressed politically by imposing the idea of democracy, in the sense of parliamentary and party government, or of sovereignty, in the sense of suppression or subordination of all governmental organs to the sovereign state, or of nationality, by creating a semi-religious solidarity in support of that sovereignty. It may be expressed economically by imposing ideas of individualistic capitalism, competition and control on communities enjoying more elaborate and equitable, but less productive and progressive communal civilizations; or industrially by substituting the factory and foundry for the hand loom and home craft. It may also be expressed in education by convincing other continents of the advisability of acquiring attainments in European science to their material or even moral advantage, or by exposing the discipline of tribal tradition and training to dissipation by the gospel of the missionary, the goods of the trader and the good intentions of the administrator." But of all these aspects the core is economic penetration coupled wherever possible with political control, in short,—economic imperialism.

The history of this imperialism shows that it arose historically out of governmental co-operation and finally government co-option of the trading companies,—the famous Dutch, English East Indies and West Indies and West African companies, the latter of which took over the organization of the African slave trade. Commenting on the surprising success of this movement over all possible rivals, Hudson points out that behind the extensive trading activities of the rival civilizations there was "no driving force of politically powerful commercialism, no persistent state support for overseas expansion, no active naval ambition to promote innovations in shipbuilding and tactics."

European imperialism has been supported by, or rather has generated a particularly advantageous official philosophy, a colonial-mindedness, assuming very typically the attitude of cultural superiority, which, like the religious fanaticism of the early Moslems, has greatly facilitated the success of the expansion. It is this predominant and now chronic attitude which has stood in the way of much reciprocity of cultural exchange between European and non-European peoples. European culture contacts for this whole period, therefore, have been typically characterized by unequal rather than reciprocal cultural influence upon the other countries and races which were contacted. Thus its increased mobility, which Shapiro points out, has not increased its cultural permeability, for cultural arrogance does not favor cultural exchange. Even in the ruthlessness of ancient military conquest and empire, other societies left the door open to considerable cultural exchange. Modern policy and attitude shuts this door, and leaves only a few indirect openings for the counter-influence of divergent cultures, through the chinks of fashion, exotic curiosity and occasional movements of literary, artistic and intellectual interest. Especially have the Western artists and writers, and latterly the Occidental scientists dissociated themselves from the "official" European attitudes toward alien cultures, and often within the narrower circle of their influence have reversed the official position about the content and values of native cultures,—Oriental, Polynesian, African and Indian. From them, and an occasional enlightened missionary source, the little tradition of intercultural liberalism remaining has stemmed.

Separate strands in this great modern expansion were independent and differently motivated, especially in its earlier phases when pioneering conquest, religious proselytizing and settlement migration were also dominant motives. However, they all converged eventually in an alliance with the economic and political interests at the heart of the movement, and as Hudson comments wryly, "the divine right of trade was not to be denied." An analysis of these economic factors will come later (Part II).

For the moment, the cultural effects of this historic movement will be considered. They were most varied in specific detail, as might be expected, not only as caused by differences of state, religious and individual enterprise, but as characteristically different in some respects according to the national policy and tradition. But whether Spanish, Portuguese, Dutch, English, German or French, missionary or secular, there were certain common denominators. Chief among them was this general characteristic of producing rapid cultural disruption or displacement rather than smoother cultural fusions, thus bringing into existence border-line varieties of incompletely assimilated hybrid cultures. This was due in large part, no doubt, to the rapidity of the penetration. Yet some results depended upon cultural policy and attitude. The Latin regimes,—Spanish, Portuguese and French, although quite as ruthless politically and economically as any imperialist colonial system, seem to have exhibited considerable tolerance for cultural difference, and thus to have produced appreciable hybridization of the two cultures. Indeed they are almost everywhere characterized by a considerable degree of interpenetration of the colonizing and the aboriginal culture. The Anglo-Saxon tradition of imperialism, British that is, with somewhat parallel attitudes on the part of the former German colonial regime, has, on the contrary, the conviction of cultural incompatibility and persistently holds on, often with overt prejudice, to its own cultural tradition. This exclusiveness gives a hard cast to the culture contacts and until recently with the policy of "Indirect Rule," has keyed all educational and missionary effort to the avowed displacement of divergent cultures.

The typical effect of colonial imperialism, then, is an array either of subordinated or broken non-European cultures, dependent upon the degree of cultural resistance locally encountered. Upon the more primitive groups the impact of a highly organized civilization like that of any of the European nations or of America, which is patterned similarly, is naturally disastrous. Margaret Mead calls striking attention to this as one of the peculiar and alarming phenomena of our time. Colonial authorities are themselves becoming concerned with the problem, as one affecting both their policies of administration and their returns on the colonial investment. Little is known reliably as yet about the basic factors and the typical trends of such situations. As the Mead article points out, it is far from being a mere academic problem for the anthropologist, for the fate and fortune of millions is involved. Assuming the inevitability of the spread of Western technology and science, apart even from the continuance of imperialism, there is here a grave problem of cultural adjustment, which needs careful study and more scientifically guided policy. For merely humane motives cannot solve or save the situation, as the comparative failure of missionary activity to do so quite clearly shows. Cultural diffusion must be made more subject to the initiative of the various peoples and more carefully safeguarded from the point of view of the morally and politically responsible dominant peoples. Colonial reform is a matter of some decades of serious discussion and half-serious experimentation, but as yet the problem has hardly been objectively defined. Doubtless, as this excerpt suggests, the cultural anthropologist, as one able to see and study the problem through the medium of the affected culture, should have an important word to say as to colonial cultural policies, now that European civilization is reaching the self-critical stage on this issue for the first time in the long history of its breathless expansion.

Many competent observers do not concede it as necessary that the impact of what we call civilization upon primitive cultures should be so uniformly destructive. Pitt-Rivers, in his article on "The Effect on Native Races of Contact with European Civilization," summarizes the alternatives for widely dissimilar forms of culture confronting powerful culture bearers as the choice of dying out, being driven back or driven under. This description, true to fact in the majority of cases to be sure, is generalized too exclusively on the pattern of colonial imperialism. European forms of culture, however, do involve in prolonged contact, the extinction or profound modification of weaker cultures. Pitt-Rivers then lists eight possibilities of group interaction in the contacts of divergent cultures: extermination and cultural elimination, cross-breeding of a stock that can assimilate, partial cultural assimilation with persisting ethnic continuity, assimilation by physical amalgamation, survival as localized, encysted cultures, cultural survival by passive resistance, anomalous survival with loss of culture and subjugation and finally reverse absorption of the culture invader. The results of culture contact are thus variable enough to be unpredictable.

This is just what concrete history reveals to be the case. There is also the further contingency of the revival, even after long intervals, of cultures that seem to have been completely overlaid. A primitive culture in contact with one that is complex and advanced has slim chance of surviving in any integral way. But even the pressure acculturation of modern imperialism has its exceptions and unexpected developments. In one area, as in many islands of Polynesia, the contact may lead to disastrous depopulation, while in another, as in British India, increased food supply, sanitation, and the control of famine and epidemics may lead to accumulative over-population. In

South or Central America, the Indian culture may resistantly survive while in North America, a related branch of the same culture retreats and dies out. In one case, as with the Plains Indians, the aboriginal culture may survive more vigorously in its mixture with the settler civilization than on its own segregated reservations; in another case, it may survive in shrunken, encysted intensity, clinging on in stubborn exclusiveness like the Hottentot and Bushman cultures in South Africa, or the Surinam "bush culture":—that fugitive but surviving African culture of the hinterland of Dutch and British Guiana that has been reported by Herskovits.

One group, like the American Indian, may, on the whole, spurn the white man's culture, but another, the Negro, with domestic slavery as a different contacting base, may adopt it to the almost complete exclusion of his own. In the Rand, under the industrial system of the South African gold mines, the Bantu tribes may undergo swift and demoralizing detribalization, while in West Africa, the peasant proprietor system of cocoa planting or the "indirect rule" policy of the Nigerian Protectorate may hold intact and even intensify the tribalism of native institutions. An ethnic group under one set of circumstances may participate freely in the blending process of inter-marriage, almost to the point of losing its distinctive identity as with the Chinese in Hawaii or the "vanishing Indian," whom anthropologists tell us survives appreciably in blood admixture with the American population generally, but especially in admixture with the American Negro. The Negro himself, however, subject to considerable physical change through white miscegenation, has had his ethnic identity re-enforced by social prejudice and in certain areas even by legal restriction. All varieties of the mulatto, even those almost indistinguishably white, are accordingly thrown back upon the minority race group by a rigid and arbitrary policy of racial identification. Thus, in addition to the factors of more objective character,—race, culture type, political and economic forces, secondary factors of group attitude and social policy seriously condition the outcome in many situations of cultural contact. These in the last analysis seem to be the factors that account for what is often found historically,—quite dissimilar results from otherwise essentially parallel situations.

The directions of cultural interaction are thus not arbitrarily set, or at least not completely so. Group attitudes and policies can and do make a difference. This, so far as the future contacts of peoples are concerned, is the promising and hopeful factor. As Firth points out, the very fact that cultures constantly change provokes further differentiation and consequent cultural variation. Distinctive human types and cultures seem likely to exist always in a world dominated by cultural exchange and fusion. For even when certain mechanical aspects of what may be distinguished as material civilization spread, as did modern nineteenth and twentieth century science and technology, only superficial uniformity is established. While breaking down certain established folk-ways, these superimposed culture elements must always fit into the particular pattern of the local culture, and do not, when culturally transplanted, invariably carry identical cultural values. Within many Western nations, with a common civilization and governmental and institutional set-up, distinctive cultural traditions persist and function vitally and usefully in the lives of their sub-groups. Many varieties of this situation exist, as for example, local folk-cultures, national minorities, race minorities, language minorities. All of these form the basis of what may be generalized as the minority situation, which introduces into intra-group life almost all of the problems to which the external relations of larger culture groups are subject. They stem, in fact, from the same sources, attitudes and policies, and involve, on another scale, the same issues of intercultural exchange or intercultural conflict, as the case may be. They will be considered in greater detail later (Part IV), but they have much to gain from the application of the general principles derived from an analysis of the contacts and conflicts of major culture groups. Often, indeed, the minority issues reflect and echo the national and international problems. Their objective analysis confirms the general principles that Firth summarizes as "the one generalization of importance which emerges from the studies of culture contact and culture change," —the truth that "on the whole the people of a community tend to respond best to stimuli which have some relation to their traditional values and forms of organization." This premium upon the value of native cultures, even as bases for cultural change and transformation, points to a strong and constructive criterion in observing cultural contact and interaction.

An interesting case of this cultural pluralism, based on the relatively successful fusion of two diverse cultures is reported by Redfield. In Yucatan, Redfield found an interesting cultural situation which he describes as "a stairway leading from modern civilization down into a primitive mode of living characteristic of the past." From the coastal towns where a modern urban culture dominates, Redfield traces the gradations of intermixed Spanish and Indian culture back to the relative dominance of aboriginal culture in the hinterland. In the villages especially, Redfield found interesting cases of Spanish-Indian culture fusions, functioning congruously. He cites, as a particular instance, two altars set up, one to the "Most Beautiful Lord" and the other to the gods of the rain and the cornfield, with their respective pagan and Christian rituals almost intact. The towns he found to be more disorganized and culturally less congruous. In the city, greater variety and the dominance of the European patterns had given the culture shallower roots and organization; there was considerable sense of conflict and caste division between those who followed the Spanish and those who followed the Indian patterns of life. The total picture, however, represented typically the tendency of cultures to blend or at least to interpenetrate, especially where there was less colonial disdain of the native culture. In these areas, the aboriginal culture was still hardy and functionally sound, and had influenced the conquerors markedly. The native culture, however tenacious in fields like folk belief, religion and social habit, had wilted, as might be expected, when confronted with technological improvements and the economic organization of the invading culture, a common enough story in every chapter of contact with Western civilization. A common civilization tolerantly supporting a variety of cultures is at least not an impossibility; and can readily take shape where intercultural tolerance permits. This possibility of cultural pluralism is an important lesson for the Western world to learn, since in spite of its traditional cultural illusions, this is a world where no one general form of culture has a clear or permanent majority.

Part of our difficulty, Teggart argues, comes from the fact that our comprehension of group relations is as provincial and intellectually unsound as our political practice of group relations is unfair and inconsistent. He hints broadly at some causal connection between the two. Certainly, he concludes, we can never understand the past adequately or reliably from the angle of narrow provincialisms, whether they be national, racial or cultural. The process view of history, as he calls it,—by which we learn "not merely what has happened, but how and why," requires, he insists, a world-scale base. Thus the lessons from the scientific analysis of culture, from an analysis of the practical issues of colonial and culture contacts, and from history itself, properly gauged, converge in their more modern trends to give enlightening conceptions of cultural relativity and reciprocity. They point to a reformed theory and practice of group relations in terms of clarified conceptions of our own respective places in the total picture of human civilization.

EUROPE BECOMES SUPREME

Through sea-power the European colonial system was established, bringing about a continual flow of wealth into Europe, increasing accumulations of capital, and incessant progress in financial technique.

THE COMPLETENESS of the European ascendency on the sea from the beginning of the sixteenth century onward had led many historians to an undue depreciation of the maritime achievements of non-European peoples and to an assumption that superior seamanship is somehow innate in persons inhabiting the littoral of Europe or perhaps in the conformation of Nordic skulls. But the fact is that if we go back to medieval and ancient times the superiority is not evident. The Greeks were good sailors, yet the greatest voyage of antiquity, the circumnavigation of Africa, was the achievement of the Phoenicians. The Vikings dared greatly on the sea, yet if we are to award the palm for long-distance, open-sea voyages before Columbus, we must give it rather to the intrepid mariners of the Pacific, the Polynesians. The Greeks of Egypt in the first two centuries A.D. sailed to India, and a few even reached Tongking, but the Arab and Indian maritime enterprise of the same period was quite comparable to theirs. In the days of Islam the Arabs held for a while a naval supremacy in the Mediterranean, while on the other side of the Isthmus of Suez their range extended to China and Java in the east and to Madagascar in the south. The Chinese have traded to India by sea at several periods of their history, and in the early fifteenth century the Ming "tribute-collecting" fleets not only carried out a successful invasion of Ceylon, but even sailed as far as East Africa. The Japanese and Malays also produced bold seamen.

Altogether, Asia has no mean record to show in maritime achievement, and this makes it all the more remarkable that the Asiatic powers so easily yielded command of the sea to the Europeans. But the Asiatics, although they had developed a sea-going commerce of great dimensions in Indian and Pacific waters, could not contend with the newcomers for sea-power; there was behind their enterprise no driving force of politically powerful commercialism, no persistent state support for overseas expansion, no active naval ambition to promote innovations in shipbuilding and tactics. The Asiatic monarchies rooted in their land-revenue economy viewed the sea with indifference, and strove as far as possible to seclude themselves from it; the junk and the dhow remained what they had been, while European vessels underwent continual improvement. For a moment, at the beginning of the seventeenth century, it seemed as if Japan were about to enter the race and become a great naval and colonizing power; but the Yedo government chose instead to abolish its own mercantile marine and seclude the country from all contact with the outer world except the Chinese and Dutch trade at Nagasaki.

Thus the ocean ways were left to European supremacy. In the seventeenth century "the westerners were masters of all the seas of the world." The command of the sea was disputed between various European nations, but never seriously, from the battle of Lepanto in 1571 to the Russo-Japanese War of 1904, between Europeans and Asiatics. Through sea-power the European colonial system was established, bringing about a continual flow of wealth into Europe, increasing accumulations of capital, incessant progress in financial technique and ever greater self-confidence and independence of outlook in the commercial class. Or as J. A. Hobson more bluntly puts it: "The exploitation of other portions of the world through military plunder, unequal trade and forced labour has been one great indispensable condition of the growth of European capitalism."

In the late eighteenth century and in the nineteenth, European capitalism aided by European science applied steam power and machinery to manufacture and to transport by land and sea, thus effecting the greatest transformation in the fundamental conditions of human life since the invention of agriculture. By their new economic power and efficiency the Europeans in the nineteenth century overwhelmed Asia, not only in the military sense, but also culturally. By abandoning the sea and withdrawing to the land, where they were stronger, the great powers of Asia had put off the evil day and preserved their independence for a while without modifying their traditional modes of life and thought; even regions which had been long under European domination, such as Ceylon and Java, had remained in essentials as impervious to European cultural penetration as had Persia and Syria to the Hellenic two thousand years previously. But with the new economy all this was changed. The divine right of trade was not to be denied, all barred gates were forcibly burst open, and the engines of economic change assaulted the inmost strongholds of the mind. And Asia yielded to "westernization." Let not this process of our time be misunderstood; its decisive forces have been neither the big gun nor the Christian missionary nor the appeal of pure science, but the railway and the factory and the dynamo. These have transformed life radically in the East as in the West. Indeed the latest age may claim to be so great a variation as to supersede all former divisions of culture, to be developing a new culture of its own totally different from all that has gone before whether in West or East. This new world of machine industrialism, radio, automobiles, democracy, feminism and bourgeois-proletarian politics seems almost as alien to the world of Bourbon Versailles and "Alt Wien" as to that of the old Forbidden City of Peking, almost as remote from the age of the Spanish galleons as from that of the "great ships of Zayton." Nevertheless, the new world is European in its ancestry; the great banks and the stock exchanges and the machines are ultimately products of the city-state and the commercialism and scientific bias of its ideology.

THE WORLD IN MOTION

Aided by improvements in ship-building and in navigation, population movements and adjustments occurred on a scale new in history. Isolation vanished, and the entire world was exposed to fresh currents.

IT IS no new observation that the age in which we live is especially characterized by rapidity of communication and ease of travel. The thousands of tourists who annually wander from one continent

Excerpt from H. L. Shapiro, *Migration and Environment* (London: Oxford University Press, 1939), pp. 3-4.

to another with a speed and a comfort undreamed of a few centuries ago are symbols of a general increase in the mobility of populations. In so far as any social phenomenon can be said to have a precisely datable beginning, this extraordinary acceleration of population movement may be traced back to the Renaissance in Europe. For at that period in European history the questing spirit, freed of its scholastic toils, and stimulated by its tentative but profitable commercial contacts with a vaguely known world, filled a few adventurous men with the desire to explore and "discover" fabulous lands. Aided by improvements in ship-building and in navigation, the age of "discovery," in the egocentric phraseology of Europeans, began brilliantly and continued down to our times. It was a period when the countries of the Old World were brought into ever closer communication and when diverse races of man in both the Old and New World, hitherto unknown to each other, established a variety of contacts. In this epoch population movement and adjustments occurred on a scale new in history. Isolation vanished, and the entire world was exposed to fresh currents. These new geographic vistas, opened by exploration, and the vastly improved means of travel, introduced by science and invention, later provided accessible avenues into which vast hordes of men ventured, driven by various social, economic and individual pressures. Within the last four centuries one swollen stream of millions left Europe to populate the Americas, another of still more millions poured into South Africa and the Antipodes. Multitudes of Negroes were transported from Africa to the plantations of North and South America. Earlier movements of Hindus and Chinese were now resumed in greater number and spread over wide areas. The forgotten pools of Chinese in Southeastern Asia, marking the extent of earlier dispersions, were flooded once more and the overflow reached to the islands of the Pacific and to remote hamlets in America and Europe. In our generation, Chinese have invaded Manchuria in overwhelming numbers and with unprecedented rapidity. Recently the Japanese also have broken their bounds and have reached into the far corners of the earth.

These migrations by no means exhaust the list of peoples who have within our own times spread themselves in vast numbers over great distances. Nor are they unique as a phenomenon. They are symptomatic of a process coeval with mankind. Man has always been migratory, but never before on such a gargantuan scale. The present magnitude of the phenomenon serves to focus our attention on an ancient and significant fact.

But the facility of population movement, even in its present accelerated state, lacks all social meaning, if divorced from its consequences. And in fact, these very consequences are the reasons for our interest in the phenomenon itself.

SOME PROBLEMS OF CULTURE CONTACT

The isolated, untouched human society, secure in its own mores, with political, social, and religious structures neatly dovetailing into a secure economic base, is becoming more and more of an anomaly. Organized, aggressive diffusion, purposive attempts to induce primitive and peasant peoples to skip centuries in their development, are the rule rather than the exception today.

THE IMPACT of highly organized modern cultures upon primitive groups, or the diffusion of strongly contrasting cultural ideas such as Occidental machine culture into the Orient, provide us with the high points, the sharp contrasts, of a process which in less extreme and easily ascertainable forms is going on all over the world. To the student of stable societies, of social groups developing in isolation, or at least in peaceful self-sufficiency, the process by which a group of naked savages is converted into gold miners or ship's crew or merely robbed of all incentive to effort and left to die painlessly beside streams still filled with fish, may seem so bizarre, so alien to the nature of society and its normal functioning, as to be pathological. . . .

The isolated, untouched human society, secure in its own mores, with political, social, and religious structures neatly dovetailing into a secure economic base, is becoming more and more of an anomaly. Organized, aggressive diffusion, purposive attempts to induce primitive and peasant peoples to skip centuries in their development, are

Excerpts from Margaret Mead, *The Changing Culture of an Indian Tribe* (New York: Columbia University Press, 1912), pp. 3-8.

the rule rather than the exception today. The Soviet State's militant mechanizing of the Asiatic native is the current version of this process which has been going on, within our own immediate historical perspective, since the discovery of America. This rude contact, this uprooting of simpler peoples from their mores, is too frequent to be undeserving of serious attention on the part of the social historian.

But to the student who wishes to regularize his investigation, to define its bounds and work for definite conclusions, the study of culture contact is often baffling and nearly always discouraging. Special conditions are always so numerous that each case of contact seems to be almost a meaningless incident, a hodgepodge of accident rather than a clue to a social process. What possible coherence can be adduced from the Eskimo who trades a gun from a whaler and invents a gunlock of a new principle to replace the broken one, or from the white trader in the Trobriands slavishly taking the native pearl diver his breakfast? It is significant that most ethnologists, especially in America, who were in the best position to gather data on culture contact, have ignored these matters, or embodied them, not in their scientific treatises, but in warnings to government or missionaries—or more often still, reserved the subject for after-dinner stories.

A survey of the literature shows also divisions along nationalistic lines. The British have attacked the problem from the administrative angle primarily—the relationship between the prohibition of head hunting and the birth rate; or the effect of recruiting upon the village morale; the conflicts between native law and British law. A whole body of such literature, in which the little volume edited by Rivers, *Essays on the Depopulation of Melanesia,* is still a classic, has grown up in British countries, with the emphasis primarily practical, pragmatic, immediate. Should the native courts in this tribe continue? Is the Dukduk of the Gazell Peninsula a harmful influence which should be suppressed? Is a political disregard of women unwise in a matriarchal society like Ashanti, etc.? The need of a continued supply of native labor has also focused British attention upon demographic problems. Much of this observation is buried in government reports, other bits are immured from use by serious students in a wealth of invective against imperialistic policies or missionary influences. Although most of the observations were detailed, local, and focused to a point, the aura of controversy and expediency which has surrounded them has militated against their usefulness.

The American literature upon culture contact has been of a distinctly different variety. In British territory even such an impassioned defender of native culture as Captain Pitt-Rivers is moved to insist upon practical reforms such as the removal of the prohibition against a native policeman's having more than one wife. Such discussion of what should be done with individual peoples on special matters of government policy has been a question for the American government and the critics of government. The ethnologists have concerned themselves rather with phenomena of contact which could be treated in traditional fashion—the diffusion of European mythology and religious ideas, the influence of the introduction of beads or the horse upon the native culture. The ethnologist has insisted, historically, that the contact be in some wise regular and normal, preserve some shadow of the peaceful methods of diffusion which operate between cultures which are in some respects evenly matched. The detailed study, not of such indirect and peaceful penetration of traits, but of actual conditions where Indians are and have been in close and continuous contact with white society, is of recent origin. . . .

If, then, we are to undertake descriptions of these states of transition, of disorientation, of upheaval, which are taking place all over the world today and are becoming such a common occurrence of contemporary world history as to forfeit almost the right to be termed social pathology, what type of conclusion can we expect from this series of isolated social anomalies? . . . If the ethnologist approaches a primitive culture in transition, without thought of rendering immediate aid to government or suggesting social panaceas, but purely with a view to adding to our knowledge of history, what conclusions may the social sciences expect?

The answer seems to me to depend upon two considerations: First, to what extent culture contact may be said to follow any sort of regular course in terms of the area where it takes place, the nationality of the invading culture, the motives of the invaders, the period in history when it occurred. Are there, for example, any general statements which can be made about the results of contact in North America as compared with Dutch contact in the East Indies, about the inroads of organized Catholicism compared with organized Protestantism, about the contact with the trader as compared with contact with the colonizer, or contact with a seventeenth-century English yeoman or a twentieth-century Soviet official? Does a uniformity of attack, whether that attack be religious, economic, or social, produce some uniformity of response among the divergent primitive cultures against which it is directed? Is it possible to predict one type of conflict where the invader finds a dense native population with large linguistic units well organized politically, as in Africa, another type where he finds politically weak, linguistically diversified peoples, as in Melanesia and New Guinea; one type where he finds an agricultural population, as in Mexico; another among a nomadic hunting population, as in most of primitive North America? Will one form of conflict typically occur where the nomads occupy good lands, like the Plains Indians, another where they occupy desert, like the Navajo or the Australian aborigines? Will colonization policies, such as the Dutch approval of intermarriage and permanent settlement by officials and discouragement of missionaries, or the British toleration of missions combined with racial aloofness, always induce a certain uniformity of response? Phrased more generally, are one set of similar conditions, whether they occur among the invading or among the invaded peoples, sufficiently determinate so that general trends of culture conflict can be predicted and a detailed study here and there do duty as illumination and illustration of a wider social process? I believe this to be in some measure the case. Studies such as Christie Macleod's *The American Indian Frontier* reveal the trends in American history which were dependent upon the nationality and methods of the invader and aboriginal conditions which transcended tribal borders and ethnographic and linguistic divisions. This is partly true because culture contact tends to be so crude, because the invader relies upon a few simple methods, whether these be the Spanish mission and taxation methods, or the Dutch marrying-in method. Phenomena, such as forced labor, recruiting, or the reservation system, crop up in different parts of the world with monotonous regularity. Such educational agencies as the government schools, taught by poorly-paid employees knowing nothing of the natives, or the native catechist, with his own peculiar version of the invader's creed, occur time and again. The principal colonizing nations of the world tend to standardize their economic, educational, and missionizing methods; to interchange officials between different areas, and to concentrate final authority for native affairs in central bureaus from which emanate standardized methods of achieving and maintaining contact.

Conversely, the economic aspects of native cultures which have been used as the basis for culture area classifications fall into areas of more or less standardized response of groups of primitive peoples to white contact. So if we consider the buffalo-hunting Plains Indian, the hunting, rice-gathering Central Algonkian, or the salmon-fishing Indian of the coast of British Columbia, each has a background of common usage which must confront this organized attack of the more complex culture. The culture area concept, taking as it does, particular cognizance of economic conditions and material culture, is exceedingly relevant to this problem of contact, as the form which the economic conflict takes is so often determinate of the forms of conflict in other fields of culture. The extreme individuality of different Melanesian cultures pales somewhat in the fact of their characteristic political and linguistic disunity and magical outlook, as confronted with re-cruiting and Methodism. So we may say with safety, I believe, that the processes of organized contact between primitive and civilized man, or between civilized and simple society at the present time, show sufficiently general tendencies so that any detailed study of one group at one time will be, not an isolated record of the fate of some five hundred aborigines, but data upon much wider historical events.

TYPES OF CULTURE CONTACT

The most conspicuous difference between the culture contact in India and Indonesia and those of Oceania and the aborigines of Australia and Tasmania lies in the capacity shown by the Hindu and Moslem cultures to resist European proselytism and to preserve almost all their traditional cultural values while the barbarian cultures of Oceania and Australasia have been powerless to preserve the essential elements of their cultures.

THE EFFECTS of the contact of two dissimilar, but interacting culture-trends, can be grouped under the following classes:—

(1) Immigrant and more powerful culture-bearers may so revolutionize the environmental conditions of the native and culturally weaker people that, incapable of re-adaptation, they become eliminated and die out—examples: Tasmanians, and some Australian, Polynesian and Melanesian tribes; or

(2) The elimination of the people of a weaker culture may be disguised by substitution of miscegenated stocks, more adaptable to the changed cultural conditions, which gradually take the place of a former population—instance, the Maoris of New Zealand.

(3) A people forcibly removed from their own cultural environment and transplanted into another, where they are preserved and bred, may become adapted to new cultural conditions, with a minimum of change in ethnic continuity.

(4) Gradual culture assimilation and amalgamation of aboriginal people by immigrant people. Example, the Polynesian assimilation of Melanesian or Australoid peoples.

(5) The relative segregation of small cultural pockets maintaining themselves within the sphere of influence of a stronger culture. We might perhaps cite some of the Lolo communities near the Tibeto-Burmese border in Southern China.

Excerpt from G. Pitt-Rivers, "The Effect on Native Races of Contact with European Civilisation," *Man,* Vol. 27 (January 1927), pp. 3-5. By permission of the Royal Anthropological Institute, London.

(6) Strong immigrant culture-bearers may meet with strong and persistent opposition on the part of natives who may resist cultural contamination with great determination. I think particularly of the Balinese peaceful, but stubborn, rejection of all European cultural influences, or of the traditional Chinese intolerance of European proselytism, provoking, however, a more emphatic demonstration.

(7) Immigrant culture-bearers may succeed in extinguishing an aboriginal culture, but yet fail either to extinguish or to assimilate its bearers, who appear to survive the condition of cultural disequilibrium. May we here not cite some African examples, among, for instance, Basuto or Bantu tribes; and finally—

(8) The indigenous elements may eventually absorb the immigrants and assimilate them with or without taking over much of the culture of the latter. Here, for instance, we may think of the assimilative tendencies of the Chinese, who appear to have assimilated even the Chinese Jews who in physical features, language, dress, habit and customs, in fact in everything except their religion, appear Chinese.

In every instance where one culture strongly influences another, a condition of culture disequilibrium is engendered, followed by the extinction or modification of the weaker culture and a variable degree of re-adaptation accompanied by a greater or lesser change in ethnos. . . .

The cultural clash resulting from one racial group dominating another does not always initiate a state of depopulation—it may promote the opposite. India provides an instance. . . . The most conspicuous difference between the culture-clash in India and Indonesia with their teeming populations and the culture-clash in the depopulated islands of Oceania, or as applied to the aborigines of Australia and Tasmania, lies in the capacity shown by the Hindu and Moslem cultures of the former group to resist the European proselytism which they despise, and to preserve almost intact their traditional cultural values, however drastically their economic and political evolution may have suffered modification, whilst the barbarian cultures of Oceania and Australasia, conscious of their cultural and intellectual inferiority, have been powerless to preserve the essential elements of their cultures against proselytism.

In India native unrest became serious only in recent years. There is no question, here, of the eradication of native culture; native culture is highly evolved, complex, and resistant, and the tiny population of white colonists is quite incapable of imposing its culture upon the intellectual classes and leaders of thought, either Hindu or Moslem, who are the guardians of the culture-forms of the different races in the country; neither is it able by its influence so to modify the social organization or so to revolutionize the living conditions of the people that they are in danger of losing all interest in life and dying out, like the less highly cultured and more defenseless Polynesians and Melanesians of the Pacific. . . .

The attempts at Europeanization, to the extent in which they have met a successful resistance, have, as an inevitable consequence, produced, and been the measure of, the "unrest" that distinguishes the native problem in those countries; whilst the impotence of the more lowly and barbarian cultures to make an effective resistance has left the natives ill-equipped, and without the will, to survive the destruction of all the values that gave meaning and zest to their lives. The same forces that have in the first instance only succeeded in modifying and hampering the normal expression of native culture-forms at the cost of social disintegration, have in the other, led to the extirpation of native culture forms, with the consequence that the natives have failed altogether to adapt themselves.

THE EFFECTS OF WESTERN CULTURE UPON
PRIMITIVE PEOPLES

The great technical efficiency of our civilization, the desires for extension of sovereignty, for economic exploitation of new natural resources, for new markets for our expanding productive system, and for the religious proselytization of those whom we conceive to be lacking in certain of the higher values, all have combined to affect, and in some cases to shatter, the framework of institutions and values which primitive peoples have built up with difficulty over long periods of time.

WHEN PEOPLES are in contact with each other they may live side by side at peace, or at war, without their customs being much affected by those of their neighbors. More often they influence one another. They may, like the pastoral Bahima and agricultural Bairu of Ankole, fit into each other's mode of life while preserving each their own separate institutions. They may, like a Nupe community in Northern Nigeria, described by S. F. Nadel, consist originally of distinct cultural groups which, through sharing a common residence, have come to adjust themselves to one another so closely by intermarriage, economic co-operation, and religious interdependence that they now form essentially sections of a single small "commonwealth." For this Nadel has borrowed a term from biology, and speaks of such a state as "social symbiosis." Frequently, when the communities remain separate, they take over ideas about technical processes and ways of behaving from one another, a process that is generally known as diffusion of culture. Some primitive Australian tribes, for instance, are even now consciously adopting a more complicated system of kinship and marriage groupings from other tribes that have it, apparently because they find it useful to them in social relations with these tribes, and feel some inferiority without it.

More radical, and more important to us today, are the changes wrought by the contact of higher civilizations with more primitive

Excerpts from Raymond Firth, *Human Types* (Edinburgh: Thomas Nelson and Sons, Ltd., 1938), pp. 186-187; 188-189; 190-194.

peoples. This has often happened in the past, as the influence of Chinese civilization on the "barbarians" of its frontiers, of Rome on some of our own ancestors, and of the Mohammedan rule on the desert tribes of the Near East and of North Africa bear witness. Here it has not been merely a matter of acculturation, of adding new items to a system of which the main fabric still preserves its form, but of revolutionizing ways of life and beliefs, and imposing new political and legal institutions. Moreover, these radical changes have often been forced upon people who in the initial stages have been unwilling to accept what has been given to them. . . .

The great technical efficiency of our civilization, the desires for extension of sovereignty, for economic exploitation of new natural resources, for new markets for our expanding productive system, and for the religious proselytization of those whom we conceive to be lacking in certain of the higher values, all have combined to affect, and in some cases to shatter, the framework of institutions and values which primitive people have built up with difficulty over long periods of time. . . .

Anthropologists are able to observe in the field—what happens, for instance, in a polygynous society when monogamous marriage is made the legal or religious rule; in an agricultural system when ploughs are introduced to replace the native hoes; in a system of land tenure when titles to the soil depend upon official registration and not upon the consensus of tribal opinion or a chief's judgment; in village and house-hold economy when many of the able-bodied men go off to work for wages; or in the system of kinship obligations and mutual economic assistance when new crops are grown for an external market. To supplement this, both native traditions as to what used to happen in the olden days, and documentary records from European sources are drawn upon. . . .

An instance of the type of result obtained may be cited from the work of Audrey Richards in Northern Rhodesia. She has shown that among the Babemba the Government has recognized the chief, but the hereditary religious functionaries who formerly constituted his tribal council have been ignored, have no definite status or duties under the new régime, and receive no reward for any services that they may perform. At a time, then, when a series of new legislative

acts are demanded by the Government from the chief, he is left
without the advice or check of a body which represents tribal opinion.
And since many former economic assets of the chief have disappeared
under the modern conditions, with the abolition of war, and of ele-
phant hunting for ivory, the discouragement of tribute labor, the
introduction of some of the European standards of a money economy,
the chief can no longer afford to run his native advisory and administrative service as before. And the revenues he receives from the
Government are not sufficient to supply this deficiency. The result
is that successive governments in Rhodesia have complained that the
chiefs are failing to make new enactments to better the condition of
their people—though it is difficult to see how in the present conditions
they could be effectively enforced, despite the fact that the tribal
councils still do a great deal of unpaid work.

Another instance of the disintegrating influence of cultural com-
pulsives from an external source comes from Samoa, in a study by
F. M. Keesing. In olden days every Samoan community had as its
mistress of ceremonies a high-born virgin known as the *taupo*, who
was the pride of the village, and in some degree the center of its
political and social organization. The *taupo* was given the foremost
place of honor in ceremonies, she mixed the kava drink of chiefs and
orators on high ritual occasions, she had charge of the entertainment
of visitors, she was carefully guarded until marriage and her hand
was finally sought by chiefs for her powerful connections as well as
her beauty, when the wedding took place with huge exchanges of
valued property. The institution of the *taupo* thus served as a means
of enhancing social display and hospitality, of intensifying economic
life and the distribution of goods, and of securing strategic alliances
and valuable kinship connections in the political sphere. Nowadays,
however, few *taupo* are to be found, and even in the more conservative communities where one exists, her activities have become much
attenuated. The reasons for this show the changes that have come to
Samoan life in general, even though the people pride themselves on
their conservatism. The missions that were established in Samoa a
century ago attacked the *taupo* institution directly. Her entourage of
young women was frowned upon because they were suspected of
loose living, and certain of the dances in which she took the most

prominent part were prohibited entirely for a time. The method of preparing the kava drink by having the girls of the *taupo's* entourage chew the root was abandoned in favor of having young men pound it up with stones. The custom of polygyny under which the chiefs took many of the *taupo* as wives was abolished, so that there became "a glut in the *taupo* marriage market." Again, the custom of publicly testing the virginity of the *taupo* at her marriage came under the missionary ban. Other indirect factors played an important part. Owing to outlets in Church and other activities the position of women in Samoa has subtly changed, giving them more independence and power in public life. As a result, other women, especially those of high rank, have secured privileges that have militated against the preeminence of the *taupo* in village life. Then the frequent journeyings from one district to another and one island to another, which gave occasion for elaborate entertainment and exchange of wealth, have tended to be frowned upon by the European authorities, and attempts have been made to curb "wasteful expenditure" that seemed to hamper economic development. Moreover, with the coming of European government and the passing of local warfare, there was no longer the same function for the *taupo* to fulfill in cementing political alliances. The passing of the *taupo* system is not unregretted. A Samoan said, "It is hard not to be ashamed before visitors if we have no *taupo* to entertain them."

Such examples give us generalizations of a narrow range, but of suggestive value for comparison. They show how institutions in the native life are bound together, so that changes in one may have deep and often unsuspected repercussions upon others. They show also how radically an institution which is well established and vital in the old native life may break down under the impact of external forces, and yet while there are still traditional needs to be satisfied the people will cling to what remnants of it they can. In this cultures appear to differ; some are much more resistant to the processes of change than others, though we are not yet able to say with certainty in all cases why this should be so.

But one generalization of importance which emerges from the studies of culture contact and culture change is that on the whole the people of a community tend to respond best to stimuli which have some relation to their traditional values and forms of organization. The recognition of this principle has been put into practice by some governments in the form of the system of Indirect Rule. The importance of traditional forces is seen in the way in which after a long subjection to external forces and apparently a radical alteration in their way of life or thinking a people often break back once again to their ancient practices, or mingle ancient practices and beliefs with modern forms. An example of this is given by the many native religious cults which have sprung up in part as a reaction against European influence, and which combine elements of Christianity with old beliefs and customs in a way which strikes the casual observer as a travesty of religion. Often these tend to acquire a political and anti-European bias. Such are the Hauhau cult of the Maori, the Watch-Tower movement in its local African form, the Pa Chin Hao of the Chins of Burma, and various other prophetic cults of New Guinea and elsewhere. These must be regarded not as mere delusion, or the product of political "agitation," or a reversion to savagery, but as phenomena resulting from culture-strain, and the difficulty of making the old and the new institutions and values meet in a harmonious solution.

Culture change is not a mechanical process; it depends on the ideas of the people who are affected by it, and successful adjustment is not a simple matter of introducing "development," "enlightenment," and "progress" to backward races. Careful study is required in order to bring about the results that are aimed at. This is so even if there be complete and clear agreement as to the kinds of results that are most to be desired. But in many cases this agreement does not exist; there is conflict of opinion as to what the ultimate aims of culture change should be on the broadest issues—for instance, whether we want an educated Christian Africa, or an educated Africa not bound to any one religious faith; whether we want a democratic Africa with Negroes in Parliament, or representation of native interests in the partnership of black and white through some other channels.

CULTURE CONTACT IN CENTRAL AMERICA

When the Spaniards came to Yucatan, they performed a major operation on the native culture. Upon it they transplanted new organs, new customs, and new beliefs. Where isolation allowed it to happen the graft took, and the re-made organism grew, flourished, developed, and elaborated its parts; and the parts became intimately interdependent upon one another. Some of the parts were Spanish grafts; they, like the Indian elements, developed and merged into a single new structure. But changes occurred; technological improvements and economic events stirred even the distant forest dwellers. Now the disorganizing influences are increasing, both in city and in village.

THE INTENSITY of early Spanish influence upon Maya culture decreases as one goes down the stairway of Yucatan.[1] But the two most remote communities, peasant village and tribal village, have

Excerpts from Robert Redfield, "The Second Epilogue to Maya History," in *Supplementary Publication No. 28* (Washington: Carnegie Institution of Washington, 1937), pp. 12-22.

[1] Dr. Redfield gives us the setting for this discussion as follows: "Think of Yucatan as a sort of stairway from modern civilization down into a primitive mode of living characteristic of the past. The stairway runs southeastward. On the topmost step, in the northwestern corner of the peninsula, is Merida, the one city, eight times as large as the community next in size. Here the Spaniards established the center of the new civilization and authority they brought to Yucatan, and from here ever since have emanated practically all influences for further culture change. We have made a study of the mode of living of the people of this city. The roads and railroads of Yucatan spread fanwise out from Merida, serving the area of dense population in the northwest, where the sisal fiber is cultivated. We have made a study of a town on the railroad in this area, the second step on the stairway. The people of this town, mixed-bloods and Indians like those of the capital city, have been in contact with the city, especially in the last thirty years, since when the railroad has connected them with Merida. But compared with the city dweller, these townsmen are isolated provincials. Beyond the railroad, still further southeastward, there is a higher, denser bush where no sisal is commercially produced. The settlements here are occupied by Indians who are truly rustic peasants. They pay taxes, have simple schools, and even vote. But to the village on this third stair which we chose for study, it is four hours' walk through the forest from the nearest road. The villagers here, much more than do the townsmen, cling to the ancient ways. Beyond this group of villages there is a zone of

a similar heritage of almost pure Indian blood and of mixed Indian-Spanish culture. It was the War of the Castes that separated these two Indian village groups, and made two cultures out of what, a hundred years ago, was probably one culture. Second, the degree of isolation of the communities since the expansive period of early Spanish occupation and missionizing, increases as one goes down the stairway. As I have said, the tribal village has remained out of touch with civilization for generations. But new ideas, from baseball and Paris fashions to communism and theosophy, keep the way of life agitated in the city. In this respect, the town and peasant village occupy two intermediate points.

When the four communities are compared, first, to see the extent to which there is a common culture throughout the peninsula, one is struck by the great degree to which modes of living are the same, even in tribal village and in modern city. If a lower or middle class city dweller were to go to the remotest village, he would find a rude settlement of half-hostile primitive people, and would probably dislike it very much and wish to be back home. As they would speak Maya, and he, perhaps only Spanish, he could not talk with them. Nevertheless he would find much of their mode of living familiar. Indian ways have penetrated into the city, and Spanish ways into the Indian villages to such an extent that there is a great deal of customary life which the native of either city or remote village would find perfectly commonplace and understandable in the culture of the other. I cannot here take the time to depict for you in detail that world of conventional meanings which the Spanish-Indian contact has

---

uninhabited forest. It has been a sort of no-man's-land ever since the war between Indians and whites which broke out in the 1850's and never really came to an end. Beyond this zone one reaches the bottom step on the stairway of Yucatan: a group of villages of Indians that never capitulated to the government after the War of the Castes. Although the natives here were christianized by missionaries in the colonial period, and although at one time a Spanish road, lined by Spanish estates, ran through this territory, European occupation was later forced to withdraw. And today the natives live secluded in a forest penetrated only by chicle gatherers, traveling-merchants, and an occasional archaeologist. They are the last Maya Indians to preserve tribal independence.

Four communities, one on each step of the stair, have been studied. To avoid the use of the unfamiliar place names, I will refer to them as the city, the town, the peasant village, and the tribal village."

made general and more or less uniform throughout Yucatan. City-born laborer and distant tribesman have much the same knowledge of how to measure and prepare a cornfield, how to sow, harvest, and store the maize, and how to prepare it in the most usual edible forms. So also are general many elements of clothing—sandals, which are Indian, and hats and short trousers, which are European. General throughout are the methods of animal husbandry, of raising sugar-cane, and the use of many metal tools, rice, coffee, chocolate beaters and pots, certain herbal medicine, the making of and sleeping in hammocks, the raising of turkeys and the feeling that they are appropriate for festal eating. But less tangible elements of living are as widely and generally understood. Everywhere the same names and something of the personal and religious qualities are given to God, the Virgin, Christ, and the principal saints; the chief Catholic prayers are known; the sign of the cross has religious or magical power, there is understanding of vespers, octave, and novena. Everywhere oaths may be taken by kissing the cross, and kneeling is a sign of respect. The Christian calendar, including the week, and alphabetic writing, are known and to some degree used everywhere. In all the communities the danger of the evil eye is recognized. So also it is believed that sickness and other misfortune may come with intangible "winds" that invest persons on certain occasions. All babies are carried on the hip after they are about three months old, and it is thought appropriate, or at least traditional, to make a certain little ceremony the first time this is done. So, too, it is correct to rinse out one's mouth before and after eating, and it is known how to whistle a certain whistle when you want wind to come. It is everywhere understood that foods and medicines fall into one of two curious and non-rational categories: "cold" or "hot."

The essentials of kinship organization are basically the same throughout the area. Tribal Indian and city workman of Spanish blood can equally understand the notions of the proper subordination of women to men, the propriety of respect of elders by young people, and especially the institution of godparenthood with its concomitant relationship between parents and godparents of a baptized child. Whether Maya or Spanish be spoken, the terms used for kinsmen, with a few small exceptions, denote the same categories of relatives everywhere.

This may be summarized by saying that the Indian techniques of raising and cooking corn, of building thatched houses, of making sandals or hammocks, and a number of other things, have survived and become a part of the present culture of Yucatan. With these elements have also persisted, even in the city, bits of belief, little domestic rituals, and fragments of lore. These latter have no doubt been carried on by Indian women, as wives, mistresses, household servants, and nurses of Spanish children. On the other hand, while much European material culture has been completely assimilated, the striking fact is that the general basis of European social organization and the chief forms of the Catholic religion have also been assimilated, even by the most remote Indians of Quintana Roo.

I turn now to a comparison of the four communities with respect not as to how their cultures are alike, but as to how they differ in the presence or absence of Indian or of European elements. It is to be expected that pagan culture will be found best represented in the peripheral villages. This is true. In both the peasant and tribal villages, the pagan gods of the bush, of the cornfield, and of the village itself, are felt to be very real and close. In both communities, there is a series of agricultural ceremonies, the most important of which are carried on by special shaman-priests. These ceremonies include features which are beyond doubt Indian in origin. A special bark-beer is made and offered to the deities, as are certain ritual breadstuffs, made of maize and squash seeds. These are grouped on altars in an order symbolic of a quadrilaterally conceived cosmos, and of a hierarchy of rain and forest gods especially associated with the natural wells, and with the east. Women are excluded from ceremonies; sacred water is brought from a hidden cenote, or well; turkeys are strangled with bark-beer in their throats, as they are held by four men who bear the same names as those borne by the ancient priests who held down the arms and legs of a sacrificed human victim. There is a special group of bee-gods, and special ceremonies to these.

These remarks only begin to mention the Indian elements that are still present in the peripheral villages. Furthermore, there are pagan elements present in the remotest of the four communities, that are not to be found in the others: a dance of women, with gourd rattles, around a table-altar; lustrative retreat for the shaman-priest; the use of what are apparently men's houses, one for each tribal band.

This is to be expected. What is more surprising, at first, is that some elements of Catholic ritual are more vigorously and completely present in the most peripheral community than in any of the other three. If we except from our comparison the relatively few strictly pious and conforming Catholics in the city, and confine our comparison to the lower and middle class mixed-blood people who constitute most of the population of the city and all of that of the town, it may be declared that, in matters of religious form, the tribal village is both more pagan and more Catholic than is any of the other communities. Only in the remote village is there a daily recitation of Catholic prayers (some in Maya, some in Spanish, and some in Latin), and only there are Masses frequently celebrated. These Indians have been without direct contact with priests of the church for several generations. Their supreme religious officer is a native, with an admixture of white blood, who received from his father and his grandfather the authority and the oral lore to carry on the ritual. The laymen of this community are familiar with all the principal prayers of Roman liturgy. Special communion maize bread is used, and a communion liquor made of honey and water. These people observe the principal, and even lesser saints' days, and all the essential elements of Lent and Holy Week, including Ash Wednesday and Palm Sunday. Only these people practice penance by approaching a shrine on their knees.

We recall the progressive decline of the Catholic church in Mexico, the spread of secularization and rational philosophy in recent years, and the curb upon the clergy. Meanwhile, out in the forest, a Maya people preserve both the Christian lore and practice that the priests taught them long ago, and so much of their own more ancient native belief and ritual as survived the destruction of the temple-cities and of the upper levels of their priestly hierarchy.

But now another general fact must be brought forward. The fusion of such Spanish and Indian elements as are present is more nearly complete in the communities farthest from the city. The town is a heterogeneous sort of place, containing half-hearted Catholics who, upon occasion bring in from some village queer but powerful medicine men to perform rites that will assure a successful crop. In the peasant village, there are two cults, one carried on by the shaman-priest and directed to the pagan gods, and the other by a reciter of Catholic prayer and addressed to the saints. The two cults are parallel, complementary, and non-competing; they are separate aspects of what the natives feel to be a single body of pietistic practices. Finally, in the tribal village, Catholic and pagan ritual are intimately blended into a single cult. There, in a native hut that serves as a church, two altars are erected. One bears a cross, and represents the Most Beautiful Lord in that heaven called "Glory"; the other represents the gods of the rain and the cornfield. A single ritual involving both pagan and Christian prayers is carried on at these altars. The ancient pagan ritual maize breads are placed on both. There is one body of celebrants, who are participants in a Mass, and also votaries of the agricultural spirits. On Holy Friday, new fire is kindled at the door of this rustic temple, as is the practice in the Roman ritual. And it is said by the Indians that the kindled flame represents the rebirth of that ancient heroic personage, one Jesus, who was betrayed and destroyed long ago. But the fire is not kindled with flint and steel, but with the Indian fire drill, as was new fire kindled by the ancient Aztecs, and probably the ancient Maya. A special group of men, known as men with "hot hands" kindle the fire. And the new fire, it is thought, must be brought to all the domestic hearths and there kept alive till the evening of Good Friday on the following year. This periodic renewing of the domestic fires from a new fire ceremonially kindled is a well attested aboriginal Indian rite.

The fact I have last cited—that Spanish and Indian elements are intimately fused in the peripheral communities—leads to a reformulation of our problem. What strikes one, as one goes from the city to the town, to the peasant village, to the tribal village, is not that life becomes more Indian and less European, but that life becomes more like that which is characteristic of isolated, non-literate, long-established peoples. One might say that the peripheral peoples are more primitive than the others, except that "primitive" might connote only simplicity of technology, and might suggest a rude or disorganized life. Much more than simplicity of technology is involved here. As one goes from the city to the tribal village, as one goes from a literate, mobile people to a non-literate, immobile people, one finds not less organization, but more. In the remote villages, customs,. beliefs, and institutions are organized into a self-consistent whole. Rite expresses belief, and is carried on as the collective utterance of a people whose fears and aspirations find an expression that is for them proper and inevitable. And as one goes from city to tribal village the homogeneity of behavior within the group increases; what is right for one man, is right for all the others. In the city there is so much variety, change, and superficiality that people are bewildered; the town is less confusing, but it is a house divided; the village life, however, has so much inner consistency that I think of its mode of life as a sort of structure, and feel that it could be diagrammed, or expressed in a three-dimensional model.

We might call the simple, isolated, established people with well organized cultures the "folk" and say that the "folkness" of life in Yucatan increases as one goes southeastward down the stairway I have imagined. The "folkness" of a culture is not dependent upon the historical source of its component elements. I have spoken of the institution of god-parenthood as a feature of culture generally present in the peninsula. Although it may in part rest historically on some Indian custom of selecting sponsors for children, so far as inspection will reveal that institution is Spanish in form. This institution is more fully developed, more complexly and completely involved in other aspects of culture, in the villages than in the town. In the villages, the god-parental institution is expressed in solemn ritual, and endorsed by mythology and belief. In town and city, it is a weaker, a more secular, thing. A Spanish custom, inculcated by the early priests, helps to give the primitive culture its essential character and organization.

There is an antithesis between the building-up of a cultural organization in isolation, and the breaking-down of that organization in the course of invasion and contact or of internal invention. When the Spaniards came to Yucatan, they performed a major operation on the native culture, removing, let us say, half the organism. Upon it they transplanted new organs, new customs, and new beliefs. Where isolation allowed it to happen—and the isolation was enough everywhere in the peninsula to allow it to happen to some degree everywhere— the graft took, and the re-made organism grew, flourished, developed,

and elaborated its parts; and the parts became intimately interdependent upon one another. Some of the parts were Spanish grafts; they,
like the Indian elements, developed and merged into a single new
structure. The re-made ways of life, with little or no distinction as to
Spanish or Indian origin recognized by the people, came to take on a
feeling of rightness, to rest under moral and religious authority. This
was the phase of culture growth. But meanwhile the appositive phase,
that of civilization, was also present. New changes occurred; the
colonial period came to an end; technological improvements and economic expansion penetrated the peninsula; schools, revolution, political and economic events stirred even the distant forest dwellers. In
the city, as in all cities, the stir has always been so great as to restrict
the culture process. In the remote villages, the re-made culture was,
until recently, little disturbed by civilization. Now the disorganizing
influences are increasing, both in city and in village.

Part II

VARIETIES OF CULTURE CONFLICT

4

POWER POLITICS AND DOMINANCE

CULTURE CONFLICT, although often associated with cultural difference, does not arise from differences of culture, but from the conflict of group interests. It has accordingly a political not a natural history, for it is of historical origin and manufacture. Typical of its operation, however, is the assignment of some cultural divergence, often relatively accidental or innocuous in itself, as the origin, cause, or symbol of the group issue and its associated conflict. Difference, in this way, is so readily convertible into antagonism and hostility, that many think the dislike of the unlike is the basis and origin of culture conflict. That seems sometimes to be true, but under circumstances where unlikeness conjures up fear. The normal reaction of dislike without fear is aversion, whereas the attitudes back of culture conflict are more the products of the desire to dominate rather than the wish to withdraw, of the will to power rather than the wish to exclude.

Relative status and advantage are, then, the core of the culture conflict situation in all of its varieties, whether the struggle be between groups within a society or between societies as competing units. Given such a situation, cultural difference, through becoming associated with status of dominance and subordination, becomes a cleavage plane of culture conflict. Superiority becomes associated arbitrarily with dominance and subordination gets itself stigmatized as inferiority—and the distinction of the "majority" and the "minority" has crystallized.

The potency of the majority is not numbers but power. Often the "majority" is in reality a powerfully situated minority, acting either with the direct force of power or the indirect force of authority. The

latter makes prestige or the tradition of dominance almost as important as actual overt political, legal or economic power. For prestige,
as the heritage of power, is so closely associated with it as often to
enable dominance to prolong its control considerably after the lapse
of the original capacity to dominate by overt force. In the interims
of open struggle, majorities really govern by prestige, and so the pursuit of prestige becomes one of the chief objectives of power groups.
Power, prestige and caste become the majority ideals, and in these
reinforcements of power cultural differentials take on the significance
that more or less permanently associates them with status and converts them into symbols of superiority or inferiority. Within and without a society, they mark off the boundaries of privilege, and to be on
the wrong side of these cleavages means minority status in one degree
or another.

There is usually considerable difference, however, between the
power politics of a dominant class, caste or elite in relation to the subordinate classes and minorities within a given society and the more
obvious and ruthless rule and exclusion practiced upon a subordinate
nation or people outside the social system of the ruling power. And
yet, upon occasion, just as much ruthlessness and exclusion can be
visited upon an internal minority and cultural differentials just as
rigidly insisted upon. Normally, internal minorities are granted certain
concessions of partial inclusion and cultural participation. A majority
frequently obtains sanctions for power by giving them a shared participation in the prestige of some national or racial tradition, though
frequently this confers little besides vicarious satisfaction. By such symbolic identification, the majority power group acquires a wide and
influential sanction in the name of the state or the church, the race
or the civilization, through which as "defenders of the faith," "carriers
of civilization," or "guardians of the race," they acquire acceptance
and support both of their leadership and of their policies. In such
ways interests and programs have become historically associated with
causes of culture and civilization although in origin they may have
represented only the interests and initiatives of relatively few. Nothing
is more effective as rationalizing instruments for power politics than
the traditional symbols of the group culture or civilization, which

usually evoke the unquestioned mass support that comes from any inveterate sense of group solidarity.

Whenever historic groups are threatened from the outside, they immediately minimize all internal distinctions, and minority discriminations are held in abeyance. This crisis-patriotism is recognizably different from the normal variety. Under imperialistic regimes, it is extended at such times even to the subject peoples, who, like the internal minorities, are then brought closer in shared affiliations of the nationalist or cultural bonds of solidarity. Such hectic courting and inclusion of minority groups is in marked and often ironic contrast to the more normal "divide and rule" policy and tradition of dominant groups, to which they are apt to revert under conditions of assured dominance and control.

Such in the main is the majority profile. It is not an attractive picture, but realistically it does represent on the whole the ways of the majority, their general technique of dominance, their characteristic historic behavior.

MacCartney sketches in his article the historical forces that have produced the tradition of the European political majority. Its power politics derives primarily from military conquest, organizing and re-organizing itself in the structure of the political state as this or that subject group is added to or lost from its orbit of power. In all the elaborate historical succession of political combination and re-combination, MacCartney thinks, essentially the same principles of majority organization hold, though on widely different scale and pattern. The core foundation, whether large or small, nation or empire, is the majority-minority situation, in which subordinate groups are organized and incorporated into some unit whose solidarity is dictated by the majority and patterned after their tradition of culture.

Constantly at the heart of this system of ruling power is the problem of maintaining unity, on the one hand, and subordination on the other. The subject groups tend to assimilate and in course of time, usually do. This confronts the ruling group with what MacCartney styles the "rival national philosophies of assimilation and segregation." In Europe, from the time of the Romans on, various regimes have confronted this problem. As the subject peoples have constantly shifted in their alignments with the ruling groups, the patterns of political structure have changed. Though always ruled, the subordinate groups are sometimes subjects merely, at other times, subject minorities. As subject minorities, they confront, in addition to some political system by which they are subordinated, some national solidarity from which they are excluded.

The latter depends upon some cultural difference or tradition of cultural difference that has assumed social and historical importance. The Middle Ages, MacCartney observes, "pursued no conscious policy toward national minorities either of differentiation or of assimilation, being essentially universal and regarding the question with a tolerance born of indifference." But when, for example, France must be officially maintained as a Catholic country in the struggle against Protestantism, the French Huguenots become a national religious minority, or similarly when the English are settling Ireland, the Irish suddenly become a national racial minority, so much so that to "prevent the settlers from merging into the Irish, intermarriage, and the use of their language, laws or dress were forbidden."

Since the Renaissance, the national state based on the identification of the culture of the majority with the state, has gradually developed in Europe and brought culture difference openly into the area of power politics. Significantly enough from almost the same century, European imperialism, that other political entity which uses culture difference as an instrument of policy, was in the making. The minority issues of today are the dual heritage of this historical movement toward the national state and the extension of national culture and institutions to empire. So that today culture is the "strongest stimulant to national feeling" and cultural difference the most characteristic basis of cleavage for all minority groups, internal or external.

Especially as an expanding Europe reached out to conquest and settlement in the New World and in other continents, hitherto inexperienced varieties of peoples and culture provided a fertile ground for the development of culture bias and its erection into a justification of ruthless dominance and exploitation. Sample historic cases of this relentless investment of new areas of dominance, as portrayed in the excerpts from Darwin, Means, Vesta, MacCrone and Frederici, reveal tragic but not untypical illustration of these expansion conquests which laid down the keel of modern empire.

Ruthless and almost incredible cruelty and deception characterized many of them. Cultural difference was utilized to justify the complete repudiation of any ethical code. Whether in South or Central or North America, Polynesia, West, South or East Africa, or Asia, ruthless and inhuman tactics of subjugation prevailed. Counter-rationalizations—atrocity concepts of the "brutal and treacherous savage," "the wild Indians," "the perfidious enemy and infidel," "the benighted and conscienceless pagan," were used to cover over the terrorization and decimation of conquered peoples, so that it might receive support and sanction. The early annals of these invading movements, objectively studied, show that the atrocity characterizations applied more aptly to the conquerors than the conquered.

With pacification and subjection this initial ruthlessness subsides, but then principally because some of the subject groups must be preserved in the interest of the phase that succeeds conquest—economic exploitation. Untractable groups continue to receive harsh measures. The double code persists throughout, in that minority interests are considered only in so far as they are compatible with dominant interests. Repressive measures are reserved for any crisis in the relations of the groups, and restrictive measures govern the normal *status quo*. But any threat or disturbance to that *status quo*, and tactics of suppression immediately follow—punitive expeditions, pogrom terrorization, succeeded by fresh restrictive curbing and legislation, like disfranchisement, Ghetto or reservation segregation, the South African "color-bar" and native "passes" and curfew.

MacCrone gives a clear portrait of the European "frontier" psychology, as it confronts on the far borders of imperial encroachment the strange environment and stranger peoples. His profile of the South African frontiersman facing the Zulu, Hottentot and Bushmen parallels illuminatingly Stanley Vestal's analysis of the American immigrant farmer facing the Plains Indians. Much of their harshness and cruelty is the by-product of fear and some of their intolerance is due to the sparse hold which they have on their own culture. Nevertheless behind them is the political machinery of empire and the national state, and they conceive themselves to be the chosen representatives of the dominant race and civilization, act in their name and with their sanction. They also relay back to the dominant groups their crudely distorted picture of the aboriginal civilization. Ignorance and cultural intolerance culminate in stereotypes quite agreeable to those who wish to dispossess the natives.

Vestal calls attention to the fact that it hardly becomes the settler, who took what the Indian possessed, to call him a thief, nor, considering how often he broke his own word and treaties, to brand the Indian as treacherous. But by the perverse logic of conquest, what is a virtue with the conqueror becomes a vice for the minority. The Indian, for example, was called a nomad, although he only wandered seasonally in a well-grooved cycle adapted to his living necessities. It was the white settler who was more formidably nomadic, a prospecting adventurer, projected from a secondary base in the East, where he had paused only a generation or so after an adventurous leap across the Atlantic.

Friederici gives an even closer analysis of the repercussions of frontier contacts from a point of view of cultural influence. He traces the history of scalping, trite libel of the Indian and popular symbol of Indian barbarism. Scalping is shown to have entered its most formidable phase through the introduction of the steel and iron scalping knife, which became one of the most profitable barter items of the frontier trade. The trade in firearms, horses and intoxicants, moreover, was mainly responsible for the terror of the Indian raider, and intensified the traits for which the Plains Indians were blamed and nearly exterminated. But, as Friederici also documents, the white colonists took over the complex of scalping, systematized it, and by systems of legally enacted scalp bounties turned it into a formidable new method of repression and terrorization. This neglected chapter of colonial history throws a searching light on frontier morality, which set the key and stereotypes and precedents for colonial native-white relations. It is a tradition, which, however modified and moderated, has never been fully outgrown. Similar motives and tactics characterize economic imperialism, which in some respects is merely the organized second phase of what begins in frontier conquest.

HOW THE MINORITY PROBLEM AROSE IN EUROPE

Western Europe as a whole, throughout the entire Middle Ages, regarded the national question with a toleration born of indifference, and pursued no conscious policy towards its national minorities. When the power of the nobles was broken and the process of systematic centralization began, the unified national institutions which now come into being were modelled on customs of the majority and the minorities were required to bring their own customs in line.

IF A COMMUNITY were at once purely nomadic and purely pacific, the problem of national minorities would not exist for it. There are, indeed, even today, a few shy and gentle wandering tribes who simply ignore the rare strangers settled in their camping-grounds, as irrelevant to their politics. Most of our early ancestors, however, were forced by sheer shortage of desirable land to come into closer contact with their neighbors. Battle ensued, and of two nations one emerged the conqueror.

The conquered nation might be exterminated wholesale; but for most men of an earlier age, work was a greater terror than death. The defeated people was therefore kept in subjugation, and there now came into existence a formation which may be called the aristocratic-national state; a formation in which two or more nations coexist, but not on equal terms, the one, as a body, retaining exclusive control over the state, while the others exist merely for the benefit of their rulers. Such peoples, even where numerically more numerous than their conquerors, are yet genuine national minorities.

Since humanitarian considerations are an innovation in human affairs, the fate of these minorities in old times was assuredly no happy one. Their conquerors treated them with a single eye to their own advantage. And since the state was thus composed of two elements, one of which enjoyed all the advantages, while the other bore all the burdens, it was natural that the conquerors should be at pains to make the dividing-line between the two classes as clear-cut as pos-

Excerpt from C. A. Macartney, *National States and National Minorities* (London: Oxford University Press, 1934), pp. 22-28, 30, 33-54, 66-70, 82-83.

sible. . . . Hence the normal policy of the aristocratic-national state toward its minorities was one of rigid segregation, conquerors and conquered living side by side, perhaps for centuries, yet remaining entirely distinct.

This form of the nation-state seems to be the natural one for most early communities. Probably almost every state in Europe can trace its ancestry back to some such origin, except the few which a single nation has founded on a soil so inclement as to tempt no rivals. . . . If the association is very prolonged, the old sense of distinction between conquerors and conquered is bound with time to grow weaker in relation to the political sentiments of unity derived from common territorial and economic interests and a common history.

Finally, if a high state of civilization is reached and a complicated administrative and military machinery evolved, there will be definite and conscious efforts toward assimilation, to ensure the smoother working of that machinery, especially for purposes of defense. The last-named consideration is probably the most powerful of all. A migrant people remains fundamentally military. War is the principal preoccupation of the free citizen, his chief source of profit and of honor, and he reserves it to himself, turning over the laborious pursuits of peace to the subject minorities. But a sedentary people which has learned to appreciate the delights of civilization and has discovered that the road to wealth lies even more surely through trade and industry sees less romance and far less comfort in a soldier's life. The defense of distant frontiers is gladly left to rude and barbarous men, such as minorities; but as it is essential that they should fight for the state, and not for their own private nationality, assimilation of them becomes desirable.

This was the policy followed by Rome to an extent without precedent in recorded history. Rome herself adopted it only gradually, and in the face of considerable resistance. The ancient institutions of the *populus* and the *plebs* are a significant reminiscence of an older policy of differentiation; nor, when Rome began empire-building on a large scale, was the change-over to assimilation either speedy or systematic. Many of Rome's rulers, down to Augustus and his immediate successors, held to the principle of "Rome for the Romans," and Latin literature contains ample record of the dislike with which the old

Romans viewed their new, exotic fellow citizens. In her earlier conquests Rome left quite intact the language, manners, and institutions of the peoples which she subdued; to do otherwise would, indeed, have been quite beyond the powers of the comparatively small number of conquerors. . . . Romanization spread outward, ever farther, from its first center, until, as time went on, bringing with it one prodigious success after another, the idea was born of unifying the whole civilized world under the scepter of Rome. "Italy," wrote Pliny, "has been selected by God to collect dispersed power, to soften customs and to unite, by the communion of one language, the diverse and barbarous dialects of so many peoples, so that all the races of mankind should have one fatherland." . . .

The assimilation seems to have been largely painless, after the first savage resistance of the barbarians had in each case been broken. There is record enough of rebellions against Roman rule, and especially against the harsh tributes imposed and the conscription of manpower for foreign service in the legions. There is, however, little evidence of any tenacious struggle for the retention of national individuality as such. The main reason for this is that with Rome assimilation was only a means to an end. The right on which she based her titles was that of conquest. Having extended her frontiers to include more and more barbarians, she was satisfied, politically, with securing their loyalty. She cared very little what language her new subjects spoke, or what customs they followed, provided that they did not rebel, and their assimilation was due less to any systematic denationalization than to the automatic effects of the centralized Roman administration, the Roman army, and the superior Roman culture. Forcible assimilation, in its own sphere, was left to the less tolerant Church Militant. . . .

Thus the rival national philosophies of assimilation and segregation were already in force in eastern and western Europe respectively when they were brought into strong and active conflict by the fall of the Empire beneath the pressure of immigrant hordes from the east and the north. For a while it looked as though the sedate and well-ordered world which Rome had built up had perished irretrievably . . . The world was once again a mere welter of contending nations. . . .

Thus even where the Roman tradition had disappeared, the conditions which had given birth to the Roman system continued to operate, and with much the same effects. There was, indeed, one important difference. The great Roman world empire, with its unified system and centralized administration, in which all roads led to Rome, had disappeared forever. The ideal might be recovered later, but never the practice which cast all southern and western Europe in the same mold. None of the Germanic nations was at that time strong enough to aspire to world power, and instead the old Empire dissolved into its great natural units, within which the modern nations—even if they had to wait long for their political unification—were bound to evolve.

For the superimposition of the different Germanic tribes upon the different native peoples had laid the solid foundations of the nations of the future. These could have been overthrown only by more prolonged and more extensive national migrations, and from these most of western Europe was spared. Spain and southern Italy were indeed overrun by Moors and Saracens, Scotland and Ireland by Danes, and precisely in these countries the formation of the nations was longest delayed, so that their development lagged for centuries behind that of their more fortunate neighbors. Elsewhere, however, the migrations were much less important, and where they occurred, as in Normandy and in England, the newcomers soon blended with the native populations.

Important, too, is the fact that western Europe was now definitely established on a settled basis. With the advent of settled conditions, natural assimilation soon began to do its work. In England and France in particular, the difference between the various peoples, where they did live intermingled, was not usually great, either as regards origin, culture, or even language. Thus while it is true that the same settled existence and localized life also tended to produce minor differences of dialect, habit, and the like which probably had not existed at an earlier date, yet these developed along a different line of cleavage. In each geographical unit the population tended to become homogeneous, even if it differed increasingly (although in a minor degree within the great national boundaries) from area to area.

Now, minority problems only arise when peoples of different na-

tionality are united in the same political unit, and in particular when
they are the rivals of one another within it. But these cases arose very
rarely in medieval western Europe, owing to the new administrative
systems which developed there. The feudal system which took the
place of the great centralized, bureaucratic Roman Empire was organized on quite different lines from its predecessor.

Firstly, the new administrative divisions which sprang up tended
to coincide with the actual ethnographical conditions. . . . Secondly,
even within the larger areas, which included settlements of different
nationalities, there was an almost infinite subdivision, under a system
of delegated authority, so that where the people came into direct contact with authority it was usually in small, uninational groups. One
valley might be inhabited by Celts, another by Germans; but each
would be under its own local overlord, who administered its affairs,
and it would have little or no contact with its neighbor. And the
affairs of the people had become now almost exclusively local. The
old free national communities were gone. . . . Settled on their peasant holdings, they seldom moved afield, seldom saw even a strange
face, were cut off altogether from the current of national affairs. What
happened outside their own immediate neighborhood had ceased to
concern them.

And even if they had felt that it concerned them, they could have
done nothing to affect it. A national minority, by definition, implies
a majority. Now, within the larger units, majorities still existed in
the physical sense, but not in the political. Under the feudal system
all the peoples were equally disfranchised, and thus, with the best
will, incapacitated from oppressing one another.

Naturally, the situation was different for the politically active class
of knights, barons, princes, and kings. But here too the introduction
of feudalism had altered the whole problem. When the old free
national communities lost their sovereignty, the *raison d'être* of a
national policy had, for the time, vanished. Sovereignty now proceeded from above, and it was consequently unconnected with questions of nationality. The ultimate source of sovereignty, God, was
multi-national—or un-national, as you prefer it. Equally so, in theory,
were his two vicars on earth, the Pope and the Emperor, who claimed
authority (in what relationship to one another is immaterial to our

purpose) over the Realm Universal of humanity. From them the system of delegated authority spread downward, but each man always held his office in virtue of power conferred from above; a point was never reached where this power was invalidated by the principle of nationality. Thus there was nothing illogical in any man's ruling over subjects who were alien to him. Germans lorded it in Italy, Frenchmen in Spain, Englishmen in France, with complete equanimity and limpid consciences; even such bizarre spectacles as English or Flemish knights installed in charge of Greek, Bulgarian, or Armenian communities in the Balkans were part of the natural order of things.

Where the foreign nationality of his subjects was no theoretical bar to his domination of them, the ruler was naturally not interested in denationalizing them, even if he had been in a position to do so, which was seldom the case; for real denationalization, to be effective, must be systematic and thorough and requires both a complicated administrative system, and, ultimately, the co-operation of the people. But the feudal system, by depriving the masses of an active political existence, had excluded precisely the possibility of such co-operation.

Finally, another very important factor was constituted by the exclusively ecclesiastical character of medieval culture. Nearly all schooling was in the hands of monks, who, firstly, used as medium the "universal" language of Latin, and, secondly, were interested mainly in theological questions unrelated to national problems. Thus "culture," today the strongest stimulant to national feeling, was during the Middle Ages essentially universal. This fact did much to retard the development of nationalism.

In the absence, then, of definite reasons to the contrary, "western Europe as a whole, throughout the entire Middle Ages, regarded the national question with a toleration born of indifference, and pursued no conscious policy toward its national minorities," either of differentiation or of assimilation. It was only with the age of the Renaissance that the national question again became one of the first importance.

Throughout the long era of the Middle Ages geographical influences had been doing their work. The great natural divisions of Europe had marked out as clearly distinct from one another certain areas within which the forces of natural assimilation had led to the formation—crude as yet, and with innumerable local differences of dialect and custom—of recognizable nations. Within these areas there were certain minorities, such as the Bretons and the Welsh, who were clearly and uncompromisingly different from the majorities and defied assimilation. These had been subdued savagely enough, where need be. Indeed, eastern Europe offers no story more grievous than that of the English rule in Ireland, where, interestingly enough, the policy of segregation had to be adopted and carried through in the face of a strong tendency among the conquerors to grow assimilated to their victims. The Anglo-Norman settlers of the Pale parceled out the land among themselves, "till in title they were owners and lords of all, so as nothing was left to the natives." The latter, however, could not be exterminated, as they were required to cultivate the land for their new masters; but to prevent the settlers from merging into the Irish and acquiring their rebellious mentality, they were forbidden all trade or intercourse with the Irish, or the use of their dress, language, or laws. When, despite all precautions, one generation after another of settlers compromised with the "Irish enemy," recognized the Irish system of land tenure, employed Irishmen in positions of confidence, and even themselves adopted Irish dress and language, new reinforcements of uncorrupted men were sent over from England.

But such extremes of severity as were practiced by the English upon the Irish were not usually necessary; they were forced upon the English, in this particular case, by the fact that the conquest of Ireland was an attempt, dictated by lust of spoil and conquest, to join together what geography and history had decreed should be separate. The case of the Bretons and the Welsh was different. Here Nature indicated their incorporation in the larger political unit. The Bretons struck a bargain with the French king, becoming politically a part of France, while their local usages and privileges were to be kept intact. The Welsh were rather less fortunate, but they, too, were spared any attempts at forcible denationalization. . . .

Gradually the Middle Ages passed away, and a new form of economic life took the place of the old, narrow feudal system. The main trade routes of the world shifted to the west, in which fresh sources of wealth were opened up. Cities sprang up, a middle class came into being, culture and learning grew. But the interests of the new bourgeoisie were far different from those of the countrified land-

owners. The feudal noble stood for immobility, particularism, restriction, privilege; the capitalist demanded simplification, mobility,
unification; and his influence began to work, smoothing over local
customs, withering up little-used dialects, hastening on incomplete
processes of unification.

Now, too, the medieval universalist theories began to crumble.
While in Germany and Italy the tradition of them was destined to
linger on for centuries, greatly retarding the national unification, yet
even here, and particularly in Italy, a genuine national sentiment was
born. In France and England (the development in Spain had been
retarded by the Moorish invasions) it grew far more rapidly, largely
as a reaction against universalism, which had tended in practice to
center political power in Germany and spiritual authority in Italy.
The leaders of the reaction against these theories were the national
monarchs.

They had a twofold warfare to wage. On the one hand, they were
fighting the universalist Papacy and Empire, on the other, the feudal
régime of delegated authority and particularism. Against both they opposed the theory of a unified and unlimited national authority, owing
no allegiance above and unhampered by any restriction below; and the
obedient political philosophers, never at a loss to provide a theory to
fit the facts, duly evolved the fiction of absolute national sovereignty,
vested in the monarch. . . .

This theory of national sovereignty, it is important to observe, was
a purely political conception. It was formulated to fit actual circumstances, which were those of kings who were ruling over territories
which were not racially homogeneous. . . . Thus, although the
monarchs of France and England were the great unifiers of their
nations, they worked, not in order to create any theoretical right to
their position, but to strengthen their practical grip upon it. . . .

The primary considerations of the monarchs, in their work of
domestic unification, were political. They were anxious, that is, to
break local authority which impeded and rivaled their own, and their
efforts were directed quite as much against the great feudal lords of
their own nationality as against the chieftains of the minorities. If,
for example, the Estates of Brittany had to complain of repeated violations of their original pact with the King of France, the Estates of

other, purely French, provinces suffered no less heavily. It was true, of course, that the minorities, where they were still imperfectly subdued, were particularly rebellious and recalcitrant, thus necessitating special measures against them. . . .

The real turn of the minorities came when the power of the nobles was broken, and the process of systematic centralization began. The unified national institutions which now came into being were, naturally, modeled on those of the majority, and the minorities were required to bring their own customs into line. It is worth noting that in some cases, at least, this was not done as a repressive measure against the minorities, but rather by way of removing exceptional disabilities under which they had been placed. . . .

The monarchs of both France and England conferred considerable benefits on their national minorities. The point on which they went astray was really that on which all rulers of other peoples fail. It is the deep-rooted proclivity of most men, and of all Englishmen, to regard their own customs as "laudable" and the usages of all foreigners as "sinister," and the idea that an inhabitant of our little isle, set in its silver sea, should not wish to speak, dress, think, and eat like the usual standardized Englishman seems to him unreasonable and perverse.

The age of the two monarchs practically wiped away the differences in law and status between the majorities and the national minorities. It did not, oddly enough, extinguish the minority languages, thus preserving till the present day the basis for a national revival. The general indifference to linguistic questions seems strange today; it was, no doubt, largely due to the fact that the upper and middle classes of the minorities, with whom the monarchs had mostly to do, were already half-assimilated. The Breton Estates, for example, transacted their business in French, and outside the Estates, in the absence of an educational system, there was little public life at all. The "Act of Union for the defence of the Liberties of Brittany," of 1719, while enumerating a long list of Breton grievances, does not refer in any way to linguistic questions, which also do not figure among the complaints of the peasant spokesmen. In Wales, Queen Elizabeth actually reversed the trend of her father's legislation by enacting the translation of the Bible and Prayer Book into Welsh and ordaining that

Divine Service should be held in Welsh in all Welsh-speaking districts—an action which, as a modern writer puts it, "vitally influenced the religious and literary life of the Welsh nation; gave a new stimulus to the continuance of the Welsh language; produced a demand for education; and laid the foundations of the modern national movement in Wales."

This action of Queen Elizabeth's was due to no special tenderness for the Welsh tongue. For England and France, however, the languages of their minorities—poor, small nations, inhabiting the remotest recesses of their territories and not identical with any nations under the rule of another sovereign—were in no sense whatever a matter of international concern. What was international was the question of religion, especially in the form of the universalist Catholic Church, and it was in the national struggle against this that Elizabeth's real interest lay, as we see from the explanatory note which accompanied her decrees. The Bible and Prayer Book were to be translated in order that the Welsh who, understanding no English, were therefore "utterly destitute of God's Holy Word, and do remain in the like or rather more darkness and ignorance than they were in the time of Papistry," might partake of the same "unspeakable joy" with which the English had received the Prayer Book in "the vulgar English tongue"—and undergo, of course, the same political reactions.

Almost everywhere the worst excesses of the Renaissance period (and, in such cases as that of Ireland, well on into the nineteenth century) were directed not against languages but against religions. The darkest stain on the name of Renaissance France is the massacre of the French Huguenots. In Spain, where the minorities had for centuries enjoyed a golden age of toleration, the state suddenly turned against them. Many attempts were made to assimilate by force the large Jewish population, and when these failed, and the Inquisition reported that even nominal converts were secretly practicing their ancestral religion, they were expelled as a hopelessly bad job. The Moslem "mudéjares," who had previously been well treated and allowed the public practice of their religion, were confronted with the same alternative of expulsion or conversion; and when the converts (now known as Moriscos) were suspected of insincerity in their new religion, harsh penal ordinances were first issued against them; then, after a debate which had wavered between the alternatives of general massacre, of sending them to sea and scuttling the ships, or of shipping them off to work in the mines in America, the vast majority of them were expelled, in circumstances of great brutality.

It was reserved for the methodical Germans to lay down the principle of state sovereignty in religious matters in the famous formula *cujus regio, ejus religio* [Religion goes with the soil, i.e., the sovereign power in any country may prescribe the form of worship of its citizens BJS]—perhaps one of the most cynical phrases in history. It served its immediate end; it broke the power of Catholicism as a universal religion and for a short while, perhaps, it did give each state a national feeling based on religion. Ultimately, of course, it simply eliminated religion as a national influence altogether.

Thus, after centuries of struggle, the old universalist theories of the Middle Ages were broken down, and in their place was set up the new idol of the sovereign state; and those states which had led the revolt—England and France—had by the eighteenth century achieved a very high degree of political and administrative concentration. . . .

Thus it was the "political" and not the "personal" theory of nationality which predominated in western Europe, and particularly in France, when the most important change in political philosophy came about. This was the transference of sovereignty from the absolute monarch to the "nation" itself.

The theory evolved, or revived to fit the facts, was, this time, born in England, when the revolution of 1688 substituted one dynasty of monarchs for another. The only justification which could be found for this was that the ultimate sovereignty rested in the nation, which was thus able to transfer it from one ruler to his successor. This doctrine of the sovereign nation was elaborated in America where the colonists needed a theory to justify their secession, and in France, first by Rousseau, then by the thinkers of the French Revolution, who, first in Europe, made any far-reaching practical application of it.

The political conception of nationality was absolutely predominant in France when the Revolution broke out. . . .

The French revolutionaries were not concerned with "national" questions in the narrower sense of the word at all. The hopes entertained by the Court that national, or even regional, interests would divide them, were disappointed. They found no reason to discuss the relations of the French with the Bretons, Alsatians, or Flemings, and the only occasion on which they concerned themselves with the position of the national minorities was when, at practically the last sitting of the National Assembly in 1791, they admitted Jews to complete equality with other citizens. The establishment of the same treatment for all appeared to them to meet the whole case; the suggestion that a minority might wish for differential treatment does not seem to have arisen.

The idea of national self-determination in the modern sense of those words seems also to have passed them by lightly enough. Their principle of no conquests and no annexations would in its purest form have meant a maintenance of the existing historical frontiers. The Constituent Assembly even hesitated, for this reason, to receive Le Comtat and Avignon when they rose in rebellion against the Pope, but there, for the first time, the Left advanced the modern claim of the "nation" by asking whether the Revolution was more timid than the Monarchy, and whether it would refuse to "complete France." The other side of the question did not arise, since the inhabitants of Alsace and Lorraine shared enthusiastically in the fortunes of the Revolution, and made no attempt to free themselves from France. Merlin of Douai, presenting the report of the Comité Féodal on October 2nd, 1790, remarked: "The Alsatian people has united itself to the French people because it willed to do so; it is then its will alone and not the Treaty of Münster that has legitimized this union." . . .

Without doubt, the revolutionaries realized the existence and sympathized with the aspirations of certain historical nations, then temporarily submitted to a foreign sovereignty, such as Poland and Hungary. They believed, however, that justice would be satisfied if such states were restored their liberty, and if, within each political unit, the sovereignty were transferred from the monarch to the "nation." . . .

In western Europe the more important national migrations ceased, except in Spain, Scotland, and Ireland, with the arrival and settlement of the Germanic tribes—the "Great Migrations" usually so called. In central and eastern Europe, on the other hand, they have hardly closed today. . . .

We may divide the population of eastern Europe into three main groups.

Firstly, there is the assorted group of small nationalities which appear to be truly indigenous; to have maintained their footing since earliest historic times in approximately the areas (although not necessarily within the exact limits) which they now inhabit. These nationalities have, of course, undergone certain changes, owing to amalgamation with later immigrants; but they have preserved throughout a recognizable national type. They are comparatively few in Europe: the Greeks, Kutzo-Vlachs, and Albanians in the Balkans; the Roumanians in the Transylvanian Carpathians; and, along the Baltic seaboard, the Finns, Estonians, Latvians, Livonians, and Lithuanians.

All of these are comparatively small and weak nations. All of them owe their survival, at least in part, to the difficult and inhospitable character of their territory, or to the inability of their conquerors to adapt themselves to the method of life natural to that territory. All of them, moreover, have passed many centuries under alien rule, during which time they only constituted national minorities within a larger empire. Nearly all of them, however, which survived that rule, without the complete extermination which overtook the remaining primitive races known to the classical geographers, have today recovered their independence, and formed sovereign national states of their own.

In Asia the indigenous nationalities have been less fortunate. The Kurds are divided between Turkey, Persia, and Irāq; and of the seventy nations of the Caucasus (this was the computation of the medieval geographers) all are now included in the giant Soviet Union, with varying degrees of autonomy.

Secondly, there are two other great national groups: the Germans and the Slavs. Each of these may be regarded as genuinely indigenous within certain limits, which are not, however, those of today. Our early records show Germans holding, not only the present Germany, but also the valley of the Vistula and that of the Upper Dniester. The Slavs at this time (i.e., about the birth of Christ) were somewhere in the region of the Pripet marshes, and were probably a united people. Since that date, the two races have advanced and retired in an extraordinary alternation. . . .

From the ninth century onward, it was again the Germans who

were advancing, the Slavs who retreated. The Germans gradually recovered the modern Austria, pushing into the edges of Slovenia, and strengthening their numbers and position in Bohemia, in which, from the seventeenth to the late nineteenth centuries, they acquired such a predominance as to make it seem almost a Germanic state. . . .

The nineteenth century saw the beginnings of another Slavonic revival. The Slavs had already been gaining ground at the expense of the Finnish nations in northern and eastern Russia and southward toward the Black Sea and the Caspian, and even colonizing Siberia. They had also definitely split into several distinct nationalities. Now a national revival took place among their westernmost branches. . . .

The existence of this perpetually swaying, ever-debated frontier line between Slav and German is responsible for many of the most difficult and dangerous minority problems of today. . . .

So much for the effects of the system of personal law, as applied throughout eastern Europe. Itself the consequence of the more pro-longed character of the national migrations, it perpetuated and rein-forced the consequences of that fact by preventing the natural force of assimilation from coming into play in the areas of mixed population. Instead of the different nationalities blending within the political units, they continued to live side by side, each under its own dispensa-tion, and with comparatively little intercourse, while such movement as there was toward assimilation, usually came, not as in western Europe from above, as the expression of a desire to consolidate the state, but from below, in the ambition of the subjected nationalities to share the privileges of the conquering nation.

For although in exceptional circumstances the effects of this system might actually prove more favorable than that of the west to the con-quered nationalities, yet in general the line of cleavage remained clear between the conquerors, whose national institutions were a symbol of power and privilege, and the conquered, whose nationality was a badge of servitude. And if we ask how it was possible for such a system to be maintained for centuries without perpetual national wars, the an-swer must be sought in those circumstances to which we have referred in commenting on the curious indifference to nationality characteristic of the Middle Ages in western Europe. The same localization of interests and decay of the true national spirit had operated through the east upon the conquered peoples, and perhaps to an even greater degree, since with few exceptions they were reduced almost entirely to serf status. Such of their nobility as survived the conquest deserted to the enemy camp and changed their nationality; the middle classes (far less developed in the east than in the west, owing to the more backward state of economic life) were composed again of the conquerors, more frequently of the colonists; only the remnants remained to represent their nations with all the tenacity, but also the passivity, characteristic of the peasant.

Thus even as late as the eighteenth century it was possible to divide the population of the mixed areas into two quite distinct classes: the conquerors—Magyars, Germans, Swedes, Turks, Poles—and the conquered—Czechs, Slovaks, Slovenes, Vlachs, Ruthenes, and White Russians, the Finnish and Lithuanian nations of the Baltic, and the non-Turkish races of the Balkans; and of these, only the former were politically active and nationally self-conscious, while the latter were "nations without a history" whose nationality was passive and defensive. . . .

The importation in bulk of alien racial elements is not a practice confined to eastern Europe. It has been done all over the world. In the British Isles, for example, Ulster was colonized with Scots at the end of the seventeenth century. More lately still, the United States imported large numbers of Negroes as slaves. Both of these examples show, incidentally, that where the west has to face problems similar to those which occur in the east, it finds them at least as difficult as does the east itself. . . .

In eastern Europe, where sudden and extensive depopulation, owing to invasion and other causes, has been more frequent, the custom of colonization has always been exceedingly common, and the descendants of these colonists are responsible for a large number of the minority complexities of today.

Although foreigners, and thus belonging from the first to the notoriously unfortunate class of national minorities, the colonists were yet, as a rule, far more advantageously placed than the conquered peoples, often, indeed, being privileged beyond the native majority of the states of which they formed part. It is true that immigrants sometimes entered a state at their own risk, as fugitives or, under compulsion, as prisoners of war. If they were few or weak, they might then be condemned to slavery or to some harsh form of serfdom. The gipsies of Moldavia and Wallachia, for example, were legal slaves until their emancipation in the nineteenth century, and although they were more fortunate farther west, they were universally regarded as outcasts, ranking even below the serfs. In Bohemia, to mark their status, each of them had his right ear cut off; in Moravia (by a nice distinction) his left ear. In Hungary, until the eighteenth century, Jews, Armenians, and members of the Orthodox Church were ineligible to become nobles, or even burghers of the free cities, and as early as 1222 King Andrew of Hungary was forced, much against his will, to agree that no Jews or "Ishmaelites" should be chamberlains, or employed in the mint, salt monopoly, or customs service. In an age, however, where the great and perennial difficulty was not, as today, that of over-population, but that of defenselessness, owing to a too sparse population, anybody capable of serving the state effectively could make good terms on entry. Most commonly the immigrants undertook the obligation of military service, either binding themselves to serve directly under the sovereign (who was often at a loss for troops of his own, especially when the feudal system was highly developed and the great barons powerful and unruly), or else to guard the frontiers against all aggressors. In either case, the usual compromise was liberty, land, and exemption from all feudal dues against military service, and its effect was the establishment of an alien population along the state frontiers (precisely the territories which modern governments are so inordinately anxious to reserve for their own patriots). . . .

Naturally, where colonists entered a state upon invitation, their position was even more favorable, especially when they did so in bulk. Such immigration was frequent in eastern Europe until recent times, especially after some Oriental raiders—Turkish or Tatar—had wrought devastation and depopulation. A great part of southern and eastern Hungary (within the frontiers of 1918) was populated in this way. . . .

Racial intermingling came to characterize all Europe from the line where the solid bloc of German population ended to that where the solid Russian bloc began—a confusion which was the product of prolonged and frequent national migrations, combined with widespread practice of colonization, while the differences thus engendered were kept alive by universal application of a system of personal law.

There was, naturally, an infinite variety of gradation; but in the main, the populations in this area fell into three distinct and perfectly recognizable classes: the privileged, conquering races; the despised and humble serfs; and midway between the two in legal status, the colonists. The social division coincided with the racial, the conquerors occupying the position of landowners and administrators; the colonists supplying the urban and artisan classes, and in some cases the military, while the conquered tilled the land. And of these three the conquered, who were numerically the majority, were socially and legally in by far the least enviable position.

This situation endured throughout the Middle Ages, which in eastern Europe lasted until a far later date than in the west. Gradually, however, there arose here, too, absolute monarchs comparable to the kings of France and England, and discernibly animated by the same ambition to break the power of the feudal lords and of the Estates, and to unify their dominions under a centralized, bureaucratic rule.

DARWIN OBSERVES A WAR OF EXTERMINATION

Everyone here is fully convinced that it is the most just war, because it is against barbarians.

I SAW a troop of banditti-like soldiers start on an expedition against a tribe of Indians at the small Salinas. The Spaniard who brought the orders for this expedition was a very intelligent man. He gave me an account of the last engagement at which he was present. Some Indians, who had been taken prisoners, gave information of a tribe living north of the Colorado. Two hundred soldiers were sent;

Excerpts from Charles Darwin, *Journal of Researches into the Geology and Natural History of the Various Countries Visited During the Voyage of H.M.S. Beagle Round the World* (London: J. M. Dent and Sons, Everyman's Library, 1912; published in the United States by E. P. Dutton and Co., Inc., New York), pp. 96-98.

and they first discovered the Indians by a cloud of dust from their horses' feet, as they chanced to be traveling. The Indians, men, women, and children, were about one hundred and ten in number, and they were nearly all taken or killed, for the soldiers sabre every man. The Indians are now so terrified that they offer no resistance in a body but each flies, neglecting even his wife and children; but when overtaken, like wild animals, they fight against any number to the last moment. One dying Indian seized with his teeth the thumb of his adversary, and allowed his own eye to be forced out sooner than relinquish his hold. Another, who was wounded, feigned death, keeping a knife ready to strike one more fatal blow. My informer said, when he was pursuing an Indian, the man cried out for mercy, at the same time that he was covertly loosing the bolas from his waist, meaning to whirl it round his head and so strike his pursuer. "I however struck him with my sabre to the ground, and then got off my horse, and cut this throat with my knife." This is a dark picture; but how much more shocking is the unquestionable fact, that all the women who appear above twenty years old are massacred in cold blood! When I exclaimed that this appeared rather inhuman, he answered, "Why, what can be done? they breed so!"

Everyone here is fully convinced that this is the most just war, because it is against barbarians. Who would believe in this age that such atrocities could be committed in a Christian civilized country? The children of the Indians are saved, to be sold or given away as servants, or rather slaves for as long a time as the owners can make them believe themselves slaves; but I believe in their treatment there is little to complain of.

In the battle four men ran away together. They were pursued, one was killed, and the other three were taken alive. They turned out to be messengers or ambassadors from a large body of Indians, united in the common cause of defence, near the Cordillera. The tribe to which they had been sent was on the point of holding a grand council; the feast of mare's flesh was ready, and the dance prepared: in the morning the ambassadors were to have returned to the Cordillera. They were remarkably fine men, very fair, above six feet high, and all under thirty years of age. The three survivors of course possessed very valuable information; and to extort this they were placed in a line.

The two first being questioned, answered, "No sé" (I do not know), and were one after the other shot. The third also said, "No sé"; adding, "Fire, I am a man and can die!" Not one syllable would they breathe to injure the united cause of their country! The conduct of the above-mentioned cacique was very different: he saved his life by betraying the intended plan of warfare, and the point of union in the Andes. It was believed that there were already six or seven hundred Indians together, and that in summer their numbers would be doubled. Ambassadors were to have been sent to the Indians at the small Salinas, near Bahia Blanca, that this same cacique had betrayed. The communication, therefore, between the Indians, extends from the Cordillera to the coast of the Atlantic.

General Rosas's plan is to kill all stragglers, and having driven the remainder to a common point, to attack them in a body, in the summer, with the assistance of the Chilenos. This operation is to be repeated for three successive years. I imagine the summer is chosen as the time for the main attack, because the plains are then without water, and the Indians can only travel in particular directions. The escape of the Indians to the south of the Rio Negro, where in such a vast unknown country they would be safe, is prevented by a treaty with the Tehuelches to this effect—that Rosas pays them so much to slaughter every Indian who passes to the south of the river, but if they fail in so doing, they themselves are to be exterminated. The war is waged chiefly against the Indians near the Cordillera; for many of the tribes on this eastern side are fighting with Rosas. The general, however, like Lord Chesterfield, thinking that his friends may in a future day become his enemies, always places them in the front ranks, so that their numbers may be thinned. Since leaving South America we have heard that this war of extermination completely failed.

THE FALL OF THE INCAS

Thus did Christianity prove its superiority to the pagan faith.

FRIDAY NIGHT of November 15, 1532, found the little band of Spaniards in the blackest despondency. From their bivouac in the plaza, where the sinister shadows of deserted buildings crowded upon them and the massive shapes of two great fortresses hung over them, they could see the countless fires of the Incas' camp, so numerous that they looked like "nothing else than a very starry sky." During the night the Governor first cheered on his dejected men with all the manly eloquence which distinguished him at his best, and later he held a council of his officers in which the plans for the next day's action [when the Inca: Atahualpa, would make his promised visit] were drawn up.

The hour of sundown was approaching when, on the next day, to the pulsing rhythm of drums and the plaintive wail of trumpets and flutes, the Inca with only a few thousand troops drew nigh the city. First came bands of servitors bearing brooms with which they carefully swept the highway over which their lord was to be borne. Afterwards, arranged in companies, came contingents of soldiery bearing massive clubs with star-like heads of copper, silver, or gold, and singing wild, triumphant war-songs which sounded to the Spaniards like the yells of hellish demons. Last of all came the Cañari guard, arrayed in richly ornamented azure, who surrounded the imperial litter as it was carried by trained bearers. Seated on a golden throne under a canopy blazing with gorgeous feathers and plates of gold and silver, Atahualpa, with the Lord of Chincha at his feet, rode onwards in silence. His dress was of becoming brilliance, for around his neck were enormous emeralds and to the imperial fillet on his head had been added many embellishments of gold.

In complete silence and with perfect decorum some six thousand

Excerpt from Philip Ainsworth Means, *Fall of the Inca Empire and the Spanish Rule in Peru: 1530-1780* (New York: Charles Scribner's Sons, 1932), pp. 31-33.

Indians filed into the plaza, leaving a pathway clear for the imperial palanquin. Arrived at the center of the square without seeing a single Spaniard (for, upon order, they were all lurking within the houses), the Inca at last broke that ineffably majestic silence of his, asking: "Where, then, are the strangers?"

As if in answer Friar Valverde now scuffled forward to the imperial litter, a Breviary in one hand and an upraised Crucifix in the other. Being completely ignorant of practical psychology, the Friar plunged at once into a long-winded theological discourse in which he set forth the more absurd sacerdotal dogmas of his day, linking the Apostle St. Peter to Pizarro through that sordid fellow, Pope Alexander VI, and relating how he, Alexander, had given Peru to King Charles, whose vassal Atahualpa was now blandly invited to become. Not only was the Friar's address supremely ridiculous from the standpoint of common sense, but also its general obscurity was enhanced by the translation given to it by the mischief-making interpreter, Felipillo. To Atahualpa, rigidly maintaining an imperturbable mien upon his lofty litter, the whole thing must have sounded like the ravings of madmen, the only clear points in it being that an individual styling himself the Pope had given his, Atahualpa's, realms to some king or other and that he, the Inca, was being bidden to become that other king's vassal.

Naturally enough Atahualpa was furious. But he held his peace until the verbose Valverde was quite done. Then he exploded. In spicy language he voiced his scorn for the God "who was three persons and one more, which makes four"—such being Felipillo's version of the Trinity—for the silly Pope who gave away things that did not belong to him, and for that distant king who had the colossal impudence to put himself above the Inca. Pausing in his raging tirade only to catch his breath, he went on to say that he would make the scoundrelly outlanders pay dearly for all the damage they had done since coming into his empire, and he wound up by asking Valverde what authority he had for all the arrant nonsense with which the imperial ears had been insulted. The Friar indicated the Breviary and handed it up to the monarch. The volume was closed with clasps, and the Inca, being inexpert in bookish matters, could make nothing of the lumpish object which he found in his hands. Becoming bored he nonchalantly dropped the holy tome upon the pavement.

This "sacrilege" served as an excuse for the attack upon the Inca's person which Pizarro and his officers had planned to make. In the short, sharp scuffle which ensued, with guns barking, horses prancing, and steel armor, swords, and trappings flashing in the sundown light, Spain, represented by her handful of adventurers, rolled a proud empire in the golden dust of the plaza of Cajamarca. Mere numbers, though great, were of no avail to Atahualpa's cause in the presence of firearms and horses and of the raucous shouts of "Santiago and at them" which the Christians constantly uttered. Valverde, who had paused only long enough to snatch up his book, rushed hither and yon yelling out absolution to the attackers. In the scrimmage the bewildered Inca was tumbled out of his splendid litter, his sacred imperial llautu was snatched from his head by the soldier-chronicler, Estete, and he was almost stripped of his glittering apparel before Governor Pizarro himself, at the cost of a wound from one of his own frenzied men, rescued him—from policy, not mercy—and led him into captivity. Even then the carnage did not cease; for hundreds of unarmed or lightly armed native warriors were hacked to pieces with swords or trampled into slime by the horses without being able to deliver one effective blow for their lord. Thus did Christianity prove its superiority to the pagan faith which Atahualpa had scorned to betray.

THE ENGLISH POLICY OF CONQUEST

The English exterminated the local provincials in the provinces they overran. On both frontiers the attitude towards the "Natives" —whether "Wild Highlanders" or "Wild Irish" or "Red Indians" was the same.

THE WHOLESALE extermination of the previously established population, which has distinguished our English method of overseas settlement from the method of overseas settlement practiced by most other West-European peoples in modern times, is a trait which

Excerpt from Arnold J. Toynbee, *A Study of History* (London: Oxford University Press, 1934), pp. 465-466.

likewise distinguished the settlement of the English on the territories of the Roman Empire from the settlement of the other Barbarians during the interregnum which followed the break-up of the Empire and the dissolution of the Hellenic society. In that Völkerwanderung, most of the Barbarian war-bands from beyond the former frontiers simply stepped into the shoes of the former Roman soldiers and officials—taking their places in ruling and exploiting the provincials, in the same fashion as in the New World, a dozen centuries later, the Spanish conquistadores took the place of the Aztecs and the Incas. The English war-bands alone more or less exterminated the local provincials in the provinces which they overran, and re-populated the country themselves, instead of being content to rule and exploit the population which they found there, just as, a dozen centuries later, it was the English settlers alone who exterminated the population which they found in the New World. . . .

In the seventeenth century of our era, the governments of England and Scotland under all régimes—in the reign of James I and under the protectorate of Cromwell—were as active in "planting" Ireland and the Hebrides with settlers from England and the Lowlands of Scotland as they were in "planting" the Atlantic seaboard of North America; and on both frontiers the attitude toward the "Natives"—whether "Wild Highlanders" or "Wild Irish" or "Red Indians"—was the same. The "Natives" were to be uprooted, in order that the settlers of English stock, from England and the Scottish Lowlands, might be planted in their stead. Thus, for a century or more, the border warfare which had never ceased in the British Isles since the time of the Völkerwanderung was going on in the British Isles and in North America contemporaneously. In the British Isles, this border warfare was brought to an end, during the half century between the Battle of the Boyne and the Battle of Culloden, by the complete union of the Kingdoms of England and Scotland and the complete subjugation of the Scottish Highlanders and the "Wild Irish" to the authority of the United Kingdom. Therewith, the frontiersmen found their occupation gone, and their craft at a discount, on all the extinct frontiers—in Ulster and on the Border and along the Highland Line—and many of them emigrated to the Indian frontier of the North American plantations, where, in following their habitual pursuits, they would still be looked upon as performing a public service rather than as leading a life of lawlessness and crime.

These were the ancestors of the "Indian-fighters" who, in less than a century, carried the frontier of the United States from the Appalachian Mountains to the Pacific coast, exterminating the Indians as they advanced. It has been remarked that these English-speaking Protestant frontiersmen became assimilated to their Indian foes and victims—in dress, in habits, and above all in ferocity—and that, as soon as they had completed the extermination of the Indians, they died out themselves (except in the fastnesses of the Appalachians, where their descendants are living the old life to this day).

THE FRONTIER AND RACE ATTITUDES IN SOUTH AFRICA

The Bushmen were considered to be so utterly beyond even the pale of humanity that they were looked upon as some kind of noxious wild beast, and like wild beasts they were exterminated. In the performance of this service the frontier farmers were firmly convinced of the righteousness of their cause since the Lord God was undoubtedly on their side.

THE STOCK farmer when he crossed the mountain barrier into the interior and finally committed himself to his new way of life was at the same time extending the boundaries of European occupation into new territory. He lived on a frontier that was constantly advancing as the result of his own dispersion and, by the very nature of his way of life, he remained a frontiersman. For several generations there was no obstacle that could put a stop to his advance. During that period of time the frontier was not a boundary that prescribed a limit beyond which he could not go, but simply the last stage of an advance that was constantly being succeeded by the next and further stage. In such a process, "the frontier (was) the outer edge of the wave—the meeting-point between savagery and

Excerpt from I. D. MacCrone, *Race Attitudes in South Africa* (London: Oxford University Press, 1937), pp. 99-101, 105-106, 119-125.

civilization," and thus constituted an environment entirely different from that found in the settled area from which the stock farmer originally derived. Isolated in such an environment—for communication of any kind was a long and tedious business—the frontier farmer had to adapt himself to conditions of life that were crude to a degree. Hence his clothing, his diet, the shelter which he erected for himself and his family, were reduced to the bare minimum required to satisfy his needs. There was no scope for the refinements of life, and once they had been stripped away he soon learned to do without them. In the long run, and under such conditions, the frontier subdued the farmer and stamped him indubitably as its product. Outside his own environment and in the presence of strangers, the frontiersman was like a fish out of water, who would, as soon as he could, escape to his own habitat. On the frontier, the farmer felt free, he moved in familiar surroundings, he suffered from no sense of inferiority, and he claimed a status that placed him far above the level of those by whom he was surrounded. Thrown upon his own resources, the frontier farmer had learned to incorporate those ways of life as habits, those organizations of group activity as institutions, those modes of thinking, feeling, and behaving as attitudes, which were conditioned by his experiences and which enabled him to come to terms with, and to adapt himself to, his environment.

When we bear in mind that the frontier farmer had come from a community organized on a basis of slavery, a community in which the European belonged to the slave-owning class, we expect to find the slave-owning mentality carried over into the new environment and playing some part in shaping the attitudes, and determining the behavior of the individuals concerned, in further racial contacts on the frontier. Although the farmer was not, as a rule, a slave-owner, his immediate forebears in many cases had been slave-owners, and the slave-owning tradition dies hard. Even when reconditioned by the environment, it persisted as a part of his mind, as a mental background against which racial attitudes more directly determined by his immediate experiences would be developed. When we bear in mind, further, that the frontier farmer had come from a social environment in which Hottentots already occupied a status even below that of the slave and, therefore, immeasurably lower than that of the European, by whom they were regarded as some sort of inferior race without any caste and with no rights of their own to speak of, we expect to find that further contacts with the members of this race under frontier conditions would merely accentuate existing race attitudes almost to a morbid degree. The legal fiction that the Hottentots as the original inhabitants of the country were not amenable to the law of the land, led in practice to a denial of any legal right or protection. Since they were neither free men nor slaves nor serfs, the closest analogy seems to be simply that of outcasts. And, finally, when we bear in mind that the frontier farmers were engaged over wide areas in a constant struggle with the Bushmen, a struggle which increased in intensity and bitterness during the century and which was conducted in a merciless fashion on both sides, we expect to find that this species of border warfare would tend to stiffen the race attitudes of the European. The cardinal offense of the Bushman in the eyes of the European was that he refused to submit, that he was actually aggressive and a constant thorn in the flesh, and that, to the very last, he resisted the frontier farmer's encroachments until he was driven out or exterminated. . . .

The attitude of the farmers who took an active part in this border warfare can only be compared with that of men who were engaged in dealing with some pest that would make life intolerable unless it could be got rid of. The Bushmen were considered to be so utterly beyond even the pale of humanity that they were looked upon as some kind of noxious wild beast, and like wild beasts they were exterminated. In the performance of this service the frontier farmers were firmly convinced of the righteousness of their cause since the Lord God was undoubtedly on their side.

So I went with this small party of 12 men on the 3rd . . . and thence to Tavel Berg, where on the 10th I found such an assemblage of robbers, that we had not the courage to attack them; but reflecting that we have the promise in our favour, that they have the threats against them, and that the Lord does what seems good in his eyes, we advanced upon them and they were put to flight by the powerful hand of the Ruler of heaven and earth, and 17 of them killed there. From the smallness of my party we could not surround them, so they escaped from me. I found there great numbers of hides and skins of cattle and sheep, of which the flesh had been eaten.

By the end of the eighteenth century, only a few surviving kraals, containing the last remnants of those Hottentots who still retained some semblance of their former mode of life, were to be found existing precariously here and there on sites, especially along the coastal belt, from which they had not yet been evicted by the European.

In the 26th article of General Janssens's ordinance for the country districts, it is declared that the aborigines of the country, the Hottentots, must be considered and treated as a people who have a lawful right of residence in the colony, and who must therefore, as all other free people, be protected in their persons, property, and possessions. Such a declaration, needless to say, flatly contradicted the public opinion of the country districts, according to which the Hottentots were neither a free people nor entitled to any protection either in their persons, property, or possessions, but a form of cheap and docile labor at the disposal of the farmer, whose personal authority to treat them at will was to be final. . . .

The Bastards, or Bastard Hottentots, especially those who could lay claim to white blood, regarded themselves as a class who were very much superior either to the aboriginal inhabitants or to the slaves. The designation "Bastard" was not, as one might imagine, a term of abuse but one in which the owner took a proper pride, for it distinguished him from the despised Hottentots kinship which he was only too anxious to conceal. Bastards, as a rule, remained unbaptized and for that reason alone could never hope to enter the charmed circle of the European or Christian community. As a class, they were closely associated with that community without actually being accepted or regarded as part of it. In some respects they might be regarded as the nearest approach to that European laboring class which was lacking at the Cape. In the role of a superior and confidential type of servant, they could be relied upon in positions of trust and responsibility, such as taking charge during an owner's absence or acting as overseers on a loan farm. In the frontier districts one of their most important roles was the part they played in frontier fighting and defense. It was in this respect that they approached most closely to the status of the European, for they were allowed the use of

horses and firearms which were the prerogative of the latter, a fact
which shows the confidence placed in the Bastards as a kind of inferior European. They were expected to join in the expeditions against
the Bushmen, since they were a valuable addition to the fighting
strength of the commandos in that particular kind of warfare. We
find frequent references in the reports of field commandants, field
sergeants, and field corporals to Bastards and Hottentots who were
enlisted for commando service. The increasing demands made upon
them for this purpose, especially when many Europeans themselves
were unwilling to serve or made use of them as substitutes, led in
some parts to a general exodus in order to evade going on commando.

The race which was to become so familiar to several generations
of frontier farmers under the name of Bossiemans, Bosjesman, or
Bosjesman Hottentots, constituted the most serious obstacle to the
occupation of the country on the northern frontier, where they were
most numerous and aggressive. Over a distance of more than 300
miles, an incessant border warfare was carried on that was finally
ended only when the last Bushmen were either exterminated or
expelled. By the frontier farmers who came into contact with the
Bushman under these circumstances, the whole race was regarded as
sub-human, more akin to the baboon tribe with whom, indeed, they
were believed to have more in common than with the human species
as represented by the European himself. . . .

In the eyes of those of the frontier farmers who suffered most from
the constant depredations of these incorrigible "banditti" the only
good Bushman was a dead Bushman. That, in a sense, the Bushman
might claim to be the injured party and that their depredations were
the inevitable reaction to the invasion of their country by the Europeans who were depriving them of their means of subsistence, was
a point of view that would have seemed quite incredible to any
frontier farmer who had just been deprived of his own means of
livelihood by a Bushman raid. What particularly infuriated the
farmers and made them utterly merciless in shooting down those
whom they could overtake was the Bushman practice of maiming or
slaughtering the stock which could not be driven off or which had
to be abandoned when the pursuit became too hot. To a stock farmer
this kind of behavior must have appeared particularly atrocious. And

if we add the strain upon the nerves of those who were exposed to the full fury of the Bushman tactics of constant raids, it is clear that the policy of extermination, as a solution of the Bushman problem, would have appeared to the majority of those concerned as the only possible policy under the circumstances.

Even after the edge of the first and most immediate menace of the Bushman attacks had been blunted, the attitude toward them remained, and the policy of extermination, inherited from a previous generation, persisted as an *idée fixe* in the minds of a later generation of frontier farmer.

An interesting illustration of the contrast between the frontier and the non-frontier points of view is given by the following quotation by a contemporary: "It struck me as a strange and melancholy trait of human nature, that the Veld-Commandant [Nel], in many other points a meritorious, benevolent, and clear-sighted man, seemed to be perfectly unconscious that any part of his own proceedings, or those of his countrymen, in their wars with the Bushmen, could awaken my abhorrence."

There were some among the frontier farmers, however, who tried other methods of dealing with the Bushmen, when it was realized that a policy of violence only increased the virulence of their resistance. When General Janssens, in the course of his tour, paid a visit to the Bushmen in the neighborhood of the Seacow River, he found the greatest friendliness existing between them and the colonists settled beyond the Sneeuwberg.

The friendly intercourse was here carried so far, that the colonists, when they had anything to say to the Bosjesmans of the neighbourhood, or had little presents to make to them, could always collect them together only by lighting a fire upon one of the surrounding hills.

The veld-commandant, Johannes van der Walt, whose farm lay nearest to these Bushmen, had succeeded in winning their complete confidence. In the Little Roggeveld, and in the neighborhood of the Zak River, there also existed at one time some sort of understanding between the colonists and the Bushmen. These Bushmen who were on friendly terms with the farmers were known as *mak*, or "tame," Bushmen to distinguish them from the "wild," or "Jakhals," Bushmen who took to flight immediately they caught sight of a European.

THE AMERICAN INDIAN FRONTIER

The emigrant farmer marched with a rifle in one hand, the Old Testament in another. He always had a grievance and knew nothing and cared less about the feelings and customs of the Indians. He was alternately arrogant and panic-stricken.

THOSE FOOTLOOSE farmers who trekked up the Oregon Trail beside the white tilts of their prairie schooners brought with them a ready-made notion of the Indian, a notion gained in the long struggle for the Dark and Bloody Ground east of the Mississippi, a notion that every Indian was a lying, thieving, skulking murderer, who would delight to torture any unfortunate wretch who fell into his clutches. It was a notion which did not fit the Plains Indian at all, but it was a mighty agreeable notion to all those who wanted to dispossess the Indian, and the emigrants passed too quickly through the Plains to discover how false it really was.

As a matter of fact, the Plains tribes were generally men of their word, scrupulously honest, and too courageous to rejoice in wanton cruelty. It hardly becomes white men, who have taken everything the Indian possessed, to call him a thief. Nor, considering the way white men broke the treaties, can the Indian be branded a liar. Time and again I have left all my possessions lying on the prairie in the middle of an Indian camp of three thousand persons for as long as a week, and when I came back found everything just as I had left it. Unless whisky is flowing, a town of Plains Indians is the most law-abiding community in America. When gangsters have made our cities uninhabitable, there will still be peace and order in Sitting Bull's home town. Moreover, though atrocities did sometimes occur during the Sioux campaigns (as in all wars), the Sioux never reserved prisoners for torture. They either killed them at once, put them to ransom, or adopted them into the tribe.

Excerpts from Stanley Vestal, *New Sources of Indian History 1850-1891* (Norman, Oklahoma: University of Oklahoma Press, 1934), pp. 188-193; 195-197; 76-77; 79; 90-91.

Another droll idea cherished by these homeless farmers was that the Indian was a "nomad." Now Sitting Bull died within twenty miles of his birth-place, and but for a flood which prevented him crossing Grand River, would have built his house on the very spot where he was born. He loved his home country, and fought for it with a stubborn tenacity which has made him memorable among the patriots of all ages. Yet these wandering farmers, who had changed their base at least once in every generation for a century, and were even then jumping clear across a continent, called Sitting Bull's people "nomads." As a matter of fact, a farmer cannot love the soil as a hunter does, because he is bound to it. The cities are full of farm boys now, but you will find very few Indians there.

The emigrant farmer was, as a rule, a man of small imagination, hard and thrifty, who marched with a rifle in one hand, the Old Testament in the other, and a jug of "likker" in the wagon. He always had a grievance, and knew nothing and cared less about the feelings and customs of the Indians. He was alternately arrogant and panic-stricken, and tried to make up for the boredom of plodding along the endless trail by writing home highly-colored accounts of imaginary Indian raids. Who can blame him? Any officer who censored soldier mail overseas during the World War knows how often bored soldiers behind the lines wrote home glowing accounts of battles they never saw. Evidently, the emigrant did the same thing, and by 1850 the tribes along the Santa Fe and Oregon Trails had received a thoroughly bad name in the East.

The number of white persons killed by Plains Indians before that date was negligible, and the tribute exacted by the tribesmen from emigrants was rather less than the motor tourist pays when passing through the same region today. But the emigrant was tight-fisted. He aroused the nation. Uncle Sam decided that something must be done, and sent the Reverend Father Pierre-Jean De Smet, S.J., to summon his red brothers to the council. And when the Black Robe, as the Indians called the good father, asked them to attend, the Prairie Sioux could not refuse.

Those Indians who lived by the side of the road to Oregon were anxious to attend. They wanted to adjust their growing difficulties. They were surrounded by enemy Indian nations with whom they must fight, if they left their own hunting grounds for game. The buffalo had vanished from the Platte. White men were cutting their scanty timber, burning off their grass, turning what had lately been a great meat-producing country into a barren desert. Yet when the Sioux hunter, hungry and poor because of these same white men, ventured to approach a wagon train and ask for a little present of food or tobacco, these inhospitable devastators of his country warned him away, or even fired on him.

When white Americans visited Sioux camps, the people always entertained them freely for as long as they chose to remain, with no thought of asking payment: the evidence of the white men themselves, as shown in early Western books, is absolutely clear on that point. And it seemed pretty rotten when the men who were ruining the Sioux country, men rich beyond the dreams of Indian avarice—men with *guns* and *steel knives*;—refused to do the same for them. They could see no reason for that. Among the Sioux any man was welcome to drop in at meal-time and eat his fill, quite without invitation. Stinginess was the lowest, meanest vice they knew. Yankee thrift, Yankee caution, Yankee sharp practices were all alike abhorrent to the Sioux. And seeing how the white man behaved, the Sioux could only decide that this stranger was a mean, stingy, inhospitable rascal. The Sioux did not like the way he treated them, and they began to resent it. If, today, hordes of Chinese millionaires passed through the States, consuming our supplies, wasting our resources, enjoying our hospitality, and then—when an opportunity offered to return our entertainment—treated us as spongers, beggars, and thugs, what should we do? Probably we should be less patient than the Sioux were under like conditions.

The proud Oglala Sioux, the touchy Brulé Sioux, the friendly Cheyennes, the unstable Arapahos—all these were willing and eager to smoke with the chiefs sent out by the Grandfather from Washington.

Sitting Bull's people, however, away north on Grand River, cared little about the treaty. They went down to Laramie because the Black Robe asked it, and to see their relatives. They were always ready for a holiday. As for white men, they saw very few and wished to see none—except traders. "All we want from the white man is his hatchet, his knife, and his gun," they said. "We made one treaty; why make another?" That was what the Hunkpapa said. In fact, the sorriest vagabond in the Hunkpapa camp, with only a gee-string and a piece of old tent-cloth to cover him, thought himself infinitely better than any white man. He despised the traders as a lot of unwarlike, timid weaklings, who brought trade goods produced by more cunning people beyond the big water. Why trouble to go all the way to the Platte to smoke again with them?

Why indeed?

The civilization of the Plains Indians was established long before white men saw their country. It was ancient then. But with the coming of the horse from Europe, every phase of it received, as it were, a shot in the arm. Life became freer, richer, bolder, more picturesque, colorful, prosperous. The change wrought by the introduction of the horse in Indian life can only be compared with that brought about in our own civilization by the invention of the automobile. A static world became dynamic. Men who had lived laborious lives, plodding after game with heavy packs on their backs, who had slept huddled in wretched, leaky bark lodges or cramped tents barely ten feet across, men who had and hoped to have no property, who never traveled, never traded, never had enough to eat, and to whom war was little more than self-defense, now suddenly found themselves emancipated in a grand and glorious world.

Their range now extended from the Rockies to the Lakes, from Mexico to the Barren Grounds. They packed their burdens on animals, enlarged their dwellings to stately dimensions, got food with ease and in abundance, had something to trade, something to give away, and their warfare developed into a glorious sport. For more than a century they lived like kings.

This rich, colorful, free life of the Plains Indians entranced all men who beheld it. It penetrated the eastern forests: farmer tribes (like the Cheyennes) took to hunting again, and even the most sedentary nations hunted and lived in tents half the year. The horse, the tipi, the camp circle, the *coup*, the Sun Dance—all the typical traits of Plains Indian culture spread like wildfire; into the woods eastward, over the mountains westward; northward almost to the country of the Eskimo; southward into the Spanish settlements, where (early in the eighteenth century) the Spanish governors had to issue edicts to *compel* their subjects to till the soil and to hunt buffalo *only* at stated seasons.

Plains Indian culture bade fair to sweep the continent—until the coming of the English-speaking ploughmen. It had absorbed some of the Spaniards, had swallowed the French Canadians bodily. The Hudson's Bay Company men, and other trappers, were hardly more than Indians in thought and habit. Old Bill Williams is said to have offered his corncob pipe to the sun, like any shaman. Kit Carson lived in a tipi and counted *coups*.

To this very day, when an Indian in New York or California wishes to dress the part, he puts on the scalp-shirt and war-bonnet of a Plains Indian. So great is the prestige of that far-flung civilization still. Now, the Prairie or Teton Sioux formed the very hub and center of that civilization, and of the most powerful Indian nation on the continent. Why should they care for the wishes of a far-off white Grandfather? Not all of them could be induced to attend the treaty.

Yet many of the Sioux went. . . .

To Sitting Bull much the most interesting sight was the white man and his belongings. Long before, his people had bestowed various descriptive epithets upon the white men. In the first place, the name Was-e-chun, or Guardian Spirits, had been given them, because of the wonderful things they had and did. But after familiarity bred contempt, other nicknames were applied.

It was noticeable that one white man smelled like two porcupines, that many of them were apparently in mourning, with hair cut short, and that they had much hair on their faces and bodies. Hair on face or body was offensive to the Sioux, perhaps because he went naked so much. Because of this hirsuteness, the Sioux sometimes called the whites Dog Faces—an uncomplimentary title. Sitting Bull's people also had noticed that the white men turned out their toes in a ludicrous manner, and therefore dubbed them Crooked Feet.

Perhaps it was only their short hair which made the ears of white men seem to stick out so far, but the Sioux thought it must be due to ill-treatment received when children. While visiting caravans along the Oregon Trail, some of the Sioux had seen white parents punish their own children by pulling their ears until they cried, and the terrible cruelty of people who could so abuse their own flesh and blood profoundly shocked the Indians. An Indian who punished his own child would have been considered crazy; such a thing was almost unknown. Therefore, when a Sioux called the white men Flop Ears, it was no mere derisive nickname: it suggested that dark cruelty of which no decent Indian parent was ever guilty.

The Sioux had heard terrible tales of how white men, when starving, would eat each other (as sometimes happened among the trappers, or in the case of that unfortunate Donner party). And so, when pork was offered to the young men, an old chief advised them not to touch it. . . .

The white man's beef seemed very insipid to him, and he found that a few pounds of it made him sick. And so Indian dogs continued to go into the kettle by the hundred. All in all, Sitting Bull saw little at Fort Laramie that attracted him to the white men, though he admired their guns, their knives, their big, strong horses. For the sake of trade goods, he was quite ready to be friends; in fact, he considered that his people had always been friends—ever since the treaty of 1825. So far as white men's society went, he could be quite happy without that. . . .

Following is an anonymous letter written to Sitting Bull, Chief of the Sioux Indians, Pine Ridge Agency Standing Rock, South Dakota, postmarked from Augusta, Georgia, December 8, 1890:

"Sitting Bull, old boy, of course you are aware of the newspaper notoriety you have gained through your cussedness, and the uneasy feeling you have caused as an agitator—a worse 'tater' could not be found.

Now, I will proceed to express the object of this letter, which is to inform you that if the Military Authorities do not punish or cause the troops of the Regular army to quench your bloodthirstiness, there are 20 or 30 of us Georgian 'Corn-Crackers' who will go up there & do you up in a brown rag. We mean business, & don't you 'fordoubt' it.

I tell you this as a friend & hope you will accept it as advice, for

I don't want to see you hurt, and 'I would hate to have to go up there to hurt you myself.'

You have danced a long jig now. You had better let somebody else have a chance.

I will close now by telling you that if we hear any more of this monkey business; we are coming and the first thing we do will be to cut your right leg off & beat your brains (or horse sense) out with the bloody end of it.

Hoping these few lines will be a valuable warning to you, I await results of my effort to save you & your tribe from being wiped from the face of the earth like hogs with the measles. If there is any more moon-light hops, you will be swept away like the chaff before a jimmy-kane.

With due respect, I am, A preventor of cruelty to (you) animals.

P. S.—If you have time 'when you have time' I would be glad to hear from you by letter. Give my love to Misses Sitting Bull & all the other cows."

Newspaper clipping from the *Chattanooga Times* of January 11, 1891, headlined "History of Sitting Bull," reads as follows:

Sitting Bull, or "Tatankaiyotaka," was killed on the morning of December 14, 1890, by Bull Head, Lieutenant, and Shave Head, Sergeant, of the Indian Police of Standing Rock Agency, N. D. This is very generally known, and there is universal satisfaction over the fact. But especially is his death gratifying those parties in charge of Indian affairs. This satisfaction does not arise from the fear of any great danger impending from him, but because he was arrogant, obstinate, conceited.

Another newspaper clipping sent by C. N. Herreid on Sitting Bull, dated September 13, 1891, reads:

When the news was telegraphed from the Standing Rock Agency last winter that the great warrior and chieftain, Sitting Bull, was dead, I instinctively exclaimed, he has been murdered! I was then nearly two thousand miles from the wigwam where the famous chief of the Sioux nation met death at the hands of the Indian police. A few days ago I visited Ft. Yates and there, unsolicited, heard expressed the deliberate judgment of men who were familiar with all the circumstances, that the killing of Sitting Bull was nothing more or less than cold blooded, premeditated murder. Not satisfied with the life of the old patriarch himself, we were told that his son, a mere youth, was aroused from his innocent slumbers in his aged father's tepee, dragged from his bed and shot dead while the agonizing cries of his mother and sister were piercing the silent night air imploring mercy from the judgment seat of the Great Spirit. We were also told that the feeling of disgust among the Indians for a government that tolerates such atrocities is universal and enduring.

Blinded by prejudice, intensified by perjured reports, the popular feeling against this remarkable red man was that of intense hatred.

THE BUSINESS OF SCALPING

While firearms and steel knives gave strong impetus to scalping in North America, the acme of the custom was reached after the institution by whites of scalp premiums, accompanied by the employment of the natives by the whites for scalp gathering, and scalping by the whites themselves.

IT IS a well-established fact that the conflicts of primitive peoples, while very frequent, are in general not attended by many fatalities. The same was true of the Indians, with the exception of the very infrequent instances of a success of an attack by surprise, which was followed by a general massacre.

The introduction of firearms changed this state of affairs. The guns became not only the direct cause of a greater number of fatalities, but they also served to demoralize the party armed in a more primitive manner and facilitated pursuit. In consequence the wars became more bloody and there were more scalps.

In North America the natives were supplied with firearms by the colonists themselves, in some cases surreptitiously, in others openly.

Excerpt from Georg Friederici, "Scalping in America," *Annual Report of the Smithsonian Institution, 1906,* (Washington: Government Printing Office, 1907), pp. 432-437.

They were also furnished with the iron or steel knife, which greatly facilitated the removal of the scalp lock. Formerly the scalping was done with knives made of various materials. The reed knife was found in Brazil, Guiana, and the southeastern part of North America; the shell knife was used along the entire Gulf and north along the Atlantic coast as far as the territory of the Huron-Iroquois, also to some extent on the Pacific coast and among the Araukanians; a fist-toothed knife existed in the Chaco, throughout Brazil and the Guianas; and a stone knife prevailed in Mexico and neighboring regions, in California, the Rocky Mountains, on the Plains, and in Texas. The Apache knew how to sever the scalp lock with the sinew cord of the bow. All of these implements possessed disadvantages when compared with the white man's knife, and the latter was eagerly adopted. It became a much desired article of commerce and exchange and was soon used in scalping, upon the frequency and development of which it must have exerted a stimulating effect. . . . In the beginning of the nineteenth century, during the height of the power of the fur companies, $7.50 was paid in their territory for a knife which in England was worth 3½ pence.

"While firearms and steel knives gave a strong impetus to scalping in North America, the acme of the custom was reached after the institution by whites of scalp premiums, accompanied by the employ-ment of the natives by the whites for scalp gathering, and scalping by the whites themselves."

The first to offer premiums for the heads of their native enemies were, in 1637, the Puritans of New England. They asked for the heads, scalping being as yet unknown in that part of the country. As a result, heads of the Pequods were brought in by the colonists and allied Indians in large numbers.

Thirty-eight years after the Pequod war, began that against King Philip, and head premiums were again established. At this period the custom of scalping had already extended into New England, and most of the trophies obtained must have been scalps.

On the 15th of July, 1675, the Connecticut colonists made with one of the Narragansett chiefs a treaty in which they promised for the person of one of the feared Wampanog chiefs 40 cloth coats, or 20 for his head alone, and for each of his subjects 2 coats if living or

1 if dead. To their own troops they paid 30 shillings for each head. To the "heroine," Hannah Dustin, who with her own hands is said to have taken and brought in the scalps of 2 Indian men, 2 women, and 6 children, the colony paid 50 pounds, besides which she received many expressions of thanks and numerous gifts, including a substantial one from Governor Nicholson.

In 1680 scalp prizes were offered by the colonists of South Carolina; in 1689 they offered the high sum of 8 pounds for each scalp of an Indian warrior. About this time we hear for the first time of scalp premiums offered by the French. In 1688 the French Canadians paid for every scalp of their enemies, whether white or Indian, 10 beaver skins, which was also a high price, equivalent in Montreal to the price of a gun with pounds of powder and 40 pounds of lead. Later on, about 1691, the governor of Canada paid 10 crowns for every scalp, 20 crowns for every white male captive, and 10 crowns for a white female captive. Later on the scalp as well as the captive price was lowered to 1 crown each, though the government officials declared that 10 crowns for the scalp of every existing Iroquois would be a good investment for Louis XIV.

We have seen that it was the English who offered the first scalp premiums, and it was the French who first extended such rewards to the scalps of whites. This latter custom was, however, also adopted before long by the English colonists, and in 1693, but particularly in 1696, premiums were offered specifically for French scalps. The price per scalp, perhaps on account of the poor Canadian treasury, was always higher among the English than among the French. In 1707, during Queen Anne's war, the English increased the Indian scalp premium for those who were not employed by the government of the colonies to 100 pounds.

In 1703, during Queen Anne's war, the young French colony in Louisiana began also to offer scalp rewards, commencing with 10 crowns for each scalp. After this the prices ranged conformably with those in Canada.

In later wars in which the colonists were concerned scalp hunting was incited to still greater intensity. The premiums were large, ranging up to 100 pounds for one scalp; and they applied to Indians as well as to white enemies. The alluring profits and the growing difficulty of securing the trophy led some to skillfully make two or even more scalps out of one, and to other, more grave, abuses; members of friendly tribes and even the white countrymen of the scalpers were not safe, and even graves were made to yield victims. In June, 1755, General Braddock guaranteed his soldiers and Indians 5 pounds for every scalp of the enemy. A reward of $200 was prescribed for the head of the Delaware chief Shingask and 100 pounds for that of the Jesuit Le Loutre. Scalp prices were offered by the State of Pennsylvania. On the 7th of July, 1764, Governor Penn announced the following rewards: For every captured Indian more than 10 years old, $150; for every scalp of a killed Indian, $134; for every captured woman or boy under 10 years of age and belonging to inimical tribes, $130; and for every scalp of a slain squaw, $50.

The employment by the various colonies of friendly tribes as allies in war fostered scalping. In 1693 Frontenac ceremoniously received from Indians some scalps of the English. In 1746 Governor Clinton received and counted in an open meeting some scalps of Frenchmen, honored with a *nom de guerre* the Indian leader whose band secured them, and then had the Indians perform a war dance before him, in which William Johnson, then the Iroquois agent and later on a baronet and English general, appeared painted and half naked with the Indians. In the French colonies the conditions were similar. Scalping was also practiced during the War of the Revolution, and that on both sides. Serious complaints were made in this regard against the English, and Hamilton, "the hair-buyer general," was on this account for a long time the object of a bitter hatred. There is no doubt that the English, who incited some of the Indians against the colonists, also offered pay for scalps, though this does not seem to have been the subject of any special law or public ruling. English commanders and generals, among others Burgoyne, received scalps in festive gatherings. In the north the English, following Sullivan's expedition, paid $8; in Georgia occasionally 3 pounds for a scalp. So far as the colonies are concerned, among the border population scalping was general, besides which some of the legislatures offered direct premiums. Thus the legislature of South Carolina promised 75 pounds for every scalp of the fighting men of the enemy, 100 pounds for every captured Indian and 80 pounds for every captured Englishman or Negro.

In Mexico, the first offers of head premiums of which the writer could find a record date from 1616 to 1618, preceding, therefore, by twenty years similar rewards given by the New Englanders during the Pequod war. The occasion for the Mexican offers was the Tepehuane rebellion in the State of Durango. During the eighteenth century, particularly toward its close, and in the beginning of the nineteenth, scalps, which to prevent frauds had to show both ears, seem to have had a definite market value in northern Mexico, but exact data on the subject are wanting. During the second third of the nineteenth century reports concerning scalping are more frequent. . . .

Such a state of affairs lasted for several decades, continuing past the French invasion and well up to the eighties. The rewards offered reached, in 1863 to 1870, the large sums of $200 to $300 for each ordinary scalp and $500 for that of a chief of the Indians.

In Central and South America we find no scalp premiums and no scalp hunting.

The part of the white population most directly concerned in scalping were the frontiersmen, with the hunters, trappers, and miners. Their mode of life and their frequent dealings with the Indians, of friendly as well as unfriendly nature, developed in these men and even women, who were for the most part the descendants of the Scotch-Irish, manners which were not always in accord with those of civilization.

In some cases the Indians and after them the whites severed not only the scalp, but also other hairy parts of the skin or other pieces, and some of these were utilized for tobacco pouches, straps, belts, etc. Such pieces of skin became even, in some instances, articles of trade. In the summer of 1779 the farmers in the neighborhood of Prickets Fort, in West Virginia, killed an Indian who was wounded in a fight, and the body was scalped and skinned. The skin was tanned, and from it were made a saddle, ball bags, and belts. One of the bags is said by Mr. Thwaites to be preserved to this day by a grand-uncle of one of the farmers who did the skinning. But even the whites were not always safe before other whites in this respect; thus we read in Norton's *Redeemed Captive* that during the war of 1746 a French youth cut off an arm of a slain New Englander for the purpose of making himself a tobacco pouch.

It is but natural that a custom of such force and duration as scalping left some permanent traces, which are best recognizable in the language. The word scalp is commonly used as a synonym for the hair-covered skin of the head. It was applied to animals, and one hears to this day about the "scalp" of the puma, bear, wolf, etc. Premiums for wolf scalps were an important item of income and expense among the colonists. In ordinary conversation the term found, and to some extent still finds, many applications; thus "may I never see a scalp" was a form of oath; and there were the expressions "There can be no scalping between us," "To go a-scalping," "A company of expert hair-dressers," etc. The railroad ticket "scalper" is still a well-known figure. Figuratively, the word was used to denote social conquests, etc.

At the present time, scalping in North America has ceased to exist. It has been prohibited, under heavy penalties, by the law, and had to be given up by the conquered Indians with other parts of their former culture. Curiously enough the trophy formerly so common has become a rare article, even in American ethnological museums.

5

THE ROLE OF IMPERIALISM

MODERN IMPERIALISM is the heir of the conquest invasions of the European nations and of the exploration and frontier settlement of their nationals. From its sixteenth century beginnings to the present, it has gradually become the most considerable politico-economic movement of its supporting groups. They construe it as a part of their national welfare as it is so vital an extension of their political and economic interests. As MacCrone points out, there have been two traditions in this expansion, one idealistic and the other realistic, the one, stemming from the crusader, the explorer and the missionary priest, and the other, from the trader and settler. A fundamental conflict has prevailed between the practical interests and political objectives of the power politics involved, on the one hand, and on the other, the idealistic motivations of propagating the faith, exploring the unknown, and civilizing the heathen and primitive peoples. The mercenary motives have become increasingly dominant, due to the connection between the European industrial system and the progressive organization of colonial markets and the source supplies of raw materials. Trade rivalries have combined with national rivalries to bring imperialism to a stage where it is an organized system of power politics, carrying over some of the worst features of the frontier phase into more elaborate economic programs of exploitation.

The excerpts from MacCrone, Scholes and Toynbee in addition to showing an interesting series of contrasts and comparisons between the various branches and phases of European imperialist expansion, offer convincing proof of its basic common character in spite of all superficial variation. Imperialism's forms and official policies are modified, of course, by marked differences in the cultural set-up of its sphere of invasion. Its rationalizations and emphases also vary from time to time and from one national tradition to another. But, as MacCrone writes, "whatever the form of European expansion, the nature of the contacts between the European and the non-European tended to be, from the beginning, of a violent and aggressive kind." In spite of the contrasts Scholes notes between the Spanish and the British colonial regimes in America, he too agrees that "the fate of the Maya was essentially the same as that of other aboriginal populations which have been brought into contact with a more advanced civilization."

Scholes corroborates the judgment that from as early a date as the sixteenth century there has been conflict between the economic and the ecclesiastical and humanitarian motives of empire, and that gradually the economic motives gained complete ascendancy. Religious scruples against slavery, especially the enslavement of fellow-Christians, the zeal for proselytizing, all gave way to the priority of the interests of trade, economic expansion and political control. In the Spanish-Portuguese zone of influence that Scholes reports upon, zeal for the missionary propagation of Christianity retarded and for a time countered the worst features of the slave trade, which went on unchecked in the Protestant zones of influence in North America and the British West Indies. Finally African slavery was taken up by the Spanish to obviate the enslavement of the Indians, for whose conversion there was at the time a well-organized campaign. But Negro slave labor was insufficient, and the economic needs of the conquerors eventually dictated a system of forced labor for the Indians, for which the tribal Indian chieftains were forced to serve as intermediaries. This, with land peonage, became the equivalent in the Spanish colonies for the chattel slavery of their Northern neighbors.

Scholes's article also illuminates the way in which difference between the aboriginal cultures of the southern and the northern American Indian tribes caused marked difference in the adaptations and reactions of the invading civilizations. The semi-nomadic character of the North American Indian cultures enabled the British to deal with these tribes as block units and force them back, in the main, outside the colonial system. Their economy was not particularly suited to useful incorporation. On the other hand, the strong agricultural economy and rootage of the South and Central American Indians, with its greater resistance, forced their incorporation as an integral part of the colonial society. There was, accordingly, greater fusion of the two cultures in this area than in the North. Similarly with the people themselves, there was freer intermixture both with the whites and with the African Negroes, who were later introduced, and the half-caste attained at least an intermediate status. In the North, however, with slavery and sharper lines of race prejudice, there was, in spite of much miscegenation, rigid social exclusion that extended to the mulatto as well as to the full-bloods, so that there was less cultural interchange and fewer elements of the native cultures survived. Contemporary society in these areas still reflects this cultural divergence, but the stamp of political dominance and the effects of economic exploitation are marked upon both regions and their subordinated minorities.

In Africa, imperialistic penetration has been even more dominated by direct and overt motives of gain. Not only was this due to the slave trade, in which wholesale traffic in human beings was put on a par with the trade in gold, ivory and other commodities, but to the fact that the really effective colonial penetration of Africa is the work of the mature and latest phase of economic imperialism. As late as 1877, only one-tenth of the vast continent of Africa was under white domination, but by 1925, nine-tenths had been formally partitioned among the leading European nations,—Britain, France, Germany, Italy, Belgium, Portugal and Spain. African groups have thus met the full force of the last phase of overseas capitalistic expansion, and suffered the triple pressure of the search for raw materials and for markets, the search for settlement lands, and the increased demand for native labor necessary for all of these self-seeking enterprises. Cultural disintegration has been accelerated by the rapidity of this encroachment, and intensified by the employment of the more recent technological developments of European civilization. Physical and cultural resistance has been reduced to a minimum, and as the competition among the several nations grew, native life and resources were subject to directly proportional strain. All this has made the modern partition of Africa the most typical instance of economic imperialism, in which its political, economic and cultural motives and policies have become most evident.

Woolf generalizes them, not merely as they relate to Africa but to the whole non-European or non-industrialized world. The current forms of imperialism rest, he shows, on a far-flung industrial economy linked to the political power of a modern state. This tacit alliance of the capitalist, the trader, the manufacturer, the financier, the government and the colonial administration is the elaborate politico-economic system that has slowly been built up on the foundations of the early European culture expansions.

Direct participation of the national state in economic imperialism has not only brought about this coalition of political and economic interests, but has given the enterprise an aggressive character which economic expansion alone may never have acquired. The simultaneous pursuit of common ends by competitive national states has given imperialism also a formidable international character, along with which has gone a characteristic ideology more or less standardized and reinforced by them all. There has been a wholesale identification of the "cause of civilization" with any and all phases of European-non-European conflicts of interest, which has emphasized racial and cultural bias. But on the other hand, national rivalry has several times threatened large sections of the imperialist structure, and largely because of the political involvement, these eventualities are still inherent in the system and still threaten it far more than any counter-resistance of the subject groups can possibly do.

George Young's article treats particularly these actual and potential repercussions of imperialist tactics. Especially in its maneuvers for markets and spheres of influence, European policy has been less successful in the case of the more organized non-European nations, as also in its auxiliary extensions of non-political Europeanization. Resentment of its superiority pretensions have particularly characterized the second-generation reactions of educated non-Europeans, and Asiatic groups generally. Inconsistencies between professed code and practice have begun to weaken the once overwhelming prestige of the European political system and culture. More threatening still is the imitative imperialism of other non-European nations,—Japan particularly, which threatens from the double angle of competition and of challenge to the European cultural supremacy. All this would seem to indicate that imperialism is approaching a period of unprecedented stress, even to the point, some think, of prospective liquidation.

TRADE AND CULTURAL CONFLICT

*The overseas activities of the Protestant countries, although en-
couraged by the State, were for the most part the result of private
enterprise undertaken by companies which were granted a charter
for the purpose. But whatever the form of European expansion,
the nature of the contacts between European and non-European
tended to be, from the beginning, of a violent and aggressive kind.
The European who initiated and established contact was always
the intruder from without, the stranger at the gates, ever ready to
seize by force what he could not secure by peaceful means.*

THE RISE of the nation-states in Europe prepared the way for
an expansion overseas of European control over, and European
contacts with, non-European countries and their inhabitants which
by the sixteenth century was already well under way. Led by Portugal
and Spain, and followed in the seventeenth century by Holland,
England, and France, the European expansion to the West and to
the East was the result of many, sometimes even conflicting, motives
and assumed many different forms. It is the character, however, of
the Protestant European expansion, and more particularly of Dutch
expansion overseas, that is of special interest for our theme. As contrasted with the expansion of the Catholic countries which in the
beginning, at any rate, was to some extent permeated by a crusading
and missionary spirit, the expansion of the Protestant countries was
from the beginning far more secular and mercenary in spirit. While
the representative figures of the former were the soldier and the
Jesuit priest, those of the latter were the colonist and the trader.
Then, as now, trade rivalries and national rivalries were closely intertwined and quarrels which had originated in Europe were carried
overseas as well, where they were fought out with even greater bitterness and unscrupulousness.

For the Catholic countries, expansion overseas was regarded as a
form of State enterprise whose activities were directed and supervised
by a royal representative or viceroy. The overseas activities of the

Excerpt from I. D. MacCrone, *Race Attitudes in South Africa* (London:
Oxford University Press, 1937), pp. 3-9.

Protestant countries, on the other hand, although encouraged by the State, were for the most part the result of private enterprise undertaken by companies which were granted a charter for the purpose. This difference in organization was to lead in the case of the trading companies, both Dutch and English, to a concentration upon the trading side of their activities and to a subordination of those functions of control which were properly exercised by a State authority over its subjects. Although the great East India Companies by virtue of their charters could, and did, exercise sovereign powers, those powers were exercised more completely in the interests of their commercial aims than might have been the case had a State authority, with wider interests, been responsible for overseas expansion. When State control did finally step in, as, for instance, at the Cape at the end of the eighteenth century, the effects of Company rule, although relatively only a minor and, in a sense, negative factor in the total situation, had already been fully realized. It was not so much what the Company form of expansion did as what it failed to do, that indirectly played a part in affecting the relations of European and non-European.

But whatever the form of European expansion, the nature of the contacts between European and non-European tended to be, from the beginning, of a violent and aggressive kind. The European who initiated and established contact was always the intruder from without, the stranger at the gates, ever ready to seize by force what he could not secure by peaceful means. . . . Although Henry the Navigator, who never sailed a ship, might give the first impulse to European expansion overseas in order to extend the Christian faith, most of his life was spent in leading a last, long crusade against the Moors. Although the Portuguese ships that followed one another down the coast of Africa beyond the Moorish sphere might never sail without their complement of priests, there was no hesitation about attacking and seizing as slaves the Negroes of the West Coast who, on occasion, gave as good as they got. Although Spain, as the elder daughter of the Church, might, under Isabella, support the enterprise of Columbus in order that the blessings of the Catholic Church should be extended to the New World, that did not prevent the depopulation of the West Indian islands or the exploitation of the mainland and its inhabitants in spite of all the efforts of a Las Casas to invoke State aid for their protection. His remedy, which consisted in the importation of thousands of Negro slaves from Africa, was no better than the disease. . . .

Speaking broadly, we may say that there was hardly a single instance in the early history of European expansion overseas by way of conquest, trade, or colonization where the first contacts between Europeans and the inhabitants of the newly discovered countries did not, sooner or later, lead to conflict. And with the exception of a very rare case like the venture of William Penn, the same generalization appears to be equally true of the later contacts with the native inhabitants, especially of those countries that could be readily exploited and settled by European traders and colonists. . . .

While the main stratum of the European attitude toward non-Europeans was largely a matter of religion, there were considerable variations in the expression of that attitude corresponding to the obvious differences among the non-Europeans or non-Christians themselves. At one end of the scale were the Mohammedan and Hindu peoples, as highly civilized as any European nation, and often far wealthier and more powerful, organized into states under their own rulers and princes and with their own religions, laws, and customs. The European, under these circumstances, could at times only achieve his aims by negotiation and conciliation, by treaties that secured him special privileges or concessions at the expense of his commercial rivals. He was, and remained, an intruder who was only tolerated because of his value as a trader. Under such circumstances, there was no question of the European imposing his will upon the non-European —the most that he could hope for was to be granted the necessary facilities for carrying on his trading activities.

The Dutch merchants to Japan who succeeded the Portuguese in 1639 were isolated on a small island off Nagasaki and treated like the inhabitants of a ghetto. They were obliged to trample annually upon the Cross in the presence of a Japanese official and to make themselves objects of public derision by cutting capers for the entertainment of the Court on an annual visit to the capital. No wonder that the Dutch *koopman* gained the reputation of being ready to go through Hell for the sake of trade.

In actual practice, as often as not, the European found himself at a disadvantage since his opportunities as a trader were so entirely dependent upon the favor or goodwill of the ruling prince. The picture of Sir Thomas Roe, ambassador of King James at the court of the Grand Mogul, endeavoring patiently for months on end to negotiate a favorable treaty on behalf of the English East India Company may serve as an illustration of one kind of contact between European and non-European and of their relative positions in those days. The belief of the European in his own innate superiority over everyone outside Europe, and the fashionable dogma of mankind's division into superior and inferior races—those characteristic products of eighteenth-century European domination and nineteenth-century evolutionary theory—were, as yet, non-existent in the minds of Europeans, since the circumstances of the time did not favor their development. The only bar to intermarriage was one of religion, and when that was removed miscegenation took place freely enough. It was, in fact, encouraged on grounds of policy, since it enabled the European to gain a stronger foothold in the new countries. Albuquerque, for example, did everything in his power to encourage his Portuguese to marry Indian wives, and the same policy was followed later by the Dutch to strengthen their hold on Further India.

At the other end of the scale were the primitive races who were, for the most part, inhabitants of Africa. They were regarded as wholly savage, without religion, law, or morals, and hence more like wild beasts than human beings. It was usually taken for granted that they were cannibals. From the very beginning, the relations between them and the Europeans were entirely anarchical. Since they fell outside the pale of humanity, they could be freely kidnapped, enslaved, or massacred, for, apart from their value as "black ivory," they could offer little or no inducement to the European trader who, with his eyes fixed upon the wealth of India and the East, avoided contact with them as far as possible.

SPANISH POLICY AND THE YUCATAN

The original impelling motive of discovery and colonization was economic, and the exploitation of the resources of the colonies for the benefit of the Crown and of the colonists who supported the imperial system always remained the paramount factor in determining the character of administration.

ALTHOUGH THE Spanish colonies were for the most part within the tropical and sub-tropical zones, they contained large areas suitable for European settlement. Colonists in considerable numbers migrated to specially favored regions in New Spain and Peru, where they engaged in farming, stock raising, mining and trade. But the Spaniards found most of these areas already occupied by a numerous aboriginal population with highly developed civilizations based on an advanced agricultural economy. In this respect Hispanic America contrasted rather sharply with the temperate zones in which the British colonies in North America were founded for the vast expanse of what is now the United States was lightly populated and the Indians were much less strongly rooted to the soil than those of Mexico, Guatemala and Peru. The British were able, therefore, to deal with the Indian tribes as independent units, as nations outside their own colonial system, whereas Spain was forced to incorporate them as an integral part of colonial society. Thus social evolution in Hispanic America has been characterized by the interaction and partial fusion of two races, and two sets of culture patterns, European and aboriginal.

The forces which influenced the formulation of policy dealing with the aborigines and their relations with the Spanish colonists were economic and religious, selfish and humanitarian. The original impelling motive of discovery and colonization was economic, and the exploitation of the resources of the colonies for the benefit of the Crown and of the colonists who supported the imperial system always

Excerpt from France V. Scholes, "The Beginnings of Hispano-Indian Society in Yucatan," *Scientific Monthly*, Vol. 44 (June 1937), pp. 530-538.

remained the paramount factor in determining the character of administration. But the long crusade against the Moors had identified the cause of Catholic orthodoxy with national interests, and a militant zeal for the faith inspired the Spanish nation. It was inevitable, therefore, that when the Indies were conquered, the conversion of the aborigines and the extirpation of the older pagan religion and ceremonial should become one of the dominant aims of empire. Moreover, the Spanish jurists of the sixteenth century were inspired by a broad humanitarianism and an increasing interest in the relations between nations and peoples. The question of the aborigines raised important problems of theoretical and practical justice and the influence of the jurists contributed much to the formulation of legislation for the preservation of the liberties of the Indians within the limits imposed by the introduction of a new faith and the maintenance of Spanish supremacy.

The attempt to combine the economic and the ecclesiastico-humanitarian motives of empire created problems of tremendous historical significance. The Crown was obliged to recognize the demands of the colonists for the right to exploit Indian lands and labor, but it sought to limit abuses by protective legislation that would preserve at least the legal status of the Indians as free beings and prevent the total expropriation of Indian property. It sought also to ensure the conversion of the Indians to the Christian faith, at the same time preserving the traditional folk culture in so far as it did not conflict with Christian standards of morals and orthodoxy. Hispanic America became in effect a sociological laboratory where experiments in human relationships were made on a vast scale. The final result was the creation of a Hispano-Indian society characterized by the domination of the masses by a small privileged minority, the hybridization of culture and the existence of unsolved problems of land and labor. . . .

The basic pattern of Hispano-Indian society in Yucatan was clearly marked out by the end of the sixteenth century or about sixty years after the conquest. By that time a new ruling caste of foreign origin, extremely jealous of its privileges, had obtained firm control over the destinies of the Maya race; the exploitation of Indian labor for the benefit of this caste had become an important problem of interracial relations; and a considerable amount of fusion of culture, especially in the realm of religion, had taken place. During the remainder of the colonial period these basic problems of provincial society remained essentially the same. The methods of exploitation of Indian labor changed according to the needs of the ruling class. The proportion of Christian and pagan elements in the total content of belief and ceremonial by which the Indians made their adjustments with the invisible world varied from place to place and from time to time. But there was no essential change in the fundamental character of Hispano-Indian society.

Several centuries prior to the Spanish conquest the Maya of Yucatan had established a measure of political unity. However, rivalry between the chieftains had caused the disintegration of central authority, and at the opening of the sixteenth century Yucatan was divided into a number of petty states or cacicazgos which frequently engaged in interstate warfare. Political leadership within each state tended to be concentrated in the hands of a ruling family, such as the Xius in Mani or the Cocoms in Sotuta. The unifying forces were cultural rather than political—a common language and a common fund of folk tradition.

The Spanish conquest destroyed the independence of these states and re-established territorial and political unity within Yucatan, but the reins of government were held henceforth by an alien race. Supreme political and military authority was exercised by the Spanish governors appointed by the Crown. Subordinate to the governors were various local officers and the governing councils of the Spanish towns.

A measure of self-government was retained by the Maya in the Indian villages where local affairs continued to be controlled by native officers. In the beginning the Spanish authorities recognized the claims of former native lords and lesser nobles, and retained them as governors and principales of the pueblos. Moreover, during the sixteenth century certain chieftains even continued to exercise some leadership over areas that approximated the former petty states. But in the course of time the old rulers and their direct descendants were gradually removed from positions of influence and leadership.

This does not mean that the former ruling families lost all their old prestige. The Xius, for example, were recognized as having noble rank, and they obtained certain concessions and privileges, such as exemption from tribute, free labor on their farms and the right to possess firearms. They were also able to retain considerable holdings of land. But their influence as political and cultural leaders of the race was at an end.

The real governing class in Yucatan subsequent to the conquest was a group of about 125 families, made up of conquerors, first settlers and their descendants. Control of the local councils gave the conquerors and their descendants the means for resisting measures limiting their vested rights. They were frequently able also to force the provincial governor or the defender of the Indians to abandon policies for the amelioration of abuses of native labor and other reforms detrimental to the interests of the ruling caste. Occasionally a provincial governor would try to strengthen his own position by the appointment of relations or personal retainers to local offices, but the conquistador caste would immediately present a forceful protest to the Crown and would usually be upheld.

In so far as possible the conquistadores sought to keep their blood clean, at least the line which inherited property. A few formally contracted marriage with Indian women, but most of the unions between the two races were extramarital. Mestizo children born out of wedlock were sometimes legitimized, but the ruling caste used all its influence to prevent them from holding office.

The most important privilege granted to the conquerors and their descendants in all parts of the Indies was preference in appointment to encomiendas. During the first half of the sixteenth century an encomienda grant was essentially the right to use the labor of a stated group of Indians without pay. But this led to such abuses that a fixed tribute usually payable in kind was introduced in lieu of service, with the result that the encomiendas became a form of pension. The encomenderos were always able, of course, to obtain a considerable amount of labor from their Indians by extra-legal means, but subsequent to 1550 the essence of the system was tribute.

In return for the tribute payments the encomenderos were supposed to assume responsibility for the indoctrination of their Indians, but this obligation became a mere formality in so far as personal assistance in the missionary program was concerned. The most important obligation imposed by a grant of encomienda was military service, and in Yucatan the encomenderos were frequently called upon to defend the coasts or the port of Campeche against foreign corsairs. Grants of encomienda were made for two lives or generations, but a third life was usually permitted by dissimulation on the part of the governing officials.

In Mexico proper, i.e., in the area northwest of the Isthmus of Tehuantepec, about 55 per cent of the Indian pueblos were held in encomienda, the remaining 45 per cent paying tribute to the Crown. In Yucatan more than 90 per cent of the towns were granted as encomiendas. This fact may be explained by the limited resources of Yucatan and the lack of opportunity for profitable enterprise other than agriculture. There were no mines; trade was limited mostly to dealings in those very native products of which the tribute payments were comprised, viz., cotton cloth, maize, poultry and wax. In the sixteenth century grants of encomienda were practically the only means available for gratifying services performed during the conquest or for attracting new settlers to the province.

It is not surprising, therefore, that there was keen rivalry for appointments to encomiendas, that the tendency of a governor to fill vacancies by choosing new arrivals in preference to members of the old families was always bitterly resisted, or that protests were made against every attempt by the Crown to bring the system to an end. Grants of encomienda continued to be made until 1785, when the Crown finally ordered all tributes to be paid into the treasury, but even then payments continued to be made to former holders of encomiendas during the remainder of their lives. . . .

When the Crown ordered the abolition of the labor phases of the encomienda system, it had to provide some substitute, as the colonists were dependent on the natives for house servants, unskilled laborers for various services, burden bearers and semi-skilled artisans for house building and public works. The Spaniards were free to employ all the labor they needed at the current rate of wages, but the supply of Indians willing to work, even for pay, was often inadequate. Consequently, the Crown found it necessary to authorize a system of forced labor by which quotas of workers were summoned periodically from the Indian pueblos to serve in the mines, on farms, on building operations or in workshops of various kinds. For this labor they received wages at a fixed rate. This system of forced labor was generally applied in all parts of the Indies.

IMPERIALISM INTENSIFIES THE CONFLICT

Behind the capitalist, the trader, the manufacturer, and the financier, who had emerged from the industrial revolution and who were now led to stretch out their hands to the markets and produce of Asia and Africa, stood the highly organized, efficient, powerfully armed, acutely nationalist modern State which had emerged from the French Revolution and the Napoleonic Wars.

RIGHT UP to the nineteenth century difficulties of communication and transport effectively isolated and often protected continent from continent and civilization from civilization. There were, of course, migrations and conquests and colonizations, but these were sporadic, and normally the inhabitants of Peking or Buenos Aires could ignore the inhabitants of London and Paris as completely and safely as any inhabitants that there may be upon the planet Mars.

There was an element in the new Western civilization, issuing from the industrial revolution, which inevitably made it, outside Europe, predatory. Economically it required ever more markets and ever more raw materials; the more industrialization proceeded, the more necessary became the opening up of new markets and new sources of raw material. The economic exploitation and penetration of Asia, Africa, Australia, and South America followed, and this was the first way in which the inhabitants of those countries felt the impact of the new civilization. In Asia and Africa this exploitation and penetration took a peculiar form which has made the imperialism of the nineteenth century a very different thing from the imperialisms, conquests, and clashes of civilizations in previous ages. The mechanical inventions in communication and transport put into the hands of Europeans the power of rapidly opening up distant and difficult

Excerpt from Leonard Woolf, *Imperialism and Civilization* (New York: Harcourt, Brace and Co., 1928), pp. 10-16.

countries for the purposes of industry and commerce. The same processes of invention and the new industry had also completely altered the balance of physical power in the world. Up to the nineteenth century the civilizations of the different continents materially were not so widely separated as to give to one an overwhelming preponderance over the other. An Asiatic army could always make a fight of it with a European army, and the African could trust his poisoned arrows, his swamps and forests and mosquitoes, to protect him against the European with a muzzle-loading gun and a bottle of gin or brandy. But suddenly all this was altered. The Asiatic, living and fighting as his ancestors lived and fought in the twelfth century, found himself confronted with the modern rifle, the Maxim gun, the gunboat, and the light railway, while behind these, invisible and still unknown to him, was·mobilized the colossal organized power of modern industry in a modern State. Asia and still more Africa were powerless to resist the will of Europe.

The words "the organized power of modern industry in a modern State" point to another important characteristic in the imperialism of the nineteenth century and in the changed relationship of Europe to the rest of the world. Behind the capitalist, the trader, the manufacturer, and the financier, who had emerged from the industrial revolution and who were now led to stretch out their hands to the markets and produce of Asia and Africa, stood the highly organized, efficient, powerfully armed, acutely nationalist modern State which had emerged from the French Revolution and the Napoleonic Wars. Sometimes deliberately and sometimes haphazardly and unconsciously, the power of this terrific engine of force and government was invoked by the capitalist to aid him in developing or exploiting the other continents. The effect was stupendous. There was a sudden, rapid, and ruthless world-conquest on a scale such as previously was unknown in human history. Between 1815 and 1914 practically the whole of the continents of Asia, Africa, and Australia, with all the islands of the Seven Seas, was subjected, directly or indirectly, to the power of the European State. The subjection of Asiatic and African peoples to European States was sometimes direct, sometimes indirect. Direct subjection took place in Africa, which was partitioned among the Great Powers, Belgium, Portugal, Italy, and Spain, and in India, Ceylon, Burma, the Malay Peninsula, parts of China, and considerable stretches of Asiatic territory absorbed by Russia. In all these cases the territory itself was annexed, usually by force, and incorporated within the European State in the form of an imperial appendage. The country was administered by Europeans; the Government was a European government and the inhabitants were subjected to European laws. But there was also, in the rest of Asia outside Japan, an indirect process of subjection. Turkey, Persia, Afghanistan, Tibet, and China all remained nominally independent and sovereign States. But in fact their sovereignty no longer existed and their independence was illusory. All of them, in varying degrees, were brought under the tutelage of European States or groups of European States. Within limits they were allowed to manage their own affairs; but in economic and military matters and in their relations to Europe and Europeans they had to take their orders from Europe, in the knowledge that disobedience would entail extinction.

In no other period of the world's history has there been such a vast revolution as this conquest of Asia and Africa by Europe in less than 100 years. Until very nearly the end of the nineteenth century, Europeans themselves regarded it with complacent pride as one of the chief blessings and glories of Western civilization. The white race of Europe, they held, was physically, mentally, and morally superior to all other races, and God, with infinite wisdom and goodness, had created it and developed it so that it might be ready, during the reign of Queen Victoria in England, to take over and manage the affairs of all other peoples on the earth and teach them to be, in so far as that was possible for natives and heathens, good Europeans and good Christians. Indeed, until the very end of the century the natives and heathens themselves seemed to acquiesce in this view of the designs of Providence and the blessings of being ruled by Europeans. It is true that in almost every case originally a considerable number of Africans and Asiatics had to be killed before the survivors were prepared to accept the dominion or, as it was often called, protection of a European State; but once the dominion was established there were few revolts against European rule which could not be met with a punitive expedition.

EUROPEANIZATION AND ITS CONSEQUENCES

With the nineteenth century there came in the East an epoch in which the Europeans resembled concessionaires rather than crusaders. The Anglo-Saxon attempt to educate Asia in the principles of a creed which it preached but did not practice and of constitutions which it worshiped but could not work has produced rebellions.

THE TERM Europeanization is intended to express the effects on Asiatic, American and African cultures and civilizations of permeation by the peculiar social system set up in modern Europe as a consequence of the classical Renaissance, the Protestant Reformation and the industrial revolution. Europeanization may be expressed politically by imposing the idea of democracy, in the sense of parliamentary and party government, or of sovereignty, in the sense of suppression or subordination of all governmental organs to the sovereign state, or of nationality, by creating a semireligious solidarity in support of that sovereignty. It may be expressed economically by imposing ideas of individualistic capitalism, competition and control on communities enjoying more elaborate and equitable, but less productive and progressive, collectivist or communal civilizations; or industrially by substituting the factory and the foundry for the hand loom and home craft. It may be expressed in terms of education by convincing other continents of the advisability of acquiring attainments in European science to their material or even moral advantage, or by exposing the discipline of tribal tradition and training to dissipation by the gospel of the missionary, the goods of the trader and the good intentions of the administrator. . . .

Not only Asiatics but also Africans and, so far as they survive, American natives possess cultures and social constitutions that are more ancient than those of Europe and better adapted to the pursuit

Excerpt from George Young, "Europeanization," in *Encyclopaedia of the Social Sciences*, Vol. 5 (New York: The Macmillan Co., 1931), pp. 623, 628-630.

of happiness in their communities, especially in the climates and countries concerned. They regard the supersession of these by the simple social systems of Europe much as Europeans regard the subversion of the Roman or the Byzantine by simpler Asiatic societies. The Asiatics have always had little to learn from the Europeans in ethical and religious matters and could teach them much in matters of social morality. It seems probable that the period of direct educational Europeanization passed with the last century. Asia now educates itself in Europe and for every European who has a knowledge of Asiatic languages, literature or life there are hundreds of Asiatics who have learned not only the strong but the weak points of European civilization and culture. Competition in educational Europeanization has been transferred from Asiatic colleges to European universities. America, Eurasia and Europe, New York, Moscow and Paris, now compete for the responsibility for teaching the young of Asia and Africa how to shoot—and whom to shoot. The Christian missions are making no more progress abroad than before and are enlisting even less support at home, while the propagandists of the communist creed are undoubtedly a most formidable factor making for Eurasian education. As against this there is the individualistic education in competition, capitalism and scientific production provided by the impact of European industrialism on the arts and crafts of the East. So far this education has been mainly destructive, and it has therefore a temporary and tactical advantage over the more constructive and conscious propaganda of communism.

The earliest epoch of Europeanization was one of militarist conquest and mass colonization characterized by the expulsion of the native races. But the regions where this was possible were restricted and lay rather to the west than to the east. With the nineteenth century there came in the East an epoch in which the Europeans resembled concessionaires rather than crusaders. The European presented himself indeed in many friendly guises as mandatory, missionary, merchant and money lender. It was the last of these, the money lender, who was responsible for the most significant political consequences, consequences that produced a Europeanization not of expulsion but of exploitation of peoples, from the Morocco Sultanate in the west to the Chinese Empire in the east. The Europeanizer adopted the money lender's policy of granting loans to the successor of the self-made man for his youthful dissipations and then foreclosing on his estates before he came to years of discretion. For example, a century ago in Turkey Mahmud II, who was half French, and in Egypt Mohammed Ali, an Albanian, broke up the ancient Asiatic system and Europeanized their estates. Their inferior successors, however, squandered not only their accumulations but also the apparently unlimited resources of European credit offered them at usurious rates. The sultans Abdul Mejid and Abdul Aziz in Turkey, the pashas Mohammed Said and Ismail in Egypt, the beys Ahmed and Sadok in Tunis, pawned their realms to Europeans and only too late discovered that British or French controllers and tax collectors were installed. Such control, the modern form of conquest, led in the case of the weaker states to armed occupation, as in Tunis by the French in 1881 and in Egypt by the British in 1882. Such occupation and imperialist Europeanization was delayed in Turkey and Morocco by the able rulers Abdul Hamid II (1876-1908) and Muley Hassan (1873-94) and was eventually ended in Turkey and Egypt by post-war nationalist risings and the Eurasian eruption. Turkey has altogether freed itself from the political servitudes of the Ottoman debt administration and almost freed itself from its financial service. In other countries, such as Egypt, financial contracts of this kind are still respected, although the political controls based on them have been repudiated. In China the foreign control of the customs revenue for the service of foreign loans is one of the most controversial issues in the emancipation of the Nationalist government. . . .

Next to the commerce and capitulations of the foreign colonies there comes, as a Europeanizing factor, their culture and, associated with it, the Christian missions and the colonial administrators. These while superficially in conflict with one another nevertheless co-operate substantially in Europeanization by education, a procedure which, now that executive control and even exploitation are passing, is the most prominent and most promising. Even when executive control and exploitation were at their height, there was always an educative element. The Spanish conquistador in the West Indies or the Portuguese crusader in the East expressed the most moral motives for extermination or enslavement. Later Dutch, British and French Europeanizations in a milder and less medieval age and with a less missionary mandate helped to transform Europeanization from enslavement to education, although it is questionable whether their education is not as deadly to the souls of the Asiatic and American races as enslavement was to their bodies. In either case such Europeanization defeated itself by exciting rebellion. Spanish and Portuguese domination was overthrown, in spite of the devoted educational and spiritual missionizing of the Jesuits, by an absorption of the ruling race in a miscegenation that may have a future of its own. The Anglo-Saxon attempt to educate Asia in the principles of a creed which it preached but did not practice and of constitutions which it worshiped but could not work has produced such rebellions as that of the British educated babus in India, who prosecute their Eurasian emancipation of India from the British by preaching the immediate and unmitigated introduction of British industrial civilization and political institutons.

The educational epoch of Europeanization has passed through phases. The role of the Catholic missionaries in the early epoch of conquest was reproduced later both by Protestant missions and by political proconsuls like Stratford Canning and Cromer, Henry Lawrence and Charles George ("Chinese") Gordon. With the new imperialism of the end of the last century there appeared a less sincere and more sanctimonious Anglo-Saxon attitude in the "white man's burden" of Kipling, "the yellow peril" of Wilhelm II and the A and B mandates of the Peace Conference. It is this later assumption of a moral supremacy and a mental superiority that has already raised Asia in revolt and that will some day raise Africa. The same ideas and interests that have caused twentieth century imperialism to attempt to conserve the existing customs and constitutions of Asia have also caused African administrators to try to revitalize African tribal and communal societies rather than revolutionize them. Such Eurafrican experiments as those of the British in Nigeria or the Sudan have so far a vitality and virtue that are wanting in the more revolutionary educative efforts of Americans in Liberia or the more exploitative enterprises of Belgians in the Congo. The Europeanization of central Africa is in any case in its earliest stages.

The Europeanization of north Africa is still in a first phase of conquest which has been prolonged for over a century. The latest and probably the last of these conquests was that of the Riff tribes of Morocco Berbers who rose against, and for years resisted, the whole force of France and Spain. From this there emerges a remarkable difference in the development of Europeanization in northern Africa from that in western Asia. The Berber tribes of north Africa, a virile and versatile stock of European type, whose development has been delayed by Asiatic imperialism and Islamic institutions, have so far been partitioned into Spanish, French and Italian protectorates under military regimes. Since the French finally broke the piratical power of Algiers in 1830 the revolts of the Berber tribes, from that of Abd-el-Kader in the years from 1836 to 1847 to that of Abd-el-Krim nearly a century later, have been crushed.

6

THE ECONOMIC BASIS OF CULTURE CONFLICT

FOR PRIMITIVE cultures, in fact for non-industrial societies of all levels of cultural development, the impacts of modern imperialism have been unusually severe and disruptive. Neither the age-old drain of military plunder and tribute, nor the trade in precious metals, products and raw materials, even when carried on in exploiting barter, nor even the consistent raiding of the slave trade appears to have disorganized these native societies half so much as the superficially less rapacious contacts of the present-day colonial system. One reason already noted is the intrusion of new culture patterns with overwhelming prestige and penetrating force. But by far the major force of the colonial impact today is that of the economic system. The modern colonial system calls for elaborately organized economic contacts, with secondary bases thrust deep into the zones of native life. Where this is not the case, there is systematic transplanting of considerable sections of the native population into the orbit of European civilization as laborers.

While mere penetration of the products of Western machine production can bring about considerable cultural disintegration, particularly a decay of native craft arts and skills, it is the labor aspect of modern industrialism which most seriously disrupts native society and culture. In a modern imperialist system subject peoples are geared both to the export market and through the channels of labor to the ever-expanding production system of Europe. Forced trading and forced labor both involve forced acculturation, which ties in the economic factors with the increase in culture conflict.

Monica Hunter details very carefully some of this economically induced culture conflict and breakdown in a typical colonial area—

South Africa. "The clash," she says, "is primarily economic. There is a struggle for land and a conflict of interests over labor." There is cultural disintegration, then, no matter what the character of the colonial economy whether under the export of the labor supply outside the tribal life as in the gold, copper and diamond mining industries of the Rand or in the importation of native servant labor into the white settlements, or in the organization of agricultural production through European type farming or plantations.

Much of this occurs through lack of any consideration for the native systems, which in some cases could be reorganized to effective fulfillment of the European needs. But that would require more patience and scientific study and more respect for native life than could be expected of an economically dominated system. Yet in this very respect Miss Hunter observes a degree of tribal disorganization which threatens even the economic interests involved beyond those immediately dependent on the native labor. But consideration of the possibilities of the native consumption market, which would develop if native culture were prospering instead of retrogressing, seems almost below the horizon of the typical colonial point of view. Yet in order that the native group may have enough vitality to function in their role of enforced service to the European economy, they must have cultural support and development in exchange for their helpfulness in the colonial system. The effects of colonial contacts on native cultures will determine not only the fate of the natives but also the ultimate success of the original objectives of the colonial economy itself. This interdependence of economic results upon cultural policies and their effects is just beginning to be realized. Destruction or serious disorganization of the native cultures eventually means the undermining of the base of the colonial system.

In the island possessions of the British in Polynesia, Pitt-Rivers discovers the same correlation of economic exploitation with cultural disruption. He finds detribalization taking place rapidly under both of the two labor systems in vogue, so that as far as this area is concerned neither the free labor nor the indenture policy has proved satisfactory from the point of view of native interests. Voluntary contract opens the unsophisticated native to the beguilement and deception of the labor "recruiter," usually leads to a prolonged term in plantation service or the native labor compound, where in addition to hardship and unnatural living, he becomes alienated from tribal life. On the return to the native villages, the detribalized native serves to disorganize the life of natives not yet required in the colonial economic system, thus undermining native society. One of the most serious features is the displacement of the native idea of working on a communal rather than an individual basis, a shift which sometimes subverts their whole social system.

Detribalization as an experience is shock enough, but in situations where cultural and racial prejudices block any progressive incorporation of the transformed native into a European scheme of life, the aftermath is gravely serious. This, however, is just what happens in spite of professions of tutelage and training for a new civilization. At the present stage, missionary programs are ineffectual because they too are committed for the most part to the majority mores and their values. Indeed, detribalization under the good intentions of the missionary can be just as damaging to native morale and social adjustment. Pitt-Rivers cites the false association of European clothing with morality as a sample of this warped cultural perspective and its effect on native life. A vicious circle of maladjustments is started, beginning in a breakdown of native moral values, leading through bewilderment and imitative prudery to no constructive new morality, and ending, ironically enough, in little but profit to the European clothes merchant.

On the land and wages questions, the economic odds against the native are similarly bad. Special low rates of pay for native labor are rationalized on the supposition that the native scale of needs is much lower. This policy lacks consistency, for under typical circumstances the native system of living is broken down, and changed areas and modes of living substituted. Under such conditions the differentials doom the native to living not in an isolated, unassimilated native sphere, but to the status of an exploited dependent in a submerged stratum of the European economy. As to the land, where a European settlement policy is pursued, and the great majority of the colonies maintain that—the native communities are dispossessed of their habitual areas of living. The cultural disorganization is magnified immeasurably, particularly because large areas are required for many of these primitive cultures. In South Africa, the encroachment of the

European settlement and mining districts restricts the native population to living within one-fifth of their previous scope. This is a weighty factor in the cultural breakdown, and is, as well, one of the primary causes of the trek of the native laborers to the industrial and white settlement centers. On these scores, the economic indictment of colonial imperialism is unchallengeable.

The selection from Dover continues the economic analysis along historical lines, going into very interesting parallels of national prejudice stemming from political rivalry and conflict of economic interests. He cites the practices and codes of the British in Ireland during the period of settlement and the struggle for landholding control at that time. Dover here suggests that economic interests are the actual controlling base of most historic group prejudice and hostility. With respect to imperialism, he finds the economic factor so characteristic that he regards situations of national and racial antipathy practically identical, and thinks close historical analysis will substantiate that conclusion. Dover practically gives as his definition of prejudice an active group antipathy generated by a conflict of economic group interests and persisting or subsiding according to its group profitableness.

In an interesting memorandum on the variability of movements of group antagonism in America, that is—organized anti-foreign or anti-minority campaigns, Donald Young finds them correlated with periods of depression and sharpened economic rivalry. His figures tentatively suggest a "direct correlation between the peaks of nativist spirit in America and the valleys of economic difficulty." Certainly, in an instance previously cited—the change of attitude toward the Chinese in the West—one can definitely see such an economic connection, when prior to the exclusion phase, Chinese immigration was encouraged and even subsidized. Extremist nationalism and anti-foreign prejudice are shown by Young to have had relatively greater vogue during every successive period of depression and hard times since the mid-nineteenth century. Certain at least it is that, wherever diverse groups have become involved in economic rivalry, whatever cultural differentials may happen to be involved have been used to symbolize the issues and rationalize the struggle. Such racial factors are well-known features of many labor disputes, and operate frequently to prolong and aggravate the issues.

Charles Johnson, in discussing *Race Relations and Social Change*, comes to the conclusion that the economic base is the neglected factor in the analysis of the race problem. In spite of the strong tradition of distinctive difference, the racial situation, analyzed objectively, has so many common denominators with class and other group conflict situations, that little distinctive difference seems to remain. In this perspective, only degrees of intensity and complexity seem to distinguish both the attitudes and the historical factors of race conflict from those of some other group antagonisms. As a case in point, when in the early colonial economy the white indentured servant class occupied about the same status as the Negro, similar restrictions, legal and customary, were in vogue for both. The early codes made little distinction between them; and there was such considerable intermarriage that special legislation was called for. It was the divergent economic fortunes of the white manual worker and the Negroes, who for several generations were indentured servants rather than chattel slaves, which brought to the one improved status and closer social acceptance and carried the other to a position of serf and chattel, with marked stigma and social aversion.

Certainly there is noticeable in the fluctuation both of discriminatory treatment and intensification of group hostility a significant parallelism between periods of economic rivalry and of racial tension. The series of race riots around 1919 came significantly at the height of the Negro's forward surge into new centers and channels of industrial labor, and occurred, in centers like Chicago and East St. Louis, where the labor incursion and rivalry had been particularly intense.

The Johnson article puts forward the interesting contention that today many of the traditional problems and issues of race relations are resolving themselves into class and economic issues. The more realistically the racial situation is analyzed the more this linkage with the economic situation stands out. Certain it is, at least, that the hub of the majority treatment of the Negro minority is a policy of extreme and open economic discrimination. These differentials in employment, wages, types of employment, chances of advancement are the effective instruments of the reactionary racial policy. Without question, the economic policy, more than the political or even the social, bears the brunt of the American race conflict in the technique of majority dominance. Johnson concludes that "further changes in race relations in America will depend not only upon fundamental domestic economic readjustments, but also to some extent upon world economics."

CONTEMPORARY EUROPEAN-BANTU RELATIONS IN SOUTH AFRICA

The clash is primarily economic. A society poorly developed economically, and laying emphasis on the importance of common rather than of individual wealth, meets a highly developed, industrialized and economically individualistic society. The restriction of land and the introduction of money and of new goods alters the internal economy of the reserves, and large numbers go out to work for Europeans in labor centers. Economic changes react upon the social organization.

EUROPEANS FROM their first contact with the Bantu had a strong feeling of their superiority over them. They came as a conquering race, and the watchword of the Voortrekkers in matters regarding Natives was "no equality in Church or State." Although the humanists joined issue with them over their slogan, and civil rights for all civilized men were secured in the Cape, yet the vast majority of Europeans still maintain such a strong belief in the superiority of their race as such, that they hold that any European is necessarily "superior" to any Bantu. The social and industrial color bar, by accentuating the difference between the races, confirms the European in the belief in his superiority. Moreover, European and Bantu almost always meet as master and servant. The majority of the contacts are economic, and the European is almost always the employer. The less sophisticated Pondo cannot conceive of the European as anything but an employer. Again and again I was asked, "Are there really no brown people in England? Who then does the work?" The only words of a European language which many Pondo know are "damn fool" or some more violent epithet. Even in contact with officials and missionaries the relationship is always that of governor and governed, or master and pupil. The Europeans have always been numerically few in proportion to the Bantu, but because of the

Excerpts from Monica Hunter, *Reaction to Conquest*, (London: Oxford University Press, 1936), pp. 7-10, 546-551.

superiority of their material culture they have been able to dominate them.

There was never any very great disproportion between the sexes among the Europeans, and social feeling is strongly against inter-marriage between European and Bantu; so although there is consider-able miscegenation, intermarriage, which establishes conditions favor-able to the rapid transference of culture, is rare.

The Bantu first encountered the European as a conqueror who fought and defeated him in the struggle for land. Submitting to the inevitable he acquiesced in the confiscation of lands he had occupied, and in the establishment of British rule. Aware that he had been defeated by the superior armaments of the European he was from the first impressed by the European's material culture, and anxious to acquire European goods. The trade in guns and blankets expanded rapidly. The generation of Xhosa who had fought the Europeans and been driven from their lands were slow to forget that the Europeans were enemies, and conquerors, but the Fingos who were protected by, and became the allies of, the British, and later the Pondo, were pre-pared to make the best of the domination by a stronger power, and turned toward the government the attitude of a people toward a superior chief. The personal prefix U is used before government, and it is still thought of in remote districts of Pondoland as a person, an old man with a white beard. The people were prepared to be loyal to this new chief, but in return expected to receive benefits from him.

Conservative tendencies in Bantu society are strong. Power is in the hands of the elders, and piety demands that there should be no departure from the ways of the ancestors, who by reason of their age must know better than their children. Non-observance of certain customs (amasiko) may result in sickness sent by the ancestors. But the forces making for change are too strong even for the conservatism of the Bantu when the European is the dominating power, and new ways and ideas are forced upon him through administrator, trader, and missionary in the reserves, and by the necessity of going to work outside the reserves and living in a European environment. One sec-tion abhor the new ways; another wish to be as like the dominating European as possible, and favor European education, languages, dress, styles of housing and furnishing, manners, diversions, as means toward this end. A Pondo believes that by becoming like a European he will acquire power like a European, and the fact that the most Europeanized usually get the best-paid jobs as teachers, clerks, interpreters, and ministers, fosters this belief. The European educated have prestige in the community. I have seen a chief's son swagger into the store ignoring everyone there except the local teacher with whom he shook hands politely.

There is growing criticism and often dislike of Europeans, and discrimination between friendliness toward Europeans, and European rule, and the desire for European culture. There is a growing nationalist feeling showing itself in the sinking of tribal differences, the rise of purely Bantu churches, of an "African National Congress," of a Bantu Trades Union with a strong political bias, and movements such as the "Pioneers" organized on similar lines to European initiated movements (Pathfinders and Wayfarers, the Bantu equivalent to Scouts and Guides) but claiming to be purely African, and refusing to co-operate with movements in which there is any European control.

This section is keenly aware of the fact that European material development has given them power over Africa, admires that material development, and is determined to have European education; but the growing sense of nationalism makes them place more value on old Bantu custom and organization than did the first generation to receive European education. They are consciously outgrowing the stage of wanting to ape Europeans, and are anxious rather to absorb elements of European culture and blend it with Bantu culture.

The clash is primarily economic. A society poorly developed economically, and laying emphasis on the importance of common rather than of individual wealth, meets a highly developed, industrialized, and economically individualistic society. There is a struggle for land and a conflict of interests over labor. The restriction of land and the introduction of money and of new goods which are wanted alters the internal economy of the reserves, and large numbers go out to work for Europeans in labor centers. For the Bantu agricultural and industrial revolutions are telescoped—the necessity and possibility of developing agriculture, and the growth of a large population employed in industry, and entirely dependent upon wages, come at once, and radical changes follow one another with even greater speed than they did in Europe. All through three forces of change may be traced.

First the economic, which alters the internal economy, and drives many out to work; secondly the political, which even non-Marxists may argue was historically but an offshoot of the economic, since the extension of political control in Africa was engendered by the desire to secure, or to prevent other nations from securing, economic control, but which may be distinguished in working from the economic; and thirdly the religious, which includes evangelistic, medical, and educational work. . . .

Although different contact conditions have produced differences in the communities subject to them, similar tendencies are observable. Very rapidly European trade goods are replacing old home-made utensils and clothing. Foreign material objects are assimilated so completely that certain of them, such as white beads and scarlet blankets assume ritual value. Indigenous arts and crafts are disappearing. After an effervescence in the early stages of contact, when new materials, such as beads, cloth, tin, etc., are utilized for artistic ends, artistic talent seems to be smothered. "School people" are given over to the horrors of Victorian furnishing, and shabby European clothing. They tend to dance fox-trots in place of dramatic solos and round dances.

The *umzi* [the local kinship group] ceases to be an independent economic unit. Everywhere there is an increase in trade, and a rapid transference to a money economy. Practically all men are employed temporarily or permanently as wage-earners, and a class solely dependent upon wages is emerging. Famines are averted, and the standard of living of a minority has been raised, but for many there is a poorer diet, increasing poverty, and no security of support during periods of unemployment. Improvement in agriculture has not kept pace with increase in population. Many are landless. Land in the reserves is deteriorating; in some formerly fertile areas desert conditions now prevail. The majority of those on farms have to work harder and live on a poorer diet than their ancestors. Many, both in town and country, are ill-nourished, and the general physique of the people is probably declining.

There is increasing economic individualism. The co-operative economic unit, the *umzi*, is decreasing in size, and more and more families of a man, wife, and minor children, tend to become independent groups. Economic values are becoming dominant. Status tends to depend more upon wealth spent on the owner and his immediate family, and less upon generosity, than formerly. Whereas formerly, a big *umzi*, many adherents, and the giving of many feasts carried prestige; now a man tends to be judged by his house, his clothes, his food.

Economic changes react upon the social organization. An attempt is made to fit the new economic life into the old social structure, and up to a point is successful. The use of the plough necessitates a slight modification in the division of labor, but it is successfully fitted into the existing social structure. New work groups are formed, centered in the plough. Men living in their fathers' *imizi* [pl. of *umzi*] hand over their earnings to their fathers. Money is used as *ikhazi* [groom's gift to bride], but spoken of as if it were cattle. But the new wine is bursting the old bottles.

The decrease in the size of the *umzi* entails change in attitudes and behavior toward kin. Where the father's brothers with their families do not live even for a time in the same *umzi*, but in a separate *umzi*, behavior toward father's brother and his children tends to approximate less nearly to behavior toward own father and own brothers and sisters. This change, together with the decline of the influence of the ancestor cult, helps to blur the sharp distinction between mother's kin and father's kin.

Youth is becoming emancipated from parental control. The possibility of earning by working for Europeans, gives young men and girls economic power; a man sets up his own *umzi* at a much earlier age than formerly, and so he and his wife are less under the authority of elders than formerly. Certainly in town, and probably in the country, there is an increase in premarital pregnancy, which is attributed by Native informants to the loss of parental control. At the same time a new ideal of sexual relations has been introduced by Christian missionaries, and this ideal is lived out by some. New social groups, based on common occupation, common religious belief or common taste in diversion are being formed. They cut across the old social groups, and impair their solidarity. Class distinctions based on wealth and education are becoming more marked. Economic changes are weakening kinship bonds, and political changes deprive tribe and district of all military and many administrative functions, and weaken the power of the chiefs, with whose office the solidarity of district and tribe is bound up. . . . The difference in the degree of change in different areas is obviously very largely due to the difference in the degree of external pressure. There is a marked correlation between geographical features and the degree of change. External pressure is least in the fertile river valleys, and broken coastal country, in which roads are not easily made, and from which men were slow to go out to work for Europeans, and these are the most conservative areas. There is more change in town where the Bantu is in a European environment than anywhere in the country. The Fingo on the Border have absorbed European culture more quickly than any other community; while the amaDifa, a clan related to them, living in Pondoland, are a by-word for conservatism.

The degree of resistance to change also varies in different communities. The Fingo, who never fought the British but were protected by them, absorbed European culture more quickly than the Xhosa who were enemies.

External pressure and internal resistance are the main forces making for differences in reaction of different areas, but there are conservative islands, and "advanced" islands in the reserves, the existence of which cannot be due to either of these forces. The differences between communities on different farms are not entirely explained by differences in outside influences and the fact that the same type of people tend to congregate on one farm. Probably these variations are to be explained in terms of personality. In one district a chief favors change, or a missionary or teacher is a strong personality and popular. In another the chief is conservative or the contact agent is a weak man, and not personally liked.

Besides this difference in the degree of change between areas there are differences in the degree of change in various aspects of culture in the same community. Certain aspects of Bantu culture are changing much more rapidly than others. There are revolutionary economic changes and social modifications follow the economic changes. Religious beliefs are slow to alter even in town, and belief in witchcraft and magic is even more tenacious than belief in the power of the ancestors.

The degree of external pressure and of internal resistance are forces determining the liability of different aspects of a culture to change, in the same way as they determine the liability of different communities to change. There has been most pressure on the economic aspect of Pondo life, and it is the aspect which has changed most. Material objects, and new techniques have been quickly absorbed because they met with little emotional resistance to change. Even when a new technique involved modification of the division of labor between the sexes (as that of European thatching) the change has been quite easily made. Only in connection with cattle have the tendencies toward economic adjustment met strong emotional resistance. So strong is the resistance that some once fertile districts are almost reduced to desert by overstocking.

When a tendency to change comes up against some emotional resistance a compromise is often effected. For example, the plough was recognized as a useful tool, but women who did most of the planting were forbidden to work with cattle, so a satisfactory adjustment was made by change in the division of labor. In town, where one room may lead off another, it is often impossible for the old avoidance taboos to be observed. They are modified so that only the bed of a person avoided is taboo.

The belief in magic has its roots in psychological attitudes which are unchanged (although sometimes re-oriented) by contact. Conflicts and jealousies remain. Belief in witchcraft and sorcery is in part a symptom of social disintegration, and therefore it is not surprising that it should flourish under contact conditions. Powerful alien influence in the form of Government prohibition of "smelling out," or of killing those smelt out, and the teaching in Church and school, has only modified belief and practice to the extent that those accused are not killed, and that "school people" mostly refrain from consulting diviners.

Strong external pressure and internal resistance tend to send customs underground. . . .

The selection of elements, whether material objects, techniques, beliefs, or rituals, from the intruding culture, depends upon the degree to which they enhance previous methods, and serve ends fully congruous with the old order. Cultural elements find a footing in an alien society by being attached to tendencies already operative in that society. What is taken is what arouses the interest of individuals.

New hut-building and thatching techniques have been rapidly assimilated. European patent medicines have a wide sale because they are new and powerful magic to put to traditional ends. European magical beliefs and Christian myth are readily absorbed because they fit in with old beliefs. Sunday observance was quickly taken over because the idea of it being taboo to work on certain days was part of the old culture.

Since Africa is subject to economic contacts with Europeans, change in African communities is inevitable. The problem is how, when contacts take place, chaos may be avoided. The danger lies in the breakdown of old institutions as the result of contact with Europeans, and the failure to replace them or the failure of institutions substituted by Europeans to function. In town the Pondo institution of marriage has broken down. The old sanctions enforcing laws regarding marriages are no longer effective. The European institution of civil or Christian marriage does not work either. The sanctions which are effective in the European community are not effective in the Bantu community. Again, in towns the old system of administration through chiefs does not operate, and the system introduced by Europeans of rule through Legislative Assembly, Municipal Council, and police fails to secure order. There is danger both of old forms being retained without their content, and of new forms being borrowed without their content. The old Pondo form of administration and the new form taken from European culture are equally useless when neither work. The urgent necessity is to secure institutions which will work. . . .

THE DETRIBALIZATION OF THE NATIVES OF THE PACIFIC ISLANDS

The native is taught to work for monthly pay instead of for the clan, the ethics of individual responsibility, new wants and habits that can only be satisfied by payments in kind or by service to white traders who alone can provide the articles which gratify these new wants.

OF THE two systems of labor recognized in the British possessions in the Pacific—the "indenture" system and the system of "free labor"—the indenture system still prevails in the Solomons, Fiji, and New Guinea. Under the indenture system a native is bound under a contract for a fixed period of service which cannot be terminated at the option of the laborer—usually three years—to an employer, the employer being obliged to maintain him and pay him a small monthly wage. The system by which planters employ traveling agents who induce natives to enter into the contract is known as "recruiting." In British New Guinea no person may recruit natives unless he is the holder of a recruiter's license.

The widespread recruiting of natives, which has sometimes in certain districts resulted in the depletion of the villages of their young manhood, is frequently pointed to as a prime cause of the native decrease. The system of recruiting men for indentured labor on plantations in many ways adversely affects the life of the villages from which they come. In the first place, a large and unrestricted exodus of young men from the villages to work on plantations leaves an insufficiency of hunters, fishers, and agriculturists, and in consequence the native food supply suffers.

All the young men recruited from their villages for plantation work are destined eventually to be returned to their homes; for it is the settled policy of the Governments in the British Possessions and

Excerpt from George Henry Lane-Fox Pitt-Rivers, *The Clash of Culture and the Contact of Races*, (London: George Routledge & Sons, Ltd., 1927), pp. 58-60, 62-65.

Protectorates in the Pacific, in furtherance of the benevolent ideal of making the natives themselves benefit by all measures only *secondarily* designed (so we are invited to believe) to promote the commercial advancement of European settlers, that the education and training in civilization that natives must necessarily acquire during their experience on plantations and in the service of the white man's Government shall fit them to become pioneers in the civilization and "uplift" of their savage fellow tribesmen when they return to them.

Not satisfied merely with endeavoring to obtain sufficient labor with which to run plantations, mines or workshops, a benevolent white Government insists upon devising means whereby this process may be made to serve what it chooses to call the natives' own highest interests. The white man does not, therefore, remain content with ensuring for the proper treatment and care of those natives actually engaged in work under him, but hastens to use his influence upon the natives he involves in his economic system as a step toward revolutionizing the life of the natives he still does not require, and in subverting their whole social system. Native labor, it is admitted, must be secured somehow. If natives were recruited in districts in the proportion in which they could really be spared, and with the sanction of the native chiefs, the village life need not suffer much, the drain upon the young men need be little or no greater than in the old days of warfare and head-hunting; but these conditions could only be insured by the authorities controlling and themselves directing the recruiting. This course, it is pointed out, would appear like compulsion to the natives, and for this reason is rejected in place of "free" recruiting. "Free" contract gives the least sophisticated natives the liberty to be beguiled and duped by the blandishments and bribes of the recruiter, so it is preferred as being more consistent with the higher ethics and professions of white control. Again, if the men, or a large proportion of them, were recruited with their women, their lives on the plantations would be happier, and having once become alienated from their tribal life, their service would be extended, while their progeny would gradually become available for work and so lessen the drain upon the tribal communities. This solution is usually rejected because of the fiction that the native drawn into our economic system, educated and inculcated with the elements of European ethics, must be benefited and "uplifted," therefore he must suffer certain deprivations during his term of service in order that he may return to his tribal unit and help to "uplift" his own people. This he accomplishes by being taught to work for monthly pay instead of for the clan, by being taught the ethics of individual responsibility, by being taught new wants and habits that can only be satisfied by payments in kind or by service to white traders who alone can provide the articles which gratify these new wants, by being taught to forget his own language and learn a new universal one (Papuan native dialects are so various and distinct that natives drawn from many districts and congregated on one plantation have habitually to talk "pidgin" English to one another in order to make themselves understood). He is taught that his own customs and moral inhibitions are contemptible superstitions, that the transgression of the new codes he is told to respect does not bring automatic punishment like the consequences of his own violated tribal taboos, but only such punishment as can be meted out to him by his white masters when his transgression is discovered, and that, consequently, observance of the moral code of the white man consists in not being found out, this lesson he also learns in time is the white man's own way of looking at sins and transgressions. In short, he is thoroughly and in every way detribalized, and having been detribalized he is considered fit to be sent back to his tribe, to the life he is no longer well adapted to. Here, if he has learned his lesson, he becomes a functionless and discontented rebel against the tribal life and the authority of the clan or tribal chiefs. . . .

The evil consequences of the adoption of European clothing by native races is generally admitted. When cotton clothing, singlets and trousers, is adopted in place of the simple native loincloth of bark cloth, or the fiber or grass skirts of native manufacture, or in place of no clothing at all, these badges of "civilization" are habitually worn day in and day out, wet and dry, until they rot to pieces. While a few of the more enlightened missionaries realize the harmful effect of introducing clothing, missionary influence as a whole has been the most powerful agency in enforcing this custom.

It is not difficult to understand why European clothes should have become associated in the native mind with Christianity. The missionary arriving amongst naked or half-naked savages, with his own mind saturated with the idea of "sinfulness of the flesh" and of the vileness of the human body, finds that in his "flock to be converted" there is an almost complete absence of bodily self-consciousness and an (to him) indescribably shocking openness and joyful acceptance in sexual matters. His first efforts are directed toward inculcating "decency" and "modesty" by creating a sense of "shame." In other words by inculcating "flesh-consciousness" and the virtue of concealment, the two sign-posts of Christian culture. In this endeavor great insistence is placed upon the importance for a woman to cover her breasts. Many, in fact most, missions insist, as a condition of their admission into their churches, upon the women being supplied with the hideous and unhygienic cotton "blouses" that form a common article of trade in the South Seas. Some missions make clothing a condition of baptism. The Church of Christ teaches its adherents that no one can be a Christian who does not wear shorts and trousers. In analyzing the *raison d'être* of missionary insistence upon clothing and of their horror of nudity, it is not only the real or supposed influence of clothing upon the native mind that is relevant, but also the influence that contact with nudity has upon the missionary's own mind. That this motive should influence his attitude, the missionary is probably seldom conscious, for few missionaries practice psychological self-examination. A French Catholic missionary in New Guinea, however, once admitted to me that of all the difficulties that try the strength and temper of Europeans in their prime who set out to lead a celibate and devotional life in that torrid and sex-inflaming climate, the daily sight of, and contact with, bare-breasted young women was one of the most trying and most conducive to nervous strain.

Next to missionary encouragement and pressure, the greatest factor in encouraging the use of clothing amongst natives is the needs of the trader. The first object of the trader in his dealings with the native races is to teach them new tastes and wants which he alone can supply. Cotton cloth and steel knives are objects out of whose sale and barter the trader finds the greatest profit. In order that the natives shall become dependent upon him, the trader must create a want for these articles, and this he assiduously attempts to do. The Government authorities have, with some exceptions, usually put their seal of approval upon both missionaries' and traders' efforts to clothe the native.

ECONOMIC FACTORS IN GROUP PREJUDICES

The dominance of color prejudice in the social scene must be attributed primarily to the unmoral economic relations between technically advanced and backward groups, and not to ethnic differences which are deliberately used to rationalize aggression.

COLOR PREJUDICE occupies the stage of human relations so conspicuously that our discussion has inevitably clustered around it. But it is essentially comparable with national, communal or minority, and class prejudice, which evidently increases the argument for eliminating the concept of racial prejudice. They are all, so to speak, overlapping varieties of the same species, the differences being quantitative rather than qualitative, and determined by changing social values and the intensity of the conflict involved.

The dominance of color prejudice in the social scene must therefore be attributed primarily to the unmoral economic relations between technically advanced and backward groups, and not to ethnic differences which are deliberately used to rationalize aggression. The English, for example, are perhaps as nearly related to the Mediterranean peoples of Northern India as they are to the Welsh, but prejudice against the more exploited Indians is very different in magnitude from that against the Welsh. Moreover, anti-Indian feeling in England has risen conspicuously in response to successive injuries to British trade, through Congress boycotts and restricted scope for opportunism in India.

Among the British Islanders themselves, to illustrate the qualitative similarity between color and national prejudice, the manifestations of internal hostility appear to have increased with the growth of the spirit of self-determination. For, rightly or wrongly, the manifestations

Excerpt from Cedric Dover, *Half-Caste* (London: Martin Secker and Warburg, Ltd., 1937), pp. 70-73.

of young nationality and introversion in Ireland, as in India or Wales, such as rhetorical insistence on the indigenous culture, are associated with belief in economic gain and desire to retaliate against a protracted domination injurious to the prosperity and self-respect of the people. The factor of race-building is obviously unimportant where two nations of similar ethnic stock are concerned, though a false racial concept may be used by the Irish to stimulate national solidarity, and by the English to cover up their atrocities in Ireland. To an impartial observer, self-determination within the British Islands is therefore an utterly ridiculous spectacle, which has been created by clashing capitalistic and religious interests. In Soviet Russia, for all the ethnic and cultural divergences of its component parts, race-building and race mixture are not contemporary issues.

In communal prejudices, the influence of similar economic factors is again observed. Eurasians, for example, are often ridiculed for their attitude toward other natives and color prejudice among themselves. But it is human enough, as V. Latorre-Bara states, for the half-caste to make "every effort to affiliate himself as closely as possible with the dominant race, to which he will proclaim his kinship, while categorically denying his ties with the race that is dominated, and which, from that very fact often repeated, finds itself more and more disadvantaged all round. Consequently it is nowise strange that the dominant race attempts to and succeeds in drawing the maximum of profit from this tendency of the half-caste."

He rightly adds that this strategy is achieved by "the handing out to him of sundry small, flattering jobs which allow him to believe in a certain measure of superiority on his part over the "inferior" race. These jobs, naturally, come under the heading of minor State offices (public force, governmental clerkships, etc.). Or else the same kind of employment is found for him in private or business enterprises, employment that carries with it a certain measure of responsibility, jobs such as overseers, foremen, etc. In this manner the half-caste is used as an instrument of oppression by the ruling races. . . ."

In other words, the half-caste not only derives compensatory satisfactions from his prejudices, but uses them to resist reduction to the lower level at which the other natives are deliberately confined, and to maintain himself in the reserved occupations which he "enjoys."

He is prepared for these key-positions of continued exploitation by a priest-ridden and ridiculously expensive system of "European Education," which teaches him to despise his colored ancestry and to take a ludicrous pride in the "great traditions" of his white heritage.

But fortunately this method of supporting aggrandisement is only partly successful. For it involves "keeping the half-caste in his place," thus failing to make of him a whole-hearted ally. He will despise natives and protest his loyalty to the whites, but he also develops a considerable hatred for the rulers, its intensity being correlated with the extent to which he feels the discrimination against him. In India, one may hear Eurasians speak contemptuously of "damned niggers" and "white bastards" almost in the same breath. In that country, too, the economic *motif* of allegiance is emphasized by the changing attitude of Eurasians, associated with declining economic privileges and the inspiration of the Indian struggle for freedom, toward the motherland they had previously ignored. Tomorrow they may abandon the fatherland on which their predecessors glued their vision and their hopes.

It appears, then, that any kind of group prejudice functions inefficiently as part of the machinery of sexual and economic competition in a capitalistic world. It helps, on the one hand, to provide some measure of protection against exploitation and cultural invasion; and, on the other, to safeguard exploiters from the assimilative power of the exploited. Naturally, therefore, it is most acute where minority rule or severe social conflict is involved.

MINORITIES AND THE DEPRESSION

Not only has there been evidence of a pronounced degree of inverse correlation between the strength of political movements with the objective of preserving America for the Americans and the height of general prosperity, but there also have been similar correlations within internal regions whose economic history has not entirely paralleled that of the country as a whole.

THROUGHOUT the history of the United States there seems to have been a direct correlation between the peaks of nativist spirit and the valleys of exceptional economic difficulty. Not only has there been evidence of a pronounced degree of inverse correlation between the strength of political movements with the objective of preserving America for the Americans and the height of general prosperity, but there also have been similar correlations within internal regions whose economic history has not entirely paralleled that of the country as a whole. Nativist movements of national significance include the rise of the Native American Party in the 1830's, the Know-Nothing Order in the 1850's, the American Protective Association in the last two decades of the nineteenth century, and the modern Ku Klux Klan following the World War. These major movements achieved remarkable successes, if on the whole local and temporary, in view of the flimsy nature of their anti-minority slogans; successes which by geographic location might probably be shown to have a relation to the intensity of hard times in areas of noteworthy minority population. Less widespread minor nativist movements, such as those directed against Chinese, Japanese, and Filipinos on the West Coast, Italians in Louisiana, and the French Canadians in New England, show no serious departure from the rule.

Much has been written concerning such movements, but most of

Excerpt from Donald Young, *Research Memorandum on Minority Peoples in the Depression* (New York: Social Science Research Council, Bulletin 31, 1937), pp. 133-141.

it is historical description paying little or no attention to the possibility of generalization in terms of minorities in depression. . . .

Comparisons of contemporary with historical instances of tides of nativism should not be confined to cases found in the experience of the United States. Not to go back into earlier times, attention may be called to Italian Fascist behavior toward minorities of alien origin, or of Nazi treatment of Jews, Poles, and Catholics in Germany. There is no scarcity of comparable situations on any of the continents, and all have their contribution to offer to the understanding of nativism.

The high value placed upon unification within the state by nationalism, whether it be conceived as a political or as a cultural ideal, seems likely to lead to the limitation of the activities, rights, and privileges of minorities judged to be incompetent or unwilling to participate fully in the movement. Suggestive of such a tendency is the following quotation from Carlton J. H. Hayes:

In Europe the newest national states almost instantly [following the World War] passed from liberal pronouncements to illiberal conduct and speedily vied with older national states in establishing nationalist tariffs, armies, schools, and other agencies of propaganda and in discriminating socially if not legally against dissident minorities. In connection with this last statement it should be remarked that while the new map of Europe conformed in general to the principle of nationality, the population in some parts of the continent was so mixed in nationality or a particular region was so insistently demanded by one of the victors for commercial or strategic considerations that all the new national states (and some of the old) embraced minorities of alien nationality. To those states the temptation of "nationalizing" their minorities was strong, while states like Germany and Hungary were at least equally tempted to regard the populations and areas which they had lost as "irredentas" which must be regained as soon as possible. Agitation for the recovery of "irredentas" and movements for the "nationalizing" of minorities are alike dangerous to internal and international peace.

Then too, taking advantage of economic distress and of the enhanced nationalism of the post-war period, demagogues and dictators have risen to positions of influence or power in several European countries and have used their position to preach or enforce an ever more intensive and exclusive nationalism. The most striking illustrations of this have been the conversion of Mussolini from socialism to nationalism and the establishment and maintenance of his Fascist regime in Italy and the ascension to power of Hitler and the Nazi movement in Germany with their hostility to Jews, Poles, the French, Catholics and any other groups at home or abroad who are assumed to belie or belittle German nationalism. Somewhat similar phenomena have attended post-war dictatorships in Poland, Lithuania, Hungary and Jugoslavia and, on widely different intellectual levels, the propaganda of the Ku Klux Klan in the United States and the Action Française in France. . . .

The problem, in essence, is to determine any relationship which may exist between the degree and possible peculiar characteristics of a depression and the development of nativism in various forms. Specific subordinate questions and sources of evidence are legion. Case histories of societies, clubs, political parties, and other associations, with nativistic elements in their programs need quick reporting if they are not to be largely lost or allowed to dry down to bare documentary bones in the passage of time. Legislative proposals and enactments with "America for the Americans" objectives require less haste in study. What was the legislative trend in such matters as special requirements for or the actual prohibition of licenses for hunting and fishing, or for practicing various professions and skilled trades? Were there any changes in the restrictions on land ownership by aliens? Was there any tightening up in the enforcement of laws applying especially to aliens? What was the strength of the agitation for prohibiting some forms of or all public relief to aliens? To what extent was the amount of actual relief given to minority unemployed different from that obtained by members of the majority group? Did public employment offices offer the same opportunities to all? What was the extent of discrimination against minority employees and applicants for work in private industry and on public projects in comparison with previous years? Why did deportations increase so heavily? To what extent were voluntary repatriations of aliens publicly encouraged and subsidized? What modifications were there in naturalization regulations and procedure? What can be inferred concerning changes in public opinion regarding minorities from study of the press and as measured by attitude tests? What information may be obtained from analysis of voting records in contests where a minority issue was involved?

It will be observed that of the subordinate questions just raised, practically all may be subsumed under some other category of minority-majority relations.

A parallel question to that concerning the development of majority nativism in time of depression asks about the relation between general economic hardship and minority reactions in terms of political thought and action looking toward group unity and preservation. Are majority appeals to national or racial unity as a means of battling starvation accompanied by similar increased emphasis on minority symbols of group action?

Although there is good evidence, evidence which is reasonably convincing without having been worked into proper shape by social scientists, that majority nativism in the United States has become an increasingly powerful political factor since 1929, the corresponding minority picture is a confused blur. It does seem clear, however, that there has been no more than a slight tendency for minorities to fight their case politically with a united front, yet it would be valuable to know to just what extent Negroes and Jews, say in New York City, or Chinese, Japanese, and Filipinos on the West Coast, have banded together, if at all, because of their common plight. In spite of the common belief to the contrary, it seems that little success has been achieved by the few minority leaders who have advocated such co-operation. Minority groups have too little in common except their treatment by the majority, and too many points of serious difference, to permit their standing shoulder to shoulder except in sporadic instances, particularly since it is possible to derive some psychic satisfaction out of the presence of other peoples in the same boat and on a lower deck.

A probable hypothesis is that the harder minorities are pressed to get a living, the more they tend to emphasize defensively their minority qualities and traditions. On the other hand, it seems from purely general observation that such an hypothesis can stand only when oppressed individuals find it impossible to pass over into and identify themselves with the majority. Certainly there are tendencies toward both escape from and defensive retreat deeper into minority status. In either case, the possibility of an effective political program for even a single minority is minimized.

Instead of attempting to gain protection through the ballot, a procedure not adapted to the use of numerical minorities unless they happen to hold the balance of power between two major factions, those who can neither escape from minority status nor endure it without compensating adjustments give some evidence of a tendency to resort to compensatory idealized tradition.

THE ECONOMIC BASIS OF RACE RELATIONS

Race problems are an incident of world economics and the race relations a code of behavior developing out of the contact and conflict of economic interests of the groups identified as racially different. All the psychological phenomena of group tensions, taboos and fears, direct and indirect aggression urges, jealousies and hostilities, are incidental to this basic fact.

RACE RELATIONS, as we conceive them today, may in many respects be said to be only incidentally racial. They reflect a state of mind and a social or political philosophy shaped to expediency. The race relations themselves are, for the most part, stereotyped patterns of behavior representing efforts to find the most comfortable basis of adjustment between groups whose interests are directly or indirectly in conflict. This group conflict may become a part of the social heritage to such an extent that the basic motivations to conflict are obscured. The patterns of behavior and the motivating attitudes, however, are frequently the same whether the element of race is absent or present; or even when the race factor is erroneously assumed to be present. . . .

The race line, during the recent war in which France and Germany fought on opposite sides, was held to divide the people of Baden from those of Alsace though in bodily form they both belong to the same Alpine sub-race. Race prejudices are entertained against the Irish who are not a race. The early stages of migration of Italians and Poles provoked the familiar group cleavages which took on all

Excerpts from Charles S. Johnson, "Race Relations and Social Change," in *Race Relations and the Race Problem*, edited by Edgar T. Thompson, (Durham, North Carolina: Duke University Press, 1939), pp. 271-291; 302-303.

the features of race prejudice. Similar manifestations appear in some areas in regard to Catholics, who represent a religious denomination, and Jews, who represent a religious culture.

Race problems, in like manner, may be said to be not so much an expression of biological race differences as of the underlying forces that give prominence to the external group differences, such as they are. Race problems which are the structure of present-day race relations are an incident of world economics, and the race relations a code of behavior developing out of the contact and conflict of economic interests of the groups identified as racially different. All the psychological phenomena of group tensions, taboos and fears, direct and indirect aggression urges, jealousies and hostilities, are incidental to this basic fact.

The present customary practices recognized as race relations are merely social mechanisms brought into use to facilitate control of one group by the other. The social mechanisms regulating group relations may vary geographically, or change over the years, but when they change it is in response to those racial sentiments which are born of basic conflicts of interest. Rarely, if ever, does the group psychology, whatever the degree of intensity of emotion, or the ideological content, operate independently in the social situation.

Economic changes, whether construed as progress or disorganization, both induce and are, in themselves, social changes, and the race relations are dependent upon these economic changes to a much greater extent than upon any other single element. Race attitudes are only one element in the constellation of group attitudes. Religion is another, and it is remarkable how closely these two have been related in the recent history of race relations. . . .

Lord Olivier traces the rise of self-conscious sentiments and antagonisms based on color to the period of the beginning of the British slave trade. Viscount Bryce says that "down to the days of the French Revolution there had been very little, in any country, at any time, of self-conscious racial feeling." The expansion of Europe began with the opening up of the New World, and this coincided with the early stages of development of the Industrial Revolution. The slave trade and the colonization of America were, significantly, the first big business, and accompanied the first large-scale extension of Europe.

The really serious implications of this expansion, however, and the necessity for ever increasing markets did not become acute until the last half of the nineteenth century.

In the era of feudalism Europe had contacts with other parts of the globe. There had been constant conflict with the Slavs and Arabs. There is also evidence of contact between Africa and Europe in the presence of Africans on the Continent. Hannibal at the Court of Peter the Great, Capetien in Holland, Juan Latino and Sebastian Gomez in Spain, and Alessandro in Italy, are notable historical examples. Throughout the Middle Ages the cleavage between the nobility and the common people provided the psychological and social patterns familiar today under the classification of race.

There are traces of this cleavage in the claim of the nobility of Europe that the peasants, who of course were not Negroes, were descended from Ham and condemned by Noah to slavery. Before the notion of race was introduced as an explanation, the French nobles, seeking some justification for their class position, had referred their origin to certain legendary heroes. Hertz cites instances of French scholars, as late as the seventeenth century, tracing the ruling class back to François, a son of Hector. In England, where, incidentally, the Industrial Revolution was more advanced than in the rest of Europe, the social chaos which followed the drastic economic reorganization converted impoverished children into the "pieces" that the African slaves were, later, to become. The new inventions had created a demand for child labor, and under this economic urge these children of the same blood and race stock, in the words of the Hammonds, were "even more powerless and passive in the hands of a master than the stolen Negro, brought from his burning home to the hold of a British slave ship." . . .

The expansion of Europe was impelled by the necessities of a rapid industrial expansion, and with this went the extension of the economic system which supported industrial expansion and commerce. This industrial expansion, however, had its own social complications. It tended to concentrate populations in cities and towns, and accelerated the growth of these populations. This in turn created a demand for raw materials and markets for the benefit of the people at home, and new areas for population expansion.

Contact of Europe with new territories, whether in Africa or India or America, created new social and cultural problems. One of these problems has been the rapid increase in the European peoples as compared with the native populations of the newly discovered areas. Another has been the creation of mixed blood populations who are both biologically and culturally marginal. Wherever Europe has penetrated, these mixed blood populations have developed into race problems. The patterns of the relations have tended to follow the economic pressures inherent in the nature of the contact.

When the British first extended their economic interests into India, and at the time of the founding of the pioneer English factors in India in the early seventeenth century, they encouraged intermarriage with the native population. From this contact the Eurasian population developed. The Court of Directors of the East India Company, in 1687, addressing the President of Madras, urged that the marriage of their soldiers to the native women was "a matter of such consequence to posterity" as to be encouraged at some expense. When the Eurasians became numerous and threatened to outnumber the Europeans, and the competitive demand for positions became pronounced, the racial policy changed and with this change the relations shifted to acute racial discrimination. The Indians and mixed bloods were relegated to a fixed economic subordination, and their consequent poverty and degradation were used to justify the judgment of an inherent degeneracy and shiftlessness and unfitness for the society of the English.

In Java, during the early settlement by the Dutch, the natives were readily assimilated into the Dutch population. With improvement in transportation and communication and the competition of newer job-seeking Dutch with the Javanese-born population, the natives were subject to increased pressure and discrimination. With these changes came changes in attitudes and in the patterns of association. Only in more recent years has there developed among the native population a resistant countermovement in the formation of a nationalistic organization to defend their interests.

Africa is the new seat of European rivalry, and of some of the most acute race problems to be encountered anywhere in the world today. One type of race contact is that between European settlers in Africa and the native population. The Union of South Africa offers a good example of this. The present area of the Union, which covers four territories, Cape, Natal, the Transvaal, and the Orange Free State, is 417,917 square miles. The white population numbering about 1,800,000 owns 80 per cent of the best land, while 7,000,000 Bantu have been given back 8 per cent of the land, for the most part unfertile and waterless. What was once regarded in the language of imperialism as a native problem is now rather flagrantly regarded as a racial problem.

Leaders of the country have proclaimed and translated into law a policy of complete racial segregation, with the full formula of racial dogma and doctrines of white supremacy. The policy extends even to the Church where, by an Act of Parliament, natives are excluded from membership in the Dutch Reformed Church, the semi-official religion of the State. Color bar legislation attempts to adjust economics artificially to racial dogma and policy; social-minded individuals who seek a more humane relationship are drastically ostracized; and by deliberate means the doctrine of an unalterable racial inferiority is being implanted. Here is, altogether, the most complete arrangement of racial dominance and exploitation existing anywhere in the world today.

Sarah Gertrude Millin says of the Boer that his "colour feeling has something almost religious about it. He considers it his *duty* to hate black blood in all its manifestations." Sir Thomas Watt, a white South African, is responsible for this interpretation of the attitude of his fellows, in an article in the London *Times*: "To those who say England cannot be a party to a great act of injustice, I would reply that this matter is to us in South Africa such a vital and fundamental matter, that no ethical consideration, such as the rights of man, will be allowed to stand in the way."

According to the Carnegie Commission Study in 1933, of a total white population of 1,800,000, over 500,000 are below what is termed a "subsidized" level, 150,000 are permanently unemployed because of lack of skill and inability to compete with natives. In turn, the Government subsidizes municipalities that dismiss natives and employ whites, which costs them about 200 per cent more. Nevertheless, white unemployment increases. Taxing natives for the social relief of poor whites and turning the returns of mining to aid agriculture have failed, and the curious result of this has been to give ominous importance to the racialists who preach the threat of the natives to white civilization, and who in turn insist upon large military budgets.

In South Africa there is a mixed population of 600,000, known as the Cape Colored. They are the result of the early contact between the Portuguese, and later the Dutch, with the Hottentots. After the abolition of slavery there, in 1833, the Cape Colored had legal equality with the white population. They escaped acute competition with the poor whites and, as a result, retained a relatively high status. And although the Cape Colored population has escaped much of the social discrimination that has been the lot of the competing black, the rise of the poor whites is beginning to increase anticolored prejudice as the traditional jobs become attractive.

In the British West Indian island of Jamaica the unmixed native has not been in as direct competition with representatives of the colonizing power as the mixed blood, and, . . . the most intense racial hostility of the white is directed against the mixed blood.

In the early American colonies before the country became economically promising, close personal relations with native Indians and Africans were encouraged. As numbers increased and slavery crystallized . . . the racial policy was reversed, and the attitudes which had been founded upon religious grounds shifted to a racial basis. Racial stratification of the society followed this shift of attitudes.

In South America, Brazil in particular, the Portuguese colonizers who sought gold rather than the settled art of agriculture, developed a mild slavery and a fluid social structure which was characterized by absence of racial stratification. Portugal, although an active colonizing power at this period, was an underpopulated country and did not need new areas for population expansion. As a result, few women accompanied the colonists and this encouraged the taking of native women for wives. Today racial amalgamation is a part of the accepted policy of Brazil, and there are comparatively few unmixed Negroes. . . .

Lord Olivier points out, that the institutions of civilization disguised the self-seeking and violence of economically aggressive nations by organizing social injustices under constitutional and legalized forms and corporate class interests. This frees the individual from the appearance and commission of personal responsibility. His personal interest may thus present itself as his legitimate profession and duty, his class interests as essential to social order, his national conquests as something akin to divine right and duty.

The first Negroes brought into the English colonies in America in 1619 were not slaves, but indentured servants. The English people had in their culture no pattern of slavery such as that of the Portuguese and Spanish who settled in the New World. This latter form, inherited from the Middle Ages, was comparatively mild. It had not been a slavery to control labor so much as it had been a result of conquest in war, or for the purpose of replenishing the harems. It was indiscriminate in its sources, and no implications of racial incompetence were used to justify it. Moreover, it was possible for slaves to attain high occupational rank. There were philosophers, teachers, and poets among them. For the English the pattern was indenture, which had developed out of the necessity for adjusting a surplus urban population to the exigencies of the new industrial system. The grist for the New World expansion were these indentured servants and, as the demand for labor grew, other redemptioners, ex-convicts and beggars, kidnaped from the grog shops around the English wharves. The first Negroes who by accident were brought into the colony were accepted on the same basis as the other indentured servants who were white.

The muster roll of the settlement of Virginia in 1624 and 1625 found twenty-three Africans listed as "servants," as were the whites of that class. Thirty-four years after the Negroes came, Anthony Johnson, a Negro, and undoubtedly one of the first twenty arrivals, got a court judgment sustaining his claim to the perpetual service of John Casor, another Negro. . . . Around the period of the Revolutionary War it is probable that slavery would have been abolished had not cotton and slave labor become more valuable, following the invention of the cotton gin.

With the eventual failure of tobacco, rice, and indigo culture, the colonists had become lukewarm on slavery. As Patrick Henry remarked to Lafayette, they held onto slaves more from a habit of dependence than any other motive. Lafayette himself had observed that white and black seamen and soldiers had fought and messed together in the Revolutionary War without apparent race consciousness. In Granville County, North Carolina, a full-blooded Negro, John Chavis, educated at Princeton, conducted a private school for white children, and was a licentiate under the local Presbytery, preaching to white congregations in the state. One of his pupils became Governor of North Carolina, another was the state's Whig Senator. Two were sons of the Chief Justice of North Carolina. He was not stopped until the Denmark Vesey uprising in South Carolina (the first state to show promise of economic prosperity through the cotton industry) threatened the whole structure of slavery.

In the North there were free Negroes. The favorable experience of Virginia with slavery had tempted colonies in the North at first to try it, but conditions were not conducive to the use of such labor and in time slavery disappeared. Free labor drove out slavery in Pennsylvania, and slavery drove out free labor in Virginia. The free Negroes in the North had a difficult struggle, but it was with the immigrant Irish of their own economic level. Oliver Cromwell, the Puritan dictator, while traffic in black slaves was on, sold all of the Irish not killed in the Droghada massacre into Barbados. It might be in place to mention that the Irish, although white, were accorded by the earlier Americans no more consideration than the Negroes. As far south as Kentucky, they were mobbed and murdered when they menaced the natives' work. Speaking of the Irish during the 1850's, one Northern commentator noted: "An Irish Catholic seldom attempts to rise to a higher condition than that in which he is placed, while the Negro often makes the attempt with success." And this was used as an argument in favor of the Irish as laborers. They were the "dirty Micks," "shanty Irish," "Paddies," and "yellow bellies." As their economic position improved and they moved into political positions, the tight little isolated communities began to dissolve, and with them the social attitudes which all along had been regarded as thoroughly racial. . . .

Between 1845 and 1860 cotton prices rose, the value of slaves increased 100 per cent, and with them the land values; and with every increase in value the difficulty of breaking the status of Negro slavery increased. It was the clever young political scientist, Thomas

R. Dew, just back from study in Germany, who began to rationalize and sanctify the racial inequality which was proving so profitable.

The birth of these stereotypes which represent a crystallized contempt and disrespect for Negroes can be traced to the necessity for establishing the inferiority of Negroes and thus proving their sole fitness as slaves and essential parts of the existing economic system. The proofs of the subhumanity of Negroes, their incapacity for education and civilization, merely reflected the economic necessity that they be given no more education than was required for the menial tasks they were called upon to perform. Christianity and the Bible were brought in to solidify this position—"A servant of servants shalt thou be." . . . The defense of slavery, however, had to rationalize the perpetual subjection of the Negro. Slavery, as indicated, had been merely tolerated in the early years of the Republic. . . .

Calhoun reconstructed the Aristotelian doctrine that some men are slaves by nature, and attacked the American theory that "all men are created equal." Not only are they not born equal, he argued, but their very inequality must be regarded as one of the essential conditions of the progress of civilization. . . .

The race problem became important only after the emancipation of Negroes into the free status of citizenship. Under slavery there was a labor issue, a moral and political issue, but the problems were not, strictly speaking, race problems. Emancipation and Reconstruction marked the coming to power of the nonpropertied and long suppressed poor whites of the South. President Andrew Johnson himself was born of the so-called "poor white" stock of the South. It was during this period that the ogres, "The Solid South," "Blood will tell," "White domination," were born. Through such leaders as Tillman, Vardaman, and Smith, they articulated a long festering hatred for the Negroes and their first acts were directed at the favorable economic position as artisans and workers in which Negroes were left by slavery. Then followed a period of the most bitter open competition in history and, naturally enough, the highest lynching rates, the segregation laws, which aimed not against contact (for domestic service and miscegenation were not interfered with) but at disabling, economically, the Negro workers. This was an attempt to provide artificially a protected status for the Southern white workers.

Between 1881 and 1907, all the Southern states enacted laws separating the races on railroad cars, street cars, and in schools, from jury service and the primaries. South Carolina forced cotton manufacturers by law to institute such separation as to exclude Negroes completely from textiles, the only new and characteristically Southern industry since the Civil War. The Census of 1880 showed for the first time a decrease in the absolute number of Negro artisans in spite of an increasing Negro population.

For those who wonder why the fervor of the North cooled so suddenly and there came to life the new formulas, "The South's peculiar problem," "Noninterference," "Let the South settle its own problem," it is to be remembered that among other things the North was impatiently awaiting through the period of Reconstruction a new field for its capital; and only the pride of the South had held it off to that point. . . .

In the North for several decades prior to the World War much was heard of the virtues of the "melting pot" and the rich heritage which immigrants brought to America. The Americanization societies came to be almost as popular and widespread as the present-day American Legion. Pageants glorified the contributions of the varied racial and national groups of other parts of the world to the great American cauldron. It is no accident that this spirit of tolerance of racial and national diversity corresponded with the demands of manpower of our rapidly expanding industries. Immigrants came to these shores in increasing numbers until they reached the stupendous total of more than a million a year; and this high total continued for some ten or more years ending with the World War. When the industries began to reach the saturation point, and new recruits were no longer needed, new sentiments developed against these immigrants. These sentiments grew in intensity as a result of increasing competition with American labor and finally reached a climax in our drastic immigration laws.

Coincident with this development was the change in the behavior pattern toward the Negro. So long as they were not needed in the North for labor, they were held bottled up in the South where, at the same time, an oversupply of this labor invited the harshest racial treatment. With the withdrawal of immigrant labor, due to a war emergency, and with a new need in industry appearing, attitudes regarding Negroes changed swiftly. Their merits were praised. They were welcomed in the North, and most of their extreme crudities of behavior in the new environment graciously tolerated. In the South, on the other hand, the withdrawal of this labor, and the consequent threat of a removal of cheap labor did much to revise attitudes in that section, prompting greater consideration for Negro workers and their families, the building of schools, and the development of a sentiment which would support interracial bodies looking to co-operative effort.

Within a brief period, following the Negro migration to the North, there was a series of brutal race riots which resulted in the death of hundreds and the injuring of thousands of Negroes and whites. It is well known that the first of these clashes in East St. Louis, in 1917, was caused by the importation of Negro workers who were becoming a menace to the jobs of the white workers. . . . The responsibility for these outbreaks might well have been shared by the industrial managers and the municipalities which encouraged the labor power, but took no account of the social setting or requirements of workers who were also legally and socially citizens. The real bitterness of the Chicago riot centered in two spots: the area about the stockyards, where Negroes had entered the industry in thousands and were accused of taking white men's jobs while the whites were away in the army; and in the Hyde Park area, where the chief grievance was the financial loss to white owners in Negro residence areas, allegedly through depreciation of property values. The Arkansas riots, around Helena, in 1917, grew out of efforts to curb the Negro cotton tenants who wanted to get more for their cotton. The Tulsa riot had in its background the resentment against Negroes for their growing independence, their accumulation of money, their so-called arrogance and impudence, and the desire of certain interests to gain control of the valuable property and desirable sites which Negroes owned. In the Atlanta riot of 1906 one of the chief incitements to violence was the circulation of cards showing Negro carpenters and bricklayers building houses, thus menacing the economic security of white men. . . .

The professed reason also for the limitation of Negro school funds, when the white masses came into power, was that of cost, and the feeling of bitterness toward such Negro facilities as existed was because they deprived the equally disadvantaged white children by that amount. . . .

It is to be remembered, too, that education was opposed at first because it made Negroes less useful as slaves. Later, industrial education was supported to make better domestics in positions which were regarded as Negro jobs, and as such, outside the range of competition. When industrial education became established as necessary to the requirements of the new industrial order we had the curious situation of bricklayers' unions petitioning the City Council of one Tennessee city to stop teaching the trade to Negroes in the public school; and the school board being suddenly willing to let Negroes have the inexpensive classical education, while the expensive equipment of technical high schools was supplied to white children only.

There are evidences of the operation of economic forces in determining race relations in the present changes occurring generally in the South. This area is particularly interesting because it still holds four-fifths of the Negro population of the country. The South was, historically, the nucleus of the nation. If the country could have been developed without black labor it probably would have been. But under the circumstances Negro labor became a most important support of the economic life of the area. The social and cultural problems which so conspicuously mark the Negro population are in large part a result of the status of slavery imposed upon them. The social and cultural lag of the South itself may be said to be in some part, at least, a result of the social necessity felt for keeping this status fixed. The Negro question, and the persistent attitude toward it, have contributed to backwardness of the white population. . . .

There has been an accentuation of economic problems incident to the presence of the Negro in the social structure. The cost of separate schools, churches, transportation facilities, imposes a burden of many millions annually. The almost universal illiteracy of the Negroes at their emancipation imposed the burden of their education, as well as that of millions of unpropertied nonslaveholding whites, from the very beginning. Social and cultural institutions, such as schools, hospitals, libraries, welfare agencies, which had flourished to some extent in the North, had to be started from the base line. The important observation here is that the tensions inherent in a state of general insecurity, heightened emotionally by the racial attitudes generated, have been reflected in the race relations of the area. Any effort on the part of the Negro to change his status would be expected, inevitably, to provoke resistance, since it carries with it the implication that this would further intensify the insecurity and further endanger the status of the dominant race.

The complex of economics, social institutions, and the Negro has kept the section acutely conservative on most of the social programs that could reasonably be expected to make advancement. Consistent with its social dogmas, the South was bound to resist, and did resist, compulsory education for years, because it meant an added financial burden and threatened to unsettle the racial alignment. It had to oppose woman suffrage, because it threatened to add the unwelcome Negro woman vote, and also because it threatened to disturb the domestic role of women generally. It had to oppose labor legislation because this would discourage factories being drawn by a plentiful market of cheap labor. It had to oppose labor organization because it threatened the free rights of employers, and reflected radical ideas. It had to oppose, and continues to oppose, legislation preventing child labor.

Because the region has been burdened historically with the caste system, growing out of slavery, and a sharp class system for whites, it has had to condone dual codes of justice against its moral judgments and even, in some areas, to condone lynchings. It has been forced to put a ban on liberal thinking and discourage social movements of any sort which might mean the emancipation of the whole people. Its scholars and scientists who rose above the provincialism of the area frequently had to seek more congenial atmosphere for unshackled minds.

There have, however, been signs of changes in the large over recent years. Not always is this evident in direct personal relations, such as could be measured by the sudden expansion of individual Negro personalities, or in the sloughing off of race prejudices on the part of individual whites, but in a diffused, though unmistakable, breaking of many of the old taboos, and a breaking of the fixation of attention on the Negro problem, as such. Recent studies now reaching the general public have shown, for example, that the cotton tenancy problem, assumed for decades to be purely a Negro problem, is basically a Southern problem involving, actually, more white than Negro tenants and sharecroppers. They show, also, that the Negroes have been moving away to the North to escape economic death in the South. They reveal that the vast wastage of the soil is not Negro ignorance and negligence, but the responsibility of those who own, control, and direct the labor of the land; and only a few of these are Negroes. They show that the poverty wages simply mean no purchasing power for the people, on which the industries must thrive, and that the undernourishment so prevalent means, eventually and early, nonproductive illness and costly death.

It is the recognition of the serious economic plight of the South, perhaps, more than anything else, that is prompting a new approach to the problems of the area, and bringing about a new order of race relations. Race problems are being viewed by the new leaders, not as a separate and lamentable phenomenon, but as an element of the total economic structure and situation. This suggests that there will be economic backwardness as long as race and economics are kept separated, and that economic improvement will bring adjustments in the race problems. The strength of this new conviction has been sufficient to tolerate new racial patterns of relations. . . .

Race problems as here described take on curious characteristics—characteristics that belong to economic imperialism, to nationalism, and to religious emotionalism. They are, nevertheless, real, and confusion of the issues is further evidence of the fictitious nature of race and color as political instruments. We have noted how the specter of race arose as a new emotional urge to conflict, conquest, and exploitation—and the excuse for it. It is now evident that belief in the fundamental racial differences is less the cause than the result of a desire for exploitation.

Race, as one of the most convenient rallying points of the emotions of peoples, has great significance for the economic orders and political through of present-day Europe. The U.S.S.R. has made an important bid for the allegiance of subject peoples to its economic system by repudiating racial philosophies and penalizing the expression of racial antagonisms. The totalitarian states, by a confusing of race with nationality, have invited the opposition of other peoples, and fostered antagonistic aggression of their own nationals in the advancement of economic practices of doubtful feasibility. In the fusion of racial, political, and economic ends they have stirred emotions to a fervor adequate for the purposes of a crusade. . . .

Further changes in race relations in America will depend not only upon fundamental domestic economic readjustments but also to some extent upon world economics. Increase of education, which is now inevitable as a phase of the general cultural development, will make a fixed status for the Negro improbable. New technical developments will continue to disturb the social and racial mores, creating new situations in which the racial etiquette will be undefined. Urbanization and industrialization will continue to shift the basis of relations from a caste to a class structure. In the end there will be less emphasis on the significance of race difference than upon the solidarity of class interests.

7

TYPES OF SOCIAL CLEAVAGE

Aʟʟ SOCIETIES have their patterns of social cleavage, and each is characteristic. Many of these group cleavages are functional, and mark off the working sub-groups of the society in question. But although associated with the organic structure of the society, many of them represent distinctions in the invidious sense of the word, and reflect lines of social stress and conflict. The group may take them up into some comprehensive organized unity, but beneath the surface of this rather formal solidarity, these separatisms persist and color the social attitudes and relations of their respective members. In the practical round of everyday living they bulk large and importantly, especially when they are separatisms associated with some sense of cultural difference, actual or even historical. The naturalized citizen, for example, assured of full legal and constitutional equality, may yet have an apologetic uneasy citizenship because of being received with some majority reservation as a newcomer or as not quite belonging. Every minority group member particularly knows some sectarian line, all the more real in actual group living for being founded on traditional difference or distinction of custom or unwritten law.

Minority distinctions are invariably negative and restrictive. They range through a wide gamut from relatively trivial and tolerable distinctions to grave, handicapping and almost intolerable discrimination. Despite such infinite variety, group conflict cleavage has certain significant common factors and possibly common motives and objectives. The social distinctions of caste, class, race and sect, and even those of sex, seem to have interesting common denominators. The reactions and devices of religious sectarianism have very close analogies with those of racial prejudice and persecution, and many of the usages of caste repeat themselves with shadings of degree in class and minority hostility and discrimination.

In historical origin, many of these distinctions of group separatism were functional. But as the society matures, they become traditional and stereotyped. The tradition then operates to stratify the group, and limit individuals and sub-groups by well-defined and often very arbitrary codes and conventions. These prescribe minutely intra-group status and through the custom and etiquette of group relations, limit the occupations, social scope, privileges and association of the sub-ordinate groups. All who do not belong to the privileged or ranking groups are affected seriously by these prescriptions, which as far as their lives are concerned, become proscriptions. Meanwhile, the privileged group or collective set of privileged groups constitute the "majority," which, irrespective of its numbers, dominates. These proscriptions and restrictions apply not only to the basic social relations of the various groups, but extend through social ritual and etiquette to the secondary cultural aspects of life, to social standing, prestige, to the privileges of social affiliation and cultural participation. The sense of belonging or of sharing the culture is, after all, one of the primary bases of social solidarity. Exclusion from it, even in the presence of other partial integrations, represents a status of definitely restrictive and negative social character. Individuals and groups may suffer acutely in terms of lack of status and its imputed disparagements, even when otherwise fairly successfully accommodated to the social environment.

Cultural discrimination of this sort is peculiarly arbitrary, in that, being traditional, it frequently ignores acquired status, withholds recognition as determined by the normal criteria of the society, and operates with a stringency that tolerates little or no exceptions. Such discriminations, however, vary considerably in degree, from the extreme of outcast ostracism and pariah exclusion to the comparatively milder and more superficial exclusions of class and cultural snobbery. Some minority status is even self-imposed, but unless it can counter-assert superiority, in the presence of the dominant majority tradition, it still connotes some shade of not belonging, some degree of subordinate status.

As these types of social cleavage are studied intensively, it becomes increasingly clear that there are common denominators running through them. The term *caste* is frequently used, out of its original and strictly historical meaning, to denominate the basic character of all these restrictive social and cultural exclusions. There is warrant for this extended usage, since many of the group distinctions are as arbitrary and restrictive as primitive caste was, and all associate social stigma with restricted privilege and association. The taboos and code traditions of colonial and of American race prejudice, for example, so closely approximate caste in extreme practice that they need only the addition of "untouchability" to be identical. In spite of considerable miscegenation, prohibited intermarriage is officially maintained, and the taboos of restricted association, relaxed only to suit the majority interests and convenience, as in labor and personal service relations, amount in practice to "social untouchability." The fanatical exclusions of anti-Semitism, with its Ghettos and "identification badges," is in many respects, similar. Comparable also is the code of the colonial officer, whose political caste status puts insuperable barriers between him and all "natives." Ironically enough, many a maharajah, looking down through centuries of caste tradition on subordinate layers of Hindu society, now finds himself the victim of superimposed political caste, with the minister resident or colonial "adviser" its obdurate symbol. This cannot be construed as mere political restriction and hierarchy as prevails between rulers of varying rank, for accompanying it is the arbitrary dictation of the governing group mores and etiquette as a symbol of cultural superiority superseding the traditional native etiquette. Both in intra-group and inter-group relations, caste is a very considerable modern phenomenon.

Gallagher, analyzing the American racial variety, concludes that race prejudice, like class and caste prejudice, is merely one variety in a general species and also comes to the conclusion that race prejudice is a particularly virulent variety of cultural prejudice. As a result, race becomes significant not as a biological description or ethnic identification, but primarily as a symbol of group conflict between cultures or between culture groups within a culture. He finds that its real significance lies in the employment of the concept of race as "a culture symbol of group conflict and group organization." This is not to ignore the distinctive differences between class and race or between the concrete variety of this or that type of minority situation, but to point out the significant similarities and over-lappings. Rationalizations of cultural group prejudice exhibit the same analogies. The latter, in fact, shift base periodically between religious, cultural and racial grounds of distinction and discrimination, as, for example, the medieval stress on the Jew as a religious sect and the modern distorted emphasis on the Jewish difference as racial.

Gallagher then proceeds to a specific analysis of American racial prejudice. The historical origin of American color prejudice lies in the slave system. Its present-day traditions are the modified prolongation of the slave codes. Gallagher demonstrates clearly, however, that the perpetuation of race caste in the South is due to the South's economy, with its continued exploitation of a cheap labor supply rather than due to the mere weight of the historical tradition. The cultural and other differentials are maintained, then, for only slightly altered objectives. The status quo of subordination and its accrued vested interests support the tradition and code. Economic conflict supports attitudes of antipathy rather than friendliness, and the racial distinctions persist as protective and rationalizing devices for the majority interests and status.

Gallagher also shows how a tradition, derived historically from the ante-bellum regime and the interests of the planter class,—a relatively small and now almost defunct group, has become the dominant social tradition of the "solid" South. This occurred through the strategic inclusion of large sections of the white population in the emotional satisfactions of superior caste status, whether they shared the actual social status and economic privilege of the slavocracy or not. The vicarious satisfactions of the poor whites, with a small share in the benefits of restricted labor competition, have been used to create a specious solidarity of interests based on the perpetuation of the discriminations of color caste. Yet these allied interests are not in fact identical. Close observation of racial attitudes and practice reveals variation in these attitudes as between one class and another on both sides of the color line. Although a steady alignment and policy of majority-minority relations has been maintained, this variance of attitude from class to class within the society is a symptom of split motives and interests, and forecasts the possibility of a break in the traditional alignment should group interests among the whites divide sufficiently.

But in the present situation it is regarded as almost axiomatic that the "white man's floor is the Negro's ceiling," that certain symbols of superiority and inferiority should be maintained strictly, in order to preserve the status quo and keep the system intact, and that caste should obliterate class lines and all other distinctions to place "all Negroes below all whites." This is insisted upon, although economic class lines would put all upper-class Negroes and some of the middle-class Negroes higher in economic status than most of the lower-class whites. These paradoxical attitudes and policies, in addition to obstructing many lines of social change and cultural advance, add to the emotional stress of the majority-minority conflict, and are in large part responsible for the irrationalities and fanaticism in the majority psychology.

The etiquette code of race relations as it functions today in a typical Southern community confirms the judgment that a vigorous caste system based on color operates in this section. What to the outsider would seem to be trivialities of social intercourse,—such as minutiae about handshaking, modes of salutation, use of the "front door," eating together and the like, are so uncompromisingly prescribed by the unwritten rules of the race relations code that they have the force and character of genuine "taboos." In this way what has been traditionally characteristic of relative racial status is bulwarked against any possibility of change by this elaborate conventionalized paraphernalia of superiority-inferiority symbols. No matter how trivial, these symbols are invested with the force and loyalty of the whole social system, and the least infraction is met with the total resistance of the entire majority. Thus the prescribed social etiquette assumes practical importance beyond its superficial ceremonial meaning, for it reinforces the majority policy of dominance as expressed more realistically in economic exploitation, disfranchisement, group intimidation and social ostracism.

Psychologically, especially in the minds of the majority, this order of things is accepted as almost inevitable and beyond question. The stereotyped distinctions stand like frontiers, across which much inter-racial commerce and intercourse must flow, but which are reserved for any eventuality of conflict of group interests as intrenched positions of exclusion and defense. In the shadow of this hostile tradition, what Romanzo Adams reports as "the unorthodox race doctrine of Hawaii" would seem quite unattainable, and untenable if it were. Yet another pattern and tradition of group contact in a multi-racial situation operates, as he shows, to secure the almost complete absence of race prejudice and sustained social tolerance and cultural reci-procity. In addition to the absence of serious group antagonism and friction, Adams reports that the "code of racial equality makes it possible for men of superior character and ability to attain to positions of power and dignity and to exercise authority, without limitation as to race." Race in that sort of social context is merely what it is to the scientist, a specific inheritance of family stock. It exists under such circumstances to be recognized but not to make a difference, as a basis of preferred loyalties not of prescribed limitations.

Toynbee's selection reports further historical instances where a strong tradition of solidarity has neutralized the negative sense of racial difference. He shows, first, how the strong proselytizing interest of late medieval Christianity gave effective religious sanction to the ignoring of race difference. In this era, embassies were received at European courts from the pagan African kingdoms, important political relations were maintained with Ethiopia, and the one of three magi was traditionally represented as Negro. Toynbee considers the more liberal racial attitude of the Latin peoples and their comparative free-dom from race prejudice to be an historical carry-over of this earlier Christian cosmopolitanism, with the substitution, in the case of the French tradition, of a commonality of institutions and culture for the old commonality of religion. These historical data show that, whereas religion can in some cases be the most stubborn and divisive of all the organized social interests, it can also in other instances be a strong force in the opposite direction. In Moslem tradition and practice, the excerpt goes on to show, the bonds of religious solidarity take pre-cedence over racial difference in all cultural and social relations, even to the point of unrestricted intermarriage. In this case religious cleavage and its loyalties cut squarely across racial and other cultural cleavages and resolve them.

Golding's account of the religious persecution of the Jew is an illustration of religion in the other role. The religious prejudices of medieval Europe were intense, and precipitated against the Jews a century-long campaign of religious and social persecution, culminating here in mass expulsions, there, in exploitation and Ghetto restrictions. The Ghetto laws, with their residential segregation, prohibitions of intermarriage, political and legal disabilities, ostracism, symbolic insult and periodic terrorization, as described in Golding, are very comparable to much that is reported in Gallagher and MacCrone of the pattern of racial prejudice against the Negro. The rationalizations used follow also the same patterns. The Jew is blamed for his cultural difference, but blocked in all attempts to assimilate. He is adjudged inferior, but carefully and elaborately disarmed for effective competition. He is urged into exclusive group organization but denied its normal privilege of freedom from external regulation and intrusion. In medieval times, religious difference was used to justify these practices, but when religion no longer had a forceful appeal as a ground of rationalization, the sectarianism became "racial" as in contemporary German anti-Semitism. The Jew now comes to be considered a member of an inferior culture group instead of an offending religious sect. He is accused of being an unfair competitor economically and professionally, of being a parasitic element in the body politic, and an alien strain in the culture. The techniques of restriction and persecution remain substantially the same. The political and economic motivation of contemporary persecution gives special directions and emphases to the persecution, as might be expected, in line with these interests.

But medieval anti-Semitism, with all its religious assertions, was also insistent upon economic and political disabilities,—drastic restriction of occupations, periodic confiscation of wealth, exclusion from full citizenship and from positions of leadership and honor. Whether the division of group interests starts historically in religious difference or in politico-economic rivalry or in colonial contact and imperialistic domination, eventually the full complement of caste cleavage and persecution comes into play, if the issues of the conflict become sufficiently acute.

There are differences, of course, between these social situations and their severally different alignments of interests and grounds of conflict. Particularly are there differences to be noted between the controls of caste, class and dominant groups who share a social order with their subordinates and the controls exercised over peoples as in imperialism, overseas or continental, where the dominant power maintains an external and more arbitrarily coercive relation to the ruled. Yet even this general difference has considerable exception. Even as internal situations, intra-group sectarian issues may become as acute as any major extra-group conflict, as the Jewish question, in some instances, or the "race problem" in the United States or the "native question" of colonial South Africa. Yet a large-scale divergence, which is crucial and critical elsewhere, can be so altered by a policy of assimilation or by attitudes of reciprocity as to become less acute than many internal minority issues. Cases of this are the racial fraternalisms of certain French associations, particularly in the Old Colonies, or the cultural situation in several South American countries, particularly Brazil, and the close welding of a variety of races, nationalities and cultures in the religious solidarity of Islam.

MacCrone, reporting on religious and racial issues in the Union of South Africa, details a contrasted situation even within its borders. In the early Cape Colony, he finds, there was a subordination of racial to religious cleavage. At that time conversion to Christianity conferred freedom from slavery and social acceptance of natives and mixed-bloods to the extent of legalized intermarriage. The Cape Colony "colored" population is part product of this regime. On the South African frontier, however, the identification of race with religious difference made "pagan," "black" and "non-Christian" synonymous and lumped racial and religious prejudice into a particularly stubborn cleavage line. Under stress of that frontier antagonism, it was for a time legally forbidden to attempt to christianize the natives. There was a comparable brief interval, incidentally, when such a dilemma confronted the slave masters in the United States, and then the christianizing of the slaves was hotly debated. On the South African frontier cultural intolerance has been acute for generations, and this is partly to be accounted for by the intense religious sectarianism which characterized this frontier farmer culture, and to the fanatical use of religious difference to justify the dispossessing of the pagan natives. Color prejudice under these conditions became particularly intense.

The unusual severity of racial cleavage is largely accounted for by the high degree of visibility of skin color as a very obvious sign of group membership. It facilitates the drawing of the lines of demarcation when racial groups are involved in opposition or conflict. But although there is a constant projection of the conflict to the plane of "racial competition," the real issues are never solely those of race difference. Historically the prevailing forms of color prejudice have acquired their particular invidiousness from the background of slavery and its stigma, and from colonial contacts with very diverse cultures attendant upon the slave trade and later, imperialistic European expansion. Color difference has thus acquired historically an association with primitiveness and low cultural accomplishment, as well as with inferior economic and subordinate political status. Once so associated, dominant groups maintain culture differences and the tradition of them to facilitate their dominance. To do so, they must perpetuate in arbitrary symbols and fictitious stereotypes distinctions and generalizations about whole peoples and races, which in some cases have been factual in the past, but which assimilation and acculturation have tended to break down. Attitudes and doctrines of caste are formidable resistance mechanisms in the path of such changes, but ordinarily they only succeed in delaying, not preventing the changes due to social interaction and cultural contact.

Any handy distinction, aside from color, however, can be singled out as a symbolic basis for group discrimination and antagonism, other distinctive physical features, dress, folkways and manners, and language. One of the most paradoxical but also most inveterate, is sex. Here, where there is neither difference of culture, ethnic stock or interest relations, culture differentials have been traditionally maintained that make women one of the most seriously conditioned of all "minorities." An inheritance perhaps from the patriarchal form of social organization, the status of women has been arbitrarily and restrictively defined for centuries. Only in the last century did a woman's rights' movement discover the full extent or the full implications of the tradition. At that time, in spite of slow improvement over generations, the legal, economic and social equality of woman,—if social equality be construed as parity of personal liberty of action and a single standard of values, was far from attainment, and has not been fully attained as yet after a generation or so of hotly contested reform. Stern gives a retrospective review of the movements and forces that have propelled the changing status of women and the trends toward full emancipation. He concludes that the cause of women's rights is vitally linked to the causes of other disadvantaged minorities, and has often moved forward and backward with other phases of social reform and reaction.

It is interesting to note in passing how deceptive is the apparent exemption from affront in the case of the sex minority. Much of the intolerance and prejudice of sex dominance gets itself expressed by indirection, sometimes under the guise of banter and humor. However in situations of serious competition, ruthless majority attitudes and doctrine have often been promulgated. Indeed an interesting parallelism can be shown between the stock arguments put forward for feminine inferiority and those asserting racial inferiority. With slight reservations, it is the same position basically;—the insistence on the innate difference of capability, of the necessity for protection and guidance because of inherent irresponsibility and dependent nature, the presence of "special" aptitudes interfering with such traits as would warrant open competition and rivalry in majority reserved spheres,—in sum, all the clichés of a strong and intrenched cultural prejudice.

Language is another differential of importance in a review of group discrimination and culture conflict. No more accurate than the other arbitrary symbols, language is one of the most frequently used devices both for symbolizing and propagating cultural solidarity and in reverse use, for symbolizing group exclusion and hostility. Later, it will be seen as the crux of many of the present-day minority problems in Europe. For the moment, its general use as a cultural differential is under consideration. Elin Anderson gives in her study a careful clinical picture of this type of cultural cleavage in a New England city. Wisely, she does not connect the attitudes of the cultural minorities she found there immediately with their historic backgrounds in the Old World Europe. For in spite of an unquestionable carry-over of some of the loyalties and the historic quarrels of Europe into minority situations in the United States, the core of most of these antagonisms can be traced to local interests and factors. She finds that the "old settlers" in this community form the nucleus of a group who have assumed self-appointed status and responsibility as a local "majority." They are the "charter members," the "real Americans," and the newcomers in order of succession become the lesser breeds, the influx, the snubbed minorities. A local aristocracy has thus set up a framework of minor caste distinctions and invented a new set of rationalizations from the available traditions of national and racial traits and ascribed characters. Language figures prominently; they distinguish socially between one accent and another. Religious difference also figures substantially, the Catholic-Protestant divide most particularly. Back of both, however, it is pointed out, are economic stratifications and distinctions between the owner-employer class and the others.

Since the center studied is by no means a minority storm-center, and not even particularly intolerant, there is all the more reason to regard the analysis as diagnostic. The answers of those who belong to the minority groups clearly indicated that it is not they who reflect the most un-American or undemocratic attitudes, but rather those of the majority who persist in stereotyping other ethnic groups and misinterpreting cultural difference. This, because there is no basic cultural difference involved: the frame of the minority life is culturally that of the majority in this and most American communities. What few differences there were, were in process of rapid resolution through cultural assimilation.

Even this process of minority assimilation is often complicated by the intrusions of majority intolerance. The Cassidy excerpt points out the second-generation immigrant problem and its tragic cleavages between the cultural loyalties of two generations. This conflict, like the similar dilemmas of the racial half-caste, are of course the reflex of majority prejudice, and are by-products of the struggle for status in terms of its false but very real and arbitrary values. Minority experience sometimes compensates eventually for this inner division against itself; however, the basic corrective can and should be an enlightened majority tolerance.

The most serious fact about all these invidious cultural distinctions, throughout all their variety, is their conservative lag behind the trends of cultural change. Modern imperialism, for instance, while committed theoretically to conservative doctrines of race and culture, is from economic necessity committed to opposite trends in its practical effects. The wide extension of its range of contacts, its mechanical intrusion of its own forms of culture both through economic penetration and agencies of cultural communication create, along with unusual cultural disruption, accelerated trends toward cultural assimilation and standardization. By humanitarian movements also, Western civilization is paradoxically leveling off its own cultural differences and making its traditional cultural distinctions increasingly contrary to fact. Out of conflicting policies of penetration and exclusion, of assimilation and separatism stem certain peculiar dilemmas, which confront contemporary civilization with peculiar force. These are the subject of consideration in the next two sections, which deal respectively with majority and minority policies and attitudes.

AMERICAN CASTE AND THE NEGRO

When two groups of people are engaged in a chronic conflict of interest, largely economic, centering around the problems of security and status, each group having a high degree of visibility in skin color or other group characteristics there is a conscious drawing of racial lines of demarcation and the use of the concept of race as a tool in the struggle. Race prejudice is a convenient device for the exploitation of one group by another. The old social patterns which were fashioned in ante-bellum days in accordance with the economic processes of that time became so thoroughly a part of the group thinking of the white caste, that a shift in the economic pattern has not yet appreciably altered the social pattern. The white man's floor is the Negro's ceiling.

IT DOES not appear from scientific study that racial antipathies are "instinctive," something to be charged to a mysterious, immutable "human nature." Each child has an experience of race feeling which is peculiar to him, built upon experience or lack of experience with members of other groups, but "the nature of these contacts is largely determined by a much larger and more inclusive influence: the adult-made environment." Lasker concludes tentatively that "the evidence makes it probable that the attitudes unconsciously transmitted are much more effective than those deliberately taught."

Some writers on this question have made a good deal of the fact that children tend to fear the intrusion of strange and unaccustomed factors in experience. A strange face, a strange noise, may call out a violent reaction of fear or aversion in the child. In the youth this may be changed to disgust or to amusement. Such reactions, it is said by some, indicate an instinctive base for race attitudes. The point does not need argument. The close and intimate relationship between the white infant and the Negro nurse, common practice in thousands of the best homes throughout the South, and the cementing of genuine lasting attitudes which are at least cordial on both sides, indicates that the alleged instinctive attitude of aversion is not opera-

Excerpts from Buell G. Gallagher, *American Caste and the Negro College* (New York: Columbia University Press, 1938), pp. 21-26, 49-50, 86-99.

tive in these cases at least. Moreover, it is clear that while the new or the strange may call out fear it may also evoke curiosity. Which of the two attitudes will be called into play depends upon a complex of factors, not least important of which is the attitude of adults and older children present. The adult attitude determines whether the child will build up habits of friendliness or of withdrawal. Both attitudes are possible so far as human nature is concerned. This appears to apply to all races and to all situations. . . .

If race prejudice is not instinctive, then why is it prevalent? The first answer is that attitudes of antagonism or of discrimination between racial groups are not universally prevalent. The French, for example, during the World War seemed to show little or no race prejudice toward the Negro American.

A reasonable hypothesis for as much prevalence as we see in particular societies is that there are conflicts in society which, by their continuance, support attitudes of antipathy rather than of friendliness; and that these basic conflicts fasten themselves upon the individual members of the several groups, calling out the responses of antagonism and prejudice rather than of understanding and friendliness. "Race" then becomes important not as a biological description or ethnic classification, but primarily as a symbol of conflict between groups in the culture. Race is not itself the cause of conflict; but men organize themselves for conflict according to observable lines of demarcation such as skin color and hair texture. Having so organized, they rationalize the division, call it "racial," and use the symbol thus created as a device for furthering covert ends.

Racial antagonisms are therefore not unlike other group antagonisms between classes or nations.

When cultures which have marked surface differences come into contact, conflict is likely to result, because the habit patterns of the individual are formed in terms of his own particular group culture, and any effort at adaptation, implying loss of status on his part, is unwelcome. Or, within a given culture, groups with noticeable physical differences may come into sharp competition in the economic sphere, with resulting conflict and the organization of sentiments and emotions around the central fact of struggle for a livelihood and for comparative status on the economic ladder. "Race prejudice is like class and caste prejudices—merely one variety of a species."

The focal point of race antagonisms is likely to be some threat to existing status. To quote R. E. Park:

Every change in status, whether of an individual or of a group, involves a change in social organization. Prejudice—that is, caste, class and race prejudice—in its more naïve and innocent manifestations, is merely resistance of the social order to change. Every effort of the Negro, for example, to move, to rise and improve his social status, rather than his condition, has invariably met with opposition, aroused prejudice and stimulated racial animosities. Race prejudice, so conceived, is merely an expression of conservatism. . . .

Prejudice expresses itself in the acceptance by the individual of the stereotype or social norm which appears to fit the needs of his group in the conflict. If the basic pattern is that of the economic structure, then the lines of economic conflict determine the racial conflict, and the racial attitudes conform to the economic processes. "Racial animosities supplement group symbols, or fictions, and make possible connected group activities. Group prejudices are rationalizations by which the individual maintains his self-esteem and advances his economic and other interests." It is this line of thought which leads Herbert A. Miller to conclude, "I am convinced that practically all race concepts are not race at all, but concepts derived from economic situations. There are certain economic advantages to be derived from having one group subordinated to another." Following the same line of thought, Reuter states the same conclusion a little more moderately. "Race is made the symbol of cultural status, and thus serves to justify the exploitation of the weaker group with the inevitable political and cultural consequences. Being a symbol of cultural status, it serves to classify individuals, and so to retard their advance by limiting their freedom and determining the cultural values to which they have access."

When two groups of people are engaged in a chronic conflict of interest, largely economic, centering around the problems of security and status, each group having a high degree of visibility in skin color or other group characteristics, there is a conscious drawing of racial lines of demarcation and the use of the concept of race as a tool in the struggle. Feeling, strong emotion, is called into play, and race prejudice results. In this sense, race prejudice is a convenient device for the exploitation of one group by another. . . .

Lessening of race tension may be looked for as the general level of economic and cultural life for whites and Negroes alike is raised. From the standpoint of better race relations, or even from the more limited point of view of the advancement of the Negro, it appears that raising the standard of living of lower-class whites is fundamental to any improvement in circumstances for the Negro. Since economic competition is the most important of the social factors causing race antipathies; and since race attitudes of paternalism also root in economic patterns; and since overt expressions of race tension come with fluctuations in economic conditions; we are justified in inferring that any comprehensive attempt to improve the condition of the Negro must include a realistic treatment of (a) the fact of economic exploitation of the Negro working classes by the white middle and upper classes: (b) the fact of economic pressure which frequently thrusts great numbers of whites and Negroes below the poverty line; and (c) the fact of economic competition between Negro and white working classes, a competition which is made desperate by the low wage level and rendered chronically bitter by fluctuations in the economic process. . . .

Part of the emotional difficulty of the South today grows out of the contradictory situation of two different caste patterns operating simultaneously. When an individual occupies one relationship in economic matters and another in "social" matters, the etiquette of social observance becomes hopelessly complicated. For the white man who is sensitive about the maintenance of the "proper" social distance, the closer and more nearly equalitarian relationship of the economic status is abhorrent. He tends to demand that Negroes should all stay in the lowest economic brackets, thereby simplifying the problem by making economic status permanently identical with the old social status of slavery. But for the Negro upper-class member, the situation is equally abhorrent. He feels that his economic classification should be reflected in his social status; and when he finds himself thrust unceremoniously from the economic to the social status, he feels that violence is being done to his personality. The "social ground" on which he stands as a producer and consumer is suddenly taken from under him as a citizen, and he is dropped to a status below that of the lowest white person, with the trap door of caste clamped over his head, while the white caste draws itself together to give its united weight to the defense of the closed door.

This dual configuration is an interesting illustration of the tenacity of a stereotype. The old social patterns which were fashioned in ante-bellum days in accordance with the economic processes of that time became so thoroughly a part of the group thinking of the white caste, that a shift in the economic pattern has not yet appreciably altered the social pattern. The rigid enforcement of the caste line of separa-tion in both economic and "social" patterns makes possible the modi-fication of relative status in the economic sphere at the same time that the inferiority of the old stereotype is maintained unmodified in all other relationships.

By the 1930's, the number of Northerners actively engaged in furthering the cause of the Negro in the South had become so small as to be statistically negligible; the few Yankees remaining in the South are either merged in the Negro upper class or absorbed by the white caste, in accordance with the conformity of the individual Yankee to one or the other group standard. The typical attitudes across class and caste lines are tabulated below. One important modi-fication needs to be borne in mind as this tabulation is read, namely, that the expression of a given attitude through contacts in the economic realm will tend not to be the same as the expression of that attitude in noneconomic "social" contacts. This is particularly true of race attitudes where Negroes in the upper- and upper-middle-class groups are involved. If it is an economic relationship (white seller, Negro customer, for example), the economic status of the Negro may be taken into account. But beyond this recognized economic realm, the old differences of caste inequality are enforced.

Characteristic interclass attitudes of the 1930's. Interclass attitudes within each of the respective castes follow closely the same general patterns, with the upper class setting the pace, the middle class emulating, and the lower class envying. The picture is substantially the same in both cases.

1. The white upper-class attitude toward
   —Negro upper class: puzzled appreciation, not unmixed with open tolerance as long as caste lines are rigorously adhered to;

—Negro middle class: pleasant and paternalistic benevolence, which helps to preserve the self-respect of the white at the expense of that of the Negro;

—Negro lower class: paternalism shading into indifference.

2. The white middle class attitude toward

   —Negro upper class: hostility and resentment of threat to status, sometimes softened into philosophical acceptance of status as long as sophistry of caste line preserves fiction of superiority;

   —Negro middle class: active opposition to Negro business and trade development which seems to undermine economic security of white middle class, resultant antagonism;

   —Negro lower class; indifference except to Negro as purchaser or laborer, merging into hostility, with latent oppression and terrorism.

3. The white lower-class attitude toward

   —Negro upper class: undisguised antipathy and resentment, including unadmitted inferiority complex which must be vehemently denied in action;

   —Negro middle class: same as preceding, differing only in degree;

   —Negro lower class: day-to-day tolerance as long as caste line is rigidly observed, but latent terrorism lurking underneath calm exterior.

4. The Negro upper-class attitude toward

   —white upper class: extremely self-conscious race consciousness, with resentment over lack of social recognition of class status through superimposition of caste line;

   —white middle class: much the same as preceding;

   —white lower class: resentment that inferior class occupies superior caste position, with antagonism, contempt, fear, and acute race tension at all times.

5. The Negro middle class attitude toward

   —white upper class: general adjustment to caste system and acquiescence in superior status of upper- and middle-class whites, with refusal to consider the plight of the lower-class white, and resultant effect that Negro middle class maintains position of dominance over Negro lower class by accepting caste division as its own limit;

   —white middle class: much the same as preceding, but confused by competitive conflict of two middle classes for business and income, though not for caste status;

   —white lower class: secret contempt, open indifference.

6. The Negro lower-class attitude toward
    —white upper and middle classes: the perpetuation of the slave psychology with its acceptance of inferior status, emulation of white aristocracy, and eager receipt of paternalism in exchange for observance of caste;
    —white lower class: antagonism, friction, resentment, an easy, day-to-day adjustment glossing over the deeper antipathies, and renewed competition for jobs stimulating latent race feeling.

These tabulations of attitude are not intended to be definitive or all-inclusive or infallible. It is readily granted that there are many exceptions to even these general attitudes, and that the permutations and combinations of attitudes are not limited to the mathematical possibilities of these tables. We are dealing here with the devious processes of human beings, and each individual tends to weave his own pattern of action. These individual variations sometimes amount, in the aggregate, to group exceptions to the generalizations which are here offered merely as a convenient means of suggestive analysis. One of the important sets of exceptions which should be noted here has to do with the numerically small but potentially important group of individuals whose attitudes do not conform wholly to those of the class and caste to which they belong. Not a few of the present generation of white college students in the South, to cite but one example, will be molders of new patterns which will be at variance with the accepted race attitudes of their own social groups.

Let it also be pointed out that the variety of attitudinal patterns made probable by the cross-currents of caste and class sheds additional light on a phenomenon which is puzzling to many persons not intimately acquainted with the South. Many Southern whites can say with complete truthfulness that they feel no antipathy toward Negroes, that they know no antagonism or unfriendliness. But we have seen that antagonism is not a necessary concomitant of acceptance of caste; there may be other forms of prejudging (prejudice) than those which result from sharp conflict. Indeed, one of the most widely prevalent patterns of prejudice is this pattern of paternalism which expresses itself in kindliness and condescension. It is probable that this attitude is much more effective in perpetuating the caste system than are the more vigorous and explosive tactics of the direct actionists. It is no reflection upon the character or good intentions of a benevolently inclined white person to point out that his assumption of an attitude of benevolence results in cultivating a corresponding attitude of dependence on the part of the Negro. At best, this paternalistic "looking out for" particular Negroes is an enheartening relief in a difficult situation.

Individual white persons, particularly those who have a family tradition of former ownership of slaves, are quite likely to take a genuine and sincere interest in the welfare of certain Negroes. They are quite likely to extend to them a regard and affection which they would deny to many white people. Occasionally this may even carry over into formal and public action, such as burying a favorite servant in the family burial plot (white) in defiance of caste usage. Quite commonly, it means that the white person assumes a responsibility for the Negro at crucial moments of financial or legal trouble, or at times of sickness and the like. There is a carry-over of much that was good in the old master-slave relationship when paternalism is benevolent. But at its worst, this attitude can become a cloak of hypocrisy. The white person permits charity to take the place of justice; he "looks out for" the Negro who is faithful to him, but he wishes to be free from any involvement in the question of social justice for an oppressed race. Two baleful effects of this attitude of paternalism need to be put down to its debit: it tends to perpetuate the old plantation legend, by giving plausibility to the idea of the contented darky and the kindly master; and it inevitably saps the self-respect and undermines the independence of the Negro who is involved in it. Viewed from this angle, the benevolence of the well-intentioned white person who wants to "take care" of certain Negroes is on a par with the misdirected zeal of the social uplifter who is out to "do them good" rather than to work alongside Negroes for the solution of common problems. The attitudes and status of the members of the submerged group are in large part a reflex of the outlook and stance of members of the white group with whom they happen to associate. If in the white person's attitudes there is any recognition of difference in status, that is fairly certain to make its impress upon the Negroes concerned; and if the social stance taken by the white person suggests the posture of condescension, the caste system is being subtly and effectively maintained. This last is important; for stance is not so much a matter of where one stands, as how he stands. One can move from a former position of opposition to a new position of tolerance, but if the posture of superiority remains unchanged, the fact that the person stands on new ground does not alter the basic relationship. The important thing to note about the caste-class complex of psychological attitudes we are here examining is that, although many diverse, and sometimes contradictory, attitudes are included in the whole matrix, each of these attitudes does in some way recognize the caste line, and on the whole the attitudes of whites tend to insist on caste. . . .

It appears, then, that prejudice is the reverse of the coin whose obverse is group loyalty. Loyalty to one's own kin and caste are exalted into virtue; and the corollary of antagonism to another caste is seen not as a vice but as the natural expression of the virtue. Race attitudes can therefore be defended with peculiar tenacity and complete self-righteousness. Stereotypes are built up and gain credence without regard to scientific verification or lack of verification, because they tend to bolster the caste division and to win continued acceptance for it. As these defense rationalizations grow, they fulfill a threefold purpose: (1) they become shorthand expressions of accepted social patterns; (2) they serve readily as rallying cries for the maintenance of caste, and of other components of the *status quo*; because (3) they obscure the real issues involved and appear to appeal to high motives and loyalties. There is an extensive literature which rationalizes the alleged racial differences which are the defined boundaries of caste. Largely a product of the last two centuries, this literature has, through the control of stereotypes, tended to fix the status and to control the relationship of the two castes. . . .

Judging the caste system by its operation, however, instead of by its rationalization, certain pragmatic axioms of operation can be described. First, the white man's floor is the Negro's ceiling. . . .

The second, and more obvious, meaning of the "separate but equal" notion is that wherever the Negro does win his way upward, that progress must be interpreted as an improvement in condition but not in status—the caste line may be dented but it must not be broken. To return to the simile of the white man's floor being the Negro's ceiling, we point out that when the Negro does break through to a new level, he finds that the whites have been busily erecting a new partition, so that he has let himself into a new and vaster prison house, more terrible in some respects than his former confinement, because he had hoped for larger freedom on the new level. Let a contemporary struggle for educational opportunities at the graduate level illustrate this point. In recent months, legal struggles have resulted in a court decision compelling the state of Maryland to admit Negroes to certain branches of its state-supported graduate schools because the segregated school system did not provide these graduate opportunities. Similar action is pending in several other states. It is interesting to note that, closely synchronized with the announcement of these legal rulings, several of the border states are taking a suddenly active interest in establishing "graduate schools" in connection with the segregated state institutions of higher learning. This is in addition to the long-term interest in education for Negroes at the graduate level which has been exhibited by many fair-minded persons throughout the South. It is the expression, conscious or implied, of the old insistence on the integrity of the caste line. It says, in effect, "If the Negro *must* have education which is equal to the white, it must be separate." This is the other meaning of "separate but equal."

A second pragmatic axiom of the caste system is the importance of etiquette in preserving the system. Observance of the etiquette implies acceptance of caste status. Failure to observe caste etiquette implies at least lack of sympathy with the racial division, and may imply refusal to conform to caste distinctions.

A third axiom of the caste system as it operates in America is that in making comparisons across race lines, no distinctions within either caste are to be permitted to operate disadvantageously to the white or advantageously to the Negro. Colloquially phrased, this notion is, "Any white man is better than every Negro." The caste line places *all* Negroes in a social position inferior to *all* whites, even though the economic class lines would operate to put all of the upper-class Negroes and some of the middle-class Negroes higher in economic status than most of the lower-class whites. In this sense, caste becomes the compensation mechanism whereby the poorer white achieves a status which his position in the economic scale denies him. It also operates as a psychological force of high potency in establishing and maintaining the Jim Crow system of providing public conveniences and public services. Since any white man is "better" than every Negro, it follows that no Negro should be permitted to go into railroad stations, cars, theaters, etc., on a par with any white person. To admit a Negro to the white coach would be to deny white superiority and to endanger white supremacy. Thus, in actual practice, the Negro who is cultured, refined, and in all ways (except ancestry) a desirable social companion, may not enter the church or the school or the theater with white persons of similar background and sensibilities; he may not purchase a railroad ticket except by going to the Jim Crow window and waiting until all white patrons have been served (which may be rather disconcerting if the train is pulling into the station); he must wait for "his" turn, keep in "his" place. As the caste system defines "his" turn, it is: after all whites; and as the caste system defines "his" place, it is: below all whites. . . .

The anomalous position of the upper- and middle-class Negro under the caste system is reflected in the maldistribution of professional services for Negroes. Since the caste system is somewhat more rigid and pronounced in the South than it has yet become in the North, there is a marked tendency for Negroes of the professional classes to gravitate northward in an escape from the onus of caste. The 1930 census reports show Illinois, with a total Negro population of 328,972, reporting 192 lawyers, judges, and justices; while the whole tier of states constituting the Deep South (Florida, Georgia, Alabama, Mississippi, Louisiana, Arkansas, and Texas) with approximately half of the total Negro population of the nation (5,567,258) report only eighty lawyers, judges, and justices for the entire area. New York and Illinois, with a combined Negro population of 741,786, have 323 Negro dentists; while the Deep South with its five million Negroes has a grand total of 354 dentists. The contrast with reference to physicians and surgeons is: Illinois and New York, 541; the Deep South, 892. But in clergymen, the South carries away the banner: Illinois and New York combined can muster only 1,376; while the Deep South reports eight times that number—10,328. This last fact not only reflects the decidedly inferior professional preparation of the typical clergyman as compared with other professions, which accounts in part for the tremendous disproportion of professional religious services to the other three professions listed. It raises a further question as to whether the type of activity carried on by clergymen is more nearly compatible with life under the caste system than the type of activity required of other professions. Alabama, with its 1,653 Negro clergymen in 1930, lists only four lawyers who cared to struggle against the caste system in Alabama's courts. With the recent death of one of these four, there are but three lawyers of color in a state which has a Negro population near one million people. Are the hazards of law practice before Alabama's courts and under Alabama usage such as to discourage Negroes from establishing themselves in that state? Or is it to be assumed that the colored clientele is so adequately and satisfactorily served by white lawyers that Negro competitors are discouraged on that account? And is the Negro clergyman more free to practice his profession under the caste system than is the Negro lawyer? If so, is this relatively greater freedom due to the leniency of the caste system in matters of religion, or to the lack of anything in religion as it is preached and practiced which seriously challenges the caste system? . . .

UNORTHODOX RACE DOCTRINE IN HAWAII

In Hawaii, under the code of racial equality, it is possible for men of superior character and ability to attain to positions of power and dignity and to exercise authority without limitation as to race.

WHEN A TRAVELER familiar with race doctrines and practices in other places visits Hawaii, he is impressed with the apparent absence of what is commonly called race prejudice. One man said, "humanly speaking, you have no race prejudice in Hawaii." The things observed relate largely to ritual. A man of any race is addressed as "Mister" in Hawaii. A man from Texas saw and heard a Negro in the legislature—a Negro treated with respect and as an

Excerpt from Romanzo Adams, "The Unorthodox Race Doctrine of Hawaii," in *Race and Culture Contacts*, edited by E. B. Reuter (New York: McGraw-Hill Book Co., Inc., 1934), pp. 145-146; 148.

equal—and he went away in disgust. If our visitor has traveled in China he knows that the Chinese are not admitted as guests to Shanghai hotels intended for whites. But in Honolulu a Chinese man or a man of any other race may be entertained in any hotel and white men may sit at the table with him. In cities of the United States, Negroes occupy a separate section in theaters, away in the rear. In Hawaii a man of any race may be seated in the best section. If our traveler were to visit the public schools he might find a Negro woman as principal of a school in which she is the only Negro, or he might find one whose principal is an American Indian. He might be shocked to discover that men of dark complexion can and do arrest white criminals and act as their jailers. If he goes to the governor's reception he will see men of all colors shaking hands and holding friendly conversation with each other. If he is entertained at the home of a leading citizen, and if he is believed not to have sentiments antagonistic thereto, he may sit at the table with guests some of whom are not of his own race. If he is taken to a university social affair he will see young men and young women of several races and mixed races dancing on the same floor and to the same music. Should our traveler visit the industrial or the commercial sections of the city, he might find a white man who takes orders from a man of some other race or a white man who deposits his money in a bank with a Chinese or a Japanese manager. If he consults the report of the Bureau of Vital Statistics he will find that men and women of all races are intermarrying and that, in the general process of interracial amalgamation through marriage, the white race is taking an important part. Possibly our traveler may attend a church wedding to witness a white young woman marry a man of some other race, while the friends of both or several races give their sanction by sitting in the pews. . . .

In short, the race mores of Hawaii are, or tend to be, the mores of race equality, and the doctrines are, therefore, unorthodox from the standpoint of white people, especially of most English-speaking white people.

At this point no question is raised as to equality of stature, beauty, strength, inborn mental ability, temperamental traits, education, or technical skill. It is just a question of what the social ritual symbolizes. The use of the title Mister, the front-door welcome, the sitting together at dinner, and many other things symbolize equality of social status in Hawaii, just as the denial of the title Mister, the back-door entrance, and other rules of similar import symbolize social inequality in other places.

In the long run, the ritual affects the relations of a more directly practical sort in a very important way. Under the code of racial equality, it is possible for men of superior character and ability to attain to positions of power and dignity and to exercise authority without limitation as to race. Personal status comes to depend more on personal merit and less on racial antecedents.

WHEN RELIGION CUTS ACROSS RACE LINES

In our western society color prejudice was once unknown and is not now universal. Moreover the Arabs and all other white Muslims have been free from color prejudice toward the non-white races as was the medieval western Christian. They divide mankind into believers and unbelievers who are all potentially believers and this division cuts across every difference of physical race.

IN THE eyes of the medieval western Christian, when he looked abroad upon the world, the heathen, wandering unkempt in the wilderness, were neither incurably unclean nor irretrievably lost. Potentially, they were Christians like himself; and he looked forward to a time when all the lost sheep would be gathered into the fold. Indeed, he looked forward to this with assurance as the foreordained consummation of terrestrial history, the fulfilment of God's purpose in the world. In this spirit, medieval western artists used to portray one of the three magi as a Negro. How different from the spirit in which the white-skinned western Protestant of modern times regards his black-skinned convert. The convert may have found spiritual salvation in the white man's faith; he may have acquired the white man's culture and learned to speak his language with the tongue of an angel;

Excerpt from Arnold J. Toynbee, *A Study of History* (London: Oxford University Press, 1934), pp. 224-226.

he may have become an adept in the white man's economic technique, and yet it profits him nothing so long as he has not changed his skin. Surely he can retort that it profits the white man nothing to understand all mysteries and all knowledge and have skill so that he can move mountains, so long as he has not charity.

This medieval western freedom from the prejudice of race-feeling has survived among western peoples who have remained more or less in the medieval phase of our western civilization: for instance, the Spaniards and Portuguese and the descendants of Spanish and Portuguese settlers who have established new western communities in America. Among these rather backward western peoples, the racial criterion has never superseded the criterion of religion; but it is more interesting to observe the same freedom from race-feeling surviving among another western people, the French, who have ever been in the forefront of western progress and have distinguished themselves (for good or evil) by the radical thoroughness with which they have secularized their national life.

The French have discarded, as decidedly as the English-speaking peoples, the medieval western dichotomy of mankind into Christians and heathen; but the dichotomy which they have substituted for it is one of the same humane and significant kind. When the modern Frenchman looks abroad upon the world, he divides the human family into people who possess, and people who lack, the modern French version of the western culture; and in his eyes everybody, whatever the color of his skin, as potentially a cultivated Frenchman. A Negro from the Senegal who possesses the necessary qualities of intellect and character can rise, and does rise, to positions of power and honor in French society, without being made to feel that he is being enfranchised grudgingly or esteemed with reservations. The freedom of the French from race-feeling has been a fact of common knowledge all through the modern age of western history. In the seventeenth and eighteenth centuries of our era, in North America, when the English settlers were expelling or exterminating the Red Indians, the French settlers were intermarrying with them and assimilating them. During the general war of 1914-18, the Negro citizens of the United States who were serving in the American army in France were astonished at the social liberality with which the French whites treated the

African Negro subjects of the French Republic serving in the French army, whose cultural level was much lower than that of the North American Negroes on the average. The justice of this observation can be verified by any English-speaking white man who takes the trouble to visit a garrison town in a French colony or in France itself and watch the white and black soldiers of the Republic passing the time of day together when they are off duty.

We may next point to the fact that while, in our western society, race-feeling was once unknown and is not now universal, there are other societies in which the prejudice has taken shape on different and sometimes diametrically opposite lines.

For instance, the primitive Arabs who were the ruling element in the Umayyad Caliphate called themselves "the swarthy people," with a connotation of racial superiority, and their Persian and Turkish subjects "the ruddy people," with a connotation of racial inferiority: that is to say, they drew the same distinction that we draw between blonds and brunets but reversed the values which we assign to the two shades of white. Gentlemen may prefer blondes; but brunettes are the first choice of Allah's "Chosen People." Moreover, the Arabs and all other white Muslims, whether brunets or blonds, have always been free from color-prejudice *vis-à-vis* the non-white races; and, at the present day, Muslims still make that dichotomy of the human family which western Christians used to make in the Middle Ages. They divide mankind into believers and unbelievers who are all potentially believers; and this division cuts across every difference of physical race. This liberality is more remarkable in white Muslims today than it was in white western Christians in our Middle Ages; for our medieval forefathers had little or no contact with peoples of a different color, whereas the white Muslims were in contact with the Negroes of Africa and with the dark-skinned peoples of India from the beginning and have increased that contact steadily, until nowadays whites and blacks are intermingled, under the aegis of Islam, through the length and breadth of the Indian and the African continent. Under this searching test, the white Muslims have demonstrated their freedom from race-feeling by the most convincing of all proofs: they have given their daughters to black Muslims in marriage.

RELIGION AND THE PERSECUTION OF THE JEW

Anti-semitism is essentially European. Because the Jew was a religious minority, he was segregated from the rest of humanity and distinguished from them by a special badge of shame. However long his ancestors had been settled in any particular country or city he was considered a stranger. He was segregated not only socially but economically. Accusation based on religious tradition led to spoliation and frequently massacre.

UNTIL THE fourth century, Christianity itself was fighting for existence. At last, by the Edict of Milan in 313 A.D., Constantine the Great, without troubling to adopt Christianity himself, gave it nominal tolerance, and actual supremacy, in the Roman Empire.

On the position of Judaism, the results of this change were instantaneous. Hitherto, the bitternesses between Judaism and Christianity had been those of rival sects. But now, the Christian policy and the Christian point of view were taken over bodily by the State. Henceforth the religious teaching that the Jew was to be segregated and degraded became part of civil doctrine. In earlier Roman law, Judaism had been characterized as a "most illustrious faith, certainly legitimate." The early Christian emperors adopted the clerical vocabulary, and called it, instead, a "sacrilegious gathering" or "nefarious sect." And their legislation reflected the change in attitude. The citizenship which the Jews had been granted, together with other inhabitants of the Empire, by the Edict of Caracalla, began to be modified; but whereas they had shared the privileges with others, they stood virtually alone when it came to discrimination. For the first time in history the full enjoyment of citizens' rights became dependent on adherence to a certain religious system. The ecclesiastical code, which had been unimportant while it was ecclesiastical only, came to be embodied in the code of the State, which joined the Church in degrading and segregating this nonconformist element.

Excerpts from Louis Golding, *The Jewish Problem* (West Drayton, Middlesex, England: Penguin Books Limited, 1938), pp. 35-41, 43-49, 58-70.

It was not merely a question of a change of vocabulary. At every turn the Jew found his position affected. From the beginning, the Church had naturally encouraged conversions, which the Jews had equally naturally opposed; now, only six years after the Edict of Milan, by a law of Constantine (himself not yet baptized!) the latter were threatened with burning if they dared to molest (i.e., dissuade) converts to the faith of the true God. Conversely, the daughter faith disapproved of its followers going over to Judaism; this now became a civil crime, punishable by death, as also was intermarriage between Jews and Christians. (Small wonder that the Jews, making a virtue of necessity, now stopped considering theirs a missionary religion. Thus, however, they opened a way to yet another reproach, that they were intolerably exclusive—one of the last offences of which the ancient world could have accused them.)

The Church loudly objected to the presence of Jews in positions of trust which might give them authority over true believers. This, too, now became part of civil law. The Church had always frowned on the possession of Christian slaves by Jews; now, it was forbidden by the State, this being the prelude to a wider prohibition. Constantine's son, Constantius, went so far as to prohibit the Jews from owning not only Christian, but even pagan, slaves. There was no question of humanitarianism in this—slave-owning was regarded as a normal and proper state of affairs. But, as most agricultural and manual labor was performed by slaves, this was tantamount to a prohibition to Jews to employ labor in any shape or form, and was a powerful impulse toward their exclusion from normal economic life.

The reaction reached its climax under the Emperor Theodosius II (408-450), author of that famous code of law which formed the basis of later European jurisprudence. This embodied all the prevailing anti-Jewish conceptions and regulations, which thus became as it were implicit in the legal background of the medieval world. The Roman legal system is the only part of Roman civilization which post-dates (and reflects) the triumph of Christianity. . . .

Hence, with the progress of time, there was no relaxation in the official anti-Jewish policy. The reverse, indeed. The struggle against Paganism was over in Europe, until the twentieth century. Greek hedonists, Teutonic barbarians, and Slav idol-worshipers had alike been converted nominally to Christianity. There remained only, as the personification of misbelief and as the whetstone whereby the zeal of simple Christians might be kept keen, the Moslems and the Jews. But (except as regards certain areas of the south of Europe—where, incidentally, as a natural consequence, religious prejudice was not quite so strong) the Moslems were a remote contingency, living in distant lands on the misty border of Christendom. The Jews, unfortunately for themselves, were to be found everywhere. They formed accordingly the object of a perpetual campaign. Kindly, pious, zealous votaries of the religion of love found, in fact, in the hatred of the Jew, and at times in the massacre of Jews, the psychological outlet for sentiments which in themselves may perhaps have been pure and high-minded.

This legislation proved, in the course of the Middle Ages, a double-edged weapon. For, when the Arabs made their triumphant incursion against what had once been the Roman Empire, they found this system for the regulation of relations with non-believers in force, and adopted it themselves without any very great modifications. To the shocked dismay of Christendom, however, the non-believers in question were now not the Jews alone, but the Christians, too. Thus the laws of Constantine and the Codex Theodosianus, which had embodied the current anti-Jewish prejudices of the Church, became the basis of a code under which the Church, too, groaned. . . .

The Mohammedan was, of course, subject to waves of xenophobia and religious fanaticism in which the Jew suffered, but no more than his Christian neighbor. (The experience of recent years, when in Palestine and elsewhere the Arab was vented mainly on the Jew the resentment which he feared to express against the European generally, is a completely fresh phase, easily explained.)

On the other hand, there were interludes—the most famous was in Moorish Spain in the eleventh and twelfth centuries, or Turkey in the sixteenth—when Islam provided medieval Jewry with its nearest approach to an earthly paradise this side of Palestine, with Jewish freedom, Jewish statesmen, and Jewish achievement. And, if there was anti-Jewish prejudice, there was none of its rationalization by accusations of ritual murder, of commercial exploitation, and there was no enforced economic segregation so marked as to create a "Jewish problem." Indeed, the feelings which made for anti-Semitism in Europe became canalized (in Turkey, for example) in another direction. "It takes ten Jews to make a Greek, and ten Greeks to make an Armenian," ran the Turkish proverb; and it was against the unhappy Armenians (whom Zangwill considered to have an even greater title to the crown of the martyr people than the Jews) that the pogrom spirit of the Turk vented itself. Anti-Semitism, therefore—fanaticism and stranger-hatred *plus* a little something that the others haven't got—is essentially European. Farther East, moreover, beyond the sphere of the Mediterranean religions and the Mediterranean spirit, resentment against the Jewish religious and ethnic difference was so slight as to be unnoticeable, and the very ancient Jewish communities of China and India—yellow and black respectively (so much for the Jewish "race"!)—wilted away as a result of the sheer placidity of their existence.

At the period of the growth of Islam and of the consolidation of Christianity, a great change came about in the Jewish people—a change which was to be of vital importance in the history both of the Jews and of the world. It may be summed up in five words. *The Jew became a European.*

In a sense, he had always been. For the demarcation between Europe and Asia is largely an artificial one, and what we term "European civilization" is, in fact, that civilization that had its cradle in the eastern Mediterranean as a whole (not necessarily on the European littoral). But it is one of the remarkable facts in history that the Jews, alone of all peoples have had the faculty of following the tide of culture—not once, nor twice, but time after time. As its center moved westward, so the Jews moved with it—first from the eastern to the central Mediterranean, then to western and finally to northern Europe and the Atlantic seaboard. Thus they were influenced by European civilization, and in turn were able to influence it (a unique phenomenon) at every stage in its development. . . .

Indeed, of all the peoples of Europe today, the Jews have by a long way the longest and most continuous settlement. Centuries before the ancestors of many of the present nationalities of the Western world had emerged from the steppes of central Asia, Jews were living in Europe and playing a part in European cultural life. To think of them as strangers and aliens is to contradict history itself.

Precisely when the change which brought the Jews from Asia into Europe reached its culminating point is not very easy to say. But, from the year 1000 A.D. onwards, the greater and more vital part of Jewry was definitely settled in Europe, and henceforth associated preponderantly with European life, European ideas, and European intolerance. . . .

It is a typical conception of nineteenth-century liberalism that religion is a private affair. In the Middle Ages the case was different. Religion was a public affair. It was everybody's business, and it affected every activity. In consequence, the hatred of nonconformity did far more than to exasperate religious prejudice. It invaded, and it infected, every branch of life.

The Jew [it was ordained] must not be in a position of superiority over any Christian. It followed that he must not be admitted to a share in the Government. The extensions of this disability were enormous. The Jew must not occupy any administrative post, however lowly; he must not be a customs collector or an administrator, for in either of those positions he may issue orders to non-Jews. Finally, he may not even be an employer of labor. If, therefore, he were a master craftsman, he could not employ Christian assistants. He could not even have a Christian lad apprenticed to him to learn the trade. He must work by himself, or at the most employ fellow-Jews as artisans. And what would be the feeling of his Gentile neighbors when they witnessed the progress of this Semitic "cell" in their midst, when they found the unbeliever perfecting trade processes which he could not communicate to others through the normal channels? The segregation was an invitation to the eviction which ultimately followed, when this particular problem was solved by the disappearance of the Jewish craftsman.

At home, too, the Jew was not allowed to have a non-Jew in his employment. He could not even have a Christian housemaid. More than that. When his wife was in travail, no Christian midwife was allowed to attend on her. Nay, if she died in child-bed, no Christian mother was permitted to serve as wet-nurse for the child. On the other hand, it was considered grossly improper for the Jew to act as physician, as then he might acquire influence over his patient's soul as well as his body.

Your Jew and Christian must be kept apart, for fear of improper influence. Then they must not live together in the same house—or even in the same street. No non-Jew may live among Jews, and no Jew among non-Jews. There must be in each town a special quarter, or street, or courtyard set aside for the habitation of the Jews. (Later, these Jewish quarters will be termed *"Ghetto,"* after the one-time foundry (*ghetto*) at Venice, in which the local Jewish community was segregated in 1516.)

It goes without saying that the Jewish quarter would not necessarily be situated in the most salubrious quarter of the town; at Rome, for example, it was in the low-lying area near the river, which was inundated almost yearly by the winter floods. Herded together like animals, they bred like animals and died like animals; and it was ony by reading the Bible, and observing the traditional Jewish agricultural festivals, that the Jewish child realized that such a thing as the countryside really existed. It was in central Europe, particularly in Germany, that the Ghetto system was developed to its extreme, and in certain parts continued to apply until the middle of the Victorian era.

Even more far-reaching in its results than the ecclesiastical objection to seeing Jews in positions of superiority was the objection to friendly association with them on terms of equality. In the first place, in order to avoid such intercourse, how were you to know your Jew? It was Pope Innocent III, inspired by a Muslim innovation from which Christians, too, had suffered, who thought of the solution. At the Fourth Lateran Council, it was solemnly ordered that the unbelievers should wear a distinctive badge. The form and color of this differed. In medieval England it was a piece of saffron cloth in the legendary shape of the Ten Commandments. In France and Germany (in the latter case, down to the close of the eighteenth century) it was in the form of a yellow circle, worn on the outer garment over the heart. In Italy, the wearing of a hat of distinctive color became the rule. The badge came to be in effect a badge of shame. It marked off the Jew for contumely from other men. From a long distance off he could be recognized. He became the butt for jeers, for practical joking, for assault,

Marked off as another being, he became considered (as was inevitable) an inferior being.

The Jew represented a religious minority, in an age when religion was taken more seriously than today; more than this, he was held to be responsible for the Crime to which Christianity owed its origin, and regarding which the passions of Christians were periodically stirred to fever pitch. Because he was a religious minority, he was segregated from the rest of humanity and, indeed, distinguished from them by a special badge of shame. Hence, however long his ancestors had been settled in any particular country or city, he was considered a stranger, and subjected to all the ferocious xenophobia of the Middle Ages.

He was segregated, moreover, not only socially, but economically, too. He was driven into various urban occupations, more especially money-lending, in which profit would have been considerable had not spoliation followed so rapidly on its heels. Hence he was envied by the poor, who were convinced there must be money in the Jewish quarter; hated by his clients, who saw in him the instrument through which the king denuded them of their property; resented by the baronage, who recognized in him the agent of royal exactions, and hence of royal absolutism; and protected by the Crown only when the slow process of taxation seemed more lucrative than the catastrophic one of spoliation. It was to the interest of no one else to protect him; it was to everyone's to attack him. Moreover, that spirit of religion which should have been a restraining influence provided in most cases (owing to the special circumstances) the initial impetus, if not the actual cause, for the onslaught. . . .

Once a section of the population was set aside for prejudice and contumely, and was barred off from all normal intercourse with its neighbors, it was natural for the most preposterous ideas about it to be evolved and the most absurd misconceptions to arise. It was thus held (the belief still lingers in remote districts even in England, to the present time) that the Jews were endowed by a beneficent providence with tails. It was believed, too (Sir Thomas Browne thought it necessary to classify it as a common superstition), that they had a special odor, over and above the all-pervading unwashed odor of medieval humanity, which disappeared automatically when the waters of baptism were administered to them. Finally, Jews were thought to be subject to a perpetual bloody flux, a reminder to all generations of their share in the Crucifixion.

Now, it was clear that persons endowed with these physical characteristics were capable of practices to match, however abominable. It was widely believed, therefore, that the Jews were in the habit of sacrificing Christian children at intervals, in mockery of the Passion of Jesus. The blood thus procured (it was said) was used in their Passover rites, its consumption being held to relieve them of the special odor with which they were endowed.

This sort of fable was an old one. Renan once called attention to the uninventiveness of human malignity, pointing in particular to this specific charge, which is constantly brought up against unpopular religious minorities, of every creed, all over the world. It was, as a matter of fact, raised against the early Christians during the first persecutions, against the monks of Mt. Sinai by the Arabs, against the Jesuit Missionaries in China in the sixteenth century, against the first European residents by the Japanese, and against the Christians in the Far East at the time of the Boxer Rebellion. In every case it was unfounded and absurd. In the case of the Jews, however, it was peculiarly so. For the reiterated Biblical prohibition to consume animal blood (Leviticus, xvii, 10-14; Deuteronomy, xii, 16, 23-5) received at the hands of the Rabbis an extravagant interpretation. Every animal had to be slaughtered for food in such a manner that it instantaneously lost the maximum amount of blood; every remaining drop was drained off before the meat was permitted for food; and a man was even forbidden by the ritualists to eat a piece of apple which showed the slightest trace of his own bleeding gums! A conforming Jew would thus submit to unheard-of torture rather than consume a particle of blood. He considered human flesh—moral questions aside—as technically forbidden. Yet he, of all persons, was accused of making a practice of consuming human blood, criminally obtained, as a regular religious rite!

Yet, however preposterous the charge, it was in the Middle Ages believed in almost universally. . . . Time after time, century after century, in place after place, the accusation was renewed, and led in almost every instance to mob justice, to mass condemnation, and a trail of bloodshed. . . . Upwards of 150 recorded episodes of the sort are listed by the historians; yet probably these do not constitute more than a fraction of the whole. In almost every case the accusation was followed by wholesale arrests and spoliation—frequently by massacre.

A wave of blood accusations swept over Poland in the eighteenth century, which was responsible for the dignified Report of Cardinal Ganganelli (afterwards Pope Clement XIV), in which he completely exonerated Jews of all conceivability of blame for such outrages. Nevertheless, throughout the nineteenth century there were other sporadic outbursts—though seldom, by a curious coincidence, in any place where an impartial trial could be assured. In the twentieth century it has been revived in Nazi Germany, under semi-official auspices, in the famous Jew-baiting organ, *Der Stuermer*, with a plethora of revolting and chimerical detail. . . .

The Ritual Murder libel, fantastic though it was, was followed by another even more preposterous. It was in 1215 that the Fourth Lateran Council recognized officially the doctrine of Transubstantiation—that is, that in the ceremony of the Holy Communion, the consecrated elements become the actual body and blood of Jesus Christ. Now, it so happens that a microscopical scarlet organism (known as *micrococcus prodigiosus*), having an appearance not unlike that of blood, may sometimes form on stale food kept in a dry place. This similarity to blood led in the Middle Ages to the assumption that it was blood, and was regarded as a proof of maltreatment. In such cases the prodigy was generally believed to be the outcome of a fiendish plot of the Jews, who, desiring in their satanic hatred to renew upon the body of the Lord the agonies of the Passion, had somehow obtained access to the consecrated element and tortured it with knives and pincers until it bled.

The idea was rather more insane than fantastic, for no one would have gone to the trouble and risk of doing this unless he actually believed that the wafer was the body of the Saviour—in which case he would not have remained a Jew, nor could he conceivably have desired to perpetrate such an outrage. Yet this self-contradictory extravaganza caused the loss of the lives of thousands from the period when it was first mooted, at Beelitz near Berlin in 1243, when scores of Jews and Jewesses were burned at the stake upon this charge. Later, cases of the sort, with their accompaniment of pillage, bloodshed, and banishment, were recurrently brought up all over Europe, culminating in *causes célèbres* (which are still commemorated locally) at Paris in 1290, at Brussels in 1370, and elsewhere. And in 1420 a charge of this type led to the extermination, with a horror of cruelty unequalled until 1938, of the entire Jewish community of Vienna.

For a thousand years, therefore, the record of the Jews in Europe was a protracted martyrdom. In all history there is little more harrowing than this bloodstained record. The continuous record begins with the First Crusade, when the eager soldiers of the Cross were persuaded that they could gain paradise by the slaughter of a single infidel, of whatever religious persuasion, and began to save the sepulchre of Christ by onslaughts on the Jewish quarters all along the Rhineland. With the Second Crusade, the infection spread to France, and with the Third to England, where the entire community of York immolated itself rather than fall into the hands of the assailants. In 1391, the Lenten sermons of a zealous archdeacon at Seville were the pretext for the beginning of a wave of massacres in Spain, from the Pyrenees to the Straits of Gibraltar, in upward of a hundred cities, the number of victims being reckoned at 70,000 souls. In Germany—the classical land of Jewish martyrdom for a thousand years—no fewer than 146 flourishing communities were wiped out in 1298 alone in consequence of a charge of ritual murder in one city. Thirty-eight years later, almost the whole Jewish population of Alsace, Swabia, and Franconia was exterminated. The climax was reached at the period of the Black Death, when the relative immunity of the denizens of the Judengasse led to a widespread allegation that they had poisoned the wells with a concoction manufactured of spiders, frogs, lizards, Christian beards, and consecrated Hosts, and the Jewish communities of some 350 places were butchered in consequence.

In eastern Europe, the outbreak of the Ukrainian Cossacks against Polish misrule in the seventeenth century was accompanied by a series of onslaughts on the Jews. The toll of Jewish lives between 1648 and 1658 may be reckoned at 100,000. A hundred years later, bands of "Haidamack" rebels rose again in the Ukraine, perpetrating atrocities which at least rivalled these.

Thereafter, with the French Revolution and the Industrial Revolution and the spread of Western ideas, it was thought that a new era had set in. But in 1881 a series of outbreaks took place in Russia which added a new word—"pogrom"—to the vocabulary of Europe and devastated no fewer than 160 Jewish centers. It was these Russian pogroms, of the late nineteenth and early twentieth centuries, which sent wave after wave of refugees to seek a new home in the lands of freedom in the West.

RELIGION AND RACE CONSCIOUSNESS

Membership of a religious group was an exclusive privilege of the frontier farmer in South Africa which distinguished and separated him by an immeasurable distance from those who did not share it with him. By virtue of his religion, he justified his right to dominate the heathen by whom he was surrounded. He fell outside the pale, and their claims therefore, could never compete on equal terms with those of the Christian group.

THROUGHOUT the early, as well as subsequent race contacts, the great dividing line which ran between European and non-European was that of religion. It mainly determined the attitude of the European toward the non-European since that attitude was always some variation or other of the basic group attitude, either in its Catholic or in its Protestant form, of Christian toward non-Christian. Although the inhabitants of Africa and of India, not to speak of other parts of the world, were of different shades of skin-color, of different levels of culture and of civilization, of different religions or of no religion at all, they were all alike with respect to that fundamental difference which yawned like a gulf between them and the professing Christians.

The significance of this difference is well illustrated by the institution of slavery. All born outside the Christian community, especially

Excerpt from I. D. MacCrone, *Race Attitudes in South Africa* (London: Oxford University Press, 1937), pp. 6-7, 40-43, 125-135.

those who were captives of war, could lawfully be enslaved. Thus, of Prince Henry the Navigator we read that

'in pursuit of his crusading purpose he did not hesitate to sacrifice himself, and his zeal for religion led him to rejoice when a company of adventurers brought back cargoes of natives, because of the salvation of those souls that before were lost. He gave away those that fell to his share, for slavery was not in his design, though it was then, and for centuries later, considered lawful.'

No Christian could, of course, hold a fellow Christian in slavery, and a slave who had been baptized was entitled, therefore, to claim his freedom. For a Christian to be held in slavery by a non-Christian was intolerable—hence the Christian duty of ransoming or rescuing those Europeans who had fallen into the hands of the Moors of North Africa. The slave-trade, which was first started by the Portuguese and later monopolized by the English, was originally justified on the ground that the West African Negroes were either "lost souls," in which case it was the Christian duty to rescue them, or "savages and pagans," in which case they probably had no souls to lose and were, therefore, born to be slaves. In other ways as well, the European professing Christianity considered himself entitled to enjoy the privileges of his faith at the expense of those who did not share it with him. In the early days of European expansion,

'the mere act of discovering a country in which heathens lived, was strongly held to give the discoverers a lawful title to the soil, and dominion over all its inhabitants. The duty of converting the native people to Christianity was, however, the condition annexed to this power of acquiring new territories at will.'

The race attitudes which were characteristic of frontier society toward the end of the eighteenth and at the beginning of the nineteenth century cannot be fully appreciated until they are brought into relation with the whole spirit and outlook of that society.

Under frontier conditions, every society is engaged in a more intense struggle either against the forces of nature or of man or of both than is usually the case with a more firmly established society; and the "atmosphere of war" so engendered must affect, to a greater or less degree, the individual expression of attitude. In such an atmosphere the attitudes that are brought into play tend to assume extreme or exaggerated forms of expression as a means of coping with, and ending, the conflict. The insecurity, therefore, which infects the whole of frontier life only serves to strengthen the attitude in the individual, to stamp it in more firmly, as a means of defending the society against the threat from without. Hence we do not expect to find the operation of group attitudes, particularly race attitudes, qualified by other considerations and, least of all, by any consideration for the opposing group. The absence of status relationships between groups, such as exist in an older society, will, under the unsettled conditions of frontier life, necessarily involve the dominant group, or group that seeks to dominate, in conflict with the other group or groups. Passive resistance, even if it merely takes the form of a failure to comply on the part of the latter, is sufficient to render more intolerant the attitudes of the dominant group, while hostile action or aggressiveness will make them more violent and embittered.

Since the race attitudes are only one element in a pattern of group attitudes, we find that all the social attitudes of the group, racial, religious, social, and political, come into play in a mutually supplementary way. In the inter-group conflict, therefore, in which race attitudes play the major part, no intra-group conflict between these attitudes and the other attitudes of the group can be tolerated, since such an internal conflict can only be a source of weakness. And of all the elements of the total attitude pattern of frontier society, race and religious attitudes were most closely and intimately associated with one another. The term "Christian," which, in this context, meant, in the first place, that the individual to whom it applied had been accepted and was recognized as a member of a group professing a particular religion, was universally used as synonymous with the terms "European" and "white man." The great importance attached to the profession of Christianity was very largely a persistence of the attitude brought by the first Europeans to the Cape. Generations of contact with non-Christian natives and heathen had only served to enhance that attitude and to give it a more vigorous exclusiveness.

Of all the elements in his social heritage, there was none to which the European of the frontier clung with greater fervor or which he prized so highly as his religion. Although he might have lost touch with the main stream of contemporary European culture, the frontier farmer still retained the peculiar tradition of his seventeenth-century European background in its original form. It was the tradition that played a fundamental part in determining his race attitudes and in making him race conscious, for membership of his religious group was an exclusive privilege which distinguished and separated him by an immeasurable distance from those who did not share it with him. In the absence of any kind of opportunity for public worship, the religious exercises conducted by the head of the family took on an added significance, and even in the poorest or most remote household of the frontier, the Bible was to be found occupying the place of honor. . . .

For the frontier farmer, then, his religion was, first and foremost, a social fact—and a jealously guarded group-privilege. By virtue of his religion, he justified his right to dominate the heathen by whom he was surrounded. They fell outside the pale, and their claims, therefore, could never compete on equal terms with those of the Christian group. The idea that Christians and non-Christians were, in any sense, equal, even before the law, or that an offense by a Christian against the person or property of a non-Christian should be taken as seriously or be dealt with as vigorously as a similar offense by a non-Christian, was entirely foreign to frontier mentality. When the revolutionary doctrines of liberty, equality, and fraternity arrived on the frontier toward the end of the eighteenth century, they were warmly welcomed, not merely because they served to justify the repudiation of the Company's authority, but also because they were a genuine reflection of the democratic spirit of frontier society. But outside the closed circle of that society they abruptly ceased to have any validity— a limitation which, in view of the relations prevailing with those to whom these doctrines were not considered to apply, appeared as a paradox even to contemporary observers. But, from the point of view of the frontier farmer, there was no real inconsistency in his attitude. In fact, to have taken up any other attitude would have been tantamount to undermining the whole foundation upon which his society rested. It would have been equivalent to an admission of defeat, the reversal of a tendency that had been steadily developing for generations. Under the circumstances in which he was placed and with the whole weight of his social heritage upon him, the frontier farmer was literally forced into adopting the attitude which he did toward those who fell outside his group. The inconsistency lay rather on the side of those who, failing to appreciate the total situation to which his attitude was the response, attempted to apply standards of social behavior which would have made his continued existence on the frontier impossible. . . .

The comparative failure of the first missionary efforts was regarded as a proof that such people were not fitted for Christianity, while the actions of men who married women of color were an awful example of the social consequences that would follow from the breaking down of the religious barrier.

The negative aspects of the Calvinistic creed, its doctrine of predestination, its emphasis upon the community of the elect, the exclusive twist that could be given to its teachings, were all perfectly adapted to the interracial situation of the frontier. The conclusion was readily drawn, and applied, that the heathen fell outside the scheme of salvation. Attempts to christianize them were not merely not sanctioned by, but actually contrary to, the teachings of the Bible. . . .

Under such circumstances, the intense and exclusive group consciousness of the frontier found expression in a consciousness of race and social supremacy which coincided almost uniformly with the distinctions based upon creed and color. Christianity and skin-color, membership of a particular group and social superiority, became so closely associated with one another that any one by itself could serve as a criterion of group membership. And, conversely, the absence of any of these carried with it the stigma of religious, social, and racial inferiority which almost automatically excluded the individual so distinguished from membership of the group. The group had, in fact, become, to all intents and purposes, a kind of caste into which the individual was born, or from which he was excluded as the result of the same accident.

Of all these criteria, that of skin-color was the most pervasive and the most consistent in its operation. In spite of the fact that an individual, especially if he were light colored, might achieve some kind of religious, racial, or social equality which would enable him to secure admission into the caste-group, inferiority was always found associated with a dark or black skin, but never with a white skin, which, on the contrary, was everywhere associated with religious and social superiority. Because differences of skin-color are so obvious, they can, more readily than any other physical difference, become attached, by a process of "conditioning," to the prevailing social attitudes of the group. When once such a color difference becomes the sign of a distinction which either includes or excludes, the result is a group-color prejudice.

Although color prejudice, as such, was not so rigidly exclusive in its operation as it has since become, there is some contemporary evidence to show that it was already firmly established before the end of the century. Distinctions of color, even when they came into conflict with those other distinctions with which they usually coincided, and to which they originally owed their existence, were certainly by now, and probably had been for some time, more important than any other criterion as a means of group inclusion or exclusion. But it was not a criterion that always worked with complete consistency nor was it an all-or-none affair. Since color prejudice, as a social attitude, can have no reality apart from the existence of the group, much of its operation will depend upon the circumstances in which the group has developed and the conditions under which social contacts take place. On the frontier, as we have seen, contacts with other groups were more or less of the anarchical kind that is characteristic of frontier conditions. Under such circumstances, group attitudes were more violent, more intense, and brought into play the more hostile and aggressive tendencies as the result of the local situation. In the older established parts of the country, such as the slave-owning agricultural districts of the Cape, where social contacts between whites and people of color were, to a far greater extent, regularized by status, and where relations on that basis were, on the whole, of a far friendlier and more intimate kind, distinctions of social position or of skin-color were likely to be far more conspicuous than distinctions based upon race or religion. In the one case, the very closeness of social contact tended to emphasize what differences there were in skin-color since other differences were less conspicuous; in the other case, these other differences were so obvious that they tended to overshadow the difference in color as such. . . .

Skin-color became associated with an inferior or servile status in the community as well as with a "Heydensche afkomst." Whereas formerly persons of color had been freely admitted into the European or Christian community, on the ground that they were of mixed parentage in addition to having been baptized, they were now, more and more, being excluded on the very same ground even in spite of having been baptized. Thus, ever since slavery had been introduced at the Cape, it had been taken for granted that a baptized slave could claim his freedom. The inevitable result was

'that the children born in slavery are neither baptized nor given any religious instruction. There is a common and well-grounded belief that Christians must not be held in bondage; hence only such children as are intended for emancipation, are baptized.'

When, in 1792, the question was explicitly raised by the Church Council of Stellenbosch, whether owners who permitted or encouraged their slaves to be baptized would be obliged to emancipate them, the matter was referred to the Church Coucil of Capetown for its opinion. That body replied that neither the law of the land nor the law of the church prohibited the retention of baptized persons in slavery, while local custom strongly supported the practice. . . . Within, and upon, the boundaries of the Cape settlement there had come together the most heterogeneous collection of human elements that ever constituted a psycho-social situation. There were the Company officials who combined the functions of trade and of government; there were the Company workmen and soldiers engaged in fulfilling their contract; there were the freemen, all ex-soldiers, sailors, or workmen of the Company, who were engaged in tempting fortune on their own; there were the slaves and the Hottentots; and, finally, there were the ships' crews who from time to time appeared upon the scene to enjoy the benefits of the refreshment station. Within this complex situation the pattern of relations is not easy to define in any positive way. But with regard to the relations between Europeans and non-Europeans, there appears to be ample evidence to show that the factors of race and skin-color as such played little or no part in determining the attitude of the former to the latter. As we have already pointed out, the line of distinction between groups was less affected by differences of race or color of skin than by differences of religion. The effectiveness of religion in this respect was, no doubt, due partly to the fact that it happened so frequently to coincide with particular race and color groups, and even with particular national and social groups, but cutting across these divisions were the distinctions created by differences of religion. Men were, in the first place, Catholics or Protestants, Christians or non-Christians, Mohammedans or Kaffirs; and the greatest prejudice existed where there was the widest difference.

At the Cape, there was opportunity enough of bringing into play attitudes, both positive and negative, which were rooted in religion and which would affect the whole pattern of relations between European and non-European. Thus, a non-European at the Cape, once he had been baptized, was immediately accepted as a member of the Christian community and, as such, was entitled to his freedom, if a slave. The marriage bond, at a time when the marriage ceremony was an exclusive Church monopoly, was only legal when both the parties had been baptized. Even extra-marital relationships were affected by the baptismal condition of one or other of the partners. . . .

We find that baptism not only conferred upon the individual a legal status but a social status as well which, in the case of women of full color, frequently led to marriage with European men. In a community in which white women were at a premium, some sort of connection with other women, whether slave or native, was inevitable. But in addition to these illicit or casual relations which might exist in spite of social disapproval, there were also regular unions that took place with full social approval and religious sanction. The fact that the men were of a class that would not, and, in any case, could not, exercise any particular choice in the selection of wives is not by itself a sufficient reason to take these marriages for granted. . . . These early mixed marriages are all of European men and women of pure blood, either liberated slaves or daughters of slaves from the East, especially from Bengal. On aesthetic grounds there could be no objection to these Bengalese women, and since there was certainly no objection on grounds of skin-color, they and their children were simply absorbed into the predominantly white community. On the other hand, intermarriage, as distinct from cohabitation, between European men and Hottentot women at the Cape was extremely rare.

ATTITUDES IN CLASS RELATIONS

Class barriers are erected at the portals of the home. A man who regards another as of an inferior social class is experiencing on grounds of cultural differences a disinclination to invite the other into his family circle.

WHEN WE review the conventions of address, the principles of etiquette and all the unformulated rules and customs which govern the behavior of members of one social class in relation to members of another the impression is derived that these rules and conventions constitute an elaborate mechanism of defence against intrusion and intimacy—against *familiarity* when we use the word with a full consciousness of its etymological suggestions. These defences are erected not so much in the interests of the individual but in the interests of the family.

In his business affairs a man deals with others of differing social class with a relative absence of class consciousness. He will eat and drink with his social inferiors provided he is not called upon to present them at his family table. It is, perhaps, on account of the peculiar sanctity of the family circle that the status of the domestic servant is more affected by class considerations than is that of other workers of economically similar grade. The fact that class barriers are erected at the portals of the home engenders distinctive problems when circumstances require that members of an inferior class should find a place within the domestic organization.

Defences against intrusion into the family circle are, of course, mainly in the interests of the younger generation in that circle. The chief danger against which provision must be made is the danger of

C. A. Mace, "Beliefs and Attitudes in Class Relations," in *Class Conflict and Social Stratification*, edited by T. H. Marshall (London: Le Play House Press, 1938), pp. 157-160.

the "injudicious" marriage. Broadly, we may say, that by the time a man has reached a position in which he has children approaching marriageable age his own social status is pretty definitely fixed. It will not be fundamentally affected by the achievement of a title—which merely accords social recognition to a status in principle established—or by the loss or gain of a fortune. Such changes, however, can affect the status of his children. Accordingly, so far as parents may have social ambitions, they are ambitions on behalf of their children, and so far as they have social anxieties they are anxieties regarding their children. Apart from the commission of crimes there are few things that are so *de-grading* as the inappropriate marriage. It is a much more serious matter if a youth marries out of his class than if he marries a woman of a different nationality or of a different religion.

If this analysis be correct, class consciousness is primarily a consciousness associated with a set of "avoidance reactions." A man who regards another as of an inferior social class is experiencing on grounds of cultural differences a disinclination to invite the other into his family circle. He is conscious of social inferiority in encountering similar resistances to intimacy in others.

How far, we may next inquire, are these avoidance reactions associated with specific positive attitudes to members of his own social class? How far do they involve a positive sentiment with regard to that class?

Here we must distinguish, even more sharply than elsewhere, between different social classes. There are many reasons why a sentiment for one's own class will differ at different levels in the social hierarchy.

Commonly the apex of the social pyramid is constituted by a relatively small group with distinctive characteristics, characteristics on the basis of which lay opinion will substitute in the place of the conception of a whole series of classes, the simple distinction between people who have "social standing" and those who have not. Probably every advanced nation has its "two hundred families" distinguished by the more or less long-standing enjoyment of power, united by continuous inter-familial association, and, still closer by intermarriage. Such conditions are conducive to the formation of a sentiment of typical constitution, a sentiment intermediate between patriotism and the sentiment for one's family or clan.

THE STATUS OF WOMEN

The problem of women's rights has been but a part of the larger problem of minority rights.

HISTORICALLY, cultural changes and in particular, economic changes have had decisive effect upon women's place in society and in the family. Throughout history class lines have cut across sex lines with the result that women of the ruling classes have enjoyed privileges denied to men as well as the women of the submerged classes. Within each class, however, women have been at a disadvantage as compared with men. Likewise women of dominant races as a rule have had rights and privileges not shared by either the men or the women of minority races. Women's rights have been inextricably bound up with the broader problem of human rights, and improvements in the status of the masses, through changes in productive relations, have had repercussions on the status of women. When the dominant ideology of an era has been humanitarian and rationalistic and geared to the enlargement of freedom and the release of human potentialities, woman's status has advanced, if not always formally through legislation, none the less in practice. On the other hand, in periods of cultural retrogression, as under fascism, when human rights are curtailed, the earlier institutionalized restrictions which sanctioned and enforced the subordinate status of women are revived and intensified.

In western society, the patriarchal social organization prevailed for centuries. Although there had been permutations in degrees of dominance, women unquestionably had been subordinate to men within the family throughout the ancient and medieval world. When in early modern times the bourgeoisie began to develop its attitudes, the sub-

Adapted from Bernhard J. Stern, "The Family and Cultural Change," *American Sociological Review*, Vol. IV (April 1939), pp. 199-208.

jection of women was accepted by both the Church and aristocracy. The exalted formalism and passionate eroticism of romantic chivalry were merely veneer that did not interfere with the application of corporal punishment to wives as permitted by canon law. It was a manifestation of woman's changing relations when, beginning with the thirteenth century, the bourgeoisie began to exhibit in some respects more regard for the personality of the woman than did either the aristocracy or the Church. The wives of the bourgeoisie had entered into trade, both independently and as shopmanagers and assistants, and also the wives of artisans were admitted to some guilds on an equal footing with men. As a result, borough regulations permitted them to go to law and provided that their husbands were not to be held responsible for their debts. The middle class and artisan husband was, moreover, dependent upon his wife's assistance in these days of family and domestic industry. Neither husband nor wife could prosper without each other's help and it was to his interest that she be trained in some skill which would make her economically proficient. Traditional attitudes were tenacious but by the sixteenth century the cloistered life of woman of feudal days had begun to disappear.

These changes in outlook toward women cannot be ascribed to the Reformation, although it liberalized the canonical view of divorce. Luther still regarded marriage as "a physic against incontinence" and declared that women "should remain at home, sit still, keep house, and bear and bring up children."

That women's prestige had not been greatly heightened among the clergy in England, is illustrated by Bishop Aylmer's characterization of them in a sermon before Queen Elizabeth:

Women are of two sorts; some of them are wiser, better learned, discreeter, and more constant than a number of men; but another and a worse sort of them, and the most part, are fond, foolish, wanton flibbergibs, tattlers, triflers, wavering, witless, without counsel, feeble, careless, rash, proud, dainty, nice, tale-bearers, eavesdroppers, rumor-raisers, evil-tongued, worse-minded, and in every wise doltified with the dregs of the devil's dunghill.

The improved position of women in the family that came with the rise of the middle class resulted in a large part from the desire of the thrifty citizen to make his life a success according to mercantile ideals. As Wright declares of this citizen:

Like all true believers in the divine right of property, he was aware of the positive service rendered by so important a functional unit as the home to the organization of that society which made his goods safe and gave his accumulated possessions continuity. Hence, he was seriously concerned to maintain a code fostering ideals useful in the efficient conduct of the household, so that the home might make the greatest possible contribution to the happiness of its component parts, without friction and waste, either material or emotional. In this middle class code of domestic relations, the husband was recognized as the primary earner of wealth while upon the wife devolved the duty of the thrifty utilization of the income for the comfort of her household. Therefore the wife became, acknowledged or unacknowledged, the factor determining the success of the individual home. If the wife were a railing shrew, a slattern, an extravagant, gossipy, or faithless creature, the domestic efficiency and happiness so earnestly desired by every worthy husband would be jeopardized.

The Elizabethan tradesman considered it his duty to be well informed on the domestic relations that might lead to the stability of the home. There arose a vast literature of handbooks and printed guides which gave advice to the middle class on family happiness and crystallized attitudes independent of the tradition of the aristocracy. In these manuals, a gradual improvement in women's position is discernible. They repeatedly insist that the woman must be treated as the lieutenant of her husband, sharing his confidence and trust, and not as his chattel and slave. The husband retained his powers of discipline and his authority, but there was an increased emphasis on woman's rights. Family industry and domestic economy, however, by its very nature offered a limited horizon to women and perpetuated men's dominance in all essential respects.

With the introduction in England of industrial capitalism which broke away from the family system and dealt directly with individuals, husbands were freed to some extent from whatever economic dependence they had had on their wives. The ideal of the subjection of women to their husbands could be put into practice without the husband fearing the consequent danger of his wife's inefficiency. Women no longer were given specialized training with the result that one of the first fruits of capitalist individualism was their exclusion from the journeymen's associations. Excluded from the skilled trades, the wives of the men who became capitalists withdrew from productive activity and became economically dependent and to a large degree parasitic. The wives of journeymen either were obliged to confine themselves to domestic work, or to enter the labor market as individuals in competition with their male relations. The competition which had previously existed only between families in which labor and capital had been united within the family group, was now introduced into the capitalist labor market where men and women struggled with each other to secure work and wages. Capitalist organization tended to deprive women of opportunities for sharing in the more profitable forms of production and confined them as wage workers to the trades where they were obliged to accept lower wages than men and thus to depress labor standards.

As a reflection of the development of capitalist economic life, the political theories of the seventeenth century regarded the state as an organization of individual men only, or of groups of men, not as a commonwealth of families. Consequently, educational, scientific, economic, and political associations formed for public purposes did not include women as members, which underscored their postulated inferiority and made their functioning in the larger community difficult.

It is erroneous to overestimate the rapidity with which domestic industry and the family life which centered around it disintegrated. As late as the mid-eighteenth century, the population of England remained mainly rural and women continued to be engaged in productive work in their homes and in some form of domestic industry, but from that time forward, agrarian and industrial changes deprived them of their employment. There was great distress and unemployment among women as well as men at the turn of the century. The laborer's wage remained below the level of family subsistence, and women and children were urgently obliged to work to supplement the father's income.

Development of the family in the United States paralleled in many respects that of the Old World. With the culture of colonial New England dominated by the Puritan clergy, the patriarchal regime of

Biblical tradition prevailed. Woman's status is clearly defined by a seventeenth century document:

The dutie of the husband is to travel abroad to seeke living: and the wives dutie is to keepe the house. The dutie of the husband is to get money and provision; and the wives, not vainly to spend it. The dutie of the husband is to deale with many men: and of the wives, to talke with few. The dutie of the husband is, to be entermedling: and of the wife, to be solitaire and withdrawne. The dutie of the man is, to be skilfull in talke: and of the wife, to boast of silence. The dutie of the husband is, to be a giver: and of the wife, to be a saver . . . Now where the husband and wife performeth the duties in their house we may call it College of Qyietness: the house wherein they are neglected we may term it a hell.

According to Calhoun, for nearly 150 years after the landing of the Pilgrims there were practically no women wage earners in New England outside of domestic service. Later, however, theory and practice did not always coincide, for some women of the poor classes went outside of the home to work and others of the middle class engaged in independent enterprise. An analysis of advertisements from 1720 to 1800 reveals that women were teachers, embroiderers, jellymakers, cooks, wax workers, japanners, mantua makers, and dealers in crockery, musical instruments, hardware, farm products, groceries, drugs, wines and spirits. Hawthorne noted one colonial woman who ran a blacksmith shop, and Peter Faneuil's account books show deals with many Boston tradeswomen. Mrs. Spruill has recently shown that the same situation prevailed in the southern colonies where women's function was likewise conceived as being limited to that of childbearing and serving as housekeeper.

The ferment created by the discussion of human rights that accompanied the American revolution penetrated into the home. Abigail Adams asked her husband that he see to it that the new government should not "put such unlimited powers into the hands of the Husbands." In John Adams' jesting response there was recognition of the fact that the problem of woman's rights was but a part of the larger problem of minority rights. He expressed surprise that the British ministry, after stirring up "Tories, land-jobbers, trimmers, bigots, Canadians, Indians, Negroes, Hanoverians, Hessians, Russians, Irish, Roman Catholics, Scotch renegadoes," had also stimulated women to demand new privileges. It is significant that the organized woman's rights movement in the 1840's was associated with the antislavery movement, which was women's recognition of the fact that their own inferior status had sociological implications comparable to the oppression of the Negro people. The campaign for the removal of woman's disabilities in the home as well as in the state became a part of a broader program for the extension of democratic rights.

As in Europe, it was the factory system that accelerated changes in the functions of the family by bringing women from the household into the larger industrial world, for the majority of the employees of early American factories were women. The basis was thus laid for a changed status of woman in the family derived from the fact that she contributed to the family income, and in some instances was the major source of family support.

Recent economic developments have not checked the increase in women's participation in industrial life. The unemployment census revealed that between 1930 and 1937, 2,740,000 additional women workers had entered the country's labor market. Women are not merely entering industry in larger numbers than ever before, but more of them are remaining in industry permanently. There is, as a result, an unprecedented approach of equality between the sexes and a less coercive discipline of the children. The participation of women in industry has, however, not resulted in actual equality for women in the United States because women have been at a disadvantage in their bargaining power with men and they have had the double burden of home and work. Traditionally, women have been paid less for their labor and have been obliged to combat historically derived attitudes that they are less capable than men of developing skills and attaining man's level of productivity. There have been many impediments to women's social equality both in law and in practice, and social services and legislation have been insufficient to cushion the effects upon the family of women's entrance into industry.

In the Soviet Union, industrialism and urbanism and the mechanization of collectivized rural areas are now involving women in all phases of economic, social, political, and cultural life. Women's equality is implemented by its legalization in the Soviet constitution and facilitated by a vast network of state social services that relieve tensions and anxieties that have been the traditional lot of the working woman. Through these services, the difficult problem is solved of how women can enter industry on a par with men, and at the same time be the nucleus of satisfying family life. With economic security and improved living and working standards assured in an expanding collectivist economy, the basic cause of marital unhappiness is removed. The family is thus more firmly established, with its cohesive force resting primarily on the affectional relations between parents as equals and parental authority over children derived not by force but by responsible guidance. These advances in the status of women, associated as they have always been historically with the extension of rights to other submerged groups such as national minorities, are penetrating remote areas, although they involve drastic shifts in older institutionalized values.

The threat of retrogression in the family comes from fascist countries, where monopoly capitalism in crisis has abolished democratic forms. There has been an outspoken and organized effort to subordinate women once more to an inferior status and to confine them to childbearing and domestic work under the indisputable authority of the male members of the family. In spite of its announced plan, it has not been able to eliminate women from industry, for in a highly industrialized country like Germany, women are required in economic life, but the fascist program has worked to their detriment. Employment of women in civil service, in the professions, and in skilled trades is barred. Men have displaced women at their lower wages with the result that the entire wage structure is depressed and insecurity is intensified. The patriarchal family is glorified, and family life, dominated by the husband and father, reinstitutes those qualities of coercion the elimination of which had been the achievement of centuries of progressive thinking. The regressive developments in women's role in the family and society are but a part of a larger picture which includes as well the denial of rights to minority peoples.

CULTURE CLEAVAGE IN A NEW ENGLAND COMMUNITY

The small Old American group has been helped to maintain its predominant position by the strength of its traditional feeling of the racial superiority of the Anglo-Saxon. The newer peoples on the whole accept the Old Americans at their own valuation, perhaps partly because the premium placed on conformity to standards already set has not permitted them to value their own standards and interpretations of America. The influence of the Old Americans tends to preserve the status quo and puts a check on too rapid an invasion from the lower ranks into their society.

THE ROLE played by each of the main ethnic groups in the life of the community is in part dictated by its historical place in the development of the city and in part by the essential motivation of the group—what it selects out of American life to make its own, what essentially it contributes to the larger community. In order to appreciate the life of the community and the place of each group in that life, it is necessary to make some analysis of the role of each.

Every community contains its corps of people who consider themselves its charter members. They have determined its nature, created its organizations, fostered its development. In Burlington [Vermont] this corps consists of Old American Protestants—the Yankees, as they still are called. They have always lived there, they love the place, they own it. No matter what changes may come over the city, no matter how far it has lost its early character, they watch over its development and growth with a certain sense of responsibility born of the feeling of proprietorship. This feeling is justified in a sense by the fact that most of the institutions around which the life of the city centers today were founded by their forefathers. These had, immediately upon their settling in 1763, set up a town government and public schools, and, as early as 1791, the University of Vermont.

Excerpt from Elin L. Anderson, *We Americans. A Study of Cleavage in an American City* (Cambridge, Mass.: Harvard University Press, 1937), pp. 21-34.

After these agencies symbolic of the principles of free government had been established, they turned their attention to the organization of a religious society, which was formed in 1805. Today the descendants of these Old Americans have to a large extent retreated from the commercial life of the city, but they still control the banks, most of the city's manufacturing, the University. Furthermore, they have through their institutions, and aided by the fact that the immigrant invasion was never great enough to threaten their position of dominance, set an indelible stamp upon the life of the community. . . .

The small Old American group has been helped to maintain its predominant position by the strength of its traditional feeling of the racial superiority of the Anglo-Saxon. As one woman, concerned about a more successful interrelationship between the various ethnic groups of the community, explained: "Of course you do believe that the English are the finest people yet produced on earth. You do believe that they have the most admirable human qualities and abilities that any people have ever had!" Interestingly enough, the newer peoples on the whole accept the Old Americans at their own valuation, perhaps partly because the premium placed on conformity to standards already set has not permitted them to value their own standards and interpretations of America. At any rate, they always speak highly of the Old Americans as fine people with superior ability, shrewd business men, and leaders of the community; though some qualify their appreciation by commenting that the Old Americans tend to be snobbish and ingrown, and that they place undue emphasis upon the forms of their culture, which they expect all newer peoples to emulate.

Traditions of family and name, of power and influence in the financial and civic life of the community, of race-consciousness, plus a very deep conviction that the Protestant traditions of their forefathers are basically important to the development of free institutions in America, set the Old Americans apart as a group distinct from other people. Within that group there are the usual divisions of classes and cliques, of rich and poor; but the common elements of culture and tradition give an impression of a common unit in relation to other ethnic groups in the community. The Old Americans are charter members; they give a kindly welcome to newcomers, as behooves people of their position, but they expect in return the respect that is due charter members. One who can claim even remote blood connections with any of the group is cordially welcomed without question; he is "one of us," while one who cannot claim such connection is "accepted" only as he obeys the forms and the codes of the group, because, after all, he is "not one of us."

Freed from the kind of economic pressure that is known to a great proportion of the people in the other groups, the Old Americans are concerned primarily with "nice living." Their interests and activities connect them with persons outside the community more than with those within; thus they have broad views, wide interests in the arts, literature, and even international relations. In the community, however, their interest is in keeping their place and their prerogatives; their influence tends to preserve the *status quo* and puts a check on too rapid an invasion from the lower ranks into their society.

The Irish are the leaders of the opposition. With the same fighting spirit that they showed in Ireland against the English, under the banner of their religion and their political party they aggressively assert their difference from the Old Americans and take it upon themselves to champion the rights of the immigrant, casting their lot not with the dominant element but with the "have nots." This role for a people who speak the English language and identify themselves more or less with the English tradition has made for a conflicting situation even more complex than that known to their forefathers in Ireland.

Their criticism of all things English and their loyalty to the Roman Catholic Church went deeply against the grain of the descendants of the Yankee settlers, who were proud of their English origin and traditions and of the independence of religious thought expressed in Protestantism. As a result, to many Old Americans the Irish have epitomized differences in social philosophy which are deeply opposed to the English and Protestant principles upon which this country's institutions were built. To be an Irishman—a Papist and a Democrat—is as a red flag to a bull to many a Puritan Yankee. The failure of each to appreciate the other or to understand the principles for which the other stands is the basic tragedy which disturbs the equanimity of any community where Irish and Old Americans are found together.

In Burlington also the Irish have assumed the role of champions of political justice for the newer immigrant groups and leaders of the Catholic Church in America, while at the same time they have a strong conviction that as the Old American political leadership diminishes the Irish will be the inevitable leaders in the political and civic life of the community. As one of their leaders pointed out: "The Yankees today aren't the people that their fathers were. Their fathers were God-fearing men who were real leaders. Their sons seem somehow to be going to seed. They don't have the life in them. They don't have their fathers' convictions."

The role chosen by the Irish is beset with many difficulties. On the one hand, the newer elements at times find the leadership of the Irish officious and irksome; on the other hand, the older elements sometimes find them pushing, and carry over from their English forebears a distrust of their dependability. As a whole, however, the Irish are spoken of highly by all groups, with qualifications such as those indicated in the comment: "The Irish are loyal and faithful first to their church, second to their kind. When these obligations have been fulfilled, they make excellent citizens, contributing to the best interests of the community."

The difference between the French Canadians and the other groups in Burlington cannot be understood without a recognition of the attitude with which the French Canadians regard the territory itself. They may not proclaim it from the house-tops, but to them Burlington is a French city and they are its true citizens. To all of New England they have felt a peculiar claim. After all, they say, was it not French explorers and priests who opened up much of the country? Did not Samuel de Champlain discover this very territory, and were not the French the first white settlers on the shores of Lake Champlain? Certainly a military conquest could not entirely take away the feeling that they have a right to this territory. Some of their leaders, at least, have continued to dream of the day when New England will again be New France.

With this belief deep within them, their settling in New England has differed from that of other people. Their migration has been a "peaceful penetration" across an imaginary line; indeed, at first their migration was largely seasonal. Some Burlingtonians still recall the trainloads of French Canadians, through with their work on the farms, who would arrive each fall to work in the lumber yards and mills and after staying for a short season to earn, as they said, some of the gold and silver that America had to offer, would return to their poor Canadian farms. On the farms of Quebec, as in Europe, "The States" was pictured as a land with streets of gold. Gradually they began to lengthen their stay here from one season to two, from two seasons to three; then they came for a period of two or three years, until they settled permanently. When they did, it was not so much like settling in a new land as extending the boundaries of the old. The tie with Canada has always remained strong, partly because the short distance to the home land makes close contact possible, partly because the continued migration without restriction of French Canadians has constantly re-enforced the Canadian national spirit.

Although they are French, they differ markedly from the Frenchman of today and are, in habit of thought and behavior, more closely akin to his forebears. They have been separated from France for over 170 years and have known nothing of the great liberalizing movements, such as the French Revolution, the great literary revolution, and other upheavals which have so greatly influenced modern France. Their way of life in Canada has therefore remained essentially that of a simple peasant folk whose most vital cultural element has been their religion; as in any primitive society, the forms of that religion govern every aspect of their lives. This circumstance has made far more for docility and obedience to rules than it has for the quality of individual enterprise and responsibility considered characteristic of America. They have willingly accepted the leadership of the parish priest as their forebears did two centuries ago. In the French-Canadian community around the cotton mill in Burlington, today, the priest is spiritual guide, lawyer, doctor, friend, and comforter, to his people. Such complete acceptance of a single cultural force has resulted, in the estimation of many students, in a lack of interest in other forms of development, a result manifested in the lack of schools and free libraries in French Canada.

In Burlington those of French-Canadian descent form a bloc of nearly ten thousand people. Although individually volatile, they are as a group unassertive, concerned primarily with maintaining what they have in the way of national integrity—their religion, their language, their customs. They have never had to fight for these in the same way as the Irish. The right was granted them by the British at the time of the conquest and they have preserved these characteristics by constant passive resistance to outside influence whether British or French. Even in Burlington they seem less perturbed than others by the course of outside events; they put their faith in God and quietly produce the future population of the city.

In contrast with the Old Americans and the Irish, however, as one of their number said, "the French don't stick together. They act as if they felt inferior and ashamed of their nationality. They don't speak up for themselves, and they have nobody to speak up for them. If they had strong leaders, they would be more proud of being French; and that would be good." Their spokesmen in America, sensitive to the fact that the French Canadians have by comparison with other groups contributed but little to America in terms of material success, in all their newspapers point out that French Canadians have a very special contribution to make to American life, a contribution of spiritual rather than material wealth. In the midst of a materialistic world, they say, the French-Canadian group stands for religion, things of the spirit. Admitting that the group will probably never have much of material wealth or power, they point out that the way of poverty is the way to heaven, and that the spiritual mission of the French Canadians is to show materialistic America a way of life which is the way of Jesus.

As a peaceful, unaggressive people, they have won to some extent the sympathy of the Yankee group, whose social and economic position is not threatened by their advancement. This Yankee sympathy is based partly on the belief that they have had to submit to Irish leadership in religious organization and partly on the belief that they have been held back in Canada as a conquered people. There is also in it, however, something of the attitude of an adult to a child, an appreciation of their warm, earthy simplicity and a delight in the "quaint" aspects of their behavior, as presented in the poems of

Rowland Robinson. But this attitude is accompanied by a rejection of some of the very qualities which make them charming.

The Jews, destined to be dispersed among all peoples on the face of the earth, have a quota of 800 in Burlington. With a long history of persecution and suffering behind them, they have sought to find a place of freedom for the oppressed. Perhaps the principles on which this country was based have meant no more to any group than to the Jews. The intensity of feeling may be seen in part by the remark of one Jewish woman who said: "The first thing I did when I came to America was to kiss the ground. This was a free land—my country. Here there would be no more pogroms."

In Burlington they have pursued the dual role the Jews have had to assume in America as much as in any other country. On the one hand much of their life is within the group, centered around the synagogue and the Talmud Torah, for even in America, though they may enjoy equality before the law, they know discrimination born of prejudices ingrained for centuries in the Gentile mind. On the other hand, showing their appreciation of the liberty that America offers, they actively participate in all civic and philanthropic enterprises. In Burlington their presence is being more and more felt, and some people worry that their influence is becoming an irritant in the life of the community; but their role essentially is that of the impersonal outsider whose support is sought in times of intra-community conflict between the two main branches of the Christian faith.

The Germans have nearly as much right as the Yankees to the claim of first citizens of Burlington. When Ira Allen came in 1773 he found two Germans settled on the shores of Shelburne Point. According to Allen, they "had the appearance of peaceable men, and on their promise to behave were suffered to remain undisturbed." Whether because of this "peaceableness" or because their numbers have never been large, the Germans have quickly become almost indistinguishable from the rest of the community. Today they number 300 persons, but it was not until 1880 that enough of them found their way from the surrounding towns to form a little German neighborhood in the city. Those who came were largely from one section of the country, Silesia, where they had been farmers, weavers, and artisans; in Burlington they fitted into the lumber mills and trades.

The German love of music, of intellectual discussions, and especially of *Gemütlichkeit* led them to organize as early as 1891 a German club,—a branch of the National Order of Harugari, which is still the center of German social life in the town. It aims to preserve and transmit to the second and third generation an appreciation of German culture.

Two Italians reached Burlington in 1890. A few years later, while working under their padrones on the Delaware and Hudson Railroad on the New York side of the lake, some came over in search of a suitable location for their families. When they found that in Burlington they could secure work in building some of the streets and sewers, they decided to settle. For some time, while there was work on the roads and in building the near-by army post, there were more Italians in Burlington than there are at present. Now, though few in number, they are not a compact group—the three or four families from northern Italy distinguishing themselves from the majority who have come from the southern part. Unlike the Irish or the French Canadians, they have made no effort to center their life around a church of their own. This is due partly to their small number, but also partly to traditions of a state-supported church which make Italians slow to establish and support a church of their own. They are more or less lost in the English-speaking parish; and only at times of baptisms, funerals, and marriages do they feel the need of seeking the services of a French-Canadian priest who is well versed in Italian. In 1934, for the first time, they organized an Italian club. This has been an important social center for all the Italians in Burlington and Winooski, and an educational force aiming to make them feel at home in America and understand its ways and laws.

Representatives of other peoples have added their peculiar qualities to Burlington, but they are too few to form distinctive groups, or they have already fused into the larger blend. The English and English Canadians, with traditions so similar to those of the Old Americans, have merged with that group. Syrians and Greeks, part of the last great migration from southeastern Europe, are few in number. The Syrians comprise some thirty families, the first of whom came to Burlington in 1895; they have established no church of their own but have become members of the English-speaking Roman

Catholic parish; their unity is expressed through the social activities of the Lady of Mount Lebanon Society. The Greeks number some twenty families, or 130 persons; one or two Greeks were in Burlington in 1902 in small fruit stores and restaurants. The Greeks remain individualistic, and come together as a group only on special occasions, as when a Greek Orthodox priest comes to town; ordinarily they attend the Episcopal Church, which has been the most hospitable to them as well as nearest in teaching to their own. The American Hellenic Educational Patriotic Association is an important force in uniting all the Greeks of Vermont, emphasizing pride in the Greek heritage. Other people, such as Norwegians, Swedes, Finns, Armenians, Turks, Negroes, and some representatives of seventeen other nationality groups, are too few in number to do much more than add a touch of color to the pageant of peoples who have found their way to Burlington.

The life of all these people is the story of the process of becoming at home in the ever-changing, increasingly complex, American world. They are all intent on realizing the hopes and dreams which America has symbolized to them or their forebears. Each group, according to its need, clings to its customs and traditions as to things assured in an unsure world; each has had to realize that this country has welcomed not only its own group but also those that have been its traditional enemies. Only slowly has each realized that the large economic and social forces affecting all America are drawing them all together in common concerns: all are concerned with earning a living, bringing up their children, keeping up their religious practices; all hope that their children may realize what they did not enjoy; all hope for a little fun; all worry over their old age.

In the process of adjusting to their new American environment, different potentialities within the groups have been brought out—special interests in educational training, in the kinds of jobs they have taken. Thus, slowly, new divisions are arising within the groups; and those with similar interests have begun to reach across barriers of nationality or religion which once were all-important in American life. New divisions are being formed. The old, however, those of nationality or religion, may often color these new developments, especially as each group has not fully realized the sense of freedom that it hoped to find in America.

In Burlington it is possible to observe the advances and checks experienced by each group in its attempt to share in the common life of the community and to see therein the part that these early differences in America play in the new cleavages which inevitably form in a more settled society. It is possible to see the advantages and the disadvantages of preserving the old lines against the rapid social change in the world about us.

SECOND GENERATION YOUTH

The second generation problem is created by social conditions and attitudes which make the child constantly aware of a sense of difference.

THE MERE fact of having parents who were born abroad does not create the so-called second generation problem. It is created by social conditions and attitudes which make the child constantly aware of a sense of difference. It is intensified when children grow up in families having standards quite at variance with the standards which the children see in the world outside their homes; when they are subjected to and at the same time rebel against a kind of home discipline that tends to become more and more authoritative as the parents feel their own position socially and economically less and less secure. As a result the children often copy the things that are least lovely in American life and discard the things that are best in their own nationality community, on the theory that by so doing they will gain status in the American community. The problem grows in acuteness according to whether the child belongs to a nationality group or to a family that seems conspicuously different from the general pattern of American life about him. Conversely, the problem is least acute in nationalities whose manners and customs are most like our own. . . .

Excerpt from Florence G. Cassidy, *Second Generation Youth* (New York: The Woman's Press, 1930), pp. 32-36.

The immigrant groups which are most foreign (1) because of differences in political traditions, social life, religion, stage of industrialization, and economic security in country of origin, and (2) because of the comparatively recent date of establishment as nationality communities within the United States, with all that means in terms of economic position, housing, education, political power, and social recognition, are *peasant groups* from the countries that before the war furnished the so-called "recent immigration," and, since the war, more especially since the 1924 quota law, unskilled laborers from the countries not subject to quota, such as Mexico. Again, we must add new arrivals from Porto Rico and the Philippine Islands, who technically are not immigrants at all but who have to encounter as difficult problems of adjustment as those faced by true immigrants.

No generalization can be made safely about the foreignness of any individual merely on the ground of his nationality, or on the ground of the recent arrival of his nationality or matrix group in America. It is also necessary to know how recently the family came to join that group and how recently the individual came to join the family. We have to consider the age at which the individual emigrated, his general adaptability, previous experiences, and general education.

Parents whose nationality *mores* are at variance with what seems to be the pattern of American life at the moment are much disturbed by the way in which America, consciously or unconsciously, tends to pull their children away from them. In their efforts to pull them back they often but widen the breach. The children, on the other hand, with no understanding of their parent's situation, with little respect for them (oftentimes a reflection of the unwarranted remarks of Americans), but with a consciousness only that "they are different," seek escape from an unpleasant home situation in exaggerated recreation, dress, manners, and social behavior. At other times there may be constant friction and open rebellion at home. Still more often there may be little open conflict but uneasiness and unhappiness in the lives of both parents and children, an indication usually that both are suffering from a lack of adequate recognition at home and in society outside the home.

Despite this somewhat gloomy picture there are of course innumerable families in which there is deep understanding and sympathy between parents and children. We do not see the picture of parent-child relationships in proper perspective unless we realize that there are gradations in attitudes which shade all the way from violent physical cruelty to most imaginative and affectionate understanding. There is the ignorant and inarticulate parent who meets what he calls the "wildness" and "freshness" of his child with repeated beatings. There is the parent who understands very little about the strange ideas which America has put in the mind of his child, but who stands mutely aside, suffering but not criticizing or interfering. Then, lastly, there is the parent who has insight and understanding, who treasures what was good in old-world ways, understands what will carry over into American life, and appreciates what is good in new-world ways. We have observed that often the greatest conflicts between parents and second generation children come when the children have reached what seems to the parents to be a marriageable age. This is but natural, as it is in this realm that we find the greatest difference between the parent's idea, and the ideas expressed by American teachers, friends, writers, and neighbors. Furthermore, all people tend to be more or less conservative in preserving their own peculiar marriage customs.

Part III

THE WAYS OF DOMINANT PEOPLES:
DEVICES OF POWER

8

TECHNIQUES OF DOMINANCE

ONCE THE majority has acquired its status through power, the problems of its maintenance arise. Auxiliary weapons are more useful for that, with overt power and force held in reserve for the emergency. Prestige has already been shown to be one of the main devices of power, but behind that, even, there is need of tradition and rationalizations. These are the cultural and ideological weapons, and they take on larger significance the more inclusive the orbit of majority power becomes. For the large units of power are the great nations, the empires and their adjuncts. World-scale religions also come into the picture at this point. They all capitalize their form of culture and tend to identify it with civilization itself.

No branch of civilization is as adept in such majority ways as the European; it has a chronic habit, as Toynbee remarks, of egotistically identifying itself with human civilization. European civilization has had, it is true, both a remarkable development and a remarkable expansion. Its cultural success has been beyond precedent, for it has achieved a political and cultural dominance far out of proportion to the number of its adherents. It is without doubt a great world civilization, but as Toynbee points out, it is not the only world civilization of our day. Even though its agencies of economic imperialism extend into the areas of its rivals, they, rather than European civilization still dominate these areas culturally, and in the long run cultural dominance has its importance. These other grand-scale cultures—Byzantine, Islamic, Hindu and Far-Eastern, control at least the minds and loyalties of their hundreds of millions, and are far from being decadent or dormant. Several of them, after having been somewhat under the spell of the idea of European ascendancy, are challenging that ascendancy either in resentment or competitive and imitative assertion. This is the situation, little thought of by many partisans of European dominance, which moves Toynbee to characterize the Western civilization's tradition of itself as, on the whole, an illusion of dominance.

The expansion of European civilization has occurred largely by reason of its political and economic organization. On that and other specific scores, its superiority is to be conceded. But it is the claim of general superiority that is found to be unwarranted by any fair and objective history of human culture. Like all world civilizations, its cultural base resulted from the historical fusion of many cultures, with heavy borrowing of many of its culture elements from non-European sources. Such step-ladder theories of culture as conceal these facts, Toynbee shows, have been outmoded in other fields and need to be in any sane and scientific view of culture. So in the first place, the criterion of these grandiose claims, ignoring the great collateral branches of civilization, is untenable and in the second place, granting that even, the true story of human civilization does not substantiate the claim. The ethnocentric version of civilization is more untenable even than the equivalent national superiority claims. Moreover, this historian thinks that the stage has been reached where the European pretensions are provoking more resentment than assent, and ironically in the parable of the Chinese Emperor Ch'ien Lung's arrogant letter to George III of England counsels the West against false pride of civilization.

On both national and racial frontiers, the majority devices of dominance assume analogous tactics, with similar creeds of superiority and the over-idealization of their values. Since majority group interests and policy are basically so similar, it is not surprising to discover that majority rationalizations have so much in common. Back of them all is the prevalent tendency to personify social groups and dramatize ideologically social issues and conflicts. This calls for contrasted dichotomies of group traits and characters to symbolize the issues involved. Whether sect or nation or ethnic groups are concerned, these contrasts polarize, in sharpened contrasts, favorable and unfavorable characterizations. Around these stereotypes of rivalry and conflict, elaborate historical rationalizations are built, the most elaborate of which are ethnic or racial myths. Nationality symbols belong to the same tradition and often indulge in similar fictions. These stereotypes as ascribed to minorities do not arise from any realistic characterization of alien or opposed groups, but from reversed contrasts of the traditional virtues and supposed superiorities of the groups who invent and use them. Detailed analysis of any of them will reveal that they are far too conventional to be concretely descriptive, and of too various a character to be characteristic.

Majority groups, of course, have no monopoly on such stereotypes. Minorities indulge in them also. But wherever they are associated with actual dominance, they have formidable force and wider currency and acceptance. They can be analyzed in any of the rival national myths either of yesterday or today; yet they display their mechanisms and motives most clearly in the more extreme characterizations of the racialists. This is illustrated by Copeland in his interesting analysis of the majority use of the Negro as what he calls a "contrast conception." The long-sustained issue in the South between the two races has led, he construes, to "a distinct delineation of each in contrast to the other." The social separation is reflected in the concepts and beliefs white people came to hold about the "opposite race." Popular thinking, through this use of the Negro as a foil for the white race, has created a concept of him as a "counter-race." This exhibits not only the psychological mainspring of Southern race prejudice, but the dominant motivation, at least so far as their working symbols of superiority and inferiority go, of most group prejudices, —sectarian, racial, national and cultural. Without such concepts of contrast there could be no dramatization of the social conflict in idealistic terms. Its statement in realistic terms, particularly from the majority viewpoint, would lead to unstrategic disillusionment. The South has thus created "two sociological races"—"white" and "black," in irrevocable conflict with each other except under a situation of control. This belief about the relative merits of the races gives an ultimate sanction to the status quo, and at the same time provides a basis for white caste cohesion.

The same psychological tactic, on another scale, is to be seen in the use of social symbols and majority stereotypes in the literary, artistic and stage characterizations of minorities. Not only do literature, art and drama particularly, reflect the social tradition in these matters, they serve in an important way to sharpen these symbols and to propagandize them. Adams shows how minority stage caricatures, in addition to diverting popular interest from concern over the serious social problems of minorities to the enjoyment of the comic aspects of their lives, serve to reinforce majority notions of superiority by propagandizing postulated minority non-conformity. On the American stage, the stock Irishman, the comic German or "Dutchman," the minstrel characterizations of the Jew and the Negro have been superficial and irresponsible, and have led to derogatory stereotypes that have become more deeply rooted in the public mind by reason of the offguard approach of recreational fun and unsuspected farce. It is noteworthy that these types often reach a peak in periods of antipathy and group hostility; at all times their enormous popularity is due to their indirect flattery of the conformist majority. They are thus influential adjuncts of the group feuds, and propagate their antipathies. Resulting from ethnocentric majority attitudes, they lay a base for formidable minority depreciation and name-calling, which the more serious social conflicts readily utilize.

The sociological roots of minority stereotypes and caricatures in the light of the majority-minority situation and its issues are analyzed by Sterling Brown in his study of the Negro character as seen by white authors. He shows that the favorite Negro stereotypes are not in all cases innocent or hasty generalizations, but that many are subtle rationalizations and deliberate majority propaganda. The myth of the contented slave was invented, in spite of the historical record of many slave insurrections and periods of great insecurity in certain sections because of them, to justify enslavement and placate the conscience of the slaveholder. Its greatest currency in literature and public opinion, oddly enough, was during the Reconstruction period when the myth was used deliberately as a rationalization of the lost cause of the Confederacy and an attempt, partly successful, to undermine the pro-Negro sentiment of that period. The stereotype of the "wretched freeman" is to be regarded also as a pro-slavery device at the height of the period of the fugitive slave, designed to stem the tide of slave desertions and buttress the paternalistic Southern fiction of the Negro's helplessness and need for protection. The still current tradition of the comic Negro, Brown shows to serve the same function of majority flattery and of conscience appeasement, and he proves it to be a typical majority device by tracing a close parallel in the English tradition of the comic Irishman, built up originally at the time of Ireland's greatest persecution. The stereotypes of the tragic mulatto, the brute Negro, and the slightly more subtle recent stereotype of the exotic primitive are all shown to be primary reflections of majority "racism," indirectly flattering the superiority complex of the dominant group and perpetuating the tradition of wholesale and inescapable "natural" inferiority or peculiarity on the part of the black minority.

In exalting the virtues of the majority, these stereotypes sometimes go beyond minimizing the minority by projecting fictitious faults and even slanders upon them. In situations of tension, when supremacy is threatened, such legends and attributions become bogeys of violent fear, hostility and hate. Golding shows how in the case of the Jew this reaction has gone to the length of deliberate libel and calumny. The "ritual murder" myths of anti-Semitism, the "rapist" bogey of extreme anti-Negro prejudice, the clichés of the "atrocious Hun," the "Yellow Peril" and the like, exhibit the extremities of majority attitudes when they reach the proportions of a psychosis. Throughout history it has been the sad fate of many minorities to serve the role of scapegoat through the use of such majority rationalizations of past exploitation and present persecution.

"Twentieth Century Ghetto," detailing the documentary history of the latest of these minority mass persecution campaigns, leaves no doubt about the lengths to which majority intolerance and persecution can go even under modern conditions. The medieval age has probably been libeled in the use of the term "medieval" to denote such stages of intolerant hate and violence and such degrees of fanatical cruelty. For the documents prove that the traditional extremities of persecution can be transposed to modern techniques and multiplied in their swiftness of execution and scale of operation. The implications of acquiescence on the part of so many of the "majority," permitting the inner core of leadership to function so on its behalf and with something more than a passive role of bowing itself to superior force, is commentary on the previous receptivity and conditioning of the public mind built up by intolerance years before the actual crises come. Here at any rate, if we take the clinical point of view, is a classical though extreme case of majority behavior, available for study in all its concrete detail and immediacy.

In certain extreme situations, the majority reactions actually do develop into a social psychosis, with definite states of social fear and hysteria and accompanying delusions of "race peril." Demagogic manipulation of group feeling can induce such states, as is evidenced by the history of many "hate campaigns," among them the "Popery riots," the Ku Klux campaign of the mid-seventies and its modern revivals, the Polish "pogroms," and scores of other localized race riots and lynchings and attacks upon minorities. Here one sees merely the climactic explosions of accumulated tensions and antipathies with deep historical roots and long periods of gestation. They are the acute flares of relatively chronic rivalries and animosities. MacCrone traces, for example, the social history of an intense and chronic racial hatred in South Africa, and shows its base to be simply an inveterate habit of disregard for any but majority interests. This disregard grows by social indoctrination into a fetish of superiority which brooks no question, and ranges through a gamut of superiority, dislike, hostility, contempt, and fear. "Kaffir" finally becomes the symbol for everything undesirable and evil, is so used as a derogatory adjective, generating an attitude ready for any situation of tension or crisis to translate itself into exaggerated feelings of group fear and anxiety. The preponderance of numbers of the native population enhances this, and then, "the white man projects his own hostility on to the black man and comes to fear that hostility as a threat directed against himself." Any clash or even any sign of resentment or progress on the part of the native is interpreted emotionally as a situation of race peril from "a rising tide of color" or as a threat to "white supremacy" or of "being swamped by the blacks." Restive signs in the masses or a warrantable demand of advancing sections of the subject population for more recognition or less restriction, or even single incidents of crime can then under such circumstances precipitate general social hysteria, campaigns of repressive legislation, spasms of mob violence and persecution. Supplementary delusions then arise in the perspective in which any movement of the minority is viewed, and reactions which would normally be received sympathetically or at least without alarm, become abnormally impudent and threatening. Minority and majority by this time have become involved in mutual recrimination, and relays of rationalization and counter-rationalization ensue. The stage has been set for the resumption of open conflict relations in a cycle of reactions which the majority dominance has unwittingly generated against itself.

ILLUSIONS OF DOMINANCE

We are no longer conscious of the presence in the world of other societies of equal standing; and we now regard our society as being identical with "civilized" mankind and the peoples outside its pale as being mere "natives" of territories which they inhabit on sufferance, but which are morally as well as practically at our disposal, by the higher right of our assumed monopoly of civilization, whenever we choose to take possession. We have hardly yet begun to suspect that our own civilization may not, after all, be the consummation of human history or a synonym for civilization itself.

WE ARE NO longer conscious of the presence in the world of other societies of equal standing; and that we now regard our society as being identical with "civilized" mankind and the peoples outside its pale as being mere "natives" of territories which they inhabit on sufferance, but which are morally as well as practically at our disposal, by the higher right of our assumed monopoly of civilization, whenever we choose to take possession. Conversely, we regard the internal divisions of our society—the national parts into which this society has come to be articulated—as the grand divisions of mankind, and classify the members of the human race as Frenchmen, Englishmen, Germans, and so on, without remembering that these are merely subdivisions of a single group within the human family.

It is no accident that our common name for ourselves became extinct, and our separate names for our various national allegiances became prominent, toward the beginning of the so-called "modern" period of our history, when our society began to establish what seemed until lately to be a secure and permanent ascendancy over the other living societies of the same class. The historical fact, however, which is implicit in this oblivion of our common name is chiefly a feature of our own microcosm. The other societies have not ceased to exist simply because we have ceased to be aware of their existence; and we can hardly advance further in our search for an "intelligible

---

Excerpts from Arnold J. Toynbee, *A Study of History* (London: Oxford University Press, 1934), pp. 31-35, 151-163.

field of study" without reviving or inventing some name to denote our society as a whole and to distinguish it from other representatives of the species. Since the word "Franks" has always been inaccurate and has now become exotic, it seems preferable to revive the name "Western Christendom." The objection to this is that, since the Reformation, religious allegiance has not only ceased to be the principal expression of the unity of our society, but has actually become one of the principal factors in its internal differentiation. It is therefore perhaps more accurate, as well as more concise, to omit the word "Christendom" and to speak simply of "the West" or "the Western Society" or "the Western World."

As soon as we bring our mental image of our own society into focus by finding a name for it, the images and the names of its counterparts in the contemporary world come into focus side by side with it, especially if we keep our attention fixed upon the cultural plane. On this plane, we can distinguish unmistakably the presence, in the world of today, of at least four other living societies of the same species as ours: first, an "Orthodox Christian" or Byzantine society—whichever title we prefer—in South-Eastern Europe and Russia; second, an "Islamic" society with its focus in the arid zone which stretches diagonally across North Africa and the Middle East from the Atlantic to the outer face of the Great Wall of China; third, a "Hindu" society in the tropical sub-continent of India, south-east of the arid zone; fourth, a "Far Eastern" society in the sub-tropical and temperate regions between the arid zone and the Pacific.

On a closer inspection, we can also discern two sets of what appear to be fossilized relics of similar societies now extinct, namely: one set including the Monophysite Christians of Armenia, Mesopotamia, Egypt, and Abyssinia and the Nestorian Christians of Kurdistan and Malabar, as well as the Jews and the Parsees; a second set including the Lamaistic Mahayanian Buddhists of Tibet and Mongolia and the Hinayanian Buddhists of Ceylon, Burma, and Siam, as well as the Jains in India.

It is interesting to notice that, when we turn back to the cross-section at A.D. 775, we find that the number and the identity of the societies on the world-map are nearly the same as at the present time. Substantially, the world-map of societies of this species has remained constant since the first emergence of our Western society. In the struggle for existence, the West has driven its contemporaries to the wall and has entangled them in the meshes of its economic and political ascendancy, but it has not yet disarmed them of their distinctive cultures. As Headlam-Morley writes,

'In the valley of the Rhine, throughout the whole of France and the Latin countries, one can never be far away from the consciousness of the Roman period, which is the matrix from which all later stages have sprung. In Cologne or Trèves, that which is of the tenth or eleventh century already begins to wear the air of modernity; in Danzig or in Cracow, anything before the fourteenth century is remote antiquity. And, as you go still farther east, new, strange and foreign elements intrude themselves upon you—the cupolas and minarets of Russia and the Moslem—but nowhere do we find anything comparable to the succession of the Gothic and the Renaissance. Here we find that our familiar formulas no longer serve us.' . . .

While the economic and political maps of the world have now been "Westernized" almost out of recognition, the cultural map therefore remains today substantially what it was before our Western society ever started on its career of economic and political conquest. On this cultural plane, for those who have eyes to see, the lineaments of the four living non-Western civilizations are still clear. Even the fainter outlines of the frail primitive societies that are being ground to powder by the passage of the ponderous Western steam-roller have not quite ceased to be visible. How have our historians managed to close their eyes lest they should see? They have simply put on the spectacles—or the blinkers—of their generation; and we may best apprehend what the outlook of this generation has been by examining the connotation of the English word "Natives" and the equivalent words in the other vernacular languages of the contemporary Western world, e.g. "indigènes" in French; "Eingeborenen" in German. The following extract from the *New English Dictionary* speaks for itself: *Native, substantive.* 4. One of the original or usual inhabitants of a country, as distinguished from strangers or foreigners; now *esp.* one belonging to a non-European and imperfectly civilized or savage race.

When we Westerners call people "Natives" we implicitly take the cultural color out of our perceptions of them. We see them as trees walking, or as wild animals infesting the country in which we happen to come across them. In fact, we see them as part of the local flora and fauna, and not as men of like passions with ourselves; and, seeing them thus as something infra-human, we feel entitled to treat them as though they did not possess ordinary human rights. They are merely natives of the lands which they occupy; and no term of occupancy can be long enough to confer any prescriptive right. Their tenure is as provisional and precarious as that of the forest trees which the Western pioneer fells or that of the big game which he shoots down. It may be observed that the Westerners of our age are not the only people who have ever taken this view of the rest of mankind. The Mongols once had the same outlook on the world, as witness the following conversation which took place in the year 1254 of the Christian era, at Mangu Khan's Court at Quaraquorum, between the Great Khan's secretaries and the envoy of St. Louis, King of France, the Friar William of Rubruck:

'And they began to question us greatly about the Kingdom of France, whether there were many sheep and cattle and horses there, and whether they had not better go there at once and take it all. And I had to use all my strength to conceal my indignation and anger; but I answered: "There are many good things there, which you would see if it befel you to go there." '

These passages are illuminating from more than one point of view. They show how once a Westerner felt at being treated as a native at a time when Westerners were themselves exposed to a treatment which it is at present their privilege to inflict upon others. We may also reflect that the Mongols, in their time, enjoyed the privilege for not much more than one century. Is our own tenure of "the Lordship of Creation" likely to last much longer? And how shall the "civilized" Lords of Creation treat the human game, when in their own good time they come to take possession of the land which, by right of eminent domain, is indefeasibly their own? Shall they treat these "Natives" as vermin to be exterminated, or as domesticable animals to be turned into hewers of wood and drawers of water? All this is implicit in the word "Natives," as we have come to use it in the English language in our time.

The present derogatory connotation of the word is less than a century old. Its original color was neutral, and in that stage of its history it was given a laudatory connotation as often as not: for instance, in such phrases as "native land," "native valor," "native hue of resolution." The devaluation of all non-Western culture in our Western estimation may have been a consequence of the rather sudden and sensational victory of our Western society over all other contemporary societies on the economic and political planes. In this connection it may be observed that the derogatory usage of the word "Natives" became current about the same time as this condescending attitude, and it may be inferred that the attitude and the usage both reflect the influence of the same change in the social environment. In India, where the change in the economic and political relations of the parties within the same span of time was still more sudden and sensational than it was in the Far East, the change in the attitude of the Westerners was still more striking. Its extent can be measured by reading *The Travels of Mirza Abu Taleb Khan in Asia, Africa, and Europe during the years 1799-1803*. When this Indian gentleman visited the British Isles on the eve of the British conquest of India, it is evident from his narrative that he was received in "Society" as an interesting and honored guest, and his memoirs reveal no shadow of an "inferiority complex."

Evidently the word "native" is not a scientific term but an instrument of action: an *a priori* justification for a plan of campaign. It belongs to the realm of Western practice and not of Western theory; and this explains the paradox that a classificatory-minded society has not hesitated to apply the name indiscriminately to the countrymen of a Gandhi and a Bose and a Rabindranath Tagore, as well as to "primitives" of the lowest degree of culture, such as the Andaman Islanders and the Australian Blackfellows. For the theoretical purpose of objective description, this sweeping use of the word makes sheer nonsense. For the practical purpose of asserting the claim that our Western civilization is the only civilization in the world, the usage is a militant gesture. It signalizes the fact that all the non-Western societies which are alive in the world today, from the lowest to the highest, have been swept up into our economic net, and it postulates the contention that this common predicament is the only important fact about any of them. In short, the word "Natives" is like a piece of smoked glass which modern Western observers hold in front of their eyes when they look abroad upon the world, in order that the gratifying spectacle of a "Westernized" surface may not be disturbed by any perception of the native fires which are still blazing underneath.

The dogma of "the Unity of Civilization" requires the historian to ignore the difference—of kind rather than mere degree—which distinguishes the continuity between the histories of two related civilizations from the continuity between two successive chapters in the history of a single civilization. By shutting their eyes to this, our historians enable themselves to regard Hellenic history as just an earlier chapter in the history of our Western civilization (which they have already equated with "Civilization" *sans phrase*), and Minoan history in the same way. Thus they telescope three civilizations into one, and trace the history of this singular "Civilization" back in a straight line from the ubiquitous Western civilization of their own day to the primitive society in the "Neolithic" stage of material technique out of which the Minoan civilization emerged about the beginning of the third millennium B.C., and thence, through the upper and lower strata of the "Palaeolithic" technique, to the pre-human ancestors of mankind. It is true that, in presenting the evolution of civilization in this figure of a single straight line, they are compelled to admit the entrance of one tributary from a separate source in order to account for the germ of creative activity, derived from the Syriac society, out of which the internal proletariat of the Hellenic society generated the Catholic Church. Yet, however important they may acknowledge this contribution to be, they insist upon treating it as exceptional; and in any case they derive "Modern Civilization" from no more than two sources: the main stream from "Greece and Rome," the tributary from "Palestine."

They ignore the histories, or the chapters in the histories, of civilizations that do not happen to fit into the frame within which they have confined their picture—dismissing them as "semi-barbarous" or as "decadent" or as belonging to "the Unchanging East" which is declared to be without significance for "the History of Civilization."

On such grounds they ignore, to begin with, all those chapters in Syriac history which are subsequent to the fertilization of the internal proletariat of the Hellenic society with the Syriac germ of the Catholic Church. They ignore, for example, the Nestorian and Monophysite movements in which the Syriac society attempted to turn the Christian syncretism to its own account; they ignore Islam, the universal church which the internal proletariat of the Syriac society eventually succeeded in creating for itself out of indigenous elements after Hellenism had been expelled at length from the Syriac world; they ignore the Umayyad and "Abbasid Caliphates," the political instruments by which the final expulsion of Hellenism was accomplished and by which a barbarian "successor-state" of the Roman Empire was then converted into a reintegration of the Syriac universal state of the Achaemenidae. Again, they ignore the histories of the Egyptiac, Sumeric, Babylonic, and Hittite societies, except in so far as these civilizations influenced the Minoan or the Syriac of the Hellenic. Finally, they ignore the histories of all the other civilizations completely. Orthodox Christendom, for instance, is either tacitly subsumed under Western Christendom on the strength of the common element in their names, or else it is disposed of, in terms of Western history, as a sort of temporary excrescence on the body of our Western society which served it in its infancy as a shield against Oriental attacks and which afterwards atrophied and dropped off in the course of nature when its services had ceased to be necessary. As for the other three living non-Western civilizations—the Islamic, the Hindu, and the Far Eastern—they are refused recognition and their members are disposed of by being tied, as "Natives," to our Western chariot wheels. Moreover, Indic history is telescoped into Hindu history and Sinic history into Far Eastern history by the same high-handed manipulation that is applied to Minoan, Hellenic, and Western history; and thus the Indic and the Sinic civilizations are eliminated likewise. This only leaves the four civilizations of the New World—the Mayan, the Yucatec, the Mexic, and the Andean—and these are explained away as irrelevant phenomena of an *alter orbis*, or more bluntly as abortive attempts at civilization which fell too far short of success to be taken into account. . . .

A census of opinions would almost certainly reveal that, in the actual circumstances of the world, there are still at least as many Orthodox Christian and Islamic and Hindu and Far Eastern observers who each regard their own respective society as the consummation of human history and as severally synonymous with Civilization itself, and who hold this view with the same assured conviction that sustains the corresponding but incompatible view among their Western contemporaries. The same assurance proclaims itself in the utterances of all the extinct societies, in all the chances and changes of their mortal lives, wherever a record survives. The pyramid-builders of Egypt possessed this assurance in greater measure than the most triumphant captain of industry in the Western world of today; the revivalists of the Twenty-Sixth Dynasty, and the priesthood which continued to preserve the long-since petrified tradition of the Egyptiac culture under the Achaemenian and Ptolemaic and Roman regimes, inherited the assurance of the pyramid-builders, regardless of the fact that in their times the Egyptiac society was in contact with other representatives of the species to which any unprejudiced observer would have given precedence over the Egyptiac society unhesitatingly if he had been asked to pick out the Chosen People of the age. Doubtless the last scribe who knew how to write the hieroglyphic script and the last sculptor who knew how to carve a bas-relief in the Egyptiac style cherished the same illusion, when the Egyptiac society was *in articulo mortis*, that had been cherished by their predecessors at the time when the Egyptiac society was still holding its own among its kind and at the still earlier time when, for all that its members knew, it was the only society of the kind that ever existed or was destined ever to exist in the world. All this suggests that the current Western misconception of "the Unity of Civilization" through its assumed identity with the Western society has deeper psychological roots than those which are grounded in the momentary state of our social environment. . . .

On the cultural plane, we have hardly yet begun to suspect that our own civilization may not, after all, be the consummation of human history or a synonym for civilization itself. Indeed, we people of the West, so far from shaking ourselves free from the illusion as it besets us in this form, have apparently sunk deeper into this slough of error in the course of our history. In the so-called Middle Ages we portrayed one of the three Magi as a Negro and looked forward to the intervention of an Oriental champion of Christendom called Prester John. In the eighteenth century, when we had degraded the Negro to the role of a slave, we were still capable of admiring the culture of the Far East. Today, after dismissing the artists and philosophers of China to the limbo—or corral—which we have constructed for "Natives," we are apparently even losing our admiration for Hellenism, the civilization to which ours is "affiliated." When we have closed this last door against the humanities, we shall have touched the nadir of our fall from grace.

We can observe how exquisitely ridiculous our "Anglo-Saxon attitude" looks when it is struck by other people. Consider, for instance, the following missive which was presented in A.D. 1793 by the philosophic Emperor Ch'ien Lung to a British envoy for delivery to his master the mad King George III of Britain:

'You, O King, live beyond the confines of many seas; nevertheless, impelled by your humble desire to partake of the benefits of our civilization, you have despatched a mission respectfully bearing your memorial. . . . I have perused your memorial: the earnest terms in which it is couched reveal a respectful humility on your part, which is highly praiseworthy.

In consideration of the fact that your Ambassador and his deputy have come a long way with your memorial and tribute, I have shown them high favour and have allowed them to be introduced into my presence. To manifest my indulgence, I have entertained them at a banquet and made them numerous gifts. . . .

As to your entreaty to send one of your nationals to be accredited to my Celestial Court and to be in control of your country's trade with China, this request is contrary to all usage of my Dynasty and cannot possibly be entertained. . . . If you assert that your reverence for Our Celestial Dynasty fills you with a desire to acquire our civilization, our ceremonies and code of laws differ so completely from your own that, even if your Envoy were able to acquire the rudiments of our civilization, you could not possibly transplant our manners and customs to your alien soil. Therefore, however adept the Envoy might become, nothing would be gained thereby. Our Dynasty's majestic virtue has penetrated into every country under Heaven, and kings of all nations have offered their costly tribute by land and sea. As your Ambassador can see for himself, we possess all things. I set no value on objects strange or ingenious, and have no use for your country's manufactures.'

The Emperor's attitude evokes a smile today when we read his words in the light of all that has happened during the period of rather more than a century that has elapsed since those words were indited. It seems scarcely credible to us, here and now, that a Manchu philos-opher-king, receiving a plain announcement of the approaching impact of the West newly armed with the tremendous weapons of indus-trialism, should have shown himself so blind to the signs of the times. Yet there is no doubt that Ch'ien Lung was an able and experienced statesman with a distinguished mind; and the sequel to the episode does not really expose him as a fool. Rather, it suggests that a contemporary Western statesman of equal ability, if he had been standing in Ch'ien Lung's shoes, would have reacted in the same way; and this suggests, in turn, that our own attitude toward "Natives" may come to appear equally obtuse a century hence.

Again, we may recall the story of the Sharif of Morocco who, returning home after a visit to Europe at some date which was later than the establishment of the French protectorate over his country, was yet heard to exclaim, as he sighted the Moroccan coast: "What a comfort to be getting back to civilization!" When our great-grand-children make the same remark as their ship enters the Solent or the Mersey, will the joke be published in the comic papers of China and—Morocco?

THE FUNCTIONS OF A RACIAL IDEOLOGY

Racial ideology and its counter-conception have tended to create a black sociological race which in all respects is compatible with the social wishes of the white caste. Racial ideology operates to draw white people together, while at the same time it distinguishes and sets Negroes apart from whites, and the sharper the contrast the better the purpose is served.

RELATIONS between white and black people in the South have given rise to a distinctive conception of the Negro. As a natural outcome of the juxtaposition of two divergent ethnic groups, white people have sharply distinguished themselves from black people. It is

Excerpts from Lewis C. Copeland, "The Negro as a Contrast Conception," in *Race Relations and the Race Problem*, edited by Edgar T. Thompson (Durham, North Carolina: Duke University Press), pp. 152-155, 156, 158, 160-161, 163-164, 170-175, 175-177, 177-179.

not surprising then to find that there has been a marked tendency to conceive of the Negro in terms of contrast. In fact, one may speak of the Negro as a "contrast conception." . . .

In the traditional social philosophy which arose out of the planta-tion economy of the South there appears to be just such a polarization of social values and beliefs regarding the white and Negro peoples. White master and Negro slave were set apart from the beginning. During the history of the South the discussion growing out of the long-sustained opposition between the Negro and white groups led, in the realm of belief, at least, to a distinct delineation of each in contrast to the other. The social separation is reflected in the concepts and beliefs white people came to hold about the "opposite race." In popular thought black and white have become conceptual antipodes. The black man and his appurtenances stand as the antithesis of the character and properties of the white man. The conception makes of the Negro a counterrace. The black race serves as a foil for the white race, by which the character of the latter is made all the more impressive.

Voegelin and others show how the Jews in Germany are being used in a similar manner. Tacitus long ago made use of racial contrasts in his portrayal of Roman decadence by posing the Germans as an ideal race. Moralists and theologians frequently point to "pagans and heathens" to establish a point of view by reference to its negation.

The contradistinction between white and black is still an important element in Southern thought and literature. Though it has long been subjected to severe criticism, and rejected by many, its logical implica-tions have so thoroughly insinuated themselves into the mind of the masses that it exerts an unconscious influence upon general public opinion. The conventional idea of the Negro forms the fundamental premise in public discussion of "the Negro problem." As such it conditions contacts and relations between the races, and must be taken into consideration in formulating any racial program. Citizens and institutions who would adopt a liberal program must continually ask, "What will the public think?" or "What will be the social or political reaction?" Certain elements of the older beliefs have become crystallized into social rules which people generally obey whether they agree with the underlying principle or not.

Here we are concerned with the functioning of the traditional concept of Negro people in social relations. In calling attention to its influence on public opinion we by no means intend to imply that it is still held universally. Our primary interest in the beliefs is the manner in which they portray the concept and its function and not as evidence of race prejudice and discrimination. Our materials were selected on this basis, and in quoting the statements and developing their implications no personal agreement or disagreement is implied. The analysis is based upon interviews and published works from which quotations are given to illustrate prevalent beliefs without any assumption as to their scientific or ethical validity. It is important to keep in mind also that we are assuming the standpoint of the white masses and viewing the "opposite race" through their eyes. We are looking out from the white world across the moat separating the races. From this point of view certain things white people say are relevant. They may be regarded as social facts in themselves and as facets of an underlying social race relation. . . . They are important only in so far as they reveal the total structure of the ideology and the common assumptions diffused through the public opinion of the community.

If the presentation is not to be misunderstood, it is necessary to keep in mind that the racial beliefs do not by any means reveal a total picture of race relations. Indeed, one of the most interesting phases of race relations is the manner in which the beliefs and conceptions fail to take account of the intricate web of social and economic ties that bind the groups into a common social order. . . . In discussing Negroes white people often unconsciously impute their views to other areas where different conditions prevail. Likewise, clashes between the races are so impressive that frequently they are felt to be generally prevalent, and thus the amicable relations are obscured. Moreover, conventional beliefs, like all traditions, are slow to change and may persist long after the social milieu giving rise to them has disappeared. They may intrude themselves into the social consciousness in such a manner, however, that one does not recognize their origin or anachronistic character. When a body of beliefs becomes so totally out of harmony with the changing present that it distorts the world view and misrepresents social relations we may justifiably speak of a "false social consciousness." . . .

The beliefs concerning the physical traits of the Negro constitute one of the most conspicuous phases of the conceptual contrast. White Southerners have been very greatly interested in the anthropology of the black man in America and elsewhere, but the popular mind was primarily interested in the traits that pertain to the Negro's participation in society. Natural universal sanctions are sought for social relations. The characteristics assigned the Negro are symbolic for social relations. The characteristics assigned the Negro are symbolic of the status given him in the social order. This explains why the black man has been conceived as subhuman and brutish, and altogether unlike white men. . . .

Since the moral beliefs and sentiments diffused through a society constitute the ultimate sanctions of the social organization, it is not surprising to hear so much talk about the morals of opposite races and classes. These characterizations are to be understood symbolically, however, as representative of the opposition that runs through the community. Moral distinctions are the final rationalizations of racial contrasts, for through these collective representations the counter-ideas of race are reduced to feelings and sentiments; they become emotive in nature. . . .

Thus the racial beliefs function to create two sociological races and to set them apart as two social orders and moral universes. One method of maintaining the distinction between them is through a feeling of resentment. Now, it is significant that the atmosphere within which the conception of the Negro arose is permeated with this feeling and likewise that the conceptual framework is ideological in nature. Only from this standpoint can we understand the *raison d'être* for the antithetical beliefs about Negro and white people and the emotive nature of the ideas. Wherever groups and classes are set in sharp juxtaposition, the values and mores of each are juxtaposed. Out of group opposition there arises an intense opposition of values, which comes to be projected through the social order and serves to solidify social stratification. . . .

The popular conception of Negro character is dramatically portrayed in folk beliefs, fables, anecdotes, jokes, songs, and literature. To sound natural the anecdote must be told in the dialect which whites attribute to Negroes and which is believed to be peculiar to them. In striking contrast to the colored characters, the white characters speak in the most polished and stilted phrases. The things white people laugh at in Negro life are significant, for these are the traits that are considered distinctive. The blackface comedian is so different, so far apart from whites that he has little claim for their sympathy; hence they can laugh at him. Even his moral life is made the point of ribald jokes. Some Southerners protested against the portrayal of the lower class in the play, *Tobacco Road*. It was regarded as a travesty against the whole South. But there is little compunction against playing up the unattractive features of the Negro community in any connection, for by implication these represent what Southern white people are not. They reveal the reverse of the "true South."

We can now understand some elusive aspects of the diametrically opposite way white and Negro women are regarded. The white woman is one of the most conspicuous symbols of white racial values. She stands for the home, domestic relations, and intimate contacts. To protect her is to make secure the inner social circle and to forestall race mixture. Thus, she is made to exemplify the virtues of the race and is enshrouded with the symbols of purity. Her status is made all the more exalted by the conceptual polarity of comparison with the black woman. In contrast to the ennoblement of white women, Negro women stand as the symbol of degradation. Here, above all, the distinction is absolute. There can be no basis of comparison between the two. Everywhere in public one sees and hears the contrast implied in the terms, "white ladies" and "colored women." In white parlance the Negro is not ordinarily a lady or a gentleman. . . .

We have characterized the beliefs about the Negro as ideological. By this we mean that the outlook and conceptual orientation are an expression of white-caste consciousness in its effort to legitimatize prevailing or desired race relations. It is essential to take account of this in understanding one of the motives for casting the Negro in the conventional role as the counterpart of white men. The South has been forced to "explain" constantly its "peculiar institution." During most of its history outsiders have criticized its racial customs. Hence much of its literature has been polemical rationalizations and defenses in answer to its critics. In "explaining" Southern race relations writers, such as Harris, Page, and Dixon, inevitably portrayed a character who was naturally inferior and subordinate to white people. In this litera-ture the black man is made the converse of the white man. Through it there runs a sharp racial distinction, a contrast so definite that racial assimilation is made obviously impossible and repulsive.

In commenting on the books current in his youth Booker T. Washington was struck by the manner in which they "put the pic-tures of Africa and African life in an unnecessarily cruel contrast with the pictures of the civilized and highly cultured Europeans and Americans." In one book a picture of George Washington was "placed side by side with a naked African, having a ring in his nose and a dagger in his hand. Here, as elsewhere, in order to put the lofty posi-tion to which the white race has attained in sharper contrast with the lowly condition of a more primitive people, the best among the white people was contrasted with the worst among the black." Washington relates that he unconsciously took over the prevalent feeling that there must be something wrong and degraded about any person who was different from the customary. . . .

One of the most persistent patterns of belief in Southern thought is the heritage from the slave regime. It is through this phase of the social consciousness that the racial ideology is given one of its most potent expressions. Here we find a mentality that preserves the racial contrast by insistence upon adherence to the patriarchal relations of master and slave in contemporary race relations. In commenting on the contrariety between the two races a white man said, "These Negroes aren't anything but animals anyway. It hasn't been long since they were all just slaves, and one would go out and buy a big husky Negro like he would a good mule."

Though Negroes are competing with whites for many jobs, there still prevails much of the pattern of the plantation economy. Manual toil and menial tasks tend to be reserved for the Negro. A common laborer said, "They work right many Negroes at the tobacco factories. Don't nobody mind Negroes working there, 'cause it's known that them are jobs that no white man can stand. Just ain't healthy for them. Course you know a Negro can stand anything. That dust doesn't hurt him a bit. The thing that's ruining all of us is that Negroes are given jobs that white people ought to have."

Southerners cannot get along without the Negro because the whole economic system is dependent upon his labor. One of the chief problems has been to keep the Negro on the land. His labor is the chief reliance of planters, and when he leaves the planter stranded, crops go to ruin. Furthermore, depressed Southern agriculture has not been able to keep up with the rising wage scale. Every wave of Negro emigration and every advance in wages have brought crises in the South. The reaction to the situation finds expression in such remarks as "We can't get the Negroes to work" and "They demand too high wages," which transmute the relation to another level. One is still told that "Negroes are too undependable and are temperamentally unfit for factories. He hasn't the aptitude for mastering the intricacies of machines. The monotony puts him to sleep." It is out of this situation that there has arisen the popular belief that "cultivation of the soil is natural to the black man." It is thought that his native habitat is the country and that he is at home in the cotton fields. There he is contented, for "the cabin in the cotton" is his heritage. He cannot stand the city and dies off at an early age.

The South's dependence on the Negro is further obscured by the belief in the complete dependence of the black race upon the white race for moral as well as economic support. The Negro is thought of as a child race, the ward of the civilized white man. We are told: "The savage and uncivilized black man lacks the ability to organize his social life on the level of the white community. He is unrestrained and requires the constant control of white people to keep him in check. Without the presence of the white police force Negroes would turn upon themselves and destroy each other. The white man is the only authority he knows." We frequently heard remarks that "the best Negroes have been trained by white people." In contrasting city and country Negroes one person remarked, "Out in the country the Negroes work hard and can be depended on. That's because they have been trained by white people. They're not used to mixing with their kind much." Again it was said, "White people in the South have learned that a Negro is no good without a white man over him."

The conviction that Negroes are utterly dependent upon whites is a natural expression of the benevolent paternalism inherent in the class organization. This spirit is reminiscent of the master-slave relation and serves to create and preserve the aloofness and opposition characteristic of that regime. . . .

It is apparent that through the endless discussion of the Negro there runs a basic pattern of ideas. The beliefs are facets of an ideology, the central theme of which is the natural and inevitable quality of the social order. They are oriented toward the social logics of a caste order, and have for their purpose the sanctioning of race relations on that basis. The system of beliefs contributes to this end by giving to Southern society a mythical background. It brings over to the present the traditions of the past out of which the pattern of race relations has grown. The tremendous interest in the Negro and his traits is ideological. It is significant that it is out of this philosophical milieu that the conception of the Negro has grown, for herein lie the logical motives which have determined the nature of that concept. The ideology, of which the counteridea is the fundamental premise, tells us little about the Negro per se, but much about the white people, their wishes and struggles, and what they want the Negro to be like.

The traditional racial ideology has thus given rise to a "false social consciousness" which tends to distort everything that comes into its sphere. Negro life and character are made the antitheses of that of the white man. The contemporary flow of Negro life and the status of his community are obscured in deference to a pattern of behavior belonging to the plantation economy of the past. By casting a glamor of pathos over the patriarchal relations of the old regime they are posed as ideal patterns for the present. We may venture to assert that the racial ideology and its counterconceptions have tended to create a black sociological race which in all respects is compatible with the social wishes of the white caste. Then the counterbeliefs about the Negro are expressions of the social sentiments and antipathies of the superior caste.

This point of view gives us an insight into many of the remarks white people make about Negroes. We are told: "The Negro loves the South. No one understands him like the Southerner. When you see a Negro in the North, you'll find he's homesick for the South. There's no one in the North to help him out like we do in the South. . . . Negroes do not want equality. I've never seen but one

Negro who demanded that I refer to a colored person as mister. We had a very faithful old janitor, and we thought the world of him. Once when he was sick I went out to look him up. I asked a Negro woman where I could find Uncle Skids. She replied, 'I don't know where you'll find any Uncle Skids, but Mister Jones lives over there.' That made me mad, for I could never think of calling Uncle Skids mister. He'd think that I didn't like him any more." This man was speaking from the perspective of the prevailing racial philosophy and was oblivious to the fact that the Negro might have, in his own community, a social personality or role compatible with the title of address. Even the élite Negroes who are at the head of state institutions and national business concerns are conceived in the conventional role of the servant. In commenting on Negro leaders a white man said: "They are just as submissive as they can be. They know how to get along with white people. When you go over to see one on business they get up and stand. When, you go up to one on the street he'll take off his hat and say, 'Yes suh, mister, what can I do for you?' "

Here we see one of the fundamental aspects of the racial ideology: it obscures Negro life and attitudes. This arises from the dual function it serves, for it operates to draw white people together, while at the same time it distinguishes and sets Negroes apart from whites, and the sharper the contrast the better the purpose is served. The opponent must be depreciated and made a nonentity. In this manner the ideology makes of the Negro an alien that cannot be assimilated to the white group. . . . Assimilation is made repulsive, for the out-group is portrayed as physically and morally unclean.

We are now in a position to understand more fully the symbolic character of the beliefs which tend to take from the black man the elements of social personality. Now we can understand why Negroes do not always participate in those events in which the community celebrates its collective life and ritualizes its interests and values. In the early eighteenth century when Negroes were chased from Independence Square on the Fourth of July, it was said that "They have no part in it." Wherever and in so far as the race has been excluded from those ceremonials in which the common feelings are created and expressed, it has been thereby excluded from full participation in the community life. It is not surprising then to see that the black man has little part in public opinion, and that there has been a tendency to deny him a part in the white man's sacred tradition and myth. We were told: "In my youth people thought that the Negro had no soul. They said there is no Negro in the Bible, and the Bible doesn't apply to them."

The white-caste ideology has undergone constant change in the history of the South. When Negroes were savages and heathens no racial ideology was required to symbolize the social distinction. When the social and cultural differences between black and white were great the contrast was still obvious, and a crude simple racial doctrine sufficed. But as the Negro became civilized and threatened to invade the inner sanctity of white society, a social philosophy was built up to rationalize the social opposition and sentiment against assimilation. The contrast now became a symbolic one. As the threat of assimilation has become greater, as Negroes have become more like whites, the ideology has become more abstract, more "scientific" and "rational," more finely drawn. It approaches the recondite and occult nature of European racialism which finds expression in French and German politics.

The traditional racial ideology of the South forms a conceptual framework within which everything social is viewed. For generations Southerners have busied themselves writing a "Sociology for the South" to which task have been bent the efforts of historiography, psychology, biology, economics, etc. The racial beliefs are thoroughly diffused through the masses and pervade all forms of literature. In this manner the ideology has become a part of the world view of the masses, contributing to the formation of their goals, sentiments, and motives. Outsiders in passing judgments upon the South appear to be oblivious to this, but the emotive nature of the beliefs indicates that they are just as much a part of the mores as any other beliefs. Bailey wrote, "The race attitude of the Southern whites is not a code of cases but a creed of a people—a part of their morality and of their religion."

Once the ideology has arisen it becomes a creative factor in the social process. It reacts back upon the social milieu within which it originated. . . . It is applied to new situations, it utilizes new fictions, and it is constantly presenting new rationalizations. The beliefs are so powerful that there is a constant pressure toward consistency with the ideological pattern thus set. Negroes themselves cannot escape the pattern, but unconsciously assume the role held out to them. Newcomers subtly accept the beliefs as they do Southern dialect and etiquette. So thoroughly is the collective unconscious of the South suffused with the racial philosophy that anything may become a racial issue. The racial mores are a part of the ultimate sanction of the moral order, and they are assumed as the criteria of relevance, truth, and right. As such they constitute a Weltanschauung, which intrudes itself into the social consciousness of an authority within itself, an orthodoxy that needs no defense. . . . Thus, the ideology "naturalizes" the social order, giving an ultimate sanction to the relative status assumed by the races, and at the same time provides a basis for white-caste cohesion. In the process the Negro is posed as a counterrace, an inner enemy, the antithesis of white society.

NEGRO CHARACTER AS SEEN BY WHITE AUTHORS

The Negro has met with as great injustice in American literature as he has in American life. The majority of books about Negroes merely stereotype Negro character in seven types, the contented slave, the wretched freeman, the comic Negro, the brute Negro, the tragic mulatto, the local color Negro and the exotic primitive.

THE NEGRO has met with as great injustice in American literature as he has in American life. The majority of books about Negroes merely stereotype Negro character. . . . Those considered important enough for separate classification, although overlappings *do* occur, are seven in number: (1) The Contented Slave, (2) The Wretched Freeman, (3) The Comic Negro, (4) The Brute Negro, (5) The Tragic Mulatto, (6) The Local Color Negro, and (7) The Exotic Primitive.

All of these stereotypes are marked either by exaggeration or omis-

Excerpts from Sterling A. Brown, "Negro Character as Seen by White Authors," *The Journal of Negro Education* (Washington, D. C., Vol. II, No. 1, January 1933), pp. 180-201.

sions; they all agree in stressing the Negro's divergence from an Anglo-Saxon norm to the flattery of the latter; they could all be used, as they probably are, as justification of racial proscription; they all illustrate dangerous specious generalizing from a few particulars recorded by a single observer from a restricted point of view—which is itself generally dictated by the desire to perpetuate a stereotype. All of these stereotypes are abundantly to be found in American literature, and are generally accepted as contributions to true racial understanding. Thus one critic, setting out imposingly to discuss "the Negro character" in American literature, can still say, unabashedly, that "The whole range of the Negro character is revealed thoroughly," in one twenty-six-line sketch by Joel Chandler Harris of Br'er Fox and Br'er Mud Turtle.

The writer of this essay does not consider everything a stereotype that shows up the weaknesses of Negro character; sometimes the stereotype makes the Negro appear too virtuous. Nor does he believe the stereotypes of contented slaves and buffoons are to be successfully balanced by pictures of Negroes who are unbelievably intellectual, noble, self-sacrificial, and faultless. Any stereotyping is fatal to great, or even to convincing literature. Furthermore, he believes that he has considered to be stereotypes only those patterns whose frequent and tedious recurrence can be demonstrably proved by even a cursory acquaintance with the literature of the subject.

THE CONTENTED SLAVE. The first lukewarm stirrings of abolitionary sentiment in the South were chilled with Eli Whitney's invention of the cotton gin at the close of the 18th Century. Up until this time the *raison d'être* of slavery had not been so powerful. But now there was a way open to quick wealth; Cotton was crowned King, and a huge army of black servitors was necessary to keep him upon the throne; considerations of abstract justice had to give way before economic expediency. A complete rationale of slavery was evolved.

One of the most influential of the authorities defending slavery was President Dew of William and Mary College, who stated, in 1832, that

. . . slavery had been the condition of all ancient culture, that Christianity approved servitude, and that the law of Moses had both assumed and positively established slavery. . . . It is the order of nature and of

God that the being of superior faculties and knowledge, and therefore of superior power, should control and dispose of those who are inferior. It is as much in the order of nature that men should enslave each other as that other animals should prey upon each other.

The pamphlet of this young teacher was extensively circulated, and was substantiated by Chancellor Harper of the University of South Carolina in 1838:

Man is born to subjection. . . . The proclivity of the natural man is to domineer or to be subservient. . . . If there are sordid, servile, and laborious offices to be performed, is it not better that there should be sordid, servile, and laborious beings to perform them?

The economic argument had frequent proponents; an ex-governor of Virginia showed that, although Virginia was denied the tremendous prosperity accruing from cotton raising, it was still granted the opportunity to profit from selling Negroes to the far South. Sociologists and anthropologists hastened forward with the proof of the Negro's three-fold inferiority: physically (except for his adaptability to cotton fields and rice swamps), mentally, and morally. Theologists advanced the invulnerable arguments from the Bible; in one of the "Bible Defences of Slavery" we read: "The curse of Noah upon *Ham*, had a *general* and *interminable* application to the whole Hamite race, in placing them under a *peculiar* liability of being enslaved by the races of the two other brothers."

The expressions of these dominant ideas in the fiction and poetry of the period did not lag far behind. In fact, one influential novel was among the leaders of the van, for in 1832, the year in which Professor Dew stated the argument that was to elevate him to the presidency of William and Mary College, John P. Kennedy published a work that was to make him one of the most widely read and praised authors of the Southland. His ideas of the character of the Negro and of slavery are in fundamental agreement with those of Dew and Harper. According to F. P. Gaines, in *The Southern Plantation*, Kennedy's *Swallow Barn* has the historical significance of starting the plantation tradition, a tradition hoary and mildewed in our own day, but by no means moribund.

Swallow Barn is an idyllic picture of slavery on a tidewater planta-

tion. The narrator, imagined to be from the North (Kennedy himself was from Tidewater Maryland), comes to Virginia, expecting to
see a drastic state of affairs. Instead, he finds a kindly patriarchy and
grateful, happy slaves. After vignettes of the Negro's laziness, mirth,
vanity, improvidence, done with some charm and, for a Southern
audience, considerable persuasiveness, the "Northern" narrator concludes: "I am quite sure they never could become a happier people
than I find them here. . . ."

Shortly after the publication of *Swallow Barn*, Edgar Allan Poe
wrote:

. . . we must take into consideration the peculiar character (I may say
the peculiar nature) of the Negro. . . . Some believe that Negroes are,
like ourselves, the sons of Adam and must, therefore, have like passions
and wants and feelings and tempers in all respects. This we deny and
appeal to the knowledge of all who know. . . . We shall take leave to
speak as of things *in esse*, in a degree of loyal devotion on the part of
the slave to which the white man's heart is a stranger, and of the master's
reciprocal feeling of parental attachment to his humble dependent. . . .
That these sentiments in the breast of the Negro and his master are
stronger than they would be under like circumstances between individuals
of the white race, we believe.

In *The Gold-Bug*, Poe shows this reciprocal relationship between
Jupiter, a slave, and his master.

In 1853, William Gilmore Simms, in joining forces with Dew and
Harper in the *Pro-Slavery Argument*, writes: "Slavery has elevated
the Negro from savagery. The black man's finer traits of fidelity and
docility were encouraged in his servile position. . . ." Simms turned
from cursory references to slavery to ardent pro-slavery defense, in
company with other novelists of the South, for a perfectly definite
reason. The abolitionary attacks made by men like Garrison had
taken the form of pamphlets, and these had been answered in kind.
The publication of *Uncle Tom's Cabin* in 1851, however, showed
that the abolitionists had converted the novel into a powerful weapon.
Pro-slavery authors were quick to take up this weapon, although their
wielding of it was without the power of Harriet Beecher Stowe.
Swallow Barn was reissued in 1851, and "besides the numerous controversial pamphlets and articles in periodicals there were no fewer

than fourteen pro-slavery novels and one long poem published in the three years (1852-54) following the appearance of *Uncle Tom's Cabin.*"

These novels are all cut out of the same cloth. Like *Swallow Barn,* they omit the economic basis of slavery, and minimize "the sordid, servile and laborious offices" which Chancellor Harper had considered the due of "sordid, servile, and laborious beings." The pro-slavery authors use the first adjective only in considering free Negroes, or those who, by some quirk of nature, are disobedient; admit the second completely; and deny the third. Slavery to all of them is a beneficent guardianship, the natural and inevitable state for a childish people.

There is very little reference to Negroes working in fields; even then they are assigned to easy tasks which they lazily perform to the tune of slave melodies. They are generally described as "leaving the fields." They are allowed to have, for additional provisions and huckstering, their own garden-plots, which they attend in their abundant leisure. Their holidays are described at full length: the corn huskings, barbecuing, Yuletide parties, and hunting the possum by the light of a kindly moon.

In *Life at the South,* or *Uncle Tom's Cabin As It Is* (1852), Uncle Tom, out of hurt vanity, but not for any more grievous cause, runs away. His wife, Aunt Dinah, although loving Tom, realizes that her greater loyalty is due to her master, and not to her errant spouse, and refuses to escape with him. Tom, after experiencing the harshness of the unfeeling North, begs to return to slavery. In *The Planter's Northern Bride,* the bride, having come to the slave South with misgivings, is quickly converted to an enthusiast for slavery, since it presents "an aspect so tender and affectionate." One fears that the bride is not unpartisan, however, since her appearance on the plantation elicited wild cries of worship, and her beloved husband is a great ethnologist, proving that the Negro's peculiar skull and skin were decreed by the divine fiat so that he could pick cotton. In *The Yankee Slave Dealer,* the meddling abolitionist cannot persuade any slaves to run off with him except a half-witted rogue. . . . In *The Hireling and The Slave,* William J. Grayson, "poet laureate" of South Carolina, contrasts the lot of the industrial worker of the North with that of the slave. Gems of this widely read poetical disquisition follow:

And yet the life, so unassailed by care,
So blessed with moderate work, with ample fare,
With all the good the starving pauper needs,
The happier slave on each plantation leads. . . .

This pattern of the joyous contentment of the slave in a paradisaical bondage persisted and was strongly reinforced in Reconstruction days. If it was no longer needed for the defense of a tottering institution, it was needed for reasons nearly as exigent. Ancestor worshipers, the sons of a fighting generation, remembering bitterly the deaths or sufferings of their fathers, became elegists of a lost cause and cast a golden glow over the plantation past; unreconstructed "fire-eaters," determined to resurrect slavery as far as they were able, needed as a cardinal principle the belief that Negroes were happy as slaves, and hopelessly unequipped for freedom. Both types were persuasive, the first because the romantic idealizing of the past will always be seductive to a certain large group of readers, and the second because the sincere unremitting harping upon one argument will finally make it seem plausible. We find, therefore, that whereas *Uncle Tom's Cabin* had triumphed in the antebellum controversy, the pro-slavery works of Page, Russell, and Harris swept the field in Reconstruction days. It is from these last skillful authors, undeniably acquainted with Negro folk-life, and affectionate toward certain aspects of it, that the American reading public as a whole has accepted the delusion of the Negro as contented slave, entertaining child, and docile ward.

Mutual affection between the races is a dominant theme. Irwin Russell implies throughout that the Southern white best understands how to treat the Negro. . . . Thomas Nelson Page followed Russell's lead in poetry. In the poems of *Befo' De War*, Page puts into the mouths of his Negroes yearnings for the old days and expressions of the greatest love for old marster. . . .

Joel Chandler Harris is better known for his valuable contribution to literature and folk-lore in recording the Uncle Remus stories than for his aid in perpetuation of the "plantation Negro" stereotype. Nevertheless, a merely cursory study of Uncle Remus's character would reveal his close relationship to the "Caesars," "Hectors," "Pompeys," *et al.* of the pro-slavery novel, and to Page's "Uncle Jack" and "Uncle

Billy." In Uncle Remus's philosophizing about the old days of slavery there is still the wistful nostalgia. Slavery was: . . . "in some of its aspects far more beautiful and inspiring than *any* of the relations between employers and the employed in this day."

George Washington Cable, although more liberal in his views upon the Negro than his Southern contemporaries, gives an example of the self-abnegating servant in *Posson Jone'*. This slave uses his wits to safeguard his master. A goodly proportion of the Negro servants are used to solve the complications of their "white-folks." They are in a long literary tradition—that of the faithful, clever servant—and they probably are just as true to Latin prototypes as to real Negroes . . .

Although the realism of today is successfully discounting the sentimentalizing of the Old South, there are still many contemporary manifestations of the tradition. Hergesheimer, arch-romanticist that he is, writes that he would be happy to pay with everything the wasted presence holds for the return of the pastoral civilization based on slavery. . . . *Ol' Massa's People*, by Orlando Kay Armstrong, is one of the most recent of the books in which ex-slaves speak—as in Page apparently with their master's voice—their praise of slavery. . . . Designed originally to defend slavery, it is now a convenient argument for those wishing to keep "the Negro in his place"—out of great love for him, naturally—believing that he will be happier so.

THE WRETCHED FREEMAN: As a foil to the contented slave, proslavery authors set up another puppet—the wretched free Negro. He was necessary for the argument. Most of the pro-slavery novels paid a good deal of attention to his degradation. Either the novelist interpolated a long disquisition on the disadvantages of his state both to the country and to himself, or had his happy slaves fear contact with him as with a plague.

In *Life at the South, or Uncle Tom's Cabin As It Is*, Uncle Tom experiences harsh treatment from unfeeling Northern employers, sees Negroes frozen to death in snow storms, and all in all learns that the North and freedom is no stopping place for him. In *The Yankee Slave Dealer*, the slaves are insistent upon the poor lot of free Negroes. In *The Planter's Northern Bride*, Crissy runs away from freedom in order to be happy again in servitude. . . .

There was a carry-over of these ideas in the Reconstruction. Harris, in one of his most moving stories, *Free Joe*, showed the tragedy of a free Negro in a slave-holding South, where he was considered a bad model by slave-owners, an economic rival by poor whites, and something to be avoided by the slaves. The story might be considered as a condemnation of a system, but in all probability was taken to be another proof of the Negro's incapacity for freedom. Although Harris wrote generously of Negro advancement since emancipation, there is little doubt that the implications of many passages furthered the stereotype under consideration.

Page, a bourbon "fire-eater," for all of his yearnings for his old mammy, saw nothing of good for Negroes in emancipation: Universally, they [Southerners] will tell you that while the old-time Negroes were industrious, saving, and, when not misled, well-behaved, kindly, respectful, and self-respecting, and while the remnant of them who remain still retain generally these characteristics, the "new issue," for the most part, are lazy, thriftless, intemperate, insolent, dishonest, and without the most rudimentary elements of morality. . . . Universally, they report a general depravity and retrogression of the Negroes at large, in sections in which they are left to themselves, closely resembling a reversion to barbarism.

The notion of the Negro's being doomed to extinction was sounded by a chorus of pseudo-scientists, bringing forth a formidable (?) array of proofs. Lafcadio Hearn yielded to the lure of posing as a prophet:

As for the black man, he must disappear with the years. Dependent like the ivy, he needs some strong oak-like friend to cling to. His support has been cut from him, and his life must wither in its prostrate helplessness. Will he leave no trace of his past? . . . Ah, yes! . . . the weird and beautiful melodies born in the hearts of the poor, child-like people to whom freedom was destruction.

Modern neo-Confederates repeat the stereotype. Allen Tate, co-member with Donald Davidson of the Nashville saviors of the South, implies in *Jefferson Davis, His Rise and Fall*, that to educate a Negro beyond his station brings him unhappiness. One of the chief points of agreement in the neo-Confederate *I'll Take My Stand* by Davidson, Tate and ten others is that freedom has proved to be a perilous state for the Negro. Joseph Hergesheimer agrees: "A free Negro is more often wretched than not." "Slavery was gone, the old serene days were gone. Negroes were bad because they were neither slave nor free." And finally, a modern illustration must suffice. Eleanor Mercein Kelly in an elegy for the vanishing South, called *Monkey Motions*, pities "the helplessness of a simple jungle folk, a bandar-log, set down in the life of cities and expected to be men."

It is, all in all, a sad picture that these savants give. What concerns us here, however, is its persistence, a thing inexpressibly more sad.

THE COMIC NEGRO: The stereotype of the "comic Negro" is about as ancient as the "contented slave." Indeed, they might be considered complementary, since, if the Negro could be shown as perpetually mirthful, his state could not be so wretched. This is, of course, the familiar procedure when conquerors depict a subject people. English authors at the time of Ireland's greatest persecution built up the stereotype of the comic Irishman, who fascinated English audiences, and unfortunately, in a manner known to literary historians, influenced even Irish authors. Thus, we find, in a melodrama about Irish life, an English officer soliloquizing:

I swear, the Irish nature is beyond my comprehension. A strange people!—merry 'mid their misery—laughing through their tears, like the sun shining through the rain. Yet what simple philosophers they! They tread life's path as if 'twere strewn with roses devoid of thorns, and make the most of life with natures of sunshine and song.

Any American not reading the words "Irish nature" could be forgiven for taking the characterization to refer to American Negroes. Natures of sunshine and song, whose wretchedness becomes nothing since theirs is a simple philosophy of mirth! So runs the pattern.

In her excellent book, *American Humor,* Constance Rourke points out the Negro as one of the chief ingredients of the potpourri of American humor. She traces him as far back as the early '20's when Edwin Forrest made up as a southern plantation Negro to excite the risibilities of Cincinnati. . . . Kennedy in his *Swallow Barn,* not only reveals the Negro as delighted by the master's benevolence, but also as delighting the master by his ludicrous departure from the Anglo-Saxon norm.

It was in the early '30's, however, that T. D. Rice first jumped "Jim Crow" in the theaters along the Ohio River and set upon the stage the "minstrel Negro." Apparently immortal, this stereotype was to involve in its perpetuation such famous actors as Joseph Jefferson and David Belasco, to make Amos 'n' Andy as essential to American domesticity as a car in every garage, and to mean affluence for a Jewish comedian of whom only one gesture was asked: that he sink upon one knee, extend his white-gloved hands, and cry out "Mammy."

In pro-slavery fiction the authors seemed to agree on the two aspects of the comic Negro—that he was ludicrous to others, and forever laughing himself. . . . To introduce comic relief, perhaps, in stories that might defeat their own purposes if confined only to the harrowing details of slavery, anti-slavery authors had their comic characters. Topsy is the classic example; it is noteworthy that in contemporary acting versions of "Uncle Tom's Cabin," Topsy and the minstrel show note, if not dominant, are at least of equal importance to the melodrama of Eliza and the bloodhounds.

Reconstruction literature developed the stereotype. Russell's Negroes give side-splitting versions of the Biblical story (foreshadowing Bradford's *Ol' Man Adam an' His Chillun*), or have a fatal fondness for propinquity to a mule's rear end. Page's Negroes punctuate their worship of "ole Marse" with "Kyah-kyahs," generally directed at themselves. The humor of Uncle Remus is nearer to genuine folk-humor, which—it might be said in passing—is *not* the same as the "comic Negro" humor. Negroes in general, in the Reconstruction stories, are seen as creatures of mirth—who wouldn't suffer from hardship, even if they had to undergo it. Thus a Negro, sentenced to the chain-gang for stealing a pair of breeches, is made the theme of a comic poem. This is illustrative. There may be random jokes in Southern court rooms, but joking about the Negroes' experiences with Southern "justice" and with the chain-gang is rather ghastly—like laughter at the mouth of hell. Creatures of sunshine and of song!

The "comic Negro" came into his own in the present century, and brought his creators into theirs. Octavus Cohen, who looks upon the idea of Negro doctors and lawyers and society belles as the height of the ridiculous, served such clienteles as that of *The Saturday Evening Post* for a long time with the antics of Florian Slappey. His work is amusing at its best, but is pseudo-Negro. Instead of being a handicap, however, that seems a recommendation to his audience. Trusting to most moth-eaten devices of farce, and interlarding a Negro dialect never heard on land or sea—compounded more of Dogberry and Mrs. Malaprop than of Birmingham Negroes, he has proved to the whites that all along they have known the real Negro—"Isn't he funny, now!"—and has shown to Negroes what whites wanted them to resemble. . . .

Arthur E. Akers, with a following in another widely read magazine, is another farceur. He uses the situation of the domestic difficulty, as old as medieval fabliaux and farces—and places it in a Southern Negro community, and has his characters speak an approximation to Negro dialect—but too slick and "literary" for conviction. Irate shrews and "Milquetoast" husbands, with razors wielded at departing parts of the anatomy, are Akers' stock-in-trade. Hugh Wiley with his Wildcat, inseparable from his goat, Lady Luck, unsavory but a talisman, is another creator of the farce that Negro life is too generally believed to be. E. K. Means, with obvious knowledge of Southern Negro life, is concerned to show in the main its ludicrous side, and Irvin Cobb, with a reputation of after-dinner wit to uphold, is similarly confined.

The case of Roark Bradford is different. An undoubted humorist, in the great line of Twain and the tall tales of the Southwest, he gleans from a rich store of Negro speech and folkways undeniably amusing tales. But as his belief about the Negro might attest, he has a definite attitude to the Negro to uphold. His stories of the easy loves of the levee (frequently found in *Collier's*) concentrate upon the comic aspect of Negro life, although another observer might well see the tragic. In *Ol' Man Adam an' His Chillun* we have farce manufactured out of the Negro's religious beliefs. It seems to the writer that the weakest sections of *Green Pastures* stick closest to Bradford's stories, and that the majesty and reverence that can be found in the play must come from Marc Connelly. In *John Henry*, Bradford has definitely weakened his material by making over a folk-hero into a clown.

Although the situations in which the comic Negro finds himself range from the fantastic as in Cohen, to the possible as in "The Two Black Crows" and in "Amos 'n' Andy," his characteristics are fairly stable. The "comic Negro" is created for the delectation of a white audience, condescending and convinced that any departure from the Anglo-Saxon norm is amusing, and that any attempt to enter the special provinces of whites, such as wearing a dress suit, is doubly so. The "comic Negro" with certain physical attributes exaggerated— with his razor (generally harmless), his love for watermelon and gin, for craps, his haunting of chicken roosts, use of big words he doesn't understand, grandiloquent names and titles, "loud" clothes, bluster, hysterical cowardice, and manufactured word-play—has pranced his way by means of books, vaudeville skits, shows, radio programs, advertisements, and after-dinner speeches, into the folklore of the nation. As Guy B. Johnson urges, there is a sort of—

. . . folk attitude of the white man toward the Negro. . . . One cannot help noticing that the white man must have his fun out of the Negro, even when writing serious novels about him. This is partly conscious, indeed a necessity, if one is to portray Negro life as it is, for Negroes are human and behave like other human beings. Sometimes it is unconscious, rising out of our old habit of associating the Negro with the comical.

In pointing out the stereotype, one does not deny the rich comedy to be found in Negro life. One is insisting, however, that any picture concentrating upon this to the exclusion of all else is entirely inadequate, that many of the most popular creators of the "comic Negro," "doctor" their material, and are far from accurate in depicting even the small area of Negro experience they select, and that too often they exceed the prerogative of comedy by making copy out of persecution and injustice.

THE BRUTE NEGRO: Because the pro-slavery authors were anxious to prove that slavery had been a benefit to the Negro in removing him from savagery to Christianity, the stereotype of the "brute Negro" was relatively insignificant in antebellum days. There were references to vicious criminal Negroes in fiction (vicious and criminal being synonymous to discontented and refractory), but these were considered as exceptional cases of half-wits led astray by abolitionists. *The Bible Defence of Slavery,* however, in which the Rev. Priest in a most unclerical manner waxes wrathful at abolitionists, sets forth with a great array of theological argument and as much ridiculousness, proofs of the Negro's extreme lewdness. Sodom and Gomorrah were destroyed because these were strongholds of *Negro* vice. . . .

H. R. Helper, foe of slavery, was no friend of the Negro, writing, in 1867, *Nojoque*, a lurid condemnation of the Negro, setting up black and beastly as exact synonyms. Van Evrie's *White Supremacy and Negro Subordination, or Negroes A Subordinate Race, and (so-called) Slavery Its Normal Condition* gave "anthropological" support to the figment of the "beastly Negro," and *The Negro A Beast* (1900) gave theological support. The title page of this book runs: "The Reasoner of the Age, the Revelator of the Century! The Bible As It Is! The Negro and his Relation to the Human Family! The Negro a beast, but created with articulate speech, and hands, that he may be of service to his master—the White Man . . . by Chas. Carroll, who has spent 15 years of his life and $20,000.00 in its compilation." Who could ask for anything more?

Authors stressing the mutual affection between the races looked upon the Negro as a docile mastiff. In the Reconstruction this mastiff turned into a mad dog. "Damyanks," carpetbaggers, scalawags, and New England schoolmarms affected him with the rabies. The works of Thomas Nelson Page are good examples of this metamorphosis. When his Negro characters are in their place, loyally serving and worshiping ole Marse, they are admirable creatures, but in freedom they are beasts, as his novel *Red Rock* attests. *The Negro: The Southerner's Problem* says that the state of the Negro since emancipation is one of minimum progress and maximum regress. . . .

The best known author of Ku Klux Klan fiction after Page is Thomas Dixon. Such works as *The Clansman*, and *The Leopard's Spots*, because of their sensationalism and chapter titles (e.g., "The Black Peril," "The Unspoken Terror," "A Thousand Legged Beast," "The Hunt for the Animal"), seemed just made for the mentality of Hollywood, where D. W. Griffith's in *The Birth of a Nation* made for Thomas Dixon a dubious sort of immortality, and finally fixed the stereotype in the mass-mind. The stock Negro in Dixon's books, unless the shuffling hat-in-hand servitor, is a gorilla-like imbecile, who "springs like a tiger" and has the "black claws of a beast." In both books there is a terrible rape, and a glorious ride of the Knights on a Holy Crusade to avenge Southern civilization. Dixon enables his

white geniuses to discover the identity of the rapist by using "a micro-
scope of sufficient power (to) reveal on the retina of the dead eyes
the image of this devil as if etched there by fire." . . . The doctor
sees "The bestial figure of a negro—his huge black hand plainly
defined. . . . It was Gus." Will the wonders of science never cease?
But, perhaps, after all, Negroes have been convicted on even flimsier
evidence. Fortunately for the self-respect of American authors, this
kind of writing is in abeyance today. Perhaps it fell because of the
weight of its own absurdity. But it would be unwise to underestimate
this stereotype. It is probably of great potency in certain benighted
sections where Dixon, if he could be read, would be applauded—and
it certainly serves as a convenient self-justification for a mob about to
uphold white supremacy by a lynching.

THE TRAGIC MULATTO: Stereotyping was by no means the monopoly of pro-slavery authors defending their type of commerce, or
justifying their ancestors. Anti-slavery authors, too, fell into the easy
habit, but with a striking difference. Where pro-slavery authors had
predicated a different set of characteristics for the Negroes, a distinctive sub-human nature, and had stereotyped in accordance with
such a comforting hypothesis, anti-slavery authors insisted that the
Negro had a common humanity with the whites, that in given circumstances a typically human type of response was to be expected,
unless certain other powerful influences were present. The stereotyping in abolitionary literature, therefore, is not stereotyping of
character, but of *situation*. Since the novels were propagandistic, they
concentrated upon abuses: floggings, the slave mart, the domestic
slave trade, forced concubinage, runaways, slave hunts, and persecuted
freemen—all of these were frequently repeated. Stereotyped or not,
heightened if you will, the anti-slavery novel has been supported by
the verdict of history—whether recorded by Southern or Northern
historians. Facts, after all, are abolitionist. Especially the fact that
the Colonel's lady and old Aunt Dinah are sisters under the skin. . . .

Anti-slavery fiction did proffer one stereotype, doomed to unfortunate longevity. This is the tragic mulatto. Pro-slavery apologists had
almost entirely omitted (with so many other omissions) mention of
concubinage. If anti-slavery authors, in accordance with Victorian
gentility, were wary of illustrating the practice, they made great use

nevertheless of the offspring of illicit unions. Generally the heroes and heroines of their books are near-whites. These are the intransigent, the resentful, the mentally alert, the proofs of the Negro's possibilities. John Herbert Nelson says with some point:

Abolitionists tried, by making many of their characters almost white, to work on racial feeling as well. This was a curious piece of inconsistency on their part, an indirect admission that a white man in chains was more pitiful to behold than the African similarly placed. Their most impassioned plea was in behalf of a person little resembling their swarthy protegés, the quadroon or octoroon.

Nelson himself, however, shows similar inconsistency, as he infers that the "true African—essentially gay, happy-go-lucky, rarely ambitious or idealistic, the eternal child of the present moment, able to leave trouble behind—is unsuited for such portrayal. . . . Only the mulattoes and others of mixed blood have, so far, furnished us with material for convincing tragedy."

The tragic mulatto appears in both of Mrs. Stowe's abolitionary novels. In *Uncle Tom's Cabin*, the fugitives Liza and George Harris and the rebellious Cassy are mulattoes. Uncle Tom, the pure black, remains the paragon of Christian submissiveness. In *Dred*, Harry Gordon and his wife are nearly white. . . . Richard Hildreth's *Archy Moore, or The White Slave*, has as its leading character a fearless, educated mulatto, indistinguishable from whites; Boucicault's *The Octoroon* sentimentalizes the hardships of a slave girl; both make the mixed blood the chief victim of slavery.

Cable, in *The Grandissimes*, shows a Creole mulatto educated beyond his means, and suffering ignominy, but he likewise shows in the character of Bras-Coupè that he does not consider intrepidity and vindictiveness the monopoly of mixed-bloods. In *Old Creole Days*, however, he discusses the beautiful octoroons, whose best fortune in life was to become the mistress of some New Orleans dandy. He shows the tragedy of their lives, but undoubtedly contributed to the modern stereotype that the greatest yearning of the girl of mixed life is for a white lover. . . .

The novelists have kept them in the background. Many recent novels show this: *White Girl, The No-Nation Girl, A Study in*

Bronze, Gulf Stream, Dark Lustre—all of these show luridly the melodrama of the lovely octoroon girl. Indeed "octoroon" has come to be a feminine noun in popular usage.

The stereotype that demands attention, however, is the notion of mulatto character, whether shown in male or female. This character works itself out with mathematical symmetry. The older theses ran: First, the mulatto inherits the vices of both races and none of the virtues; second, any achievement of a Negro is to be attributed to the white blood in his veins. The logic runs that even inheriting the worst from whites is sufficient for achieving among Negroes. The present theses are based upon these: The mulatto is a victim of a divided inheritance; from his white blood come his intellectual strivings, his unwillingness to be slave; from his Negro blood come his baser emotional urges, his indolence, his savagery. . . .

Roark Bradford in *This Side of Jordan* gives an unconscious *reductio ad absurdum* of this stereotype.

The blade of a razor flashed through the air. Scrap had concealed it in the folds of her dress. Her Negro blood sent it unerringly between two ribs. Her Indian blood sent it back for an unnecessary second and third slash.

It might be advanced that Esquimauan blood probably would have kept her from being chilled with horror. The strangest items are attributed to different racial strains: In *No-Nation Girl* a woman cries out in childbirth because of her Negro expressiveness; from the back of Précieuse's "ankles down to her heels, the flesh was slightly thicker"—due to her Negro blood; Lessie in Welbourn Kelley's *Inching Along* "strongly felt the urge to see people, to talk to people. . . . That was the white in her maybe. Or maybe it was the mixture of white and black."

This kind of writing should be discredited by its patent absurdity. It is generalizing of the wildest sort, without support from scientific authorities. And yet it has set these idées fixés: The Negro of un-mixed blood is no theme for tragedy; rebellion and vindictiveness are to be expected only from the mulatto; the mulatto is victim of a divided inheritance and therefore miserable; he is a "man without a race" worshiping the whites and despised by them, despising and despised by Negroes, perplexed by his struggle to unite a white intellect with black sensuousness. The fate of the octoroon girl is intensified—the whole desire of her life is to find a white lover, and then go down, accompanied by slow music, to a tragic end. Her fate is so severe that in some works disclosure of "the single drop of midnight" in her veins makes her commit suicide.

The stereotype is very flattering to the race which, for all its self-assurance, seems to stand in great need of flattery. But merely looking at one of its particulars—that white blood means asceticism and Negro blood means unbridled lust—will reveal how flimsy the whole structure is. It is ingenious that mathematical computation of the amount of white blood in a mulatto's veins will explain his character. And it is a widely held belief. But it is nonsense, all the same.

THE LOCAL COLOR NEGRO: Local color stresses the quaint, the odd, the picturesque, the different. It is an attempt to convey the peculiar quality of a locality. Good realistic practice would insist upon the localizing of speech, garb, and customs; great art upon the revelation of the universal beneath these local characteristics. Local color is now in disrepute because of its being contented with merely the peculiarity of dialect and manners. As B. A. Botkin, editor of *Folk-Say*, has stated: "In the past (local consciousness) has been narrowly sectional rather than broadly human, superficially picturesque rather than deeply interpretative, provincial without being indigenous."

The "local color Negro" is important in any study of the Negro character in American literature. But, since the local colorists of the Negro were more concerned with fidelity to speech and custom, with revelation of his difference in song and dance and story, than with revelation of Negro character, they accepted at face valuation the current molds into which Negro character had been forced. Therefore, local colorists have been and will be considered under other heads. Page and Russell were local colorists in that they paid close attention to Negro speech, but the Negro they portrayed was the same old contented slave. Their study of Negro speech, however, was fruitful and needed—for pro-slavery authors had been as false in recording Negro speech as they were in picturing Negro experience. Kennedy, for instance, forces a confessedly wretched dialect into the mouths of poor Negroes, and W. L. G. Smith has his Shenandoah

Negroes speak Gullah, because his master, Simms, had written of South Carolina Negroes.

Cable, one of the best of the local colorists, in *The Grandissimes* goes a step beyond the mere local color formula; *Old Creole Days* is local color, but has been considered under the "Tragic Mulatto." The Negroes in Lyle Saxon's old and new New Orleans, E. Larocque Tinker's old New Orleans, R. Emmett Kennedy's Gretna Green, are in the main kinsfolk to the contented slave; in Evans Wall's Mississippi canebrakes are exotic primitives, or tragic mulattoes; on Roark Bradford's levees are primitives; and those on Julia Peterkin's Blue Brook Plantation, in Heyward's Catfish Row, and in John Vandercook's Surinam, Liberia, and Haiti, usually surmount, in the writer's opinion, the deficiencies of local color. Stereotyped, or genuinely interpreted, however, they all agree in one respect: they show the peculiar differences of certain Negroes in well-defined localities.

John B. Sale in *The Tree Named John* records with sympathy the dialect, superstitions, folk-ways of Mississippi Negroes. He is meticulous, perhaps to a fault, in his dialectical accuracy; the milieu is correspondingly convincing. His Negroes do carry on the pattern of mutual affection between the races—and yet they are far nearer flesh and blood than those of Page. Samuel Stoney and Gertrude Shelby, in *Black Genesis*, give the peculiarities of the Gullah Negro's cosmogony. Care is paid to fidelity in recording the dialect, but the authors' comments reveal a certain condescension toward quaintness which is the usual bane of local colorists. In *Po' Buckra* the authors reveal the localized tragedy of the "brass-ankle"—the Croatan-Negro-near-white caste. Much of the "tragic mulatto" theme is in this book, as well as the purely local color interest. Ambrose Gonzales in his Gullah renditions of Aesop, and in his tales of the "black border," reveals for the curious the intricacies of a little known Negro dialect, following the lead of Harris, and C. C. Jones, who recorded the Br'er Rabbit tales in the dialect of the Georgia coast.

Although most of these authors who dwell upon quaint and picturesque divergencies are discussed under other headings, it will not do to underestimate this local color Negro. The showing of Negro peculiarities in speech, superstitions, and customs has been popular for many years, and is likely to be for a long while yet. It undoubtedly has its artistic uses; but being an end in itself is surely not the chief of them.

THE EXOTIC PRIMITIVE: This stereotype grew up with America's post-war revolt against Puritanism and Babbittry. Literary critics urged a return to spontaneity, to unrestrained emotion; American literature had been too long conventional, drab, without music and color. Human nature had been viewed with too great a reticence. Sex, which the Victorians had considered unmentionable, was pronounced by the school of Freud to have an overwhelming importance in motivating our conduct. So the pendulum swung from the extreme of Victorian prudishness to that of modern expressiveness.

To authors searching "for life in the raw," Negro life and character seemed to beg for exploitation. There was the Negro's savage inheritance, as they conceived it: hot jungle nights, the tom-tom calling to esoteric orgies. There were the frankness and violence to be found in any under-privileged group, or on any frontier. There were the traditional beliefs of the Negro being a creature of his appetites, and although pro-slavery fiction had usually (because of Victorianism) limited these to his yearnings for hog meat and greens, 'possum and yams, and for whisky on holidays, Reconstruction fiction had stressed his lustfulness. He seemed to be cut out for the hands of certain authors. They promptly rushed to Harlem for color. In Harlem dives and cabarets they found what they believed to be *the* Negro, *au naturel*.

The figure who emerges from their pages is a Negro synchronized to a savage rhythm, living a life of ecstasy, superinduced by jazz (repetition of the tom-tom, awakening vestigial memories of Africa) and gin, that lifted him over antebellum slavery, and contemporary economic slavery, and placed him in the comforting fastnesses of their "mother-land." A kinship exists between this stereotype and that of the contented slave; one is merely a "jazzed-up" version of the other, with cabarets supplanting cabins, and Harlemized "blues," instead of the spirituals and slave reels. Few were the observers who saw in the Negroes' abandon a release from the troubles of this world similar to that afforded in slavery by their singing. Many there were, however, who urged that the Harlem Negro's state was that of an inexhaustible *joie de vivre*.

Carl Van Vechten was one of the pioneers of the hegira from downtown to Harlem; he was one of the early discoverers of the cabaret; and his novel, *Nigger Heaven,* is to the exotic pattern what *Swallow Barn* was to the contented slave. All of the possibilities of the development of the type are inherent in the book. . . . Van Vechten, who was already famed as a sophisticated romantic novelist, writes graphically of this Harlem. His style invited emulation from young men desiring to be men-about-town first and then novelists, just as Kennedy invited emulation from young Southerners desiring to defend slavery first. Van Vechten's novel does more than present the local color of Harlem; there is as well the character study of a young Negro intellectual who cannot withstand the dissipations of the "greatest Negro city." But the Bohemian life in Harlem is the main thing, even in this youngster's life. According to the publisher's blurb, "Herein is caught the fascination and tortured ecstasies of Harlem. . . . The author tells the story of modern Negro life." The blurb claims too much. There is another, there are many other Harlems. And *the* story of modern Negro life will never be found in one volume, or in a thousand. . . .

Van Vechten has a noted magazine editor comment pontifically on the possibilities of Negro literature:

Nobody has yet written a good gambling story; nobody has gone into the curious subject of the divers tribes of the region. . . . There's the servant-girl, for instance. Nobody has ever done the Negro servant-girl, who refuses to "live in." Washing dishes in the day-time, she returns at night to her home in Harlem where she smacks her daddy in the jaw or else dances and makes love. On the whole I should say she has the best time of any domestic servant in the world. . . . The Negro fast set does everything the Long Island fast set does, plays bridge, keeps the bootlegger busy, drives around in Rolls-Royces and commits adultery, but it is vastly more amusing than the Long Island set for the simple reason that it is *amused.* . . . Why, Roy McKain visited Harlem just once and then brought me in a cabaret yarn about a Negro pimp. I don't suppose he even saw the fellow. Probably just made him up, imagined him, but his imagination was based on a background of observation. The milieu is correct. . . .

Although these are merely the offhand comments of an editor, and

not to be taken too seriously as final critical pronouncements on *the*
Negro, still certain implications are obvious. The best Negro characters for literary purposes are suggested: gamblers, fast set, servant-
girl-sweet-mamma, etc. All are similar in their great capacity for
enjoyment—and it is that side that must be shown. The eternal
playboys of the Western hemisphere! Why even one trip to Harlem
will reveal the secret of their mystery. The connection of all this
to the contented slave, comic, local color Negro is patent. Another
thing to be noticed is the statement issued by the literary market:
Stereotypes wanted.

In *Black Sadie*, T. Bowyer Campbell, whose preference is for the
stereotype of the contented slave of the South, ironically accounts for
the Harlem fad by the desire of jaded sophisticates for a new thrill.
But Campbell does agree in some degree with the Harlem stereotype:
"Colored people demand nothing but easy happiness, good nature."
. . . "Easy come, easy go, niggers," Campbell closes his book, philo-
sophically.

Sherwood Anderson, in *Dark Laughter*, expresses a genuine Rous-
seauism. Hostile toward the routine of industrialism and Puritanism,
Anderson sets up as a foil the happy-go-lucky sensuality of river-
front Negroes, who laugh, with genial cynicism, at the self-lacerations
of hypersensitive Nordics. His "dark laughter" lacks the sinister under-
tone of Llewellyn Powys' "black laughter" heard in Africa. Anderson's
Negroes are too formalized a chorus, however, for conviction, and
are more the dream-children of a romanticist than actual flesh-and-
blood creations. . . .

William Seabrook in *Magic Island* and *Jungle Ways* writes sensational travel tales—according to some, in the tradition of Munchausen
and Marco Polo. He exploits the exotic and primitive, recording
voodoo rites, black magic, strange sexual practices, weird superstitions, and cannibalism. His work brings a sort of vicarious satisfaction
to Main Street, and advances the stereotype. He traces back to original
sources what downtown playboys come up to Harlem to see.

The stereotype of the exotic-primitive would require more than
a dogmatic refutation. Not so patently a "wish-fulfillment," as the
"contented slave" stereotype was, nor an expression of unreasoning
hatred, as the "brute Negro," it is advanced by novelists realistic in

technique and rather convincing, although demonstrably "romantic" in their choice of the sensational. But it would be pertinent to question the three basic assumptions—either insinuated or expressed—underlying the stereotype: that the "natural" Negro is to be found in Harlem cabarets; that the life and character depicted there are representative of Negro life in general; and that the Negro is "himself," when startlingly different in the sensational aspects of his life.

Unwise as it is to generalize about America, or New York State, or even Queens from the Great White Way, it is no less unwise to generalize about Negro life and character from Harlem. It is even unwise to generalize about Harlem, from *the* Harlem shown in books. Strange to say, there is a Harlem that can be observed by the cold glare of daylight.

The exotic primitives of Mississippi levees and canebrakes, of Catfish Row and Blue Brook Plantation are more convincing, as examples of frontier communities, and of under-privileged groups who are known to live violent lives. It is surely not impossible, however, to believe that observers with an eye for environmental factors might see an entirely different picture from the one presented by searchers for exotic-primitive innate tendencies. . . .

ATTEMPTS AT REALIZATION: It would be a mistake to believe that the works of all white authors bear out these stereotypes. Some of the best attacks upon stereotyping have come from white authors, and from Southerners, just as some of the strongest upholding of the stereotypes has come from Negroes. Moreover, the writer of this essay hopes that he will not be accused of calling everything a stereotype that does not flatter Negro character, or of insisting that the stereotypes have no basis in reality. Few of the most apologistic of "race" orators could deny the presence of contented slaves, of wretched freemen, in our past; nor of comic Negroes (even in the joke-book tradition), of self-pitying mulattoes, of brutes, of exotic primitives in our present. Negro life does have its local color, and a rich, glowing color it can be at times. What this essay has aimed to point out is the obvious unfairness of hardening racial character into fixed molds. True in some particulars, each of these popular generalizations is dangerous when applied to the entire group. Furthermore, most of these generalizations spring from a desire to support what is considered social expediency rather than from a sincere attempt at interpretation, and are therefore bad art.

CARICATURES OF MINORITIES

When a minority group either comes in large numbers or is sufficiently segregated to attract attention, when it is unassimilated and offers real or imagined economic competition, ethnocentric beliefs arise and shortly result in the appearance of stage caricatures.

THE PRESENCE of Negroes in the United States, first as slaves and later as freedmen and citizens, has given rise to a long series of popular stage characterizations. . . . The first really great song-and-dance sketch impersonating a Negro was that given somewhere between 1828 and 1831 by Thomas D. Rice (often called "Daddy" Rice or "Jim Crow" Rice) because of his sketch of "Jim Crow." To "Jim Crow" Rice is given the credit for the presentation of the sketches which later developed into American minstrelsy. The origin of the minstrel show was in the singing and dancing of plantation slaves and in the imitation of them by white actors whose blackface songs and skits were popular features in menageries, circuses, museums, and theaters. The Virginia Minstrels and Christy's Minstrels have disputed the honor of having staged the first minstrel show about 1843. This distinctly American form of entertainment, which was well received in England also, reached the peak of popularity between 1850 and 1870. After the Eighties, the decline in the importance of minstrelsy was reflected in the decreasing number of shows. In the 1880's there were at least thirty companies appearing simultaneously; in 1896 there were ten; in 1919 there were but three first-class organizations playing in the United States. . . .

The immigrant has been secondary to the Negro in furnishing comic material for the American stage. Certainly, neither aliens as

Excerpts from Harold E. Adams, "Minority Caricatures on the American Stage," in *Studies in the Science of Society*, edited by George Peter Murdock (New Haven, Conn.: Yale University Press, 1937), pp. 1-13, 15-17, 18-21, 22-23, 24-26.

a whole nor any particular nationality group has given rise to a theatrical production comparable to the minstrel show. Nevertheless, Irishmen, Germans, Jews, and many other nationality groups have been characterized on the stage. Frequently they have been presented in comedies, farces, and revues among numerous other character types; and perhaps much more frequently they have been caricatured in burlesque and in variety and vaudeville acts along with numerous other "turns."

While the English colonists constituted a considerable proportion of the original population of the United States, we have also had English immigrants. Certain types of Englishmen have been carica-tured on the American stage; whether they were presented as natives of England or as our immigrants is unimportant because theater-goers would regard the sketch as typical of both.

Of all the immigrants, the Irish have furnished the most comical material for the stage, standing second to the Negro in this respect. From 1828 to 1859, before and during the early period of minstrelsy, Irish plays and farces appeared in our theaters. The early plays were Irish in scene, full of singing and dancing, and very romantic in theme. Those which came in the 1840's were nationalistic and his-torical, reflecting interest in Irish freedom. In the 1850's native Irish and Yankee characters appeared together in the same plays and thus gradually the interest shifted from the native Irishman to those trans-planted in America.

The important years of Irish immigration were 1840-60, when more immigrants were coming from Ireland than from any other source; 1847 to 1854 were the years during which the greatest number of Irish arrived; and the 1850's were the peak years. This Irish "flood" was, doubtless, influential in the transformation of the stage character and play from glossy sentimentalism to hostility and ridicule.

From 1870 to 1910, the Irish immigrant was caricatured in plays, in variety and vaudeville sketches, and in songs. The Irish types were based upon the immigrants who had arrived in the United States after 1847, and did not represent the earlier arrivals who had become assimilated. Not only Irish ballads (1860's and later), but also "Dutch" slap-stick comedy (in the 1850's) were features of the minstrel olio, and many black-face soloists sang in "Dutch" dialect. The German immigrant appeared on the stage simultaneously with his first great migration to America.

For sixty-five years the comedy displayed at the expense of the transplanted German has come largely over the footlights of the variety and vaudeville stage. . . . The anti-German sentiment resulting from the World War prevented further performances by German type comedians unless their character skits depicted "touching loyalty" to the United States. With the lessening of this feeling against the Germans, in the last few years a number of German type comedians have appeared. . . .

It is difficult to determine with exactness the first appearance of the caricature of the immigrant Jew. The Jewish type appeared in the minstrel in black-face much later than the Irish and German characters, probably in the 1870's. Doubtless the most significant and certainly the most successful portrayal of the Jewish immigrant was *Abie's Irish Rose* (1922). . . . These stories of immigrant life are important not only because they contain comical types, but also because they base their comedy upon the antipathies existing between minority groups and present genuinely American social situations.

The Jew in caricature is still with us. Moving pictures occasionally present him, and certain radio programs regularly include the type. . . . There is paucity of information regarding the theatrical caricature of the Italian immigrant and the same scantiness of information exists concerning Scotchmen, Chinese, Scandinavians, and Greeks. No reference to Slavic types was found. Interest in the Italian immigrant is clearly reflected in the "Mariuch" and other type-songs, such as "Mariuch, She Take da Steamboat," "My Brudda Sylvest," and "Dorando Winna da Race." An occasional Italian organ grinder and accordion player appears in comic sketches in vaudeville and the movies, and the radio infrequently utilizes the Italian type. . . . Chinese types are portrayed in *A Trip to Chinatown* which began its long run, in 1891, and in 1896, Weber and Fields' burlesque, *The Geezer*, thoroughly distorted Chinese, German, and Irish types. Currently, Chinese characters appear in Fu Man Chu's movie murder mysteries, in Charlie Chan's mystery stories, and in Wun Long Pan, Fred Allen's occasional impersonation of a Chinese detective.

The theater, like society, depends upon expediency and follows a "prosperity-policy." . . . The types of stage characters included in this study are inaccurate representations resulting from ethnocentric majority' attitudes.

There is evidence that a half-dozen of the pre-minstrel delineators of Negroes made efforts to portray their subjects with some degree of accuracy. Most significant is the fact that these sketches were of individual Negroes whose eccentricities were so obvious that they attracted attention, or that the Negro traits seized upon were those in which he supposedly varied from other human beings rather than those which he had in common with white people. Yet it is possible that they were represented as typical of all southern Negroes, and it is likely that they were so accepted by the audience.

Evidence of the inaccuracy of portrayal of the Negro is much more abundant in the details of the minstrel show. The costumes were novel artistry and not genuine Negro dress. The burnt cork make-up standardized all Negroes as coal black, and the light circle around the mouth was an extravagant distortion of the supposedly typical lips of the Negro. A few of the pre-minstrel songs, like that of "Jim Crow," had a genuine Negro basis, but most of the minstrel songs did not. . . . The majority of minstrel songs were written by white men and were the product of their imaginations rather than of actual contact with plantation life. . . . A verse of "Old Dan Tucker" attributed to the colored man traits which had been long assigned to the bragging, "rip-roaring" frontier type. And the most extreme unreality occurred when white men in black face sang "Negro" songs in an alleged Irish brogue or dislocated German dialect. . . .

The standard minstrel portrait of the plantation Negro emphasized traits suggested by the adjectives lazy, shiftless, improvident, superstitious, stupid, ignorant, and slow, and those reflected in a fondness for watermelons, chickens, gin, crap games, razors, and big words. This stereotyped picture conforms closely to the concept of the "average" Negro which exists in the heads of many white people today. . . .

The evidence presented makes it clear that the pre-minstrel delineations of the Negro were based on exceptional varieties of Negroes, the oddities of the race, and upon the dissimilarities rather than likenesses of Negroes to white people. Touch up this picture with additional strokes by actors and song writers interested in art rather than reality, and the caricature becomes defined. The minstrel show accepted this misrepresentation and distorted it further, in a manner suggested by the evidence concerning the lack of reality, in the costumes, make-up, songs, dances, jokes, and traits depicting the minstrel Negro. As the minstrel show developed, it increased the distortion. The sources emphasize again and again how it departed more and more from the semblance of reality it had earlier possessed, until it presented a complete burlesque of the Negro.

The minstrel, however, established a type to which most actors have since conformed. Even colored actors ape their white brothers in perpetuating the myth. They sing "coon" songs, joke about "niggers," and accept their success as a gift of the gods. From the passing of the minstrel to the present time, Negro actors, such as Step'nfetchit, variety stars like Cantor and Jolson, and radio acts like those of "The Two Black Crows" and "Amos and Andy" have conformed to the stage type which had slight basis in reality but which conformed to what white people thought the Negro was or should be.

The minstrel show was a poor environment in which to originate German, Irish, and Jewish types because it blackened their characters as well as their faces. The characterizations presented by these three delineators of the Jewish and other immigrants, were sketches of individuals possessing personal idiosyncrasies, and the essence of their comicality was their variant traits. Yet it is fair to assume that theatergoers accepted these characters as typical of their respective nationalities.

Many nationality sketches have been burlesqued very candidly. The staple English low comedy characters of the 1840's were drawn eccentrically even when presented by English actors. Twenty years later, Sothern caricatured the foppish Englishman in "Our American Cousin." His interpretation was so exaggerated that it submerged the action of the play and all the other characters, including a well-drawn Yankee type. Early in the twentieth century, Vesta Victoria became the prototype of a long line of English low comediennes with broad cockneyisms, outlandish dress, and other exaggerations. . . .

Many of the sketches of minorities shown in variety halls, dime museums, beer gardens, and burlesque were very obviously not based on careful studies of immigrants. Their very intent was low comedy, not portraiture.

One actor came to present a great variety of types because the sketches are not based upon a personal study of the actual characteristics of each individual type, but upon stock figures which have become stereotyped. Stage devices like a foreign accent, a red nose, a "chin piece," a "fright wig," a monocle, green clothing, and a black face become symbols which are easily recognized by an audience and promptly associated each with its proper type. Foreign accents, ungrammatical constructions, and mispronounced or misused words are examples both of symbolism and of inaccuracy of type portrayal. An actor using a foreign accent and jumble of American words is immediately classified by the audience as a Jew, Italian, Irishman, etc., although in some cases the identification must be aided materially by other symbols, such as a low-crowned derby, a beard, or an immigrant name, e.g., Fritz, Abie, or Tony. . . .

The stage dialects attributed to immigrants, while containing some elements of truth, are largely products of imagination or necessity; yet they may be accepted commonly by audiences as characteristic of immigrants. The available evidence harmonizes with statements by several authorities concerning the distortion of immigrant characterizations.

That majority Americans have ethnocentric attitudes toward minorities is illustrated by the names they apply to the latter. The English, according to Mencken, having few aliens in their midst, have developed "nothing comparable to our huge repertory of opprobrious names for them." He presents a list of sixty-two names which Americans apply to sixteen immigrant groups. His description of our attitude toward the English, moreover, applies admirably to ethnocentrism as it affects the stage. The stage Englishman is never a hero, and in his role of comedian he is laughed at with brutal scorn. To the average red-blooded he-American his tea-drinking is evidence of racial decay, and so are the cut of his clothes, his broad *a*, and his occasional use of such highly un-American locutions as "jolly," "awfully" and "ripping." . . .

Stereotypes, once they have arisen, become so thoroughly a part of the folkways that it is exceedingly difficult to dislodge them. Ethnocentrism can be based on observable differences, but it matters not whether the peculiarities of minorities are real or imagined; as long as the majority believes such peculiarities exist, their beliefs have as much force as if they had a factual basis. Minorities do have folkways differing from those of the majority, but stage caricatures of minorities are based on many false or exaggerated differences.

The relationship between ethnocentrism and stage caricatures is further shown by the fact that the stage type which is popular at a given time represents the particular population element which is the current subject of ethnocentric obsessions. Early in theatrical history the Yankee and the backwoodsman, who looked down upon and scorned each other, were popular stage caricatures. These were soon joined by the Negro caricature, followed in turn by the sequence of immigrants—the Irishman, Jew, German, Italian, etc. It seems clear that the order of the rise and popularity of the stage types conforms closely to the order in which the respective minorities make their first great impact on the majority. When a minority group either comes in large numbers or is sufficiently segregated to attract attention, when it is unassimilated and offers real or imagined economic competition, then ethnocentric beliefs arise and shortly result in the appearance of stage caricatures. The minstrel presents some evidence in support of this. The first great series of Negro caricatures, which came between 1830 and 1870 and which culminated in the minstrel show, pictured the particular extraneous element that was then dominant. It is quite possible that the passing of the minstrel show in the North resulted from the displacement of the Negro by the immigrant as the central object of ethnocentrism, and that the minstrel lived longer in the South because there were few immigrants there. Harrigan's farces followed closely the period of the great popularity of the minstrel. It is significant that his plays depicted, not the older Irish who had become assimilated, but the recent arrivals who were not, and that, when the latter had absorbed many native folkways and were no longer conspicuous by their alien ways, a revival of Harrigan's farces found audiences unresponsive.

THE SOURCES OF ANTI-SEMITISM

Throughout the history of anti-Semitism the line of attack has changed perpetually. The child is brought up to believe that "The Jews killed our Lord." Later the prejudice is too deeply implanted to fade away. Instead, it is metamorphosed into something else. Crimes more pertinent to the contemporary scene are attributed to the Jews of the modern world, according to individual taste—that they are too nationalist or that they are international, that they are communists or that they are capitalists, that they suffer from an incurable incivism or that they are represented in excessive numbers in public life.

A NTI-SEMITISM did not come into being because some Jews, or even because all Jews, were dislikeable. Its original grounds were religious—not personal, not social, not economic, not political. It was postulated that the people who denied Christ must not be admitted to the free life of their neighbors. From time to time bloody attempts were made to avenge the Passion on helpless groups whose ancestors in a remote age and land were said to have been responsible for it. At present, that line of attack has been completely abandoned— officially, at least; and so little is the "Jewish Problem" conceived on a religious basis that now in Germany even persons whose parents or grandparents or great-grandparents were converted to Christianity, and who are themselves devoted sons of the Church, are submitted to a persecution as ferocious as that directed against their remote kinsmen who profess Judaism.

But throughout the history of anti-Semitism the line of attack has changed perpetually. When religion came to count for less in the life of the Western world, it was brought up against the Jews that they confined themselves to trade and commerce and showed no aptitude for the professions (from which they had been rigorously excluded for centuries). This was one of the principal criticisms brought forward rather more than a century ago, when it was first proposed to confer

Excerpt from Louis Golding, *The Jewish Problem*, (West Drayton, Middlesex, England: Penguin Books Limited, 1938), pp. 12-26.

the rights of citizens upon Jews. A deliberate, and successful, attempt was made by leaders of the Jewish communities to divert their young people from commerce to the professions, with a result which is well known. It later became one of the main charges against the Jews in certain countries that they occupied a place in the professions utterly disproportionate to their numbers.

One asks oneself on what basis is an ethically just proportion to be worked out. Can it be maintained that there are, for instance, too many Scotsmen who are schoolmasters or Welshmen who are miners in proportion to their total number? Is it not natural that Jews should manifest an almost indecent enthusiasm to enroll themselves in those callings from which they had been excluded for so many centuries? Is it not reasonable to assume, does not experience in fact teach us, that such enthusiasms sober down as a community finds its own level with the lapse of two or three generations? . . .

It would be easy to multiply instances of this anti-Semitic inconsistency, the pretext for which changes not merely from time to time but from place to place. In the early years of this century, when Russia was massacring the Jews in the name of Holy Church, German anti-Semites were virulently protesting against the position they had attained in the professions; Drumont, the father of French anti-Semitism, was inveighing against their importance in the world of finance; and in England (where the world of finance was properly respected) certain labor leaders were accusing them of sweated labor and overcrowding in the East End.

Finally, I cannot forbear from instancing the immemorial jibe that the Jews have no appetite to be land workers, hewers of wood and drawers of water. The jibe, of course, ignores the fact that the Jews had been evicted from the land in Palestine, where for a thousand years they had hewn wood and drawn water; where certain Jewish communities, escaping the general doom, have continued to hew wood and draw water during all these subsequent centuries. It is true, of course, that in those lands where Jews were forbidden to own or work land under the most stringent penalties, they did not own or work land. But what happened in those countries where at last the Jews were allowed access to the land? In Russia, for instance, where Jewish agriculturists began to flourish under the old régime, the

May Laws of 1882 uprooted them from their holdings. What has happened in South Germany and the Burgenland we know too well, where there were a number of old-established Jewish farmers, indistinguishable from their neighbors except by their religion. We are witnesses today of a return to the land in Palestine. We are not less witnesses of the towering difficulties which oppose them in every quarter.

The truth of the matter is summarized by Dr. Roth in his invaluable *The Jewish Contribution to Civilization*. ". . . Jewish agricultural settlements exist today all over the world. The total number of Jews throughout the world who look to agriculture is now nearly 700,000; and the number is increasing almost daily. The phenomenon is unique in the world today, where the general tendency is not towards, but away from, the land."

I think I have said enough to demonstrate the inconsistency of anti-Jewish sentiment, which veers round full-circle both in space and time. It is, I think, succinctly illustrated in the old Talmudic story of a certain Roman Emperor, who one day ordered a Jewish peasant who had *not* saluted him to be executed for disloyalty, and the next day ordered another Jewish peasant who *had* saluted him to be executed for pretentiousness.

The Jew, then, is reproached as being now black, now white, now both simultaneously. The Jew knows more clearly than the anti-Jew that there is no logic in these mutually contradictory reproaches. They are attempted rationalizations of historic and widespread prejudice, and it should be possible to trace these prejudices to their source.

In the first place, the Jews constitute, in every country and in almost every city, a Minority. That is to say, they are in one sense or another Different. Here at once is a breeding-ground of prejudice. It will be remembered how unfavorably the Man Who Could See was received in Mr. Wells's *Country of the Blind*. I am reminded, too, of a certain theological seminary in which a myopic delegation approached a new student and asked him, in somewhat menacing terms, why he did not wear spectacles.

Not, of course, that among humans the Jews are alone in being a minority. There are minorities in every country, in every environment, in every group; both religious minorities, such as (say) the

Plymouth Brethren in England; and ethnic minorities, such as (say) the Basques in France. But the Jews happen to be both an ethnic and a religious group. That is to say, those persons who profess the religious system known as Judaism are at the same time distinguished from their fellow-citizens to some extent by reason of the fact that they are Jews by descent—that they belong to the ethnic group known as Jews. It is as though all the Plymouth Brethren in England were descended from Basque refugees, and that all the descendants of Basque refugees in England professed the same distinctive, and not necessarily popular, faith. Their qualifications for unpopularity would in this case be doubled.

Ethnic minorities (one hesitates to use the term "race," now ascribed mystical reverence and a non-existent scientific authenticity) are discernible in many countries. But the Jew is distinguishable by the fact that he is so often a new arrival. Here again one must not generalize too sweepingly. Jews have been settled in Italy (for example) since the second century B.C. without a break, and have been familiar on the Rhineland since the fourth century A.D. at least. Even in England, whence they were excluded from the thirteenth century to the seventeenth, their present settlement dates back for nearly three centuries. Yet the fact remains. Since the first Dispersion, anti-Semitism has been responsible for a constant stream of wanderers from countries of persecution to countries of opportunity, so that most lands contain a greater or smaller proportion of foreign Jews. It is not surprising that strangers from another country are disliked, when we are not at all sure about a visitor from the next parish. "Look, Bill! Furriner!" observed a hero of one of Mr. Punch's most famous drawings. "'Eave 'arf a brick at 'im!" exclaimed his companion, without looking up.

The Jews are in a minority in still another direction. They are marked off from their neighbors, not only ethnically and religiously, but also to a considerable extent vocationally. The circumstances of their history have made of them essentially town-dwellers, and, as town-dwellers, largely confined to certain callings and professions. As I have already suggested, this balance is already redressing itself— apparently, if anything, too quickly. The anti-Semite gets it both ways, on the urban swings and the rural roundabouts.

The Jews, then, are a minority palpable along several lines of demarcation, though their distinguishability becomes less acute as the generations proceed, until at length Jews themselves are often at a loss to distinguish among the company they keep which are Jews and which are not. By that time, unfortunately somewhere the wheel of persecution has turned again, and a new influx of victims once again sharpens the blurred lines. But rooted or uprooted, they are human, pleasant or unpleasant people, or merely negative people, with the customary human gradations.

As, for example, the Scots are—to instance a people whose position in the modern world, or at all events in the British Empire, is in many ways strikingly similar to that of the Jews. They are legendarily imbued with some of the same characteristics so far as money matters are concerned. They have a similar historical background, in which there is a religious as well as an ethnic element. They begin life with the same one advantage—a passionate devotion to education, to secure which parents are prepared to make any sacrifice. And, equipped with this one advantage and a certain degree of ambition, they similarly have to make their way, in many instances, among people of a different background.

The results, with the Scotsman, are more remarkable by far than with the Jew. In journalism, politics, engineering, banking, and some other callings, their proportion is extremely high. The Englishman's newspapers are largely written by Scotsmen. His bank manager is probably a Scot. If he goes on an ocean voyage, there is every likelihood that the engineers responsible for his safety will be Scots. If he is of the same age as the writer of these pages, he will have spent a fair proportion of his days under the tutelage of a Scottish Prime Minister. On reaching the Dominions, he is not unlikely to find himself in a region built up by Scots and ruled by Scots.

And very properly. These men progressed by reason of their ability. They cannot be reproached for lack of devotion, of skill, or of consciousness. No one in his senses will attempt to regard this remarkable advance on their part as a menace, or will speak about the "Scottish Problem" simply because Scots do not refrain from making the fullest use of their natural abilities. True, people did once. In the middle of the eighteenth century, there was a dangerous anti-Scottish agitation in London, and even the great Dr. Johnson was as unsparingly anti-Scottish as he might have been anti-Jewish. That prejudice, a less formidable one though comparable in its causes, has died down. It is not quite imbecile to hope that some day the other will be dead, too.

For there have been similar minorities before. In England, in the first half of the eighteenth century, there were the Huguenot refugees, who had left France for conscience sake on the Repeal of the Edict of Nantes by Louis XIV. They were a religious minority, for their mode of worship differed from that which generally obtained in England. They were an ethnic minority—Frenchmen, who at the beginning did not understand the language of the majority of the population. They engaged in distinctive economic callings—they were export merchants, bankers, and above all weavers, whose skill was largely instrumental in establishing one of England's staple industries. And precisely the same accusations were brought up against them as have been brought up against the Jews. They were dirty, it was said; they overcrowded; they reduced the standard of living; they deprived the honest English workman of his job, or reduced his wages. So similar indeed were the accusations brought up against the Huguenots and allied Nonconformists at this period, that some of the pamphlet literature published against them was reprinted almost verbatim a hundred years later as propaganda against the Jews.

The reason why the prejudice against the Huguenot refugees of the eighteenth century did not survive into the nineteenth is, simply, that the Huguenots themselves barely did. They found themselves in a sympathetic environment; they were, on the whole, well treated; and there was no unsurmountable religious barrier between them and their new neighbors. Hence they were assimilated rapidly. They advanced in social status; their descendants intermarried with the noble families of the country; they entered into the peerage. Simultaneously, their Churches were gradually abandoned. At long last, there was little left but a number of magnificently endowed charities (which, it is said, render the fact of being a Huguenot orphan one of the most lucrative of all possible professions in this country) and a group of families who pride themselves on their romantic origin in a fashion which would have sounded ludicrous two hundred years ago.

The Jews, on the other hand, considered as a group, have refused to surrender their identity. They believe that the religious system evolved by their fathers retains its value to the present day. They feel that the religious prescriptions and the folkways evolved during the long centuries of their history have an importance of their own. They have ideas of decency in personal and even national relationships which have behind them the force of three millennia of history. They cherish the ideas of universal peace first enunciated by Isaiah. They are the heirs to a noble religious tradition—old already at the time when Jesus was born, and in fact basic to his own teaching. And (whatever individuals among them may do or think) the Jews, as a group, consider that this priceless religious heritage is not lightly to be surrendered. . . .

Incidentally (though Zionists consider this to be more than incidental), the Jews, unlike most other minorities, are nowhere a majority. They have no nucleus settled on the soil in their own country; they have no Government which can intervene or protest on their behalf; they have not the moral satisfaction of knowing that somewhere in the world there exists a land which is theirs, and from which no power on earth can exclude them. Even were the Zionist experiment in Palestine to be overwhelmingly successful, it would be out of the question for the Jews ever to constitute, as the Germans do, a power which, from the physical point of view at least, is great, and which is prepared to intervene vigorously to prevent discrimination, real or fancied, against its nationals in other lands.

For the Jews are a minority which is, in so far as it is Jewish, without roots in any independent land. They have, in fact, all the disadvantages of a national minority, without any of its advantages.

Thus the Jews combine all the qualifications for misfortune. Not only are they a minority. They are simultaneously a religious minority, an ethnic minority, an economic minority. And, above all, they are an easily distinguishable minority. It has been said that the part played in English economic life by the Quakers is out of all proportion to their numbers: that during the past century and a half they have taken an exaggerated share in many walks of life, amassed a very high degree of wealth, and exercised a disproportionate weight, not only in the progress of various movements, but also in the affairs of the country. If that is so, few persons are aware of it, for the Quaker names are Barclay, Bevan, Hanbury, Gurney, Richardson. No one, as he walked through Lothbury, would pay much attention to such names, or shudder at the idea that such a tiny handful of the population could exercise so great a weight in its financial affairs. If instead of such names he read Cohen, Levi, Rosenberg, Isaacs, his reactions, I fear, would be more emphatic.

If a man is jostled by a hook-nosed individual on the Underground, who may, in fact, be of Tartar or Roman extraction; if a firm with which he does business, with a purely Slav name, goes bankrupt; if he finds that a political cause which he particularly dislikes is championed by an, in fact, completely "Aryan" partner in an historic banking firm; if his slumbers in his club are disturbed by a voice which he suspects of being slightly guttural, he thinks of the offender immediately as "a Jew," and of all Jews as being in those same ways lamentable.

We all know of the admirable old system by which a prince of the blood royal was never punished by his tutor, as his person was too sacred to be molested. Instead, a Whipping-boy was appointed, upon whose unoffending posterior the prince suffered vicarious punishment. The function of the Jew is not unlike this. He is the Whipping-boy of history.

A word must be said here regarding the history of it [anti-Semitism] in the individual. The Jews are singled out adversely, for censure and for obloquy, in the education and training of the ordinary child. Careful teachers may qualify it, but all too often it is taught in school, it is repeated in conversation, it is proclaimed from the Pulpit, it is reiterated in readings from the Gospel, it is echoed in literature, that Jesus Christ was killed by "the Jews"; that is, that "the Jews" were responsible for the greatest of all crimes in history.

No palliation or explanation is admitted. It is not pointed out that, at the time of the Passion of Jesus, the Jews were under Roman rule and could not pronounce a death sentence. (They had virtually abolished the death penalty, it seems. A rabbi of the next generation asserted that a court which pronounced a death sentence once in seventy years was a "tribunal of murderers." And even when the Jews had the power of capital punishment, it could never be carried out on a Friday, the day of Jesus's death.) It is not pointed out that the main incident on which this collective accusation rests—the mob surging round Pilate and crying: "His blood be on us and on our children!" is regarded as legendary by Christian scholars; nor that at the time of the Passion of Jesus the Jewish party in authority was a Romanized group of aristocrats, false to every Jewish tradition and playing only for their own safety. It is not pointed out that the historical gospels exclude from all participation in the arrest, trial, and crucifixion the religious leaders of the people, the creators of modern Judaism—the Pharisees. (The last mention of Pharisaic contact with Jesus in Matthew comes in Chapter xxii. 41; the narrative of the plot against his life begins in Chapter xxvi. 3; the last contact in Mark is in Chapter xii. 1. In Luke the last contact is in Chapter xvi. 14; the narrative of the plot begins in Chapter xix. 47. To Christian readers for whom the word "Pharisees" is identical with "hypocrites" or "whited sepulchers" it might also be pointed out that the Epistles of St. Paul are saturated with Pharisaic teaching, as great Christian scholars like Travers Herford and George Foote Moore have recognized.) It is not pointed out that, in any event, only a minute portion of the Jewish people, a long time ago, can have been involved.

No. Elementary education admits of no half-colors, and the child is brought up to believe that "The Jews killed our Lord." Later on, he may have to read Chaucer's "Prioress's Tale," and Shakespeare's "Merchant of Venice," not to mention countless incidental allusions scattered throughout English literature, and rarely counteracted by any work of popular appeal which presents a more favorable picture.

Thus the child grows up with a prejudice early implanted in his mind. The Jewish schoolchildren with whom he mixes can bear witness to its strength and virulence, and to the fact that the query: "Who killed Christ?" is not intended academically. Later on, his attitude may alter. He may no longer believe all that he was told at school. He may not even adhere to the fundamental tenets of Christianity. But the prejudice is too deeply implanted to fade away. Instead, it is metamorphosed into something else. Crimes more pertinent to the contemporary scene are attributed to the Jews of the modern world, according to individual taste—that they are too nationalist or that they are international, that they are communists or that they are capitalists, that they suffer from an incurable incivism or that they are represented in excessive numbers in public life.

There, alas, the prejudice is, first in the mind of the child, then in the mind of the man, sometimes a rationalized prejudice, sometimes a prejudice that repudiates all rationalization.

THE JEWS UNDER THE NAZI REGIME

An enumeration of the measures, legal or extralegal, adopted by the Nazis against the Jews as a background for the more publicized violent outbursts, makes it plain that there has been no turning back but a relentless march toward the total elimination of German Jewry.

FROM TIME to time outbursts against the Jews in Germany, or repressive laws and decrees directed against them, have been given publicity in the world press, but in the intervening periods comparatively little has been heard about the treatment of the Jews under the Nazi régime. A widespread belief prevails that during the intervals between the publication of such laws or the occurrence of such outbursts the German Jews led a comparatively secure life. The facts are very different. Those who have studied the position of the Jews under the Nazi régime realize that apart from short periods in 1934 and at the beginning of 1935, and possibly during the Olympic Games in 1936, the German Jews have been constantly harassed and persecuted ever since Hitler came to power.

By enumerating the measures, legal or extra-legal, adopted by the Nazis against the Jews (as a background for the more publicized violent outbursts, which we do not mention here), in chronological order, it will be made plain that there has been no turning back but a relentless march toward the total elimination of German Jewry.

1933.

As soon as Hitler came to power the Jew-baiting started, particu-

Excerpt from "Twentieth Century Ghetto," in *The Living Age* (April 1939), pp. 154-160.

larly after the elections of March 5, 1933, had given Hitler's Government (although not the Nazi party alone) a bare majority. During the first few weeks individual actions were taken against Jews, many being killed or beaten. The first Government-sponsored action was the general boycott of Jewish concerns, Jewish lawyers, and doctors, and so on, on April 1. On account of the shaky economic position of Germany in 1933, this boycott was confined to one day, but soon the Government began to take legal measures against the Jews.

April 7.—A new Civil Service law was issued dismissing all non-Aryan officials (this term embraced, in addition to civil servants proper, teachers, university professors, judges, public prosecutors). Ex-servicemen and those who held their jobs before August 1, 1914, were excepted. On the same day a law was issued debarring non-Aryan lawyers, the same exceptions being applied as in the case of officials.

April 22.—Non-Aryan doctors were deprived of their panel practice, which in Germany is the backbone of most medical practices, the same exceptions being applied as in the case of officials.

April 25.—A law was issued creating a *numerus clausus* for Jews in secondary schools and universities. Exceptions were made for the children of ex-servicemen.

June 2.—A decree expelled dentists and dental surgeons from panel practice under the same conditions as medical doctors.

June 30.—A new Civil Service law stipulated that no one who was not Aryan or was married to a non-Aryan could be appointed a civil servant in the future. No exceptions were made for ex-servicemen.

In June prominent Jewish musicians and singers of the State Opera House were dismissed.

July 11.—It was made known that the private health insurance companies had decided to exclude from their service all those non-Aryan doctors who had been excluded from panel practice.

July 12.—It was made known that the Labor Front, which replaced both the trade unions and the employers' organizations, had adopted the Aryan paragraph.

July 13.—The organization of the film industry excluded all non-Aryans from employment in films in any capacity whatsoever.

July 14.—A law was issued enabling the Government to revoke naturalizations granted between November 9, 1918, and January 30, 1933.

September 29.—A new Peasants' Law was issued decreeing that no one who cannot prove his and his wife's Aryan descent back to 1800 can become an hereditary farmer.

October 4.—A new Journalists' Law was issued preventing non-Aryans from continuing to work as journalists, except on purely Jewish newspapers. The Minister of Propaganda was entitled, but not compelled, to make exceptions in favor of ex-servicemen.

In November, Dr. Goebbels issued a decree concerning the membership of the newly founded Reichskulturkammer, which entitled the Minister to exclude anyone whom he does not consider suitable. Exclusion from the Reichskulturkammer means total exclusion from any activity in the spheres of art, music, theater, literature.

1934.

March 14.—The Minister of Defense adopted the Aryan Clause for the Army.

June 11.—The Aryan Clause of the Civil Service Law was extended to teachers in private schools.

August 16.—Hitler's deputy, Hess, issued an order to all Party members to avoid any contact whatever with Jews.

November 8.—Minister of Education published list of books to be used in the schools for instruction in the Jewish question. These books included the notorious forgery, *The Protocols of the Elders of Zion.*

1935.

April 17.—The Minister of the Interior decreed that in the future no licenses for dispensing chemists should be issued to non-Aryans.

April 24.—A decree by the President of the Press Chamber provided that nobody who cannot prove his or his wife's Aryan ancestry back to 1800 may be in any way connected with publishing activities.

May 21.—The military conscription law provided that Jews cannot serve in the forces, and non-Jewish non-Aryans cannot rise above the rank of private.

In the early summer a great propaganda campaign against the Jews was organized throughout the country, Streicher traveling from town to town, urging the boycott of Jewish shops and the prohibition of mixed marriages and extra-marital relations between Jews and non-Jews.

July 2.—It became known that a law court had upheld a registrar's refusal to marry a non-Jew to a Jewess, although no legal prohibition existed.

July 15.—Anti-Jewish riots occurred in the west of Berlin; Jewish shops were damaged.

July 16.—The Secret Police announced that many Jews and non-Jewish women had been arrested for "racial disgrace," although there was no law prohibiting such relations.

September 10.—A decree by the Minister of Education provided that by the Easter term, 1936, all Jewish children would have to be removed from the elementary schools and special Jewish schools established.

September 15.—The Nuremberg Laws deprived Jews of the rights of citizenship, of the right to hoist the German flag, prohibited marriages between Jews and German Aryans, and made extra-marital relations between them a criminal offense. On account of the loss of citizenship, all those Jewish officials who had been exempted from dismissal in 1933 were now dismissed. The same applied to notaries.

October.—Jews were excluded from the ordinary Winter Relief organization. They were permitted to establish a special Jewish Winter Relief organization.

1936.

March 26.—A decree compelled Jewish dispensing chemists to lease their businesses to Aryans by October 1, 1936.

July 13.—The Postmaster General decided that the privilege of free telephones for war-blinded ex-servicemen did not apply to Jewish war-blinded ex-servicemen. (A similar decision applied to free radio licenses.)

October 27.—The first Jewish-owned firm was expropriated. The Berlin Suhlerrifle factory was taken over, without compensation, by the Nazi party. The banking account of the owners was confiscated.

1937.

January 1.—Jewish labor exchanges closed by Government decree.

May 15.—Jews, as well as anyone married to a Jewess, were excluded from the ex-servicemen's organization.

June 11.—A law court in Königsberg ruled that the word "Jew" applied to a non-Jew was a grave slander.

During 1937 a drive was started to expel Jews from trade and commerce. Many Jewish business men were forced by police pressure to sell their businesses to Aryans. Others were forced to do the same through the cancellation of mortgages, the withdrawal of leases, decisions of trade organizations not to supply them with goods, and so on. Whole branches of trade were thus purged of Jews.

1938.

January 1.—Jewish doctors who, as ex-servicemen, still retained their insurance practice were given three days' notice by fourteen insurance companies.

A decree concerning gramophone records prohibited all music by Jewish composers or performed by Jews.

February 6.—An amendment to the income tax law canceled allowances for children in the case of Jews.

March 30.—Jewish communities ceased to be regarded legally as bodies.

March to June.—The annexation of Austria led to various outbursts against the Jews. Jews were forced to do menial work. Many were driven to suicide, thousands were arrested. Nazi commissars were placed in control of Jewish businesses. Many of the arrested Jews were compelled to sell their concerns for next to nothing, against a promise of release. Thousands of Jews were expelled from frontier districts in Burgenland and Styria, many of them driven over the frontier without passports and made to camp, in some cases for weeks, in no-man's-land.

April 26.—All Jews possessing more than 5,000 marks were compelled to register their possessions with the Government. All real estate belonging to Jewish religious communities, which had hitherto been exempt from land tax, was to be taxed.

May 17.—A circular by the currency authorities ordered that emigrants might take their personal belongings with them without special permission only if they could prove that they were acquired before January 1, 1933.

May 19.—A circular by the Lord Mayor of Berlin decreed that Jews might in principle be treated only in Jewish hospitals.

May 23.—The Nuremberg Laws were declared valid for Austria.

May 31.—Mass arrests of Jews in Berlin.

June 14.—A decree was issued compelling Jews to mark their shops conspicuously.

June 20.—Jews were excluded from stock exchanges.

July 10.—A new decree expelled Jews from various trades, such as the real estate trade, bureaus supplying information, guides for foreign tourists, marriage brokers, itinerant trade, firms supplying watchmen.

July 10.—Government decided to withdraw from Jews all licenses to act as commercial travelers and agents.

July 22.—All Jews were compelled to obtain a special identity card.

August 2.—A new law expelled all Jewish doctors including ex-servicemen, from the medical profession, only a limited number of Jewish healers being permitted to treat Jewish patients only.

August 18.—A law compelled all Jews to adopt Jewish first names.

October 15.—All Jews, including ex-servicemen, were expelled from the bar, and only a limited number of Jewish consultants admitted for Jewish clients only.

November 10.—At 2 A.M. an anti-Jewish pogrom started in all German towns; synagogues were set on fire, all Jewish shops and stores demolished, thousands of Jews arrested.

November 12.—A law forbade Jews, as from January 1, 1939, to own retail shops, delivery businesses, or to work as independent craftsmen. The damage done during the pogrom had to be repaired by the Jews; insurance claims were forfeited in favor of the Government; the Jewish community was required to pay a fine of 1,000,000,000 marks, roughly $415,000,000.

November 12.—Jews may not possess any kind of weapon. Infringement of this regulation will be heavily punished.

November 12.—A decree by Dr. Goebbels excluded Jews from concerts, lectures, dances, theaters, cinemas, and so on.

November 14.—The Minister of Education barred all Jews from elementary and secondary schools, universities, and other high schools.

November 16.—An ordinance of the Führer deprived Jews of the right to wear army uniforms.

November 24.—Second decree was issued on the registration of Jewish property.

November 28.—A police order was issued restricting the appearance of Jews in public to certain districts and to certain times. Those violating regulation were to be fined up to 150 Reichmarks or sentenced to imprisonment up to six weeks.

December 2.—All Jewish property in the Sudeten German areas was required to be registered.

December 3.—The Reich Minister of Economics issued a decree regulating the utilization of Jewish property, exercising full control over the sale of Jewish enterprises, real estate or other Jewish property.

December 4.—Jews were prohibited to own and drive automobiles. All Jews were required to surrender their driving licenses.

December 12.—A decree permitted Jews going abroad to take along objects which are not absolutely necessary for personal use only with the consent of the proper authorities; this measure did not apply to foreign Jews.

December 14.—The Reich Trustee of Labor received power to appoint managers for Jewish-owned enterprises. Jews were forbidden to be assistant managers.

December 28.—Establishment of new Jewish clothing firms was prohibited. Butchers were arrested for kosher slaughtering.

December 29.—A decree limited purchases by Jewish concerns; Jewish physicians were barred from private insurance company boards.

1939.

January 1.—Every Jew was required to add the name of Israel or Sarah to his own name.

February 10.—Aryan landlords were required to report to official offices all dwellings free of Jewish tenants or those to be vacated in the future.

February 11.—Herr Funk ordered compulsory "Aryanization" of Jewish patent and other protective rights, including copyright.

February 15.—Seventy per cent of the "Aryanization profit" in trade and industrial enterprises and 100 per cent in real estate accrued to the Government.

February 16.—A decree was passed by the Reich Minister of Economics concerning the use of compulsory measures for the removal of Jews from commercial enterprises.

February 23.—A decree was issued by Field Marshal Hermann Göring, Commissioner for the Four-Year Plan, to the effect that all German or stateless Jews must surrender before March 7 all jewels and other objects of gold, silver or platinum as well as all diamonds, pearls and other precious stones. Violation of decree was to be punished by fines or imprisonment.

February 25.—The Jewish community in Berlin received orders from the police to produce daily the names of 100 Jews who then will receive two weeks' notice to leave the country.

THE PSYCHOLOGY AND PSYCHO-PATHOLOGY OF RACE PREJUDICE

From early childhood the white man is accustomed to look down upon the black as a member of the servant class, as one who definitely occupies an inferior status in the same system. The white child tends to regard the black as a menial by nature, an inferior to be looked down upon with feelings of superiority and contempt. The black man may readily come to represent in the mind of the white man that very aspect of his own Unconscious with which the latter is in a state of conflict. This may account to some extent for that morbid fear of miscegenation that pervades so much of the background of the European race attitude. The anxiety felt for the future of the white group may be partly the result of a fear of revenge on the part of the black man. The white man who projects his own hostility onto the black man comes to fear that hostility as a threat directed against himself.

EVEN A SUPERFICIAL analysis of the typical attitudes of the white to the black reveals it as a very complex attitude which expresses itself as a blend of superiority, dislike, hostility, contempt, fear. Further, we know that it is an attitude which is acquired. The factors which have been operative in bringing about the attitude may

---

Excerpt from I. D. MacCrone, *Race Attitudes in South Africa* (London: Oxford University Press, 1937), pp. 259-263, 287-290, 298-302, 308-310.

have occurred so early in the experience of the individual, for instance, in early childhood, that they can no longer be recalled; secondly, where through suggestion so much is done to develop the attitude, the individual may readily overlook the operation of certain factors; while, finally, some of the factors may be of such a nature that they are repressed, since the individual is not willing to admit that they play a part in affecting his attitude. . . .

In the first place, we have factors derived from the past contacts between white and black and transmitted to the present generation. Rightly or wrongly, the interpretation of such contacts emphasizes, especially in school textbooks and in popular tradition, the fact of violent conflict between the two races. Massacres of unsuspecting whites by savage blacks in this country, tales of bloodthirsty savages perpetrating outrages on parties of innocent white men, women and children, form the staple of the accounts of the first contacts between white and black presented to the younger generation and excite emotional reactions in the minds of those who know of them merely by hearsay which have no small effect on their subsequent attitude as adults. Especially among the descendants of the Voortrekkers and that section of the white community who cherish their traditions, the influence of this factor is still of considerable importance. A trace of this influence may be seen in the fact that no native is allowed to possess firearms, that the rifle is the privileged possession of the white man and that, in the last resort, it is that weapon which may be relied upon to settle any dispute between white and black. Although no one in his senses anticipates a revival of armed conflict between white and black, any isolated outbreak of violence does excite intense emotional excitement in the minds of the whole community, some of which is undoubtedly due to the operation of the factors mentioned above. Of some importance, also, for our theme was the fact that a daily paper in Johannesburg endeavored to increase its sales by issuing on two occasions within a week alarmist posters announcing further violent conflicts. Finally, it may be noted in this context that, whenever bloodshed accompanies these conflicts between white and black, the worst offenders are frequently found to be unauthorized local civilians with firearms, who consider that they are justified in turning them against anyone with a black skin.

Secondly, we find that our present economic, political and social structure invariably tends to lay upon the black the stigma of inferiority. From early childhood the white man is accustomed to look down upon the black as a member of the servant class, as one who definitely occupies an inferior status in the social system. The black man is at the beck and call of anyone with a white skin, his freedom of movement is restricted by pass laws and all the menial, unpleasant and irksome tasks are performed by his labor. From the point of view of the white man, his one supreme function is to perform the "dirty" work of the white community. The result of such a system is, of course, unavoidable. The white child growing up in such a community inevitably tends to regard the black as a menial by nature, as an inferior to be looked down upon with feelings of superiority and contempt. Hence, there can be no question of comradeship between the white and black, for that implies a feeling of equality between the two, which is rendered impossible by the present social system, while any pretension to such equality on the part of individual members of the black community is either regarded as ridiculous, or, where it has some foundation in fact, excites excessive hostility, as we see in the case of the educated native. We are only too familiar with the attitude due to the association between the black and the functions which he performs in our community. Any kind of manual or menial work is "Kaffir" work, unfit for the individual who has had the good fortune to be born with a white skin. In the same way and by a similar process of association, a "dirty" stroke in a game of tennis is called a "Kaffir" stroke, while a decent person who "plays the game" is a "white" man even if he is a "nigger."

No one could blame a visitor to our large towns if he came to the conclusion that all our convicts are black men, for whilst everywhere we see black convicts in prison garb at work in public places, black convicts being marched through the streets in charge of warders, the white convicts (of whom there must be some) are conspicuous by their absence. The ordinary white individual in South Africa, it is true to say, hardly ever sees a white convict. Here, again, we have factors at work which undoubtedly shape the attitude of a typical member of the white community toward the black, for they tend to excite fear of the black man, especially in the minds of unprotected white women and children. It is no exaggeration to say that this fear is never really absent from the minds of many white women and girls, and that it is so widespread as almost to constitute a kind of "mass" neurosis. The black man is always the villain of the piece, whether in real life or on the stage or cinema—to the small child he is the "bogey" man, who may haunt his imagination even when he is no longer a child.

A fourth group of factors affecting the attitude of the white to the black are of a pseudo-scientific nature. The native is regarded as a child in mental development. Lacking as he does the cultural equipment of the white man, he comes to be regarded as one who is incapable of acquiring that equipment. Hence arises the belief that the native is innately inferior in intelligence and lacking in a sense of responsibility. In some cases the strongly marked negroid features— thick lips, heavy jaw and broad, flat nose—and bodily odor of the black, reinforce the belief that he belongs to a lower human order, as well as excite a feeling of repulsion.

The wholesale imitation of the white man on the part of the black is regarded by the former as a further proof of his own innate superiority. Where we find imitation giving rise often to incongruous results, the white man not only despises but also ridicules. Thus, the sight of a native girl smoking a cigarette, or of letters written in poor English which are so often quoted as good jokes, not only enhance the white man's feeling of superiority, but also tickle his sense of the ridiculous. Again, the native is often made an object of ridicule as evidenced in a small way by the use of names such as "Snowball," "Sixpence," etc., given to him by the white man.

Finally, we may group together all those factors which serve as a barrier preventing genuine social intercourse and prohibiting understanding between white and black. In any case, we would not expect the white man in view of his attitude to learn the language of the black, and this fact alone, apart from other considerations, makes a sharing of emotions, beliefs and ideas impossible between members of the two races. Insofar as there is a common language between white and black, it is confined to the trivial and external affairs of the outer life of the two races—their inner and intimate affairs, a knowledge of which might lead to mutual understanding, remain unknown and both races, though in daily contact, lead a life remote from, and inaccessible to, the other.

The combined effect of all the factors so far mentioned is the formation in the mind of the white man of an image, or picture, of the black race, as such, which determines his attitude to the individual members of that race. The white sees a member of that race, not as an individual personality like himself, but as a representative of an alien group, whose most striking characteristics are an inferiority in intelligence and knowledge, an inferiority in standard of living and occupation, a tendency toward violent and criminal practices, a behavior which is childish and often ridiculous, in short, the opposite of all those qualities which form the image which the white man has in mind when he thinks of his own group. In spite of the numerous exceptions in both races, it is these images or concrete ideas strongly charged with emotion which determine the attitude of the white man both to members of his own group as well as to members of the alien group. . . .

In the South African context, and with regard to the social contacts between white and black as members of two widely divergent groups who at the present time occupy a very different social status relative to one another, any kind of social contact on a basis of genuine social equality is quite out of the question. For the representative European, even although his attitude toward the native may be favorable, the Bantu are literally a *terra incognita* of which he is quite content to remain in ignorance. Since he has become conditioned to one set of social situations in which the native is always found occupying an inferior status, he proceeds in his contacts with the native to deal with him in accordance with the social habits of his own group. The differences in the physical appearance, behavior, and habits of the native as a member of a socially inferior group, develop an attitude of aloofness and superiority on the part of the European. Not for him to take his turn after a native in a queue at the railway station, bank, or post office, or to travel in third-class carriages on a train journey, or to attend the same places of entertainment, or to be served at the same restaurant (although natives traveling on the railway in specially reserved first- and second-class compartments may be provided with a meal in the restaurant car, at the discretion of the chief steward and after the European passengers have been served), or to shop at the same establishments. The native and all his ways are relegated to a subordinate position, and social contacts are reduced to the minimum required to make the social structure function. Any closer or more intimate contact either bewilders or irritates the European, who concludes that the native must have a different and, therefore, an inferior mentality to his own.

The association between the native and his status has led to the development of a wide range of conditioned reactions on the part of the European. The term "Kaffir," which is still in widespread use (especially in Afrikaans), has become the conditioned stimulus to a great variety of emotional or visceral reactions to situations in which the native appears in some form or other and always in a derogatory sense. Since the prevailing social habits and attitudes all presuppose this association, they necessarily continue to foster it. Although resolute efforts are being made in more enlightened circles to break down the association, the process of unconditioning is likely to be a lengthy one, and for some time to come of a purely superficial nature so far as the bulk of the European population is concerned. The fact that there is a small, though appreciable, development of a class of educated natives while, on the other hand, whites are being employed on an increasing scale in manual work, such as road making and repair, which until a few years ago was only performed by natives, appears to show that the beginnings of such a process are already at work. . . . We may well inquire whether the increasing improvement in the status of a minority of the natives will provide a sufficiently potent stimulus to neutralize the effects of the present system, in which, broadly speaking, a minority of whites is striving to maintain itself at the apex of a pyramid, the base of which is composed of a majority of blacks. In order to do so, the stimulus provided by this minority would have to become prepotent, that is, it would have to give rise to effects which are more intense or more satisfying than those which are being produced by the existing social system. Otherwise the improvement in status may only have a qualifying effect, or may have a directly opposite effect to that which might be expected on *a priori* grounds, by appearing as a threat against the existing status of the whites.

The black man, who has hitherto always been identified with the savage or uncivilized person (so much so that "black man" and "savage" are in popular speech synonymous expressions), is regarded as living a life which is largely free from the conventions and restriction of the civilized or white person's life. In order to conform to the demands of his social environment, the white man has to repress those animal or primitive impulses which he believes find free expression in the behavior of the black man or savage. Of these impulses, the erotic or sexual impulse, with its various component elements, is by far the most important. It is the impulse whose control and direction constitute one of the main problems in the life of the civilized individual. It involves a constant process of renunciation, that is, of repression, and the development of a censorship so rigid that it can be evaded in many cases only in the disguised forms of dreams and neurotic symptoms. Toward one's own unconscious impulses the conscious attitude is one of hostility and repulsion. Under these circumstances the black man may readily come to represent in the mind of the white man that very aspect of his own Unconscious with which the latter is in a state of conflict. It is not surprising, therefore, to find that the hostility that is felt on other grounds by the white man toward the black is reinforced by a hostility derived from a source of which the individual himself is quite unconscious and which he would probably be the first to repudiate.

To some extent this view appears to be confirmed by the differences in attitude, both of certain groups as wholes and of individuals, to which attention has often been drawn. The differences in attitude toward men and women of color, for example, which are alleged to distinguish the Anglo-Saxon and the Latin groups may be due, in addition to a great variety of other causes, to a difference in their attitude toward sex, so that where a greater tolerance exists in the one case we may expect to find it correlated with a greater tolerance in the other. On the other hand, where social inhibitions and taboos severely restrict the gratification of sex appetites, we may anticipate a more severe color-prejudice as the result of greater sex intolerance. In a Protestant, and more particularly in a Calvinistic and Puritanical, society where sex and sin are synonymous, the intolerance in both cases is likely to be the most intense of all. When we turn from the attitudes of groups to the attitudes of individuals, there can be little doubt that the white prude, whether man or woman, is more than likely to be found displaying an intolerant or hostile attitude toward the native, since the very obsession with sex against which prudishness as a reaction formation may be expected to lead to such a result. . . .

The universal belief that natives indulge their sex appetites more freely and more promiscuously than do Europeans may, or may not, have some foundation in fact, but there can be little doubt about the effect of this belief upon the attitude of the representative European toward the native. Native life, native customs and practices, and, above all, the sexual life of natives, exercise a perennial fascination upon the mind of the white man and woman. This "call of the wild," this urge to return to nature, this tendency to regress to the unrestrained gratification of primitive man and woman, serves as a constant pull upon the civilized, or, more strictly speaking, partially civilized man and woman "to go native" and to throw aside the restraints of civilization. In actual life, as well as in the "wish" world of novel and drama, this theme is repeated with endless variations. The immense popularity during the post-war years of native, or negroid, music and dances in America and Europe was another expression of the same phenomenon. If, as we suggest, the attraction is derived from a sexual source, its influence will extend far beyond a directly sexual interest in the native. But, before we go on to deal with this aspect of the sexual factor and its influence upon the white man's attitude toward the native, a further consideration of the more directly sexual aspects is necessary in order to appreciate these indirect effects. Thus, in addition to the widespread belief that natives enjoy a freer sexual life, we also find a general belief to the effect that native men are more virile and sexually more potent than white men, while native women are more voluptuous and have more "abandon" than white women. From the crudely sexual point of view, it would appear that the native female as well as the native male might exercise an even greater attraction upon the white man and white woman than partners of their own race—an attraction which would be still further enhanced by the lure of novelty and the very contrast in skin-color. If we add to this the fact that, in many cases, men as well as women of a socially superior class find a more complete sexual grati-fication in intercourse with those who belong to a socially inferior and despised class, it is not surprising that the very idea of such intercourse between white and black should appear as a form of perversion and, therefore, revolting to the normal white man and white woman.

There is sufficient evidence on record to show that sexual inter-course between white and black, and more particularly between European men and native women, is of fairly frequent occurrence in spite of the strong social disapproval which it arouses, not only in the white community but among many members of the native com-munity as well, while cases in which white women have seduced native men or boys are not unknown. Where, as in such cases, the sex factor threatens to override the barriers which are ultimately based upon the resistance to sex itself, social disapproval with its powerful sanctions is obviously not enough, and has had, in fact, in South Africa to be supplemented by a law according to which illicit or extra-marital sexual intercourse between white and black has been made a crime.

If the general point of view from which we have so far dealt with the problem of sexual attraction is accepted, then the indirect effects upon the attitudes of white men and women, apart altogether from the direct effects which are relatively simple and straightforward, of such an attraction are bound to be of considerable psychological significance. They may account to some extent, for example, for that morbid fear of miscegenation that pervades so much of the back-ground of the European race attitude, and which sooner or later finds expression in the question: "Do you want your daughter or your sister to marry a black man?"—one of the implications being that white women would have no hesitation in so doing and, in fact, would readily do so once there was genuine social equality between white and black. . . . The same effects, no doubt, also inflame the emo-tions excited by crimes of rape committed by natives against white women, while similar crimes of white men against native women are to a large extent either ignored or regarded with indifference.

In all such cases, the very excess of the emotional reactions aroused leads us to suspect that they are the results of factors which have nothing to do directly with the situation itself. Since the actual situation does not appear to justify such emotional violence, we are obliged to find some other explanation and to look for its source in the individual himself.

When we turn to the sources of anxiety which may affect the race attitudes of members of the white community in South Africa toward the native, the most obvious appears to be the great numerical preponderance of black over white. The significance of this fact may be exaggerated, but it does excite emotional reactions in which vague fear and anxiety are conspicuous. As a consequence, the attitude in question is affected in a way which is not present in the case of attitudes toward other groups with which it has much in common, such as the attitudes toward the Cape Colored and toward the Indians, both of whom are minority groups. Thus the fears of "being swamped by blacks," of the "rising tide of color," of the differential fertility of white and black, which have led more than once to alarmist predictions even in responsible quarters, are all readily excited in minds that are prepared to accept them. How real the threat of the superior numbers of the native both within, and beyond, the borders of the Union is felt to be may be gathered from its influence upon the defense policy and the military organization of the country, which, according to a recent declaration of the Minister of Defence, does not exclude the possibility of an armed conflict between white and black. Military training and equipment, like so many other blessings of Western civilization, are so far as possible to remain a monopoly of the white man as the trustee of that civilization.

So much for the objective source of anxiety which, whatever its importance, can hardly be regarded as a sufficient explanation for the entire fund of anxiety, especially when, as at the present time, the supremacy of the white man is absolute. A remote contingency by itself could hardly be sufficient to have such a powerful effect unless it served at the same time as the conductor for anxiety derived from other, less obvious sources. Some of these have already been mentioned, and it is not improbable that contact between white and black may tend to aggravate them. Thus the past record of the white man's treatment of the native, as well as the present relations between the two groups, are not such that they can be regarded with entire equanimity even by the most self-complacent white person who is not completely blinded by race or color prejudice. In that case the anxiety felt for the future of the white group may be partly the result of a fear of revenge on the part of the black man. The white man who projects his own hostility onto the black man comes to fear that hostility as a threat directed against himself. Bearing in mind what has already been said about the role of the black man in the white man's Unconscious, we may conclude that some of the hostility felt by the white man is of that sadistic kind in which a fusion of the aggressive and erotic impulses comes to be displaced upon the man with a black skin. In that case the hostility represents an indirect gratification of impulses which leads directly to the development of a sense of guilt or fear of punishment by the white man's own Super-Ego and hence to an increase in anxiety. But this increase in anxiety will only exacerbate hostility, so that we have a vicious circle in which hostility and anxiety, as alternately cause and effect, reinforce one another. The more or less neurotic man and woman, whose own internal conflicts are only partially overcome, tend to externalize and project them in the form of a conflict between white and black, so that the mental conflict of the individual becomes the paradigm for a racial conflict. Again, the black man who, according to popular belief, gratifies his impulses more freely than the white man, is an object of envy, and, therefore, of hostility. Since he symbolizes the repressed impulses within the white man's own (black) Unconscious, such expressions as the "rising tide of color" and "being swamped by the blacks" may have more than a merely rhetorical significance for the neurotic individual who finds them emotionally so disturbing. Hence, an anxiety which is induced, in the first place, by the pressure of repressed impulses comes to be attached to the black man or black group in the form of a typical phobia or anxiety hysteria.

In his attempt to deal with, and to master, an anxiety whose main sources are subjective, the white man employs the same mechanisms in his treatment of the native as are characteristic of the conventional neurotic. Thus we find displayed in the social attitudes of members of the white group toward the native those very features of aggression and repression, of segregation and isolation, of projection and phobia formation, which represent so many duplications of the defence mechanisms of the neurotic individual. The extra-individual conflicts between the two racial groups are but the intra-individual conflicts within the mind writ large, and until the latter are removed, reduced, or modified, they must continue to exercise their baleful influence upon the race relations and the race contacts of white and black in "sunny" South Africa.

9

DILEMMAS OF DOMINANCE

FOR ALL their ruthless procedure and extravagant pretensions, majorities are not altogether unaware of the repercussions of their regimes. From time to time they face the situation realistically, sometimes at minority insistence, and make concessions. As governments, they also support auxiliary agencies of placation and remedial aid that work in behalf of the damaged minority life and interests. All of which shows an awareness of the dilemmas of the situation and some recognition of the moral responsibility involved in dominance.

Imperialist regimes particularly face such situations, for a peculiarly violent and disruptive type of relationship develops, as has been observed, when the life of a society is regulated from the outside, particularly when a new civilization is superimposed. In the first stages of improvised penetration and exploitation, wide-scale damage was done to these cultures. Missionary and governmental agencies have begun to realize the extent of this damage, and for mixed motives, some humanitarian and others selfish, have sought to slacken the force of the direct displacement of native cultures and the complete undermining of minority morale. In some instances, governments have attempted to rebuild a foundation of native customs and sanctions for cultural reconstruction. A more liberal and more scientific approach to the whole problem has combined with the bitter experience of the comparative failure of force acculturation to bring about the realization that many of the native cultures represented seasoned adaptations to their environment, and may be better suited to it than is the superimposed civilization. In some quarters, missionary and others, there was deep disillusionment with the superficiality of native Christianity; in many instances the enforcement of the Christian codes had accomplished the reverse of their intentions by uprooting native moral sanctions and not effectively replacing them. European clothing had augmented disease and, as was indicated by Pitt-Rivers, had complicated sex morality. European manufactured goods had broken down native crafts and skills. In terms even of European values and interests, the negative results were increasing.

At this stage, but only rather recently, there commenced certain reversals of governmental policies, such as the French extension of the assimilation program to her newer African dependencies, a reform colonial administration in the Belgian Congo, the "indirect rule" program of native co-operation devised for the British administration in Nigeria but since extended to a few other colonies, and most characteristic of all—the Mandates policy and system. The latter definitely professed tutelage and trusteeship as the dominant aims of colonial government, though with no compulsive machinery beyond annual reports to a League of Nations' *Mandates Commission.* The new policy of the United States Bureau of Indian Affairs for the tribal rehabilitation of the North American Indians still on the reservations is a late but promising offshoot of this same movement. Reform missionary policy also now seeks to study native pagan cultures and to build a program of Christianization based on the favorable elements of native law and custom. These are indications of enlightenment in the direction of European-non-European group relations.

Yet they are comparatively recent and on a small scale, when the total extent of colonial contacts is considered. Previously there was no attempt whatsoever at the preservation or even the correct evaluation of alien cultures and native institutions. Mere divergence was taken to mean inferiority and undesirability. That tradition of total cultural superiority still remains as a standard tradition and policy to which the movements mentioned are regarded as experimental exceptions. With this professed humanitarianism of a "mission of civilization" and for the advancement of lower cultures on the one hand, and with practical objectives of continued dominance and economic profit on the other, imperialist regimes are confronted with an almost unresolvable dilemma in their cultural policies. They, therefore, vacillate between a program of assimilation and one of cultural separatism.

Hutt's article discusses this dilemma as it applies in South Africa.

The average white South African thinks the Bantu native is either unfit for a share in the life of modern civilization or capable only of participation on its lowest economic level as an unskilled agricultural or industrial laborer. But Hutt shows that the natives are gaining a foothold in the economy of the invader's culture. He documents the development of the Africans as skilled workers, generally, and as successful traders and peasant land producers in West Africa and other sections where the economic system and the sparse settlement of the whites permits. In South Africa itself, the prolonged even though restricted contact with the patterns of European life has resulted in partial cultural transformation. The necessity for the use of native labor, Hutt believes, dictates increased contact and augmented acculturation. Even a restricted system of native education has already brought large sections of the native population to a level that can be favorably compared with the Voortrekkers—the pioneer settler-farmer forebears of the white population. But that modicum of progress has already produced opposition from the typical colonial, who faces the alternatives with distrust and conservative dissatisfaction.

Intermarriage, and its more frequent substitute—miscegenation, raise what is probably the most acute of the dilemmas of European-native relations. The half-caste seems to be an inevitable and formidable phenomenon in the large-scale contact of diverse races and cultures. There can be no doubt about the origin of this social dilemma: the European makes the half-caste and then by his attitude of racial exclusion, makes the half-caste problem. For the half-caste's hybrid character and his paradoxical status come not from his mixed blood but from his divided social heredity. In spite of his potential role as a carrier of culture and an intermediary of culture fusion and exchange, the half-caste is usually caught in the no-man's land between conflicting cultures and opposing groups.

Although there is always this common denominator problem to the social situation of the mixed blood population, there is no solid front of majority cultural policy. The very diversity of policy in this respect reveals the dilemma the white man confronts, if he is to maintain his traditional policy of caste superiority. In some situations, concessions are made, granting the half-caste intermediate status as a group more privileged than the full-blood native. But this semi-recognition results ultimately in a situation painful to the half-caste, since he is denied complete identification with the whites although he has assimilated much of their tradition and values, and is, by the very fact of his buffer-class position, resented by the subordinate group. As Dover points out, he tends to form a distinct and rather isolated social group, with increasingly unsatisfied ambitions and no fixed loyalties. Under the conditions Dover is observing—the situation of the Eurasian half-castes, his conclusion is that their lot, after a generation or two, is gradual submergence with the bulk native group. He notes, though, that this has not always been so, even in British India, where the majority prejudice has been unrelenting. In Indo-China the Eurasian's predicament is not so hard; for there the liberal French policy of inter-marriage has brought measurable cultural recognition to the assimi-lated Franco-Annamite. Between this and the rigid British exclusion of the half-caste is the somewhat intermediate situation produced by the semi-lenience of the Dutch in their areas of colonial control—the Dutch East Indies. The Dutch, however, maintain special schools for Indo-Europeans; so over most of the Eurasian zone, the half-caste lives as a marginal group, paying the price of European racialism. It should be noted in passing that in the considerable areas of Islamic society, the half-caste does not constitute a social problem, and never has, for his humanity is at par under their more tolerant system.

The other horn of the half-caste dilemma is represented by the policy of lumping the half-caste with his native group ancestry. This more militant exclusiveness throws the half-caste back on the sup-pressed group, to become, at first, a disgruntled and uncompensated outcast, but eventually in the course of cultural accommodation, the yeast of the forward advance of the entire native group in its cultural counter-offensive. The consciousness of his affinity with the privileged group and his resentment of his social treatment give the half-caste this inevitable militancy after he has once recovered from his initial cultural disorientation. These two divergent policies represent, in the main, the Latin and the Anglo-Saxon policies of race, the one pivoting its prejudice on its own form of culture and advocating assimilation, the other standing fast on separatism and advocating in its social organization, bi-racial institutions. These two traditions reflect them-selves respectively in the contrast of the race codes of South and

Central America with that of the United States. According to their historical cultural affiliations with the Latin or the Anglo-Saxon traditions, the various islands of the West Indies are similarly sharply divided in their racial attitudes.

Stonequist, who reviews the position and cultural role of the mulatto in the United States, where the Anglo-Saxon precedents have been rigidly, almost fanatically followed, finds that even under the handicap of exclusion from cultural privilege, the mulatto group has functioned typically as a "marginal Man," bridging the cultural gap between the majority and the minority groups. Historically, because of his more favored frontage on the majority culture, the mulatto, he finds, has played a constructive role in Negro group advance. In its strict exclusion policy, the majority has hurled a boomerang, so to speak, against their cultural barrier, having chosen to confront the minority without a buffer class. Pierson, on the Negro in Brazil, reports on the mulatto under the Latin system. Here, after a few generations, during which the half-caste group got separated quite far in advance of the underprivileged blacks, the general policy of assimilation has spared society in general any "race problem" as such. The blacks, even though still concentrated more heavily in the low-pay economic groups, have not experienced racial stigma and cultural restriction beyond their class handicap. They, therefore, do not constitute a self-conscious minority, and individual blacks have at all times risen to positions of merit and public recognition, according to individualized circumstances. Brazil's racial policies, indeed, set a model in the pattern of race relations.

These broad comparisons of the mulatto under differing racial policies, both agree on certain fundamental points. They show that race mixture is an inevitable consequence of the contact of races, that it occurs in spite of severe legal prohibitions and social ostracism, and that the half-caste, despite transitional cultural difficulty and maladjustment, plays, on the whole, a positive constructive role in the cultural situation. Either he serves to liberalize the situation by relaxing the racial tension, which ultimately benefits the full-blood population, or he is instrumental in leadership which facilitates the cultural advance of the handicapped racial minority. Under both circumstances, the half-caste is a focal point of cultural interchange. As a culture type, he is only regarded as negative and undesirable by the culture "purists," whose position, we shall see in the next section, is not sustained either in progressive scientific theory or by careful sociological observation. Ironically enough, the purist tradition is the one theoretically maintained most usually by those segments of the majority who stand self-contradicted in practice by the facts of miscegenation.

Racial and other group intermixture is not as exceptional as it is generally thought to be. Though cultural exogamy is seldom welcomed, even when legally permitted, it does occur frequently. Contrary to the current belief that group attitudes have remained constant against it, Stern's historical sketch of intermarriage and its legal sanctions, shows it to have fluctuated considerably from period to period. Intermarriage has often been historically interdicted between groups that now intermarry freely; occasionally the trends reverse and prohibition takes the place of previously favorable sanction. The basis of the barrier tradition changes repeatedly, at one time following religious, at others racial, or other sectarian lines. Race mixture also occurs with frequency across legal and other customary barriers of proscribed intermarriage. Finally, though still a contentious intercultural issue, intermarriage is itself decidedly on the increase because of the widespread contacts and secularization of modern forms of culture.

The primary prejudice operating in these situations is cultural, and Stern finds it to have its highest incidence in relatively solid, homogeneous social groups. Its primary factors of change, then, are those tending to break up the solidified type of community. Modern economic and political trends, tending to do just this, are normally solvents of the provincialism on which cultural prejudice thrives. Apart from marital relations, there are several serious aspects of cultural prejudice operating in the social rather than the political sphere. The problem of the immigrant is the most important of these. Indeed immigration, especially in a country like the United States, that has experienced so much of it and from such a wide variety of ethnic and national sources, is bound to supply a crop of intercultural problems.

There is, in the first instance, the question of majority regulation of immigration access to the society, then that of the reception that the migrant himself receives, and finally the later problem of cultural assimilation and its dilemmas. Several of these issues are more appropriately treated in their contemporary aspects (Part V); but here the factor of majority control needs passing consideration. Hourwich submits this factor to a searching analysis. He shows how a majority bias has developed historically in the American descendants of immigrants against the late-comers. About this cultural prejudice there has grown up a justifying legend that the type of old immigrant was superior to the more recent immigrants from Southern and Eastern Europe. Hourwich cites contemporary descriptions of the old immigrants and what their condition and cultural level was both before and considerably after their coming to America. The record smashes the legend, and gives no backing to the still popular view that the early immigrants were "accessions of strength" and those of today "accessions of weakness." America's city slums have seen a succession of tenants in order of immigration precedence; it has been an ethnic parade of one foreign minority group after the other, struggling in a squalor and penury for which American conditions have been co-responsible for an economic foothold in the new land. American nativism is in large part, therefore, unwarranted culture prejudice, and puts the native-born with a distant immigrant background in the position of historical inconsistency. His unawareness of this is, perhaps, one of the factors that, properly corrected, might possibly liberalize the current generation's mounting prejudice against the contemporary immigrant. In the light of the past history of America and of its basic tradition of being a democratic haven of the ambitious and the oppressed, the growth of this exclusionist attitude confronts the country with a dilemma that may induce a serious crisis with regard to its fundamental institutional policy.

WHITE DOMINANCE IN SOUTH AFRICA

The sons of the present settlers will find it difficult to fit into the curious economic situation we may expect to develop. Conflicting tendencies in current policy are reflected in the educational sphere. This arises from an attitude towards natives of repression tempered by reluctant liberalism or liberal-sounding formulas. The "upward march" seems to be trumpeted with the proclamation of each new restriction. Some real or apparent concessions are necessary to allay discontent.

POLITICALLY and socially [the Bantu] natives are a subordinate class. In social life public opinion ordains that natives shall be regarded as a class apart. In this respect they must be grouped with all non-Europeans. Social segregation has to be strictly upheld by politicians, for practically all uneducated Europeans cling religiously to it and their attitude is widely reflected even among persons of education and culture. Most native leaders tactfully conform to the abhorrence of the dominant race; their people are humbly courteous to whites, all of whom they conventionally address as "boss." We find thus a severe taboo on eating, traveling, or conversing as equals with persons of different skin pigmentation. Rationalized by play on the horror of miscegenation and fostered by economic interest, this has far-reaching effects on the possible range of non-European employment. It makes it extremely difficult to delegate to natives any authority over white men, even those of the lowest type. It is, indeed, usually impossible to get members of the two races to work side by side unless the white man can securely feel himself to be the "boss." There is nothing surprising, therefore, in the natives forming an economically subservient as well as a politically and socially despised race. This has made it easy for the conviction to arise that the inferiority is a natural one, that owing to an innate lack of ability to follow the occupations or share in the life of modern civilization, the

Excerpts from W. H. Hutt, "The Economic Position of the Bantu in South Africa," in *Western Civilization and the Natives of South Africa*, edited by I. Schapera (London: George Routledge and Sons, Ltd., 1934), pp. 198-203, 204-205.

native is inevitably doomed never to rise above the level of "put and carry work."

The belief is a delusion. We have the evidence of what has been accomplished in other parts of Africa where the absence of a white laboring class had enabled the rapid progress of those who, a few years ago, had been living the life typical of the most primitive tribes. We find, for example, in West Africa and parts of the East African territories native mechanics, bricklayers, printers, carpenters, and locomotive drivers. We find also that in that environment the native not only acquires an efficiency comparable to that of the European artisan but he tends to acquire their characteristics. He becomes ambitious and is moved by what we are accustomed to think of as normal incentives in civilized communities. We must notice also that in those parts of Africa in which the Europeans form an administrative and capitalist class only, the native appears to have developed all the characteristics of the typical independent peasant proprietor. In Southern Rhodesia and Kenya, where the proportion of Europeans to natives is about one to two hundred, it is unlikely that the laboring and artisan classes will ever contain many non-natives. These areas will probably become "White Man's countries" only in the sense that they will be able to support a considerable white upper and middle class. There will be no motive on the part of capitalists to attract artisan labor from overseas except as instructors. It may be that "The sons of the present settlers will find it difficult to fit into the curious economic situation that we may expect to develop." If so, it is likely that they will emigrate. The self-interest of the ruling classes there will, in all probability, lead even to clerical workers ultimately being recruited from the natives' ranks. The repercussions of developments in the North cannot fail to exercise a profound influence upon the aspirations of the same races within the Union. Many South Africans do not like to think about this.

The truth is that the native, as he is, is the product of an environment and his own tradition. But he is now in contact with the environment that has produced the modern European and we see him breaking rapidly with tribal traditions. The fact that "centuries of effort" have gone to produce the cultural heritage of white communities does not justify the very usual inference that the accumulation of social tradition or knowledge on which it rests cannot be rapidly handed over. An invention which has taken years of investigation and experiment to create may be capable of effective utilization by all and sundry. South Africans are obsessed by the fear of a native population nearly three times their size coming to approach them in material welfare and outlook. They realize the inevitable political consequences of economic equality and are distressed by the thought of those whom they have been brought up to regard as their servants becoming their equals or superiors. But by this time it is becoming increasingly recognized that the tendency for the modernization of the lives of natives is too strong to be prevented. All that those realists who fear and deplore the movement can hope for is the power to exercise some check or brake on the rate of advance. They will say that their aim is to secure an "orderly march," a phrase which might suggest that their conscious object is actually the fostering of assimilation by natives of white traditions and standards. Now when it is pleaded that the "haphazard advance" of the native must be prevented we have to recognize two sets of grounds for the argument: firstly, that which recommends gradualness in the interests of the native; and secondly, that which frankly admits that the protection of his competitors is the motive. *Prima facie* there does not seem to be much plausibility for the view that rapidity of development militates against the native's advantage. After all, the advance will follow from free choice on the part of individuals. Maladjustments in development are surely more likely to arise from restrictions on individual initiative in social change. For quite apart from the scope which freedom gives to trial and error and the cumulative experience which it breeds, the greatest plasticity in institutional innovations will not be achieved by enforced uniformity. The sheer strength of conservatism in the tribal life and outlook is probably an adequate safeguard against undue haste. It will be a minority of Bantu who will be rapidly progressing at any time. There is nothing resembling a conscious forward movement on their part as a whole. The State, controlled by capitalistic interests, has largely encouraged them through taxation and in other ways to enter into the white man's economy, whilst hardly recognizing that such is the inevitable effect of their policy. Probably the majority of natives leaving the reserves for the first time are reluctant and homesick. In so far as their progress is due to *voluntary* choice it is the individual native who is the cause. He is slowly becoming aware of new possibilities through contact with the knowledge, resources, and opportunities of the Western world. He may be regarded as seeking the fuller life that these opportunities offer. The adoption of more developed economic forms has been spontaneous and orderly but not "planned." It has been a response to competitive capitalism which Europeans introduced; but it has not been deliberately fostered by white authority. On the contrary, what has been accomplished has been in spite of considered resistance. . . .

Many natives who fall below the economic standard of "civilization" are a long way ahead of many white people from the standpoint of culture, intelligence, or physique. There are, it is true, several Bantu tribes who are still in a most raw state; and it would not be misleading to say that among natives as a whole illiteracy, ignorance, and gross superstition are common. About two-thirds are illiterate today. But we do not think of the peasantry of pre-War Russia or eighteenth-century Ireland as "uncivilized." If we made a comparison between them and the modern Bantu, clothing would be the most relevant distinction; and that is largely a matter of climate! The great hordes of natives who flock to the mines today would probably compare not too unfavorably with the Irish hordes that were attracted to England during the early nineteenth century. Christian feudalism and pagan communism produced contrasting social forms; and Western and Bantu cultures are very different. Yet as they are today they cannot be usefully opposed by the words "civilized" and "uncivilized." The natives' food, clothing, laws, customs, superstitions, and economic standards generally are different. That is all we can say. Even from the point of view of material culture it is probably correct to say that apart from the amount of meat available, the state of many natives in the reserves compares not unfavorably with that of the Voortrekkers. Tribal traditions do not render them unfit for town life although naturally the adjustment is not always easy. As urban dwellers they are remarkably law-abiding and well-disciplined, in spite of a legal code which makes criminal offenses of infringements of petty regulations. . . .

The private advantages of a knowledge of English are clearly recog nized by the natives themselves who are prepared to make strenuous efforts to learn to read. One of the main attractions of the towns is said to be the possibility of obtaining education. Where schools are denied to them we find adult men getting together in groups and teaching one another the arts of reading and writing. Parents will make great sacrifices to get their children into schools. But conflicting tendencies in current policy are reflected in the educational sphere. This arises from an attitude toward natives which those not brought up in the South African tradition are apt to regard, perhaps quite unfairly, as one of repression tempered by reluctant liberalism or liberal-sounding formulas. The "upward march" seems to be trumpeted with the proclamation of each new restriction. Some real or apparent concessions are necessary to allay discontent in the depressed class and to supply an ethical justification. The native, we are told, must be released from his laziness, for the white man needs his labor; he must be taught better agricultural methods, for that will delay his drift to the towns; he must be taught hygiene, for epidemics are no respecters of races; but he must not be encouraged to be anything but a native. If education should lead to the complete disintegration of tribal traditions, it is thought likely to cause him to think for himself as the white man's equal. This attitude is giving emphasis to a wide-spread desire to substitute Bantu tongues for English as the medium of instruction, and some move in that direction has already taken place. Moreover, there is a multiplicity of native tongues whose persistence is an effective barrier against the emergence of any common Bantu culture or unity. And solidarity among them is not welcomed.

It is almost universally admitted today that some education must be provided for natives, in spite of the common belief among those who employ them on *simple* labor that it "spoils" them. The belief is that it detracts from their servility or respectfulness and makes them less inclined to work on farms or in the mines. A little education has this effect simply because it gives them wider alternatives. It enables them to do messenger work, for example; the ability to read and write is a great advantage even to house-boys and those who do cleaning work in shops and stores; and these occupations are usually preferred by those who can get them. But there is one form of education that is practically withheld from the Bantu—that is, systematic instruction and apprenticeship in skilled trades. Some provision has been made for training them as teachers, clerks, nurses, agricultural demonstrators, and so forth, but for industrial occupations, for which they are peculiarly suited, the State at any rate has given but scanty facilities.

THE ROLE OF THE HALF-CASTES

A characteristic of the half-caste is a tendency to form distinct ethnic groups socially allied to the ruling classes. On the whole prejudice prevents social identification with the white and they are inclined to be submerged in the numerically preponderant stocks.

BOTH RADICAL and related miscegenation are much more extensive than is commonly supposed, not only between white and colored populations, but also between the colored peoples themselves, the millennia over which the processes of fusion have been spread resulting in so inextricable a mixture of racial elements that it is no longer possible to speak with precision of pure and hybrid populations. Today there are no half-castes because there are no full-castes.

The attributes and status of marginal communities are essentially functions of their physical and social environment, and not of Divine displeasure or some mysterious incompatibility of "blood," a fluid which has nothing to do with informed social discussion. Certainly, there are disharmonic and socially maladjusted individuals in such communities. Perhaps, too, their incidence is higher than it is among more integrated groups, though that remains to be proved, but they are susceptible to the same methods of improvement that are applied to "pure" peoples. . . .

The most significant characteristic of half-castes, from the Creoles and Cajuns of Alabama to the polyglot crosses of the Pacific, is the tendency to form distinct ethnic groups socially allied to the ruling classes, but inclining to submergence in the numerically preponderant stocks. This isolation is usually maintained for considerable periods,

Excerpt from Cedric Dover, *Half-Caste* (London: Martin Secker and Warburg, Ltd., 1937), pp. 138-140, 166-171, 266-267.

the cultural endowment of the economically successful stocks being perpetuated long after their physical legacies are no longer discernible. Miscegenation therefore plays an important part in cultural diffusion. . . .

In the early days of the British insinuation into India, Eurasians were referred to as "half-castes," "mixed bloods," "countryborns" and "members of the mixed races," and appear to have accepted these terms without protest. By the beginning of the nineteenth century, these names definitely acquired the value of epithets rather than descriptive terms, and in 1825 the community therefore organized a meeting at Calcutta, which resolved that "East Indian" was the "most appropriate and applicable designation." It was not universally used, however, the term "Indo-Briton" being more popular as it suggested blood relationship with the ruling class.

A few years previously (1813-1823) the term "Eurasian," attributed to the Marquess of Hastings, had been sporadically used, and in fifty years it had become so general that the Association founded by E. W. Chambers in 1876 adopted it as a communal designation. Unfortunately, it soon came to have a derogatory implication, which the Eurasians sought to elude by appropriating the label "Anglo-Indian" from the resident Britishers who had invented it for themselves. In 1897, the Secretary of State for India was petitioned by a deputation, led by J. R. Wallace, to give official recognition to the filched cognomen, but that dignitary remained unimpressed. Undeterred, the energetic doctor founded on his return "The Imperial Anglo-Indian Association," rhetorically declaring that "Britishers we are and Britishers we ever must be. Once we relinquish this name (Anglo-Indian) and permit ourselves to be styled "Eurasians" or "Statutory Natives of India" we become estranged from our proud heritage as Britishers."

The reward of these patriotic exercises was the publicly expressed sarcasm of Lord Curzon, then Viceroy of India, and the neglect of the euphuistic appellation outside the community itself. But Lord Hardinge authorized its use for the Indian Census of 1911, and it is now officially employed without being universally recognized, though it is beginning to find favor in print, often with the satirical qualification "new style." Moreover, it has not released the Eurasians from their statutory definition as "Natives of India," nor their occupational definition as "European British Subjects." The political subtlety of these terminological anomalies exposes "Anglo-Indians" to utilization according to official convenience. As natives they are excluded from certain British privileges, while as European British subjects they enlarge the British electoral and military strength, and are prevented from orienting themselves to complete acceptance of their statutory position.

The transparent diplomacy of this situation has recently been emphasized further by giving Eurasians of direct European paternity the definite status of European voters, leaving those whose European paternal connections are more remote to vote as "Anglo-Indian Natives of India," while those who derive their white ancestry from the maternal side are regarded as natives without qualification. The members of many Eurasian families therefore share with some of their West Indian allies the curious privilege of being able to exercise their vote in different constituencies. . . .

A growing Eurasian population is now separating as a marginal community in Hongkong. Twenty-five years ago, mixed breeds on the island sought alliance with, and were accepted by, the paternal groups, chiefly Chinese, British and Portuguese, a large number classing themselves as Chinese, though paternally allied to the British, to avoid prejudice and gain economic opportunity. In this way, Eurasians became the leaders of the local Chinese, and even today many of the most eminent Chinese in Hongkong, such as Sir Robert Ho Tung, are of mixed descent.

With the growth of the Chinese national spirit, however, and the educational progress of pure Chinese possessing the bilingual advantage of the Eurasians, it began to be felt that the Eurasians "should no longer be classed as Chinese, or at any rate as the leaders of the Chinese community, and the exponents to the British of Chinese thought and sentiment." And one must add to this explanation the factors for Anglophily and communal divisions that have always been created by the growth of British colonization.

Since the [World] War, the Eurasians of Hongkong have therefore found it politic to ally themselves more with the British, many changing their Chinese and Portuguese names to facilitate this ambition. But, on the whole, prejudice prevents social identification with the whites. So they are growing as a separate group along the lines of Eurasians elsewhere, though they still retain a closer connection with the natives than the Eurasians of India. . . .

Northward, in Shanghai, the Eurasians are also relegated to a marginal status, but it is said that they are being absorbed in the very heterogeneous population of that cosmopolitan city. The Hanbury School, originally established for Eurasians, has been recently consolidated with the municipal schools for Europeans, but a Eurasian Mission and Sunday School remain, along with other signs of group organization. The unusual beauty of many Eurasian women in this area undoubtedly favors the processes of absorption.

Elsewhere in China, as in every important port from the Aegean Sea to the Behring Straits, groups of Eurasiatics are springing up, but little is known about them and they do not appear to create problems like the usual Eurasian communities do. Since the Revolution, the Russians, who have always mixed readily with Mongoloid peoples from their Chinese frontiers to Alaska, have been diluting Mongolian "blood" on an unprecedented scale, both within and without the Soviets. In the Manchurian Railway Zone, for example, hordes of white Russians resident there have been compelled to accept the living standards of the Chinese, and it is estimated that the resulting relations have already produced more than 60,000 children of Sino-Russian origin. Within the Soviet Union itself, I have found it impossible to obtain information on the enormous amount of miscegenation which is proceeding there, as it is not regarded as a problem.

In areas under French and Dutch administration in the East Indies, Eurasian communities of considerable size flourish under official encouragement and the absence of any significant color bar. In the Netherlands Indies, however, social tolerance does not extend to alliances between Dutch women and native or Indo-European men as it does in the French colonies, where white women freely avail themselves of this broader ethnic sanction. The results of this attitude are shown in the status of the Franco-Annamites, who often rise to posts of authority, and are generally regarded as socially efficient and physically able by French officials and anthropologists who have been concerned with them. On the whole, however, they occupy the position of an intermediate group used for maintaining the machinery of local exploitation along more tolerable lines than is evident in India.

In the Dutch East Indies, too, the Eurasians form the backbone of colonial administration. They trace their origin to the Portuguese occupation of Java early in the sixteenth century, and form a vigorous and cultured group. They resemble the Eurasians of India closely in physical and cultural characteristics, which is not surprising since the Javanese have a pronounced Indian heritage, but they are socially more effective. This advantage is partly due to the fact that their numerical strength (175,000-200,000 according to A. Vandenbosch) is more concentrated and relatively greater, but also to official encouragement, which has enabled the Indo-Europeans, as they are called, to deal more successfully with the factors that determine the deterioration of an intermediate people, particularly those concerned with the progress of native education and competition, and the growth of a resident white group.

Early in the nineteenth century, the Dutch Government realized the political consequences of allowing an established and loyal community to slide down the social scale through declining economic privilege and the absence of compensating opportunities. In India, at about the same time, the astute Lord Canning anticipated the folly, from the imperialistic viewpoint, of a similar situation. A very few years, he wrote in 1860, "will make it (the Eurindian community), if neglected, a glaring reproach to the Government. . . . On the other hand, if cared for betimes, it will become a source of strength to British rule and of usefulness to India."

But, whereas Lord Canning was a prophet crying in the wilderness, the Dutch went wisely beyond prophecy. They saw that many Indo-Europeans had already lost their communal identity in the *Kampongs*, on which lack of education and economic foundations had thrown them, while a further leakage was created by successful parents sending their children to Holland, many of whom never returned. (It is said that there are now 20,000 Indo-Europeans in The Hague alone.) And in the remaining majority the signs of social decline were unmistakable. The obvious measures for arresting the decay were to guide a part of the population into agriculture and industry, to provide poor-relief and additional official appointments for the lower classes, and to organize an institution which would rekindle hope and help to hold the social mores together. And the obvious was not neglected. . . .

In 1886, a technical school was opened at Batavia, and soon after special provisions and credits enabled Indo-Europeans to obtain and work agricultural lands. In the 'nineties, the *Indische Bond* attempted, with the active encouragement of the Government, to co-ordinate and expand Eurasian efforts to explore new economic fields. . . .

It was not until the Indo-Europeans accepted the necessity of co-operative existence that they began to adjust themselves to the changing social complex, though the previous efforts of the Government must have strengthened their struggle. This revised outlook came after the War, when "The Indo-European Bond," which concerned itself only with Indo-Europeans and not the poor whites as well, arose out of the ashes of the previous organization. Its outlook and measures were comparatively radical. It asked for and received financial support as sound investments, and not as charitable evidence of ethnic sentiment. It runs a journal and stimulates communal endeavor in every sphere. It has created the capital for establishing numerous scholarships, a large general relief fund, several schools, and an excellent agricultural colony, *De Giesting,* in South Sumatra, which is recognized and supported by the Government as an important economic venture rather than a conciliatory means of showing paternal responsibility. And, in contrast to other Eurasian Associations, its membership includes a majority of the Indo-European population.

The undeniable success of this organization testifies to the greater than British wisdom of the Dutch Government in its policy of assisting Indo-Europeans "to attain and maintain by their own exertions a field of their own social life." But it has not been able to secure an undivided allegiance to Dutch imperialism. Already, the Indo-European community is "showing signs of an Indonesian orientation," this new nationalism, which is part of a world movement against imperialistic domination, being strengthened by economic disabilities, such as the denial of land ownership and the abolition of special salary and other official privileges, and the lack of complete cultural integration with the ruling class.

THE MULATTO AS A MARGINAL MAN

The American mulatto group does not function as a buffer group as in South Africa. Neither is it an outcast group like that of the Eurasians of India. Instead it is merged into the Negro people and contributes to its leadership.

THE SIGNIFICANT feature of the American problem is the unwillingness of the white man to make any distinction between mixed bloods and full bloods. They are all classed as "Negroes." Even the man who cannot be distinguished from the purest Nordic is a "Negro" if it is known that he has a Negro ancestor or one drop of "Negro blood." . . . To a realist it appears that America can afford to practice this extreme racial policy, since the whites constitute nine-tenths of the total population, whereas in South Africa the Europeans are in the minority and the support of every white or part-white man is needed. The American mulatto group, therefore, does not function as a buffer group as in South Africa. Neither is it an outcast group like that of the Eurasians of India. Instead, it is merged into the Negro people and contributes very largely to its leadership.

This fact is of fundamental significance in understanding the general characteristics of the American mixed blood. He is not the dejected, spiritless outcast; neither is he the inhibited conformist. He is more likely to be restless and race-conscious, aggressive and radical, ambitious and creative. The lower status to which he is assigned naturally creates discontented and rebellious feelings. From an earlier, spontaneous identification with the white man, he has, under the rebuffs of a categorical race prejudice, turned about and identified himself with the Negro race. In the process of so doing, he suffers a profound inner conflict. After all, does not the blood of the white

Excerpts from Everett V. Stonequist, *The Marginal Man* (New York: Charles Scribner's Sons, 1937), pp. 24-27, 110-112.

man flow in his veins? Does he not share the higher culture in common with the white American? Is he not legally and morally an American citizen? And yet he finds himself condemned to a lower caste in the American system! So the mulatto is likely to think to himself. Living in two such social worlds, between which there is antagonism and prejudice, he experiences in himself the same conflict. In his own consciousness the play and the strife of the two group attitudes take place, and the manner in which he responds forms one of the most interesting chapters in the history of the Negro.

Perhaps no one has voiced this inner conflict with more dramatic self-analysis than W. E. B. Du Bois, in *The Souls of Black Folk.* . . .

Since the mulatto has tended to occupy a higher cultural level and to possess more of white social and physical traits than the average black man, he has generally been looked up to by the latter. This attitude has facilitated the leadership role of the mulatto. In India and South Africa, however, the unmixed natives have a distinctive culture and social organization of their own—in India this is being strengthened in some respects by a growing nationalist movement—which creates a cultural as well as psychological gulf between natives and both Eurasians and Eurafricans. Consequently, while these Eurasians and Eurafricans face ostracism or at least indifference and social isolation from both whites and natives, the American mulatto experiences this from only the white race. As the black man progresses it becomes easier for the mulatto to identify himself with his lot, and the black man in turn profits from the stimulus of the mulatto's leadership and association. Thus a nationalistic movement of the racial type is set in motion: its unique psychological dilemma is that it must express itself in terms of the white American culture, instead of reviving an indigenous culture like the usual nationalist movement. This movement has not only a growing political and economic significance: it also means an intellectual, artistic, and general spiritual awakening. . . .

Among the educated class of Negroes, the mulattoes occupy a conspicuous position. They predominate in the higher circles of Negro society and contribute more than their proportionate share to Negro leadership. This fact has led some to assume that it is the influence of white blood which makes them superior, but others (or perhaps

the same persons) are likely to believe that race-mixture is biologically degenerating and should be stopped at all costs. The same
process of race mixture is claimed to produce two opposite effects.
Is there not some other explanation for the achievement of the
mulatto?

The history of the Negroes in the United States offers a clue to
the greater achievements of the mulattoes. From the very beginning
they secured a more favorable status in the eyes of the white man.
They were made the favored slaves, worked in the house of the
master rather than as field hands, and benefited from their closer
white contacts. The white master, if he were also the father, often
felt a moral obligation toward his mulatto children—this obligation
taking the form of providing education, bequeathing property, and
frequently granting freedom. The mulattoes thus achieved an early
advantage or start over the unmixed Negroes, an advantage which
has been maintained to the present day, although more and more
black individuals are rising to Negro leadership.

As with the mixed blood generally, there has been a tendency
for the mulatto to identify himself with the white race rather than
with the black race. But the white man refuses to accept the mulatto
and, indeed, refuses to give him a status superior to that of the black.
From the white point of view, a drop of Negro blood makes a person
a Negro, no matter how "white" he may appear. The very fact that
the mulatto is closer to the white man in cultural attainments and
physical traits renders it all the more difficult for him to accept this
extreme color line. It has meant bitter frustration and mental conflict. . . .

Continued pressure from the white world compels the mulatto to
cast his lot more and more with that of the black man. This has been
facilitated by the progress of the darker Negro since Emancipation,
and by the diffusion of white blood into the Negro population. The
mulatto recognizes that he must gain his livelihood by serving in the
Negro community. Meanwhile, his position of leadership gives him
prestige, and the lack of a special group consciousness among darker
Negroes prevents any line being drawn from that side. Consequently
the group consciousness developing in the Negro race is embracing
both mulatto and black man in a common sentiment and collective
movement.

The difference in the psychology of the mulatto and that of the educated black man is decreasing. Race consciousness and common interests are bringing them together. There is a tendency for dark men to marry light women. Most significant, perhaps, is the fact that they both live in the same dual social situation. Thus, while the educated black man, unlike the mulatto, is not conscious of having white blood in his veins, he is acutely aware of the discrepancy between his cultural achievements and rights as an American citizen on the one hand, and the white group's attitude toward him on the other. . . .

THE NEGRO IN BRAZIL

Brazilians say there is no Negro problem because the Negroes are being amalgamated and assimilated and eventually will be completely incorporated. To individuals of all classes, this eventual absorption of every ethnic unit is a matter of pride and self-commendation.

THE GENERAL tendency to absorb all diverse ethnic elements has been persistently characteristic of Brazilian society. Out of the traditional behavior which developed in response to the circumstances and conditions of colonial life emerged an informal racial policy, or racial ideology, which has served as a philosophy underlying and giving consistency to the mores, appearing only when they are challenged from without and individuals seek to rationalize and defend their customary conduct.

Thus, the race problem in Brazil, insofar as there is a race problem, is determined by the resistance which an ethnic group offers, or is thought to offer, to absorption. For example, recent opposition to Japanese immigration apparently has been largely motivated by apprehension that the Japanese would constitute a group difficult to assimilate. In an attempt to refute this imputation, the Japanese Embassy in Rio published a pamphlet to which were appended several photographs of mixed Japanese-Brazilian families. Brazilians

Excerpt from Donald Pierson, "The Negro in Bahia, Brazil," in *American Sociological Review*, Vol. 4, No. 4, August 1939, pp. 532-533.

say there is no Negro problem because the Negroes are being amalgamated and assimilated and eventually will be completely incorporated. To individuals of all classes, this eventual absorption of every ethnic unit is a matter of pride and self-commendation. A Bahian school girl of white parentage remarked: "Race mixture is an inevitable thing. We Brazilians are rapidly becoming one single people."

The operation of this racial ideology is revealed in intimate detail in the present social order of Bahia. Organization is based upon class, not upon caste, as in India; nor is there evidence of the development within the larger community of a self-conscious racial minority like, for example, the Negro in the United States. There is no deliberate segregation as one finds where races have been embittered for a long time; spatial distribution is largely the result of economic shifting. Such moral isolation as exists is due to varying educational levels or to identification with vestiges of African culture, particularly the fetish cult. The Negro and the mixed-bloods are represented throughout the entire occupational scale, although, as is to be expected, considering the original slave status of the Negro, his relatively disadvantageous position upon receiving his liberty, and the comparatively brief time he has enjoyed a freely competitive status, the darker portion of the population is still concentrated in the low-pay, low-status employments. Rise in class, however, is recognized not merely by a Negro world, as is largely true of similar advancement in the United States, but by all members of the Bahian community. Miscegenation has now proceeded to the point where Bahians anticipate, and take pride in predicting, that the Negro will, within a reasonable period of time, be completely absorbed. Intermarriage is common. Although color and negroid features are still symbolic of slave origin and still tend to be closely identified with low status and hence to constitute a considerable handicap to marriage into the upper classes, these characteristics lose their restraining character in proportion to the degree white intermixture increases or their symbolic reference is called into question by evidence of certain status-enhancing qualities in a given individual. Similarly, personal competence or individual achievement admit persons possessing considerable color into such status-symbolizing institutions as exclusive clubs. Race consciousness is at a minimum, "passing" has no point, nor are circumstances conducive to the appearance of the "marginal man." The entire organization of society tends to take the form of a freely competitive order in which the individual finds his place on the basis of personal competence rather than of racial descent.

This is not to say that there are no social distinctions in Bahia; for such are obviously common to all societies, one thing or another serving as a basis. Neither does it mean that there is no discrimination, or that the Negroes and mixed-bloods are completely satisfied with their lot. For instance, I visited in Bahia a very dignified all-Negro benevolent and fraternal society which was established more than a hundred years ago. Its members were orderly and responsible citizens. Pictures of its founders and subsequent leaders adorned the walls. Since its charter grants admission only to pretos, or blacks, the existence of this organization indicates that when it was founded there was at least some prejudice in Bahia, and this prejudice may still exist. But the important point is that a man of color not only may, by reason of individual merit or favorable circumstance, improve his status and even achieve position in the upper levels of society, but that this position then will be with reference, not merely to the darker group whose color he happens to share, but to the total community.

INTERMARRIAGE

Economic and political factors determine and modify religious prohibitions to intermarriage, which are likewise tied up with provincialisms and national and race consciousness. Where differences in color do not reflect historical or contemporary differences in culture, religion or economic status they do not hinder intermarriage.

IN EVERY society, primitive or historical, personal choice of a mate from another group is regulated by group sentiments of approval and disapproval defined by the group's vested interests and

Excerpt from Bernhard J. Stern, "Intermarriage," *Encyclopaedia of the Social Sciences*, Vol. 8 (New York: The Macmillan Co., 1932), pp. 151-154.

its desire to perpetuate or enhance its prestige. Current evaluations of the ranking of other groups, cultures, castes, classes, occupations, nationalities, religions and races determine the degree of encouragement or discouragement accorded a prospective marriage. Hostile attitudes toward intermarriage, which are constantly changing in their direction and intensity, range from ridicule and scorn to tabus involving ostracism or death. Correlated with heightened group self-consciousness, fostered by ethnocentric leadership and perpetuated by isolation, these attitudes act as means of insulating the group, of preventing the dissipation of its forces and of preserving its traditions against the disintegrating effect of alien influences. On the other hand, intermarriages looked upon with favor by the group are those that it believes will extend its social, economic and political power and improve its status.

Marriage functions in primitive society as a means of effecting co-operation between small isolated groups in conflict, barter and ritual; and such marriages are arranged as are thought to advance these ends. Distinctions based on property and rank when present, as, for example, on the northwest coast of America, regulate the marriage choice, as do occupational discriminations in east African society, where the blacksmith is held in low esteem. In Roman society political caste and occupational considerations determined the range of intermarriage relations. Romans had conubium, or legal intermarriage, with neighboring Latin groups by special grants. Conubium was also permitted with some peregrines who were not Roman citizens or Latins but members of political communities which had acknowledged Roman supremacy and which had been absorbed or had been granted a measure of autonomy. No conubium with slaves was permissible and intermarriage between patricians and plebeians became legal only after 445 B.C. A freedman could not marry his patroness or the widow or female descendant of his patron, whether the woman was of senatorial rank or not; the extreme penalty for such offense was condemnation to the mines. Senators and their descendants were forbidden to marry freed women or men and anyone who was or whose father or mother had been engaged in the theatrical profession. Soldiers, imperial officials and tutors lost certain privileges of conubium during the period of their employment. When Caracalla in 212 A.D.

made full Roman citizenship a common status for free subjects of the empire he increased thereby the range of territorial and racial intermarriage.

In societies where religious ritual and ceremony give significant sanction to marriage and where the interest of the group is oriented around sectarian beliefs religious differences interfere with free intermarriage. Religious sects demand unreserved loyalty and their emotional appeals for group cohesion develop attitudes of zealous exclusion in the marriage relation with members of other sects. The antagonisms against intermarriage are intensified if the religious leaders are seeking to counteract the assimilation process concomitant with religious tolerance or if there has been a tradition of embittered conflict between the religious groups involved. Economic and political factors determine and modify religious prohibitions to intermarriage, which are likewise tied up with provincialisms and national and racial consciousness. Christianity has since its inception established impediments to marriage with those outside of the faith. On the authority of passages in the New Testament (II Corinthians vi:14) and the utterances of the church fathers St. Cyprian and Tertullian the Council of Elvira (300-306) forbade Christian girls to marry "infidels, Jews, heretics or priests of the pagan rites." The Christian emperor Constantine in 339 prohibited all intermarriages between Christians and Jews and a statute of Valentinian, Theodosius and Arcadius enacted in 388 regarded such intermarriages as adulterous. The councils of Laodicea (343-381), Hippo (393), Orléans (538), Toledo (589) and Rome (743) reiterated the interdiction against the intermarriage of Christians with Jews, heretics and infidels and these prohibitions were incorporated in the Gratian collection. With the coming of the Reformation, councils and synods in various parts of Europe extended these prohibitions to apply to Protestants; and popes, particularly Urban VIII, Clement XI, Benedict XIV, Pius IX and Leo XIII, inveighed against intermarriage with non-Catholics in vigorous language. The secularization of marriage laws and procedures, the increasing power of the civil authority over ecclesiastical authority in the regulation of marriage and the diminishing part played by religion in contemporary life have lessened the force of marriage impediments of the church, but they are still potent in religious communities.

The revised code of canon law of 1918 reiterates the prohibition of marriages between individuals of "mixed religion" and "disparity of cult," but as a concession to the increasing laxness in the rigid enforcement of the impediments it permits such marriages if the non-Catholic party promises in writing that he will not interfere with the religious worship of the Catholic and if both parties promise that the children of both sexes will be baptized and reared in the Catholic religion. These conditions were rigidly insisted upon in 1932 in a letter issued by the church authorities who set as punishments for violations the annulment of the marriage, exclusion from participation in church activities, the denial of a church funeral and in extreme cases public excommunication.

After its secession from the church of Rome the Church of England continued to regard difference in religion as an impediment to marriage and annulled mixed marriages when made; it included among prohibited marriages those with Jew, Turk or Saracen. The Westminster Confession of Faith published in 1647 declared that "such as profess the true reformed religion should not marry with infidels, Papists, or other indolaters." Ireland in 1697 passed "An act to prevent Protestants intermarrying with Papists," which provided that no Protestant woman who either possessed or was heir to any form of real property to the value of £500 should marry a Papist under the penalty of losing all her property—the act revealing economic factors underlying prohibitions against intermarriage usually concealed by the overtones of rationalization. An Irish law in 1725 made it a felony for any Papist priest or unfrocked clerk to perform a mixed marriage and a statute in 1745 threatened those who celebrated such marriages with capital punishment. A declaration of the Federal Council of Churches of Christ in America in 1932, subsequent to the statement of the Catholic church on intermarriage, asserted that "where intolerable conditions are imposed . . . persons contemplating a mixed marriage should be advised not to enter it." Some Protestant sects have prohibited intermarriage with members of other creeds on pain of expulsion; all have brought pressure to bear upon their members to marry within their religious group.

The Mohammedan law of marriage according to the Maliki school ordains that the confession of Islam by the husbands is one of the conditions of all marriages. A Moslem may not marry a woman who is an unbeliever; but on the basis of the Koran (v:7) an exception is made of a marriage to a *kitabiyyah*, a free "scriptural woman," a term which designates Christians and Jews. Such marriages although legally valid are considered "abhorrent" especially in non-Moslem countries.

Jews have also consistently looked with disfavor upon intermarriage with non-Jews. Biblical injunctions against marriage with neighboring tribes and the demand of Ezra that the Jews after their return from the Babylonian exile put aside their foreign wives were used as authority for Talmudic prohibitions against intermarriage and by Maimonides, who incorporated the prohibition in his code. Exception was made by some rabbis if the non-Jew became a proselyte; in the codification of the *Shulchan aruch* the consensus of opinion was that such marriages should be exempt from the prohibition. The Jewish synod convened in Paris by Napoleon in 1807 decided that although intermarriages between Jews and Christians in accordance with the civil code could not be solemnized by the religious rites of Judaism they were valid and not subject to religious anathema. The declaration of the rabbinical conference in Brunswick, Germany, in 1844, that intermarriage between Jews and Christians and with the adherents of other monotheistic faiths was not forbidden if the children were reared as Jews met much hostile feeling in Jewish circles as being too assimilationist in tone. The large majority of Reform Jewish rabbis have supported the traditional orthodox opposition to intermarriage as a threat to the survival of Judaism. The food customs and ritualistic observances of orthodox Jewry concentrated in enforced or voluntary ghettos, the barriers of antisemitism and nationalistic loyalties evoked by the Zionist movement have served to maintain group cohesion. In spite, however, of the tenacious efforts of a spirited leadership the rate of intermarriage between Jews and non-Jews is increasing. Drachsler's statistics of New York City, where the Jewish population was highly concentrated, showed the ratio of intermarriage of Jews between 1908 and 1912 to be 1.17 per cent, among the lowest of the intermarrying groups; the rate varied widely, however, with the country of origin, and Jews of the second generation were found to have intermarried seven times more frequently than those of the first generation.

Extensive intercontinental migration has led to intermixture of races throughout history without biological detriment. Such intermixture was sometimes unimpeded by social restrictions and at other times took place in the face of discrimination. Because color is especially conspicuous it has served as a primary criterion of race in laws against racial intermarriage, but where differences in color do not reflect historical or contemporary differences in culture, religion or economic status they do not hinder intermarriage. In Mexico and in Central and South America, for example, whites, Negroes and Indians intermarry without restraint. There has been wide variance in the attitudes of the Spanish and Portuguese, themselves mixed groups, and the English conquerors toward intermarriage with native populations. Wherever garrisons of soldiers are stationed in colonial countries large mixed populations result. Racial intermarriage is common in Malaya and in the Hawaiian Islands. The eight hundred castes and subcastes and the approximately five thousand local castes of India are not exclusively racial divisions but have also arisen from occupational and sectarian differentiations. In the United States and in the Union of South Africa, the chief arenas of race conflict, whites, as a means of retaining their economic, political and social domination have legislated against racial intermarriage. Neither the laws against racial intermarriage, which are found upon the statute books of twenty-nine states, nor the intensity of the caste sentiment against it has prevented the merging of races in the United States, as is shown by Herskovits' findings that 80 per cent of Negroes show traces of mixture with whites or with American Indians. The miscegenation laws have, however, prevented Negroes from obtaining the legal and property rights which the marriage contract provides. The prejudice against intermarriage with orientals on the west coast of the United States is a reflection of the prevailing social discrimination against them. Racial intermarriage has increased in Soviet Russia in the wake of full political and economic equality accorded to all racial groups.

Commercial and administrative groups in foreign countries, especially in colonial lands where they are racially distinct from the native population, do not intermarry with the latter. Governing minorities, even when of the same race and with approximately the same cultures as the governed, hold themselves aloof; and when their status is threatened by intermarriage they enact against it—the Statute of Kilkenny (1366) forbidding the English of the Pale to intermarry with the Irish is typical of such legislation. Immigrant national groups transport to their new homes the national loyalties and the Old World customs, which are suffused with heightened appeal because of the immigrants' nostalgia and their impact with a hostile culture. In their segregated ethnic communities a strong sentiment prevails against intermarriage with its disintegrating influences. These are resisted most effectively if the immigrants are massed geographically, if they have effective nationalistic leaders to foster loyalties to the traditions and language of the group through systematic propaganda and education. But even if these factors are at work, intermarriage takes place; Drachsler found an intermarriage ratio of 14 per 100 with an increase of approximately 300 per cent in the second generation, an increase which ranged from 100 per cent to 1000 per cent among the different nationalities. The ratio of intermarriage was highest among the northern, northwestern and some central European peoples and, with the exception of the Jews and Negroes, lowest among the Italians and the Irish. De Porte, in his study of the marriage statistics of New York State exclusive of New York City between 1916 and 1929, found that the relative number of marriages of immigrants from southern and eastern Europe in which the bride was foreign born and the groom native increased six times in a decade and that the proportion of marriages of this group in which the groom was foreign born and the bride native was in 1929 greater than the proportion among the immigrants from Canada, northwestern Europe and Germany. With the multiplicity of cultural contacts afforded by facility of communication and mobility and with the decline in immigration it has become increasingly difficult for national groups to maintain the separatist attitudes nurtured by isolation in ethnic communities. The propinquity afforded by urban and industrial life develops personal associations that do violence to the traditional stereotypes that inhibit social relations leading to marriage. Class lines which were important in marriage selection within the national and religious groups now function as the chief determining factor—the dominant economic classes seek to maintain their prestige and wealth by looking with disfavor upon marriage with persons from the lower social and economic levels. Intermarriage is also on the increase among foreign born dispersed in rural communities remote from the cohesive pressures of foreign nationalistic agencies. The fact that in the modern world marriage has become increasingly an individual matter, less dominated by parental control, has likewise accelerated intermarriage.

ATTITUDES TOWARD IMMIGRANTS, OLD AND NEW

It has come to be accepted as an unquestionable truth, so often has it been repeated—that the type of the old immigrant was superior to the more recent immigrants from Southern and Eastern Europe. It is the old story of the Golden Age in a modern version. The cold facts of history, however, do not bear out this popular myth.

IT HAS come to be accepted as an unquestionable truth so often has it been repeated—that the type of the old immigrant was superior to the more recent immigrants from Southern and Eastern Europe: . . . It is the old story of the Golden Age in a modern version. The cold facts of history, however, do not bear out this popular myth. . . .

So great was the poverty of the early immigrants that for the sum of ten pounds they were willing to sell themselves into peonage. The last sales of immigrants are reported in 1819 in Philadelphia. Nearly a century ago, the managers of the Society for the Prevention of Pauperism in the City of New York spoke of the immigrants "in the language of astonishment and apprehension":

. . . This country is the resort of vast numbers of these needy and wretched beings. . . . They are frequently found destitute in our streets, they seek employment at our doors; they are found in our almshouses and in our hospitals; they are found at the bar of our criminal tribunals, in our bridewell, our penitentiary, and our State prison, and we lament to say

Excerpts from Isaac A. Hourwich, *Immigration and Labor* (New York: G. P. Putnam's Sons, 1912), pp. 61-67, 73, 75-77.

that they are too often led by want, by vice, and by habit to form a phalanx of plunder and depredations, rendering our city more liable to increase of crimes and our houses of correction more crowded with convicts and felons. (1819.)

Eighteen years later the Mayor of New York City in a communication to the City Council complained that the streets were "filled with wandering crowds" of immigrants "clustering in our city, unacquainted with our climate, without employment, without friends, not speaking our language, and without any dependence for food, or raiment, or fireside, certain of nothing but hardship and a grave."

This was the period when, according to Gen. F. A. Walker, the average immigrant was "enterprising, thrifty, alert, adventurous, and courageous." A contemporary writer anticipated in 1835 General Walker's parallel between the old and the new immigration in almost identical language.

"Then our accessions of immigration were real accessions of strength from the ranks of the learned and the good, from enlightened mechanic and artisan and intelligent husbandman. Now, immigration is the accession of weakness, from the ignorant and vicious, or the priestridden slaves of Ireland and Germany, or the outcast tenants of the poorhouses and prisons of Europe."

A generation later it is again reported that "the poor and the productive classes of Europe, by hundreds of thousands, have been, and are now coming to our shores, with fixed habits and modes of life. These now constitute, mainly, the army of our unskilled laborers, are ignorant and degraded, pitifully so."

Regarding the standard of living of Irish peasantry at the beginning of the Irish exodus to America, when, according to General Walker's "rightful presumption," the average immigrant was thrifty and had accumulated the necessary means to pay his way, we have the following description from the same authority:

The conditions under which they had been born and brought up were generally of the most squalid and degrading character. Their wretched hovels, thatched with rotting straw, scantily furnished with light, hardly ventilated at all, frequently with no floor but the clay on which they were built, were crowded beyond the bounds of comfort, health, or, as it would seem to us, of simple social decency; their beds were heaps of straw or rags; their food consisted mainly of buttermilk and potatoes, often of the worst, and commonly inadequate in amount; their clothing was scanty and shabby.

Congestion was a common evil in those days, as it is today, and the reason for it was sought in the fact that the Irish immigrant, born in a cabin or a garret, had been used to crowding at home. The *New York Weekly Tribune* of May 2, 1846, discussing a strike of Irish laborers in Brooklyn, said that their earnings were hardly sufficient to pay the rent of a decent tenement, so "they were allowed to build miserable shanties on ground allotted them by the contractors on the plot occupied by them in performing the work." A quarter of a century later the dwellings of the Irish immigrants in Boston were officially characterized as "sickening kennels." Says Dr. Kate H. Claghorn, comparing the old immigration with the new: "No account of filth in daily surroundings among Italians and Hebrews can outmatch the pictures drawn by observers of the habits of immigrant Irish and even Germans."

The living conditions in an Irish district in 1864 were thus described by a city inspector:

The tenants seem to wholly disregard personal cleanliness, and the very first principles of decency, their general appearance and actions corresponding with their wretched abodes. This indifference to personal and domiciliary cleanliness is doubtless acquired from a long familiarity with the loathsome surroundings, wholly at variance with all moral or social improvements. . . .

Dr. Claghorn concludes her review of the housing conditions of the former generations of immigrants with the following remarks:

The newer immigrants arrive here at no lower social level, to say the least, than did their predecessors. Their habits of life, their general morality and intelligence can not be called decidedly inferior. . . . The Italian ragpicker was astonishingly like his German predecessor, and the Italian laborer is of quite as high type as the Irish laborer of a generation ago. In some cases the newer immigrants have brought about positive improvements in the quarters they have entered. Whole blocks have been transferred from nests of pauperism and vice into quiet industrial neighborhoods by the incoming of Italians and Hebrews.

Throughout the nineteenth century relief against city poverty was sought in directing the current of immigration to the farm. As early as 1817, "the same anxiety was felt that is felt today to get the immigrant out of the 'crowded' cities into the country beyond." In 1819, the managers of the Society for the Prevention of Pauperism of the City of New York favored the plan of establishing "communication . . . with our great farmers and landholders in the interior" with a view to provide "ways and means . . . for the transportation of able-bodied foreigners into the interior," where labor could be provided for them "upon the soil." Forty years later the Association for the Improvement of the Condition of the Poor complained of the Irish immigrants that "they had an utter distaste for felling forests and turning up the prairies for themselves. They preferred to stay where another race would furnish them with food, clothing, and labor, and hence were mostly found loitering on the lines of the public works, in villages, and in the worst portions of the large cities where they competed with Negroes . . . for the most degrading employments."

The old immigrants, like those of the present generation, were mostly unskilled laborers and farm hands. . . .

The social prejudice against the immigrant which it is sought to justify by his alleged inferiority, antedates the influx of the "undesirable aliens from Eastern and Southern Europe." Suffice it to recall the agitation of the Know-Nothing days, with its rioting and outbreaks of mob violence against the Irish, the desecration of their churches, the petty persecution of Irish children in the public schools, the denunciation of the Germans, the mobbing of German newspapers and Turner halls.

Probably the most important element in this antipathy was the pure contempt which men usually feel for those whose standards of life seem inferior. This feeling was felt towards all immigrants of the poorer class, irrespective of their race. To the mind of the average American the typical immigrant was a being uncleanly in habits, uncouth in speech, lax in the moralities, ignorant in mind, and unskilled in labor. . . . The immigrant bore a stamp of social inequality.

The manifestations of this social prejudice in the industrial field seventy years ago were much the same as today.

About the year 1836 to 1840, very material changes took place among . . . the general laboring help in all departments of industry. The profuse immigrations from Ireland . . . crowded into all the fields of labor, and crowded out the former occupants. Under the prejudice of nationality . . . the American element, the daughters of independent farmers, educated in our common schools . . . re-tired from mill and factory, and all the older establishments, and can no longer be found therein. Their places were taken up in the old, and all the new were filled by the new immigrants. . . .

Even the vexed problem of "assimilation" appears to be as old as immigration itself. Benjamin Franklin, in a personal letter dated Philadelphia, May 9, 1753, characterized the Germans of Pennsylvania in the following terms:

Few of their children know English. They import only books from Germany, and of the six printing houses in the Province, two are entirely German, two half German, half English, and but two are entirely English. They have one German newspaper and one half German. Advertisements intended to be general are now printed in Dutch and English. The signs in our streets (Philadelphia) have inscriptions in both languages, and some places only in German. They begin, of late, to make all their bonds and other legal instruments in their own languages which (though I think it ought not to be) are allowed in our courts, where the German business so increases, that there is continued need of interpreters, and I suppose in a few years they will also be necessary in the Assembly, to tell one half of our legislators what the other half says. In short, unless the stream of importation could be turned from this to other colonies, as you very judiciously propose, they will soon outnumber us, that all the advantages we will have will in my opinion, be not able to preserve our language, and even our government will become precarious.

Franklin's apprehensions concerning the Legislature of Pennsyl-vania were all but justified at the convention of the State of Pennsyl-vania held at Philadelphia from July 15 to September 28, 1776, whose minutes were ordered published weekly in English and German. This practice was still continued as late as 1790.

The conditions in Pennsylvania were by no means exceptional. Says Prof. McMaster of the same period:

Diverse as the inhabitants of the States . . . were in occupations, they were not less diverse in opinions, in customs, and habits. . . . Differences of race, differences of nationality, of religious opinions, of manners, of tastes, even of speech, were still distinctly marked. . . . In New York the Dutch element prevailed and the language of Holland was very generally spoken.

With the great influx of Irish and German immigrants in the middle of the nineteenth century, distinct colonies of those nationalities grow up in the larger cities.

So large are the aggregations of different foreign nationalities (says a report of that day) that they no longer conform to our habits, opinions and manners, but, on the contrary, create for themselves distinct communities, almost as impervious to American sentiments and influences as are the inhabitants of Dublin or Hamburg. . . . They have their own theaters, recreations, amusements, military and national organizations; to a great extent their own schools, churches, and trade unions; their own newspapers and periodical literature.

The Irish were accused of "clannishness," like the "immigrants from Eastern and Southern Europe" in our day, although "to a large extent this going apart of the Irish was but natural in view of the contemptuous manner in which the 'nativist' Americans treated them." It took three generations to raise "the Celts and the Teutons" to a place among the "more desirable immigrants from Northern and Western Europe."

10

SUPERIORITY CREEDS AND RACE THINKING

OF ALL THE theoretical rationalizations of modern group conflict, the concept of race has become the most frequently used, especially so since the concept of nationality has come to be tinged more and more with the idea of race. Its prevalence and the particular force of its appeal are surely symptomatic of something deeply characteristic of our time. Originally invented as a concept for scientific description of human group differences, of interest only to a narrow circle of specialists, it has by some extraordinary shift been brought over into the popular thinking even of the masses. In an age that worshiped science, a scientific term that could be taken over into politics was destined to have wide currency. From its use in majority group politics, it then came to serve a similar function in the counterassertions of minority groups, and its career as a stock concept was fully launched.

As a term of majority manufacture, it must first be considered in the majority frame of reference. The majority use of race proceeds from the disposition to group personification that has already been discussed. Racialism incorporates these ethnic fictions and gives them historical perspective, and to the layman, apparently convincing scientific standing. If it were not for the competitive character of the nationalist aspects of the racialist doctrine, there would be an overwhelming unanimity on the subject in the European majority thought. But, as Barzun remarks, "more and more the national cultures are seeking to exclude one another on the ground of the racial incompatibility of minds. The idea of race, so used, makes easy the transition from cultural to political ill feeling." And so, by stages, the term race has passed from a term of scientific classification to a concept of cultural rationalization and from that, finally, into a political weapon of group conflict.

Never any too sound either as a scientific term or as a philosophy of history, race and racialism are still shabbier, intellectually, in international and interracial politics. In the last stage of partisanship to which the idea has deteriorated—Nazi German race history, it has become obvious race politics. The sinister aspect of this, though, is what Barzun notices, that racialism has become so emotionalized with many racial and national groups as scarcely to need any closely reasoned support. "It has become," says Barzun, "rather a mode of thinking than a set of doctrines, and one so entwined with the culture of modern Europe as to constitute an ingrained superstition."

But though the racialist point of view may seem to have come to the crest of its career in this wide vogue and popularity, it has really reached a point of culminating confusion and imminent self-contradiction. For it is identified with too many conflicting causes; they cannot compete much longer without discrediting their ideological basis. From other quarters, also, racialism is under heavy contemporary challenge; its pseudo-scientific character has aroused the progressive scientists; geneticists, anthropologists, historians and sociologists are definitely repudiating doctrines which, in the heyday of specious generalizations, threatened to discredit the sciences from which the racialists borrowed their terms. So at the height of its vogue, racialism faces two sorts of vital contradiction, theoretical repudiation from the scientists and practical self-contradiction from the competitive claims and counterclaims of its devotees.

Contemporary racialism involves biological, sociological and anthropological misapprehensions not supported by the best knowledge and scientific theory in these several fields. Racialist doctrines with such contrary-to-fact implications are:

1. that historic groups, like peoples and nations, are true racial groups and represent "pure races,"
2. that intelligence and capacity for cultural development are determined by factors of race, and are thus transmitted by inheritance as group characteristics, and
3. that human cultures and civilizations, being racially character-

istic, are thus proprietary possessions of specific races, nations or classes.

Quite opposite to these tenets of racialism, it is the consensus of the best scientific opinion that,—

1. All historic peoples, especially the larger European nations, are ethnically very mixed, and do not represent "pure races" or even significant racial types,
2. that there is no scientifically demonstrable correlation between intelligence and race or between race and group cultural capacity,
3. that the identification of culture with race traits and nationality claims is, therefore, unwarranted both by the scientific and the historical facts.

This identification of race and culture, which has been the root assumption of racialism since the early days of Aryanism as a culture theory, Boas carefully examines and disproves. He also disproves the companion assumption that racial descent determines mental and social character and capacity. Not only are most national groups composed of mixed biological strains, but these are rapidly becoming more mixed. They are also subject to biological variation, which would give us no permanency of racial types, even where we start out with them. History, carefully traced, suggests social causes and historical explanation for practically everyone of the group traits commonly assigned by racialist doctrine to biological and hereditary factors.

Racialism has become so inveterate a habit in popular thinking, however, that it carries on unabashed by scientific contradiction in many instances. Toynbee devotes passing but devastating attention to some of the more popular brands of race bias. So trivial or contrary to fact are most of these, that it is quite obvious that they not only originate on the level of uncritical thinking, but remain there throughout their use and acceptance. They are entertained as unquestioned tribalisms, building up the norm of the group into a criterion for universal application. These are the equivalents in the sphere of physical qualities of the social contrast-concepts previously analyzed. The opposite of the preferred or familiar in physical appearance, manners and behavior is then regarded as undesirable, and should any group antagonism arise, the contrast trait will immediately become a focus of the dislike and the symbol of the other's inferiority.

The excerpt from Klineberg takes up the psychological implications of racialism, its assertions of the intellectual inferiority of other racial groups. He first proves that the criteria of intelligence in use, even those which are supposed to be scientifically objective, have limitations of reliable comparison. They are reliable tests of relative ability only among those who have had approximately similar cultural experience. For they have such a definite cultural basis as to be completely unreliable with groups having radically diverse culture patterns. Each group will show high proficiency relatively in those reactions which have high emphasis and survival value in their respective cultures. This principle applies even to widely different regions of the same culture, so that all these tests and their scores need anthropological or sociological weighting to be fair comparisons.

Intelligence testing, moreover, of the most accurate kind has failed to substantiate any of the race superiority claims with respect to intelligence. Comparing racial or national or class groups in equal numbers, there are only differences of averages, which instead of showing a correlation with the race or cultural group show direct correlation with cultural exposure, training and opportunity. Comparisons were made between the scores of comparable groups of American whites and Negroes, with results like these: the averages of Negroes with favorable cultural background, although below those of the whites for the same areas, were above those of the whites from less favorable environments. Here, even though the general Negro average was considerably lower than the general white average, what was responsible was evidently factors of environmental advantage rather than racial inheritance. Moreover, the overlapping of both high and low scores counterindicated any group limitation in range of variation either way; there were exceptional high-score intelligences in both racial groups.

Klineberg concluded from his test analysis that social and economic level had more to do with the variations than any other set of factors. His comparisons were between Northern, Southern, Negro and white groups, and the sectional differences were as marked or more so than the racial. All the differences could be scientifically explained without recourse to any hypothesis of innate racial capacities or disability. Such scientific conclusions invalidate both the innate superiority and the innate inferiority arguments of the racialists, as they relate to intelligence. As it has been aptly put—there are no intellectually superior or inferior races or nations or classes with regard to ability, but only superior and inferior individuals. The higher or lower average incidence of certain groups, in certain times and places, is due to complex but definitely environmental factors, or where hereditary factors are involved, individual inheritance rather than social group inheritance.

The estimation of peoples in the lump aggregate is, therefore, unscientific. As habitually made by majority groups, it is usually weighted in their own favor by being based on their cultural values and patterns, misapplied as an absolute standard. Often, too, this partisan comparison takes place in terms of a double standard which takes as characteristic for the majority group, the best examples, and for the minority group, selects as typical not the best but often the worst. That any such comparison can be seriously entertained as fair or objective is only indication of the almost complete reign of emotional thinking in this field.

Group traits are, as a matter of fact, very tricky characters, and usually are generalizations not acceptable in careful thinking. However, by cultural selection and emphasis, certain types do come to characterize, on the average, certain groups, and become typical group characterizations. But the important reservations it is necessary to make about typical group traits is their purely composite character as indicating, like composite photographs, certain group preponderances, and always to remember in addition that what are called racial or national characteristics are only the results of historical factors and often change radically with historical changes in those same factors.

Some of the very groups accused particularly by prejudiced majorities of having fixed group traits and characteristics have undergone historically the most extreme cultural transformation. The Jews and the Negro, as peoples transplanted from culture to culture, have historically proved a variability and capacity for assimilation which belies any attribution to them of fixed traits and strictly racial character. The Jew in the course of his long and tortuous history has been forced by social circumstance, and often by pressure of persecution, into one transforming change after the other. He has been in turn predominantly pastoral, agricultural, mercantile, remolded back from a dominantly urban type to a successful agriculturalist, so that as the case proves, all that type can possibly mean in his case is a predominant mode of living and an historic group adaptation based upon it. The Negro, likewise, in assimilating American culture, has shed many basic and characteristic African habits and taken on quite different adaptations and reactions. Only in majority stereotypes are these minority groups so "unique" and so "unchangeable." National traits also, to the extent they exist at all outside patriotic imagination, are similarly just historic adaptations, subject to considerable historical variation.

With regard to the matter of physical type, that, too, has been proved significantly variable. Shapiro reports, in his study of Japanese immigrants in Hawaii, marked change in their physical characteristics without intermarriage, apparently from adaptation to a new environment and change in mode of living. These results parallel those obtained by Boas several years back in observations on the children of recent immigrants. Such scientific proof of the instability of physical group characteristics takes the last vestige of foundation from under the racialist's assumption about the permanency of physical race types. Together with the historical disproof of fixed social and cultural characteristics, the theoretical structure of racialist doctrines practically collapses.

There remains only one further tenet of racialism, and that—the doctrine of natural antipathies, which, likewise, is easily disproved. Even if miscegenation were waived as an effective disproof, that there is any such instinctive aversion between widely different racial types is counterindicated by the commonly observable behavior of children when not indoctrinated with prejudice reactions by adult groups. Quite obviously they learn to be prejudiced, and so does the group, for it is by the same process of indoctrination that the historic prejudices of all varieties perpetuate themselves.

Finally it is necessary to note that the stereotypes of minority groups by majorities have somewhat conservative character; they and the antipathy vary little from generation to generation. But the rationalizations are baffling in their contradictory changes, as they shift about in the tactics of historical clash and conflict. Historically they often cancel themselves out, but in these respects the majority mind fails to remember. As the Golding excerpt shows, the Jew has been persecuted during different periods for diametrically opposite traits and behavior. At one time, the unassimilated Jew will be the target of anti-Semitism, at another, the assimilated Jew, or as today in Nazi Germany both may become the object of attack. He has been accused of being "too nationalistic," and then again, as "too internationalist." All of which proves the basic irrationality of the whole apparatus of majority group glorification and minority group depreciation. These irrationalisms are, unfortunately, often picked up by minorities and used as the basis of their own counterassertions and group compensations. Such imitative and retaliatory imitation of majority behavior is one of the tragic sequels of majority intolerance. The main historical result of majority superiority creeds and attitudes has been to provoke minority struggle for status, and thus to accelerate social change in the direction of offsetting the inequalities. To follow this, we must turn to the analysis of the inter-group situation from the angle of the minority which Section IV takes under consideration.

THE NATURE OF RACE THINKING

Race thinking does not consist merely in believing a particular theory about human races. It is a passion for labeling and classifying large groups of people on insufficient evidence. What should we think of a chemist, or of a druggist, who would class all white powders as bicarbonate of soda and dispense with them on that convenient principle.

AMONG THE words that can be all things to all men, the word Race has a fair claim to being the most common, the most ambiguous, and the most explosive. No one today would deny that it is one of the great catchwords about which ink and blood are everywhere spilled in reckless quantities. Yet no agreement seems to exist about what Race means.

No argument is needed to prove that race and the feelings connected with race are one of the powers shaping the world. One European nation of seventy million inhabitants is governed by men whose main policies involve certain hard-and-fast race-beliefs. Another European nation not long since found it useful to whip up animosity against black-skinned men to help justify an imperialistic war. In the Balkans, in Turkey, in Persia, in Scandinavia, in Holland, sizable groups of the population work with or without government backing to boost their own "racial type" at the expense of all the others. . . .

Race may indeed be a mere pretext or it may be the aegis of a sincere fanaticism. In either case it is a reality in the minds of millions who hold the lives and fortunes of their neighbors in their hands. . . . The very vagueness of the concept of race adds to its protean power, for to the racialist and to his victims the "facts of race" are a scientific truth as well as a belief satisfying deep mystical impulses.

This threat to a world order is no less strong in the intellectual realm. More and more the national cultures are seeking to exclude one another on the ground of the racial incompatibility of minds. The idea of race makes easy the transition from cultural to political ill-

Excerpts from Jacques Barzun, *Race. A Study in Modern Superstition* (New York: Harcourt, Brace and Company, 1937), pp. 3-25.

feeling. This pattern of judgment is familiar to contemporaries of the World War, whose sincere and passionate belief in the wickedness of Kant, Hegel, and Nietzsche—cultural enemies—was as strong as their hatred of political foes like Bismarck or the Kaiser, and as useful to the Cause as poison gas or tanks.

Within national boundaries, race as a basis of judgment in matters of art and thought helps carry on the critics' war. It nourishes smug self-approval, stiffens factions, and decides among the imponderables: Russian music, jazz, atonality, and other live issues are discussed by critics as conservative as Ernest Newman and Olin Downes in terms of "barbarian races," "racial strain," "Celtic melancholy," and "Afro-American harmonic elements." In the cooler regions of mathematics and philosophy, abstract and passionless subjects (as one thinks), "races" are discovered by ingenious scholars—not all of them Germans by any means—and "threats" or "dangers" to the national culture are staved off by dismissal, boycott, or exile.

Recent manifestations of the race-spirit have led observers of the ever-spreading intolerance to believe that it originated exclusively in Germany, more particularly in Nazi Germany. It is quite true that the Third Reich has become the most blatant apostle of racialism in the modern world, but the movement has deeper roots than that régime. Present-day race-propaganda in Germany betrays plainly enough that it uses words and ideas by no means novel in Western culture, and that its ammunition is largely borrowed from the European science, art, and history-writing of the past century, without distinction of nationality . . . or race.

Equally important, though generally overlooked, is the fact that articulate minorities in other countries than Germany are fully as much engaged in thinking and talking about race. The only difference is that no other government has yet gone so far as the Nazi régime in adopting race as a popular slogan, despite its obvious value as a means of diverting attention from economic problems and as a satisfaction of the ever-latent zest to persecute. But read attentively the press and political literature not only of England, France, Italy, and the United States, but also of Mexico, Turkey, Rumania, and Scandinavia: you will not read very far before you are told or left to infer that the whites are unquestionably superior to the colored races; that the

Asiatic Peril is a race-peril; that the Japanese of late seem to have become very yellow indeed, so much so that the Chinese have almost become white brothers in comparison; that the great American problem is to keep the Anglo-Saxon race pure from the contamination of Negro (or Southern European, or Jewish) "blood." The quarrel about race and blood is often carried even closer home, as when we are informed that among the whites the tall blond Nordics are a superior breed destined to rule the world and that brown-eyed, round-headed Latins, whether in Europe or in South America, are a degenerate, revolutionary lot. . . .

Above the babble of the fanatics one can distinguish a few voices vainly shouting that the notion of race is a myth which all intelligent people should discard. Yet the quarrel about race is certainly not between the uneducated, on the one hand, and the cultured élite on the other. Brains, birth, high station, or success in a particular profession do not prevent a man from holding fast to race-prejudice. A British Foreign Secretary with a Biblical surname feels it necessary to dispel doubts about his race. "I am not a Jew," says Sir John Simon, recklessly adding, "I am just an ordinary Briton of Aryan stock." The well-known scientist, Sir Arthur Keith, spends a great deal of time and energy stressing the value of race-prejudice in modern life and urging the necessity of conflict among races as a means of improving the species. It is not the German professors alone who make the printing presses grind and groan under the weight of treatises proving that the authors and their friends are Nordics, heirs of the Greeks, and creators of all that is good, true, and beautiful. In France, where it is often thought that race-ideas can take no hold, the most impenitent form of race-superstition thrives, namely, that which is unaware of itself. Indeed, race-controversies raged in France long before they became a constant preoccupation in the rest of Europe. In seventeenth- and eighteenth-century France, race was already a political weapon in the struggle between absolutism, aristocracy, and the middle class. The warfare spread to the arts and philosophy in the nineteenth century, by which time independent shoots in other cultures had also borne fruit, leaving the grand harvesting on a world-wide scale to our generation.

Viewed in the light of its antecedents and world-spread, the race-question becomes a much bigger affair than the outburst of palaver and persecution observable in present-day Germany. It becomes rather a mode of thinking so intertwined with the culture of modern Europe as to constitute an ingrained superstition. Other outstanding forces of the epoch—Romanticism, Nationalism, Political Democracy, Science, and Imperialism—have reinforced the power of race-thinking in popular as well as educated opinion. It adorns or defaces, as one chooses, every type of mental activity—history, art, politics, science, and social reform. . . .

Suppose for a moment that the word and concept Race were wholly alien to our vocabulary and thinking, and that someone to whom it was familiar were trying to tell us what it meant. How could he go about it? He might begin by saying that a race was a group of people of all ages and sexes who were found in one place and resembled one another. We should certainly object to that definition as being too vague. How large is "one place" and what does resemblance amount to? In some ways all men and all animals resemble one another; but in another way, no two individuals are alike. The query would open up a broad field of argument, for even supposing that our interlocutor mentioned a white skin and light hair as the signs denoting a given race, we should find it difficult to agree on the precise point where white skin ends and dark begins among individuals. The Berbers of North Africa are blue-eyed and lighter-skinned than the Sicilians, and as Shaw has pointed out, a really *white* man would be a horrible sight. The same difficulty would arise about light hair or brown eyes; indeed all the characteristics of the human body that might be named as criteria would be found in actuality to merge into a finely-graded series which one can break up into groups only by being arbitrary and saying, as of skin, "I shall call this man white, and that one, a shade darker, black." Moreover we should find that contrary to common opinion, no set of fixed characteristics occurs in human beings as a constant distinguishing mark of race. So-called Nordics have long skulls but so have many so-called Negroes, the Eskimos, and the anthropoid apes. The "Mongolian" birth-spot occurs among the whites and the Ainos in Japan frequently show features that should class them as "Nordics."

This lack of conformity is bad enough but we could also stump our informant with another query. What if the striking differences of skin and hair and eyes were more striking than significant? A knowledge of the normal life of men in society suggests that a Japanese scientist is in many ways more like an American scientist than either is like a manual laborer of his own color. In other words, it is fallacious to consider human beings as mere arrangements of organs, apart from their functions, their habits, and their minds.

If we voiced this objection, the word Mind would probably recall to our friend the great differences among the shapes of the human skull, thought to be related to mental differences, and expressible in index numbers, but if we forced him to be a little clearer about what is meant by *dolichocephalic* and *brachycephalic* and what can be inferred from this classification of skulls, we would soon find ourselves in a labyrinth of contradictions fit to make us despair of discovering a reliable token of race.

To be sure another word than Mind is for many people the clue to race and it might be advisable to examine its merits. That word is Blood. For the French and German racialists the word is the infallible oracle, the original Logos containing the answer to all questions. . . . To less ardent mortals blood is merely a tissue like any other, except that it is carried in a serous fluid and that it circulates through the body. The blood of neither parent is directly communicated to the offspring and the properties of any individual's blood are not ascertainable without fairly complicated tests, none of them infallible. In any case, these tests, according to competent serologists, have nothing to do with determining race.

The idea of race does not make sense until we know a great deal more about the transmission of individual and family traits. To build racial anthropologies without a solid genetics is like starting a house with the roof. This self-evident proposition has, nevertheless, not deterred even the best scientific minds of this and the last century. That is why we cannot stop the discussion of race here, but must show in detail how absurd and unsubstantial, and what a confused wreckage, all the unsupported roofs of the nineteenth-century anthropological erections really are.

We are no nearer finding out what a race is by asking biology than we were by measuring skulls or judging at sight on the basis of pigmentation. The remaining methods are even less promising. First comes history. We can arbitrarily go back to the time of the Germanic invasions in the fourth and fifth centuries A.D. and find in the struggle of peoples after the Fall of Rome the origin of modern races. We shall then juggle with the names of Celts, Gauls, Iberians, Ligurians, Helvetii, Belgae, Brythons, Latins, Franks, Normans, Saxons, Angles, Jutes, Lombards, or Burgundians. But when it comes to determining who these were, where they lived, whether they survived, what they looked like and whether in our day, the French writer, Rémy de Gourmont, is a Gaul or a Norman—one man's guess is nearly as good as another's. Next we can try nationalism. We can assert, with Sir Arthur Keith, that a race and a nation are synonymous; that several hundred years of a common history and a common way of life have welded people of divergent physiques into one race. That definition hardly defines. Under it, the "renegade Englishman" Houston Stewart Chamberlain, who elected Germany as his Fatherland would be of German race. The language spoken is an equally unsatisfactory criterion. By that token Henry James and Joseph Conrad would be of the same race, though one was born in New York, and the other in the Ukraine. Some people are bilingual, and the race of a headwaiter would be beyond conjecture.

As for "centuries of common history" that is a common metaphor, but it is an inexact statement of fact. Human beings do not live through centuries of common history and what they pick up of the past through education or common report varies greatly according to social class and intellectual powers. The "common way of life" is equally fallacious, except in self-contained, one-class communities; and this is true in spite of the tremendous power over mass emotions which the press, the cinema, and the radio have acquired in the recent past. They are powerful agents of assimilation but they have hardly had time to create distinct breeds of men. The fact that one can make forty million Britons believe for a time in the German atrocities is no test of their belonging to the same race. We are still far from our original goal, which was to understand what a race of men, in contradistinction to other races of men, might be.

But if we give up the pursuit on our own account, we must still see what men who have thought and written about race think it is.

Their ideas form, not a definition of race, for they all disagree among themselves, but a type of thinking, which I shall call race-thinking, and which bears certain easily recognizable features.

Race-thinking does not consist merely in believing a particular theory about human races, and to refute the Nazi believer in Nordic or Aryan supremacy would not suffice to show up the basic error involved in the notion of a Nordic or Aryan race. It would only let the disillusioned racialist fall into the arms of the Celtist, the Yellow Peril fanatic, or the dolichocephalic anthropologist. What must be extinguished is the passion for labeling and classifying large groups of people on insufficient evidence. That remarkable urge to lump together the attributes of vast masses with which we can have no acquaintance is common to everyone. "The Japanese are a crafty and imitative race." "Isn't that typically American?" "That is a Jewish trait." "Nordic self-control."

Race-thinking is exhibited not only by anthropologists and ethnologists, not only by historians and publicists who make up systems of race-discrimination, but likewise by everyone who in a casual or considered remark implies the truth of any of the following three propositions:

1. That mankind is divided into natural types on the basis of certain recognizable physical features, transmitted by the process of generation and leading to distinctions among "pure" and "mixed" races.

2. That mental and moral behavior can be referred to the physical structure of the individual and that knowledge of the structure or of the racial label which denotes it provides a satisfactory account of the behavior.

3. That ideas, capacities, art, morals, and personality are the product of social groupings variously termed race, nation, class, family, without further defining of the group intended, or inquiry into the particular relation between the group and the product under discussion.

These three generalized types of race-thinking lead and merge into one another. Few writers limit themselves to one of these premises, and mankind at large entertains all three with equal readiness according to their suitability for the occasion. The reason for distinguishing among them is primarily to show that the formal rejection of type one, two, or three is no guarantee against succumbing to the basic fallacy of race-classification. What this assumption is, can perhaps be best described in its ordinary manifestations. In everyday usage the ascription of race takes no account of particular facts; it merely appeals to common knowledge. It considers, for example, the nation a natural force that selects and organizes human qualities and defects into certain patterns. From so considering the nation it is easy to shift to the family, class, college, or tradition. We thus get not only the German mind or the Greek mind but also the bourgeois mind and the Harvard mind, and, as we see daily in novels, plays and biographies, the X-, Y-, or Z-family mind which supposedly accounts for the hero's personality.

It may sound as if this criticism of a common practice were a denial of the obvious fact that people who belong to the same family, nation, climate, class, or "race" have a tendency to think alike, even to look alike. No such denial is asserted or implied. . . . What is asserted and implied is that *these tendencies to think and look alike, if they exist, must be proved.* They must not be merely presumed. The particular individual of whom the group quality is predicated must be studied in his own person and in his relation to the group before the label can be affixed. The necessity for so doing is obvious. The problem of when and how similarities of body and mind occur, and to what degree, is extraordinarily complex, and man's fatal tendency is to assume greater simplicity and regularity in nature than actually exists. The race-thinker, whatever his affiliation, takes the ready-made names by which we refer to the factor in question and from the name deduces arbitrarily what he wishes to find. The Mongolians are crafty; the British have no sense of humor; brachycephalic people are excitable; the Aryan is a born leader. Finally, persuaded by his own glibness, the race-believer comes to see only those instances that seem to bear out his preconceived notion. He does not consciously suppress evidence against his thesis, he becomes blind to its presence and immune to its presentation by others.

The connection between this habit and scientific method is especially paradoxical. One would think that the so-called scientific habit of thought would tend to make us extremely careful in dealing with details and differences. It should seem as if the object under consideration, be it a man or a group, would be looked at from every angle, seen as it really appears. The very opposite has happened. The modern passion is to lump individuals together on the most superficial, unverified grounds of similarity and describe them *en masse*. What should we think of a chemist, or even of a mere druggist, who would class all white powders as bicarbonate of soda and dispense them on that convenient principle? When a habit of thinking conducted on these lines becomes quasi-universal, sinks out of the conscious mind to reappear in everybody's mouth as the most obvious of truths, then it is no exaggeration to term it a superstition, ranking honorably in history with the belief in witchcraft and horoscopes.

To sum up our attempt at finding a satisfactory definition of race, one that will really define and yet correspond to the facts, we may say that so far we have seen only its practical and intellectual difficulties, which ought to make any prudent man suspend judgment until Genetics can offer a more complete body of knowledge. But to expect prudence in thinking about subjects with emotional content is folly, too; and so we shall find that the racialists of the last 150 years leap over the initial obstacle to race-theorizing, make assumptions to suit their object and do not define their terms any more than the man in the street who borrows their language without questioning its validity.

THE FALLACY OF THE CONCEPT OF PURE RACES

The belief in hereditary racial characteristics and the jealous care for purity of race is based on the assumption of non-existing conditions. Since a remote period there have been no pure races in Europe and it has never been proved that continued intermixture has brought about deterioration.

UNTIL THE first decade of our century the opinion that race determines culture had been, in Europe at least, rather a subject of speculation of amateur historians and sociologists than a foundation of public policy. Since that time it has spread among the masses. Slogans like "blood is thicker than water," are expressions of its new emotional appeal. The earlier concept of nationality has been given a

Excerpt from Franz Boas, *The Mind of Primitive Man* (New York: The Macmillan Company, 1938), pp. 253-260.

new meaning by identifying nationality with racial unity and by assuming that national characteristics are due to racial descent. It is particularly interesting to note that in the anti-Semitic movement in Germany of the time of 1880 it was not the Jew as a member of an alien race who was subject to attack, but the Jew who was not assimilated to German national life. The present policy of Germany is based on an entirely different foundation, for every person is supposed to have a definite, unalterable character according to his racial descent and this determines his political and social status. The conditions are quite analogous to the status assigned to the Negro at an earlier period, when licentiousness, shiftless laziness, lack of initiative were considered as racially determined, inescapable qualities of every Negro. It is a curious spectacle to see that serious scientists, wherever free to express themselves, have on the whole been drifting away from the opinion that race determines mental status, excepting however those biologists who have no appreciation of social factors because they are captivated by the apparent hereditary determinism of morphological forms, while among the uninformed public to which unfortunately a number of powerful European politicians belong, race prejudice has been making and is still making unchecked progress. I believe it would be an error to assume that we are free of this tendency: if nothing else the restrictions imposed upon members of certain "races," abridging their right to own real estate, to tenancy in apartment houses, membership of clubs, to their right to visit hotels and summer resorts, to admission to schools and colleges shows at least that there is no abatement of old prejudices directed against Negroes, Jews, Russians, Armenians or whatever they may be. The excuse that these exclusions are compelled by economic considerations, or by the fear of driving away from schools or colleges other social groups is merely an acknowledgment of a widespread attitude.

I may perhaps restate in briefest form the errors which underlie the theory that racial descent determines mental and social behavior. The term race, as applied to human types, is vague. It can have a biological significance only when a race represents a uniform, closely inbred group, in which all family lines are alike—as in pure breeds of domesticated animals. These conditions are never realized in human types and impossible in large populations. Investigations of morphological traits show that the extreme genetic lines represented in a so-called pure population are so different, that if found in different localities they would be counted as separate races, while the middle forms are common to races inhabiting adjoining territories, excepting the occurrence of small groups that may have been inbred for centuries. If the defenders of race theories prove that a certain kind of behavior is hereditary and wish to explain in this way that it belongs to a racial type they would have to prove that the particular kind of behavior is characteristic of all the genetic lines composing the race, that considerable variations in the behavior of different genetic lines composing the race do not occur. This proof has never been given and all the known facts contradict the possibility of uniform behavior of all the individuals and genetic lines composing the race.

Added to this is the failure to see that the many different constitutional types composing a race cannot be considered as absolutely permanent, but that the physiological and psychological reactions of the body are in a constant state of flux according to the outer and inner circumstances in which the organism finds itself.

Furthermore the varying reactions of the organism do not *create* a culture but *react* to a culture. On account of the difficulties involved in defining personality and separating the endogene and exogene elements that make up a personality it is difficult to measure the range of variation of biologically determined personalities within a race. The endogene elements can only be those determined by the structure and chemism of the body and these show a wide range of variation within each race. The claim that a race is in any way identical with a personality cannot be given.

The diversity of local types found in Europe is a result of the intermingling of the various earlier types that lived on the continent. Since we do not know the laws of intermixture, it is impossible to reconstruct the early constituent purer types, if such ever existed. We may not assume on the basis of a low variability that a type is pure, for we know that some mixed types are remarkably uniform. This has been shown for American Mulattoes, Dakota Indians, and made probable for the city population of Italy. It is also not certain in how far exogene elements may be partly determinants of local types or how social selection may have acted upon a heterogeneous population. In short we have no way of identifying a pure type. It must be remembered that although by inbreeding in a small local group the family lines may become alike, this is no proof of purity of type, because the ancestral forms themselves may be mixed.

Setting aside these theoretical considerations we may ask what kind of evidence is available for the claim that there is any pure race in Europe or, for that matter, in any part of the world. European national types are certainly not pure stocks. It is only necessary to look at a map illustrating the racial types of any European country—like Italy, for instance—to see that local divergence is the characteristic feature, uniformity of type the exception. Thus Dr. Ridolfo Livi, in his fundamental investigations on the anthropology of Italy, has shown that the types of the extreme north and those of the extreme south are quite distinct—the former tall, short-headed, with a considerable sprinkling of blond and blue-eyed individuals; the latter short, long-headed and remarkably dark. The transition from one type to the other is, on the whole, quite gradual; but, like isolated islands, distinct types occur here and there. The region of Lucca in Tuscany, and the district of Naples, are examples of this kind, which may be explained as due to the survival of an older stock, to the intrusion of new types, or to a peculiar influence of environment.

Historical evidence is quite in accord with the results derived from the investigation of the distribution of modern types. In the earliest times we find on the peninsula of Italy groups of heterogeneous people, the linguistic relationships of many of which have remained obscure up to the present time. From the earliest prehistoric times on, we see wave after wave of people invading Italy from the north. Very early Greeks settled in the greater part of southern Italy, and Phoenician influence was well established on the west coast of the peninsula. A lively intercourse existed between Italy and northern Africa. Slaves of Berber blood were imported, and have left their traces. Slave trade continued to bring new blood into the country until quite recent times, and Livi believes that he can trace the type of Crimean slaves who were introduced late in the Middle Ages in the region of Venice. In the course of the centuries, the migrations of Celtic and Teutonic tribes, the conquests of the Normans, the contact with Africa, have added their share to the mixture of people on the Italian peninsula.

The fates of other parts of Europe were no less diversified. The Pyrenean Peninsula, which during the last few centuries has been one of the most isolated parts of Europe, has had a most checkered history. The earliest inhabitants of whom we know were presumably related to the Basques of the Pyrenees. These were subjected to Oriental influences in the pre-Mycenaean period, to Punic conquest, to Celtic invasions, Roman colonization, Teutonic invasions, the Moorish conquest, and later on to the peculiar selective process that accompanied the driving-out of the Moors and the Jews.

England was not exempt from the vicissitudes of this kind. It seems plausible that at a very early period the type which is now found principally in Wales and in some parts of Ireland occupied the greater portion of the islands. It was swamped by successive waves of Celtic, Roman, Anglo-Saxon and Scandinavian migration. Thus we find change everywhere.

The history of the migrations of the Goths, the invasions of the Huns, who in the short interval of one century moved their habitations from the borders of China into the very center of Europe, are proofs of the enormous changes in population that have taken place in early times.

Slow colonization has also brought about fundamental changes in blood as well as in diffusion of languages and cultures. Perhaps the most striking recent example of this change is presented by the gradual Germanization of the region east of the Elbe River, where after the Teutonic migrations, people speaking Slavic languages had settled. The gradual absorption of Celtic communities and of the Basque, in ancient times the great Roman colonization, and later the Arab conquest of North Africa, are examples of similar processes.

Intermixture in early times was not by any means confined to peoples which, although diverse in language and culture, were of fairly uniform type. On the contrary, the most diverse types of southern, northern, eastern and western Europe, not to mention the elements which poured into Europe from Asia and Africa, have been participants in this long-continued intermixture. The Jews also have been proved by physical examination as well as by blood tests to be of highly mixed origin.

In Europe the belief in hereditary mental qualities of human types finds expression principally in the mutual evaluation of the cultural achievement of nations. In present-day Germany the hatred of the Government against the Jew is a relapse into cruder forms of these beliefs.

Since we have not been able to establish organically determined differences in the mental faculties of different races, such as could claim any importance as compared with the differences found in the genetic lines composing each race; since furthermore, we have seen that the alleged specific differences between the cultures of different peoples must be reduced to mental qualities common to all mankind, we may conclude that there is no need of entering into a discussion of alleged hereditary differences in mental characteristics of various branches of the White race. Much has been said and written on the hereditary character of the Italian, German, Frenchman, Irish, Jew and Gypsy, but it seems to me that not the slightest successful attempt has been made to establish causes for the behavior of a people other than historical and social conditions; and I consider it unlikely that this can ever be done. An unbiased review of the facts shows that the belief in hereditary racial characteristics and the jealous care for purity of race is based on the assumption of non-existing conditions. Since a remote period there have been no pure races in Europe and it has never been proved that continued intermixture has brought about deterioration. It would be just as easy to claim and to prove by equally valid—or rather invalid—evidence that peoples which have had no admixture of foreign blood lacked the stimulus for cultural progress and became decadent. The history of Spain, or, outside of Europe, that of the remote villages of Kentucky and Tennessee might be given as striking examples.

The actual effects of racial mixture cannot be answered by general historical considerations. The adherents of the belief—for it is nothing else—that long-headed groups lose their bodily and mental pre-eminence by mixture with round heads, will never be satisfied with a proof of the improbability and impossibility of proving their cherished beliefs, for the opposite view also cannot be proved by rigid methods. The real course of race mixture in Europe will never be known accurately. We do not know anything in regard to the relative number and composition of mixed and "pure" lines; nothing in regard to the history of the mixed families. Evidently the question cannot be solved on the basis of historical data but requires the study of strictly controlled material showing the movements of population. With all this nothing in the known historical facts suggests that preservation of racial purity assures a high cultural development; else we should expect to find the highest state of culture in every small, secluded village community.

RACIAL FEATURES AS A FACTOR IN RACE ANTAGONISMS

Our color prejudice has not a shadow of physiological justification but is an instance of an irrational aversion from whatever is different. The Japanese are sensitive to the general hairiness of the human body because, in Japan, this is a more significant feature than the color of the skin.

IT IS an established fact of physiology that, in all human beings, the pigment secreted in the skin is qualitatively the same; and that the different shades of color which strike the eye and affect the feelings and give rise to theories and classifications correspond to mere differences in the quantity in which this qualitatively uniform human pigment happens to be present beneath the skin of any given specimen of the human race. We can verify this on the body of an African Negro; for the palms of his hands and the soles of his feet are of a different shade from the rest of his skin and of practically the same shade as the whole skin of a white man—the explanation being that, on his palms and soles, a Negro has about the same quantity of pigment that a white man has all over, while on the rest of his body the Negro has rather more. This fact indicates that our color-prejudice has not a shadow of physiological justification. "Nordic Man," who rejoices in the rather low quantity of pigment in his skin, eyes, and hair which happens to be normal in human beings of his

Excerpt from Arnold J. Toynbee, *A Study of History* (London: Oxford University Press, 1934), pp. 227-229.

kind, is repelled by the abnormal case in which this quantity is reduced to zero and "the Blond Beast" transformed into an albino,
though logically, if colorlessness is the pink of perfection, the rare
albino ought to be hailed by his commonplace Nordic relatives as a
king of men. Again, even the relative lack of color which is normal
and therefore comely in the sight of a white man is abnormal and
therefore unbecoming in the sight of a Red Indian, who expresses
his aversion by calling the white man a "pale-face." It even happens
that a human being comes to regard his own color with aversion if he
lives for some time in a minority of one among people of a different
color—the color of the majority setting the norm. For example, it is
said that David Livingstone, on one of his expeditions, after passing
many months in Central Africa with no white companions and
none but Negroes round him, began to find that the sight of his own
naked skin turned him sick, as though he were looking at some
deformity of nature.

This craving for the normal in physical appearance (whatever the
normal may be in the particular circumstances) is not of course confined to the single feature of color. For example, in the United States,
where the physical appearance of the white people is the norm for the
colored people, the colored women try to lessen their unlikeness from
the white women by straightening their hair. On the other hand, the
white women, who have no fear of looking like Negroes, take pleasure,
as white women do in other countries, in having their hair waved or
curled. Thus, in the same American town at the same moment, some
barbers may be busy straightening women's hair in the Negro quarter
while others are busy curling women's hair in the white quarter—in
both cases alike, for the satisfaction of the universal human craving to
be "in the fashion."

Hair, indeed, is just as good—or just as bad—a criterion of race as
pigment. The North American whites and Negroes are sensitive to
the straightness or curliness of the hair on the head. The Japanese
are sensitive to the general hairiness of the human body, because, in
Japan, this happens to be a more significant feature than the color of
the skin. The Japanese people (like almost every other people that
has ever distinguished itself) is of mixed race; and its original racial
components must have differed widely in color; for there is a consider-

able diversity of color among the Japanese people to this day. In the same district and in the same social class and in the same family you may find skins varying from copper-color to what white people call white. Hence, the differences of color within this range do not excite race-feeling among the Japanese any more than this is excited among Europeans by differences in the quantity of hair on their bodies. On the other hand, Japanese of all shades of skin are alike in being more or less hairless except on their heads, in contrast to the aboriginal inhabitants of the Japanese Islands who, like Nordic man in the un-shaven state of nature, have bushy beards and hairy chests. For this reason, the Japanese call these aborigines (the remnant of whom are now philanthropically preserved, on the northern island of Hokkaido, in "reservations") "the Hairy Ainu." In the local circumstances of Japan, it is just as natural to emphasize the hairiness of the inferior race as it is in the United States or in the Union of South Africa to emphasize their color; and as the people of European origin supply the color-classification, which suggests itself in their own local circum-stances, to the whole of mankind, so we might expect the Japanese to divide the human family, not into a "White Race" and a "Colored Race" but into a "Hairless Race" and a "Hairy."

Logically there is nothing to choose between one classification and the other; but it may be edifying for us to glance at the classification with which we are less familiar. It yields what, to our minds, are dis-concerting results. It brackets "Nordic Man" with the hairy Ainu of Hokkaido and the Blackfellows of Australia and the Veddahs of Ceylon and the Todas of the Nilgiri Hills in Southern India, as one of the representatives of a race whose abnormal hairiness makes them not as other men are. . . .

Another racial feature which acts as a stimulus of race-feeling, no less powerfully than hairiness or color, is smell.

"I hope you have been enjoying yourself," said an English dramatic critic to a celebrated Japanese actress who had been having a season in the West End of London. "Yes, on the whole," the lady replied, "but of course there have been hardships to put up with." "Hardships? I am sorry to hear that," the Englishman exclaimed (rather taken aback, for the Japanese artist had been received enthusiastically by the English public). "Oh yes," she burst out. "And the worst of all

was the smell. The people in this country smell like lions and tigers.
. . . But not you, of course," she added hastily, solicitous for her
own manners and for her interlocutor's feelings, "you only smell of
mutton-fat and scented soap." The truth is that the Japanese, whose
national odor is kept sweet and wholesome by a mainly vegetarian
diet, are considerably distressed by the rank and fetid odor of the
carnivorous peoples of the West—an odor of which we are hardly
conscious ourselves because we are living in the reek of it all the time.

It is not only the Japanese who are upset by the white race's smell.
A highly cultivated and fastidious English lady of my acquaintance
once went to stay for several months in South Africa and engaged a
staff of native servants—among them, a little Kaffir maid. It happened
several times that the maid, on being summoned into her employer's
presence, fell into a sudden faint; and the lady, who was kind-hearted,
felt some concern. What could be the matter with the girl? Was it
heart-disease? Or was it just acute nervousness at finding herself
tête-à-tête with a member of the superior race? The lady questioned
the other servants, only to have her questions parried and eluded in
the usual provoking fashion; but at last an older servant, who saw
that her mistress was becoming really upset and alarmed, succeeded
in conquering her own reserve and embarrassment. "You needn't
worry, Madam," she assured my friend, "there is nothing serious the
matter with the girl. The fact is, she has come straight from her village
to you; this is her first place in white people's service, and she isn't yet
quite used to the white people's smell. But don't you worry. She will
get used to it soon enough. Why, look at us! We all used to faint at
first, but now we have quite got over it. It will be the same with her,
you'll see!"

WHAT PSYCHOLOGICAL TESTS SHOW

Until we can be certain that the same opportunities have been given to the Negro and the foreign-born white as to the native born white, any direct comparison of average test scores will be meaningless.

IN THE FIELD of racial psychology no other problem has attracted so much attention as the question of the inherent intellectual superiority of certain races over others. This problem has been approached in a great many different ways, but usually with so much obvious bias as to make the scientifically minded student very sceptical of the conclusions. With the development of the first intelligence scales by Binet and their use in the quantitative measurement of individual differences, it was felt that perhaps an instrument had finally been devised which would make it possible to study with complete objectivity the relative ability of various races. Terman, one of the early authorities in this field, expressed the opinion that the Binet scale was a true test of native intelligence, relatively free of the disturbing influences of nurture and background. If this were so, the difficult problem of racial differences in intelligence might be solved as soon as a sufficiently large body of data could be accumulated.

The data are now available. The number of studies in this field has multiplied rapidly, especially under the impetus of the testing undertaken during the World War, and the relevant bibliography is extensive. The largest proportion of these investigations has been made in America, and the results have shown that racial and national groups differ markedly from one another.

Negroes in general appear to do poorly. Pintner estimates that in the various studies of Negro children by means of the Binet, the I. Q. ranges from 83 to 99, with an average around 90. With group tests Negroes rank still lower, with a range in I. Q. from 58 to 92, and an

Excerpt from Otto Klineberg, *Race Differences* (New York: Harper & Brothers, 1935), pp. 155, 162-164, 166-167, 174-176, 182-189. By special permission of Harper & Brothers.

average of only 76. Negro recruits during the war were definitely inferior; their average mental age was calculated to be 10.4 years, as compared with 13.1 years for the White draft.

In the case of the American Indian, the I. Q.'s are also low, the majority being between 70 and 90. Mexicans do only slightly better. Chinese and Japanese, on the other hand, show relatively little inferiority to the Whites, the I. Q.'s ranging from 85 to 114, with an average only slightly below 100.

Among European immigrant groups, Italians have in general made a poor showing. In a series of studies their I. Q.'s ranged from 76 to 100, with an average about 87. Poles do equally poorly and in the Army tests were even slightly below the Italians. Immigrants from northwestern Europe have in general been more successful, and the demonstration by the Army psychologists that in the test results the immigrants from Great Britain, Holland, Germany and the Scandinavian countries were superior to others has been corroborated by more recent studies.

If we had absolute faith in tests of intelligence, we should have to regard this evidence of racial differences as conclusive. In recent years, however, more work has been done on the tests themselves, and little by little the conviction has grown that Terman's statement was an exaggeration, and that environmental factors cannot be ignored in any valid interpretation of these results. There may still be some controversy as to the extent to which these factors enter, but material has accumulated which leaves no doubt that they play an important part. In a recent critical survey, Garrett and Schneck write that "the examiner must always remember that comparisons are permissible only when environmental differences are absent, or at least negligible." . . .

This selection will be concerned with a critical discussion of some of the environmental, or non-racial, factors affecting the results, and individual studies will be cited only where they help to clarify the argument.

One preliminary caution is necessary. The problem of heredity versus environment, nature versus nurture, as it is here being considered, does not refer to individual, but to group, differences. This needs to be kept clearly in mind. It may be decided, for example, that heredity does not account for the observed intellectual differences between Negroes and Whites, and that the conditions of the environment are alone responsible. It would not follow that heredity did not enter into individual differences. There would still be room for wide variability within the Negro or within the White group, part of which at least could be explained only by the superiority or inferiority of individual or family germ plasm. The fact that persons living in almost the same environmental conditions will still differ widely from one another in intelligence, and the fact that identical twins living in very different environments will yet resemble each other closely, argue strongly in favor of an hereditary basis for part of the differences in intelligence between individuals and family lines. The problem of group differences, however, cannot be so easily dismissed. . . .

Many studies testify to the close correspondence between standing in the tests and the social and economic status of the groups tested. This was revealed in the study made by the Army testers, and it has been amply verified by subsequent investigations in England, France, Germany and Japan, as well as in the United States. There are marked differences, not only between adults in various occupational levels, but also between their children,. the professional and moneyed classes ranking higher than skilled and unskilled laborers. . . .

The obvious difficulty in the interpretation of these findings is the question as to what is cause and what is effect; whether people are in the upper economic levels because they are more intelligent, or whether they do better on the tests because of their superior opportunities. The answer to this question is of great significance in the problem of racial differences. Most of the groups who rank low in the tests, for example, the Negro, the Mexican, the Italian, come largely from the lowest economic levels; if economic status affects test scores to any extent, they are very definitely handicapped in a comparative study.

Intelligence may be regarded as the cause of economic status only if opportunities are equal and competition is entirely free. Even within a relatively homogeneous, native-born White American population, this is not altogether true; the handicaps are not evenly distributed. In the case of the Negro, however, the difficulties in his way are so great that any inference from industrial status to intelligence is completely unwarranted. The kind of competition the Negro has to face in his search for a job leaves no doubt as to the additional handicaps he must overcome. The same is true, though not to so great an extent, of some foreign-born White groups, who tend to enter the occupations at the lowest economic level, emerging from these only after a generation. That their economic inferiority is only temporary is made clear by a report of the U. S. Immigration Commission, which indicates that although at the start the immigrants have much lower occupations than the native-born, in the second generation the majority rise to the average native-born level. "Until we can be certain that the same opportunities have been given to the Negro and the Italian as to the native-born White, any direct comparison of average test scores will be meaningless. . . ."

The effect of relative familiarity with the language in which the test is administered is of obvious importance, and was recognized very early in the history of testing. This resulted in the construction and use of a large number of performance tests in which language does not appreciably enter, but the feeling seems to have persisted that language tests are somehow superior. In spite of criticism, most studies of racial differences have been made by means of linguistic tests. . . .

There is no doubt of the rather close correspondence between amount of education and standing in the tests. This was first demonstrated clearly by the Army testers. A number of studies followed with similar results. . . .

It has sometimes been urged that amount of education is an effect, rather than a cause, of intelligence, the more intelligent children staying longer at school and doing better in their school work. This is certainly true in part, but there is no doubt that opportunity, as determined mainly by economic status, also enters. In addition, there is direct evidence that schooling is important in determining the level of the I. Q. . . .

It is clear that merely equating two groups for school grade and assuming that therefore their training has been substantially identical can hardly be justified. Four years of schooling in a southern rural Negro school are certainly not equivalent to four years in a White school in New York or Chicago. It would be difficult to overemphasize the frequent discrepancy in per capita expenditures, in equipment and facilities, in the training of the teachers and in the length of the school term. In spite of this, many of the comparisons upon which the conclusions regarding racial differences are based involve groups whose schooling is equally disparate. The study by Foreman has demonstrated a close correspondence between scores on achievement tests and expenditures for the schooling of Negro children in a number of southern rural communities. It would be interesting to repeat this study with tests of intelligence. In any case, there seems to be little doubt that the inadequate schooling of the average southern Negro child may also be regarded as playing an important part in test performance. . . .

Although it is true that Negroes rank below Whites in most intelligence test studies, it must also be kept in mind that Negro groups may differ markedly from one another, and that they are by no means invariably inferior. It is well known, for example, that during the war the Army testers found Negro recruits from the North far superior to Negroes from the South, and, in the case of certain of the northern states, superior also to southern Whites. This is shown in the following table.

SOUTHERN WHITES AND NORTHERN NEGROES, BY STATES,
ARMY RECRUITS

Whites		Negroes	
	Median		Median
State	*Score*	*State*	*Score*
Mississippi	41.25	Pennsylvania	42.00
Kentucky	41.50	New York	45.02
Arkansas	41.55	Illinois	47.35
Georgia	42.12	Ohio	49.50

It was suggested at the time that one of two factors might account for these results: 1, the superior environment of the northern Negro, or 2, a selective migration of the more intelligent Negroes from South to North. The Army testers did not decide between these alternatives.

More recent studies, for the most part conducted upon children rather than upon adults, have in general corroborated these findings. There is on the average a difference of about seven points in the I. Q.

of northern and southern Negro children. Usually the northern Negroes are still below the White norm, but in some studies they show no inferiority whatsoever. Clark, for example, gave the National Intelligence Test to 500 Negro elementary school children in five schools in Los Angeles, and obtained a median I. Q. of 104.7, which is slightly above that of the White children with whom they were compared. Peterson and Lanier gave a series of tests to twelve-year-old White and Negro boys in three different cities, Nashville, Chicago and New York. They found in general that whereas in Nashville there was a marked superiority of White over Negro boys, in Chicago this was not nearly so great, and in New York it disappeared altogether. Their conclusion was that these results could best be explained on the theory that there had been a selective migration northward, and that New York in particular had attracted an especially intelligent class of Negro migrants. Incidentally, they interpreted Clark's results in Los Angeles in a like manner.

This problem of selective migration appears to the writer to be crucial in the present status of Negro intelligence testing. If there is such a selection, the superiority of the New York and Los Angeles samples will prove nothing as to the intelligence of the average Negro; these groups will then be exceptions. If, on the other hand, there is no selective migration on the basis of intelligence, their superiority can mean only that an improved environment may raise the test scores of the Negro to the White level. In that case the whole argument for a racial difference as based on tests of intelligence will have no foundation.

A series of studies recently completed at Columbia University has been directed toward a solution of this problem. In one study the attempt was made to discover whether those Negroes who left the South for the North showed a measurable superiority in intelligence over those who stayed behind. For this purpose the school records in three southern cities, Birmingham, Nashville and Charleston (South Carolina), were examined carefully to see how the marks obtained by those children who had migrated to the North compared with those who remained behind. The records for 1915-1930 were studied in this manner. When it was discovered that a particular Negro boy had left Nashville, let us say, for New York or Chicago in 1927 after finishing the fifth grade, the records were examined to determine where he had ranked in comparison with the other members of his class. A simple statistical formula was used for transmuting his rank into a score based upon percentile position in the class, so that the ranks of all the children could be placed on a comparable basis. The destination of the migrant was usually learned from the school authorities. In this way over 500 cases were collected of migrants who were known to have gone to one or another of the large northern cities, and the results were analyzed for any indication of their superiority.

There was no evidence in favor of a selective migration. As it happened, the migrants from Charleston were a somewhat superior group; those from Nashville were just about average; those from Birmingham were definitely below. The migrants as a group were almost exactly at the average of the whole Negro school population in these three southern cities. Whatever the selective factors in migration may be, they appear to differ markedly for the different communities. To the extent that school marks are a measure of ability, the use of the blanket phrase "selective migration" is obviously unwarranted, as it is by no means invariably the superior persons who leave. . . .

So far then, we have no right to assume that the superiority of northern Negroes is due to selection. On the other hand, we have very direct evidence of the degree to which the northern environment may affect the test performance of southern-born Negro children. In our series of studies over 3000 Negro school children in Harlem in New York City were tested, the measures including a number of different linguistic and performance tests—the Stanford-Binet, the National Intelligence Test, Otis Intermediate, Pintner-Paterson, Minnesota Form Board. In each study the children examined were of the same sex, the same age, attended the same or similar schools in Harlem, were all southern-born and of approximately the same social and economic status. They differed as far as could be ascertained only in one important respect, namely, the number of years during which they had been living in New York. In each case they were compared with a New-York-born group which was taken as the standard.

It was argued that if the superiority of the northern over the southern Negroes is entirely due to selective migration, the length of residence in New York City should make no appreciable difference in the test scores, since all the migrants have presumably been selected for high intelligence. If, however, the environment has an effect, this should show itself in a gradual improvement in the test scores at least roughly proportionate to the length of time during which the superior environment has had a chance to operate. It was felt, therefore, that this procedure might make it possible to choose on strictly experimental grounds between the two alternatives.

The results vary slightly in the different studies, but almost without exception they agree in showing that the lowest scores are obtained by the groups which have most recently arrived from the South. There is a close though by no means perfect relationship between test score and length of residence in New York. . . .

There appears to be no doubt that an improvement in the environment, with all that that implies, can do a great deal to raise the intelligence test scores. Interestingly enough, this improvement seems to take place most markedly in the first five or six years; those children who have lived in New York for a longer period seem to show little further advancement. The subjects in these studies were all ten- and twelve-year-old children; and the results probably mean that when the school years have been spent entirely in New York City, the environmental opportunities may be said to have been equalized. It should be added that with the performance tests this result is not so clear, and that the environmental effect appears largely to be restricted, as far as these studies go, to tests with a definite linguistic component.

Two further checks were applied to this material. In one of the studies, anthropometric measurements were taken in order to determine whether the various migrating groups differed from one another in their possession of Negroid characteristics. It was found that the New-York-born group was a little less Negroid than those born in the South, but there was no difference between the groups corresponding to their length of residence in New York. This factor therefore can obviously not account for the observed differences in intelligence. In the second place, the question was asked whether there was any indication that the quality of the migrants was deteriorating, and that this fact rather than the change in the environment might account for the better showing of the earlier migrants. This was studied by comparing in two successive years two groups of twelve-year-old boys who had lived in New York the same length of time. The results showed that almost invariably the later migrants were superior. There is therefore no indication of a deterioration in the quality of the more recent migrants, and the correspondence between test score and length of residence in New York seems to be due to the influence of the better environment.

This finding is in agreement with the results obtained by Long and McAlpin. Long studied third- and fifth-grade Negro migrant children in the city of Washington, and found a similar rise proportionate to length of residence. McAlpin used the Kuhlmann-Anderson test on Negro school children in Washington and found a difference of about six I. Q. points between those born in the city and those who had migrated from the South. Peterson and Lanier in their important study also found New-York-born Negro children to be superior to those born elsewhere (although the difference was not entirely reliable statistically).

Even in the northern cities the Negro children are usually below the White norms, although Clark's study in Los Angeles and Peterson's and Lanier's in New York showed no such inferiority. The real test of Negro-White equality as far as intelligence tests are concerned can be met only by a study in a region in which Negroes suffer no discrimination whatsoever and enjoy exactly the same educational and economic opportunities. Such a region is difficult to find, although there may be an approximation to it in Martinique or Brazil. . . . It is safe to say that as the environment of the Negro approximates more and more closely that of the White, his inferiority tends to disappear.

It is the writer's opinion that this is where the problem of Negro intelligence now stands. The direct comparison between Negroes and Whites will always remain a doubtful procedure because of the impossibility of controlling the various factors which may influence the results. Intelligence tests may therefore not be used as measures of group differences in native ability, though they may be used profitably as measures of accomplishment. When comparisons are made within the same race or group, it can be demonstrated that there are very marked differences depending upon variations in background. These differences may be satisfactorily explained, therefore, without recourse to the hypothesis of innate racial differences in mental ability.

THE INSTABILITY OF THE HUMAN ORGANISM

The assumption of stability in man's physical characters is no longer tenable without qualification. Indeed, from the evidence of the Japanese in Hawaii man emerges as a dynamic organism which under certain circumstances is capable of very substantial changes within a single generation. Not only may migrant populations undergo modification when transposed to a sufficiently different environment, but physical changes may also occur in fixed populations if their environments alter in the course of time.

ALTHOUGH BIOLOGISTS have exhibited some interest in the effect of migration on the lower organisms, students of man have lamentably neglected this aspect of their investigations of human biology, even though migration has always been and is especially now profoundly characteristic of his behavior. Boas, a generation ago, brilliantly demonstrated in a pioneer work, which unfortunately had few followers, that the children of immigrants to the United States underwent modifications in stature and cephalic index under the influence of their new environment. The material of his study, however, limited to immigrants and their children, could throw little light on the relationship of the immigrants to the stocks from which they sprang.

The present investigation was designed not only to discover what immediate effects a change of environment might produce in the physical habitus of a migrating population—in this case the Japanese born in Hawaii—but also to obtain a control on the physical characteristics of the Japanese immigrants. These ends were achieved both by comparing immigrants with their offspring born and bred in Hawaii

---

Excerpts from H. L. Shapiro, *Migration and Environment. A Study of the Physical Characteristics of the Japanese Immigrants to Hawaii and the Effects of Environment on their Descendants* (London: Oxford University Press, 1939), pp. 4-6, 184-188, 194-195, 198-202.

and by obtaining for comparison members of the same families in Japan who were raised in the very villages whence the Japanese in Hawaii migrated and who were nurtured under the same conditions which surrounded the immigrants.

Environment, as generally used, is a loose expression to cover the large number of variable factors that constitute the milieu in which an organism exists. In its broadest sense it includes everything outside the individual organism. Although, in human terms, we speak of physical, social, economic, spiritual and intellectual environments beside many others, these are merely subdivisions of the totality of factors material and immaterial which lie outside the organism and sustain or stimulate it.

Accepting the convenient differentiation of environment and organism, we find in nature an infinite variety of environments. In fact what we regard as a constant environment is constant only in its tendency to change. It changes with the seasons, in the succession of night and day and even from minute to minute. It changes in temperature, humidity, barometric pressure, circulation of the atmosphere, solar activity, food supply, water supply, mineral content of the soil, presence and concentration of bacteria, health regulations, culture, and in numerous other ways. Some of these changes are slight and insignificant; others are of presumably greater import. Most of these variables occur in all human environments, although they may differ widely in their particular expression. Recognizing the ever constant change and flux of environment, certain ranges and combinations do form patterns which are distinguishable from each other even though the gradations from one to another are often very fine. What precise effect differences in any or all of these variables may exert on the biology of man is practically unknown. . . .

The differences between the environment of a Japanese village and life in Hawaii are not only physical and climatic but social and cultural as well. Besides obvious changes in temperature, rainfall, humidity, soil conditions, food supply there are innumerable alterations in cultural and social conditions involving the regulations of health, labor, economics and a multitude of other factors. Our immediate problem is rather to demonstrate whether or not bodily modifications do occur under environmental changes, whatever may be the specific environmental factor involved. . . .

Although the individuals of a group vary within fairly wide limits, their average characteristics have commonly been regarded as unchanging over long periods of time. In fact, the vast bulk of comparative racial studies rests on this tacit belief in the stability of the statistical balance of the component variables of a population. This traditional view became so firmly entrenched in practice that it assumed the guise of an article of faith beyond the necessity of examination. In recent years, however, dissatisfaction with this dogma has slowly been gaining headway, without, however, actually attaining sufficient force to affect the established methodology. . . .

Were methodology the only consideration at stake, it would still be of great significance to examine the bases of such a belief in the stability of human populations. But other consequences of this dogma likewise come into question. If populations have remained unchanging during millennia of time and through wide fluctuations in environment, it is legitimate to ponder the logical consequences of such an hypothesis on the general theory of human evolution. Such an interpretation would minimize the effect of environmental shifts which we know have on occasion been considerable. It would deny all but the minutest effects to the accumulation of mutations. It would erase from practical consideration the working of differentials in a given population. It would render man static in a world of flux and change. To doubt the accuracy of this representation of man does not thereby impose an acceptance of a state of affairs in which man is a completely unstable organism constantly veering like a weather vane with the winds of environment. It does, however, impose the necessity of reexamining the basis for such a belief by testing it against the reality as we find it in nature.

Although in actuality the methodological approach to the comparative study of human groups and the theoretical discussion of their origins and classification are merely different phases of the same problem, in practice they have been completely severed from each other. The extent of this divorce of theory from practice is illustrated by the fact that proponents have never been lacking to defend the theoretical significance of environment in shaping the organisms of nature, even including man, while on the other hand a critical attitude toward the philosophy underlying comparative methods in racial studies, if it existed at all, escaped exact formulation. In fact, it was not until Professor Boas published his classical investigation of the bodily characteristics of the descendants of immigrants to the United States that most physical anthropologists were even aware that their methodological premises could profitably bear closer scrutiny. This was the first detailed and reliable research into the stability of the bodily characteristics of a migrant population born and bred in one environment and producing children in another. And the data amassed by Boas showed incontrovertibly that in the population he examined the children born in this country showed slight but definite modifications from their immigrant parents. These modifications, moreover, were greater the longer the residence here of the parents before the birth of the child. Despite the widespread discussion which this work provoked, the criticism of current practices implied in it failed to affect the traditional procedures of racial studies. Even the vistas of research which it opened remained neglected.

The present study is an attempt to determine the physical consequences both of migration and of a marked change in environment on a specific population. In this instance the population is Japanese and the migration is from Japan to the Hawaiian Islands, an environmental change of considerable magnitude both physically and socially.

In one sense our data fall into two divisions, based on country of residence: the Japanese living in Hawaii and the Japanese resident in Japan. But since the Japanese in Hawaii actually consist both of a group who were born in Japan but who migrated to Hawaii and of a succeeding generation of Japanese who were born and bred in Hawaii, we have chosen to divide the total data into three distinct groups, based both on country of birth and on country of residence. These three major divisions, therefore, are the following: 1. Hawaiian-born Japanese of Japanese immigrant parentage. These are subjects who were born in one of the Hawaiian Islands and have continued to live there up to the time of this study. 2. Japanese immigrants now resident in Hawaii but born in Japan. 3. Japanese sedentes. This last group are the relatives of the immigrants and Hawaiian-born who have remained in Japan, in the villages from which the immigrants migrated. They represent the stock of which the immigrants were originally a part and they live under conditions similar to those which surrounded the immigrants until their departure for Hawaii. To ensure obtaining strict comparability throughout, special efforts were made to include as many relatives as possible in all three groups. In Japan the villages from which the Japanese in Hawaii took their origin were visited and in most instances the living members of the families of our Hawaiian Japanese were measured for inclusion in the series of sedentes. In this manner the sedentes provide a control on the two groups in Hawaii. Although they represent the original population, they are contemporary with the Japanese in Hawaii.

It was necessary to deal with contemporary groups as far as possible since the Japanese appear to be undergoing size changes comparable to those well known in Europe and America. For that reason alone it would have been unwise to attempt to dispose our subjects in successive generations, even assuming that the grandparental generation in Japan had been numerous enough to provide an adequate representation. . . .

The Japanese male immigrants now resident in Hawaii entered almost entirely as laborers for sugar and pineapple plantations. They came almost exclusively after 1898, the earlier immigrants having for the most part returned to Japan. Most of them came single, but were joined later by "picture brides." Those who successfully established themselves in their new homes remained to rear their families in Hawaii. Obviously, the economically and socially well endowed were not candidates for migration. The vast majority of the male immigrants were laborers, landless or impoverished, who by virtue of economic pressure envisaged an opportunity to better their lot in a new country. Physically, however, no evidence exists of any deliberate selection either by the recruiters or by plantation managers; and, considering the pressing need for labor in Hawaii and the wholesale nature of the movement, none was to be expected. It might be argued that since the immigrants were economically and socially selected, they might have been derived from differentiated elements in the general Japanese population. This reasoning, however, loses its force because the sedentes employed for comparison form part of the same socio-economic level from which the immigrants were secured and genetically belong to the same stock. The sedentes are, in fact, members of the same families to which the immigrants belong. They represent the inheritors of small family holdings and those who for one reason or another preferred to remain at home despite economic pressure.

A statistical summary of the 50 characters and indices for which the total series of immigrants and sedentes are compared reveals an astounding degree of significant divergence between the two groups genetically so closely linked. The male immigrants deviate significantly from the sedentes in 72.4% of the measurements and in 76.2% of the indices. Similarly the immigrant females diverge from the sedentes in 67.9% of the measurements and in 45.0% of the indices. With some exceptions both the male and female immigrants tend to deviate in the same characters. . . .

Economic status has long been recognized as a probable differentiating factor in a physically homogeneous population. Children from prosperous homes tend not only to be taller and heavier but to vary in other anatomical and even in physiological traits from the norms of the general population. The assumption here, supported by evidences of differences in diet, is that with an increase in the family income the diet as well as other environmental factors improve.

Besides the more passive elements of environment, the more active factors such as the degree of physical labor at various economic levels also assume significance with economic differentiation. . . .

The assumption of stability in man's physical characters is no longer tenable without qualification. Indeed, from the evidence of the Japanese in Hawaii man emerges as a dynamic organism which under certain circumstances is capable of very substantial changes within a single generation. If a Japanese population may thus alter its aggregate characteristics, then the probability certainly exists that other groups in other parts of the world have undergone similar physical changes in the past, since migrations and radical shifts in environment have been not infrequent events in man's history.

Not only may migrant populations undergo modification when transposed to a sufficiently different environment, but physical changes may also occur in fixed populations if their environments alter in the course of time. In fact, abundant evidence is spread in the recent literature demonstrating marked size and associated proportional changes in established European and American populations. The specific environmental factor producing these alterations is not universally agreed upon, but the phenomenon itself is unquestioned. And it bears witness to the dynamic potentiality of the human organism to respond to environmental changes.

This recognition of the dynamic and plastic character of the human organism and, by logical extension, of human populations raises a serious methodological problem. For if populations may be altered by changes in environment then identical populations reared in different milieus may develop physical divergencies. And the simple test of identity or similarity of group-means becomes inadequate as the sole criterion of relationship. By such a test, for example, the present data in the absence of their historical setting could not have been satisfactorily appraised. . . .

The available evidence suggests that a given type is characterized by only a limited plasticity, and that the patterns of change are fixed by the nature of its fundamental structure. Consequently we may hardly expect to find that any population may be altered in any direction, or that by some form of transmutation through the agency of environmental alchemy we may transform one stock into the semblance of another. We have no evidence to support such a deduction. Nature, in fact, furnishes abundant evidence to the contrary. But should further investigation corroborate our hypothesis of a dynamic human structure, plastic to environmental influences, but limited in its plasticity both in direction and extent, then our methods of comparison must be adjusted to recognize these possibilities.

The preceding discussion springs mainly from a consideration of the changes undergone by the Japanese born in Hawaii. But our data also indicate that antecedent to this expression of plasticity, some form of selection governed the type of immigrant who ventured to Hawaii. It would appear, therefore, that the difference between the Japanese sedentes in Japan and the Japanese born and bred in Hawaii rests not entirely on environmental factors but is attributable in part to the differentiation which characterized the immigrants. I confess that it is difficult to understand the mechanism which might select such an immigrant type. I have already explained that no physical selection was exercised by recruiters. Economic pressure did, of course, govern the composition of the human stream of laborers who migrated to Hawaii. But that does not explain why the immigrants differ from the sedentes, since the subjects in the control series of sedentes are close relatives of the immigrants and they have both been bred under similar conditions. . . .

If, admitting the inefficacy of a social or economic basis for the selection of an immigrant type, we turn to a psychological explanation then we are faced with other difficulties. It becomes necessary to assume that the immigrants are differentiated not only physically but psychologically as well, and that physical differences are associated with innate psychological ones. While innate psychological drives no doubt exist, it is extremely doubtful that they are genetically linked with special physical variations within a mixed population. Moreover, it also becomes necessary to explain the similar selection found among the immigrant women. Although they are not as definitely differentiated from the sedentes as are the immigrant males, nevertheless they do parallel the male pattern. The immigrant women either accompanied their husbands or were sent to Hawaii as "picture brides." In neither case does individual choice appear to have been especially open to the women. Consequently, the psychology of the immigrant does not appear to have determined their migration.

Still another explanation of the immigrant differentiation suggests itself. It may be argued that the divergence of the immigrants from the sedentes is not so much an original difference as it is the result of a modification induced by the Hawaiian environment. But this is unsatisfactory for corollary reasons. In the first place, the immigrants with few exceptions were adult on their arrival in Hawaii. And secondly, changes of the degree shown by the immigrants are contrary to our knowledge of the plasticity of adults. It is true men and women show some alteration in their dimensions during the period of maturity and senility but these changes are usually relatively slight in comparison to the numerous significant differences which distinguish immigrants from the sedentes. It would, for example, be highly improbable to expect that the marked drop in the absolute and relative trunk height among the immigrants be achieved in maturity and as a consequence of an environmental change. Furthermore, it is perhaps significant that whereas the Hawaiian born reflect environmental changes only in their quantitative or size characters, the immigrants, on the other hand, show definite evidence of differentiation in their qualitative traits as well. . . .

If migratory groups represent selected strains of a population which may later undergo additional modification through environmental influences, then a mechanism is provided here to explain some of the variation which is encountered among related populations. I do not suggest that selective migration and environmental modification are the only or even the major forces in evolution or in producing group variations, but they do offer contributory factors to the complex process of differentiation and evolution. I see no reason why evolution and variation need necessarily be confined to a single mechanism. It seems to me that a truer picture would include the combined inter-action of a large number of factors and circumstances.

Part IV

THE WAYS OF SUBMERGED PEOPLES: TACTICS
OF SURVIVAL AND COUNTER-ASSERTION

11

THE PREDICAMENTS OF MINORITIES

THE MEETING and mixing of peoples has almost completely eliminated the independent, isolated group, but the number of minorities has been multiplied as originally separate groups have become incorporated in some larger national or colonial unit. The larger national units into which minority groups are incorporated politically and economically do not completely absorb them culturally and socially. Many are converted into repressed and excluded groups, living in the shadow of the dominant majority. Out of this situation the minority problem arises in all its increasing acuteness of culture clash and conflict. Minority group consciousness, although it may have originated in cultural distinctiveness, becomes increasingly a product of enforced relations to a majority treatment and policy. A minority group, irrespective of size or constituency, is thus best characterized as a social group whose solidarity is primarily determined by external pressure, which forces it to live in terms of opposition and ostracism.

With group status the crux of the minority position, the minority situation becomes nevertheless highly complex and variable. In the perspective of history, groups are seen subject to extreme and sometimes sudden change of status, passing from majority to minority status or the reverse, and sometimes assuming, even while in minority status, typical majority attitudes toward other minority groups. It is this subtlety and variability that makes general analysis of minority issues difficult. Yet only from comprehensive analysis can the basic factors of the minority situation be reached. With all their superficially baffling differences and complexities, minority situations do have essentially the same basic common factors and similar reactions and predicaments.

Minority and majority attitudes are intimately connected, so that the minority profile is more or less the complement of the majority profile. To explain minority behavior and attitude one has to scrutinize majority attitudes and policies as well. From this point of view, for example, the Negro "problem," as has been aptly said, becomes "a problem of the white mind." Minorities, of course, initiate attitudes and policies of their own, but even here, more often than not, the explanatory factors are to be found on the majority side, with the minority reaction a paired effect.

Certain groups, living in isolated and self-imposed group independence, are very special cases of the minority situation. The position of certain small "ethnic communities," particularly religious sect colonies, approximates that of an independent minority. They live in terms of distinctive difference and a preferred orthodoxy which separates them from their fellow communities. But in origin very often they go back to some historical majority-minority conflict, and have acquired their exclusive and sometimes fanatical separatism, in trying to escape the threat, remembered from the past or dreaded for the future, of majority discrimination and persecution. The American colonial scene, and the Canadian, as Dawson's article will show, was full of such nonconformist minorities and their refugee settlements. Most of them were destined to an ultimate minority lot through absorption back into larger communities.

Caroline Ware throws light on general minority behavior in her study of ethnic communities, of which she finds a large variety—religious settlements, trading communities or foreign settlements, settler colonies, refugee colonies, yet unabsorbed immigrant colonies, and racial, language and cultural minorities. Different as these are from one another, they are all subject to the common lot of cultural separatism and militantly contrasted status. The effective factors of conflict and hostility are not so much the cultural divergence itself, as it is the sense of difference and exclusion. The status and attitude of a minority group thus depends primarily on the reception it receives and the sort of barriers that are raised against it by the larger or more established or dominant community. Race, nationality, language and religion can all be sharp and serious issues of difference and hostility. Yet none of them need be. The Swiss confederation, for example, has reconciled language and national traditions still hostile to one another in other situations. The truce of races in the Moslem religion or under the French tradition has already been pointed out. There is also the comparative truce of religious animosity in the contemporary alignment of Catholics and Protestants as compared with their earlier open feuds.

Issues which seem, however, to have been resolved may turn out to be dormant merely, with fresh outbreaks of rivalry and hostility from time to time. Many of these issues have become intensified under conditions of the modern nationalist state, where, as Ware points out, minority groups can retain or assert their self-determinant identity only against the drive of the dominant majorities for a uniform culture and a single loyalty. The nation-state, by making this demand for an all-inclusive, paramount loyalty has sharpened the minority situation into one of the most critical issues of our time.

It is only in frontier situations that ethnic communities have any real chance for independent self-determined living. In Dawson's description of Western Canada, with its Doukhobor, Mennonite, German Catholic and other sectarian communities, one can achieve a realization of the colonial United States, with its Huguenot, Baptist, Quaker, German Pietist, Moravian, Mennonite refugees and the more recent Mormon and other sectarian settlements. Even in the vast, sparsely settled Canadian West, Dawson finds their separatism breaking down with the passing of frontier conditions and the intrusion of the railroad, the highway, urbanization, nationally organized education and the radio. The trend of a highly organized urban civilization is against their persistence, and they appear as relics of an age of separatism surviving in an age of fusion. As their physical separatism vanishes, their rigid cultural differentials dissolve in the process with only remnants remaining. Group settlements which seemed in irreconcilable conflict with the world and sought to exclude it by every known device have in one or two generations had to renounce rigid separation, although they may hold loyally to parts of their tradition. Their problem then becomes the same as that of the more definitely subordinated minorities and their minority traditions. They all seem destined to live in terms of a common civilization, with historical cultural differentials taking secondary place. The minority problem resolves itself more and more, then, into the alternative of whether these cultural differences of race, national tradition, language and religion are to be reconciled in practical reciprocity and mutual respect or maintained as barriers of proscription, prejudice and group hatred. Both Ware and Dawson agree on the inevitable assimilation of ethnic communities, and an integrated economic order and common material civilization as the prevailing trend in modern society.

The full predicament of the minority situation emerges in the case of minority groups subject to forced separatism while living in close juxtaposition or even subordinated incorporation with the majority group. Such is typical of both the Jewish and the Negro minorities, both of them subject to intense and sustained cultural proscription and prejudice. Wirth analyzes the force of cultural exclusion and group animosity upon the Jew, with particular reference to the Jew who does not identify himself with the Jewish orthodox community. Under some majority policies, different segments of the Jewish minority have been subject to different treatment; under others, as in the present Nazi persecution, practically the same disabilities and proscriptions have been meted out to all. Wirth points out how arbitrary and undiscriminating these majority prejudices are, and the particular handicap which they place upon the minority group that aspires to cultural assimilation and conformity. The Jew under these circumstances is made acutely conscious of difference, labeled arbitrarily with a group status, traits and attitudes not necessarily his as an individual. Such coercive group identification is bound, at first, to associate negative values with his group or racial consciousness. The experience of the Negro and members of other racial minorities is very similar. In the case of the Negro, the attitude is more acute by reason of the ease of his social identification, and the added irony that in the American situation, he has no separate religion and little racial tradition surviving into which to retreat. Under such majority persecution, morbidity, supersensitiveness, and an initial projection of resentment to one's own minority are understandable reactions. So, too, is that phenomenon common to highly restricted minorities, "passing" or concealment of group identity when possible and advantageous.

Individuals differ, according to temperament, in the degree of these minority group reactions; with some, positive hatred and aversion for his own group may predominate; with others, intensified loyalty and externalized projection of the animosity reaction back to the majority. Negative reactions develop ranging all the way from an oppression psychosis of hopelessness and despair, with all sorts of escapist mechanisms, to bitter cynicism and counter-hatred. Enhanced minority consciousness and a hectically reinforced group solidarity are inevitable developments in due course of time. Wirth points out how the culturally snubbed Jew has often become the apostle of nationalism and racial consciousness, and shows the extent to which anti-Semitism has been responsible for the development of Zionism. There are close analogies in other minority experience, particularly the Negro; Garvey-ism, as one example. Excessive factionalism, recurrent panaceas of solution, ultra-racialism often ensue, and a sensitive, at times fanatical minority group patriotism is generated.

All of these extremes and aberrations in minority behavior trace directly to majority treatment, although often as not, they are charged against the minority by the majority extremists. But in spite of all the pull and counter-tensions of conformity and non-conformist reactions, the average minority group manages somehow to adjust its life to the imposed social handicaps and paradoxes. In many cases they adopt conformity for advantage and recognition, while building, on the other hand, their separate tradition for compensation to enhance minority morale and solidarity. Morale is continuously necessary, for even after the cruder phases of majority segregation and persecution subside, later generations of minority groups have to meet the ordeals of ostracism and cultural disdain. In societies where prejudice prevails, members of minority groups are forced to accept mass rather than individual appraisal, and to learn to expect mass condemnation from a society that, as Wirth puts it, "imposes collective responsibility from without."

Such is the typical predicament when an intense racial or religious prejudice motivates the majority. The initial effects tend, naturally enough, to stagnation of hope and effort or attempts on the part of individuals to escape the minority lot. But the secondary effect is a challenge to fight the handicap of the situation. Minority progress, even though it may reap fresh prejudice from its success and its threat of rivalry, pivots on the motive to disprove the majority libel and to demonstrate the abilities and possibilities of the minority group. This enters in as a strong component in the individual ambition of many minority-conscious individuals. The dominance of this type of motivation is significant of the second, more positive phase in the group history of minorities.

Frazier, in a panoramic review of the Negro family, traces the American Negro minority experience in what amounts to two parallel stages of minority demoralization and minority compensation and reconstruction. In the Negro's case, in addition to the complete loss of his traditional patterns of culture and family life, there was the almost complete demoralization which slavery wrought, complicated by extensive concubinage and miscegenation. The gradual achievement of majority patterns and standards of family life, therefore, represents a double accomplishment, assimilation of an alien majority culture and recovery from deep social disorganization under majority suppression. The close incorporation of the institution of domestic slavery facilitated this process in one respect, but hampered it greatly in the other. The Negro still finds majority imposed obstacles, social and economic, blocking the path to complete cultural conformity. But he has made no reservation in his program of complete assimilation, and the results are remarkable in respect to the cultural gap that has been successfully bridged and the short space of time during which the adjustments have been made.

The advance, as Frazier shows, has had to be made at disproportionate cost. At every stage the minority predicament has complicated the already difficult process of adjustment, since the process of culture assimilation required values of conformity and procedures of imitation, while the majority prejudice imposed separatism and differential standards. The present degree of conformity is retarded only by the resistances to complete social and economic integration which still persist. Yet the majority has set in motion forces which it cannot completely halt. The dominant forces now affecting the Negro family organization, and increasingly operating on the Negro masses, are those of rapid urbanization. These have brought an inevitable toll of economic maladjustment and discrimination, but also an acceleration of cultural assimilation, that in the judgment of the author, seems to overbalance the social costs, and promise much closer integration of the black minority.

Allen details a little known and partially successful effort on the part of the Negro during Reconstruction days toward constructive assimilation. For a short decade or so after the enfranchisement of the Southern Negroes, black and white members of the Southern state legislatures participated together in such a movement. In spite of statements to the contrary, the numerical ratios of Negroes and whites in these legislatures show that there was no real threat of Negro domination. What eventually wrecked the system and brought back disfranchisement of the bulk of the Negro population after a reign of Ku Klux terrorism was an intolerance of anything approaching equality. The enactments of these legislatures were not confiscatory or vindictive and much of the legislation was in the general interest. Progressive measures issued from many of these bodies, often at Negro initiative—among them, attempts to break up the large agricultural landholdings (but with proposed compensation), the abolition of property rights for voting, the establishment of civil rights' bills, and most important of all provisions, the establishment for the first time in the South of free public education of any kind. There was here a temporary coalition of minority interests—those of the recently freed Negroes and of the upland or poor-white farmers, which together constituted the real numerical majority of the South. This coalition, hardly aware of itself and its potential power, was attacked by a propagandist white "majority" movement which speciously raised the "Negro domination" bogey, called these heavily mixed bodies "black Parliaments" and labeled this progressive agrarian and educational program "Negro rule" and "black dominance." The success of this propaganda in gaining the support of the poor whites is another indication of the operation of traditional majority racialism and its popular appeals. With the lapse of the political and civil rights guarantees granted by these legislatures, the Negro minority slipped back almost to its old status in the South, from which there has as yet been no mass recovery, but only the hard gains of individual achievement and progress.

Foreman tells of a comparable unsuccessful struggle of the Seminole Indians to make an adjustment in the framework of the majority culture. These tribes over a period of decades made continuous effort to incorporate the white man's political, economic and educational institutions. They were only to be thwarted by majority mismanagement and persecution, the record shows, and not from any inability to reconcile the newer with their traditional culture. It was this type of mismanagement that led to the messianic Ghost Dance religion which swept through the Indian tribes of the country, the philosophy of which is illuminated by the interview with the Indian chief, described by McGillicuddy. The minority group, on the whole, is inclined to be set in the groove of imitativeness by the very process of assimilation; and this was probably more general among the Indian tribes than is recognized, certainly where the white majority civilization gained prestige in their view, and before the type of bitter disillusionment set in which this incident records. A good portion of Indian intransigence was really a matter of cynical disillusionment and withdrawal in the face of obvious hostility and deception.

Monica Hunter reports on a primitive minority people, the South African Bantu, who, in some of their tribal branches have chosen the alternative of withdrawal, but in others have been incorporated into the dominant social system. She records acute and cynical disillusionment of the latter group with the majority motives and policy. Only the power of the majority regime seems to be respected; it has lost almost completely its prestige and sway over the minds of the thinking elements of the minority. The attitude of the educated Bantu is marked by bitter resentment, with group attempts, here and there, at counter-assertion and aggressive nationalist organization. Where such extreme repression prevails, as in South Africa, even the merest beginnings of native nationalist programs and organization is deeply significant and all the more so when, as is cited, a conference based on a minority coalition of native Bantu, half-caste "Colored" and Indian (Hindu) groups is in active organization.

W. O. Brown similarly reports on what he calls "an immature racialism" in South Africa, among the native population which according to its growth within a single decade, will "ultimately grow into a matured race consciousness." For several generations after the military subjugation of the Zulus, there was almost complete submissiveness on the part of the leaderless and heavily exploited South African natives. Their condition, though not nominal slavery, approximated that under the American slaveocracy, with local variations of forced labor, agricultural and domestic peonage and similar subordinations. Brown reports, as does Hunter, that while the white man still has power and status, he is rapidly losing prestige among the natives in this area. There has gone along with this the rapid rise of race consciousness, the emergence of labor and nationalist organizations among natives, and the sporadic outbreak of protest and aggressive movements, the latter pivoted on racialist programs. Some of these movements are ephemeral and escapist, but others are marked by dawning realism and practicality. The rising tide of racialism seems to find expression on many fronts, religious, economic and political, and as a symptom of minority counter-assertion is far from being negligible.

Repressive policies of labor contracts and taxation and wholesale detribalization have operated to give impetus to native solidarity. Tribal, caste and cultural lines which originally would have put barriers in the way of common interests and co-operation have been swept aside, leaving wider scope for more inclusive organization. So even in the depressed minority situation of South Africa, reactions show nascent minority developments which are but the early phases of that mature type of minority counter-assertion of which Indian Nationalism today is a classical example. Indian nationalism, likewise, started from the contrary and unreconciled pressures of majority policies, particularly because the path of the English educated Indian is blocked through denial of the advantages of full cultural participation. In line with such inevitabilities, Brown states it as his opinion that in time Bantu racial consciousness will be sufficiently strong to constitute a serious challenge to the majority policy and program as soon as a knowledge of more developed movements and their tactics of organization reach the receptive soil of native resentment and reaction.

Majority repression of minorities is only securely successful so long as it succeeds in having the minority accept itself in the dictated terms of the imposed subordination. As soon as there is a beginning of the re-definition of self-determined group objectives on the part of the minority, a second phase of relationships has really begun, even though it may take a considerable while to take root and develop. This counter-assertive phase of minority life is the consideration of Chapter 12.

ETHNIC COMMUNITIES

*The persistence of ethnic communities is due in part to the degree
of divergence between the dominant and the minority culture, in
part to the size of the group and the nature of the bonds which
hold it together but primarily to the reception which the group
receives, the status which it is accorded and the barriers which we
raised against its members by the larger community. The fate of
the ethnic communities depends further upon the leadership they
generate and their isolation or contact.*

ETHNIC COMMUNITIES are groups bound together by common ties of race, nationality or culture, living together within an alien civilization but remaining culturally distinct. They may occupy a position of self-sufficient isolation or they may have extensive dealings with the surrounding population while retaining a separate identity. In its strict meaning the word ethnic denotes race; but when applied to communities in the above sense it is loosely used, in the absence of any other comprehensive term, to cover the more general concept of culture. Purely religious communities, such as the Mormons or the Shakers, or economic communities, like the New Harmony or Brook Farm groups, do not fall under the term although they are in many respects similar to the groups here discussed.

Such communities vary according to their origin, their cohesive factors, the attitudes of the outer community, and the nature of the civilization of which they are a part. They tried to survive by reason of self-consciousness produced by divergence and through the tenacity of their social institutions. In major group migrations ethnic communities may be created because the exodus of one people to make way for another is rarely complete. Very frequently the remnant of the old does not lose its identity, and although it becomes merged with the oncoming multitudes it retains its ancient customs, its language and its group consciousness intact. Eastern Europe is full of such communities surviving from the waves of Teutonic and Slavic migration in the early centuries of the Christian era. Efforts to rectify

---

Excerpt from Caroline F. Ware, "Ethnic Communities," *Encyclopaedia of
the Social Sciences,* Vol. 5 (New York: Macmillan, 1931), pp. 607-613.

boundaries at the close of the World War were impeded, especially in Transylvania, by the presence of just such self-conscious communities, owing their origin to population movements more than a thousand years before. Still older communities are to be found in the Near and Middle East, where centuries of population movement have left their traces in a tangled mass of unamalgamated units living in close juxtaposition to one another. The Turkish Republic has found these communities a major obstacle to the development of its national character and has endeavored by exchange of populations to rid itself of elements which the old empire had been unable to assimilate.

Communities originating from migration movements survive chiefly through their own cohesion and their resistance to assimilation. Where communities are created through military conquest they are more apt to be forced into existence by the command of the dominant group, as when conquering invaders expropriate a subjected land and set aside an area to which the native population is segregated. In the United States, Indian reservations were created in this way and were so completely endowed with a community character that until recent years American law dealt with them only as tribes, not as individuals. Native quarters are familiar features of cities where an alien has taken forcible possession. Such communities tend to hold a definitely lower social status than those arising from migration, as they are conquered groups and not simply minorities. Where a people has been sent into captivity as a group, as the Jews in Babylon, or have been individually enslaved, as the Negroes in America, ethnic communities may develop in quite different ways. The Jews in Babylon drew closer their tribal bonds, defined more consciously their culture pattern, recorded their history, laws and customs and emerged from captivity with their traditional culture strengthened. The American Negroes, however, isolated and without leadership, drawn from different tribes which did not even speak the same language and bound together only by a common color and status, have built out of the culture of their captors a new culture.

Administrative and trading groups in foreign, usually "backward," countries may be considered ethnic communities. With a personnel which is largely transient and a status equal if not definitely superior to that of the general community, they deliberately and as a matter of political policy set themselves apart in order to maintain their prestige and conserve their culture. The largest and most famous of such communities are to be found in the Far East, where the English quarter of an Indian city is as distinct as a Chinatown in America. In most modern European colonies this policy is aided by racial distinctiveness, but in the absence of marked dissimilarity it becomes necessary to resort to force. The famous Statute of Kilkenny forbidding the English of the Pale to intermarry with the Irish whom they were administering was prompted by fear that the governing body would be absorbed into the country and political control be lost. The color legislation of the Union of South Africa, distinguishing the whites, the colored and the natives, is a similar effort on a larger scale to keep the governing group from being undermined by the encroachments of a growing mixed element. Trading colonies, although not backed by the same political force, have been similarly imposed upon the area in which they are located and remain separate because of superiority, not simply because of difference. The "factories" of the East India companies in India, the outposts of progress along the jungle rivers of Africa and the imposing settlement of Shanghai with its European laws, its English speech and its complete separateness from the corresponding native town, all represent a more powerful material culture and are indirectly allied to more powerful political states. . . .

The shifting of boundaries between modern nationalist states inevitably creates communities culturally allied to their former and distinct from their new nationalities, as in Alsace-Lorraine and the southern Tyrol. Such communities have a distinctly different status from any of the separatist groups described above. Because they claim identity with a still independent national group they receive external support and look forward hopefully to the time when the turn of the political wheel may carry them to the other side of the frontier. Efforts to Germanize Alsace after 1870 could hardly hope for success while the statue of Strasbourg in Paris stood draped in black.

Communities of fugitives or of voluntary emigrants are familiar types today. Of the two a body of involuntary exiles is more apt to make a positive effort to retain its cultural identity. Among the more potent reasons why Jewish communities have remained distinct from their environment in eastern Europe and elsewhere is the fact that they have been communities of fugitives, not of voluntary emigrants; and their presence in any land has usually been due to the desire to escape from a worse situation elsewhere. Certain of the settlers in the American colonies, notably the German sects, and some of the groups going more recently to the interior of South America have set out with the intent of maintaining their own community life in the land of their adoption, but usually when emigrant communities retain their distinguishing features it is more by accident than by design. Such groups entering a wilderness may count on isolation to permit the survival of their own culture, but where the isolation of the wilderness has given way to the contacts of an industrial civilization the tendency of the alien to seek the reassurance and guidance of his own kind is responsible for community development. Such immigrant ghettos have been accepted in Canada as more or less permanent and have been encouraged by permission to use the language of the group in the schools, but in the United States these "little Italies" and "little Polands" have been denounced as evidences of the failure of the process of assimilation called for by national policies. By the act of immigration the immigrant voluntarily accepts the country to which he goes and he is expected to become an integral part of it. The persistence of ethnic communities under these circumstances is due in part to the degree of divergence between the dominant and the minority culture, in part to the size of the group and the nature of the bonds which hold it together but primarily to the reception which the group receives, the status which it is accorded and the barriers which we raised against its members by the larger community. The survival of immigrant groups as ethnic communities may be very generally attributed to the attitudes of the country which they have entered.

Physical difference which cannot be changed or concealed sets one group apart from another and marks any man who seeks to leave his community and become part of the surrounding culture. The Chinese who seeks to leave his Chinatown is under a severe handicap not experienced by the Italian who emerges from little Italy. Differences in color are conspicuous and count for more than those involving head form, which may interest the anthropologist. The importance of race varies not only with the degree of racial divergence but with the strength of race prejudice in the dominant group, a fact clearly displayed in the contrast between Anglo-Saxon and Spanish or Portuguese colonies. Race becomes more potent as a differentiating factor when reinforced by differences of culture or status. The American Negro is confined to certain occupations and excluded from full participation in American life partly because he started as a slave. . . .

Where no marked racial differences exist, cultural difference forms the basic cohesive bond and appearance merely supports cultural barriers. The cultural unit may be a tribal one, as in certain groups in the Near East, or it may derive from local tradition, as in the Tyrol and Alsace. Elsewhere a submerged national group such as the Poles, Slovaks or Czechs preserves its national culture. Most commonly, however, the cultural differences are those that obtain between the culture of the home state of the culture community and that of the new state, differences involving language, tradition, common interest in the land of origin, common pride and common customs. In the case of European quarters of eastern cities the culture represented is compositely occidental rather than the peculiar heritage of a single national group.

Supplementary to race and nationality the strongest reinforcing factors are language and religion, both of which are apt to be essential parts of the national culture complex. The development of national languages, coterminous, for the most part, with national states, has made language a symbol of nationality as well as the vehicle of tradition. The retention of the traditional tongue is often the principal aim of those who seek to prevent an ethnic group from losing its identity, while the loss of that language is taken as a measure of amalgamation. It was largely through the preservation of the Polish language that the Poles retained their common identity for a hundred and fifty years under Russian, Austrian and German domination. In attempting to mold the Tyrol into an undifferentiated province of the Italian state the principal drive has been against the use of the German language and has been carried to the point of changing the place names to their Italian form or an Italian substitute.

Religion, although less outwardly distinguishing than either race or language, is a peculiarly cementing force because of its institutional character and its possibilities for intellectual leadership. Its sustaining force is outstandingly displayed in the case of the Jews. . . . Other groups show the same experience in a modified form. To the Armenians their church has been for centuries the symbol of their nationality. German Mennonites, Dunkers and other sectaries in the United States have remained distinctly German communities, while neighboring German farmers have lost their separate identity. Among the French of Canada the Catholic church has undoubtedly been the strongest factor in preserving their cultural community intact, while among recent immigrant groups in the United States it has played a similar role. Polish churches and parochial schools form the central institutions of many Polish communities in America. Even among the Irish, where no language factor has operated to keep the group apart, the identification of Irish with Catholic and the teaching of Irish history in parochial schools have helped strongly to prevent loss of identity and to keep the Irish after several generations a partially if not wholly distinct culture group.

Other elements of cohesion and differentiation support those already described, although none have the separative force of race, nationality, language or religion. Differences of economic organization are occasionally important most notably in the case of the gypsies, who have maintained their tribal organization, nomadic character and primitive economy in the midst of a sharply contrasting industrial civilization. More frequently it is difference of economic status rather than of organization which maintains the barrier between groups and prevents amalgamation. Those who wish to keep the American Negroes a distinct group recognize that the latter's economic status aids this purpose and oppose economic and professional advance on the part of the Negroes, knowing that it will weaken the barriers raised against them.

Tradition is a very strong factor in communities that have remained in a fixed place to which traditions are attached—principally those communities created by conquest or political transfer. It is very much weaker in immigrant communities, where the traditions are often ill adapted to the new environment, where they do not have the place association which might otherwise keep them alive and where there is often no literate group necessary to perpetuate them.

Given these lines of cohesiveness as a basis for survival, the fate of ethnic communities depends further upon the leadership they generate, their isolation or contact, the attitude of the majority group and the economic and political texture of the society of which the community is a part. A major difference with regard to the pressure that has been exercised from the outside exists between ethnic communities of ancient or medieval times and those situated within modern nationalistic states. During the Middle Ages, when political and economic life was organized locally, the survival of ethnic entities was a matter of course. Trading communities of English in the Netherlands or the German Hanse in London were set up by definite agreement. The Venetians demanded in return for assistance to the crusaders the right to establish trading posts within the cities of the East where their measures, laws and tongue should prevail. Throughout the western world the isolation of economic life and the particularism of political organization permitted the survival of self-contained, diverse units. With the beginnings of nationalist sentiment in the West the situation changed. Minority groups could retain or assert their self-determinant identity only against the drive of the dominant majorities for a uniform culture and single loyalty.

Ethnic communities produced by immigration are subjected to similar types of pressure as soon as they become large enough to awaken a sense of fear—not fear lest they rise in active political revolt but lest they deflect the development of a nation from its traditional channels and cause power and control to pass from the dominant to the submerged groups. In their relations to the indigenous Indian population the countries of the New World have encountered problems similar to those of the ancient migration-founded communities of Europe, but with respect to later immigrant groups radically different relationships have arisen. In Canada the presence of an established French population which antedated the English induced a policy of tolerance toward other groups, their cultural autonomy being in a measure acknowledged through permission to retain their language for some official and educational purposes. In the United States, on the other hand, the system of public education with its almost universal use of English established the principle that the nation was to be unilingual and unicultural at base. The successful operation of this principle was taken for granted. It remained for the events of the World War to bring out the fact that the nation was not of one culture and one language and that neither Jacksonian democracy with its assertion of the similarity and equality of all nor the later theory of the melting pot had worked effectively. While the public schools were teaching in English, private schools, particularly certain parochial groups both Protestant and Catholic, were carrying on instruction in various foreign tongues; and both industrial centers and rural regions contained communities culturally distinct from their American surroundings and conscious of their separate identity.

These communities had developed and survived in part through the constant additions to their ranks from the stream of newly arrived immigrants and in part through the fact that the American people did not carry into practice their national theory of equality. Branding the members of these communities as "wops," "hunkies" or "kikes" they exerted social pressure to force them back into their ghettos, where they might seek their place among their own kind. Of low economic status, without an intelligentsia (except in the case of the Jews), leaderless and with a tendency to lose successful members, since the price of success is often the severing of group ties, these immigrant communities hung on in most American cities, ignored by many and condemned by others as un-American. They have all developed certain characteristic features. In every case mutual benefit societies have been formed to assist members at times of sickness or death and incidentally to serve as social gathering places. In practically every case food stores and restaurants purveying the type of food familiar at home have served as centers where gossip is exchanged, news shared and the stereotypes of thought and action reinforced and preserved. In most communities a church follows the first signs of prosperity when the group is able to support a priest, for to many an immigrant his religion is the only experience which he can carry unchanged from his old home to his new. Whether or not a school follows the establishment of the church depends largely upon leadership, for the demand for education is far from universal among immigrants, who are often illiterate. The development of schools is most apt to be stimulated by religious authorities seeking either to preserve the religious affiliation of a group exposed to alien ways or to enable a particular church with its leaders to survive. Thus in certain communities Polish priests, seeking to retain their parish membership among the second generation of immigrants, have established parochial schools presided over by Polish nuns where the Polish language, history and traditions are taught. When not supported by religious leaders such schools are usually the work of organization officials who see in the younger generation the only way to maintain organizations which originally grew up to protect newcomers. Where a community is sufficiently large and literate, a press in the native tongue brings in the news of the old country, the gossip of the community itself and an interpretation of the affairs of the nation at large. Although it can hardly remain so complete for more than one generation in a city, a new generation does not see the end of the old isolation.

These communities consist of a solid, group-conscious nucleus, surrounded by a fringe which is gradually being worn away by intermarriage, education, participation in such activities as sports and by economic change. They are torn within themselves by conflicts between the generations, for the first generation of native-born children, subjected to external influences, differs sharply in ways and attitudes from its parents. The internal factors holding the communities together are weakened wherever immigration has been reduced, and the attitude of the outer group bulks larger as a perpetuating force.

The World War had a very distinct effect upon the ethnic groups in America. It revealed to the American people that these communities not only had continued to exist but were of such proportions as to threaten the continued dominance of the old group. It called attention to the role that these communities may play as centers for propaganda by enemy or by radical groups and showed them as bases for European operations by elements interested in political change in the old country. In consequence, it stimulated an active program of Americanization which developed into the campaign to assert Nordic superiority and resulted in the passage of the quota immigration law based on the assumption that certain ethnic groups can be assimilated into the American body politic more easily than others. At the same time the emphasis on self-determination and the birth of the many post-war nations that grew out of the ethnic communities within the Hapsburg, Hohenzollern, Romanov and Ottoman dominions gave the nationals of those countries greater self-confidence. While removing from these groups the necessity of keeping alive the national sentiment for which they had been responsible when their nations were only countries of the mind, it gave backing and standing to members of these rejuvenated nations abroad. In response to talk of Nordic superiority, leaders within immigrant communities have arisen to demand recognition for their groups, not merely for the exceptional individual. Such leaders are insisting that the amalgamation of ethnic groups into the American community must be by incorporation, not by suppression, and must proceed on the basis of respect for differences of inherited tradition and culture.

While America was becoming conscious of her ethnic groups, the nations of Europe proceeded on the assumption that ethnic communities are to remain characteristic of European life. The principle was recognized in the formation of the Minorities Commission of the League of Nations and in the treaty clauses requiring the defeated states to recognize their minority groups, although the victorious powers imposed no such obligations upon themselves. Soviet Russia has fostered cultural autonomy within the Soviet Union, encouraging Tartars, Cossacks, Jews or Armenians to develop their group consciousness and their cultural institutions upon their inherited soil or in newly created communities on land set apart for them by the government. Acceptance of the communist economic system is the only conformity required.

Meanwhile, the force of economic pressure is constantly at work, breaking down isolation, producing physical mobility, causing contacts between members of different groups and rewarding those who are successful at the economic game, with scant regard for the group from which they come. The same factors which are wearing down cultural differences between nations are at work to eliminate ethnic communities within states. Although a standardized, international language makes slight headway and although international bitterness keeps alive national self-consciousness between and within states, the diffusion of a standardized material culture, elimination of distance and the common language of business are all at work to make the ethnic community a relic of a separatist age. Its greatest opponent is the unconscious pressure of an integrated economic society and a leveling material civilization.

SECTARIAN SETTLEMENTS ON THE CANADIAN PRAIRIES

In situations where cultural invasion threatens religious and nationalistic minorities manifest a sectarian tinge and seek to retain their identity by isolating themselves in a measure from their neighbors. This is done by settling in homogeneous groups and maintaining their own language and institutions. Participation in the outside labor market, the entrance of the railway, the penetration of commercial towns and the secular institutions which accompanied them and the entrance of new settlers operate to diffuse outside ideas and practices within the settlements.

GROUP SETTLEMENT, too, has been much in evidence in the prairie region of the Canadian West. In Manitoba, Saskatchewan, and Alberta homogeneous groups have taken possession of specific areas where their members comprised from half to all of the population and where a sense of communal solidarity was experienced from the outset. . . . Some of these groups exhibit more individualism in community building than others. The Germans and French are the most individualistic, but their individualism is held in check by a common desire to maintain their cultural distinctiveness. The collective *motif* is dominant in the sectarian settlements of the Doukhobors. . . .

In the sect a spontaneous enthusiasm for an ideal "way of life" unites the members, regardless of how divergent their original backgrounds. Conscious of their solidarity, they pursue their objectives with a fervor which is often fanatical. They ardently oppose compromise because they are convinced that all others should be possessed of their "way of life." While at its inception the purposes of the sect

Excerpts from C. A. Dawson, "Group Settlement, Ethnic Communities in Western Canada," in *Canadian Frontiers of Settlement*, Vol. VII, edited by W. A. Mackintosh & W. L. G. Joerg (Toronto: The Macmillan Company of Canada Ltd., 1936), pp. xiii-xx, 378-380.

and their means of attainment are vague, they are emotionally compelling. In time they become defined in a "way of life" which prescribes for every member what he should unalterably do in the most intimate affairs. Later, under the impact of more secular and individualistic societies this "way of life" becomes less irreconcilable and more tolerant of the ideal aims of other groups. Such has been the life history of political parties and all or most of our major religious denominations. They emerged in emotional turmoil, were in conflict with the world, and sought to exclude it by every known device.

As just indicated, sectarian behavior is not limited to the field of religion. Political groups are often as emotionally intense and uncompromising in respect to an ideal order they seek to establish as are religious groups in their espousal of a "way of life." Each type of sect represents a radical departure from the established definitions of situations on which others continue to rely. Yet it is possible to distinguish between them. It is noteworthy of political sects that they soon begin a revolutionary attack upon the social and economic order about them. They seek not to withdraw from the world but to change it for themselves and for all others. The religious sects, with whom we have been most familiar, have endeavored to withdraw from the world and perfect their mystically conceived "way of life." If those about them would be saved they must flee the world and join the sect. The religious sect gives vent to its emotions in experience meetings, through ritual, and by spontaneous assent to its asserted verities. It is ecstatic rather than aggressive. However, if political groups are effectively frustrated in their efforts they may either be dissolved or become emotionally expressive like the religious sect. The Doukhobors and Mennonites had, at least during the early decades of their life on the Canadian prairies, the characteristics of the religious sect described above. The Mormons represent a middle stage in the evolution of the sect. Their somewhat radical departure from the Bible of the Christian churches, their espousal of polygamy for a period of their history, their recent emergence, and their protracted geographical isolation in the commonwealth of Utah have combined to retain for the Mormons much of their original zeal. Nevertheless, in many respects they have developed an elaborate and mature type of religious organization and in a large measure have become accommodated to the secular world after the fashion of other major religious denominations. This has been facilitated by the possession of the same language as their neighbors.

The other groups studied belong to the Roman Catholic Church whose sectarian stage was outgrown during the early centuries of the Christian era. Long ago this church learned how to deal discriminatingly with secular forces. Its "way of life" and the philosophy of a competitive and individualistic order have become adjusted to each other. As a religious group it is mature and wise in the ways of two worlds. In a large measure ritual and technique have taken the place of the unconventional enthusiasm of the early centuries of expectancy. The Roman Catholic Church has had its periods of revival when emotional urgency was great. At times it has become identified with linguistic and cultural revivals and received a transferred emotional quickening in some respects akin to sectarianism. Thus the Roman Catholic Church is linked with linguistic and nationalistic sentiments in German Catholic communities in the prairie region. Similarly, the Catholic Church is associated with French-Canadian nationalism in facing Anglicization and the marked secularization which accompanies it. In situations where cultural invasion threatens, religious and nationalistic minorities manifest a sectarian tinge and seek to retain their identity by isolating themselves in some measure from their neighbors. This is done by settling in homogeneous groups and maintaining their own language and institutions.

Such congregate settlement is known as *segregation*. Racial and religious groups may have blocks of land allocated to them as had the Doukhobors and the Mennonites, and in large measure also the German Catholics and the Mormons. Without prevision, however, segregation may take place through the natural desire of migrants to settle beside neighbors possessing the same language, religion, and general culture. To some degree this natural process was present in all groups studied, but it was most active in the case of the Mormons, Germans, and French-Canadians. In these latter groups it was reinforced by the colonizing urge of a sponsoring institution, a land-settlement organization, or a nationalistic society. Furthermore, leaders in these homogeneous communities were active in stimulating the entry of population elements possessing their own ethnic backgrounds. Consequently, these minorities became distinctive societies occupying their own land-base and further separated from neighboring communities by language, institutions, and nationalistic and sectarian sentiments. For varying periods these "culture islands" enjoyed a "splendid isolation." During such isolation, distinctive sects like the Mennonites and Doukhobors remained at a stage of arrested development in their life cycle. The world was shut out and they retained their initial fervor and their "way of life" unmodified. Such a situation could not continue when active railway building and the rapid entry of new peoples from outside regions took place. Portions of these sects moved again to new isolated areas. Those who remained experienced an invasion of peoples, institutions, and ideas which profoundly changed their mode of life.

The factor most significant in initiating the invasion of people and institutions within the confines of these "colonies" was the railway which was later supplemented by the permanent highway. The extension of the railway to the vicinity of the colony ordinarily means an intensive settlement of the land in proximity to the latter, as well as an invasion of its margins by outsiders who in time demand that their language, school system, and nationalistic sentiments prevail, not only on the margins, but throughout the colony. This was particularly true when these newcomers belonged to the region's English-speaking majority. Their active demand was a signal for the provincial government to extend its school system to "colony" districts. Thus the process of Anglicization moved forward. With the penetration of the railway within the precincts of the colony Anglicization was intensified because the railway was accompanied by the village which displaced the agricultural or church villages as the main centers within the colony. This displacement took place gradually, as the various studies will demonstrate. The commercial villages became the main points of entry for commercial institutions and professional services, manned in many instances by representatives of the region's English-speaking majority. Furthermore, since the commercial village is part of a constellation of villages and towns which is linked with the focal cities of the region by a permanent network of transportation and communication systems, it constitutes a major channel for the diffusion of outside culture in its ethnic constituency. Through the various avenues of social and economic penetration these ethnic groups are led to speak the official language of the region and to adopt its prevailing methods of making a living, its expenditure practices, and its loyalties. This assimilation of the colony as a unit gathers momentum through the children of immigrants and may require two generations or more for its completion. Knowing their young people's susceptibility to the cultural penetration of the surrounding communities, the sectarians respond to the situation by perennial opposition to government schools and to extensive contacts between their children and non-colony people.

Assimilation to the more secular world surrounding and invading these colonies calls for a consideration of the subsidiary processes of *secularization*. Secular values, as distinguished from sacred, are calculable, utilitarian, and mundane. They are largely divested of emotion and sentiment, and involve attitudes which reflect, in a measure, the critical detachment of science. There are aspects of church organization that have a secular emphasis, as for instance the administration of its finances, and there is a patriotic verve to sections of the public school curriculum which has much in common with sectarianism. Thus secular matters are not simply those which are dissociated from the dominance of the church, although such dissociation has ordinarily enhanced secularization and narrowed the field of religious control. These studies indicate how colony schools come under the direction of the secularly-minded provincial administrators of education and how minorities adopt the official language of the region as a utility and not as an object of sentiment. Evident, too, is the way in which play and recreation come under the direction of those who provide opportunities for participation in them on a pecuniary basis. Whether commercialized or not, colony play-activities are, increasingly, the outcome of human impulses controlled by the experimental standards of a secular society. Secularized play and recreation make their appeal more particularly to young people in these ethnic groups. They are a means of emancipation from strict patriarchal family authority and from the absolute control of a closed group society.

Secularization in these colonies is manifested, also, in the detachment of religion from a mother tongue and from the nationalistic sentiments associated with the latter: this means a wider use of the English language in religious services; it signifies the partial transfer of sentiment to non-traditional community objectives; and, in consequence, religious feeling freed from its previous ethnic affiliations becomes more tolerant of these new loyalties and is eventually aligned with them in new social situations. In short, the religious group re-defines its role in Anglicized communities with their marked secular emphasis. Sectarians of whatever type tend to make their peace with the plain facts of the extremely competitive society which has surrounded and invaded their colonies. . . .

The Doukhobors . . . differ most from individualistic Canadian communities. They live in farm villages, are a sect with a very distinctive "way of life," are collectivistic in ownership and operation of land, and differ from their neighbors in language and social practices. The Mennonites, like the Doukhobors, are quite distinctive from their Canadian neighbors in all major items except that they are individualists in ownership and operation of their land. The Mormons are still more like their fellow Canadians than are the Mennonites, since the former speak the English language. Furthermore, although religious traditions separate the Mormons from the religious denominations of Canada, they were somewhat tolerant of the latter at the time of migration and were moving toward a social adjustment with their non-Mormon neighbors. Some of them, also, were British in birth and sentiment.

The German Catholics . . . like the French-Canadians, differ from English-speaking Canadians in language and social practices; they were not Canadians. Yet the Germans differed from the latter only in language and certain cultural heritages, which had been somewhat changed during the previous sojourn of many of them in the United States. The French-Canadians . . . are Canadians by birth, language, and sentiment. They are, however, a minority group in the region studied and subject to many of the forces which are transforming other minority groups into individualistic English-speaking Canadian communities. . . .

The cultural factors which conditioned the productive efficiency of these ethnic groups also facilitated their social contacts and the establishment of their own institutional services. The loneliness of the pioneering period was lessened in an atmosphere of sympathy and understanding which made neighborly visits so frequent. In these homogeneous groups, too, more formal institutional services sprang into being quickly. Religious leadership, church buildings, and varied forms of religious organization emerged at the outset. Schools also were soon established among most of these groups upon their own insistence and very often through their own provision. In varying degrees they developed their own forms of economic organization. To these basic services the members of these colonies soon added a system of social and recreational organization. These institutions were accessible, received a minimum of subsidy, and were not readily displaced by invading institutions at a later date. The evidence makes it apparent that community organization developed readily in these communities and gave to the pioneers a sense of security and permanency during the early stages of their pioneering. It is, of course, true that these colonies were self-centered and stood aloof from the more secular aims which prevailed in the majority of other communities in the Canadian West.

It was to be expected that these separatist communities would arouse the antagonism of those settlers who belonged to neighboring communities in which a more secular pattern of life prevailed. Many of the social and economic movements which had received the ready support of other settlers were met with stout opposition in these colonies. The politics of the latter were uncertain; they seemed to be opposed, in some instances, to public schools, to avoid the official language of the region and, in certain groups, to be antagonistic to the nationalistic sentiments of the linguistic majority. In other instances, while the members of a colony spoke the official language, they adhered to religious tenets which seemed strangely alien. In such a situation the members of outside communities felt uncomfortable and insecure. Naturally they brought pressure to bear on governmental representatives to bring these *blocs* under school, homestead, and all other regulations without delay or compromise. In many instances these ethnic minorities were made extremely self-conscious and resentful by the antagonistic attitudes of their neighbors. In consequence, representatives of governmental departments found the task of extending their activities in certain of these colonies extremely difficult and costly. A similar strain was imposed on other administrators who sought to unite the members of these *bloc* communities with their neighbors in bringing about improvements in communication, marketing, banking, and many other matters which extended far beyond any colony. All these ventures involved deprivation, waste, and delay. Thus the incorporation of these ethnic communities in the social and economic structure of the prairie region placed a heavy burden upon all its inhabitants. This burden, particularly evident in the case of the Doukhobors, was manifest in some degree of all the groups studied.

All these communities have been subject to the play of forces which operated to break down the barriers which separated the homogeneous groups from their neighbors. Participation in the labor market outside, the entrance of the railway, the penetration of commercial towns and the secular institutions which accompanied them, and the entrance of settlers very different in outlook from the original colonists were some of the means by which the ideas and practices of the outside world were diffused within these colonies. While the public school did not make its entrance as unobtrusively as did certain other secular services, it soon became an effective means of extending the channels of contact with other peoples in the prairie region. It seems clear from the evidence analyzed that the unplanned play of external forces in the long run tends to eliminate much, perhaps all, of the distinctiveness of separatist colonies. School and other governmental regulations, when wisely administered, facilitate enormously the apparently inevitable assimilation of these ethnic minorities. Some of those who have attempted to hasten this assimilation by ill-chosen means, have unwittingly retarded it by arousing the self-consciousness and recalling the receding solidarity of these colonies. Assimilation may be facilitated by extending types of social organization to these ethnic communities if administrators learn how to work with the inevitable tide rather than against it.

WHY THE JEWISH COMMUNITY SURVIVES

In the past it was the influx of a constant stream of orthodox Jews that was relied upon to hold the community together and to perpetuate the faith. Today, however, this force can no longer be depended upon. The revival of prejudice against the Jew has served as a substitute. It has immensely stimulated group-consciousness and strengthened solidarity. It has turned a great number of Jews who were in the advanced stages of assimilation back to the fold.

N O SOONER does the Jew venture forth . . . into the broad cosmopolitan life of the outer world than he encounters external obstacles and experiences inner conflicts. The transition from one culture to another, and from one personality to another, is a process that requires not only time but demands the co-operation of both groups. . . .

The rebuffs administered by prejudice and exclusion serve to make the Jew keenly conscious of his separateness. He finds that the outer world will not receive him as an individual, but insists upon attaching the label "Jew" to him and to his children, not taking cognizance of the fact that he feels himself no more a part of his people than they consider him a part of themselves. He stands on the map of two worlds, not at home in either. His self is divided between the world that he has deserted and the world that will have none of him.

Having been successful in business or in his profession, the Jew who has tasted some of the fruits of the gentile world in free association with his more intimate circle of associates, with fellow-students in the university, or with the members of his professional group, at first seems to find the stories of prejudice and exclusion either exaggerated or at least not applicable to himself. His personality expands, and he relaxes somewhat in his studied manners and courtesies, just to be natural and act the part of one who is at home and feels at home. All the time, however, he is conscious of a bit of formality,

Excerpts from Louis Wirth, *The Ghetto* (Chicago: The University of Chicago Press, 1928), pp. 263, 264-266, 269-270, 271-272, 279.

sometimes overcordiality, which puts him on his guard. Stories of the prejudices and rebuffs that others of his faith have suffered reach him. Secretly he hopes that he will be able to put an end to all these unfounded rumors and will be able to return to his people to tell them that prejudice against the Jew is either a fiction or a justified reaction on the part of the Gentiles to the coarseness, the aggressiveness, and lack of tact of the Jews themselves. And sometimes he succeeds. But more often his hopes are shattered before he has even entered halfway into the outer world.

It takes an extreme courage to "face the music" of hostility as an individual. More often the tendency is to return to one's own people, to the small but human and sympathetic group of the family and the *Landsmannschaft*, where one is appreciated and understood. . . .

What has held the Jewish community together in spite of all disintegrating forces is, not only the return of disappointed Jews who have sought to get out, and, failing, have returned to become apostles of nationalism and racial consciousness, but also the fact that the Jewish community is treated as a community by the world at large. The treatment which the Jews receive at the hands of the press and the general public imposes collective responsibility from without. . . .

Until recently the German Jews, i.e., the reform element, and the Russian Jews, or orthodox element, each had its separate set of communal institutions. Consolidation for any length of time of the more important communal enterprises invariably was frustrated by the internal dissensions of the factions. Again under the impetus of external pressure the group was welded into a solid mass.

Nothing probably has done more in this direction than the revival of anti-Semitism. The attacks of Henry Ford and the organization of the modern Ku Klux Klan have mobilized the Jewish community into numerous organs for combat. The immigration legislation has called into existence national and local organizations for political action. And the cataclysmic changes in the economic condition of Eastern-European Jewry have produced international Jewish relief organizations which collect millions of dollars annually. Finally, the revival of anti-Semitism on a world-wide scale, with the heightened social consciousness of the Jews, has turned the utopian Zionism of the nineteenth century into an active nationalistic movement with practical objectives and organized political action. The alarming rate of intermarriage has turned the Jewish community inward and caused it to scan its social structure with a more critical eye. The unbounded faith in nostrums so characteristic of the Jew is shown by the promptness with which he turned to a reconstruction of what he considered the weak spots in this structure. . . .

While the ghetto has been emptying, there have been few new recruits to fill the vacancies. In the past it was the influx of a constant stream of orthodox Jews that was relied upon to hold the community together and to perpetuate the faith. Today, however, this force can no longer be depended upon. The revival of prejudice against the Jew has served as a substitute. It has immensely stimulated group-consciousness and strengthened solidarity. It has turned a great number of Jews who were in the advanced stages of assimilation back to the fold. It has given impetus to the Jewish nationalistic movement and to orthodoxy.

THE NEGRO FAMILY IN A WHITE MAN'S SOCIETY

After emancipation Negroes began to build their own institutions and to acquire the civilization of the whites through the formal process of imitation and education. Despite their high hopes that their freedom would rest upon a secure foundation of land-ownership, the masses of illiterate and propertyless Negroes were forced to become croppers and tenants under a modified plantation system. In their relative isolation they developed a folk culture with its peculiar social organization and social evaluations. The urbanization of the Negro population has brought about the most momentous change in the life of the Negro since emancipation.

DURING SCARCELY more than a century and a half of history, the Negro, stripped of the relatively simple preliterate culture in which he was nurtured, has created a folk culture and has gradually taken over the more sophisticated American culture. Although only three-quarters of a century has elapsed since the arrival of the last

Excerpt from E. Franklin Frazier, *The Negro Family in the United States* (Chicago: The University of Chicago Press, 1939), pp. 479-488.

representative of preliterate African races, the type of culture from which he came was as unlike the culture of the civilized American Negro today as the culture of the Germans of Tacitus' day was unlike the culture of German-Americans. . . .

When the Negro slave was introduced into American economic life, he was to all intents and purposes, to use the words of Aristotle, merely an "animate tool." But, as in all cases where slavery exists, the fact that the slave was not only animate but human affected his relations with his masters. To the slave-trader, who had only an economic interest in the slave, the Negro was a mere utility. But, where master and slave had to live together and carry on some form of co-operation, the human nature of the slave had to be taken into account. Consequently, slavery developed into a social as well as an economic institution. The lives of the white master class became intertwined with the lives of the black slaves. Social control was not simply a matter of force and coercion but depended upon a system of etiquette based upon sentiments of superordination, on the one hand, and sentiments of submission and loyalty, on the other. Thus the humanization of the slave as well as his assimilation of the ideals, meanings, and social definitions of the master race depended upon the nature of his contacts with the master race. Where the slave was introduced into the household of the master, the process of assimilation was facilitated; but, where his contacts with whites were limited to the poor white overseer, his behavior was likely to remain impulsive and subject only to external control.

Yet, social interaction within the more or less isolated world of the slave did much to mold his personality. Although in some cases the slaves retained the conception of themselves which they had acquired in their own culture, their children were only slightly influenced by these fading memories. Consequently, their personalities reflected, on the whole, the role which they acquired in the plantation economy. Individual differences asserted themselves and influenced the responses of their fellow-slaves as well as their own behavior. The large and strong of body and those of nimble minds outstripped the weak and slow-witted. Some recognition was shown these varying talents and aptitudes by the slaves as well as by the masters. Within the world of the slave, social distinctions appeared and were appreciated.

When the sexual taboos and restraints imposed by their original culture were lost, the behavior of the slaves in this regard was subject at first only to the control of the masters and the wishes of those selected for mates. Hence, on the large plantations, where the slaves were treated almost entirely as instruments of production and brute force was relied upon as the chief means of control, sexual relations were likely to be dissociated on the whole from human sentiments and feelings. Then, too, the constant buying and selling of slaves prevented the development of strong emotional ties between the mates. But, where slavery became a settled way of life, the slaves were likely to show preferences in sexual unions, and opportunity was afforded for the development of strong attachments. The permanence of these attachments was conditioned by the exigencies of the plantation system and the various types of social control within the world of the plantation.

Within this world the slave mother held a strategic position and played a dominant role in the family groupings. On the whole, the slave family developed as a natural organization, based upon the spontaneous feelings of affection and natural sympathies which resulted from the association of the family members in the same household. Although the emotional interdependence between the mother and her children generally caused her to have a more permanent interest in the family than the father, there were fathers who developed an attachment for their wives and children.

But the Negro slave mother, as she is known through tradition at least, is represented as the protectress of the children of the master race. Thus tradition has symbolized in the relation of the black foster-parent and the white child the fundamental paradox in the slave system—maximum intimacy existing in conjunction with the most rigid caste system. Cohabitation of the men of the master race with women of the slave race occurred on every level and became so extensive that it nullified to some extent the monogamous mores. The class of mixed-bloods who were thus created formed the most important channel by which the ideals, customs, and mores of the whites were mediated to the servile race. Whether these mixed-bloods were taken into the master's house as servants, or given separate establishments, or educated by their white forebears, they were so situated as to assimilate the culture of the whites. Although a large number of this class were poor and degraded, fairly well-off communities of mixed-bloods who had assimilated the attitudes and culture of the whites to a high degree developed in various parts of the country. It was among this class that family traditions became firmly established before the Civil War.

Emancipation destroyed the *modus vivendi* which had become established between the two races during slavery. Although the freedmen were able to move about and thereby multiply the external contacts with the white man's world, many of the intimate and sympathetic ties between the two races were severed. As a result, Negroes began to build their own institutions and to acquire the civilization of the whites through the formal process of imitation and education. Then, too, despite their high hopes that their freedom would rest upon a secure foundation of landownership, the masses of illiterate and propertyless Negroes were forced to become croppers and tenants under a modified plantation system. In their relative isolation they developed a folk culture with its peculiar social organization and social evaluations. . . .

The stability and the character of the social organization of the rural communities has depended upon the fortunes of southern agriculture. Up until the opening of the present century, the more ambitious and energetic of the former slaves and their descendants have managed to get some education and buy homes. This has usually given the father or husband an interest in his family and has established his authority. Usually such families sprang from the more stable, intelligent, and reliable elements in the slave population. The emergence of this class of families from the mass of the Negro population has created small nuclei of stable families with conventional standards of sexual morality all over the South. Although culturally these families may be distinguished from those of free ancestry, they have intermarried from time to time with the latter families. These families represented the highest development of Negro family life up to the opening of the present century.

However, the urbanization of the Negro population since 1900 has brought the most momentous change in the family life of the Negro since emancipation. This movement, which has carried a million

Negroes to southern cities alone, has torn the Negro loose from his cultural moorings. . . . During and following the World War, the urbanization of the Negro population was accelerated and acquired even greater significance than earlier migrations to cities. The Negro was carried beyond the small southern cities and plunged into the midst of modern industrial centers in the North. Except for the war period, when there was a great demand for his labor, the migration of the Negro to northern cities has forced him into much more rigorous type of competition with whites than he has ever faced. Because of his rural background and ignorance, he has entered modern industry as a part of the great army of unskilled workers. Like the immigrant groups that have preceded him, he has been forced to live in the slum areas of northern cities. In vain social workers and others have constantly held conferences on the housing condition of Negroes, but they have been forced finally to face the fundamental fact of the Negro's poverty. Likewise, social and welfare agencies have been unable to stem the tide of family disorganization that has followed as a natural consequence of the impact of modern civilization upon the folkways and mores of a simple peasant folk. Even Negro families with traditions of stable family life have not been unaffected by the social and economic forces in urban communities. Family traditions and social distinctions that had meaning and significance in the relatively simple and stable southern communities have lost their meaning in the new world of the modern city.

One of the most important consequences of the urbanization of the Negro has been the rapid occupational differentiation of the population. A Negro middle class has come into existence as the result of new opportunities and greater freedom as well as the new demands of the awakened Negro communities for all kinds of services. This change in the structure of Negro life has been rapid and has not had time to solidify. The old established families, generally of mulatto origin, have looked with contempt upon the new middle class which has come into prominence as the result of successful competition in the new environment. . . .

The most significant element in the new social structure of Negro life is the black industrial proletariat that has been emerging since the Negro was introduced into Western civilization. Its position in industry in the North was insecure and of small consequence until, with the cessation of foreign immigration during the World War, it became a permanent part of the industrial proletariat. This development has affected tremendously the whole outlook on life and the values of the masses of Negroes. Heretofore, the Negro was chiefly a worker in domestic and personal services, and his ideals of family and other aspects of life were a crude imitation of the middle-class standards which he saw. Very often in the hotel or club he saw the white man during his leisure and recreation and therefore acquired leisure-class ideals. . . . But thousands of Negroes are becoming accustomed to the discipline of modern industry and are developing habits of consumption consonant with their new role. As the Negro has become an industrial worker and received adequate compensation, the father has become the chief breadwinner and assumed a responsible place in his family.

When one views in retrospect the waste of human life, the immorality, delinquency, desertions, and broken homes which have been involved in the development of Negro family life in the United States, they appear to have been the inevitable consequences of the attempt of a preliterate people, stripped of their cultural heritage, to adjust themselves to civilization. The very fact that the Negro has succeeded in adopting habits of living that have enabled him to survive in a civilization based upon laissez faire and competition, itself bespeaks a degree of success in taking on the folkways and mores of the master race. That the Negro has found within the patterns of the white man's culture a purpose in life and a significance for his strivings which have involved sacrifices for his children and the curbing of individual desires and impulses indicates that he has become assimilated to a new mode of life.

However, when one undertakes to envisage the probable course of development of the Negro family in the future, it appears that the travail of civilization is not yet ended. First it appears that the family which evolved within the isolated world of the Negro folk will become increasingly disorganized. Modern means of communication will break down the isolation of the world of black folk, and, as long as the bankrupt system of southern agriculture exists, Negro families will continue to seek a living in the towns and cities of the country. They will crowd the slum areas of southern cities or make their way to northern cities where their family life will become disrupted and their poverty will force them to depend upon charity. Those families that possess some heritage of family traditions and education will resist the destructive forces of urban life more successfully than the illiterate Negro folk. In either case their family life will adapt itself to the secular and rational organization of urban life. Undoubtedly, there will be a limitation of offspring; and men and women who associate in marriage will use it as a means of individual development.

The process of assimilation and acculturation in a highly mobile and urbanized society will proceed on a different basis from that in the past. There are evidences at present that in the urban environment, where caste prescriptions lose their force, Negroes and whites in the same occupational classes are being drawn into closer association than in the past. Such associations, to be sure, are facilitating the assimilation of only the more formal aspects of white civilization; but there are signs that intermarriage in the future will bring about a fundamental type of assimilation. But, in the final analysis, the process of assimilation and acculturation will be limited by the extent to which the Negro becomes integrated into the economic organization and participates in the life of the community.

WHEN NEGROES PARTICIPATED IN THE GOVERN-MENT OF THE SOUTH

There was active participation of the freedmen in democratic government only a few years after the abolition of slavery. The participation of the Negro in the Reconstruction government even to the smallest degree was considered "Negro Domination." These governments established the basis for democratic legislation in the South and some of their outstanding innovations still stand.

THE CONSTITUTIONAL Conventions elected by the new voters in the Reconstruction Period [following the Civil War] were the first really representative bodies of the people to meet on

Excerpts from James S. Allen, *Reconstruction, the Battle for Democracy* (New York: International Publishers, 1937), pp. 116-122, 126-144.

Southern soil. They were also the first state assemblies in which Negroes participated as elected representatives of the people. In the South Carolina Convention there were 48 white delegates and 76 Negro, fully two-thirds of whom had once been slaves, while the white up-country was represented by some substantial farmers and "low-down whites." In Louisiana 49 delegates of each race participated. The "Black and Tan" Convention of Mississippi had 17 Negro delegates out of a total of 100. Negro delegates were also elected to the other constitutional conventions. But only in South Carolina and Louisiana did the Negroes participate in proportion to their ratio in the population or in the electorate.

Most of the conventions were predominantly agrarian and directly representative of the poorer sections of the population, especially in South Carolina. Almost half of them had toiled on the plantations as slaves, others had scratched out a bare living in the uplands.

Contrary to the general impression created by highly prejudiced accounts that the Reconstruction bodies consisted largely of "carpetbaggers," at least 70 of the delegates [of the Alabama Convention] were native Southerners. Likewise in Mississippi, where Negroes had evidently been discriminated against in the selection of delegates—the so-called carpetbaggers only had some 20-odd representatives, nearly all of whom had been soldiers in the Union Army and who had been elected from the Black Belt counties. On the other hand, there were 29 native white Republicans. Of the 17 Negro delegates, at least seven were ministers. The Negroes had supplied the necessary majority for calling the Convention, while it was dominated by the white delegates. In Louisiana, many of the Negro delegates were propertied free Negroes under slavery, while a good proportion once tilled the soil as slaves.

These people's conventions, the overwhelming majority of whose delegates were newly awakened peasants, proceeded to write state constitutions which would revolutionize the South if put into effect today. . . .

The new constitutions provided for Negro suffrage and for complete equality of civil rights. They disfranchised and barred from office the leaders of the Confederacy, as already stipulated in the Fourteenth Amendment. . . .

Other measures passed by the conventions reflect the thoroughgoing nature of the democratic overturn. The South Carolina constitution provided that no person be disqualified for crimes committed as a slave. Property qualifications for office were abolished and representation in the Lower House was to be apportioned by population and not property, as had been the case under slavery. No one could be imprisoned for debt nor prevented from enjoying property rights. A system of universal public education was to be created. Rights of women were extended. The system of county government was reorganized, providing for the election of all county officials and enlarging county self-government. In Mississippi and Louisiana additional provisions were included to assure equal rights on all public conveyances. The University of Louisiana was opened to Negroes. Other state conventions passed similar constitutions, which embodied a complete transformation of the old social structure.

The conventions also struck at ideological remnants of the slave system. One resolution passed by the South Carolina body demanded that steps be taken to "expunge forever from the vocabulary of South Carolina, the epithets, 'nigger,' 'negro,' and 'Yankee' . . . and to punish this insult by fine and imprisonment."

The proceedings of the conventions show their deep roots in the soil. In Mississippi, General Gillem co-operated with the big planters and refused to permit the execution of a number of resolutions passed by the Convention. One of these would have levied a high poll tax for the relief of destitute Negroes but the General held that there was plenty of work for the freedmen if they would only go back to the plantations and not wait for the convention to pass a law giving them the land. He also objected to other resolutions requesting tax collectors to suspend collection of all taxes assessed against freedmen before January 1, 1868, and providing for the abolition of all debts, contracts and judgments that had been made early in 1865. These demands were aimed at the system of contract labor and peonage on the plantations. Still another request that all property taken from the freedmen by their former owners be returned was vetoed by the commanding General.

The land question was the most frequently discussed in the South Carolina Convention. A Southern historian informs us that "some of the reforms proposed by the colored delegates" were "born of ignorant self-assertiveness; for example, the suggestion that landlords be required to pay wages from January 1, 1863," the day of Emancipation. A similar resolution had been passed in the Alabama Convention.

Although radical land reform was not proposed by the South Carolina body, the cry for the partition of the large estates was raised again and again. An extended debate raged around a proposed stay law designed to prevent the sale of large plantations for debt. R. H. Cain, Negro leader who later served in Congress, opposed the law because it was class legislation which would help the rich only and he favored relieving the poor of both races. F. L. Cardozo, another leading Negro Reconstructionist who was later Secretary of State and State Treasurer, opposed the stay law on the grounds that nine-tenths of the debts on the plantations were contracted for the sale of slaves. By taking this opportunity to throw the plantations upon the market, he held, they would be striking at the plantation system by breaking up the estates and selling them in small lots to the freedmen. "One of the greatest bulwarks of slavery was the plantation system," he declared. "This is the only way by which we will break up that system, and I maintain that our freedom will be of no effect if we allow it to continue. . . . Give them an opportunity, breathing time, and they will reorganize the same old system that they had before the war. I say, then . . . now is the time to strike." The speaker, however, made it clear that he did not mean confiscation, the only effective measure which would have assured the destruction of the estates. "Let the lands of the South be divided," he said. "I would not say for one moment that they should be confiscated, but if sold to maintain the war, now that slavery is abolished, let the plantation system go with it." The proposal to sell out the large plantation owners was repeated often in this and later bodies.

The convention did not take a definite stand for wholesale confiscation. . . . Even the most advanced Reconstruction body was not ready to press the most fundamental demand of the freedmen. The convention, however, legislated in favor of the small farmers and thus established a basis of co-operation between the Black Belt and the uplands.

The high point of the revolution in the South was the extension of civil and political rights to Negroes and their participation in government. Other democratic reforms were made, such as the establishment of a public school system and the reorganization of state and county government permitting fuller political activity to white small-farmers. But Negro suffrage and participation in government was undoubtedly the most important innovation.

The Negroes, however, did not hold the dominant position in any of the state governments, even in those states where they formed the majority of the electorate. The Reconstruction Governments were maintained for varying periods only as long as the alliance between the Negro people and the upland farmers existed and was not disrupted by the reaction. From the start the Negroes were handicapped by totally inadequate representation in the state and national governments. Even in South Carolina, where the revolution reached its highest level, the Negroes did not dominate the state power. Although the Negro people played a decisive role in maintaining these governments and in initiating and carrying through democratic reforms, the administration was largely in the hands of their Northern and Southern allies.

In Mississippi and Louisiana, the two other states in which Negroes were in the majority of the population, Negro representation was even less and it was still less in other states. . . .

The post of the superintendent of education was filled by a Negro in many states, eloquent testimony to the striving of the illiterate freedmen for education. Between 1871 and 1901, there were 22 Negro members of Congress, two of whom were Senators.

Today, when government in the South is based upon white domination and the ostracism of the Negro, and when there is only one Negro representative in Congress, these facts may appear startling. In one sense they are: they reveal an active participation of the freedmen and their representatives in democratic government only a few years after the abolition of slavery and, as events showed, they exerted a powerful progressive influence. Yet at the height of popular democracy in the South the Negro was still inadequately represented in the assemblies and in the offices of power. This was an important contributing factor to the defeat of the Reconstruction governments.

To the Bourbons the participation of the Negro in government, even to the smallest degree, was already "Negro Domination." One Negro legislator immediately was multiplied in their startled eyes to a hundred. The press raged against the "Black Parliaments." It certainly rankled to have their former slaves, or even some of their working field hands, pass some of the most progressive legislation the South has ever had, or tax the rich to provide an education for the poor.

In South Carolina, Mississippi and Louisiana the "Black Parliaments" were more completely assemblies of the people. The social composition of the first South Carolina Reconstruction legislature, 84 of whose 157 members were Negroes, is revealed by the fact that the taxes paid by all the legislators amounted to $700.63, of which six members paid $309.01. There were not many men of property here. Negroes who but three years before had been slaves were legislating for the public welfare.

Through the eyes of James S. Pike, a leading Northern Republican who visited South Carolina and returned home to launch a campaign of slander and vituperation against the Reconstruction governments, we can at least catch a glimpse of the legislature of 1873. . . . Despite Pike's condescending jibes, even from his description of the members of the assembly as they left the State House, it is apparent that this was primarily an assembly of landless peasants and small landowners,

About three quarters of the crowd belonged to the African race. They were of every hue, from the octoroon to the deep black. They were such a good looking body of men as might pour out of a market house or a court-house at random in any Southern state. Every Negro type and physiognomy was here to be seen, from the genteel serving man to the rough hewn customer from rice or cotton field. Their dress was as varied as their countenances. There was the second-hand frock coat of infirm gentility, glossy and threadbare. There was the stovepipe hat of many ironings and departed styles. There was also to be seen a total disregard of the proprieties of costume in the coarse and dirty garments of the field; the stub-jackets and slouch hats of soiling labor. In some instances, rough woolen comforters embraced the neck and hid the absence of linen. Heavy brogans and short, torn trousers it was impossible to hide. . . . These were the legislators of South Carolina.

Pike had never seen the like of it in any Northern state, where legislators were men of property and "substantial citizens." He was even more alarmed at the leading role of the Negroes in the legislature.

The Northerner, accustomed to the finished perorations and well-turned phrases of constitutional lawyers in sedate legislative bodies, was taken aback at the homespun fashion in which this people's body conducted its business, although he could not help but sense their intense seriousness.

The leading topics of discussion—wrote Pike—are all well understood by the members, as they are of practical character, and appeal directly to the personal interests of every legislator, as well as those of his constituents. When an appropriation bill is up to raise money to catch and punish the K.K.K., they know exactly what it means. . . . So, too, with educational measures. The free school comes right home to them; then the business of arming and drilling the black militia. They are eager on this point.

The laughing propensity of the sable crow is a great cause of disorder. . . . But underneath all this shocking burlesque upon legislative proceedings, we must not forget that there is something real to this uncouth and untutored multitude. It is not all sham, nor all burlesque. They have a genuine interest and a genuine earnestness in the business of the assembly which we are bound to recognize and respect.

. . . They have an earnest purpose born of a conviction that their position and condition are not fully assured, which lends a sort of dignity to their proceedings.

Most of the Negro leaders in the Reconstruction governments were men who had received education and training in the Abolition movement. Quite a number were Northerners who had come South with the Union troops as soldiers, ministers, teachers or agents of the Freedmen's Bureau. New Orleans supplied many leaders who had been free colored men of property under slavery. There were not a few Negro mechanics and artisans, who either as free or slave workers had had the opportunity under slavery for self-education.

Negroes were also energetic in municipal and county affairs. . . . The coastal and Sea Island region of South Carolina was visited in 1879 by Sir George Campbell, a Member of Parliament, and he was surprised to find that the Negroes had maintained many of their gains. Although their title to the land was then again being attacked, they had established independent and self-supporting rural communities, while many of the men also worked in the ports and the phosphate beds. At Beaufort the Negroes still controlled the elections and sent their own people to the municipal and county offices, as well as representatives to the State Assembly. "It has the reputation of being a sort of black paradise," wrote Campbell about the Beaufort area, "and *per contra*, I rather expected a white hell. . . . To my great surprise I found exactly the contrary. At no place that I have seen are the relations of the races better and more peaceable."

The energetic participation of the Negro in politics was certainly a complete reversal of the old situation. In the words of a ditty current among the Negroes of South Carolina:

> De bottom rail's on de top,
> An' we's gwine to keep it dar.

The new legislation [of the Reconstruction governments] was generally along the lines laid down by the Reconstruction Constitutions and covered (1) civil rights for Negroes, including the ratification of the Fourteenth and Fifteenth Amendments; (2) the establishment of a public school system; (3) reorganization of state and county government; (4) revision of the system of taxation; (5) land and labor relations; and (6) aid to railroads and other capitalist undertakings. . . . In some cases the Radical governments lasted only two or three years: in Virginia, North Carolina and Georgia, conservatives and reactionaries already controlled the state by the end of 1870. In still others, such as Alabama and Texas, the Radicals had only a slight edge on the Conservatives.

Black Codes and the old slave laws were repealed and in most cases Civil Rights Bills were passed to enforce equal rights for Negroes on conveyances and in public institutions. When the Civil Rights Bill passed in Louisiana, a Bourbon paper warned "any Negro, or gang of Negroes" attempting to exercise the privileges it conferred would do so "at their peril." The mere passage of such measures did not assure equal rights and many were the battles waged by Negroes to maintain the rights conferred by their legislatures. For example, when the Common Carrier Bill, providing for equal accommodations on street cars and railroads, was before the Alabama body, hundreds of Negroes and a number of their white allies held demonstrations against the street cars in Mobile (which discriminated against Negroes) and boarded all the cars.

The Negro members of the state assemblies were naturally most adamant in fighting for equal rights. When the Civil Rights Bill was before the Alabama session of 1872-73, the Negro representative Merriwether declared that his people intended to assert their rights everywhere. In reply to a conservative who charged that Negroes wished to use these rights as stepping-stones to something beyond, he declared: "They are stepping-stones, and the colored people intend stepping along upon them until they stand side by side with the gentlemen who oppose them."

In Georgia, the Negroes waged an unequal struggle against a strong Conservative alignment, which included a number of anti-Radical Republicans. The first legislature refused to seat the Negro members on the ground that Negroes were not eligible for office in the state. The Negro Republicans met in militant convention at Macon "to inaugurate war against the foul and base action of the so-called Legislature and to oppose the principles of all men who oppose equal rights." With the aid of Congress, which refused to seat Georgia members until the right of Negroes to hold office was recognized, Negro members resumed their seats in a legislature which was already under the control of reactionaries. The Negroes formed the Left of the assembly and pressed a number of progressive measures, such as bills for female suffrage and prison reform. The latter was directed against the practice of leasing out convicts to private contractors.

A common school system was established, for which the Negro delegates in the legislatures fought the hardest and which they insisted on maintaining at all costs. As long as they had a voice in the state governments these systems were maintained for both whites and Negroes. As soon as the reactionaries began to get the upper hand, they were curtailed as, for example, in Alabama where the schools were closed down because funds could "not be found" to pay teachers.

The establishment of the schools constituted one of the largest items in the state budget and was a social duty of which the old slave-masters knew nothing. To them it was foolish extravagance to supply free education to "poor whites" and Negroes, to provide funds for the election of county officers (who were generally appointed under the oligarchy), to establish asylums for the handicapped, etc. It was considered even greater squandering and corruption when the new governments set about raising these funds from among all men of property, including the big planters. While fraud undoubtedly existed, especially in connection with railroad subsidies, the cry of corruption was a political weapon used against the legislatures which carried through measures for the public welfare on funds raised by taxing the planters.

This becomes evident when the methods of taxation before and after the war are compared. In South Carolina, for example, the system before the war placed a low valuation on land and slaves and taxed heavily the merchants, professionals and bankers. The middle class businessmen paid taxes five and six times as great as the planter. When the planters were overthrown and the middle class controlled the state power, the situation was changed. The system of taxation was revised on a uniform basis applying to all property at its full value. . . . The Reconstruction governments established the basis for democratic legislation in the South and some of their outstanding innovations, such as the democratization of administrative machinery and the public school system, still stand. But in its comment upon the work of the reconstructionists, the *Fairfield* (S. C.) *Herald*, for example, characterized the policy of the Reconstruction legislature as:

a hell-born policy which has trampled the fairest and noblest of states of our great sisterhood beneath the unholy hoofs of African savages and shoulder-strapped brigands—the policy which has given up millions of our free-born, high-souled brothers and sisters, countrymen and country-women of Washington, Rutledge, Marion and Lee, to the rule of gibbering, louse-eaten, devil-worshipping barbarians, from the jungles of Dahomey, and peripatetic buccaneers from Cape Cod, Memphremagog, Hell and Boston.

THE PLIGHT OF THE AMERICAN INDIANS

The Seminole defied the efforts of the white people to drive them from their country to which they clung with a tenacity and desperation that have no parallel in our humiliating annals of Indian spoliation.

THE SEMINOLE Indians defended their liberty and homes in Florida at an appalling cost of life. They defied the efforts of the white people to drive them from their country to which they clung with a tenacity and desperation that have no parallel in our humiliating annals of Indian spoliation. By their courage, strategy, and resourcefulness they exposed to ridicule an invading army of more than ten times their number. Their homes and settlements destroyed, driven into well-nigh inaccessible swamps and hunted like wild animals out of their hiding places during a six-year reign of terror, they were carried from time to time as prisoners to the Indian Territory.

They were at last conquered by a long and expensive war of attrition, and except for a few hundred who escaped the soldiers, the removal was completed in the year 1842. By resistance to removal from their homeland these indomitable people had incurred the wrath of our Government that imposed punitive and humiliating measures upon them. One of the most harmful of these was the stupid policy of requiring them to be merged with the Creeks in their western home. So-called treaties had been entered into in 1832 and 1833 wherein the Indians were made to say that they agreed to the terms. All the available evidence shows that they were not favorable to this plan, but on the contrary were bitterly opposed to it for reasons fundamental in their history and conflicting interests.

The Creek domain assigned to the Seminole for their occupancy was the area lying between the Canadian River and the North Fork

Excerpts from Grant Foreman, *The Five Civilized Tribes* (Norman, Oklahoma: University of Oklahoma Press, 1934), pp. 223-224, 226-229, 237, 276-278.

of the Canadian and extending west to the Little River. . . . When the Seminole emigrants arrived they found their country already occupied. They were brought by water from time to time, and nearly all disembarked at Fort Gibson, where they were mustered by the agents whose duty it was to count the survivors of those tragic journeys and provide for the issue of their rations.

They had been dragged from their homes, compelled to abandon their meager possessions and arrived at Fort Gibson destitute, cold, and hungry and were dependent on the rations issued there for their existence. The difference in climate, soil, resources and living conditions between their former home and the strange country into which they were thrust was so great and forbidding that these bewildered, embittered, and broken-spirited people preferred to remain in camp around the fort and receive rations, rather than to venture upon the uncertain hazard of extracting a living from the soil of a new country. Subsistence was furnished one party of Seminole near Fort Gibson in 1842 at a cost to the Government of three and one-half cents each per diem, which must have provided meager fare for these wretched people.

Chief Mikanopy was somewhat more tractable than many of the subchiefs, and he was induced to remove with some of his followers to the Deep Fork; in 1841 this band had nearly eight hundred acres of land fenced and planted in corn. They also were raising beans, pumpkins, and melons and small quantities of rice. . . .

Nearly fifteen hundred Seminole Indians under Alligator and Wild Cat, and other chiefs, were encamped around Fort Gibson in a distracted condition, homesick and discouraged, inflamed by their forcible removal from their homes in Florida; destitute and bewildered; for want of tools, helpless to cultivate the land or build homes; without means of transportation to the land provided for them even if they wished to go there; but above all else resolved not to locate in the country of the Creeks, become subject to their control, and risk the loss of their slaves and free-born Negroes who accompanied them.

These helpless and wretched people were living on the lands of the Cherokee who took pity on them and permitted them to cultivate the soil; but some of them rewarded their friends by killing stock to keep their families from starving. In 1842 Alligator and a large number of his followers at Fort Gibson waited on George W. Clark, their issuing agent; they desired to know when the Government would give them the axes, hoes, and rifles promised by the officers to whom they surrendered in Florida. They said that before they were marched to the boats, General Jesup, in order to lighten the burden of removal told them to throw away their old rifles, kettles, tools, and other cherished possessions, which would be replaced by the Government when they arrived in their new home. This promise had not been redeemed in the more than four years since the arrival of most of them in the West. . . .

The year 1843 was a particularly distracting one for these unfortunate, homeless people. Spring, the season for planting was passing, and it was nearly June when some of the Seminole immigrants indignantly and vigorously protested to their agent and condemned the faithlessness of the Government that had promised them axes and hoes and had failed to provide these most necessary tools so they could cut the timber, clear the land, build their humble log cabins and plant crops for their sustenance. . . .

Agent Judge visited the various depots where during the summer of 1843 he issued corn and salt to some of the Seminoles who had located in the Creek Nation. On this occasion he had an opportunity of observing some of the earlier settlers in their new homes and "noticing their domestic arrangements; and in every instance their Cabins were Clean and Comfortable, and content seemed to be manifest in all their Countenances and a large vessel of sofka to which all who called were welcome, which for the first time I tasted, and it was very good; they dress corn in a great variety of ways, some of which would be considered a luxury in any Civilized society." He was surprised at the progress they had made: "I found them in possession of as good land as any in the country, and generally satisfied; and things comfortable around them; they had raised a considerable surplus of rice which they sell at $3.00 per bushel and good demand for it. . . . They are very desirous of having a school established; they have frequently named this subject. . . . Wild Cat and Alligator both have agreed to move next fall." However, a drought that summer reduced by one-half the corn crop of the immigrants, but to offset that loss some of them had good crops of rice and potatoes. . . .

[After this, Wild Cat wrote:] ". . . We have been conquered. Look at us! A distracted people, alone without a home, without annuities, destitute of provisions, and without a shelter for our women and children, strangers in a foreign land, dependent upon the mercy and tolerance of our red brethren the Cherokees; transported to a cold climate, naked, without game to hunt, or fields to plant, or huts to cover our poor little children; they are crying like wolves, hungry, cold, and destitute." . . .

The Seminole Indians had been reduced in population nearly 40 per cent in thirty years, by the war of extermination waged against them and the fugitive manner in which they had lived in the swamps to escape capture. As usual, none of the $2,000 promised in the Treaty of 1856 for agricultural assistance had been advanced to the Indians who were becoming restless for a fulfillment of that engagement. There was no school in the Seminole Nation but a few of the leading members of the tribe were anxious that the treaty stipulation on the subject be carried into effect. . . .

"By improving their education facilities, [Agent Rutherford urged] all the ignorance and superstition which now characterize them as a tribe will vanish, and a few years will find the Seminoles an intelligent race, worthy to be considered a part of our common country, and fully competent to aid in sustaining its reputation for intelligence and Christian philanthropy; for the Seminoles are by no means deficient in native force of character and keenness of wit. It wants only cultivation, a knowledge of letters, and the excellencies of moral and mental discipline; and I ask you to consider the importance of this matter and place it in a true light before the department. There seems to be among them a preference for the original customs and habits of their tribes; it is only the progress of civilization that can remove these absurdities, and render them a happy and contented race." . . .

Nearly thirty-five years after the Government by devious means secured the execution of the so-called treaty with the Seminole which drove them from their homes in Florida, they became fixed upon a tract of land of their own. Here they applied themselves industriously to farming, built cabins and fenced their lands; schools were erected, and these neglected Indians, though much behind, caught step with the other tribes, and exhibited a commendable zeal for improvement.

THE SIGNIFICANCE OF THE INDIAN GHOST DANCE RELIGION

"If the Messiah is not coming, and by his coming he will again make us a strong people and enable us to hold our own in this land given us as a home by the Great Spirit, and the white man is not afraid of that, why have these soldiers been brought here to stop the dance?"

WHAT WAS back of the Ghost Dance so far as Pine Ridge was concerned? A shortage in the beef ration, resulting hunger, and a hard winter. . . .

Late in November, when the storm was brewing, I induced my old friend Little Wound, a leading War Chief, to call on Gen. Brooke and Agent Royer, at the Agency Office, to talk over matters.

Gen. Brooke asked Little Wound if he was a Ghost Dancer. His reply was: "No, my friend, over sixty winters have passed over me and I am too old for dancing, but now that you have asked me that question I will tell what I know and have heard about the Messiah and the Ghost Dance.

"There have lived among my people for many winters the holy men or missionaries whom the Great Father has sent to us to teach us your religion, and how much better it is than ours. They bring with them the holy book, the Bible, from that book they tell us wonderful stories, they tell us of the man who went into the den of wild animals, and was not harmed because his Great Spirit protected him.

"They tell us of the men who went into the fiery furnace, hot enough to melt bullets, but their hair was not even singed.

"Then they tell us a wonderful story, of how many ages ago the white men's brains got to whirling, they lost their ears, they would listen no more to the Great Spirit, and they strayed off on the wrong road, and finally the Great Spirit sent his Son on earth to save them.

Excerpt of the testimony of V. T. McGillycuddy from Stanley Vestal, *New Sources of Indian History 1850-1891* (Norman, Oklahoma: University of Oklahoma Press, 1934), pp. 85, 87-90.

"He lived with those white men for over thirty winters, and worked hard to get you back on the road, but you denied Him, and you finally nailed Him up on a great wooden cross, tortured, and killed Him. He was known as the Messiah, and when He was dying on the cross, it was promised that He would come again some time to try and save the people. These things the missionaries tell us.

"About two moons ago there came to us from the far North, from the Yellowstone country, a young Cheyenne, named Porcupine, with a strange story. He had a vision—in it he was told to go to a large lake, in the Northwest (Walkers Lake, Nevada) and there he would meet the Messiah.

"He told me that the Messiah was a tall white man with golden hair and whiskers, and blue eyes, a well-spoken man, and He said, 'Porcupine, I am the Messiah; My Father, the Great Spirit, has sent Me a second time to try and save the people, but when I was here before, they denied Me and killed Me. When the Spring time comes with the green grass, I am going to visit the different Indian people, and the whites.

'But this time I have arranged a certain dance and signs, and in my travels if I am so received I will stop with them and try and help them. If I am not received in these signs, I will pass them by.

'Now Porcupine, I will give you these signs and this dance, and you go ahead of Me and teach them to your people.'"

Said Little Wound: "Now whether Porcupine really saw the Messiah, or only had a pleasant dream, I do not know. I got my people together and said, 'My friends, if this is a good thing we should have it; if it is not, it will fall to the earth itself. So you better learn this dance, so if the Messiah does come he will not pass us by, but will help us to get back our hunting grounds and buffalo.'"

Then the old chief turned to me with these words, "My friend Little Beard, if the Messiah is *not* coming, and by his coming he will again make us a strong people and enable us to hold our own in this land given us as a home by the Great Spirit, and the white man is not afraid of that, *why* have these soldiers been brought here to stop the dance?"

I could not but remark to Gen. Brooke as follows, "Little Wound's remark, 'if this is a good thing we should have it; if it is not, it will fall to earth itself,' is the key to the whole situation. It means that they will dance through the winter. The green grass comes, with it no Messiah, and the thing ends.

"If I were agent here, I would let them dance themselves out. What right have we to dictate to them on a religious belief founded on the teaching of the religion of the white man? If the Seventh Day Adventists get up on the roof of their houses, arrayed in their ascension robes, to meet the 'second coming,' the U. S. Army is not rushed into their field." . . .

I remember the remark of my old friend Mark Twain, in talking with him on the Indian question:

"Our Pilgrim Fathers were a Godly people; when they landed that day on Plymouth Rock, from off the Mayflower, they fell upon their knees, they thanked Almighty God for the many blessings he had vouchsafed them that day, in enabling them to reach the land of liberty and free thought.

"Later on they fell upon the aborigines."

THE BEGINNINGS OF BANTU NATIONALISM

Bantu nationalism is developing rapidly, but nationalist leaders tend to concentrate on attempting to secure the same political rights and economic opportunity for Bantu as are enjoyed by Europeans. The Bantu has now no share in the government of the country. The causes of the emergence and success of various religious, political and trade union organizations are clearly discontent with existing economic conditions and European domination.

SOME BANTU regret the old days, feeling that life before the coming of the Europeans was preferable to life nowadays, and that Europeans have brought nothing of value. The belief that Europeans will be swept into the sea, and Bantu have South Africa to themselves again, recurs periodically. Most "school people" admire elements in European culture, and are themselves too different from

---

Excerpts from Monica Hunter, *Reaction to Conquest* (London: Oxford University Press, 1936), pp. 557-562, 573-574.

the "raw" tribesmen to wish to return to the old way of life. Whatever their feeling toward Europeans they are eager to absorb something of European culture. Many of them deplore the dropping of most old Bantu customs, believing that their decay is in part responsible for the increasing laxity of parental control and immorality, by which they are greatly concerned. They are proud of their people's past, but they resent bitterly being lumped together with "raw Natives." They are struggling for recognition as civilized men. South Africa as a whole refuses to recognize any of Bantu stock as such. Her refusal generates a very keen sense of racial disabilities, and views on the results of contact with Europeans tend to be a list of grievances. Since race is a ground of social, economic, and political disability, there is naturally suspicion of any "differentiation policy," in education or political organization. There are traces of a reaction against European culture; of a desire to reject it, and conserve Bantu culture; but this tendency is not strong. Bantu nationalism is developing rapidly, but nationalist leaders tend to concentrate on attempting to secure the same political rights and economic opportunity for Bantu as are enjoyed by Europeans. There is a desire for emancipation from European control, but eager acceptance of European culture. The Wellingtonites preached that Europeans would be swept into the sea, but stores were to remain and be taken over by Bantu. . . .

In the Bantu press the following points are dwelt upon: 91 per cent. of the land of the Union of South Africa is owned by under 2 million Europeans, 9 per cent. by 5 million Bantu. Under the Land Act of 1913, which made it illegal for Bantu to hire land (outside certain areas) except in return for services, many Bantu have been expelled from farms in the Northern Provinces, and also in the Cape Province until 1917, when the courts ruled the law to be *ultra vires* in the Cape. No provision has been made for those expelled. They have gone to already overcrowded reserves, or to towns. The Act further prohibited the purchase of land outside certain areas, pending the demarcation of open areas in which Bantu might buy land. Reports of commissions appointed to demarcate "open areas" have been disregarded, and up till 1934 no further provision has been made. The Native Service Contract Act of 1932 reduces labor tenants in the Transvaal and Natal to the position of serfs. . . .

The land question is the most bitter of all. ("The land is the chief." —Proverb.) "If the Government has no hole to bury us in it should send us to Heaven."

Under the Mines and Works Act (1911) and the Amendment Act (1929) Bantu, by reason of their race alone, are excluded from certain skilled occupations. Under the "white labor policy" posts in public services, formerly filled by Natives, are now being given to Europeans. This policy costs taxpayers, including Bantu, much. Native wages are very low, European wages high compared with standards in Europe. The refusal to grant Bantu trading rights in certain town locations further restricts their economic advance. The bargaining power of Bantu is hampered by the Masters and Servants Laws under which breach of contract is a criminal offense for Bantu employees, and which makes strikes by Bantu, except day and weekly laborers in the Cape, illegal.

Taxation is unequal. All Bantu males over 18 years are liable for an annual tax of £1, those in reserves for an additional local tax of not less than 10s. No other section of the population pays any direct tax unless earning over £150 p.a. if single, £250 if married. In 1930, 76.5 per cent of the European population paid no direct taxes. Bantu failing to produce a poll tax receipt are imprisoned, and after imprisonment have still to pay their tax even though unable to secure employment.

Benefits from taxation in the form of state services are unequal. Grants for European and Colored education are given a lump *per capita* basis. Grants for Bantu education are given in a lump sum, and there is no adequate provision for their increasing with increasing needs. . . . In 1923-4 the amount spent per head on the education of European children was £17 18s. 6d.; on Bantu children £2 8s. 5d. in the Cape, less in other provinces. Many schools eligible for grants are without them, and Bantu teachers' salaries are extremely low. European and Colored persons are eligible for old age pensions: Bantu are not. Old Bantu men in very poor circumstances still have to pay poll tax. The widespread poverty is the root of bitterness against Europeans.

The Bantu view of European economic policy is expressed in the proverb, "The white man's envy forbids us the red clay, although he does not paint himself." . . .

Bantu have no share in the government of the country, and are not adequately consulted in legislation concerning themselves. In the three Northern Provinces Bantu have in effect no vote. In the Cape the qualifications for Bantu male voters are higher than for European voters, and Bantu women have no vote. Bantu are not eligible as members of the Legislative Assembly or Senate. Under the Native Affairs' Act of 1930 provision was made for summoning representative Natives to consult with the Government on proposed legislation affecting Natives, but in eight years (1926-34) Native representatives have been summoned only once (when they were expressly warned not to mention Native grievances), although a number of Acts directly affecting Natives have been passed.

"The ox is skinned on one side only." The proverb is applied to European courts, which it is complained do not mete out even justice. In cases in which one party is Bantu and the other European, the jury (composed solely of Europeans) is not impartial. For the same crimes widely different sentences are passed on Europeans and Natives. A Native is hanged for assault of a white woman, a white man may get only a short term of imprisonment for assault of a Native woman. Europeans flogging to death, or "shooting by accident" Bantu have, in some instances, only been punished by small fines. Fines imposed are out of proportion to Native earnings. Cases of ill-treatment of Bantu by police are common. Under the Riotous Assemblies Amendment Act, 1930, "inciting to race hatred" is a criminal offense. . . .

The endless social annoyances to which Bantu are subjected arouse bitter feeling. Men with university degrees speak of inconvenience caused them by not being allowed to travel on trams or buses in some towns, of difficulty in getting any but third-class accommodations on trains, of rudeness of officials, of the way in which Bantu customers in stores, or public offices, have to wait until Europeans who have come after them have been served, of the rude manner of many Europeans when speaking to Bantu, of their refusal when speaking in English or Afrikaans to give any courtesy title. As Dr. Moslema remarks, it is the educated Bantu who bears the brunt of racial feeling, because many of them come in close contact with Europeans without being their servants. So long as the Native is a servant "he may move among them (Europeans) as much as he likes, he may handle their food, and their children, enter their houses, and sit on their couches, travel with them in the same compartments"—but "the moment he becomes independent he is ostracized by Europeans."

Bitter comments are made on the hypocrisy of Europeans who claim to be Christians, and yet enforce a color bar even in their churches. The same parliament which passed the Color Bar Bill inserted in the constitution the clause, "The people of South Africa acknowledge the sovereignty and guidance of Almighty God." Because of this attitude of some of those who profess Christianity some Bantu leaders are urging their people to throw over Christianity. "At first we had the land and the white man had the Bible. Now we have the Bible and the white man has the land." "They told you to close your eyes and pray, and the other whites came and took away the land from behind your back while you kept your eyes closed." "I appeal to you all to learn and go to night classes, and leave the Bible alone. The Bible will only teach you to be soft and easy going." . . .

Pondo and Fingo, who were later in encountering Europeans than were the Xhosa, never fought them. The armed opposition of the Xhosa ended in 1880. Since then the only armed opposition of Bantu within the Union has been the Zulu "rebellion" of 1906. Bantu are only allowed arms under special permit. They receive no military training, and were not accepted as combatants during the Great War. On the other hand, all white South African men undergo compulsory military training. Bantu leaders are well aware that Europeans have the military power. . . .

The causes of the emergence and success of various religious, political and trade union organizations are clearly discontent with existing economic conditions and European domination. All of them are inter-tribal and expressions of Bantu nationalism. They tend to have a religious flavor. The cattle killing was supposed to be ordered by the ancestors. The separatist Churches were the earliest nationalist movement of "school people." The Israelites were primarily a religious sect. The Industrial and Commercial Workers' Union and Wellingtonites which began as economic and political movements found it expedient to hold their own Sunday services. The readiness of the country people to believe in miraculous means of release from existing conditions is marked. . . .

No student of Bantu affairs in South Africa can doubt that these disintegrating forces [within these movements] will eventually be submerged by the rising tide of Bantu nationalism. The existence of a conference including practically all organizations of Bantu, Colored, and Indian suggests that Bantu nationalists may be joined by other non-Europeans.

These movements are symptoms of unrest; nevertheless, there has been less industrial disturbance in South Africa than in Europe, America, or Australia since the War. The Transkei boasts the smallest police force for an equivalent population anywhere in the British Empire. In 1914 various chiefs in the Union offered gifts of money and men for the War. Even in 1928 the Bunga voted £250 out of its small resources for relief for Europeans in drought-stricken areas.

THE RESPONSES OF THE RACE CONSCIOUS

The race conscious of the low status group are aware of past and present exploitation. They recall with bitterness the limitation of their freedom and their debasement. No race conscious member of the subordinate group can believe that his race is to suffer forever the status of an outcaste.

AT THE present time the ideology of the oppressed is developing among the natives of Africa, especially those of white-controlled South Africa. And the Negro in the United States gives frequent and eloquent expression to this type of sentiment. The following poem by James D. Carrothers is a typical expression of this feeling of self-pity and oppression:

> To be a Negro in a day like this
> Demands forgiveness; bruised with blow on blow
> Betrayed like him whose woe-dimmed eyes gave bliss

Excerpts from W. O. Brown, "The Nature of Race Consciousness," *Social Forces*, Vol. 10, No. 1 (Baltimore: Williams and Wilkins, 1931), pp. 90-97.

Still one must succor those who brought one low
To be a Negro in a day like this.

To be a Negro in a day like this
Demands rare patience—patience that can wait
In utter darkness. 'Tis the path to miss,
And knock unheeded at an iron gate
To be a Negro in a day like this.

To be a Negro in a day like this
Demands strange loyalty. We serve a flag
Which is to us white freedom's emphasis
And one must love when truth and justice lag,
To be a Negro in a day like this.

To be a Negro in a day like this—
Alas! Lord God what have we done?
Still shines the gate all gold and amethyst,
But I pass by the glorious goal unwon,
To be a Negro in a day like this.

Not always is this self-pity of the despairing type. At times it is
cool and detached. In the case of the Negro this type of attitude is
expressed in the writing of some of the younger Negroes such as
Hughes and Cullen. Notice, for example, this neat little turn from
Hughes:

I do not hate you,
For your faces are beautiful, too.
I do not hate you,
Your faces are whirling lights of loveliness, too.
Yet why do you torture me,
O white strong ones,
Why do you torture me?

Since the race conscious are sensitive they naturally resent anything
that impugns the status of their race. Hence they protest vehemently
against the notion of their inferiority as a race. Any definition of
status for the race that implies subordination angers and hurts them.
And any type of behavior on the part of members of their race that
implies the subservient attitude to other races they condemn. For

example, Negroes deplore the "Uncle Tom" type of Negro, the name "Uncle Tom" becoming an epithet that stings.

The race conscious posit their race as an entity to which they have obligations. They have a conscience about this race. They must serve it, fight for it, be loyal to it. To the outsider the race of the race conscious may appear to be an imaginative construction but to the initiated this race is a reality, in a sense, a personal experience.

Race pride is an aspect of race consciousness. It implies the tendency to place highly one's race, to exalt its virtues, to take pride in its past, its great men, its achievements. The racially proud express what Sumner has termed ethnocentrism. Their race becomes the measure of all things. It becomes the central, pivotal human grouping. Invariably race pride tends to be an expression of the sentiment of racial superiority. This is even true of subordinate racial groups such as the Negro in the United States or the natives of South Africa. Such a belief gives support to race conscious individuals. It bolsters their self-respect, exalts their conception of themselves and inures them against the pain incident to a low status. The race consciousness of a subordinate racial group is apt to be more defensive than is true of that of a dominant racial group. Psychologically its utility is probably greater for the subordinate than for the dominant, though to the statusless in the dominant racial group it proves a great boon, giving them a sense of their value that is out of proportion to reality.

This race pride is expressed in several forms. Thus racial achievements are magnified. In the case of racial groups of an inferior status memory of racial achievements compensates for the tribulations of subordination. Stress placed on the achievements of the race represents an attempt to effect a more favorable impression of the race both by its members and by outsiders. This manifestation of racial pride is a defensive gesture, being an attempt to bolster one's conception of one's race. This defensive pride is especially obvious in the case of low status racial groups. Thus the various Asiatic groups, conscious of the valuations of the West, defend in speech, press, and literature their achievements. The same tendency is to be noted among the race conscious natives of Africa, especially of South Africa. See for typical expressions, S. Plaatje, *Native Life in South Africa* (1917); and S. M. Molema, Bantu, *Past and Present* (1920). The reaction of the race conscious Negroes of the United States is typical in this respect. Some illustration of this tendency may be found in the concern with Negro history, the vogue of African art, the space given in the Negro press to events and achievements which bolster racial pride, much of the literature of Negro writers, and in the eagerness with which recitals of the Negro's attainments are listened to. And thus the race conscious individual, contemplating his great racial past, is secured in his sense of personal worth.

Glorification of the individually great of the race is another expression of the pride of the race conscious. The great man of the race becomes a symbol. His achievements typify the possibilities of the race. In a sense he is the prototype of the race. This great man, in the ideology of the race conscious, tends to become a mythological figure. Through him they vicariously achieve status.

This idealization of the great men of the race is a means of glorifying the race as a whole. It exalts the race in the eyes of its race conscious members. As a result the race conscious themselves are exalted. Negro newspaper editors exploit the achievements and personalities of the great of the race. The anniversaries of such men as Douglas and Washington are observed and given wide publicity in the press. The psychological states of depression, sense of inferiority and humility give way to those of a feeling of personal worth and pride. The much talked of "New Negro" exemplifies this fact. The phrase is used as a description of the type of Negro who demands his rights, who refuses to pay obeisance to the "superior" white man, who considers himself the equal of any man, who resents insults to him or to his race and who refuses to accept as a fixed and necessary condition a low-caste position in the social system. He is no beggar, no humble "Uncle Tom," but a self-conscious personality, aware of his worth and dignity. He would applaud the sentiment of Mr. Randolph when he says, "The time has passed when a grown-up black man should ask a grown-up white man for anything."

The race conscious of the low status group are aware of past and present exploitation. They recall with bitterness the limitation of their freedom and their debasement. Grievances are formulated, becoming a part of their ideology. The Negro poet, Claude McKay gives eloquent expression to the prejudice of the race conscious in the following poem.

Oh, when I think of my long-suffering race,
For weary centuries despised, oppressed,
Enslaved and lynched, denied a human place
In the great life line of the Christian West;
And in the Black Land disinherited,
Robbed in the ancient country of its birth,
My heart grows sick with hate, becomes as lead,
For this my race that has no home on earth.
Then from the dark depths of my soul I cry
To the avenging angels to consume
The white man's world of wonders utterly:
Let it be swallowed up in earth's vast womb,
Or upward roll as a sacrificial smoke
To liberate my people from its yoke!

Of course, the race conscious always make exceptions in their prejudicial reaction. Not all Negroes are like Negroes; nor all whites like whites in general. These exceptions become the friends of the race conscious, often objects of affection and gratitude as well as symbols of hope and security.

The race conscious easily believe in a portentous destiny for their race. . . . No race conscious member of a subordinate group can believe that his race is to suffer forever the status of an outcaste.

The race conscious of the dominant group do not monopolize the notion of being "a light to the Gentiles." Their brethren of the "inferior" races tend also to develop the ideology of saviors. They are apt to feel that their suffering has refined and spiritualized them, making them superior to their gross natured persecutors.

For the race conscious among the races of low status to believe in a better future is essential. Race consciousness otherwise would atrophy and die. Hope is essential to its vitality. And to be able to believe that while they suffer and "envision the stars" they are at the same time performing a mission satisfies the human need for the feelings of worth and superiority.

The Negro in the United States who is assimilated to the ideology of race consciousness sympathizes with the struggles of the African natives, protests against the imperialism of the United States in the Caribbean, appreciates the nationalism of the Indians and Chinese and is sympathetic generally with struggling minorities. The race conscious who belong to proscribed groups sense a spiritual unity and are aware of a common cause. . . .

In the modern world the oppressed races have a common foe, the white peoples of Western Europe and their cousins of the United States. This isolable and convenient enemy makes the emergence of sentimental solidarity among the oppressed easy. The mechanisms of modern communication aid in the diffusion of this feeling to all the oppressed children of men. The oppressed have common experiences, face the same problems, those involving racial status, and hence speak a common language, ideologically speaking. Each oppressed group is strengthened by this realization. The cause of race consciousness takes on a wider meaning and importance.

12

MINORITY REACTION AND COUNTER-ASSERTION

INVESTIGATING characteristic American Negro reactions in a town in the far South, Dollard shows how under the surface of a seemingly passive accommodation, resentment and a potentially aggressive protest can be in process of formation. He finds that the typical traditional attitudes of acquiescence and subservience are deceptively assumed by quite a few, and that while caste etiquette is deferred to, it is done so with increasing reservations. Where once the Negro took over the white man's estimate of himself as true, he now has at least grave doubts of that inferiority except by virtue of force and arbitrary control. Blocked in political behavior and overt revolt, Negro behavior uses many subterfuges of passive resistance and covert protest, not yet translated openly into the sphere of action, but nevertheless in process of psychological gestation. Internal minority organization is weak in this instance, as might be expected under so repressive a regime. But according to the sample cited by Dollard, which happens to be in the deep South representing almost the nadir of the racial situation, the Negro minority is unmistakably passing over into an incipient phase of counterassertion. Powdermaker, who studied the same community, shows further that, while the older generation still accepts the regime at face value, the succeeding generations are more skeptical and, in feeling, at least, more militant. She found that the differences in Negro attitudes is closely correlated with the age generations, and that among the youngest group, irrespective of class and educational status, attitudes of resentment, challenge and disillusionment are markedly present.

The Negro's case, then, as Gallagher points out, is distinctly transitional, with open possibilities both for forward movement and for serious future clash with the entrenched mores of caste. He finds that more considerable gains have been made without resistance on the artistic and cultural flank, with less progress on the frontal racial alignments of economic and political participation. However, to the extent that artistic and cultural recognition yield status concessions and bolster minority morale, such gains are regarded as favorable, provided they do not prove mere concessions rather than clearances of caste conventions. Prior to the eventual challenge of the primary positions of caste privilege, such cultural salients strengthen minority morale and generate an internal momentum of progressive self-assertion.

Generalizing on this type of minority experience, Elkin's paper states upon the basis of his observations of the reactions of primitive peoples to the white man's culture, a three stage cycle of minority reaction, generally true for this type of culture contact and conflict. The first stage is one of tentative and experimental contacts with the alien culture, with ready adoption of certain of its utilities and acceptance, usually, of missionary and educational guidance. With increasing detribalization and exploitation, general disillusionment is generated, followed by a stage of helpless inferiority and substantial doubt about the values of the native's own culture. According to Elkin, the hold on the aboriginal culture is not completely lost in this reaction of distrust and bewilderment, as the third stage of the reaction reveals. For this stage pivots on a return to the old culture as, after a generation or so, a positive phase of group or racial consciousness succeeds the period of helplessness and inferiority feeling before the onslaughts of the more powerful civilization. The first symptoms of the last phase are movements for the revival of the old culture. In Mexico, Australia, in India, South and West Africa, and with certain North American Indian groups, such a series of reactions is traceable. The cycle varies both in time and intensity, but seems in general to follow approximately the same general course. The return of the minority to its own culture is rarely a mere retreat back to the old conservatism and former provinciality of culture. Occasionally it may be so rationalized, but this is a protest reaction mainly. In actuality, the cultural revival is a grafting of adopted elements of the invader's culture upon traditions and symbols of the old. The cultural

potentialities of such modified cultural nationalism are more sound
and promising than the occasional more narrowly conceived nationalisms of minorities, who react so violently to the majority pattern that
they imitate it in reverse. The Garvey movement was an instance of
the latter sort.

It is very necessary to note that, in spite of the general truth of
such a cycle of minority reactions, specific situations provide a number
of exceptions to the rule. Linton's article calls attention to the wide
variability of group attitudes and cultural results, depending upon the
concrete factors involved, particularly as due to the selective reactions
of economic factors in the culture contact. The widely contrasted
results shown by his account of the course of the acculturation
process with different American Indian groups parallels familiar
discussion of the same sort of contrast in India as between the Hindus
and the Moslems. Facing the same situation of minority adjustment
to English dominance and education of the European type, these two
segments of the Indian population have reacted very differently, or at
least at very different rates in their progress toward counterassertive-
ness, although the trends of contemporary Indian nationalism may be
regarded as a symptom of a growing convergence of the Hindu and
Moslem protest of English and European hegemony.

Race consciousness on the part of minorities is an inevitable and
pardonable reaction to majority persecution and disparagement. It
is after all, however, potential minority racialism, and thus by no
means exempt from the errors and extremisms of majority racialism.
In certain versions, it has been an echo or imitation of the majority
attitudes, expressed in counter-symbols and reversed claims, but motivated by the same rationalizations. To the self-determination formula
of Pan-Ethiopianism: "Africa for the Africans," for instance, Garvey
added the concept of a "Black Empire," very obviously an imitative
imperialism. W. O. Brown in *The Nature of Race Consciousness*
calls attention to these countertraits in tracing the conversion of
minority race consciousness from self-pity to positive racialist pride
and self-assertion. Group achievements in this compensatory stage
tend to become grossly magnified, counterclaims of superiority and
of chosen mission often follow. Relatively helpful as compensations
for shattered morale and damaged self-respect, these attitudes have

potentialities, which sometimes mature, for the counterpersecution of others. The majority "scapegoat reaction" also runs in some minority history as well, and in lieu of opportunity to punish their oppressors, minorities, upon gaining power, sometimes victimize and persecute other groups.

Historically almost every large-scale majority racialism has had a minority group analogue. Zionism is manifestly a reaction to anti-Semitism; Pan-Islamism is as much a political answer to Christianity's alliance with European imperialism as it is a parallel religious sectarianism. Pan-Asiatic programs and movements are basically provoked reactions to a chronically aggressive Europe, and Pan-Ethiopianism is directly a counterassertion to colonial imperialism. In all this, there is close patterning after the majorities along both political and theoretical lines. The propagandist reconstruction of the minority tradition, predicating superiority claims and the invention of prestige myths and rationalizations involves the same fallacies and contradictions that were found characteristic of the behavior of majority groups.

The minority thus has its psycho-pathology also: a case in point being that described by Guy Johnson in his study of a mixed Indian-White-Negro group. These folk, the "Croatans" in North Carolina, predominantly Indian in blood, but without trace of Indian culture, are in an anomalous minority position. In their limited situation, they compensate by accenting their superiority to the neighboring Negroes, and are particularly sensitive about being mistaken for Negroes. The latter resentment is all the more acute because there is considerable admixture of Negro blood in the group. Thus the prejudice pressure has arrayed one minority group against another. On the slightest of claims to the Indian tradition, the author finds, the Croatans compensate in terms of their own exaggerated Indian genealogy and local myths. The same ethnic combination which here exhibits unstable and morbid social relationships, in Brazil, where a tradition of racial and cultural tolerance prevails, shows just the opposite results; a compatible society with considerable cultural fusion and reciprocal respect; evidence, one might conclude, that sounder majority attitudes provoke sounder minority reactions.

Reid's study of the Negro West Indian immigrant in the United

States shows this minority within a minority to have produced two very interesting types of reaction in West Indian contacts with the native-born Negroes. Difference of cultural background, combined with commonalty of race, has conspired in this case to rather complicated minority interactions. Initially the native Negro group responded with considerable hostility to the culturally strange newcomers in their midst. The reaction was partly American hundred per-centism, refracted from the Negro's share of typical American intolerance. But there was also, in part, that not infrequent minority compensation of finding an outlet for repressed minority resentment and pique by reacting negatively to another minority. To precipitate this intra-racial hostility, there was a certain amount of economic competition and conflict between the two groups, which got itself expressed in a cultural form of prejudice which turned the typical majority stereotypes against the West Indian Negro.

Gradually, however, there has developed mutual accommodation between the native and foreign-born Negroes, based primarily on a common cause of resistance to race prejudice, which has equally affected both. The West Indians, less accustomed to prejudice, at least of the American type, have been on the whole vigorously assertive and have thus often been in the vanguard of this movement. This leadership and its common appeal to an inclusive racialism has slowly welded both groups into a close working solidarity. Again, the Garvey movement, led by a West Indian and with a large West Indian contingent, was responsible for a considerable impetus toward a more unified racial front. The dominant factor, however, in this was the common proscription of all on the basis of color, in the absence of which the two segments of the Negro peoples would doubtless not have fused or co-operated for several more generations.

The mainspring of Indian nationalism, likewise, is a strong bond of counterassertive reaction to British dominance and subordination of multi-racial India. Before the growth of this sentiment and its organization by the Indian Nationalist Congress, India had no sense either of nationality or of common racial interest. Shridarani records how there was slowly forged the common front which the several Indian sects and peoples are coming to accept as their one hope of liberation from political domination, economic exploitation and cultural disparagement. Indian nationalism has had to bridge inveterate feuds and hostilities, most serious of all the Hindu-Moslem antagonism, and, in addition, the social separatism of the caste system. That in so culturally diversified a land an anti-British movement with so much of a following could have been organized in some thirty years' time is one of the signal examples of the resurgent wave of the contemporary countermovement against European dominance. The force of European prestige, in its heyday, was enormous; India, with its tradition and numbers, should otherwise have been able to assert at least an effective passive resistance. But after generations of almost complete prostration before the might of Britain, it was reserved for a minority leader who had learned his first tactics in a minority struggle in South Africa, to formulate the campaigns of cultural revival, passive resistance and non-co-operation (civil disobedience) which have generated the momentum of the most formidable counterassertive movement of the present day.

On the cultural front, Indian nationalism calls for reassertion of native Indian tradition, customs and culture values. That is as vital to the movement as its political objectives. In fact this cultural program first dramatized the movement on any large scale. This crucial role of a cultural program in a minority movement is demonstrable from many quarters and in the case of many people's movements, national and racial. The connection and role of the revival of minority cultures will be discussed more fully under the section on national minorities (Part V). Here it is sufficient to see the effect on minority motivation and feeling of solidarity induced by the positive pride in a common cultural tradition or movement of cultural self-expression. Such movements have become increasing adjuncts of minority counterassertion, and have been influential in implementing the various campaigns of self-determination.

Majority pressure and persecution thus make over eventually the group attitudes and behavior of the various minority peoples, often to the undoing of the status quo of majority dominance.

NEGRO COUNTER-ASSERTION IN THE SOUTH

In various ways Negroes may slight, elide, and make a mockery of the deference forms, but they must observe them nevertheless; not to do so is actually an aggressive and even dangerous act. However good individual relations may be, the experience of the Negro in dealing with whites in the past justifies him in taking a distrustful attitude. Negro deference is often the mask which conceals hostile aloofness.

MOST OF the time it is the part of wisdom for the Negro [in Southerntown] to suppress his resentment at the superior advantages enjoyed by white people. This aggression is often converted into a passive accommodation and is displaced onto persons within the Negro group. It must not be supposed, however, that Negroes show no direct resentment toward white people; they do, even though this form of reaction is not of major importance.

For the sake of contrast we should remind ourselves of the normal outlets for aggression available to a minority group which wishes to change its economic or social status. They are political behavior, in-group organization, and active protest against undesired conditions. Some members of the minority group achieve political status and are able to represent the interests of their social segment. In the case of the Negroes in Southerntown, as we know, this conventional form of striving is not available. A common result is to drive hostile protest underground, to keep it a lurking and latent force in the social order. It is doubtless the failure to describe this fact and to see in proper perspective the aggressive tensions within societies that makes so many social developments and movements surprising to social scientists.

Southern white people, however, do not make this mistake in respect to Negroes. On the contrary, they show the greatest sensitivity to aggression from the side of the Negro, and in fact, to the outside observer, often seem to be reacting to it when it is not there. Still, it

Excerpts from John Dollard, *Caste and Class in a Southern Town* (New Haven: Yale University Press, 1937), pp. 286-293, 297-303, 306-308, 312.

is very convincing to experience in one's own person the unshakable conviction of the white caste that danger lurks in the Negro quarter. Only constant watchfulness, it is believed, and a solid white front against potential Negro attack maintain the *status quo*. This behavior on the part of the whites suggests the following proposition: they realize the gains they are making from the Negroes and expect the Negro to react as they themselves would if they were arbitrarily assigned an inferior caste position. As we know, they are mistaken in this assumption since there are other ways out of the dilemma than direct aggression. . . .

Certainly the whites are attuned to notice the slightest forward pressure on the part of the Negro, and the white caste is little disposed to accept even the feeblest direct action from the Negro's side. . . . The principle seems to be that nothing justifies aggression by a Negro against a white man or woman. My informant was reluctant to talk about this issue and persistently passed on to other matters. But he later made the point in another way. He said that some white men will bait a Negro and then smash him down if he answers back. Informant does not do this; when he jokes with a Negro, he also lets it be understood that he can take as good as he gives. In the case of baiting, it seems as if there were an attempt to provoke the Negro by sadistic joking and then, when his counteraggression is mobilized, to come down hard on him. The sensitivity to any assertive move on the part of the Negro is immediately recorded in threatening judgments of his behavior of the type we already know; he is said to be "uppity" or "getting out of his place."

Since the Negro may not retaliate openly, he must have recourse to furtive means if he is to retaliate at all. This we shall find to be the case where direct aggression is expressed. It is done, if possible, so that the aggressor is unknown; the direct challenge would provoke certain vengeance. We shall find also that, since explicit hostility is so dangerous, Negroes have recourse to indirect, circuitous, and symbolic methods of conflict with whites. . . .

It is worth noting as a general point that within the caste situation Negro women can be somewhat more expressive of their resentment than can Negro men. In comparing life-history data of Negro men and women it was quite clear that much more antagonism is tolerated from the women; they can do and say things which would bring a severe penalty had they been men. . . . There are, of course, distinct limits to what a Negro woman may do, but they are not so narrow as for men.

The Negro's threat to the whites is that of furtive individual acts of violence. In this day and age an uprising does not seem a real danger; it is the sporadic individual attack or reprisal which has threatening significance for the white caste. It would seem indeed that only the rather direct forms of aggression from Negroes are feared or even appreciated; ridicule is a difficult weapon for the lower-caste member against an upper-caste man, and mere wishes do not hurt anybody. The individual reaction has not always been the only type; there have been, of course, slave uprisings and these have been of some importance in the history of American slavery. There have been no successful revolts in North America, but the occasional uprisings that did occur were the source of violent reprisals, fear, and intensive precautionary measures.

There are two possible explanations for the lack of organized hostility on the side of the Negroes at the present time. One is that the warlike front presented by the united white caste leaves no hope of success. A second is that there is an alternative available now which was available only with great difficulty in slavery days—physical mobility or escape toward the North. It is understandable that escape would be preferable to the prospect of a suicidal attack. The conflict within the Negro caste makes any type of collective effort difficult, and most of all, of course, any effort against the armed and determined upper-caste group. At any prospect of a united political front on the part of the Negroes, such as membership in Huey Long's "Share the Wealth" clubs, the white alarm is immediate and the event becomes a political issue; the vigilance which is the price of dominance is keen. . . .

Occasional surprising instances occur in Southerntown where the "circumstances of the case" are taken into account and caste solidarity is not invoked. A Negro relative of one of my informants ran a small store. A white man came in, ordered some goods, got them, and then refused to pay for them. The storekeeper brought the white man into court and forced him to pay. The white man took this as an intoler-

able affront and came to beat up the Negro. In this case the other
whites did nothing, but said the white man should have paid his bill
in the first place. A sense of fair play based on the business morality
of the community here came into effect; and there may have been
other factors, such as that the store owner had a white friend at
court, or that the white assailant was disliked. All such factors alter
cases when caste punishment of Negroes is concerned. In general,
however, the feeling of the necessity of solidarity among the whites
is so strong that the nature of the case is not examined; all that is
seen is militancy in a Negro, and this, it is agreed, cannot be tolerated.

Occasionally, of course, the spirited Negro and the intolerable
situation come together and the result is a stand against the white
man. One Negro informant told a story about his father. A fence
was down between his father's farm and that of a neighbor, and the
white neighbor persistently let his horses run into the Negro's field.
It is against the law to let horses run loose in this way. The animals
got into the Negro's corn a number of times and were destroying
a large part of it. Several times the "old man" drove them back and
finally sent one of his sons to complain. After the boy returned, the
horses were promptly back in the corn again. The Negro asked his
son what had happened. The boy said the white man paid no attention
to the warning and told his hired man to let the horses loose again.
Informant's father became intensely angry, took a gun, and walked
with it in his hand to the white man's house. He had an angry
talk with the owner of the horses; finally the white man's wife inter-
vened and told him they would keep the horses away. A lynching
party formed at the white house later in the day; the owner eventually
stopped it on the ground that the Negro did not really know what
he was doing. Informant said his father became so angry under such
conditions that he did not care what happened to him; he said he
would sooner die than have the food which he was raising for his
children and for which he had worked so hard destroyed in this way.
The would-be lynchers here were reacting on principle and not
according to the circumstances of the case.

Apparently aggression of Negro children against white children is
not taken quite so seriously as that of adult Negroes. A Negro man
recalled how he and his idolized brother went around and did

mischievous things together when they were boys. They used to fight with the white boys in the neighborhood and especially with four German boys who lived on the adjoining farm. Since there were only two Negroes and four whites, the Negroes were often beaten. They would have fist fights by rounds and "rock" each other, and once there was a near-tragedy. The Negro boys' father had a .22 rifle with which he used to shoot the heads off chickens. The boys would sneak it out when he was not at home and practice with it until both became good shots. Once they decided to even things up for good and all with the German boys, and took the gun in a bag down to the line fence where they usually fought. It was planned that the older brother would engage one of the neighbors in a fight, then step aside and let the other shoot. This very day the white boys did an unusual thing. They came up and asked the Negro boys how their grandfather was; the brothers answered that he had died the night before, which was true. "Well, then," said one of the white boys, "I think we're foolish for fighting all the time this way." Peace was made and no shooting took place. It may be noted that this story was a treasured fantasy of this informant, and its function undoubtedly was to affirm his own integrity as over against white men. He did not conceive of himself as forever passively accepting affronts from the whites. . . .

Effort on the part of Negroes to improve their socio-economic position is perceived by the white caste as an affront. Holding a prestigeful job, owning a large tract of land, having a special talent by which the Negro competes with white people are forms of activity which are defined as aggressive. It is plain to see how the caste situation tends to discourage or prevent vertical social mobility in Negroes. In Southerntown, at least, resentment at Negro "rising" is felt not only by lower-class white people, but by the middle-class people as well. Statements indicating these resentments are often and naïvely made by conservative white people. They will object to any educational or other "frills" for Negroes by saying that they do not want to do anything for "niggers"; that the only place in which they like to see them is in the fields working. In some neighboring towns, though not in Southerntown, it is said that Negroes are challenged if seen dressed up on the street during week days; again their place is in the fields. Every Negro who has achieved advancement beyond lower-class status in Southerntown has been made aware of this envy and resentment at his aggressive mobility. Such Negroes are said to get ideas beyond their station, that is, to threaten the fixed inferior and superior positions of Negro and white castes. The individuality and independence which go with landownership, for example, seem to be defined as aggressive behavior on the part of a Negro; however absurd it may seem, the fact is that Negroes believe this to be the case and whites act as if it were so. A middle-class Negro informant well acquainted with this situation was much concerned about the tendency for Negroes not to struggle to own land of their own. He said that around Southerntown in earlier days they had a great ambition to own land; now they seem just to drift with the tide. He thinks one cause is their general insecurity. If they work hard for material possessions, they never know when they will have to leave them suddenly. Although it does not happen often, the threat of being driven off one's own land is always there; "the less you have, the more easily you can leave if threatened." He said that whites often attack responsible Negroes as well as irresponsible ones when a race incident occurs; the homes or barns of the innocent and upright may be destroyed. The knowledge that this can happen has a tendency to discourage the capable Negroes from saving and building up farms of their own.

Take the cases of two Southerntown Negroes who own land to illustrate. One of them is an extremely capable man who ran a large plantation very competently; he received a good salary, saved his money, and bought a few hundred acres of land as well as some other property. He continued to prosper, would have liked to buy more land, had the money and the administrative ability to run it well, but he was cautious and thought it dangerous to "pop his head up too high." The whites did not like the idea of a Negro with a large amount of land. He decided he had just about the safe amount; he would rather operate on a smaller scale and be personally secure than own a larger tract and be in danger. The other Negro owned a large plantation; he was careful not to have the land all in one place but rather in parcels in different parts and counties so that his prosperity would not be too obvious in any one region.

Another aspect of the same problem is the conception of the

"white man's job" already referred to. For a Negro to hold such a job is viewed by white people as a threatening gesture on his part. Needless to say these jobs are the less laborious, more remunerative ones with higher prestige attaching to them. Despite these hindrances, however, Negroes are inevitably pressing toward advancement in status and therefore exhibit a kind of aggression against the caste-system in Southerntown. In this they are responding to pressures in our dominant American pattern which admit of social advancement as a goal even for the humblest individuals. All too frequently success and actual mobility of Negroes are punished as aggressive acts. Without much doubt the same envy is aroused among white people when a white man advances in status or betters himself in an economic sense; but within the white caste the face of the society is set formally against the expression of it, and a white person may not be punished for his temerity, industry, ingenuity, or luck.

Continuing our descending scale of overtness of aggression, we shall refer briefly again to withdrawal of trade from white businessmen as a form of hostility open to Negroes. A boycott is a distinctly aggressive act, as he knows who has ever experienced or witnessed one. In Southerntown, at least, it would be too dangerous for Negroes to declare a formal boycott since it could easily be broken up, but individual Negroes do withdraw their patronage if they are not treated to their satisfaction in white stores. One informant reported that she had refused to buy in stores where they call her "sister," after the church custom, or "aunty," according to the older plantation custom. She could at least show her resentment by this means. It is generally held by middle-class Negroes that one reason, though not the only one, for the success of the Jewish merchants in the dry-goods trade is that they do not draw the resentment of Negro patrons in this way; Jews do not treat business as a caste matter and do not stress the inferiority of the Negro. The boycott could be an exceedingly powerful weapon, as is obvious, but the difficulty about using it, as has frequently been noted, is the lack of in-group organization among Negroes which would enable them to stand solidly behind it. Very probably, too, if attempted, it would bring in its train forms of counter-aggression from the whites against leading Negroes which would be exceedingly unpleasant. For the moment withdrawal of trade has more significance in manifesting the aggressive self-esteem of individual Negroes than in affecting the caste situation in any general way.

We must also consider the high labor turnover among plantation Negroes in this new perspective. Moving away is a form of retaliation that exasperates planters who want an efficient but stationary labor force. It is troublesome and expensive to have a constant shifting of tenant families. But one of the few things made absolutely secure to Negroes by emancipation was freedom of geographic mobility, and this they use in part to express their discontent with the conditions under which they work. It may not be a very effective means of retaliation and it may even be against the interests of the Negro himself, but it evidently gives some satisfaction. Oftentimes just to go away is one of the most aggressive things that another person can do, and if means of expressing discontent are limited, as in this case, it is one of the few ways in which pressure can be put on. The alarm of the whites and the exultation of the Negroes at the mass migrations to the North are evidence of how effective this pressure can be; it will continue to be so long as the Negroes are needed for plantation labor, but of course no longer.

White women frequently complain that their Negro cooks and servants never have the courage to let them know before they leave. They just disappear some day after a pay day. One housewife, a good natural psychologist, said that she always suspects they are about to leave whenever they come around to praise her or "make over her" especially. It is a sort of apology in advance for what they intend to do. The only explanation of such behavior is that the Negro woman views leaving as an aggressive act and fears to confess her intention lest she be stopped somehow or argued out of going. Many of the unaccountable moves that Negroes make from homes and plantations could probably be understood if they were viewed in this light. It is as if the Negro were saying, "I may be inferior and you may have many advantages over me, but at least you do not own my body."

Another type of aggression open to Negroes is the withdrawal of deference forms and prestige acknowledgments to white people. Nothing is more immediately sensed as hostile and the whites never neglect to stress the correct behavior. A Negro who had worked in northern territory for some years gave his personal experience of this.

In the Yankee town Negroes voted as well as whites, and altercations were handled on a person-to-person, not a race-to-race basis. He said he could not get used to things when he came back to Southerntown after many years away. He would say "yes" and "no" instead of "yes, sir" and "no, sir." His wife and other Negroes remonstrated with him and warned him of the danger he ran, but he found it hard to change the habit he had built up over eight years. Whites had several times corrected him when he failed to observe the caste code.

Humility and lack of direct demands are elements of caste etiquette for Negroes. We have already noted that women are given more license than men. For example, a middle-class Negro informant was asked to talk before a women's discussion group in one of the white churches on the topic "Our Manchurian Friends." The chairman of the club introduced her as a *friend*. When she rose to speak, she said that she was glad to be introduced as a friend and hoped she was one. She went on to take as the major issue of her discussion the fact that it was nice to be interested in Manchuria, but that the club might also be interested in its Negro friends in Southerntown. Right over on the other side of the tracks were plenty of problems nearer home than Manchuria. Probably no local Negro man would be asked to speak before a group of white men, unless perhaps a Negro minister, who can always be trusted to be tactful and deferential; but if a man were invited he would hardly dare to be as lacking in humility as this woman was.

Another woman informant, strongly conscious of her middle-class status, commented openly on the cowardice of white people who do not have the courage to call her "Mrs." She said she knew herself to be worthy of the title. She felt especially that white Christian ministers were hypocritical on this point, since they ought to set a good example. Of course this informant will not be allowed her title, but she apparently gets some satisfaction from expressing herself pointedly in defiance of the caste pattern. In various ways Negroes may slight, elide, and make a mockery of the deference forms, but they must observe them nevertheless; not to do so is actually an aggressive and even dangerous act.

A middle-class Negro informant said he was no "Sambo nigger." He respected whites for what they could do, but he thought every white man respected a brave man; he said that he would not show any undue deference, smile in a servile manner or scratch his head or the like. He followed the main forms because he had to, but he would not add to them by a jot and he carried them out in a cool and reserved manner. The aggressive element is quite obvious in this, the more so when one thinks that whites expect Negroes not only not to be aggressive, but to be positively ingratiating at every turn.

The sabotage of lower-class Negroes is more passive and takes the form of slowness, awkwardness, and indecision about their work. After all, this is a slavery accommodation; the slave may not show his resistance by stopping work altogether, but he can at least slow up. It may also be that the carelessness of white time and goods often attributed to lower-class Negroes is another evidence of resistance. The fact that there is something aggressive in such behavior will readily be seen when the annoyance of the boss in the face of it is observed. This partial refusal to accept the worker's role is viewed as the equivalent for the lower-class Negro of the refusal of deference signs by the middle- or upper-class Negro. . . .

We all know that the withdrawal of the interest, attention, and love of others can be experienced as a form of aggression. If a former friend does not speak to us on the street, we are aware of hostile intent on his part, some of us perhaps more so than others. Suspicion and distrust of white people are quite marked in Negroes, although they usually lurk behind the deceitful role of caste accommodation. Open distrust is much more in evidence among middle-class than among lower-class Negroes. All white people, North and South, who deal with Negroes must count with this fact; however good individual relations may be, the experience of the Negro in dealing with whites in the past justifies him in taking a distrustful attitude. He coolly surveys the other person and his actions, implying that he has to be watched, and at the same time not accepting his apparent fairness at its face value. Thoughtless white people are constantly baffled at this attitude on the part of Negroes. . . .

Negro deference is often the mask which conceals hostile aloofness. The "good nigger" from the white man's standpoint is the one who "comes across" rather completely emotionally and in whom this protective reserve is less detectable.

Everyone has noticed at one time or another an aggressive element in jokes; for example, jokes about dictators inevitably arise once other forms of aggression are suppressed. The joke, of course, conceals its aggressive intent behind the façade of the little story, and oftentimes it takes a bit of analysis to make it clear. In sarcasm, on the contrary, the aggressive element is plain. Negroes do not omit jokes from their arsenal of reprisal against white people. . . .

Possibilities of socially effective aggression for Negroes in Southern-town do not seem to be increasing. This is all the more true since depressive economic conditions have taken a heavy toll of Negro business. A middle class informant said that Negroes used to play a much larger role in the town than they do now; this was in the days when the Negroes had a bank and business was more prosperous generally. Still Southerntown is known as a good town for Negroes and the general advance in Negro status in America is reflected here also, for example, in improved schools. One informant said that the colored people have been inching forward, asserting themselves a little more, winning this and that small concession, but he feels that the progress is very slow and that only a little gain has been made since slavery days. This is inevitable since Negroes are debarred from the more direct forms of organization and action which have the power to change status relations in a democratic society, i.e., political activity.

RACIAL ATTITUDES AND AGE GROUPS

The strongest and most consistent differences in typical attitudes of Negroes toward Whites correspond roughly to age differences. The further they get from ignorance, poverty, and the slave tradition, the more they resent and rebel against such a system imposed upon them under a democracy; the more they react as the dominant Whites would react in the same position.

THE STRONGEST and most consistent differences in typical attitudes of Negroes toward whites correspond roughly to age differences. . .

The oldest generation, those who are over sixty, were born before,

Excerpt from Hortense Powdermaker, *After Freedom. A Cultural Study in the Deep South* (New York: The Viking Press, 1939), pp. 325-333.

during, or immediately after the Civil War. This means that they were born into the traditional pre-war situation or else in the period when pre-war patterns still prevailed to a large extent, even though the slaves were technically free. For all these it seems natural to turn to Whites for assistance and advice. Reared to accept dependence and submission as their role, they are habituated to the need of help in the mere mechanics of living, the more so since many of them are illiterate. Often their trust has proved well placed. Many white people felt and many still feel responsible for the welfare of the Negroes who rely upon them. The countless tales of affection between slave and master during and after slavery have a firm foundation in fact. Today the generation whose parents were "old black mammies" and faithful family retainers usually carry over the attitudes that surrounded their infancy.

Foremost among these was the belief that black people are inferior to white people. Such a belief carries with it for Negroes a lack of confidence in their own race; and this still persists, not only among the very old, though most strongly among them. The oldest genera-tion are the readiest to conclude that "niggers will be niggers," a phrase they share with the Whites and frequently employ. They are on the whole reluctant to praise Negroes who have risen above their place. . . .

In this oldest group, belief and behavior consistently acknowledge white superiority. With the next generation, those who are now middle-aged, there is a split between the two. They do not believe that the Whites are actually superior, but in dealing with the white people they act as if they did. By dint of this accommodation they have been able to succeed, or at least to get along.

This group has grown up to have less dependence on the master class, and less contact with them. Some of the change is due to the increase of education among Negroes. Few of the middle-aged are highly educated, but far more of them than of their parents command the tools that enable them to cope with the mechanics of daily living: reading, writing, arithmetic. As a group they are no longer helplessly illiterate.

As a group, too, their horizon is less limited than that of their elders. Through newspapers, movies, radio, they have become increasingly aware of a world beyond the immediate domination of the Whites in their community. They have heard about the ideal of democracy which says all men are equal; they have been introduced to the idea of the Melting Pot; they have become identified with American institutions, and celebrate the Fourth of July as their own holiday.

They have seen their peers and contemporaries succeed, even if only a few. They know it can be done. They have acquired a measure of confidence in the powers of their race, discovering that Negroes too can maintain businesses, newspapers, banks, schools, stores, plantations, all formerly considered the province of the white man. They have seen the Negro engage in professions once deemed quite beyond his powers and his rights.

At the same time they have discerned more clearly the weaknesses of the white people. They have seen them suffer under the same economic system, have seen them make the same mistakes in business, have seen them, too, helpless to change a political situation not wholly favorable to them. Gradually and quietly they have come to the conclusion that there is not much difference between themselves and the white man, except for color, and in the case of mulattoes, not so much of that. They think that all are members of the human race with about the same virtues and the same sins. . . .

The average white person in this community seldom realizes the extent to which this group questions his superiority. The middle-aged Negro is well aware that most white adults still hold to the beliefs and attitudes of their parents and grandparents; that for them there are still two distinct worlds, the white and the black. A white man may make an excursion into the black circle to have his laundry done or to select a mistress. But for him the Negroes are still shut into their own world and out of his by the fences his forebears erected. Knowing this, the prudent colored man keeps his convictions to himself. As long as the white remains ignorant of them, he remains unruffled and unalarmed. Since so much of the Negro's trouble is due to the white man's fears, it pays to keep him feeling safe. With many middle-aged Negroes, the policy of the dual role is deliberate and articulate. . . .

Among the younger generation, those in their teens, twenties, and thirties, resentment is keen and outspoken. These agree with the middle-aged in feeling that they are equal to the Whites and in desiring equal treatment. They differ in not possessing or wanting to possess the tact and diplomacy of their elders. They loathe the admission of white superiority that such diplomacy implies, and feel the need to be deceitful as a wound to their self-esteem. Their usual solution is to avoid contact with white people whenever possible, and where it cannot be avoided, to make it as slight as may be.

Even among the less-educated young Negroes there is far more open rebellion than among those of middle age. . . .

It is partly a matter of education, partly of social self-evaluation, that the shift of attitude, as one moves from the lowest to the highest class, in general parallels, although not with quite the same consistency, the change in moving from the oldest to the youngest generation. The upper-class Negro thinks more highly of himself and therefore is the more wounded by being constantly treated as if he were on a par with the lowest members of his group. The young Negro of the upper class is the one whose social and temporal distance from the old order combine to make this feeling the most intense. He is therefore the one who finds it most acutely galling to discover anew every day and many times a day that he is still subject to the dictum, "a nigger is a nigger." He, most of all, has shown that he can learn like the Whites, can live as they do, can exercise the self-discipline considered characteristic of Whites. The realization of how little all this avails brings home to him the impenetrability of the barrier that confronts him. Moreover, he is precisely the Negro whom the Whites most resent and suspect; in addition to being more sensitive than his social inferiors, he is liable to meet more hostility. . . .

The further they get from ignorance, poverty, and the slave tradition, the more they resent and rebel against such a system imposed upon them under a democracy; the more they react as the dominant Whites would react in the same position. This is part of the acculturation process.

The parents and grandparents of the young educated Negroes in Cottonville, although not accepting the situation completely, acquiesced in it and worked out a way of living in it. Because the younger generation have done neither, life is more difficult for them. They do not have to bear the lashes of an overseer, or live in a slave shanty, or step off the sidewalk if they see a white person coming. But in countless ways their self-respect and pride daily receive blows. Expecting more, demanding more, than their grandparents ever dreamed of, they are hurt in ways their grandparents could not have imagined. It has been suggested also that some of their greater intensity may be ascribable to a comparatively late and sometimes sudden awareness of the system and its consequences, and that the attitudes of their parents have not prepared them for compliance. The convictions that middle-aged Negroes of today conceal from the Whites cannot long remain secret from their children. So far the intense and mounting bitterness of the younger Negroes is helpless and undirected. They take no concerted action toward improving conditions within their group. Some of them are even at a loss in shaping their individual behavior. They will not say "Howdy, Boss," and they do not know what to say in its place. When possible, they say nothing.

The middle-aged Negroes recognize that the younger generation feel and act differently from themselves. They regret the increased bitterness and sometimes fear the results of the young people's refusal to exercise tact and diplomacy. Due allowance must of course be made for the difference always to be found between succeeding generations, even in a less changing culture; but the present difference goes beyond that.

THE NEGRO'S PARTICIPATION IN AMERICAN CULTURE

There is a degree to which the contribution of the Negro to American culture has been successful primarily because it either has not collided with, or did not openly challenge, the dominant ideas of what was appropriate for a lower caste. The task is one of the Negro finding out how to acquire the self-respect based on the recognition of the work of Negro artists without the necessity of buying that self-respect at the price of caste-conformity.

IT IS not yet proved, or disproved, that the Negro has special talents in particular lines. The stereotypes with which the caste system operates would lead us to believe that the Negro has certain artistic abilities and talents, especially in music and the plastic arts, not possessed to the same degree or in the same kind by Caucasians. To some extent this notion is a reflex of the fact that it is in the arts, particularly the spirituals and jazz or swing music, that the Negro has attracted most favorably attention from the Caucasian. But it cannot be assumed that, merely because Caucasian ears have been pleased by the sorrow songs of slavery and by the hot rhythms of swing, the Negro has a peculiar talent for artistic creation along these lines. It might be argued with equal logic that the invention of gunpowder by the Chinese showed a peculiar talent for explosives, or that Gutenberg's press established the literary inventiveness of Germanic peoples. Whatever inferences are drawn must be established in the light of historical perspective, and must hold true when full consideration is given to all sociological and environing phenomena. There has been, for example, a general feeling among cultured persons that the German people had a peculiar musical genius. Although this notion has gone somewhat into eclipse in recent years, it was widely prevalent in the first quarter of the twentieth century. But if these same Germanic racial stocks are examined not at 1900 but at

Buell G. Gallagher, *American Caste and the Negro College* (New York: Columbia University Press, 1938), pp. 368-371.

600, what has become of the alleged musical ability? It takes a pre-Nazi Munich and Nuremberg with centuries of cultural growth and development, to produce the soil out of which genius flowers. And the flowering of genius is in large part (how large a part it is impossible to say, but certainly to a very significant degree) determined by the cultural chemistry of the social soil. No Vienna, no Beethoven, Mozart, composing at six and playing for royalty before ten, could logically be taken as an example of an alleged peculiar genius of the Germanic peoples for musical expression. But whatever explanation may be given to Mozart, that explanation cannot overlook the fact that he was born and nurtured in Salzburg, the Salzburg of the nineteenth—not the ninth—century.

So, too, with the Negro's musical expression in America. It began with the sorrow songs. It has reached its current zenith in swing music. The spirituals and the seculars were born of slavery. Stephen Foster, white, took many of the plantation melodies, cast them in wording appropriate to the pattern of master-slave relationships, and gave them to America, an America which avidly welcomed these plaintive songs of sorrow that did not challenge the caste pattern. The Fisk Jubilee Singers with their superlative rendering of the songs of aspiration and longing, of sorrow and yearning, sang their way into the consciousness of two continents, and set the pattern still used by many Negro colleges in winning Caucasian approval and contributions. The birth of jazz and the development of swing further testify to the manner in which Caucasian America welcomes the Negro as he contributes a cultural strain which is so frankly and openly "Negroid."

It is impossible to say whether the acceptance is based more on the intrinsic merit of the musical contribution or upon the fact that the marked difference between these musical forms and the established classical norms does not imply "musical equality." There is a degree to which the contribution of the Negro to American culture has been successful primarily because it either coincided with, or did not openly challenge, the dominant ideas of what was appropriate for a lower caste. On the other hand, the recognition accorded Negro artists on the basis of their work has an important bearing upon the self-respect of the group. There are those who feel, with some justification, that any activity which ministers to the self-respect of the Negro is distinctly valuable; but others will argue that self-respect which is bought at the price of conformity to caste is too dearly purchased— that self-respect ought to be a by-product of struggle against caste. These latter would sharply challenge the "rightness" of conformity to cultural and artistic stereotypes. They would not necessarily rule out the possibility of using highly stylized modes of expression which are predominantly "Negroid" in connotation, but they would object to the use of such modes if their use tended to perpetuate invidious caste implications. The task is one of finding out how to teach racial self-respect without the necessity of buying that self-respect at the price of caste-conformity; and at the same time to recover the values of a racial cultural heritage without conjuring up the sociological phenomena which are historically associated with the emergence of that heritage. How to enjoy the spirituals and seculars as folk songs, without implying that the singer is recalling with pleasure the days of slavery out of which they came; how to acknowledge the Negro's gift to America without admitting a special "Negroid" status; how to achieve the value of cultural richness and diversity through group differences without surrendering the values of freedom and enjoyment which can come only through integration; how to enable the Negro American to be both a Negro and an American—these are problems.

The particular pertinence of this racial-emphasis problem to the larger question of transmitting the social heritage lies in the fact that the answers to both questions must be discovered together. The Negro student must see that both his African and his Caucasian ancestry have shared in the making of the cultural heritage into which he as an individual is now introduced. He must appropriate the values of this inclusive human heritage, with a cultivated ability to discriminate between the transitory and the enduring, the trivial and the consequential, the ephemeral and the significant. And he must come to see that as a Negro he is also an American, and that the proper phrase is "Negro American" not "American Negro." A successful social orientation of the problem of transmission of cultures, both inherited and contemporary, would weight all problems against the counterbalance of caste. The appropriation of the cultural heritage and the enrichment of contemporary culture will go hand in hand with the attempt to make caste irrelevant.

A high appreciation of the cultural heritage of the Negro, both the African and the American background, will not necessarily rule out an equally high appreciation of the non-Negro heritage. The amalgam of civilization certainly is not Caucasoid. It is human. The Negro needs to have no feeling either of inferiority, or of resentment, or of superiority, as he enters into the fullest participation and appreciation of all that is his as an American citizen—as a world citizen.

THE REACTION OF PRIMITIVE PEOPLES TO THE WHITE MAN'S CULTURE

From the point of view of the native race, three stages can frequently be distinguished in the history of its contact with the dominant immigrant white people. The first, which corresponds to the initial years of contact, is one of bewilderment, opposition, resentment and a sense of loss; then an attitude of scorn of the past and a feeling of inferiority with regard to their native culture; and finally, finding that they do not enter fully into white culture, usually because they are not wanted but are the objects of "race" discrimination and suspicion, the detribalized natives tend to revert to the old or what they can recapture of the old.

FROM THE point of view of the native race, three stages can frequently be distinguished in the history of its contact with the dominant immigrant white people. The first, which corresponds to the initial years of contact, is one of bewilderment, opposition, resentment and a sense of loss; the adults can find life and hope only in and through their own customs, traditions and beliefs; they can see nothing of value for them in the culture of the white man except perhaps in some of his material goods and tools; they also recognize in time that they must conform to some of his requirements and make what adjustments they can in their economic and social life, even

Excerpt from A. P. Elkin, "The Reaction of Primitive Races to the White Man's Culture. A Study in Culture-Contact," *The Hibbert Journal*, Vol. 35 (London: George Allen & Unwin, Ltd., 1936-37), pp. 537-545.

putting up with dispossession of land and deprivation of the ordinary means of livelihood; they may even, in some cases, deem it wise and worth while to pay lip-service to those Whites who are zealous in religious endeavor, and they very often entrust their children to missionaries for education; but their closing days are saddened by the spectacle of the young men and women being attracted to the ways and delights of the white man, for they recognize that the attraction is not intelligently based and that the ways and life of the latter are not for them, at least, not yet; they realize that the next generation will be for the most part ignorant of the ways of their fathers, will not fully understand the new sanctions and ideals and will not be accepted into the white community. The old men of wisdom know that the young ones are forgetting that "man cannot live by bread alone," not even the bread and other delectable goods of the white man, and so they retreat into themselves, passing on but little of their old beliefs— their faith, to a doubting generation, unless it be to a few exceptional individuals; and in due time they take their knowledge and their dark forebodings to the grave.

In the meantime, the members of the next generation, being influenced by the white man and his culture before they had really been gripped by the spirit of their own faith, become scornful of the old ways and superstitions, at least outwardly, and feel that they must rise above it. Now this attitude of scorn of the past and a feeling of inferiority with regard to their native culture is characteristic of the second stage of contact. It is negative in emphasis and cannot make for individual and social integration. Indeed, such a condition seems to lead to depopulation, or at least to be associated with it, and unless a people can pass successfully out of this second stage, it has a very poor future, if, indeed, it has any future at all.

Fortunately, there are usually three factors present which make possible an escape from this impasse; they are, first, the conservative nature of beliefs, especially those of a magical and animistic nature, which have to do with health and sickness, life and death. Down in their hearts, the natives still believe that there is something worth while in the old view and explanation of life and its problems, though they may know very little about it, and feel that they should not openly admit their conviction. Once, however, such beliefs, or others which they accept as similar or related, become respectable, a pathway has been made for a return to a faith which will give courage and understanding in the face of life's problems.

The second factor is the existence during the time of doubt and denial of at least some individuals who have clung to the old traditions, myths and rites waiting, even though unconsciously, for the time of disillusionment with the foreign and exotic, and of return to the old. They may have been fully or partially initiated and instructed by the old men of the past days, and, imbued with the latter's outlook and faith, they believe that hope for their people rests solely on an appreciation of the moral and social value of their indigenous beliefs and laws, even though the expression of that faith in rites and beliefs be now somewhat modified.

This leads to the third factor which is of the nature of a reaction from the feeling of worthlessness regarding native culture in general, and which is usually held for a generation or so after the initial stage of contact. Finding that they do not enter fully into white culture, usually because they are not wanted but are the objects of "race" discrimination and suspicion, the detribalized natives tend to revert to the old or what they can recapture of the old; they make what adjustments they can apart from the white organization of social and economic life, and in some cases become leaders of discontent, though not necessarily of a revolutionary nativistic movement. They realize that, for them, contentedness and happiness lie in the ways of their forefathers or in a life in line and tune with those ways. They thus come to see the function of their own old myths and rites as a source of faith and life and to argue that what is of value in the white man's religion was already in their own. They are also ready to appreciate the worth of their indigenous arts and crafts and unwritten literature and to take a pride in them; this step, however, is not usually taken unaided or without suggestion from without. The natives find white folk showing not only a great interest in the products of their former workmanship, but in some cases an appreciation of it; this makes them wonder whether they had not been too hasty in spurning and neglecting the old, and whether they had not better return to it and so recapture a real interest in living. It is at this point that a wise policy of appreciation and encouragement of native arts and crafts and literature should be put into operation both amongst children and adults. Such a policy helps to get rid of the feeling of inferiority which has hitherto been a millstone preventing the native race from rising from the "Slough of Despond." . . .

An illuminating case comes from Mexico, where the Indians had been in a state of neglect for four hundred years, and in self-defense had retreated into inaccessible regions; but now, since the Revolution of 1910, an education policy has gradually been put into operation, the motto of which is "To educate is to redeem." This was based on a conviction that the Indian could contribute toward Mexico's growth; indeed, a tendency arose to glorify everything that was Indian. But even so, it was difficult for many people in Mexico to believe that the Indians, who had been for so long regarded as human beasts of burden and "stupid" human cattle, were worth bothering about. The reformers, however, with the eye of faith, established experimental schools for Indians, which have utterly disproved the old conceptions of the Indian people as indolent, unresponsive and so on; instead, the Indian students have clearly demonstrated their praiseworthy industriousness, their incomparable morality, their racial pride and their capability of unlimited progress.

Of course, some will scoff at such a program and say that the native will in any case "return to the mat," but the trouble has largely been that he left the "mat" too soon; indeed, instead of leaving the "mat" he should have changed its quality and extended its usefulness. Now what we see in the third stage of culture contact is a "return to the mat," a return to the old faith, though somewhat modified, and to a sense of worth regarding native arts, crafts, literature, law and custom. This is important, for it gives the dominant people another opportunity to help the native race to work out its own salvation and at the same time to contribute something of value to world civilization. . . .

Now this awakening to self-consciousness is part of the process of the "return to faith," and is brought about by disillusionment with the white man and a realization that the native is not getting anywhere by aping or living under the shadow of the white man. He must express his personality and the genius of his race in his own way and there is always an element of return to the old in this reaction. Think, for example, of the old Maori who expressed the conviction of many of his people, on realizing that the hopes of social advancement which they had formed when they first consented to share their land with the white man were doomed to disappointment; he said that the Maori was at fault for deserting his old gods, institutions and beliefs, and his only chance of survival lay in a return to the beliefs of his fathers.

The thesis of this paper was recently revealed to me in its stark reality while visiting the Aborigines of the North Coast of New South Wales. I have visited these folk on several occasions, sometimes to study problems of contact and education, and sometimes to gather the fragments that remain of aboriginal culture. On this occasion, I was concerned with the latter, especially with totemism and the secret life. I soon realized that I was not discussing memories of the past but important beliefs of the present day and an institution which is now functioning.

As has happened elsewhere in Australia, so it was in this region. During the first years of white settlement, the old men only came into contact with white culture at a few material points, such as food, work and conflict; they were deprived of their hunting grounds and sometimes of their lives. The younger generation grew up on or near the property of the Whites, and realized that their livelihood depended absolutely on the latter either directly through wages and gifts, or indirectly through Government rations. They learned a good deal about the white man's ways and to a small extent adopted them. As the years went by, settlements were set apart for the natives, each with a manager who was (and is) the schoolmaster, and often a lay missionary. Unfortunately the land was only occasionally of any productive value and so farming projects seldom came to anything; poor results, therefore, could not always be attributed to the supposed innate laziness of the Aborigines, most of whom are half- and quarter-castes. Further, here and there a number settled on land of which they thought they had permanent use; in some cases, they were quite successful, only to find that they could be removed from it (sometimes by persuasion) and that Whites settled in their stead. They have likewise been realizing, especially of recent years, that their economic future is very circumscribed, being limited to laboring work, and often only that when no Whites wanted the work.

This, incidentally, makes clear to them the futility of school training, and indeed, in many centers now, their children are not welcomed
in the ordinary State schools—a change from the attitude of a generation ago. Needless to say, it has become quite obvious to them that
socially they are a race apart, except in so far as various white men
are ready to consort with their women and girls. Their lot is to live
segregated in small communities, doing work under settlement managers, or receiving rations, and occasionally getting work away from
the settlement. True, in New South Wales they have the franchise,
but this is of little value to them; thus except for a very short period
during the past year, unemployed Aborigines have not been allowed
to share in the unemployed relief works. In other words, they are not
encouraged to move toward the status of Whites.

Finally, in spite of anything they may have heard about the Christian doctrine of the brotherhood of man, they know that the organized
Christian denominations seldom pay any attention whatever to them;
practically all religious activity amongst them is left to the members
of a lay missionary organization, who, with the best will in the world,
are handicapped through lack of training in missionary work, and in
an understanding of Aborigines; moreover, many of the preachers
are women—a circumstance which aboriginal men find very hard to
understand, and in any case, they know that the priests and preachers
of the Churches in the towns are especially trained men, which is as
it should be, for amongst the Aborigines the custodians of the religious
life are the fully initiated men.

Now, these various facts, economic, social and religious, have convinced the middle-aged men of today that they cannot really share in
the life of the white man—at least, not yet. There is discontent,
much unhappiness and a lot of apathy. Some even feel that the less
trace of black there is in them, the less chance are they given of
realizing their Australian citizenship. But, and this is most interesting,
there is a return to the old faith, a reapplication of the beliefs of the
former generation. Now this is not merely a matter of holding certain
totemic and psychic beliefs, such as the belief in the totem as a kind
of guardian and other self, in the objective value of dreams and other
psychic experiences, in the power of medicine men, in the reality of
the "sky-god" and other heroes of the tribe; those who have acquired

any understanding of our attitude to spiritual things find parallel beliefs there, and are satisfied that theirs are as rational and justifiable as ours. Their beliefs are not merely good for them, but are well grounded. This applies especially to their belief in a sky-god, or hero, and they are adamant in their assertion that they have a belief in God, just as much as we have; they likewise compare certain of their tribal heroes to Biblical characters of whom they have heard from the missionaries. Thus, they are satisfied that from the point of view of religion, they have nothing to gain from us, and can find all they need in their own faith, modified as no doubt it is. This conclusion may be the result of faulty missionary methods and a reaction to the common opinion and attitude of Whites, namely, that the Aborigines have no religion. But there is more in it than that. It is a result of disillusionment. We have failed to impart an adequate understanding of Christianity to these natives, and so they are hanging onto, reviving and exalting whatever they can, of the old faith. . . .

In this region, we can speak truly of a "return to faith," and in particular, to the old faith. It is, in a sense, a retreat from the hard facts of race prejudice and clash. But it also presents to the dominant people an opportunity, for this return marks the recognition by the Aborigines of an important element in their own culture as equal to the corresponding element in ours. If the value of this faith (cult and beliefs) were acknowledged by the Whites, something would be accomplished toward freeing the natives from a feeling of inferiority with regard to their own culture, and supplying a basis for progress.

The return to faith is then part of the process of racial and cultural contact, belonging to the third stage in that process. It is a sign of defeat, disappointment and disillusionment, but at the same time it is a sign of a return to an appreciation of indigenous culture and tradition, and in that lies hope, provided that the dominant people then play their part unselfishly, respectfully, and without prejudice.

ACCULTURATION IN SEVEN AMERICAN TRIBES

The response of American Indians to white dominance has varied significantly from tribe to tribe depending upon the nature of the aboriginal cultures and the conditions of the contacts.

IT WOULD be hard to imagine better conditions for the acculturation of a native people than those which existed during the early part of Puyallup-White contact in Washington. The Indians were accepted on terms approaching social equality, with many legal intermarriages and the mutual recognition of relationship claims in both groups. Indians and whites worked side by side at the same tasks and for the same wages, and the only direct attempts to change the native culture were those connected with the abandonment of the communal houses and the introduction of Christianity. Even the latter seems to have been in the hands of intelligent and sympathetic missionaries. The individualistic patterns of the native culture made it easy for certain Indians to take on White habits without waiting for the rest of their group to assume them. The result of all this was the rapid assimilation of the Indians into the white population, and all distinctions would probably have disappeared if it had not been for certain later developments. Among these, although of minor importance, was the introduction of attitudes of social discrimination by the white later settlers. However, this seems to have been of minor importance in comparison to the sale of the Indian lands. The deadly results of this came not from a deprivation of resources but from a sudden influx of wealth which the Indians had no patterns of dealing with. The necessity for regular work was removed, while disputes as to the ownership intensified the hostilities latent in the native culture. Dr. Marion W. Smith has pointed out the sudden access of murders under the new conditions, but it seems questionable whether these, in themselves, would have done much to diminish the Indian popula-

Excerpts from Ralph Linton, ed., *Acculturation in Seven American Indian Tribes* (New York: D. Appleton-Century Co., 1940), pp. 37, 117-118, 204-206, 256-258, 332, 461-462.

tion. More important factors were the degeneration which came with idleness and plenty of money for liquor. . . .

Aboriginal White Knife culture of Nevada, as discussed by Dr. Jack S. Harris, was so simple and amorphous that there was little to be destroyed by European contact. Their economic status was already at a bare subsistence level; their social organization scarcely extended beyond the biological family, while their religion, with the solitary exception of the Gwini ceremonies, was informal and highly individualized. For the ordinary individual Ego satisfaction seems to have been derived mainly from the response of the members of his immediate family and from diversified sexual experience, while prestige outside the family group derived from supernatural experience and the consequent ability to heal. None of their basic culture patterns have been seriously inhibited at any period in the contact continuum. Even the Gwini ceremonies, with their opportunities for widened individual contacts, have been successfully transformed into Fourth of July celebrations which serve the same purpose.

Prior to the opening up of the mines, White Knife contact with Europeans was sporadic, giving them no opportunity to familiarize themselves with any but the material aspects of White culture. It seems probable that the recognition of their own inferiority which has characterized them in recent times was already present, for they seem to have been willing to borrow at all points, subject only to the limitations imposed by their low economic status. During this period the natural environment was little affected and their old techniques of food getting retained their efficiency. The acceptance of the horse, metal tools, guns, etc., improved their condition and made possible an incipient band organization, but the period was too short for the thorough integration of this with the rest of the culture.

Real difficulties began with the influx of Whites in large numbers and the resulting changes in the environment. With the destruction of the wild food supply, many of the previous techniques no longer sufficed to meet the needs of the group. The White Knives seem to have tried to meet the situation by imitating certain White techniques, i.e., wage-labor and farming, but the attempt was largely unsuccessful. The wage-scale for Indians was too low, while land which they brought under cultivation was repeatedly seized by Europeans. Most of the tribe made the only adaptation which was successful under the circumstances. They became hangers-on of the White communities, dependent on charity, odd jobs, and the prostitution of their women. The pre-existing sex mores made the assumption of the last relatively easy. The failure of the government to keep its promises to them, and the repeated thwartings of individuals who tried to improve their own condition led to the development of attitudes of suspicion and discouragement which have persisted down to the present time.

The first attempts at directed culture change came with the agency period. These were mainly in the form of additions to the culture, with little if any attempt to interfere with aboriginal practices. The abandonment of many of these seems to have been gradual and almost unconscious, with no resulting derangement to the individual. In spite of the suspicion of the government and some actual hardships, there have been no nativistic movements. Apparently the White Knives realize the hardness of aboriginal conditions and have no tendency to glorify the past. The fact that they are increasing in numbers indicates that they have made a successful adaptation in terms of the local conditions, although new difficulties will probably arise whenever there are changes in these. Their present culture is a well-integrated mixture of aboriginal and European elements with the latter on the increase. There seem to be no internal factors which would prevent their complete Europeanization. . . .

The contrast between the acculturation process among the Utes of Colorado and among the White Knife Shoshoni, described by Dr. Marvin K. Opler, is of particular interest because the two peoples are closely related and originally had cultures of very much the same sort. However, the cultures which were called upon to meet the impact of White domination in each case were markedly different. While the Shoshoni faced the Whites from the archaic level of scanty subsistence economy and hunting group organization, the Utes faced them with well-organized bands, developed war patterns and a considerable economic surplus. This difference must be seen as primarily a result of accidents of time and geographic location. The Utes, because of their more southern position, received horses first and were able to revolutionize certain aspects of their life before White pressure became serious. The Shoshoni, on the other hand, received the horse late. Cultural modifications of the sort it produced among the Utes seem to have been under way but were still so poorly integrated with the rest of the culture that they were soon swept away. In Ute acculturation there was thus an important stage which was missing for the Shoshoni.

The results of the acceptance of the horse by the Utes are of particular interest as showing the speed with which important changes can be consummated in aboriginal cultures. Wide areas of native life were transformed within three or four generations. The horse and the equipment immediately connected with its use were, of course, borrowed, but it is impossible to say how far the changes which followed in its train were influenced by borrowing or how far they were adaptations and amplifications which arose directly out of the pre-existing culture. The rise of band patterns can certainly be accounted for on the latter basis. The nucleus was already present in pre-horse days in the recognition of units larger than the family hunting group and their periodic assembly. The war patterns may have been borrowed in part, but it is significant that if this was the case most of the honorary accompaniments of warfare among the Plains tribes were lost in the process. Ute war was not a game for individual prestige but an efficient business, a valuable addition to the subsistence economy. The curious Dog Society of this period, while faintly reminiscent of the Plains warrior societies, has so many distinctive features that only the initial impetus toward its development could have been received from them. The whole transformation of the Utes into horse nomads shows how readily a culture can adapt itself to new elements in the absence of complicating external factors.

Lacking this period of horse nomadism, the Utes would probably have submitted as readily as the Shoshoni did and accepted the new conditions with the same sly sullenness. As it was, they had to be subjugated by force of arms. Their eager acceptance of the ghost dance, as contrasted with the relative indifference of the Shoshoni, reflects the fact that they had fallen from a higher estate and had really had good old times to which they wished to return. This difference is also reflected in their differing response to White ill-treatment. While the Shoshoni seem to have remained throughout willing to accept any elements of White culture which would function under actual conditions, one division of the Utes has idealized the earlier culture and has attempted to maintain it at all points.

The present existence among the Utes of progressive and conservative groups is also important as indicating the role which particular personalities may play in the acculturation process. Both evolved from a common level of cultural inadequacy and discontent, but their subsequent course seems to have been determined by the personalities of their band chiefs. The leader of the Weminutc band, now located at Towaoc, reacted to the situation by leading his people into a region where the very poverty of the resources afforded some shield from White aggression. Buckskin Charlie, the Ignacio chief, took a more realistic view of the situation and persuaded his followers that they would have to meet the Whites on their own terms. He encouraged farming and education and the trends which he established have resulted in a fairly good adaptation for his band. Although this group still have a strong feeling of solidarity and attach high emotional value to certain aspects of their old culture, it seems probable that the acculturation process has already gone so far that it will move on to its end in assimilation. It is hard to imagine them developing into an encysted social and cultural unit like the Fox. The Towaoc Ute, on the other hand, have resisted acculturation to an unusual degree, although they have been able to do so only with the aid of government rations. The ultimate result of the increasing disharmony between their aboriginal culture and the external realities will probably be a collapse of both the culture and the society, leaving the latter's component individuals to adjust as best they can. . . .

In comparison with many of the other Indian tribes the Arapaho of Wyoming have not been badly treated by the Whites. Their warfare with the conquerors was less bitter and prolonged than that of many of the other Plains Indians. The part which the semi-legendary Friday played in this affords an example of the influence which particular personalities may exert in crucial situations. The Arapaho also had the advantage of being placed on a reservation within their aboriginal range, a condition which is usually an aid to successful adaptation. However, in this case the destruction of the buffalo by Whites eliminated the most important aboriginal resource of the territory, while the region was poorly suited to the agriculture which the

Whites offered them as an economic substitute for hunting. They were reduced at once to a condition of economic dependence upon the Whites and could not have survived without rations and the small income derived from unskilled labor.

It is impossible to say how far these unfavorable economic conditions are responsible for the present lack of adjustment, but much of the difficulty certainly derives from particular patterns within the aboriginal culture. Their social and political organization seems to have been unusually close and elaborate for a Plains tribe. There was a rigid prescription of statues and roles with a concentration of power in the hands of the old, the very group which would be least adapted to coping with new conditions. The only opportunity for individual initiative lay in war, and when this activity was suddenly inhibited the younger men found themselves condemned to long-continued inferiority. A by-product of the rigidity of organization and thorough integration of the individual into his society was the development of certain personality characteristics ably described by Dr. Elkin. The sense of "shame" served to keep the younger generation in their place and to make the highly formalized social system work smoothly. At the same time it unfitted and apparently still unfits the average member of the tribe for participation in White culture. The aggressive patterns of this culture are repugnant to the Arapaho as are those of individual aggrandizement and wealth accumulation. The latter are in direct conflict with the deep-seated aboriginal patterns of generosity and recognition of kinship obligations, and in this conflict the aboriginal patterns seem to have won, preventing even the abler individuals from achieving economic independence.

It seems that the adaptation which the Arapaho have achieved so far is of a very superficial sort. There has been a considerable loss of culture content, such institutions as the age-societies having disappeared without any replacement. Acceptance of White institutions has taken place mainly in two fields, technology and religion. In the former nearly all the old arts and crafts have been replaced by White manufactured goods, while the automobile has replaced the horse. The automobile fitted so perfectly into the aboriginal nomadic patterns that it was accepted enthusiastically. In religion there has been widespread conversion to Christianity with a preference for the more highly ritualized forms, yet this has been a simple addition to the culture, accomplished without the elimination of the older beliefs or many of the aboriginal ceremonies. Another addition to religion has been the peyote cult, borrowed from other tribes. All these superficial changes in culture appear to have left most of the aboriginal values intact. Tribal solidarity seems to have been, if anything, exaggerated by the conditions of White contact, and the social pressure exerted upon individuals who behave in ways differing from the cultural stereotype is a serious bar to successful individual adaptation. This is the more remarkable in view of the apparent loss of faith in the aboriginal culture. Individuals seem to realize its shortcomings but are too timid to risk the loss of the only emotional security they possess, that of the goodwill of their fellow tribesmen. Dr. Elkin's use of sociological concepts in analyzing this situation should be noted as an example of how much certain of these concepts aid in clarifying both cultural and personality problems.

The picture of the Arapaho which emerges from this study is that of a bewildered, frightened group who have lost faith in themselves, and are marking time. Their successful adaptation either in terms of acculturation or in those of the development of an independent culture compatible with reality must await a transformation of values and of the personality systems which derive from these. . . .

The Fox of Iowa, described by Dr. Natalie F. Joffe, present an example of a group which has become encysted within another society and culture. They have achieved a successful adaptation to their White neighbors and there seems to be no prospect of their being absorbed either racially or culturally for several generations to come. Their success in achieving this independence seems to be correlated primarily with a psychological factor, their strong sense of solidarity. However, this in itself would not have sufficed to keep the tribe unbroken. They were fortunate in having a long period of not too close contact with Europeans before the intensive contact which began with the arrival of White settlers in numbers. They were thus given an opportunity to make initial adjustments. Adjustment was also facilitated by their continued residence within the same ecological area, a condition made possible at the last by their acceptance of the European technique of land purchase. In this the diminution of the natural resources upon which they had relied in aboriginal times was a gradual one. There was no necessity for an abrupt change in subsistence economy like that which came to the Plains tribes with the extinction of the buffalo. They were thus given time to make a transition from one set of economic techniques to another and it is significant that it is in this sector of their culture that they have borrowed most extensively and most willingly from the Whites. At the same time, the integrity of their culture has been maintained by the attachment of symbolic values to those elements of the previous culture which were still unable to function under the new conditions. They seem to show little if any resistance to the acceptance of new mechanical appliances, such as the automobile or an improved farm machinery, but show a very high resistance to changes in language, religion or social organization. . . .

The San Ildefonso of New Mexico and the Carrier are the only groups described in this report in which the arrival of the Whites did not produce important changes in the natural environment through the destruction of the natural resources or the removal of the group to a new locality. Although there has been a destruction of game in the case of the San Ildefonso, their main subsistence technique, agriculture, is still effective when carried on by aboriginal methods. Moreover, the destruction of game is a recent phenomenon and was not a factor in the first phase of their White contact, that with the Spaniards.

The Spanish contact offers a situation in which the results of directed acculturation backed by force can be perceived with few complicating factors. The Spaniards attempted to introduce Christianity and a new type of village governmental organization and to eliminate the native religion. They succeeded in both introductions as far as the outward forms were concerned, but in both cases these forms were reinterpreted in the light of the previous culture and were adjusted to it. This integration was successful enough so that the forms survived even when all external pressure had been removed. The attempt to eliminate the native religion failed altogether. It was met by the development of techniques of reticence and concealment which have also survived long after the necessity for them has disappeared. Although we have no direct information on this point, it seems probable that the Spanish attacks on the native religion actually heightened the group's attachment to it, giving it new symbolic values. The whole program of directed acculturation seems to have had much less effect upon native life than has the destruction of natural resources or elimination of aboriginal activities which we have observed in other groups.

The White contact of recent years also shows a very curious case of directed culture development by the dominant group. The encouragement of native pottery making and painting is an unique phenomenon. It has set a premium upon individual initiative and inventive ability which was altogether lacking in the aboriginal culture. A woman who invents a new style of pottery or a man who develops a new type of painting is immediately given an economic advantage. It has also destroyed the effectiveness of the old sexual division of labor. The woman potter is now the mainstay of the family and the man finds it more profitable to work on the land. With this increasing economic dominance goes an increasing social dominance which has not yet had time to reflect itself in new formal patterns. The women more and more rule but in theory are still subservient. The result is increasing stress. It seems possible that this altered position of men may also be linked with the diminishing interest in religious activities, which are predominantly masculine. Although the old ceremonies are still going on with full apparent vigor, it is noted that no young people are being trained to take the place of the old ones. It seems probable that the next few years will see a collapse of the esoteric aspects of the culture and a rapid acculturation of the society.

RACE CONSCIOUSNESS IN SOUTH AFRICA

*There is emerging among South African natives an immature
racialism which will ultimately grow into a matured race consciousness. The symptoms of race consciousness are the shift in mental
attitude of the native with reference to the white man, the
emergence of expressional activities and organizations of various
kinds among natives, and the rise of specific movements attempting
to mobilize racial sentiment to the end of elevating the status of
the native.*

RACIALLY, THE Union of South Africa tends to be organized
on a caste basis, with the non-white races subordinate and the
whites dominant. The natives everywhere are dependent upon the
European economic order and are subjected to the influences of European culture, though they are on the periphery of the social order of
the white man. The colored are definitely an integral part of the cultural system, but subordinate, adjusted in the main to their inferior
status. The Indians are clearly on the margin of the social structure
though an integral part of the economic world. They, like all the subordinate races, [the South African natives] are assimilating European
culture, and thus penetrating the European social order, or at least
asking for entrance. At the top the white man asserts his power, attempts to preserve his prestige, and struggles to prevent any appreciable rise in the status of the low-caste non-whites.

Viewing the situation externally, it would appear as if the natives
should be violently race conscious. Although nine-tenths of the natives live on the land, they own only about one-eighth of the land of
the Union. The whites control the other seven-eighths, though over
half of them are urban. On farm, in factory, and in mines the natives'
wages are notoriously low, the white worker averaging a wage six or
seven fold that of the native. Economically the native is a helpless
subordinate, and politically he is impotent. His culture is disintegrat-

Excerpts from W. O. Brown, "Race Consciousness among South African
Natives," *The American Journal of Sociology,* Vol. 40 (Chicago: University of
Chicago Press, 1935), pp. 569-581.

ing, and there is powerful resistance to his penetration of the European world. Numerically he outnumbers the white three to one. If mere exposure to exploitation and numerical strength produced race consciousness, the South African native should possess a vigorous variety of it.

But such is not the case. The native is so completely dominated by the white man that protests appear futile. Where he is in the European system the habit of collective obedience is established, or at least overtly so. The very cultural chaos to which he is heir deters racialism. The territorial and tribal divisions and the new economic and cultural distinctions incident to the growing Europeanization of the native also inhibit the emergence of native solidarity.

Yet there is emerging among South African natives an immature racialism which will ultimately grow into a matured race consciousness. In 1921 a writer spoke of the "sense of solidarity spreading among the Bantu in the Union and in its borders." And in 1925 a Commission Investigating the Native Separatist Church Movement had this to say: "Throughout the investigation, the commission has received the impression that there is a growth of race consciousness with its natural outcome of social and political aspirations among the Natives of the Union." The Native Economic Commission of 1930-32 likewise observed the growth of race consciousness among South African natives.

In the main, however, race consciousness among South African natives remains unformed. It is sporadic and ephemeral, not organized and constant, being local, not national, in its manifestations. There is no native solidarity. Individual natives experience resentment and feel hatred of the white man, but these individuals are not mobilized and afford no basis for programs and movements. We have the beginnings of race consciousness but not, as yet, its developed form.

Roughly, we may classify the symptoms of race consciousness under three heads: the shift in mental attitude of the native with reference to the white man, the emergence of expressional activities and organizations of various kinds among natives, and the rise of specific movements attempting to mobilize racial sentiment to the end of elevating the status of the native.

One indication of the shift in the mental attitude of the native toward the European is the decline in white prestige. The degree of this prestige is roughly indicated by the overt deference of the native, his observance of the ritual defining the status of the races, and the obedience of the native to the white man's commands. Undoubtedly this white prestige is still a potent factor in native-white relations. It is a strong force in the control of black, by white, notably in the purely native areas.

Generally speaking, however, the white man is losing ground. He still has power and status, and he can coerce and control. But he is losing the prestige which makes easy the exercise of his power and the securing of his status. The native does not invariably treat the white man with respect. Whites complain that natives in the native areas are no longer polite and well mannered to white people. They are often "insolent" to missionaries and traders, and even at times to officials. The trader does not always demand "respect." He will allow himself to be treated as an "equal" in order that he may get the native's trade. The missionary cannot invariably "discipline" the natives for fear of losing their church patronage. Contact with the white man, experience in his world, partial absorption of the white man's culture, and knowledge of the seamy side of white life have all contributed to the decay of white prestige. And this decay is a possible prelude to a rise in race consciousness.

The decline in white prestige is disclosed in the growing distrust by the native of the white man. Although he does trust individual white men, he is suspicious of white people as a whole. He is distrustful of the government, and watches every move with the expectation of being "exploited." Officials who seek to improve the land in native reserves are often thought to be improving it in the interest of future white occupancy. The native views new commissions and investigations with skepticism, recalling that the reports are not always acted upon. The native finds it difficult to believe that the government is intent on advancing his welfare. He remembers bills and acts which have advanced the interest of whites at his expense. The Land Act of 1913, the various masters and servants acts, certain features of the Urban Areas Act, the Riotous Assemblies Bill, the white civilized labor policy, and many items of native policy—all appear to indicate that the government is opposed to his interests. If he is educated he can cite chapter and verse in the Union native policy justifying his disbelief in the government. And the ordinary native has the distrust without being able to rationalize it. To be sure, this distrust is mitigated by individual officials and does not exist in the same degree everywhere; but it does tend to be a collective reaction.

This distrust is even directed against his traditional friends, the missionaries and the liberals. The educated native especially manifests hostility to the missionary, who is accused of not encouraging natives to share the responsibility of the administration of church and school. As a white man the missionary suffers in the face of the rising animosity to whites. The good intentions of liberals interested in interracial co-operation are often suspected by the native. Investigators of conditions among natives tell many stories of native hostility. Thus, there is the case of the native investigator who was told that the whites were merely using him as a tool, his data probably supplying the basis for increase in rents and taxes or for the imposition of some other burdens on poor natives by clever, ruthless, and untrustworthy whites.

The native not only reacts with distrust to the white man; he criticizes him pointedly and sharply. This criticism is formulated by the growing class of native intellectuals, who, if they were ever "loyal" to the racial system of South Africa, are so no longer.

This native intellectual who formulates the grievances of the native is of importance for the student of race consciousness. He is a member of a fairly large class. His education and culture are European, as are his conceptions of his rights. His union with native culture is tenuous. History has severed his connections with his folk origins, while the vested interests and the ideology of the white man have prevented his penetration of the white world. Thus the status of the intellectual is marginal. His own group not only does not supply a sufficient social base for an adequate spiritual and intellectual orientation, but also he is excluded from the European world. Naturally, he feels the pinch of the racial situation more sharply than the average native. His status as a person is more insecure. The acuteness of the problem of his position makes him keenly conscious of his grievances, and these, though probably less vividly experienced, are essentially the grievances of the common man among the natives. The pain of his position and his intelligence as a class make him the ideal formulator of native tribulations.

These interpreters of native grievances give content and form to native laments, and assist the natives to an awareness of their martyrdom. They give point and rationalization to the hostility to the white man. The list of grievances tends to be uniform. Thus, according to these interpreters, the white man has taken most of the native's land while the native lives in the poor areas under congested conditions. The white man restricts the natives occupationally, paying low wages and deliberately keeping him out of the skilled and more highly paid occupations. Color bars, restriction in trade-union membership, and the white civilized labor policy—all come in for denunciations as evidence of the white man's exploitation of the native. He protests about low wages received on farms, in towns, and on mines, contrasting his pittance with the higher wages of whites. He is told that he is the backbone of South African economic life, but he gets only a bare existence for his importance. He is reminded of his political impotence, the heavy taxes imposed upon him, the poor social and educational services provided, the humiliation pass system, the repressionistic native policy, and the hundred and one restrictive rules and laws by which the white man keeps him either out of his social system or subordinate within it. And his experience is such that he accepts these formulations as accurate descriptions of his unfortunate position.

The agitation reaches in one way or the other all natives, and there is no way to prevent its diffusion. It appeals, not because it is completely true, though it is, essentially, but because it does supply an explanation of native experiences and native problems.

A second cluster of symptoms of race consciousness among South African natives may be discussed under the general heading of expressional activities and organizations.

In its earlier stages group consciousness manifests itself in expressional activities of various sorts which may appear to the onlooker confused and ambiguous. But a closer look reveals that such activities do have a meaning, certainly among the natives of South Africa. For example, the messianism that has frequently cropped out in the Union signifies racial unrest. Such erratic manifestations express the chaos, the disorganization, and the disorientation of native life. At the same time the fact that they tend to take an anti-white form is an indication that the white man is becoming the object of collective antipathy.

The widespread belief in the Garvey idea of Africa for the Africans during the early twenties was significant. Marcus Garvey was in many instances regarded as a messiah. And natives in some places were awaiting the coming of the "Americans" led by their prophet Garvey, to rescue South African natives from the white oppressor.

On occasions the resentment against the white man has been expressed overtly and violently. Immediately after the World War there was a series of strikes, riots, and disturbances among the natives in such places as Johannesburg, East London, Port Elizabeth, Durban, and Cape Town. Natives were protesting against low wages, pass carrying, and other demeaning restrictions placed upon them by the white man. Behavior of this sort, sporadic, more or less unorganized, and inclined to die down as quickly as it flares up, is characteristic of the early stages of revolt.

There are other scattered social facts that may be classed with this cluster, which we have termed "expressional activities," symptomatic of a growing race consciousness. Thus, there is an increasing interest, notably in the larger towns, in the development of a native literature, art, and music. Poor, confused, and imitative as these forms of artistic expression among natives are, they contribute to the native's group awareness and serve to intensify his pride. The native press serves both as a medium of expression and as an organ for the formulation of native grievances. As yet its influence tends to be limited to the town native, since the low literacy rate among natives and their poverty prevent a wide circulation of native papers. But, even so, the press is of importance as a factor in the emergence of race consciousness.

One might expect the rise of race consciousness among South African natives to be associated with idealization of native languages and cultures, but such has not been the case. The native intellectual does resent slurs on his history or culture and references to his culture as "primitive" and his religion as "heathen." Now and then he will defend some aspect of native culture such as Kaffir beer or the native attitude toward cattle or Lobola. He may point with pride to great leaders such as Chaka, Moshesh, or Khama. But as yet he has developed no consistent philosophy with reference to the meaning of native languages and cultures. There are various reasons for this lack. It is in part an expression of the immaturity of race consciousness. It has some relation to the linguistic and cultural diversity among South African natives. There is no South African native language, nor, in the narrower sense, any uniform native culture. But probably most important of all, the reflective native realizes that salvation lies in the acquisition of European education and culture. He may idealize the Bantu and resent the white man's demeaning term "kaffir" when applied to native folk, but he does not face backward for his cultural orientation. He envisages a Europeanized native people competing for place in the social order which the European has come to think of as peculiarly his own.

In keeping with this tendency the organizations emerging, notably among the town natives, such as the fraternal, recreational, social, and economic, are European in form and purpose. The activities of such organizations will in time contribute to the native's awareness of his problems and intensify his ambition to become a part of European civilization. In a vague sort of way all such activities manifest and intensify race consciousness.

Finally, there are certain movements along the religious, economic, and political fronts of native life which are indicative of race consciousness, though not very far advanced. There are no genuinely racial movements attacking the problems of the native's status with any measure of success. The claim is that the somewhat embryonic racialism of the South African native is beginning to express itself in attempted mobilization of the native for the realization of certain objectives.

Important as an organized manifestation of race consciousness are the native separatist churches. In 1921 it was stated by the acting prime minister that there were 160 native Christian sects. Some of these are local and of little importance, while others have developed considerable strength. Some originated as splits from the missionary controlled churches; others are broken fragments of native churches. Many originated in quarrels between the missionary and native ministers; others merely represent the ambitions of a native religious leader for the control of a church. These separatist churches are not always anti-white in sentiment, the Shembeites of Natal, for example, seeming to lack this feeling. But the tendency is for the adherents to be anti-European in outlook. As the Native Churches Commission put it, "While no Separatist Church has been known to start with an anti-white motive, their separateness attracts to them the disaffected among natives and some of them acquire a more or less anti-white bias."

In the economic world the native feels the restrictions of the white man much more keenly than in the religious life. Not more than one-third of the natives are Christians, and the coercive element is not particularly important in religion. But all natives feel the exploitive power of the farmer, the mine-owner, and the white "baas." Naturally race consciousness finds expression in protests against economic servitude and in organizations proposing to improve economic conditions. Reference has been made to the periodic riots, and spontaneous revolts, unsupported by ideologies or organizations. The most significant of all manifestations of the tendency toward organized race consciousness are the Industrial Commercial Workers' Union and the Communist Party. The I. C. U., as the Industrial Commercial Union is called, was initiated in 1919 for the improvement of the native's economic status. It grew slowly until 1924, when it began to spread rapidly over the Union. Its followers looked upon it as a solution of their problems, believing that by joining it the town workers would get high pay and the rural people high wages and more land. For a time it was a mass movement, and its leaders were folk heroes. Whites trembled at its power, and the government feared it. But, as was natural, considering the disorganization of native life, the essential lack of unity, and the inability of the organization to fulfill its promises, the movement soon went to pieces; factionalism emerged; graft and corruption among the leaders were revealed; and the rank and file were left disillusioned. . . .

The Communist party is also at work among natives. Thus far it is more a sect than a movement. It is doubtful whether the small native following understands the Marxian ideology or whether it is reacting against capitalism. Natives are communists because communism is a form of revolt, of protest against the economic order manned by white masters, under which they suffer. Their radicalism is really racialism. The economic welfare of the native masses is always blocked by the South African racial caste system. The struggle for wages, for land, and for economic rights by necessity becomes a struggle for status, a racial struggle. And race consciousness becomes the driving sentiment of the movement. The native labor-unionist or communist is thus not in consciousness a proletarian but rather a member of an oppressed and disinherited race.

The religious and economic manifestations discussed are in part manifestations of native revolt. They suggest stirrings among the native masses and indicate some tendency toward the mobilization and organization of racial sentiment. There has likewise been some protest against the demeaning civic and political status of the native and some attempts to win civic and political rights. The African National Congress is the most significant expression of this aspect of race consciousness. It was founded in 1909, and, like all native organizations, has had a checkered career. Its main appeal has been to the Europeanized native. At present it is faction-ridden and weak. Its failures express the power of the European and the subordination of the native.

It can be assumed that as the native absorbs European culture he will attempt to penetrate the European world, economic, political, religious, and social, and that out of the conflict born of this penetration race consciousness will emerge. The disintegration of native culture, the pressure of white governments, and the repressive policies will contribute to native solidarity. Growing sophistication will give a knowledge of European nationalism and of the techniques and organizations necessary to develop it. Bantu nationalism may ultimately become a new variety of group consciousness, challenging white supremacy in Southern Africa.

PERSONALITY IN A WHITE-INDIAN-NEGRO COMMUNITY

The keystone of the problem is the white man's determination not to accept the Indian as his equal and to put him in the same category as the Negro. The Indian's wish to escape the stigma of Negro kinship, and thus to be identified with the white man dominates his behavior and determines his modes of personal adjustment to the other races.

SCATTERED THROUGHOUT the South, there are over a hundred groups of people who are classified by the Census Bureau as "Indians." Some of these groups, like the Catawba and the Eastern Cherokee of North Carolina, the Seminoles of Florida, and the Choctaws of Mississippi, are of relatively pure Indian stock and are recognized as such by the government, but the majority are "Indians" by courtesy. They represent varying mixtures of white, Negro, and Indian blood, but as a rule the white strain predominates, and Indian culture is either very weak or extinct.

Most of these groups are small, but there were at least thirty which had 100 or more members in 1930, and there was one, the so-called Croatan Indian group centering in Robeson County, North Carolina, which totaled nearly 15,000 members. . . .

What are the points of strain and what personal adjustments are made by the mixed bloods who form the middle caste of this tri-racial society?

The keystone in this problem is, of course, the white man's determination not to accept the Indian as his equal and, as far as possible, to put him into the same category as the Negro. In all of his relations with white people, this principle is either expressed or implied. The Indian is restricted to his own schools, and he is forbidden to marry a white person. He is supposed not to enter a white man's front door. He is not addressed as "mister" by white people and if he attends a

Excerpts from Guy B. Johnson, "Personality in a White-Indian-Negro Community" in *American Sociological Review*, Vol. 4, August 1939, pp. 516-523.

theater, he has to choose between one which provides a three-way segregation and one which seats him with Negroes. There is not an eating place in the county which permits him to enter the front door and eat with the white people. In numerous subtle ways, by glances, gestures, and intonations, he is reminded by whites and Negroes of the unmentionable stigma which attaches to him.

The Indian, then, is forever on the defensive. He feels that there is always a question mark hanging over him. His wish to escape the stigma of Negro kinship, and thus to be identified with the white man, is uppermost in his mind. It is this wish which dominates his behavior and determines his modes of personal adjustment to the other races.

One of the chief sources of mental conflict in the Indian arises from his realization that there are many people in his group who had Negroid physical traits. In 1885, when the Indians were legally declared a separate race and were named Croatan, they faced the problem of deciding just who was Indian and who was not. They wanted to weed out those who were considered "undesirables," but it was difficult for them to draw the line. They evidently fell back on a sort of pragmatic definition, viz.: an Indian is a person called an Indian by other Indians. It was as if they had said, "All right, everyone who is already in can stay in, but woe unto anybody with Negro blood who tries to get in hereafter." At their request, the legislature passed two laws which strengthened their position. One of these provided "that all marriages between a Croatan Indian and a Negro, or between an Indian and a person of Negro descent to the third generation, inclusive, shall be utterly void." Another provided "that there shall be excluded from such separate schools for the said Croatan Indians all children of the Negro race to the fourth generation." The Indians themselves were to be final judges on matters of genealogy.

It is certain that very little new Negro blood has found its way into the group in recent times. However, the Croatans today are undoubtedly one of the most heterogeneous groups ever brought together under one name. They range from pink skin, blue eyes, and flaxen hair to unmistakably Negroid color, hair, and other features. Many could pass for white anywhere else, and many would be taken for Negroes anywhere else. Even in the same family, the children often have a wide range of color and hair types. Every growing child notices these things and ponders over them. He learns that it is taboo to discuss such things. He learns that the ultimate insult that anyone can give an Indian is to intimate that he has Negro blood. He stands ready to defend his personal honor and the honor of his whole group from such intimations from any source. So intense is the feeling on this subject that one can only conclude that there is present in many persons a certain "sense of guilt" which arises from the observed reality and which calls for constant denial of the reality.

As might be expected, the strength of this color prejudice varies with the physical types. The whiter Indians seem to worry less over this matter. While they resent any attacks on the "purity" of the Indians as a group, they feel less than the darker people the necessity for personal justification. They travel about a good deal and find that they are taken for white or for Indian-white mixtures. Their very appearance is a badge of security. Indeed, they feel that if all of the Indians were like them there would be no problem. They blame the dark Indians for the stigma attached to the group and they hate them for it, but their hatred must be kept below the surface.

The darker Indians, on the other hand, are apt to be more sensitive on the matter of physical features. Their chances for unpleasant experiences are, of course, greater, and they feel more keenly the impulse to "whiten" their ancestry. Furthermore, they are jealous of the whiter Indians. Thus there is an incipient but never openly admitted cleavage between the darker Indians and the lighter ones.

The hypersensitiveness of the Croatans has led them on several occasions to drive out people who were offshoots from the main body and who came in from adjoining counties to take advantage of the Indian schools. The excuse was always, "We can't be sure about these people. We think they have Negro blood." Incidentally, some of these rejected people petitioned for a special set of schools for their benefit, but school officials threw up their hands and declared that three school systems were enough.

Another aspect of the Croatans' struggle for a status of respectability is their concern over their history and their group name. When the legislature of 1885 gave them the name "Croatan" and, by implication, recognized their Lost Colony legend [cf. Walter Raleigh's *Lost Colony of Roanoke Island* (1587)] it was trying to present them with a proud past and a good name, but the name "Croatan" soon went sour. For the first time, the whites and Negroes had a term which they could apply to these hitherto nameless people. They pronounced it with a sort of sneer or they shortened it to "Cro"—with the all too obvious implication. It soon became a fighting term, and for many years it has been virtually taboo in the presence of Indians.

Now the Indians were divided for a time over the merits and demerits of "Croatan," but the majority of them finally embraced a theory that there was really nothing to the Lost Colony legend and that "Croatan" was not their true name. Accordingly, they got the legislature in 1911 to strike out the word "Croatan," leaving their name simply "Indians of Robeson County." Thus, they were willing to give up their Lost Colony legend for the removal of the curse of "Croatan."

The vagueness of the word "Indian" was a challenge to them, because it was in a way an admission that they did not know what they were. So a new theory of history came to the front: they were really Cherokee. They again asked the legislature for help, and in 1913, over the protests of the Eastern Cherokee of the Great Smoky Mountains, they were legally named "Cherokee Indians of Robeson County." The law bore the flattering title, "An act to restore to the Indians of Robeson and adjoining counties their rightful and ancient name." But no one ever calls them Cherokee, and the problem of the name keeps gnawing at their consciousness. Lately, there has been a shift in tactics. Some of their more literate men have searched history and ethnology and have concluded that the group originated from the remnants of the Siouan tribes which once lived in central North Carolina. For several years now they have been egging Uncle Sam to name them "Siouan Tribes of Lumber River" and to take them under his wing as wards of the federal government. This, according to one young Indian, would settle the problem once and for all. . . .

The situations which I have discussed thus far are largely situations which can be met by subjective adjustments. The Indians can deny or affirm this or that, can invent theories to fit the exigencies of the situation, but what does he do when the realities of the caste structure call for more overt behavior? Apparently, he takes some of the sting out of the realities of caste by avoiding as far as possible those situations which are most heavily charged with caste meaning. Here, again, the answer seems to be that he "corrects" the reality in accordance with his wish. Insofar as possible, he conducts himself in such a way that the unpleasant reality is negated. He avoids theaters where his only choice is to sit with Negroes. If he must eat in town, he either takes along a lunch or patronizes an open-air "hot-dog" stand rather than sit with Negroes in the back room of a cafe.

In his work, the Indian's aim is to have as little to do with white people as possible. He thereby reduces his chances of being insulted. His economic outlook is greatly restricted because he will not engage in various menial tasks which Negroes engage in. His ideal is to own a farm and be his own master. With the exception of a handful of teachers, preachers, and small shopkeepers, the Indians are all farmers. They are especially expert in tobacco culture. When they are tenants for white farmers they advertise their difference from the Negro by refusing to take the subservient role of the Negro. I asked an Indian tenant how he got along with his landlord. "Oh, all right," he replied, "I don't have any more to do with him than I have to. I never go to his house because I don't want to have any trouble with him." By this, he meant that if he went to the white man's house the white man would expect him to go to the back door—then there might be trouble. The white farmers, for their part, recognize this independence of the Indian when they say, "If you want a tenant to take care of your land and make money, get an Indian. *But don't try to boss him.* He wears his pride like a sore thumb."

Thus, the Indian avoids some caste situations and brings about some degree of modification in others by sheer pride and belligerence; but he cannot avoid or negate everything. He knows well enough that the restrictions and prohibitions are there, whether he tests them out or not, and he carries a constant sense of frustration and tension.

In civic and political affairs the Indian meets with further frustration. He sees his vote count for almost nothing because of the wiles of the County Democratic Machine. He sees his one little town, Pembroke, his social center and seat of his normal school, taken over largely by white merchants. He sees the selection of town officers removed from his own control and placed in the hands of the legislature so that white people can be appointed. He has been, from Reconstruction days until the past year, without representation on any jury in Robeson County. He sees instances of brutality on the part of officers of the law. He sees many things which make his blood boil, and he feels utterly powerless to do anything about them. He feels that his little world is carefully guarded, controlled, and exploited by the white man. He is blocked at every point, yet he cannot give up the struggle, for to do so would be to admit that he is no better than the Negro. So he lives in this continuing state of compromise between the world of the white man and the world of the black man. . . .

In the Indian's own world, there seems to be some evidences of the disorganizing effect of his anomalous social position. There are certain families and certain neighborhoods which are known as "tough," and these produce an unusual amount of drunkenness, assault, and homicide. Whether this represents a primary result of caste status is difficult to say, but I am inclined to believe that it is in some measure correlated with the frustration experiences of the Indian and with certain cleavages in the Indian community.

These cleavages are probably of major importance for the understanding of interpersonal relations within the Indian community. They are roughly correlated with physical traits, and yet it is probable that the latter have no genetic significance. At the bottom of the social scale are the darker Indians. They are on the whole poorer than the others, they are conscious of what others think of their appearance, and they are jealous of the lighter Indians. They are credited with a good deal of what is sometimes called "hell-raising." Next come the intermediate Indians. They are a little too dark to pass as white and they are especially sensitive to physical appearance. They envy the lighter ones and resent the darker ones, and they incline to be the militant, agitating type. Finally, there are the "white" Indians. They could pass for white almost anywhere. On the whole, they have a better economic status, a better education, and higher prestige. These color cleavages are a tabooed subject with the Indians, and yet they permeate the whole society. They are no doubt at the bottom of much of the violent crime of Indian against Indian. They also have something to do with the lack of strong group solidarity, the presence of factions, and the timidity of leaders.

I should not leave the impression, however, that the Indians are typically disorganized and unstable. On the contrary, most of them lead relatively calm, moderate, and industrious lives. They have a strong sentimental attachment to their native soil, and in spite of all their troubles, relatively few of them seek escape through permanent migration. They are perhaps one more example of the well-known adaptability of the human personality. Apparently, when people have work to do, have strong community institutions and a few things to be proud of, they can adjust their thoughtways and behavior so as to absorb a great deal of emotional strain.

This situation, however, is by no means static. It is difficult to conceive of a community like the Croatan community surviving indefinitely. It seems likely that the Indian will rebel more and more against his caste status. Education, wider travel, and reading, are already beginning to have their effects. The changing situation will produce personalities who no longer see virtue in patience and compromise. The Indians are becoming more group conscious. They have recently demanded the right to serve on juries, they are talking of running for political office, and they are saying among themselves that "if things don't get better we may have to start killing." The future holds interesting and unpleasant possibilities. . . .

THE NEGRO IMMIGRANT

In the Negro community the foreign-born Negro is viewed as a threat to the native-born Negro's status. The West Indians in turn are defensively resentful, constantly looking for insults, discrimination, and evidence of segregation. Because of his resentment for the segregation patterns of the United States the foreign-born Negro is a relentless protagonist for all causes fighting the social, political and economic disabilities of the Negroes in this country.

BETWEEN 1899 and 1937 approximately 150,000 Negro aliens were legally admitted into the United States. . . .

Negro immigrants being largely from the Americas do not possess

Excerpts from Ira de A. Reid, *The Negro Immigrant* (New York: Columbia University Press, 1939), pp. 24-30, 37-41, 109-112.

many of the outward manifestations of the stranger that are common to European immigrants. This standardization of external characteristics makes for less immediate social visibility. However, alien standards do provide a sharp and distinctive cleavage between the [foreign-born, Negro and the native] groups. Being a minority within a minority, Negro immigrants disturb intragroup relations because of their partial accommodation. In times of social stress, or if the foreign Negro group is highly visible, or, when it is in competition with native Negroes this lower role is more operative. As competition and visibility disappear, the role of *immigrant* or "monkey chaser" or "Spic" or "Garveyite," tends to lose its broad identity and disappear. (A "monkey-chaser" is the United States Negro's name-calling device for all West Indian Negroes. "Garveyite" has a similar meaning. "Spic" refers to Spanish-speaking Negroes, particularly Puerto Ricans and Cubans.)

The Negro immigrant presents a field for the analysis of the intra-racial aspect of the processes of acculturation—of accommodation and assimilation. While it is generally accepted that individuals reared in one culture and migrating to another can never be completely absorbed in the new culture, it is noticeable that the old culture fades more and more as time goes on, and that there is always a residue of habits, ideas, points of view and ways of doing things which is never completely changed. Meanwhile the foreign Negro group develops special cultural norms resulting from the fact that it lives and works under special circumstances; that it is compelled to contrive patterns of defensive behavior because of its role, and also because of the inescapable confusion that results from its compulsory adoption of new and majority modes of behavior. Accompanying these changes are the less inventive devices of the Negro majority and of the white group, which render new schemes of relationships and action less than satisfactory. Techniques to maintain status, to restrict and suppress— even oppress—the immigrant deviate not one whit from those employed by other groups. Their major significance is in the changes they evoke in the pattern of social role known as Negro.

It is in this respect that the adjustment of Negro immigrants differs from that of white immigrants. The Negro immigrant undergoes a reorganization of status involving adjustment to an intra-racial situation and to an inter-racial one. Leaving communities where he was part of the numerical majority, he moves into one where he is parcel of the numerical and social minority. This change presents two distinct types of social problems which are intimately related—one involving the outer or material aspects of adjusting in the new environment, such as earning a living, making a home and looking and acting as do the native-born, and the other having to do with the less tangible differences found in cultural patterns and standards of thought and action. The former are the more easily discernible differentials; the latter are the more subtle, but of equal importance. Once the former have been determined the latter may be more easily deduced. Thus, the Negro immigrant finds his usual ways of conduct inadequate to the new environment. He discovers the native Negro's attitude of amused superiority, and, while thrilling to the incentive of the new locale, he frequently remains bewildered and self-conscious for some time. The Negro immigrant becomes a déraciné—a man without roots—who has lost something of a former self which provided the "push" for his migration and has not yet acquired a new and stabilized self. He becomes aware of his almost automatic exclusion from numerous areas of social activity because of a system of group relationships called "race." He realizes that cultural differentials within this area of "race" tend to resolve themselves into class lines and to make the immigrant group a formally recognized "out-group." . . .

In the United States, Negroes, Orientals, and Jews who can rise out of their original group membership only by hiding hereditary physical features or their origins, or by other unusual circumstances, are caste groups. Within each one of these groups there tend to arise status differences or class lines. By this token, Negroes are not "just Negroes" to each other. Cutting across their social relationships are myriad status lines that make for important distinctions within the group.

The most widely known features of such sub-class and sub-caste distinctions and social stratifications within the Negro group are those based on skin color in which higher status has been acquired within the group through the biological accident of the individual's physical resemblance to the white group. Between the days of the Civil War and the World War this sub-caste distinction was based largely upon family membership and relationship. Within the last twenty years a rather unique development has indicated that this color-caste feature is no longer a unit based on family membership but one based on the individual. Intermarriage of members of different sub-castes did not necessarily uncaste the member holding superior status. Beyond this distinction there is no outstanding sub-caste feature in the Negro group.

There are among Negroes, however, numerous class lines corresponding in structure and function to those social stratifications which characterize the majority white group. The laboring classes, the "capitalists," professional people, "middle classes," the "individualists" or self-made individuals, typify this stratification. Not least among these is the stratification based on nativity and ancestry. It is in the class stratification resulting from place of birth that the role of Negro immigrant operates.

While it may be assumed that there is a strong cohesive bond operating within the Negro group, the evidence of stratification frequently belies its existence. Struggles between sub-groups appear to have an intensity equal to, and a time sequence that closely parallels, the struggle between the majority and minority groups in relation to economic opportunity and successful competition for a stated objective. The role of the Negro immigrant then becomes significant in determining what may and may not be subsumed about the Negro group's adjustment in the United States. Young's statement to the effect that immigrant Negroes disappear among native Negroes and create no special issue of race relations states the problem too simply. The Negro immigrant's advent introduced new problems of social status and social process that throw light on many aspects of the interracial pattern. A fundamental tenet of this thesis is that those problems are not problems about a natural fact called race; they are social problems—problems of social life, of economics, and of the political state. The "race" concept is simply a framework within which these factors function. Variations in the manifestations of race prejudice against Negroes as a whole in the North and in the South substantiate the presence of this social basis. . . .

It is very easy to overweigh the importance of race as a factor in social affairs, though its influence cannot be ignored. Though it is a biological characteristic by which individuals in one group are more closely related to each other by blood than they are to members of another race, it also has a social significance. This is particularly true in any areas of pronounced social and economic problems. The mere factor of racial color has influenced the social processes of the area in which the problems are located. In the Caribbean area where there are more than 7,000,000 colored persons, including mixtures of Negro stocks, and where they form approximately 70 per cent of the total population, there is not only an increasing fusion of mixture of the racial stocks, but there is also a tendency for the races to voluntarily remain apart and socially isolated. Thus, there is a distinct role for blacks, for mixed peoples, and for whites in these areas. There is no lumping of race problems as in the United States, nor is there any clearly defined line between what is possible for colored folk and what is not possible as is true in this country. The concept of race in the Negro immigrant's background, therefore, is an important index to his adjustment, for it indicates not only how he felt and how he acted in his home environment, but it also indicates what he was prior to the migration.

This racial background indicates how the Negro immigrant feels and reacts to other Negroes and to the white population. The disgust that a Negro immigrant experiences when he sees a white American doing unskilled labor may be a profound shock to his preconceived notions of the role of the white person in society. The realization that a Negro of "good birth" and performing a "gentlemanly" role as a professional person, may be forced to suffer the same social indignities as those experienced by the Negro laborer may be an initial shock that is soon rationalized into reactions as to why any Negro should suffer such treatment. . . . Nothing could be more misleading in analyzing the racial backgrounds of Negro immigrants, than to assume that they are all Negroes, in the American sense of the word.

In the United States all persons with Negro blood, no matter what amount, are classified as Negroes. In the West Indies those persons having admixtures of white and Negro blood are recognized as colored, and form a separate, though not so rigidly defined, caste. Their social position is distinctly superior to that of the black population. Within this color maze, there is a diversified system of castes in which prestige and stratification are determined not only by the amount of "white" blood possessed, but also by the social and economic position attained. European customs have combined with racial mixtures to produce a more flexible physical and social type than is found in the United States. The colored population constitutes a real middle caste, just as the blacks constitute a lower caste. This does not mean that the darker populations are openly excluded from the larger activities of the area, rather, that they are the poorest group, the most rural, and that only the exceptional individual is able to overcome the obstacles to success. In the West Indies, it is largely the colored person who fills the responsible positions that lie between higher administrative control and menial labor. . . .

From the French and British possessions in the Caribbean have come thousands of colored persons, to whom the concept "race" has never been important. To them the badge of culture or nationality has been the outstanding symbol. The confusion of culture and race becomes increasingly significant upon migration. Their social heritage represents and includes the devices that have been utilized by Negro groups in other sections to solve their life problems. Racial amalgamation is regarded as a definite "way out." By and large their social devices are based upon procedures for establishing contacts and relationships with other groups. As a result race and culture become closely intertwined.

The ways in which the Negro immigrant groups have worked out this matter of relationships with other groups are important values. They represent an accumulated life experience. They are supported by custom, usage, tradition—and, in the homeland, even by merit. These ways are tenacious and tend to survive in both the pure and hybrid forms in certain relationships abroad. These differences in settings afforded by the homeland and the new environment may be reconciled if they are based upon reason, but if they are purely matters of convention or usage they are rather irreconcilable. Disgust arises, remains and conquers. Some of the most important of these cultural factors in the background of the Negro immigrant are of importance in analyzing his American adjustment. In religion, he has a background of ritualistic religion evidenced through affiliation with the Catholic and Episcopal faiths; in politics a profound interest in self-government among the British and in the philosophy of liberté, egalité and fraternité among the French. Yet he suffers from political stagnation and from an economic system with areas that are still productive, greatly over-populated and exploited. His moral and social usages are essentially European and bourgeois; with his social institutions patterned upon an imitation of European experiences and forms. These factors include not only those influences that Boas has classed as the "strong African background in the West Indies, the importance of which diminishes with increasing distance from the South," but also the significant factors of family institutions, leisure, food habits, education, and superstitions.

While none of these factors is a matter of race, all of them are so closely identified with the racial group that they give the appearance of having racial character. On the whole, the Negro immigrant is much more aware of them than he is of his physical manifestations of race.

This close association of language, religion, moral standards, customs, and racial identity effects a sense of nationalism that is not typical of the American Negro. The Negro immigrant brings to the racial American scene a national character that has been impressed upon him by the area in which he previously lived. Substituting the American Negro character therefore becomes assimilation, a process not too easily nor very readily achieved. He must become "denationalized" and renationalized at the same time. Doing so involves recognition of a lower status than was held in the homeland, not as a national, but as a member of a rigidly defined color-caste—the Negro. . . .

The integration of the foreign-born Negro has not yet taken place. And so long as the West Indian Negro must compromise between the adjustment processes of the old and the new environment, this maladjustment will continue to exist. For in the Negro community the foreign-born Negro is viewed as a threat to the native-born Negro's status. In New York the native complains that he can no longer get work because the West Indians are so "clannish" that once one gets work he proceeds to bring in a full crew of West Indians. It so happens, however, that the inter-insular prejudices prevent just such solidarity. The native complains that he cannot secure work-relief because of those "damn monkey-chasers"; that "they" have ruined the

Baptist Church, captured the Episcopal Church and monopolized politics. The West Indians in turn are defensively resentful, constantly looking for insults, discrimination, and evidences of segregation.

In combating discrimination and segregation the Negro foreign-born are frequently able to employ stratagems not available to the native-born. Chief among such stratagems is the use of their foreign citizenship status. The native Negro maintains that the British Negro immigrant frequently breaks down all of the former's efforts at destroying racial segregation and discrimination with his "I am a British subject! I shall appeal to my consul," whenever he runs afoul of the American segregation practices. Such individual protests, maintains the native-born Negro, while getting satisfactory personal results, do little to aid the concerted racial approach for eliminating segregation practices. An indirect outgrowth of such personal protests was the Georgia amendment of her racial integrity law in 1927 to define persons of color as "all Negroes, mulattoes, mestizos, and their descendants, having any ascertainable trace of either Negro or African, West Indian or Asiatic Indian blood in their veins, and all descendants of any person having either Negro or African West Indian or Asiatic Indian blood in his or her veins." . . .

In the problem of race discrimination and segregation the foreign-born Negro is forced to make drastic adjustment. Forming a racial majority at home, and not being accustomed to such broad discriminations on a racial basis, he revolts against segregation in the States. While color, class and caste lines tend to converge in the Caribbean, it is also true that their racial separation begins there.

Color there is a factor in, though not a final determinant of, class status. Because of his resentment for the segregation pattern of the United States the foreign-born Negro is a relentless protagonist for all causes fighting the social, political and economic disabilities of the Negroes in this country. As he participates and succeeds to leadership the foreign-born Negro faces the same type of problem faced by the foreign-born white—he frequently is refused leadership even when qualified. Yet the West Indians' major contribution to Negro life in the United States as stated by one of them, is in itself a conflict-producing one—"The insistent assertion of their manhood in an environment that demands too much servility and unprotecting acquiescence from men of African blood—the unwillingness to conform and be standardized, to accept tamely an inferior status and abdicate their humanity."

Though stemming from sharply distinctive, and, at times, conflicting cultures, traditions, aims, customs and thought-schools, the non-English speaking and the English-speaking immigrants when meeting on United States soil are forced to find a new basis for social adjustment. That basis is race. Spiritually and culturally the immigrants' bonds are more closely knit with Spain, France, Portugal and Great Britain than with the United States. Their arrival here is not always a metaphorical hand-washing to out the damned spot of their home land, rather it is thought of as an effort to preserve that which is regarded as most important in the past and link it with the profits—actual and potential—of this, their promised land. But this process involves additional struggle and accommodation.

THE RISE OF INDIAN NATIONALISM

In Gandhi's call for non-cooperation, the people were asked to withdraw their aid and support of the administration, to substitute boycotts, and perform acts of civil disobedience against unjust laws. Although his movement failed in its objective, of securing independence, it succeeded in awakening India to the consciousness of her own potential power.

THE BEGINNING of the Indo-British relationship dates back to the closing decades of the seventeenth century. Attracted by the fabulous wealth of India, which also inspired the epoch-making voyage of Columbus, the directors of the East India Company decided around 1686 to "establish . . . a large, well-grounded, sure English domination in India for all time to come." Consequently, they obtained trading rights in Bombay, Calcutta and Madras from the Indian authorities. They began to purchase land, and without provocation or permission from the rulers of India, started the fortification of their

Excerpt from Krishnalal J. Shridharani, *War Without Violence* (New York: Harcourt, Brace and Company, 1939), pp. 117-140.

trading posts. The latter were manned by armed British troops and by cannons, thus violating the trust of the natives. The subsequent friction led to the rise of Robert Clive who proposed stern measures against the resisting natives. In 1757, Clive defeated the Bengal forces at Plassey and appropriated a large portion of Indian territory in the interests of the Company.

Then ensued an era of unscrupulous plunder and exploitation by the Company men. The East India Company paid such fabulous dividends that its stocks rose to $32,000 a share. All native competition was crushed. At a later period, the silk and cotton weavers of northeastern India were forced to give up their craft so that Lancashire-manufactured cotton fabrics might enjoy monopoly with Indian consumers.

Swelling resentment finally broke down the endurance of the long-suffering natives. What was left of the Indian soldiery rallied in 1857, and struck at the British forces in India. The English retaliated with organized strength and with the aid of Christian converts turned out by various missions. The rebellion of the natives was crushed with "medieval ferocity"; some 100,000 Indian lives were taken during the struggle as well as during the aftermath. The incident came to be known as the "Sepoy Mutiny" because it was a revolution which failed. India went under the authority of the British Parliament as a result, and was completely disarmed.

The resentment remained. As another armed revolt was impossible, the energies and the discontent of the populace found an outlet in "parliamentary pursuit." This new trend resulted in the formation of the Indian National Congress in 1885. . . .

The nationalists' organization increased its membership and strength by leaps and bounds. The main activity of these leaders consisted of an annual meeting held to pass formal resolutions. Their purely parliamentary activities received their first contact with militancy in 1905. That year, the ruling Britons decided to divide the province of Bengal into two parts. The "Partition of Bengal" was to be effected with a view to securing the most beautiful and fertile land of India for the sole enjoyment of the British immigrants. This aroused the fury of the Bengalis, who, backed by the whole of India, called a vigorous boycott on British-manufactured goods. The struggle sent many to prison. The agitation of the leaders and the vigorous use of economic pressure by the people at large were not in vain. The partition plan was repealed.

The success of the movement gave the Indian a taste of his own potential strength, which resulted in corresponding changes in his attitudes and aspirations. These, however, were soon to be vastly modified by the extraordinary situation created by the World War in Europe. India was called upon to do her duty by the Allies. The tone of the British Parliament as well as that of the bureaucracy in India was unrecognizably changed. Commands were tempered, and a volley of requests and appeals replaced them. Great promises of Dominion Status and war booty were given to India if she discharged her duty in the Empire's hour of trial. . . .

Gandhi attended the War Conference at the invitation of the Viceroy and supported the resolution drafted to help the Empire in its hour of danger. He apparently felt his course to be a short-cut to Home Rule for India. . . . All in all, India contributed $500,000,000 to the Allied war machine. War loans to the value of $700,000,000 were purchased by India in addition. Finished products to the value of $1,250,000,000 were sent to the Allies' side from India. The sacrifice of India's manhood was still greater. About 1,338,620 Indians were dispatched to the various battlefields in France, Palestine, Syria and Mesopotamia. . . .

At the conclusion of the War, however, India was not only denied any part of the War booty but she was even denied admission to the League of Nations. Moreover, India was not to receive Dominion Status as promised during the War.

Discontent grew by leaps and bounds. At this point, broken soldiers returned from the trenches with accounts of injustices and unequal treatment. In spite of unprecedented heroism and military acumen, no Indian received a commission—simply because he was an Indian. And all of them, they reported, were discriminated against by Europeans irrespective of rank and station. In India itself, the war boom was over and there was a general state of unemployment. Manufacturing tycoons, who had doubled and tripled their wealth overnight, forgot their abnormal profits of war-time and began to reduce wages and personnel. Consequently, the rumbling of discontent among the proletariat, audible in pre-war days, grew louder. The teeming farming population of upper India, especially inhabitants of the Punjab, were resentful of the ravages made on their male population by enforced enlistment in the British Army. Even the upper middle class, savoring the fast-fading taste of power and profit, was resentful of the turn of events. The inevitable disillusionment had come at last, and India was again a seething volcano. . . .

A commission, composed of all Englishmen and no Indian, recommended drastic measures to deal with the growing unrest. The Rowlatt Committee advised the government to curtail the people's right to gather in large assemblies. Freedom of speech and assembly as well as freedom of the press were to be greatly reduced and in many cases forfeited. Imprisonment without trial, a distinct breach of the *Habeas Corpus Act*, was to be a common practice with the police and civil authorities. All India was aroused.

Driven to desperation, Gandhi called upon the people to resist. A day was appointed for complete *Hartal* as a sign of mourning. Each village and every city in the country was to stop all normal activity for twenty-four hours and every adult was to observe a fast. Streets were deserted and shop windows shrouded. Mass meetings were held in the evening to denounce the act. Individuals were asked at these meetings to sign a Satyagraha pledge which bound them to disobey the act and such other laws as would be recommended by the nationalist high command. Finally huge processions marched through the "main streets" of India shouting revolutionary slogans.

The government struck back at the Satyagrahis in order to nip their revolt in the bud. Processions were stopped by the military at various places and large crowds were fired on at Delhi, Calcutta and Amritsar.

Then came Gandhi's call for non-co-operation. The people were asked to withdraw their aid and support which made the administration possible. Those who had been rewarded by the government with titles and honorary offices were to surrender their privileges. Rich people were to refrain from buying government loans and the poor were asked to refuse any petty service to the local authorities. Lawyers suspended their practice and disputes were settled outside the courts. Government schools were deserted as the students decided either to go to "national institutions" or to the villages to carry on the *Swaraj* propaganda. A militant boycott of British goods was promulgated, coupled with a petition to the public to patronize indigenous products. Finally, Indians in government service, from high officials to petty tax-collectors, were asked to resign from their posts. Complete paralysis of the administration was the objective. This program was further bolstered by the nationalist propaganda at work in the Indian Army. . . .

True to the pattern of Satyagraha [non-violent direct action], more militant maneuvers were to follow. After non-co-operation had partly paralyzed the administration, the actual business of destroying the existing order was planned. This finesse was to be accomplished by non-payment of the government taxes and by civil disobedience of repressive laws. Bans on nationalist literature were to be disregarded, and the government monopoly of salt manufacture was to be broken by mass action. The Rowlatt Act, the immediate cause of all this friction, was to be completely shattered.

In spite of Gandhi's constant and eloquent appeals to his countrymen to refrain from hatred and violence, violence broke out. Gandhi then decided upon the drastic step of calling a halt. This decision produced the utmost consternation within the ranks of his colleagues. Many regarded it as a sacrifice of the people's cause on the altar of an individual's ideals. However, Gandhi's decision prevailed and the Satyagraha was called off.

After a lapse of time, on March 18, 1932, Gandhi was arrested and tried on the charge of instigating the people to violence. . . .

Thus the first experiment with non-violent direct action on a national scale suffered an abortive end. Although it failed to obtain its immediate objective, it was immensely successful in awakening India to the consciousness of her own potential power. Moreover, the experience gathered during this non-co-operation movement paved the way for India's next great movement of 1930.

A lengthy period of reaction followed the apparent failure of the non-co-operation movement of 1920-1922. On one hand the people of India were brooding over the future of the Swaraj movement and on the other the British bureaucracy was tightening its grip over public affairs. . . .

The period of demoralization over, new organizations and new trends began to revive the spirits of the people. The All-Indian Trade

Union Congress, founded in 1921, was a powerful group by this time. On the farmers' front, the National Congress party was making a heroic effort to expand its activities and to seek recruits by the thousands from among agriculturists.

The labor movement came to a head in 1929. Strikes occurred all over India. The Bombay Textile Labor Union was the first. A general strike of the jute workers followed in Bengal. The Iron Works at Jamshedpur, one of the largest in the world, was the next to be threatened by a labor war. The Iron Plate Works in the same industrial town, connected with the Burma Oil Company, succeeded in suppressing the walkout before it reached large proportions. The labor movement was becoming class conscious for the first time in India's short industrial history. . . .

About this time, a new element was gaining in importance in the Indian political mosaic. The youth of India was demanding a hearing. Their organizations spread like wildfire, and by 1928, there was hardly a town of any size in India without its unit of politically-minded young men. These societies were sincerely radical. Their guiding spirits were nationalists with overtones of Socialism. They advocated that either Gandhi launch the nation once more in direct action or give up his leadership.

Gandhi felt that the time was ripe for direct action against the British government of India. The situation called for a strong Congress president who could swing the youth leagues and the workers behind that body. Gandhi's choice was Pandit Jawaharlal Nehru. One year previously the Indian National Congress in its annual meeting at Calcutta had given an ultimatum to the government to confer Dominion Status in twelve months' time. The government failed to comply. Thereupon, in 1930, under the younger man's inspiration, India declared her independence on the memorable 26th of January. It was again a revolution, albeit non-violent; the community was rising against the state. . . .

When the plans were ready, and the scene set, it was announced to the waiting nation that civil disobedience would be inaugurated on March 12, 1930. . . .

The Satyagrahis [believers in non-violent action] attacked on many fronts and employed a variety of tactics. In big cities, they organized and led huge processions in defiance of police orders and prohibitory notices served by the warrant officers. In village and town alike, public meetings and conferences of local leaders were held in spite of the government ban. The usual boycott of British goods coupled with intensive picketing by women became general. Pickets were posted even at the gates of British banks, insurance companies, mints and bullion exchanges. As the press was now forbidden by the authorities to print campaign notices and news regarding government repression, the Satyagrahis issued their own bulletins and leaflets. Although these were regarded as illegal and revolutionary, they were freely distributed among the masses. . . .

When the movement gathered momentum, certain more drastic stratagems were included in the general program. A boycott was called on all state-owned post offices, telegraph systems, trams and ship lines. . . .

Civil disobedience of unjust laws, however, was the principal feature of the strategy. The Salt Act was taken as the symbol of British exploitation of the masses and made a test case. The most formidable forces, therefore, were arrayed against the government monopoly of salt manufacture. In the wake of the violation of the Salt Act followed a redoubtable attack on the Forest Laws. And then came a general attack on as many obnoxious statutes of the state as were found vulnerable. Picketing of liquor and opium shops ate an alarming hole in the government earnings. Finally, the city-dwelling businessmen and manufacturers were called upon to withhold certain taxes, and village farmers were asked not to pay land revenue.

Meanwhile, the bureaucracy had set free all the repressive and coercive powers at its command. First, the ranking leaders were rounded up and imprisoned. All Congress offices were decreed illegal and confiscated. However, new leaders sprang from the people, and more offices were opened in outlying areas. Then followed wholesale arrests of groups and volunteer corps. Finally, firing on unarmed crowds became a common spectacle.

The toll of suffering was tremendous. According to nationalist sources, during the one year of non-violent direct action (from March 12, 1930, when Satyagraha was inaugurated, to March 5, 1931, when the truce was signed), 100,000 Indians cheerfully forfeited their liberty to enter His Majesty's numerous prisons, detention camps and improvised jails. A modest estimate shows that no less than 17,000 women also underwent various terms of imprisonment. . . .

The coercive arms of the state were paralyzed by the tactics of the opponents. After a full year of struggle, the government gave in and began negotiations with the Congress high command. Gandhi and the members of the Working Committee of the Congress were released from jail and the former was invited to Delhi.

For the first time in history, on March 5, 1931, the representative of His Majesty signed a truce treaty with Gandhi, the erstwhile "rebel." Satyagraha on a national scale had now come to a successful ending. The main demands of the people were granted in the treaty thereafter known as the "Gandhi-Irwin Pact," and the stage was set for further negotiation with a view to evolving a free India. Gandhi was invited to London for the Round Table Conference.

Now that Gandhi was in London and the other leaders inactive, with the "non-violent army" disbanded and agitation discontinued, now that people were rejoicing in their triumph and consequently were off guard—the government broke its promises. So when Gandhi landed in Bombay, he found his pact with Irwin, now Lord Halifax, violated by the government. He also discovered that the bureaucracy was in a belligerent mood and did not mean to carry out the terms of the treaty. Thereupon, Gandhi was forced to revive Satyagraha. The renewed movement, however, died a natural death in 1934. Meanwhile, the new constitution, a substantial if unsatisfactory result of the nationalist struggle, was completed. Later it became the law of the land.

Thus the second nation-wide attempt at securing complete independence was, at best, a partial success. The movement, however, further prepared the country in the art of government and made the people confident of their strength and ability. According to all observers, foreign as well as domestic, it was a reborn India at the conclusion of the Civil Disobedience Movement.

Part V

THE CONTEMPORARY SCENE IN INTER-
CULTURAL RELATIONS

13

THE PROBLEMS OF CONTEMPORARY IMPERIALISM

MODERN INTERCOMMUNICATION and the world-mindedness which it has generated are usually thought of as forces tending to break down cultural isolation, consequently as foes of provincialism and culture conflict. But, on the whole, as Kohn points out in "The Present Scene," they have intensified culture conflict and further complicated intercultural relations by enlarging the scope of this conflict and complicating its character. The campaigns for political dominance and for cultural supremacy have thus broadened the areas of old feuds and, with new weapons of competition and propaganda, this has brought increasing tension into intercultural relations on the national, international and colonial scene. Problems and policies of minority adjustment have thereby become one of the crucial issues of our time. Comparatively few communities have resolved their minority situations to the point of stable social equilibrium, not to mention the attainment of social harmony and of social justice. Discontent and disequilibrium are so acutely present in many societies as to bring definite challenge to the entire social order. In view of the natural sequel of counter-resistance to such situations in the politically established order, few serious students today doubt that the solution of minority problems and the satisfaction of even a modicum of minority demands and interests involves less than a profound reconstruction of the social order, and some think it involves even an overturn of the dominant orders.

Kohn points out how the rationalizations of Europeanization and its own internal cultural values have been gradually adopted by the oppressed and dominated minority groups throughout the world, with pressure for concessions from the dominant groups in terms of their own principles and professed values. The growing self-consciousness of backward races surges upward in claims of self-determination and self-rule. Non-European cultures and repressed minorities seize upon such justifications as the "civilizing mission" of European civilization and all the formulas and creeds of democracy professed by the dominant orders to implement their struggle for minority assertion and its mounting claims. These principles cannot very well be repudiated in majority group theory or profession—however they may be disregarded in practice. Only a few dominant states have dared realistically to make such formal repudiation; but this is perhaps the most serious aspect and the most threatening implication of totalitarian state theory. Western civilization seems yet unready, generally speaking, for such wholesale unmasking of its practical politics, and repudiation of its social norms and cultural professions. Thus the dilemma of the present time and scene.

In contemporary Western civilization there are two sets of forces operating on an expanded and accelerated scale. One set is geared to increased technological and cultural interchange and is developing increased economic inter-dependence and cultural interpenetration. Along with this, however, has gone an extension and intensification of the divisive forces of imperialism, ethnic nationalism and the accompanying rationalizations of this struggle and clash of interests in cultural separatism and sectarianism. The modern world holds a precarious balance between these two sets of forces, one of which must achieve or be given preponderance to determine the future fate and character of Western civilization.

Dominant as they yet are, both imperialism and ethnic nationalism—root sources, as has been seen, of these divisive cultural forces, face not only serious challenge but the prospect of self-contradiction. This comes about because imperialism is forced to extend its own type of civilization, while yet practicing ethnic supremacy and alien group subordination based on cultural discrimination and exclusion. Ethnic nationalism, on its part, aspires also to large-scale political units, which become by that very process increasingly multi-racial. The continued expansion of these systems, then, makes them become more and more involved in inner contradiction, and they confront, sooner or later, the boomerang effects of their own inconsistent policies.

Economic factors, being as primary and dominant as they are or seem to be, would seem to cast the die in favor of the eventual ascendancy of fusionist trends and certainly the expansion of the industrial scientific culture beyond its sphere of origin. The divisive and separatist forces seem thus to be set against the probable predominating current, even though, for the time being, they loom large in terms of the acute contemporary culture conflicts. Many or most of these problems of contemporary civilization pivot on the issues of minority rights and aspirations as against imperialistic dominance, on the one hand, and, on the other, against the cultural uniformitarianism and ethnic intolerance of the typical modern national state.

This section takes such issues of contemporary intercultural relations under consideration first, as the problem of minorities under imperialism, then, the problem of minorities in Europe under the national state, and finally, in terms of the minority problems of America and the way they affect both the conceptions and practice of American democracy.

On the stage of colonial imperialism, the rights and interests of subject peoples has become the central issue of world politics, short only of the nationalistic rivalry over the stakes of imperialism itself. In the presence of serious dominant group rivalry, the minority situations separately or in loose coalition, might conceivably be a decisive set of forces and threaten the whole structure of European imperialism. Woolf hints this, in calling attention to the inevitable effect on subject peoples of the imposition of the patterns, standards and values of European civilization. He argues the impossibility of a permanent reconciliation of the resulting trends with perpetual political and cultural subordination of these groups. There is also a progressive weakening of the economic base of imperialism where there is prolonged disregard of the native social organization, for it involves the consuming power of the colonial markets and thus affects the profit returns on invested capital. Any adjustment of the present-day situation involves the repair of the enormous damage which imperialistic intrusion and dominance have wrought upon native and subject peoples. The exploitation of the earlier stages of the practice of imperialism has been blocked from a double direction, from the gradual increase of resistance from awakening subject peoples, but also by an even more effective economic force—the decreasing economic returns of a system that does not build up, on the part of the larger masses of the colonial native population, standards of living warranting their more extensive participation in a more advanced level of culture.

The situation in British India, according to Woolf, is signal proof that imperialism, should it be successful in imposing Western rule upon Asiatic civilization, will "introduce a violent ferment of reaction that carries the seeds of its own destruction." India represents in the field of Asiatic imperialism the most developed situation of conflict, because it has suffered less cultural disorganization in the imperialist invasion, and because the ferment of British education was introduced into certain influential sections of the Indian population. Groups of Westernized Hindus were limited in numbers and were at first detached from the masses and the interests of the native cultures. Yet, when denied full participation and privileges under the English system, they became the nucleus for nationalist and anti-imperialist agitation, and fought the imperial regime with its own ideological and political weapons. After an initial phase of denationalization, these educated Indians turned against Western civilization as well as the political system, substituted a revival of native culture and tradition, and consolidated the mass support of the depressed and exploited population, whose grievances they alone could articulate. Opportunities for fuller participation in Western privileges, cultural and material, would have forestalled, Woolf thinks, the conflict of civilizations which is now on in India.

Not all of the contemporary problem in India, however, is of imperialist origin. Parallel with the problem of reconciling Hindu and European civilization is the problem of internal religious difference— the Hindu-Moslem feud and the still older separatisms of the caste system. Ghuyre's article traces these, but shows that British policy has had deep effect upon both of these internal conflicts. In many ways the policy of cultural non-interference of Britain in India has been predominantly prudential, and in cases of crisis has utilized the traditional feuds and cleavages for a "divide and rule" strategy. Legislative abolition of customary caste differences has not, on the whole, diminished caste lines; Ghuyre maintains that in some respects it has intensified them, since, except for upper caste lines, customary caste usage was loosely administered except with regard to caste etiquette. Urbanization under British rule and the Europeanization of native life by direct and indirect contact have been more potent in breaking down or loosening the rigidity of the caste system. The revolt of large sections of the Indians of all classes and religious faiths against the English and the discovery of common interests in Indian nationalism have created forceful movements for Hindu-Moslem rapprochement and for the dissolution of the caste structure. The culmination of the latter has taken shape in the campaign for lifting the bans of untouchability and the beginning of a movement to incorporate culturally even the pariah classes. Under the spur of the ideas of Indian solidarity, some provinces have legally removed the disabilities of the pariahs, even the most stringent of all their prohibitions, entrance to the Hindu temples. Many leaders of Hindu nationalist aspirations, and officers of the Indian Nationalist Congress see no hope for resurgent Indian nationalism without a speedy dissolution of the caste system and the rapid spread of religious tolerance through Hindu-Moslem co-operation. A process of double assimilation has thus been set in motion by the reactions to the imperialist regime. A double acculturation is remotely in view, that of the greater fusion of separate traditions within the Indian culture itself and of the Asiatic-European elements of culture as well.

Such clash of cultural interests is not merely involved in Anglo-Indian, but in practically all European-Asiatic relations. The policy of "Asia for the Asiatics" is historically a direct repercussion of European intrusion and resentment to its domineering exploitation. In the case of the Japanese, there is direct imitative and competitive rivalry of European imperialism. An awakened Asia confronts Europe with a challenge both to her policies of political aggression and of cultural supremacy. In the international relations with independent Japan and semi-independent China, the culture conflict is showing striking analogies to the movement already traced in the case of India, so far as concerns the reactions toward nationalist cultural revival and the selective adoption of Western technology without the previous deference for its cultural values. In the colonial spheres of Indo-China and the Dutch East Indies, even feebly in Oceanica, belated movements of native nationalism and resistance are emerging. Burma and Siam have also shown unmistakable signs of such reactions.

Ennis traces the dilemmas in this important colonial sphere in his article on French policy in Indo-China. Indo-China has followed the general sequence of the phases of imperialism, but has detailed differences on matters of native policy. The crucial contacts of the French with Indo-China occurred during the dominance of their "assimilation" policy, calculated to extend the French basis of culture as rapidly as possible. Granting humane motives to this policy, Ennis shows that in practical results it was as disintegrative in its effect upon native Annamite society as was the British policy of direct cultural disparagement. Rationalized by certain French policy makers as a compliment to the Indo-Chinese, in practical operation it engendered depreciation of the native culture and its tradition. The assimilated natives were not given full recognition nor identical privilege and opportunity with the French colonial settlers and administrators, so that the policy of assimilation has led to resentment and native counter-assertion. An Annamite nationalist movement has arisen, which has shown little signs of abatement, even with a reversal of French policy to educational and administrative regard for native tradition and customs. There has occurred, nevertheless, in the French sphere a decided shift from the policy of assimilation and cultural displacement to the policy of "association" or cultural pluralism, paralleling the British adoption of its equivalent, the policy of "Indirect Rule."

Although less hostile and derogatory, indirect rule has its handicaps, especially when introduced after a period of ruthless penetration. Only a weakened structure of native life remains to be built upon, and there is a heritage of animus and opposition to be overcome. In taking cognizance of native interests, the new policy must stimulate its own antithesis—nativism and eventually native nationalism, which has only a short step to take from cultural to political channels. The French colonial administration, having exhibited less open prejudice and thus having generated less group animosity, even when economically ruthless, hopes to resolve their intercultural problems and difficulties by this policy. Historically the French colonial system has not, on the whole, added cultural insult to political and economic injury. The French utilize the accrued cultural goodwill as an effective appeal and sanction for their increasingly large native colonial army, which they utilize for national as well as imperial defense.

Roberts sketches the rise of a similar colonial policy in Africa. At first, except in the Old Colonies and in privileged departments of Dakar and Senegal, the French colonial policy in Africa was inconsiderate of native cultures and native interests, as were the Belgian, German and British. In rapid succession, the French and then the British effected a change which has substantially co-ordinated their colonial policies. Both moved in the direction of administering their domains through the co-operation of native chiefs and the use of customary tribal sanctions for reinforcing the administration of colonial laws and regulations. Economic interests have increasingly brought about exceptions to the policy's consistent application, particularly in the Congo mining districts, the South African mining districts, the Kenya East African plantations, in fact, in most areas where the colonial economy calls for the large-scale use of native labor. There have been flagrant displacements of native populations, particularly in Natal, Rhodesia, and Kenya, considerably after the promulgation of the indirect rule program, and in Kenya even after the promulgation of the mandates principle of trusteeship for natural resources and native interests. Regard for native rights and interests seems to depend more on whether it can be reconciled with the selfish motives of sustained profit and more effective economic collaboration than it does upon idealistic professions of principle. The obligation of tutelage is of lesser consequence, whether professed by the colonial administration or the missionaries, in the latter case, because missions typically concede the official colonial policy and aim merely at palliative effect and remedial cultural services.

The net results of the French policy of "association," of the Lugard policy of "indirect rule," and of the mandates regime of the Versailles Treaty and the League of Nations have only meant a slight mitigation of the initial ruthlessness of the colonial regimes in Africa, the Near East and Polynesia. There has been no eradication of the dominant forces and motives originally involved. These new policies have merely smoothed the rougher edges of colonial contacts, removed some of the more flagrant cultural disparagements, and checked or postponed complete cultural disorganization among the weaker native subject peoples. "Each in his own civilization" has not been a workable formula because of the necessary interpenetration of native and European life, under conditions where the European factors had preassured dominance.

From observations in the Union of South Africa, and checked on the far frontiers of native-European contact on the native reservations, Schapera concludes that the Bantu tribes, for example, have been brought "permanently within the orbit of Western civilization." However slow and resisted, there will be, he believes, an eventual interchange of civilization with diminishing cultural demarcations between native and white with each succeeding generation. Bantu self-consciousness and incipient native nationalism are beginning to reinforce certain elements of the native culture, and yet at the same time, are facilitating the assimilation of European culture by the younger natives. This means that in the process of becoming more Europeanized, by virtue of the new self-conscious minority attitudes, the Bantu are not losing completely their hold on their own culture. On the native side, promising culture fusions are to be observed, combining European customs with their own. This is true particularly, Schapera reports, in the religious and ceremonial life. Acculturation of this type has been difficult in the face of the almost overwhelming procedures and attitudes of the dominant European elements. But in missionary and other efforts, which depend for their success on the goodwill and co-operation of the natives, native customs and values are acquiring a small chance to reassert themselves and play a role in cultural change. . . . Schapera also is led to believe from his observations that enough potential influence exists in the native culture to warrant the prediction of what he styles "an eventual common South African civilization shared by Bantu and European alike."

Schapera also calls attention to the little observed and comparatively recent changes in missionary policy, especially their attitudes toward native, non-Christian cultures. Coercive measures, which can so easily dominate political colonial administration, cannot prevail so readily in a sphere like religion. The missions have exercised their coercive influence mainly through the mission schools. Now with the slow growth of state programs and the secular supervision of native education, that hold is breaking, and missionary programs are more dependent than ever on native reactions of acceptance. Missionary activity, having felt considerably the setbacks of passive resistance from the pagan cultures, and being confronted with the disillusioned nationalism of important sections of the native population, has been forced to modify its approaches very decidedly in the last decade or so. This began with the tactical divorce of remedial medical and educational work from doctrinal missionarism, and finally led to an active co-operation with chieftains still holding to the native traditions. The influence of the cultural pluralism policy of colonial reforms has led in a few cases to missionary compromises with native traditions and customs which they felt could be safely incorporated within the frame of Christianity. While not considerable enough, as yet, to be called anything but experimental, such new missionary policy and programs are significant signs of a reorientation of European cultural policies and attitudes in colonial relationships. These are streaks of light merely on a colonial horizon that in the main is still ominously dark with intercultural misunderstanding and friction.

THE PRESENT SITUATION

The rationalist gospel of Europeanization unites with the Christian gospel of missionaries and the socialist appeal of revolutionaries in creating a new self-consciousness among the oppressed or backward races. With the growing world-wide insurgence among the backward races and with their more articulate expression of resentment the policy of drift becomes impossible.

RACIAL CONTACTS and therefore racial conflicts become more general with the approach of the age of imperialism. The tendencies of restless growth and expansion inherent in industrialism and capitalism soon led Europeans to seek raw materials and new markets all over the world. They brought with them the products and the methods of a higher civilization, and the nature of the ensuing conflict was determined by whether the European conquerors met peoples with a highly developed civilization and with strong indigenous political organizations or primitive tribes. In the first case, as illustrated by China or India, the net result of the contact may in the long run prove favorable to the natives; in the second case, as in North America, Australia, and the Pacific islands, it has been irreparably detrimental; in Africa, which occupies an intermediate position in this respect, it may ultimately strengthen the Negro race. In any case the conflict of races created by the invasion of a territory by a stronger or more advanced race has tended to intensify the struggle for existence of the weaker race and to disorganize its culture and social structure. The nature of the race conflicts also has depended upon the economic conditions and the cultural background of the conquering race. In North America, where the invaders were animated by an intense race superiority complex, the Indians were driven into the less habitable areas or were exterminated, whereas in the plantation regions of Latin America, where a more humane attitude prevailed, the Spaniards allowed the Indians to remain on the land and forced them to work for their new masters, thus preserving

Excerpt from Hans Kohn, "Race Conflict," in *Encyclopaedia of the Social Sciences*, Vol. 13 (New York: The Macmillan Company, 1934), pp. 37-38, 40.

their means of subsistence and allowing for their slow adaptation to the superimposed civilization. Generally the more warlike and the more highly developed agricultural tribes have shown the greatest power of survival in contact with Europeans; governments have always treated the militant tribes with much more favor than the complacent ones. In Africa, partly because of climatic conditions, white settlement was much more restricted than in America or Australia and the Negroes have proved to be a stronger race. But the slave trade, forced labor and imported diseases, like syphilis, have led to depopulation in many parts of Africa and have destroyed Negro civilization and tribal structure. The difficult adaptation to new conditions and to forced labor brought about by the imperialist penetration of Africa since the abolition of the slave trade has not given Negro society opportunity to recuperate.

The period after the World War has been marked by a world wide effort of oppressed or backward races to change their status. The awakening of the masses throughout the East, the Bolshevik educational efforts on behalf of the racial minorities, the activities of the Republican regime in Spain, the agrarian unrest in southeastern Europe, the new spirit everywhere among the Negroes, the revolts of the long suffering Indians of Central and South America, are all movements involving dynamic change in race relations. Liberalism in its original meaning is spreading its influences over all parts of the earth untouched by its victory in Europe in the eighteenth and nineteenth centuries. The rationalist gospel of Europeanization unites with the Christian gospel of missionaries and the socialist appeal of revolutionaries in creating a new self-consciousness among the oppressed or backward races. . . .

In many countries there is a tendency to minimize the importance of racial conflict in the interests of the ruling races and frequently there is hypocrisy about the benefits accruing to the backward races by their cohabitation with more progressive races. While a semblance of tranquillity can be maintained by armed superiority the problem is ignored. But with the growing world-wide insurgence among the backward races and with their more articulate expression of resentment the policy of drift becomes impossible. Then, often under the cloak of humanitarianism or science, a policy of repression by compulsory racial segregation is frequently undertaken. Racial integrity is protected by laws forbidding interracial marriages; benefits derived from government are reserved for the dominant races; participation in government is denied to the oppressed races, who are discriminated against in all phases of social life and receive not only different but definitely inferior education and living quarters and a disproportionately small share in public services.

On the other hand, the awakening of underprivileged races is stimulated by the equalitarian and humanitarian policies of the Soviet Union, where a determined stand has been taken against race discrimination. The rational belief in the complete equality of all races has become the official creed, and energetic educational efforts are being made to raise the social and economic conditions of the underprivileged races. Whereas in many parts of the world ruling classes or imperialist governments instigate or refrain from suppressing race conflict for reasons of hegemony or exploitation, communism helps to organize backward races in their struggle for political and economic advancement and liberation. . . . The Soviet Union now is the only large area inhabited by many races, free, as far as governmental agencies are concerned, of any form of race prejudice.

The growing acuteness of race conflict has recently attracted the attention of religious and humanitarian bodies. Islam in theory as in practice has never known a color bar, which largely explains the appeal it has exercised among African races; but Christianity has not as a rule lived up to its precept of the brotherhood of man. Of late, however, Christian and humanitarian bodies have begun to recognize the necessity of a definite stand on the race question. The conference of the International Missionary Council in Jerusalem, for example, declared in 1928 that "any discrimination against human beings on the ground of race or colour, any selfish exploitation and any oppression of man by man is a denial of the teachings of Jesus." . . . Christian missions in Africa and Asia, often in the face of opposition on the part of white settlers and colonial governments, have imbued the natives with a spirit of self-consciousness and individual human dignity, have helped to develop leadership among the backward races and to train natives in different branches of social and economic activity.

GREAT BRITAIN IN INDIA

The Government of India has been an alien European government. Its standards have been the standards of Western, not Indian, civilization. Education has spread through India Western ideas of democracy and nationality, of Liberty, Equality, and Fraternity, of which imperialism and the Government of India itself have been the negation.

OUR WESTERN civilization cannot exist at all without an intricate and delicate economic and political machinery. If you compare the highly organized machinery of central and municipal government, of industry, commerce, and finance in Europe today with the simple machinery of the eighteenth century—a century in which life was as complicated and civilized as it had ever been previously—you will see the enormous difference in this respect between our civilization and all those which preceded it. And this elaboration and complication of machinery and institutions are a vital part of that civilization. Sweep them away, and we should at once go back to the kind of life and the type of civilization of past centuries.

This fact has had a great effect upon the relations of Europe to the rest of the world since the industrial revolution. The primary impulse which brought the new civilization into contact with Asia and Africa was economic. The manufacturers and traders who were the harbingers in the hills and plains of Asia and the forests of Africa went there with certain definite economic objects: they wanted to sell cotton or calico, to obtain tin or iron or rubber or tea or coffee. But to do this under the complicated economic system of Western civilization, it was necessary that the whole economic system of the Asiatic and African should be adjusted to and assimilated with that of Europe. That assimilation has been carried through by European manufacturers, merchants, and financiers, or by European governments under their influence and direction and, mainly, in their interests. In the

Excerpt from Leonard Woolf, *Imperialism and Civilization* (New York: Harcourt, Brace and Co., 1928), pp. 46-47, 67-76.

process the lives of the subject peoples have been revolutionized and the bases of their own civilization often destroyed, and they have watched all this come upon them from outside, imposed upon them by force through an alien government.

Nothing like this and upon this scale has ever happened in the world before. Vast conquests and vast empires have been frequent in history, particularly in Asia, but the immemorial and respectable methods of empire and conquest were quite impossible in the nineteenth century, if only because this assimilation with the economic system of Western civilization was necessary.

Alone of Asiatic peoples the Indians had been for long in close contact with Europeans, and to some extent under the dominion of Europeans before the development of nineteenth-century imperialism. The trade with India had for centuries been of great importance, and all through the eighteenth century there had been keen rivalry among the commercial nations of Europe to obtain for themselves a monopoly of Indian trade and Indian riches. France, Holland, Great Britain, and Portugal were the principals in this struggle, and they all obtained, at one time or another, a foothold in India and Ceylon. It is, however, important to notice that up to the middle of the eighteenth century the relations of European traders and their governments with Indian rulers were in no sense imperialist. Asiatic territory and Asiatic governments were treated in the same way as European territory and governments. Great Britain or France made treaties with Indian rulers as they did with European kings and emperors, and the East India Company and other traders conducted their operations according to concessions from Indian governments and the laws and customs of India. The footholds obtained in India were not obtained by a struggle against the Indian rulers and the European did not impose his will, his political system, or his economic methods on India; the struggle was between the European rivals, each trying to prevent the others' obtaining concessions or carrying on trade. This is a significant fact, for those who maintain that the conflict which is now taking place in India and the rest of Asia against Europeans is primarily a racial conflict must explain why it is that for two or more centuries before the birth of modern Western civilization and imperialist policy in

Asia there was continual contact between Europeans and Indian governments and peoples, and no appearance of racial conflict.

But the struggle between the Europeans themselves for the monopoly of Indian trade, as the eighteenth century went on and the first effects of the industrial revolution began to be felt, had important effects upon the relations of the Europeans to the Indians. During the European wars of the last half of the eighteenth century France, Great Britain, Holland, and Portugal were perpetually fighting one another in Asia, and it was natural that the East India Company, for instance, should develop from a trading corporation into a semimilitarized machine directed against the enemies of Great Britain and often acting in co-operation with the regular military and naval forces. It was only a small step from this to the application of force by the Company against Indians, to the acquisition of territory and virtual sovereignty in India, in fact to the beginning of the conquest of India. That is what began to happen under Clive and Warren Hastings. The end of the Napoleonic Wars left Great Britain without a European rival of any strength in India and laid the solid foundations of an Indian Empire. In Great Britain itself the full effects of the industrial revolution were already being felt and the new industrialized civilization had been established. Modern imperialism was just about to burst upon Asia and Africa, and already there was blowing the wind which presages the storm. . . .

Thus it came about that, when the real penetration of Asia by Europe under the impulse of imperialism began about the middle of the century, India was the only Asiatic territory which was not independent. It was securely held by Britain as part of her Empire. That is why the history of India during the era of imperialism has been different from that of the rest of Asia. That history is extremely interesting to the student of imperialism, for it shows both the merits and demerits of imperialism at its best and also its final impossibility. The Government of India was an alien European government, administered by Englishmen, superimposed upon an Eastern people. It was organized on essentially European lines. According to its lights, it was an extremely efficient government, but its standards were the standards of Western, not Indian, civilization. Its efforts were mainly directed to material prosperity, and with that as an ideal it accomplished much. It built roads, bridges, irrigation works, railways. It introduced English law and English conceptions of justice, and English methods of education. It did everything to forward the economic exploitation of Indian territory, particularly where such exploitation could be of advantage to British industry and trade.

In shaping this system of government and in directing its policy the Indian had no part. The ruling class was British, and as years went by, it became more and more firmly established as a ruling class. Though it was extremely jealous of its own prestige and interests, there is no doubt that it also normally governed in the interests of the people of India. But inevitably the interests of India were sometimes not the interests of Britain, and where the interests were economic, those of India were sometimes sacrificed to those of Britain. A well-known instance is the excise on Indian cotton which was imposed solely in the interests of Lancashire. The large army maintained in India was and is a serious burden on the country; and to a great extent it serves the purposes of Britain and her Empire rather than those of India and the peoples of India.

The Government of India, this typically European government, as early as 1835 took a step which inevitably determined the history of its future relations to the people of India. It adopted a policy by which the State favored the education of Indians on European lines. The effect of this policy was twofold. In the first place it meant that the Government was helping to create a large class of English-speaking and westernized Indians who could not make use of their abilities and their training unless the society in which they lived was organized on European lines and unless there was a demand for their labor in the professions, the administration, and in commerce and industry. These conditions were not fulfilled. The Government itself debarred Indians, however able and educated, from all the higher administrative posts, while the professional and economic organization of India was such that there was no demand or scope for large numbers of the new, English-speaking class. Western civilization was therefore being introduced into and imposed upon India through education while the material conditions were not provided which might have prevented a conflict of civilizations. But the second effect of European education, being intellectual, was even more disturbing. That education spread through India those Western ideas of democracy and nationality, of Liberty, Equality, and Fraternity, of which imperialism and the Government of India itself were the negation.

Such was the imperialist system of government in India. Its history between 1835 and 1927 is a signal proof that imperialism, if it be successful in imposing Western rule and Western civilization upon Asiatic civilization, must introduce a violent ferment of reaction and carries the seeds of its own destruction. Its history falls into three periods. There is the period which ended with the Mutiny, an ominous outbreak, part military, part religious, against alien rule. The second period begins in 1858 with the Queen's proclamation promising liberty and equality and ends in 1905. It was a period which saw the whole economic system of India transformed under the influence of the Administration and the entry of British capital. It saw the formation of an educated, English-speaking class at first mainly contented with British rule, but growing gradually more and more restive as it found itself denied the liberty and equality which had been promised to Indians. It saw the beginnings of a political movement for obtaining self-government in the Indian National Congress which started in 1885, and later the beginnings of a nationalist movement. It saw the development of the British Civil Service into a very efficient and loyal administration, but also into a ruling class with its own interests and prejudices. The third period began in 1905 and still continues. It is a period of complete revolt against Europe. Influenced by the example of Japan, there is a rapid and violent development of Indian nationalism. The political principles of Europe are invoked against Europe, and practically all English-speaking Indians demand self-government. A new and curious feature appears in this movement, a feature which we shall continually meet in other conflicts between Asiatic civilizations and the imperialist civilization of western Europe. The educated Indians in their struggle against the Government use all the weapons of political organization and agitation which have been developed and perfected in Europe; they have learned the lesson of efficiency and organization from Western civilization, and on what may perhaps be called the material side of things they are westernized. But this material westernization has been accompanied by a violent reaction against the spiritual side of Western civilization and a characteristic revival of Indian nationalism.

THE BRITISH AND THE INDIAN CASTE SYSTEM

The British government's passion for labels has led to a crystalliza-tion of the caste system, which, except among the aristocratic castes, was really very fluid under indigenous rule. The dethrone-ment of caste as a unit of the administration of justice was counter-acted by tendencies of the British government to use caste as a means of effective control of India.

EARLY IN the history of the British rule the practice of the rulers over the three Presidencies was not uniform. In Bengal one of the Regulations, while recognizing the integrity of caste organi-zation, allowed suits for restoration of caste to be entertained by the ordinary courts. It was held that cases of expulsion from clubs or voluntary associations were of an entirely different nature from excom-munication from caste. In Bombay, however, the pertinent regulation expressly provides that no court shall interfere in any caste question. . . . Social privileges of the membership of a caste are held to be wholly within the jurisdiction of the caste. It is only when a com-plainant alleges that a legal right either of property or of office is vio-lated by his exclusion from the caste that a suit may be entertained by a court of law. This autonomy of caste, it is further held, exists only under the law and not against it. Hence caste-proceedings must be according to usage, giving reasonable opportunity of explanation to the person concerned and must not be influenced by malice.

This recognition of the integrity of caste for internal affairs did not protect the institution from inroads on some of its very vital powers. The establishment of British courts, administering a uniform criminal law, removed from the purview of caste many matters that used to be erstwhile adjudicated on by it. Questions of assault, adul-tery, rape, and the like were taken before the British courts for

Excerpts from G. S. Ghurye, *Caste and Race in India* (London: Kegan Paul, Trench, Trubner & Co., Ltd., 1932), pp. 149-162.

decision, and the caste councils in proportion lost their former importance. Even in matters of civil law, such as marriage, divorce, etc., though the avowed intention of the British was to be guided by caste-customs, slowly but surely various decisions of the High Courts practically set aside the authority of caste. . . .

The British Government did not recognize caste as a unit empowered to administer justice. Caste was thus shorn of one of its important functions as a community. Individual members might, therefore, be expected to feel less of the old feeling of solidarity for their caste-group. But nothing of the kind is observed to have taken place. First, though a caste could not administer justice, the Government would not set aside the customs of a caste in matters of civil law unless they were opposed to public policy. Caste thus retained its cultural integrity. Secondly, many other aspects of the British Administration like the Census, provided more than sufficient incentive for the consolidation of the caste-group. Mr. Middleton observes: "I had intended pointing out that there is a very wide revolt against the classification of occupational castes; that these castes have been largely manufactured and almost entirely preserved as separate castes by the British Government. Our land records and official documents have added iron bonds to the old rigidity of caste. Caste in itself was rigid among the higher castes, but malleable amongst the lower. We pigeon-holed everyone by caste, and if we could not find a true caste for them, labeled them with the name of an hereditary occupation. We deplore the caste-system and its effects on social and economic problems, but we are largely responsible for the system which we deplore. Left to themselves such castes as Sunar and Lonar would rapidly disappear and no one would suffer. . . . Government's passion for labels and pigeon-holes has led to a crystallization of the caste system, which, except amongst the aristocratic castes, was really very fluid under indigenous rule. . . . If the Government would ignore caste it would gradually be replaced by something very different amongst the lower castes." The situation in the Punjab, cannot be taken as typical of other provinces. It is well known that the Punjab was not much influenced by rigid caste-system. Yet the process of pigeon-holing and thus stereotyping has undoubtedly counteracted whatever good results might have ensued from the dethronement of caste as a unit of the administration of justice. The total effect has been, at the least, to keep caste-solidarity quite intact.

The relations of an individual member to a group in which he is born, and to which he is bound by ties, traditional, sentimental, and cultural, in a society where almost everyone belongs to one of such groups, and none can hope to have any respectable status without his group, are such that they are not susceptible to change as a result of legal enactment, administrative rules, or judicial decisions. Though caste has ceased to be a unit administering justice, yet it has not lost its hold on its individual members, who still continue to be controlled by the opinion of the caste. The picture of the control of an individual's activities by his caste, given in 1925 by an eminent social worker of Gujarat, convinces one, by its close similarity with our description of caste of the middle of the nineteenth century, that as regards at least this aspect of caste, there has been almost no change during the course of three-quarters of a century. She observes: "On our side of the country, I mean in Gujarat, the greatest hindrance to all social reforms is the caste. If I want to educate my girl, the caste would step in and say you should not do it. If I wish to postpone my children's marriage till they are sufficiently grown up, the caste would raise its hand and forbid me. If a widow chooses to marry again and settle respectably in her home the caste would threaten to ostracize her. If a young man wishes to go to Europe for bettering his own or the country's prospects, the caste would, though perhaps nowadays give him a hearty send-off, yet close its doors on him when he returns. If a respectable man of the so-considered Untouchable class is invited to a house, the caste would deliver its judgment against that householder and condemn him as unfit for any intercourse."

It must have become clear by now that the activities of the British Government have gone very little toward the solution of the problem of caste. Most of these activities, as must be evident, were dictated by prudence of administration and not by a desire to reduce the rigidity of caste, whose disadvantages were so patent to them. The most important step they have taken is the recent regulation in some of the Provinces that a definite percentage of posts in the various services shall be filled from the members of the non-Brahmin or the intermediate castes, provided they have the minimum qualifications. This was originally the demand of the leaders of the non-Brahmin movement. And it is the most obvious remedy against caste-domination. . . . The restriction on the numbers of the able members of the Brahmin and the allied castes, imposed by this resolution of the Government, penalizes some able persons simply because they happen to belong to particular castes. When in the case of certain services recruited by means of competitive examinations, some vacancies are offered to candidates who have failed to attain a particular rank in the examination, on the ground that they belong to certain castes, which must be represented in the higher services of the country, it clearly implies that even the accepted standard of qualifications and efficiency is abandoned. The result has been the pampering of caste even at the cost of efficiency and justice. The Government of Bombay, in their memorandum submitted to the Indian Statutory Commission, 1928 (p. 94), complain that the District School Boards, where the non-Brahmins have had a majority, "have almost in every case attempted to oust the Brahmins regardless of all consideration of efficiency." Yet this action is only a logical development of the attitude of the Government which nursed, rather than ignored, the spirit of caste.

On the whole, the British rulers of India, who have throughout professed to be the trustees of the welfare of the country, never seem to have given much thought to the problem of caste, in so far as it affects the nationhood of India. Nor have they shown willingness to take a bold step rendering caste innocuous. Their measures generally have been promulgated piecemeal and with due regard to the safety of British domination.

THE FRENCH IN INDO-CHINA

An anti-western Annamite says of the French "In your papers, in your books, in your plans, in your private conversation, there is displayed in all its intensity the profound contempt with which you overwhelm us. You not only refuse to treat us as equals but even fear to approach us as if we were filthy creatures." The sense of humiliation has led to many attacks against the French.

THE ADMINISTRATIVE technique applicable to races and civilizations conquered by more aggressive nations centers about two main policies—"direct" and "indirect" rule. "Direct" rule makes a clean sweep of all native traditions and brings into existence a group of social half-breeds who have lost the feeling of kinship to their old past yet are not completely at home in their new present. "Indirect" rule, on the other hand, attempts to retain as much as possible of native institutions and aims to introduce foreign ideas without too great a change in the local milieu.

In February, 1861, when the French took over the task of controlling the vanquished regions of Indochina, the situation appeared hopeless. The first agent appointed, Admiral Charner, discovered that all high native officials had fled at the approach of the Western forces. Owing to the absence of local agents, he was obliged to utilize his staff for administrative purposes. . . . In order to protect the new masters, a militia system was instituted which has become one of the main supporters of French rule in the peninsula.

For the first fifteen years of occupation there were frequent riots and attacks against individual French officers, but the leaderless natives were suppressed without difficulty. By 1882, however, the antiforeign movements became extensive. In September of this year, the white officials in Tonkin were menaced by mobs of peasants in the pay of high Annamite mandarins who had been ousted from their

Excerpts from Thomas E. Ennis, *French Policy and Developments in Indochina* (Chicago: The University of Chicago Press, 1936), pp. 52-58, 60-67, 71, 95-98, 109.

positions. Two years later (June 6, 1884) the emperor was punished for his recalcitrance by stripping him of his prerogatives. . . . The king of Cambodia likewise came under the sway of France. The ruler, Norodom, was discovered plotting to exterminate the French, and consequently was forced to sign a treaty on June 17, 1884, which led to the installation of foreign agents in every Cambodian province.

The destruction of imperial authority did not stop at the apex of the Indochinese pyramid. The French also wiped out native initiative within the smaller units. . . . Indochinese society had not developed along the primitive line which marks the culture of the Africans and the Australian bushmen. The Annamites, to the contrary, have been influenced profoundly by the institutions of China. The nobles and mandarins of Annam were akin in position and attributes to the Chinese of the old regime. . . .

Into this highly developed politico-social organization, the French introduced the fatal policy of assimilation. The results were disastrous. The emperor closed himself within his palace, torn between fear of the white man and grief over the repudiation of the "mandate from heaven," destroyed because of his inability to cope with Western agression. Many officials fled to China, "retired" to their homes in the interior, or encouraged revolts in the hope of restoring the Son of Heaven to his throne. In the provinces and communes there was mingled hostility and bewilderment. The natives saw subordinate mandarins laboring in unfamiliar *inspections* and *bureaux*, where the principle of separation of powers disturbed their ancient organization, in which executives acted as legislators as well as magistrates. The introduction of French law added to the confusion. In the eyes of the Indochinese it was not administered with the traditional religious basis, but was dispensed in a secular, harsh, almost inhuman manner. . . .

Ignorance and apathy regarding the empire is translated into something more powerful when encountered in Indochina itself. This is the attitude of superiority evinced by the average French official, who considers his houseboy the typical representative of Annamite civilization. From the primary schools through the higher institutions of the land, the natives learn how to observe the niceties of social intercourse, rooted in Chinese traditions. Refined courtesies are seen in action and heard in speech. In spite of these relationships, it is not unsual for a Resident to receive seated, hat on head, a *tong-doc* or mandarin of his own rank in the Annamite hierarchy. As a result of this affront, the dignity of the French suffers in the eyes of the people. One of the most powerful anti-Western Annamites, Phan-Tsu-Trinh, circulated a pamphlet in 1909 among the French officials of the administration which is as true today as it was when published a quarter of a century ago:

In your papers, in your books, in your plans, in your private conversations, there is displayed in all its intensity the profound contempt with which you overwhelm us. In your eyes, we are savages, dumb brutes, incapable of distinguishing between good and evil. You not only refuse to treat us as equals but even fear to approach us as if we were filthy creatures. Some of us, it is true, employed by you, still preserve a certain amount of dignity. If these submit without complaint to your constant disrespect, they are not the less grievously affected and it is a feeling of sadness and shame which fills our hearts during the evening's contemplation when we review all the humiliations endured during the day. Caught in a machine which saps our energy, we are reduced to impotency. This explains why beggars only dare show themselves in the offices of the French.

Native discontent also is caused by the idleness of the relatively highly paid white officials who have their work done by indigent local secretaries. This situation, common in other parts of Asia, but especially noticeable in Indochina, was analyzed by an educated Annamite, who stated in 1909 that he considered inequality the main root of antagonism. . . .

Although the Indochinese of the interior have forgotten the manner in which the first whites who came to the peninsula outraged their gods by quartering troops and horses in temples, there are today other matters of more importance holding their attention. These inarticulate masses hear that roads and bridges and public buildings and great dams are being constructed with their money. Impatience, and even in Asia there is a limit to waiting, grows into mistrust, because such things are done only for the folk of the cities, under the management of "white mandarins" and some of their own kin who have wandered away and forgotten home ties.

The dwellers in rural communities are not the only ones to react in this manner to modernity. The city intelligentsia also feel that progress in the land is accomplished for the exclusive benefit of the French, that the taxes which they pay profit none but the white masters, and that the farmers, constituting 80 per cent of the population, are not given sufficient aid by the administration. . . .

The sense of humiliation, owing to a loss of self-respect which was brought about by the whites taking over the responsible administrative posts of the country, has led to many attacks against the French. (About 200 British missionaries of India similarly issued a manifesto in 1930 in which they stated that the cause of most of the insurrections is found in the realization on the part of the Indians that all authority and prestige lies with the English. This group also declared that no settlement can be satisfactory which does not make for recovery of national self-esteem.) The first revolts against French authority were not as well organized as those since 1912 but were more violent and led to greater loss of life because the natives believed at this time that their civilization could be saved from being thrust into the background. . . . These acts, together with those planned in China, such as that of Gilbert Chien in 1909, were not in themselves powerful enough to get beyond the control of bayonets, but they represented the feeling of the natives.

One of the elements of discontent, exclusive of the general sentiment that no longer are the Indochinese allowed to govern the land, is caused by the inequitable fiscal organization and taxation evasions. The taxes feeding the provincial and village budgets are joined to those which make up the general budgets. It is impossible, however, to determine the aggregate in the cantonal and communal units. Consequently, the mandarins take advantage of this weakness in the system and keep for themselves large sums intended for the general treasury. The Indochinese officials always have extracted money from the people. Before the coming of the French, "squeezes" were tolerated, because most of the amounts thus obtained remained in the area of taxation for the construction of governmental residences, purchase of food, construction of roads, etc. Today this has changed, and the French are demanding that the mandarins submit lists of money collected from the cantons and communes. In order to retain their "revenues" and satisfy their superiors, the authorities are obliged to exact higher payments from the natives. Of these remittances, little is left in the locality taxed but goes to defray the expenses of administrative areas never visited by the average Indochinese. As a result, they feel themselves doubly cheated—by their own officials, to whom they allow certain "privileges," and by the French, for whom they have slight regard. The consciousness of being ground between the stones of local greed and Western efficiency thus prompts rebellion.

Another source of discord was caused (in the past, at least) by the refusal of many Europeans to pay taxes. In Cochinchina, where the whites are concentrated, many anti-French demonstrations have been motivated by the flagrant favoritism of tax-collectors. Messimy wrote in 1910 that

there is a peculiar attitude displayed by the "whites" toward the "yellows." In contact with peoples of another race, to whom we have come as conquerors, most of the French regard themselves as members of a privileged aristocracy. In the eyes of these Europeans, the main appendage of this nobility rests upon tax exemption. Let us be careful. It is not for colonists, and above all, those in Indochina, to revive the privileges which ceased to exist in France after the night of August 4, 1789.

One of the most confusing situations, brought about by the French in their administration of Indochina, is due to the promulgation of Western law. The family being the basis for legal practices in the Orient, the father becomes the judge for altercations arising within this unit. In all questions between different families the notables act as arbiters. These relationships have been destroyed with the advent of French law. The features of Western jurisprudence, such as leases, contracts, special legal agents, and definite statutes have made unavailing the personal touch of family heads and notables. The natives have become confused and know not where to turn, viewing with consternation the abolition of their time-honored principles. Unlike the French magistrate, the Annamite chief legal official possesses no absolute institutional character but has one distinctly social or functional. It is natural in Indochina, for the agent most capable of conserving this attribute to be the mandarin who administers, because he alone knows the life of the villagers and, consequently, can arrive at an equitable decision. In a country where the plans of the French have destroyed the oriental patriarchal state in order to bring into being occidental organisms, the importance of the legislator-judge has been disregarded. . . .

French naturalization laws constitute another cause for dissolution of the Annamite family. It has been impossible to reconcile French citizenship and Indochinese mores. Problems arise continually in which an Annamite ex-soldier, naturalized for services to the Republic, appears before an administrator, with claims for citizenship clearly proved. The official discovers that he is married to two women, according to Annamite traditions. In order to satisfy the French, he must relinquish one of the wives. If he does not consent to this ruling, his children are classified as illegitimate and are prevented from inheriting his property. The Eurasian problem also is becoming serious in the French colonies. Half-breeds are the leaders of many revolts, owing to their abject status. . . . The forms of French law, however, do not stop at injuring family relations. They run also against certain minor customs and prevent the "saving of face," so precious to all Orientals. . . .

As a result of a very large number of white officials and insufficient pay of natives, the Indochinese have fallen into the pitfall of "rugged individualism." The reason for this change is not difficult to determine. Debarred from governmental posts worthy of their traditional background and refusing to labor for a pittance, the more aggressive are entering business, accumulating private fortunes, and introducing into the land a new power—the power of money, which becomes the source of ultra-individualism. In this manner their oriental milieu is being undermined. Until the coming of the French, the Indochinese had no distinct value as an individual. All his customs and institutions tended to absorb him in the collective body, with personal ambitions subordinated to the dictates of the family. The material, intellectual, and moral forces were held thus under restraint. The French have weakened this collective tie, which has resulted in the appearance of large numbers who possess no interest in serving the state, as did their ancestors, and direct their energies toward the acquisition of personal wealth.

How long will these bourgeoisie be content to merely accumulate

money, without utilizing portions of it to instigate anti-French revolts? . . .

During the "rule of the admirals" (1861-79), . . . the natives
were impressed with the force and persistency of Western imperialism.
However, with the diminution of widespread opposition, the French
government realized that anti-foreign opinion might be placated by
the institution of a non-military regime. Accordingly, in 1879 a civilian
administration was created which substituted assimilation for subjection.

The principle of assimilation was not new. It came from the belief
that French civilization was the highest and most perfect on earth.
Condorcet's dogma was accepted that "a good law is good for all men,
just as a sound logical proposition is sound everywhere." Along with
this idea appeared Rousseau's vision of savage man, virtuous and eager
to become the equal of his white brothers. Furthermore, the French
Revolution and the Convention in the Constitution of the Year III
decreed that "the colonies are an integral part of the Republic, and
are submitted to the same constitutional laws. They are divided into
départements." The Colonial Congress, moreover, as late as 1889, gave
expression to assimilation and, with but one dissenting voice, declared
that French provinces, *arrondissements,* and communes could be suitably duplicated in every colony. These ideals, to which was joined the
exalted mysticism of Louis Madelin's "Our race is expansive," thrilled
the French when they gazed upon the transformation of dirty Asian
and African streets into spotless Parisian boulevards. Reflections of
such a character had a strong economic background.

By the end of the nineteenth century, industrial nations were in
need of markets, in order to counteract the high protective tariffs of
Germany and the United States. No nation, however, could expect
to be a world-power without possessions overseas. Colonies were able
to absorb the goods manufactured by the mother-countries. They were
capable also of supplying merchant vessels, and their allies, warships,
with coaling stations. Jules Ferry expressed these sentiments in 1890,
when he said that

the colonial policy is the daughter of the industrial policy. . . . The
European powers of consumption are saturated. New masses of consumers

must be made to arise in other parts of the world, else bankruptcy faces modern society and the time will approach for a cataclysmic social liquidation of which we cannot calculate the consequences.

The assimilative policy was introduced into Algeria about 1830 and did not prove to be disastrous when it shattered tribal customs. Applied, as it was later, to Indochina, anarchy was produced because Indochina is no primitive settlement but a highly developed civilization. Fortunately for the continued progress of Western control, by the end of the nineteenth century imperialism had learned some lessons from Asiatic failures. . . . Instead of the "noble savage," a "back-to-the-native" movement was started. This took the form of association. . . .

These opinions were voiced in June, 1901, before Parliament by Waldeck-Rousseau, when he said that "each should develop in his own civilization." This policy also was in harmony with the tendencies of economic development. Many leaders of industry now realized that assimilation was incapable of winning the natives to the ways and goods of the white man. They felt that association, in time, would increase the respect of "backward" peoples for the "progressive whites" and eventually enhance the sale of factory articles, made possible through the judicious application of Western capital in every region suitable for the construction of railroads and factories. Association also was hastened by the growth of labor and socialistic organizations.

The first signs of opposition to the French technique of assimilative imperialism were evident in 1876, when trade-union bodies convened for an international conference in Paris. For the first time since the defeat of the Paris Commune in 1871, anti-imperialistic and anti-capitalistic movements disturbed the vested interests. Socialistic agitations grew with the return from exile of the old Communards and the release from prison of Blanqui in 1879. National and municipal elections were contested by Socialist candidates, who criticized the government for its colonial methods. Led by the "Tiger," Clemenceau, sentiments were expressed which held up to ridicule the Republic's expensive overseas experiments. Consequently, the French government was obliged to compromise in order to retain power, doing so by modifying imperialism, by rounding its sharp edges, by toning down its garish colors of a Manchester and a Marseilles into the soft ink-brush strokes of a Peiping and a Penang. And so, association of the East and West in the great work of making the world bigger and better became the motif of empire-building. . . .

The French sincerely believe that association in time will eliminate opposition to white control. They reason that even left-wing factions will be confined to impotent anti-French fulminations and that all their promises of better days will fall unheeded upon the Indochinese, enjoying a "jug of wine and a loaf of bread" under sympathetic masters. . . . The French think that Indochina will furnish about one-fourth of the armed forces needed in future conflicts, provided the natives are taken as associates in the development of the land. The acceptance of association by the Republic is felt to be the cure for recalcitrance, in view of the fact that more opportunities are being offered every year for the educated natives. Furthermore, the French already see signs that point to the region as becoming the most perfect colony on earth, where the nationalistic utterance of "Indochina for the Indochinese" is being diverted into the more reasonable channel of an entente between East and West.

THE DILEMMAS OF COLONIAL POLICY

During the periods of trading and the commercial and imperialist exploitation of Africa, European nations paid little heed to native welfare in their colonies.

UNTIL THE closing years of the nineteenth century native policy in Africa, which during its earlier stages had displayed many similarities to that prevailing in other spheres of colonial and imperialistic exploitation, continued to be in the main spasmodic and incoherent, manifesting pronounced variations both as between regions and within a given area. Around the turn of the century a significant revolution was initiated by English and French colonial administra-

Excerpts from Stephen H. Roberts, "Native Policy," in *Encyclopaedia of the Social Sciences*, Vol. 11 (New York: The Macmillan Company, 1933), pp. 273-275, 276-279.

tors, but despite their several efforts in the direction of a more co-ordinated and far sighted policy, designed to carry into effect the untried principles of association and indirect rule, not a few of the basic dilemmas have persisted. For no other continent possesses such a congeries of races at different stages of development or has been subject to such varying degrees of European penetration. The policy of the French toward the Hamito-Semitic peoples in the Moslem countries along the Mediterranean fringe shows marked divergences from the Boer and the British treatment of the strikingly homogeneous Bantu races in southern Africa; while the general economic exploitation carried on by the representatives of France, Belgium, Germany, Great Britain, Italy and Portugal against the heterogeneous tribes scattered over the center of the continent and constituting what is generally referred to as black man's Africa involved, especially after "the grab for Africa" in the 1870's, still a third set of problems. Despite these disparities, however, a few broader trends of policy may be detected, particularly in northern and central Africa.

For more than half a century after the occupation of Algiers in 1830 the French colonial administrators concentrated their military strength on breaking the resistance of the virile Arab and Berber tribesmen. Tribal organization and institutions were viewed as barbaric survivals, and in the slow process of driving back the natives to the borders of west and central Africa the methods of *cantonnement* and *refoulement* became generally accepted. Committed to a program of progressive annihilation, the military forces aimed at segregation based on continuous withdrawal. Islam was attacked root and branch; native lands and religious *habous* were confiscated; and tribal organization was destroyed. Even an intelligent theorist like Leroy-Beaulieu said that the three bases of native life—the tribe, collective property and the polygamous family—had to be wiped out. This policy was carried out not only in the Algerian Tell but in the occupied parts of the Congo and west Africa, except in four privileged Senegalese communes where the natives were all enfranchised.

The vast extent of territory which had been acquired in northern and central Africa by 1890 made the French pause. The humanitarian and rationalistic temper of eighteenth century France was beginning to emerge once more, reshaping French policy according to older patterns. Invoking again the time-honored shibboleth of natural rights, the Colonial Congress of 1889 proclaimed the policy of assimilation as the new order of the day for Africa. Since French civilization constituted beyond cavil the quintessence of life, it devolved upon responsible administrators to convert "the absolute man," whom the philosophers had created to include even the least gallicized savage of Africa and the Pacific, into a model Parisian. Logic and reason could tolerate no alternative, and despite the opposition of Gustave Le Bon the Congress agreed to ignore such aberrations as racial endowment, ancestral tradition and geographical peculiarities. The colonies were to be French departments; the French local commune was to be introduced; and the natives were to be encouraged to become French citizens. Algeria and the Congo were to have the same organization, however great the differences in native society. The only exception was to be Tunisia, where the peculiar status of the protectorate of 1881 limited French efforts.

The results soon became clear in all of French Africa. In most of the colonies the system could be applied only at the expense of ruthless destruction of native organizations. An attack on one part of a closely interrelated native structure usually meant the collapse of the whole. Uncongenial institutions, such as fee simple and individualization, were introduced in flat defiance of the maxim that a race can evolve only in conformity with its own traditions and mentality. The 1890's witnessed the nadir of French native policy in Africa. The Arabs refused to renounce Mohammedanism: those of the coast obtained a veneer of civilization but the dwellers in the interior watched the destruction of their own tribal institutions and laws with smoldering apathy. In the northern colonies the French encountered all the difficulties involved in attacking a polity wherein state and society were linked with religion; while in the Negro lands of central Africa the development was still more premature and the goal still more unwise.

Around the turn of the century, however, evidences of the breakdown of the older system were becoming increasingly apparent not only in practice but also in theory. Practical experts . . . protested . . . against the stupidity of assimilation as applied to the natives of Africa. Cambon's success in preserving native institutions in Tunisia had brought into more striking relief the maladministration and de-population resulting from assimilation in such areas as Algeria, the Congo, Madagascar and West Africa. On the other hand, the evils of the old policy of uncontrolled exploitation were dramatically re-vealed in the scandals involving the French Congo, where in the 1890's the natives had been terrorized and enslaved under a company regime ruthlessly engaged in draining the country of its ivory and "red rubber." Attention began to be directed to the experience of the Malagasian Horas, the Tunisians and the mountain Berbers of Algeria, all of whom had been allowed to preserve their native institutions. . . . Whereas the Colonial Congress of 1900 had contented itself with adopting a skeptical attitude toward assimilation, the Congress of 1906 openly repudiated the older policy in favor of the new theory of association which is defined as "the systematic rejection of assimila-tion, and tends to substitute for the necessarily rigid and oppressive system of direct administration that of indirect rule, with a conserva-tion—albeit a well watched and well directed conservation—of the institutions of the subject people, and with a respect for its past." . . . "Each in his own civilization!" was the slogan, and after the reform of the Congo in 1907 each African colony saw the strengthening of native councils and other agencies. Along with these changes went an emphasis on the new moral values of colonization and a striking development of native plantations—in other words, economic as well as political association.

The Belgians had practically repeated the French experience, first in the indiscriminate destruction of native life in the Congo, then in the awakening of national conscience by the scandals to which it gave rise and, finally, in the turn toward native co-operation. Unfortunately the destruction of the chiefs' system had been too complete, so that by 1917 the Belgian officials stood face to face with a native rabble. This very extremity emphasized the failure and led the colonial min-ister to announce in 1920: "We claim that the native society should freely develop after its own manner, its own nature, its own *milieu*. We must respect and develop native institutions, and not—as hereto-fore—break them." Another factor was the new concept of colonization as primarily an industrial process—a concept which involved a pros-perous native population as an essential contributory element.

The German experience had been a mixed one. Being comparatively late in the race, they obtained the poorer lands. Moreover they were not at first concerned with human values, so that they carried the French and Belgian theory of exploitation to its extremes. The colonies were factories, handed over to concessionaire companies; and the natives were so ground down that frequent revolts occurred in southwest Africa, in the Cameroons and in east Africa. . . .

During the earlier periods of trading and the commercial and imperialistic exploitation of central Africa, Great Britain, like France, paid little heed to native welfare. . . .

The situation which the British faced in southern Africa was particularly complex. In the first place, a less highly developed European population, composed of Boers, outnumbered the British in every province but Natal. There were five natives to every white, unevenly distributed and with sharp differences between those living in towns, mines and farms. Moreover each province had a different policy toward the natives, the divergence being particularly marked as between the older British colonies and the former Boer republics. The existing confusion was still further aggravated by the policy of compromise pursued by the Union government in its handling of the native problem. As time went on, a population of poor whites emerged, numbering as high as 10 per cent of the whole and living side by side with the natives; while another distinct element of half castes called the Cape colored people was made up mostly of European-Hottentot mixtures. Then there were certain outer lands, such as Bechuanaland, Basutoland and Swaziland, set aside for the natives and presenting problems distinct from although influenced by those of the industrialized areas. Finally, the needs of a rapid partial industrialization led to grave interferences with all classes of natives and to the introduction of Portuguese East African natives and 170,000 Indians.

The problems of contact between the various races center mainly around the 900,000 natives who live on "urban locations" in town areas and the hundreds of thousands employed in the mines, particularly in the Transvaal. Both of these groups are divorced from the normal conditions of native life in South Africa—the life of small cultivators and herdsmen; and both represent the economic thrust outward due to the fact that there is not enough good land to provide sufficient food for all. Both present somewhat similar problems. Those natives who live on the special locations set aside for them in the towns suffer from improper housing, abnormal sex relations, epidemics and illicit liquor traffic, evils which have social repercussions on the other inhabitants of the towns. All of these conditions are present also among the mine boys, with the added complications arising from the system of recruiting and control. Since the recruiting of natives living on European farms is virtually forbidden by law, the mines depend on labor supplies from outside the Union provinces: a third of the Transvaal laborers come from Portuguese East Africa, half from the Transkei and a tenth from Basutoland. The drain is partly on foreign lands, but mainly on those very regions in which special efforts are being made to bring about native regeneration. The laborers are recruited under a contract which compels them to live in compounds and renders them liable to imprisonment for desertion; and experience has shown that no system of this kind can be freed from various abuses.

All of the industrialized natives have to face the "color bar," for the South African system is based on the existence side by side of a few overpaid whites and many underpaid natives. Since 1890 color bar legislation in the Transvaal has forbidden competition between the two sections of the population; and in 1911 a similar act, while not explicitly mentioning the color bar, secured the same result for the Union of South Africa by introducing a system of certificates to be held by all laborers using machinery. The owners wanted cheap labor and asked for a removal of the prohibition on recruiting natives north of 22°; the unions upheld the color bar and wanted a ratio "progressively favorable to the white race" in every industry except agriculture. In Parliament the Labor party fought for the color bar; the Nationalists, largely agricultural, advocated it on broader cultural grounds; while the manufacturers advanced it as an argument for high wages and high tariffs. In addition to actual legal discrimination, such as the Wage Act of 1925, a conventional color bar exists in most industries in Cape Province and Natal, and the Jim Crow principle is widely, if tacitly, assumed. In all four provinces natives have to submit to the pass system, are denied military training and cannot acquire crownland or use the Land Bank. There is a distinct racial feeling directed against the town natives by the great bulk of Europeans, who are convinced that they should remain in a state of inferiority and are inclined to use any degree of political or economic pressure to secure this result.

The same bitterness does not operate so keenly against the country natives. The problem here is one of numbers, for 5,000,000 natives are scattered through the country districts, 3,250,000 on native reserves and over 1,500,000 on European farms. All native lands were originally expropriated; but the Cape led the way in making reserves, for the most part, except in the Transkei, in small locations. Similar crown locations and mission reserves were made in Natal and most of Zululand was set aside as a trust. The Transvaal was not as liberal, and the Orange Free State took practically no steps in this direction. . . .

In recent years, however, the political question has attracted much more attention than the economic. The present policy is an anomalous one, based on historical accidents and laissez-faire, and reveals no uniformity from province to province. The Cape allows unqualified and unrestricted civil and legal equality; Natal makes certain theoretical concessions; while the other provinces confer practically no rights of this kind on natives. The Union itself represents a compromise, for when it was formed the northern provinces would not consent to the extension of rights to the natives, while the southern provinces would not consent to their penalization.

The resentment of the native population, directed at first against economic inequality, has been extended since the Boer War to the political sphere. Commissions have revealed the dissatisfaction of the Bantu at the dislocation of their customs, without compensatory privileges as enjoyed by the new race of intruders. The Zulu rising of 1906 confirmed the existence of the discontent, and the Native Affairs Commission of 1906-07 showed its urgency. The World War distracted attention from this problem, but it has since become ever more pressing. A new racial consciousness is aided by the fact that a fourth of the native children now go to school; and, although tribal and personal rivalries stand in the way, the feeling of frustration acts as a constant incentive to united action. Resenting the piecemeal or repressive policies applied to them, the natives recall skeptically Rhodes' formula of "equal rights for all civilized men south of the Zambezi." . . .

Neither a standardized native policy nor a co-ordinated movement of segregation is feasible for such a variety of social and economic conditions as prevail in the different regions of southern Africa. At the same time the natives, in their new racial consciousness, have found difficulty in comprehending the fortuitous and arbitrary divergences of policy and status as between adjacent territories. The general atmosphere of racial malaise which colors the South African native problem is, however, more intense in the case of the natives who have worked for Europeans and who themselves despise their kraal compatriots than in that of the pastoral natives on the reserves. Accordingly it is in the Free State and in the Transvaal that the question of cultural disintegration resulting from European contact is most immediate. . . .

THE OUTCOME OF EUROPEAN DOMINATION OF AFRICA

Of the Bantu as a whole it can be said that they have now been drawn permanently into the orbit of Western civilization. They do not, and probably will not, carry on that civilization in its purely European manifestations. Variations will be within the framework of a common South African civilization, shared in by both Black and White, and presenting certain peculiarities based directly upon the fact of their juxtaposition.

THE VARIOUS agents of Western civilization, and the elements they introduced into the reserves, did not appear simultaneously. The pioneers, as a rule, apart from stray hunters and travelers, were the missionaries and the traders. They introduced material culture, trade, and religion, the last generally accompanied by education. The wars so often preceding the extension of European control over the

Excerpts from I. Schapera, "Cultural Changes in Tribal Life," in *The Bantu-Speaking Tribes of South Africa. An Ethnographical Survey*, edited by I. Schapera (London: George Routledge & Sons, Ltd., 1937), pp. 357-369, 371-372, 384-387.

Native territories brought further glimpses of material culture, and new methods of fighting. The immediate concern of the Administration, this control once established, was to demarcate the occupation of land as between Europeans and Natives; to maintain law and order among the Natives, to which end it placed among them resident officials and police; and to meet through taxation the cost of the necessary machinery of government. Education, economic development, health, and similar services generally followed much later. Fairly early, too, the Natives in some areas grew accustomed to working for European farmers and other employers, the imposition of taxation aiding in the process. But the first big impetus to labor migration came with the diamond discoveries of 1869-1870, followed by extensive railway construction. The discovery of gold in the 1880's greatly increased the demand for Native labor and intensified the activities of the labor recruiters.

The European agencies differed in their policies toward the Natives. The Administration not only introduced a new form of political control, but found it necessary, in the interests of good government, to abolish the powers of the Chiefs in regard to war, foreign policy, and certain aspects of criminal jurisdiction. It refused also to tolerate ritual homicide, the punishment of sorcerers, and similar practices held to be "repugnant to the principles of natural justice and morality." In other respects the general tendency was to interfere as little as possible with Native usages, except in the Cape, where the policy was to break down rather than to perpetuate the tribal system, a tendency reversed after Union; and indeed, especially within more recent times, the avowed policy in both the Union and the High Commission Territories has been to preserve and utilize as far as possible the tribal authority of the Chiefs and the laws and customs of the people. The medical and veterinary branches, however, have all along fought against Native magic, which they find one of the greatest obstacles to the adoption of their own special services.

The basic aim of the missionaries was to convert the heathen Natives to Christianity. . . . In their zeal to introduce Christianity along European lines they wished to do away with everything savoring of heathenism. They accordingly forbade converts to practice polygamy, inheritance of widows, *lobola* (bride-price), initiation, and other heathen ceremonies, whether or not opposed to the teaching of the Gospels. Some went so far as to insist on complete abstention from drinking beer and smoking. It is only quite recently that this uncompromising attitude has on the whole been somewhat modified.

The trader aimed simply at exploiting the Natives for his own material benefit, attempting accordingly to develop as good a market as he could for his wares; while the labor recruiter tried to bring them out to work for European employers. Both were in general indifferent to tribal custom so long as it did not actively interfere with the conduct of their business. The traders, in fact, occasionally identified themselves so completely with tribal life as to cohabit with or even marry women according to Native custom, in this way incidentally adding European blood to the many other contributions Western civilization has made to the Bantu.

The Administration was generally able to impose its wishes upon the people through physical force, in the form of punishment for revolt or disobedience. The missionaries, on the other hand, had to rely upon persuasion and propaganda, and the sanctions they introduced could affect their own followers only. They, like the traders and labor recruiters, were essentially dependent upon the goodwill of the Native authorities, especially in the early days of contact. Few missionaries hesitated, however, to stand up against Chiefs or magicians who attempted to hinder their work, whereas the traders in general tried to conciliate Native opinion and avoid giving offense. Sometimes these agencies could all rely upon not only the protection but also the active co-operation of the Administration, and so act somewhat more freely; but Native goodwill always counted with them to a predominant extent.

The aspects of tribal life most immediately affected by the impact of Western civilization were economic, religious, and political. Economic life was disturbed by the introduction of European goods, by taxation, and by labor migration, as well as by the alienation of land and the new definition of tribal boundaries. In religion the difference between Christianity and ancestor-worship was sufficiently marked to make them incompatible, while the attack upon other forms of ritual was meant to produce a definite break from tribal life. Political life generally was altered by the imposition of alien rule and by the forcible diminution of the powers and functions of the Native authorities. Social organization and domestic and communal life generally were not at first directly affected, apart from the changes in marriage and other customs attempted by the missionaries. It was only after Western civilization had been present for some time that its influence extended to these other spheres as well, facilitated by the introduction or intensification of such factors as education, labor migration, and schemes of economic development.

Certain innovations the Natives had little option but to accept. . . . The superior military strength of the Europeans enabled them to force their rule upon the people and to make desired changes in administration. The long series of Native wars and rebellions show that often the Natives bitterly resented these changes, but they were powerless to prevent them. Even at the present time many administrative measures are accepted largely through fear of the consequences of disobedience.

The wares of the trader, on the other hand, were accepted readily, even eagerly, because of their general superiority to Native products. They were more durable and efficient, and could be obtained without the effort of manufacture. The goods most sought after in the early days were almost all better substitutes for corresponding Native goods —guns for spears and clubs, ploughs for hoes, and metal goods generally for Native iron, clay, and wooden implements and utensils. Ornaments, too, such as glass beads and copper or wire bracelets exercised considerable attraction and were widely adopted. This initial tendency was accentuated by the cumulative influence of missionary activity, education, labor migration, and contact with Europeans generally. By leading to a higher standard of living, they have made trade goods indispensable.

The missionaries could neither resort to compulsion nor appeal to technical superiority. But they came to the Natives at a time when there were constant frontier wars with the Europeans. Their readiness to champion the cause of the Natives made them welcome; the message they preached undoubtedly attracted many; while in later years their virtual monopoly of education, the gateway to a knowledge of English and so to a better equipment for obtaining remunerative employment, brought many willing converts. Perhaps the greatest single factor in their success, however, was the attitude of the Chief. Where he opposed Christianity, conversions were dangerous and relatively few. Where he himself accepted it, his example was generally sufficient to bring over many of his people. . . .

The personal influence of the Chief has swayed tribal opinion in regard to other aspects also. Some Chiefs opposed the introduction of European social and economic services, fearing they would lead to the disintegration and corruption of the people. Others, realizing that Western civilization had come to stay, and that "in adapting ourselves to the same civilization lay our future," eagerly accepted such elements as they thought would benefit their people. This tendency has already been noted above in regard to the welcome accorded to missionaries. For the same reason many Chiefs have supported education and promoted or encouraged schemes of economic development. Even nowadays, as most Europeans working in the reserves have found, the active support of the Chief is a powerful influence in insuring the relative success of any new measure, while his opposition or indifference invariably creates obstacles and difficulties.

Misunderstanding of innovations has all along contributed toward resistance to change. The compulsory dipping of cattle, e.g., has been interpreted by Natives in many parts of South Africa as a device to kill off their animals and so impoverish them still further; the compulsory branding of cattle in infected areas to facilitate control of their movements is resented as "marking them off as Government property"; proposals for land development are rejected for fear that if it improves too much the white man will take it away; while suggestions for the formation of farmers' associations are regarded as just another scheme for robbing the people of their money. Many other examples of a similar nature are known. The Natives have so often been imposed upon by Europeans, and in particular have been deprived of so much of their land, that they tend to regard suspiciously any proposal, even for their betterment, and to seek for some ulterior motive behind it.

Reference must finally be made to the influence of European personalities. Governments or Missions may lay down a policy, but its application rests largely with their local representative. It is to him that the Native reacts. The Native's idea of Christianity does not come so much from the Bible or from the official doctrine of the Church as from the missionary who preaches to him and who works in his area, and by the latter's conduct and treatment of his people he judges the life of a Christian. So, too, the Government is to him primarily the local official with whom he mostly comes into contact, and his ideas of European government and justice are based largely upon his dealings with this man. It is not possible, in the present state of our knowledge, to generalize about the manner in which such Europeans have affected tribal culture. But no one who has ever lived in Native areas can doubt their tremendous importance in stimulating or delaying cultural changes.

Economic life was among the first aspects of Bantu culture to be directly affected by contact with Europeans. The resultant changes are most readily found in technology. The Bantu have taken over new goods of many kinds, whereas their own domestic industries have gradually decayed. Ironwork, formerly a specialist craft, has almost wholly died out. Ploughs, hatchets, knives, and other metal implements are bought from the traders. Leatherwork has become far less important, now that blankets, clothes, and other dress materials have been introduced. . . . Pottery, basketwork, and woodwork are all becoming more restricted in practice and scope, although in Bechuanaland a new trade in wood and bone curios flourishes along the railway line. Iron cooking pots and tin cans are replacing the more fragile pots of clay; enamel basins and plates are used by many instead of baskets and wooden eating-bowls; and hardware buckets are preferred to wooden milk-pails. Good specimens of old Native work are increasingly difficult to obtain; and the occasional attempts in the schools to revive Native arts and crafts produce articles regarded only as curios. Matches have replaced the old fire-sticks; imported beads, earrings, bracelets, and other ornaments have almost completely displaced their Native counterparts; salt, tobacco, and even such foodstuffs as tea, sugar and bread, all find a ready sale. To some extent also rectangular dwellings are replacing the old circular huts, a process most marked in Southern and Western Transvaal, but noticeable everywhere. Most of these new dwellings are built, like the old huts, with earthen walls and thatched roofs, but wealthier or more important people have brick houses with corrugated iron roofs. In more progressive households one also notices beds, tables, chairs, and other European articles of furniture. The material standards of life have thus been improved, and the range of individual possession increased.

The traditional pursuits of agriculture and animal husbandry have both become more efficient. Agriculture has been improved by the widespread adoption of the plough and by the better knowledge of technique acquired through work for European farmers. . . . Almost everywhere cattle have been put to a new use as draught animals with the plough and the wagon, and new domestic animals like horses, donkeys, and pigs have been widely adopted.

The men continue to look after the cattle, assist in hut-building, and do all the work in wood and skins; while the women till the fields, build and keep in repair the huts and welling-enclosures, make pots, look after the children, and prepare the food. To this extent the traditional division of labor is maintained. But the men no longer go to war, and hunting has become of minor importance now that the game in most parts has greatly decreased. The introduction of the plough and other agricultural implements has, on the other hand, forced them to take a more considerable part in agriculture than they formerly did. The carrying of wood, crops, and water, traditionally women's work, is now occasionally done by the men with animal transport. Moreover, many new crafts and occupations have been introduced. The government employs Native clerks, interpreters, orderlies, agricultural demonstrators, and policemen; the Missions have introduced the vocations of clergyman and evangelist; the hospitals and medical practitioners train and employ nurses and dispensers; education has created a small class of teachers, both male and female; the local European residents employ store assistants, domestic servants, and cattle herds; the Chiefs have their secretaries and chauffeurs; and some people work for themselves as traders, transport riders, builders, carpenters, licensed butchers and bakers, tailors and dressmakers, and itinerant hawkers. Most of them still herd cattle and plough in their spare time, or rely upon their families or hire people to do so for them. The new activities in which they are also engaged constitute a subsidiary even if important source of income. But others have come to rely almost entirely upon their new occupation for means of subsistence.

Progress, however, has not everywhere been as marked as these facts would suggest. Relatively few people have taken full advantage of the new farming methods. Suspicion of innovations, the recency in most areas of Government encouragement, and sheer inertia have caused the great majority to lag behind. What little progress they may actually have made is due more to active pressure from without than to enlightened self-interest. Outside the Cape the communal system of land tenure still persists; ploughing in many reserves is badly done, neither manuring nor rotation of crops is practiced, very few new crops have been brought under cultivation, and little attempt has been made to introduce seed of better quality. Cattle are still regarded primarily as an index of wealth and a source of prestige. Far more value is accordingly attached to their number than to their quality. This tendency, coupled with the marked shortage of land due to the expansion of European settlement, has resulted very widely in overstocking, with consequent underfeeding and still further deterioration in quality.

In many parts of South Africa, in fact, the Bantu are no longer able to provide sufficient food for their own needs. . . .

Native agricultural produce nowadays not merely supplies food for the household, but must also be sold to satisfy new wants. The Natives, as we have just seen, now buy far more goods from the traders than they make themselves. In addition, they have everywhere been obliged to pay an annual money tax to the Administration, an experience to which they had not previously been accustomed. In many parts, too, the Chiefs or other authorities have taken to raising levies in cash for such tribal purposes as purchasing land or building schools and churches. Church dues, school fees, and similar small obligations must also be paid in cash. To obtain this the Native has had to pass from a subsistence into a money economy.

Labor migration has come to play a prominent part in tribal life. The need for money, the shortage of land, the activities of the recruiters, and a growing desire to escape from parental control or to experience adventure and change have all contributed toward converting many tribal Natives into temporary wage-earners outside their homes. . . . Of recent years, too, women also have begun going out to work, despite the almost universal disapproval of both the Administration and the tribe as a whole. Many men go to European farms surrounding their reserves, where they do work to which they are accustomed at home. But the great majority go to the towns. Here they generally work on the mines, railways, factories, or other industrial undertakings, thus engaging in labor of a completely new type. A fair number, however, enter into domestic service, which although conflicting with all tribal ideas about the proper division of labor between the sexes appeals to them as being light work, comparatively well paid, and providing plenty of food.

The sale of their labor enables the tribal Natives to maintain the standard of living to which they have attained. Without the income obtained in this way they would be far poorer than they actually are. On the other hand, through it the tribe loses the people who remain away permanently; agriculture suffers from the lengthening absence of able-bodied men; and many other aspects of tribal life have been profoundly affected by the new experiences encountered in the towns.

Cultural changes have, of course, been most marked in the tribes which have officially embraced Christianity. Among the Kxatla of Bechuanaland, e.g., little active trace now remains of the old tribal religion. . . . Marriage, death, and other domestic rites have been considerably modified by the intrusion of Christian elements and the decay of traditional practices. The Chief no longer plays an outstanding part in ritual life, and almost all of the great tribal ceremonies for which he was formerly responsible have been discarded. Christianity has introduced Churches and a completely new ritual; it has made Sunday a compulsory day of rest for all members of the tribe; it has created new sanctions for the behavior of Church members; and its hymns have profoundly affected traditional music. The missionary himself has become not only the tribal priest, but also the guide and adviser of the people in many spheres of life remote from religion.

Where the Chief himself has not yet accepted Christianity, and where consequently the great bulk of the people still follow him in adherence to the old tribal religion, the main effect of missionary activities has been to divide the tribe into two camps. Church members not only have their worship to distinguish them. They must also conform to the social and moral ideals preached by the missionary, dress in a "respectable" manner, and abstain from certain tribal customs regarded as incompatible with true Christianity. The conflict of loyalties thus entailed is often painful; but despite occasional relapses, the effect generally is to heighten the devotion of the converts to their new faith. Nevertheless, considerable ill-feeling may prevail between them and the pagans, resulting at times in political dissension. The missionary himself is often regarded as an enemy whose activities disturb the unity of the tribe; but many instances are also known where the Chief, although rejecting his teaching, welcomes his assistance and advice in dealings with other Europeans.

Despite its rapid progress in some tribes, the Christianity of most Bantu is by no means deeply rooted. It is on the whole too recent an innovation to compel loyalty through tradition or sentiment. . . .

Christianity has not only in many cases provided an acceptable substitute for the old tribal religion, but has even created separate Bantu Churches reproducing European doctrines and organization. On the other hand, it has had little effect upon traditional magical beliefs and practices. These persist strongly, even among many professing Christians; . . . Christianity for the average tribesman is too remote from the realities of economic and domestic life to prove an acceptable substitute; and modern scientific teaching, although explaining more satisfactorily the causes of disease and economic welfare, is too recent an innovation and too limited in its scope to have been able to make much headway as yet against the traditional system of ideas underlying the belief in the efficacy of magic. . . .

New lines of difference are also becoming apparent between the sexes. The men have on the whole been more exposed to European influence, owing mainly to labor migration. They have accordingly tended more readily than the women to discard traditional practices. But the women have taken much more readily to Christianity, and almost everywhere, too, girls greatly outnumber boys in the tribal schools, for their domestic duties do not hinder them from attending school regularly, while the boys are in many cases needed to herd the cattle. As a result, women have not only improved their homes and acquired new standards of dress and cleanliness: they have also become more confident and independent in their attitude toward the men, and less willing to submit to their absolute control. Labor migration, by drawing the men away from home for lengthy periods, has increased the domestic responsibility of the women as well as their spirit of freedom. Many women, too, owing to the new avenues of employment now open to them, are becoming economically independent of their menfolk. Recognition has been given to this fact in the Union, where unmarried women can under certain conditions become legally emancipated from the control of their family head. But in the High Commission Territories their lifelong legal dependence still persists. Women, finally, still have no share in the public administration of tribal affairs, but "as teachers, nurses, and church-workers (they) play a large part in education and in leading public opinion."

Communal life generally, particularly in Christianized tribes, has lost much of its old excitements. Little has so far taken their place. Children, it is true, still have their games, old and new, and their moonlight dances and songs, while civilization has given them schools and more recently various forms of youth movement to absorb some of their energy. But for adults most of the old public ceremonies and entertainments have gone. The men no longer go to war or hunt. Domestic work is monotonous and unexacting, and with the decay of home industries many old occupations have been lost, while relatively few people have taken on new work at home. Labor migration, the principal new activity, draws away most of the young men and even some of the young women, thus creating a prominent gap in social life. The activities of the Church provide some diversion from every-day occupation; but for most people the principal alternative is loung-ing and gossip by day, with the trading stores as convenient centers of gathering, while at night there is often little to do but sit over the beer pots or indulge in sexual intrigues. In pagan tribes the change has not been so marked. Sufficient of the old ceremonial survives to give color to life; but even this soon appears tame to men who have experienced the bustle and variety of an urban environment. As we have already remarked, it is not merely economic necessity that draws them abroad, but also the desire for adventure and change.

Reviewing summarily the effects of European contact upon the old culture of the Bantu, one may perhaps venture upon certain broad generalizations. Some contrast may first be drawn between Christian-ized and pagan tribes. The culture of the former at the present time is not the traditional Bantu culture of their ancestors, nor is it the civilization of the European inhabitants of South Africa. It includes elements of both. But they have been combined into a new and distinctive pattern. The Native living under this new form of culture is no longer conscious of a sharp breach between Bantu and European elements, as were his grandfather and even his father. It is true that the few Europeans living in his reserve differ from him in skin color, mode of life, and cultural allegiance. But the institutions they represent are now fully part of the tribal culture. Christianity is the tribal religion, the trading store an essential part of economic life, and the Administration an integral part of the existing political system. The school is even more conspicuously part of the routine system of education, in that all the teachers in the reserves are themselves Natives. All these new elements have been incorporated into the tribal culture, in some cases enriching it, in others replacing corresponding elements formerly existent. The modern culture also displays far more variations in detail than its purely Bantu predecessor. But these variations, whether in marriage or in belief, in morals or in economic life, now exist within a single cultural whole, and no longer reflect two different cultures in opposition. The tribe is a single unit whose members do not feel themselves sharply divided.

In pagan tribes, a considerable majority, conflict between the old and the new is still observable. Many are in a comparatively "raw" state, in which it is possible to find the traditional Bantu culture functioning with but little disturbance. In others religious differences sharply divide the people, a division reflected also in education, clothing, and other aspects of culture. Even here, however, labor migration, taxation, and the trader have brought most of the people within the workings of the European economic system, while the European Government dominates over them all. In the High Commission Territories the Native political institutions retain sufficient authority and jurisdiction to bolster up much of the old culture, although evidence is not wanting of increasing Administrative intervention. In the Union, on the other hand, political and legal changes have been so extensive that tribal administration must now be regarded as part of the general governmental system of the country.

Of the Bantu as a whole it can be said that they have now been drawn permanently into the orbit of Western civilization. They do not, and probably will not, carry on that civilization in its purely European manifestations. It is more likely that in certain directions at least they will develop their own local variations. But these variations will be within the framework of a common South African civilization, shared in by both Black and White, and presenting certain peculiarities based directly upon the fact of their juxtaposition. Already such a civilization is developing, a civilization in which the Europeans at present occupy the position of a race-proud and privileged aristocracy, while the Natives, although economically indispensable, are confined to a menial status from which few of them are able to emerge with success. There has grown up among the Europeans an ideal of race purity and race dominance, according to which the integrity of White blood and White civilization must be maintained at all costs. And so we find special legislation and usages of social intercourse directed on the one hand against miscegenation and on the other erecting artificial barriers against the cultural advancement of the Blacks. But despite all this, the Bantu are being drawn more and more into the common cultural life of South Africa.

14

MINORITIES IN EUROPE

THE MINORITY problems of Europe focus on the development
and policies of the national state. The identification of the cultural
tradition, institutions and often the language of a dominant majority
group with the political unity and entity of the "nation" has caused
serious minority repression and oppression. The grave cultural and
political conflict of the minorities has thus arisen in Europe. Although most acute in Eastern and Southeastern Europe, the existence
of minorities with divergent cultural and ethnic strains, imbedded in
the political nations, is almost universal throughout Europe. Few nations are without a national minority problem. They have been sporadically acute in Britain, with the Irish question and to a lesser degree,
with the Scotch and Welsh, in Belgium as between the French,
Walloon and Flemish populations, and in Germany on both the
south and the east. But the storm centers of the minority issue have
been the Central European residue of the Austro-Hungarian Empire,
and Poland, Western Russia and the Balkans.

In this maze of interpenetrating and overlapping areas of mixed
populations, the exigencies of political statehood have produced unstable political and cultural alignments, which have tended to get out
of balance increasingly with every successive political move in the
Balkans and Central Europe. In this area there are at least forty
million of such dispersed and politically disunited minority peoples,
running from small but ethnically tenacious units of twenty thousand
to huge sub-national groups of from one to six millions. For this
reason, Central and Eastern Europe and its ethnic tensions has been
and remains politically and economically critical for all European
civilization.

As MacCartney points out, ethnic and political frontiers seldom coincide, and political nationalism complicates this situation by linking one culture, language and set of majority interests to the political power and prestige of the state. Under this policy, divergent ethnic and cultural groups are then relegated to subordinate status. Their traditional culture has been disparaged or segregated, and a minority grievance movement provoked. Historical political enmities have played their part in these minority-majority antagonisms, but primarily it has been the minority suppression that has kept alive and intensified the issue. The minority groups proceed to take refuge in the common bond of their native language and tradition, and, after an interval of cultural reassertion and nationalism, develop ambitions for political independence or irredentist reunion with some larger political group of like language, tradition and culture. These political ambitions accentuate the clash with the dominant state, and repressive measures and a characteristic minority situation ensue. Cultural survivals and nationalist traditions which were tolerated in the initial stages of minority subordination are, then, rigidly suppressed, often by legal enactment. Deliberate steps are finally taken for the forced denationalization of the belligerent minority.

Sapir analyzes the role of language as an arbitrary symbol of this belligerent type of politically conceived state nationalism. On both sides, it is seized upon as a convenient and obvious mark of cultural difference. The dominant group tries to suppress the minority group language, often by prohibition of its use for official and educational activities, and tries to hinder its revival after suppression. Thus in most of the European minority situations, language has come to play the role of the preferred nationality symbol, and as a result, with cultural hostilities provoked, many common institutional affiliations between the two groups are consequently ignored. The language myth, Sapir correctly shows, has taken its place beside the race myth in the conflict situations of modern times. This was not true, generally, before the modern era, and seems due to the arbitrary tradition heightening the emphasis on language as a symbol of political allegiance and group solidarity in the contemporary world. This tendency to use "culture, language and race as but different facets of a single social unity, which tends in turn to identify with a political

national entity" is, as Sapir says, the characteristic modern phenomenon of ethnic nationalism. Language thus becomes an instrument of
national policy, and the national language comes to express a constitutional function, the will of the majority culture to dominate
through the agency of the nation. The minority problem, under such
circumstances, intensifies in direct proportion with the intensification
of national feeling.

Many larger nations are, in fact, multi-national states, but refuse
to admit it, or to have a policy of nationalism consistent with a multi-
racial or composite ethnic character. After the dissolution of the
Austro-Hungarian Empire, MacCartney points out, in the attempt
to rectify some of the flagrant minority oppressions in Central Europe
and the Balkans, the Versailles treaty stressed the political principle
of minority self-determination, that is, statehood for considerable
minority groups, rather than the principle of cultural reciprocity and
the legal and economic protection of minorities within larger national
units. The latter, they only tried, with the minority treaties, in the
exceptional cases of heavily mixed populations. The emphasis was on
the new politically liberated minority states, which in many cases, as
Jaszi shows, incorporated other minority groups and started out as
new "majorities" to repress their former fellow-sufferers. This situation, aggravated by great shifts of populations and the political use of
legitimate minority grievances and ambitions to justify the expansion-
ist ambitions of many of the larger national states, has led to the
acutely complicated situation of Europe today.

MacCartney says: "The real root of the trouble lies in the philosophy of the national state as it is practised today in Europe. . . . Since
the whole conception of the national state implies a violation of the
principle of equality to the detriment of the minorities, the guarantee
of equality might be construed as involving the renunciation by the
state of its national character." The alternatives to this situation are
either the multi-national or racial state, with guarantees of legal protection and cultural freedom to minorities, and consequently the
abandonment of a politically dominant culture, or the step in the
other direction to the mono-racial state. Although the latter seems
contrary to current trends in the world relations of culture groups,
the totalitarian state theoretically takes just this latter position.

The uniformitarian cultural policy of the fascist state is the logical quintessence of ethnic nationalism. The "one race, one nation, one culture" criterion of contemporary German and Italian totalitarianism represents an extreme development of the modern practice of the sovereign national state, and, however apparently opposed, is based on principles involved in less extreme form in the practice of other nations. The totalitarian state theory insists upon the ethnic character of the state as basic, and thus must insist on the mono-racial formula, to the point of the distortion of all historical facts. The Frick memorandum shows this clearly. Nationalism must be final and paramount, internationalism is condemned and all interests, individual and group, must be subordinated to the unquestioned dominance of political interests. The Nazi regime has preached racialism from the very beginning, as well as the doctrine of specific races as bearers of specific cultures. Language and blood are held to be basic bonds of social unity instead of common institutions, and this leads in their logic to the justification of the expulsion or extermination of all alien minorities. But a nation could only consistently be mono-racial on the basis of ethnic solidarity and a non-expansionist program; and manifestly no large political nation in Europe conforms or can conform to either of these specifications. The practical policies of the nations professing the doctrine are far from a really thorough attempt to reconstruct themselves along these lines, as the Italian incorporation of African colonies and the German conquests of Slavs and demand for the restoration of African colonies only too clearly demonstrates.

The only other alternatives, as MacCartney observes in his discussion of the Minority Treaties and their design to guarantee cultural autonomy to minorities within the boundaries of larger political units, are the gradual absorption of minorities, which is hardly possible, particularly under minority persecution, or the profound alteration of the basis of the state, both in theory and practice. This is possible wherever the political state is not identified with cultural nationality. Switzerland is a federated state based, with considerable success and stability, on such a multi-racial, multi-lingual principle. Bulgaria, under its recent constitution, has included provisions for fully guaranteed cultural autonomy to its considerable minority populations—the Turks and the Jews. The new Turkish Constitution also has minority guarantees, including very explicit guarantees of equal women's rights.

But the widest departure from the prevailing pattern of ethnic nationalism is the Soviet program for minority cultural autonomy. Here the principle of self-determination has been incorporated into the basic structure of the state, which is considered permanently multi-national on a cultural, religious and institutional basis, and only politically and economically federated. The Webbs present an account of the historical background and working machinery of this drastic solution of a vexing problem. Russia was confronted with a vast array of peoples, who ran a wide gamut of types and forms and levels of civilization. The language situation was also extremely complex. The Tsarist regime had been associated with a policy of cultural restriction and suppression of minorities, particularly the Jews. The principle of federalism and local autonomy was chosen as the basis for the structure of the new Soviet state. Great stimulus was given to local initiative, local sense of pride and participation by the recognition of all native vernaculars, even those unwritten, and the policy of protecting native traditions and customs. The latter were not to be considered merely as quaint survivals or historical folk tradition, but were made the base of the newer programs of popular education and, as cultural traditions, were to undergo modernized developments in education and the arts. The titles of the federated states in most instances bore the name of the local minority and used the minority language as an official language.

It is no exaggeration to state that this policy represents an almost complete divorce of cultural from political nationalism. The Soviet policy and program, because of this, goes definitely beyond even the most liberal solutions of the minority problem by the democratic states, also through its direct representation of minorities as such in the structure of the national federation. The minority programs offer the possibility of stable cosmopolitan societies based upon cultural pluralism, and dependent for their functioning upon legally guaranteed minority equality. This is significant contrast to the fascist theory and practice of the mono-racial, totalitarian state. We thus have in both the reform democratic and socialist programs of legalized cultural autonomy and institutional freedom for minority sub-groups, two hopes for the resolution of minority conflict situations. For this reason, the fate of minority groups, in large measure, seems bound up with the crucial question of which forms of government and which of these cultural policies are to prevail in Europe, in all Western civilization, for that matter—those rooted in present prevailing majority precedent and privilege or that which is based upon such social experiment and reconstruction as will assure minority groups not only freedom and equal rights but cultural recognition and dignity.

NATIONALISM AND THE MINORITIES

*The closing years of the eighteenth century saw the commence-
ment of an extraordinary national revival which gradually swept
over Europe until hardly one of her nations escaped it. The purely
cultural movement of the national minorities was seldom more than
a first stage. Even the submerged nationalities speedily came to
entertain ambition to become independent political states.*

THE MODERN age was destined to see, not the final extinction
of national feeling in eastern Europe, but its triumphant and
irresistible rebirth. The forces of economic enterprise and intellectual
discontent which were changing the face of the west penetrated more
slowly and worked more feebly in the countries whose social structure
was still mainly composed of the feudal baron and the serf. Yet they
did penetrate, and the hope of liberty and equality toward which the
French intellectuals were aspiring appealed no less strongly to peoples
who had known but little of either blessing. The closing years of the
eighteenth century saw the commencement of an extraordinary
national revival which gradually swept over Europe until hardly one
of her nations escaped it. It came not merely to the Poles, the fall of
whose kingdom shocked them into a truer and more intense patriotism;
not merely to the Magyars, whose leaders had been almost content to
sell their birthright for Maria Theresa's pottage, till her less cautious
son threatened their social order with their national identity together,
and drove them into defense of both. It came almost as early to the
Czechs, who had not yet forgotten the glories of their old state; to the
Greeks, with their early intellectual life which their Turkish masters
had never attacked; to the canny Serbian merchants waxing rich on
the trade of the fat Hungarian lands. It came, hardly later, to the
Roumanians, the Slovaks, the Bulgars, whose life brought them into
intimate contact with the national aspirations of others. The longer a
nation's servitude had been, the later was its renaissance. The Slovenes
and Ruthenes hardly felt it before the middle of the nineteenth cen-

Excerpt from C. A. Macartney, *National States and National Minorities*
(London: Oxford University Press, 1934), pp. 92-96.

tury, even later the Lithuanians, Letts, Estonians, and Albanians, whose burden had been heavier and their life more primitive still. Among a few, such as the White Russians, the Lusatian Serbs, the Masurians of East Prussia, the revival is even today tentative and uncertain. . . .

It was a renaissance not less strong than that through which the English and the French had passed, and fundamentally the ambition was everywhere the same. It was the aspiration of the individual to cast off the shackles of political institutions alien to him, which kept him in servitude; to raise himself from the position of inferiority into which he had been thrust and take his place in a free community of his equals.

But what was that community? Here lay the essential difference between eastern and western Europe—a difference which was the inevitable result of the different processes of historical evolution through which they had passed. The Breton or Provençal felt himself first and foremost a Frenchman, no less than the Parisian; it was of a liberated France that he dreamed. It was far otherwise with the Slovenes, who had never known a state of their own; with the Bulgars and Roumanians, whose states had undergone such vicissitudes that their ancient political boundaries had altogether ceased to correspond with their actual conditions; with the Slovaks, who were accustomed, indeed, to the historic state of Hungary, but had never known the day when they had been anything better than underlings within that state.

The state, to most of them, was something altogether alien. But what they did possess (it was, indeed, almost the only possession of many of them) was the personal bond of their *nationality*. The very policy of deliberate differentiation to which they had been so long subjected had kept alive among them the consciousness of this tie. A Serb had never felt that he was a citizen of the Ottoman Empire; he was mere *rayah*, cattle. But he had known that he was a Serb. Now, when passive acceptance of his status had changed into pride and active ambition, all his hopes naturally were concentrated, not upon his state, but upon his nationality, and his first endeavor was to develop and strengthen that nationality.

In most cases, indeed, the national revival began as a purely cultural movement. Almost the only exception was that of the Serbs who, characteristically, fought before they thought. Elsewhere, nearly always, the first symptom of the new age was an eager delving into national history and philology; the collection of legends and folk-lore, the compilation of grammars and textbooks. So harmless did these pursuits, conducted usually by a handful of intellectuals and priests, appear that the Austrian Government of the most reactionary period, under the Emperor Francis and Metternich, actually encouraged the embryonic national movements among the Czechs and "Illyrians" (Southern Slavs) under the impression that they were thus diverting people's minds from dangerous thoughts of politics. Equally striking was the sympathy with which the efforts of the more backward nationalities to find their souls was regarded by foreign workers in the same field. The debt owed by Slavonic research to such German workers as Schlözer, Herder, Goethe, and Grimm is universally admitted. Not only did they, with their more exact methods, clear a path through jungles in which the untrained Slavonic thinkers were becoming hopelessly entangled; they warmly encouraged the Slavs in their efforts and contributed greatly to the revival of national feeling toward which those efforts were directed.

The purely cultural movement was, however, seldom more than a first stage. Almost everywhere it was accompanied by a political ambition. This did not, indeed, necessarily mean a demand for complete independence. For the submerged nationalities in the area of mixed populations simply to shake off the power of the monarch would often have meant getting rid of their chief protector and exposing themselves to the far more grievous tyranny of the dominant nationality. To the Estonian peasant, the real enemy was not the Czar but the Baltic Baron; to the Slovak, the Magyar landowner; to the Bulgar, the Greek monk. Against these more immediate enemies the submerged nations often combined with the monarch in the attempt to maintain the multi-national state, which was to some extent also supernational; and these two strange allies fought together against the attempts of the dominant nations to rid themselves of the monarch. It is this interplay of three, and sometimes four different forces (for the colonists were often there, to enter the struggle sometimes on one side, sometimes on the other), which makes the story of the modern national movement in eastern Europe so excessively complex.

But such alliances were temporary and pragmatical expedients. Even the submerged nationalities speedily came to entertain political ambitions of a sort. But unlike the nations of western Europe, unlike, even, the historic nationalities of the east—the Poles, Magyars, and (in the later stages of their national movement) the Czechs, who took as starting-point the territory which they occupied, aspiring at political independence and unification within those limits—the submerged nationalities necessarily took as their basis the physical nation. Before long they had worked out a philosophical justification for their claim that each nation should have the right to constitute an independent political state.

LANGUAGE AND NATIONAL ANTAGONISMS

While language differences have always been important symbols of cultural difference, it is only in comparatively recent times, with the exaggerated development of the ideal of the sovereign nation and with the resulting eagerness to discover linguistic symbols for this ideal of sovereignty, that language differences have taken on an implication of antagonism.

ANTHROPOLOGY MAKES a rigid distinction between ethnic units based on race, on culture and on language. It points out that these do not need to coincide in the least—that they do not, as a matter of fact, often coincide in reality. But with the increased emphasis on nationalism in modern times the question of the symbolic meaning of race and language has taken on a new significance and, whatever the scientist may say, the layman is ever inclined to see culture, language and race as but different facets of a single social unity, which he tends in turn to identify with such a political entity as England or France or Germany. . . . The important thing to hold

Excerpt from Edward Sapir, "Language," in *Encyclopaedia of the Social Sciences*, Vol. 9 (New York: The Macmillan Co., 1933), pp. 164, 166-168.

on to is that a particular language tends to become the fitting expression of a self-conscious nationality and that such a group will construct for itself in spite of all that the physical anthropologist can do, a race to which is to be attributed the mystic power of creating a language and a culture as twin expressions of its psychic peculiarities.

So far as language and race are concerned, it is true that the major races of man have tended in the past to be set off against each other by important differences of language. There is less point to this, however, than might be imagined, because the linguistic differentiations within any given race are just as far reaching as those which can be pointed out across racial lines, yet they do not at all correspond to subracial units. Even the major races are not always clearly sundered by language. This is notably the case with the Malayo-Polynesian languages, which are spoken by peoples as racially distinct as the Malays, the Polynesians and the Negroes of Melanesia. Not one of the great languages of modern man follows racial lines. French, for example, is spoken by a highly mixed population, which is largely Nordic in the north, Alpine in the center and Mediterranean in the south, each of these subraces being liberally represented in the rest of Europe.

While language differences have always been important symbols of cultural difference, it is only in comparatively recent times, with the exaggerated development of the ideal of the sovereign nation and with the resulting eagerness to discover linguistic symbols for this ideal of sovereignty, that language differences have taken on an implication of antagonism. In ancient Rome and all through medieval Europe there were plenty of cultural differences running side by side with linguistic ones, and the political status of Roman citizen or the fact of adherence to the Roman Catholic church was of vastly greater significance as a symbol of the individual's place in the world than the language or dialect which he happened to speak. It is probably altogether incorrect to maintain that language differences are responsible for national antagonisms. It would seem to be much more reasonable to suppose that a political and national unit, once definitely formed, uses a prevailing language as a symbol of its identity, whence gradually emerges the peculiarly modern feeling that every language should properly be the expression of a distinctive nationality. In earlier times there seems to have been little systematic attempt to impose the language of a conquering people on the subject people, although it happened frequently as a result of the processes implicit in the spread of culture that such a conqueror's language was gradually taken over by the dispossessed population. Witness the spread of the Romance languages and of the modern Arabic dialects. On the other hand, it seems to have happened about as frequently that the conquering group was culturally and linguistically absorbed, and that their own language disappeared without necessary danger to their privileged status. Thus foreign dynasties in China have always submitted to the superior culture of the Chinese and have taken on their language. In the same way the Moslem Moguls of India, while true to their religion, which was adopted by millions in northern India, made one of the Hindu vernaculars the basis of the great literary language of Moslem India, Hindustani. Definitely repressive attitudes toward the languages and dialects of subject peoples seem to be distinctive only of European political policy in comparatively recent times. The attempt of czarist Russia to stamp out Polish by forbidding its teaching in the schools, and the similarly repressive policy of contemporary Italy in its attempt to wipe out German from the territory recently acquired from Austria, are illuminating examples of the heightened emphasis on language as a symbol of political allegiance in the modern world.

To match these repressive measures there is the oft repeated attempt of minority groups to erect their language into the status of a fully accredited medium of cultural and literary expression. Many of these restored or semimanufactured languages have come in on the wave of resistance to exterior political or cultural hostility. Such are the Gaelic of Ireland, the Lithuanian of a recently created republic and the Hebrew of the Zionists. In other cases such languages have come in more peacefully because of a sentimental interest in local culture. Such are the modern Provençal of southern France, the Plattdeutsch of northern Germany, Frisian and the Norwegian *landsmaal*. It is doubtful whether these persistent attempts to make true culture languages of local dialects that have long ceased to be of primary literary importance can succeed in the long run. The failure of modern Provençal to hold its own and the very dubious success of Gaelic make it seem probable that following the recent tendency to resurrect minor languages will come a renewed leveling of speech more suitably expressing the internationalism which is slowly emerging. . . .

Of the linguistic changes due to the more obvious types of contact, the one which seems to have played the most important part in the history of language, is the "borrowing" of words across linguistic frontiers. This borrowing naturally goes hand in hand with cultural diffusion. An analysis of the provenience of the words of a given language is frequently an important index of the direction of cultural influence. Our English vocabulary, for instance, is very richly stratified in a cultural sense. The various layers of early Latin, medieval French, humanistic Latin and Greek and modern French borrowings constitute a fairly accurate gauge of the time, extent and nature of the various foreign cultural influences which have helped to mold English civilization. The notable lack of German loan words in English until a very recent period, as contrasted with the large number of Italian words which were adopted at the time of the Renaissance and later, is again a historically significant fact. By the diffusion of culturally important words, such as those referring to art, literature, the church, military affairs, sport and business, there have grown up important transnational vocabularies which do something to combat the isolating effect of the large number of languages which are still spoken in the modern world.

REVERSALS OF DOMINANCE IN CENTRAL EUROPE

The political morality of the oppressed nations of Central Europe changed completely when they attained a ruling position. The same nations, which carried on the most exacerbated fights through generations against foreign oppression and the system of a forcible assimilation and which denounced this system as wicked and immoral before the public opinion of the whole world, did not hesitate to apply this same system when they became rulers.

BROADLY SPEAKING we had two different types in the nationalistic movements of the [Habsburg] monarchy. One was a movement for the building-up of a complete national state advocated

Excerpts from Oscar Jaszi, *The Dissolution of the Habsburg Monarchy* (Chicago, University of Chicago Press, 1929), pp. 248-249, 250, 251, 252-253, 256, 257, 293-294, 309.

by the more advanced peoples of the monarchy who had a clear and continuous historical consciousness. Such was the aspiration of the Hungarians, of the Italians, of the Czechs, of the Poles, and of the Croats. On the other hand the smaller or less-developed national elements of the monarchy, scarcely awakened from the feudal torpor, were less ambitious in their desires and for a long time they would have been satisfied if a kind of national and administrative autonomy had been given to them. Such was the attitude, almost until the beginning of the war, of the Slovaks, the Ruthenians, the Slovenians, the Rumanians, and the German minorities of Hungary. . . .

The process of national awakening was initiated by the Habsburgs themselves though indirectly and unintentionally. In their fight against feudalism and particularism, the "enlightened absolutism" of Maria Theresa and Joseph II, . . . clearly felt the necessity of protecting the great masses of peasant population against misery and exploitation. With their eyes turned toward the great Western models and on the Prussia of Frederick the Great, they were convinced that the power of the modern state could be based only on the financial and military efficiency of the whole people. Therefore, they tried to mitigate the burden of the feudal oligarchy and the first steps were taken toward the emancipation of the serfs. At the same time they introduced the first comprehensive system of elementary education. In an economic order which began to eliminate barter economy, which endeavored to supplant the pastures with cultivated lands, which introduced new methods in agriculture, cattle-breeding, forestry, and other useful arts, the old type of illiterate bondsman became an anachronism and a new, more rational, and self-conscious type of peasantry was wanted. This could be achieved only in a system of elementary education in the mother tongue. . . . Generally speaking, we may say that enlightened absolutism made the first serious and comprehensive attack against feudal Latinity under which the national languages became servant languages whereas the Latin remained the social and diplomatic language of the nobility. At the same time the imperial policy was very anxious to educate a sufficient number of officials from all the various nations of the empire because a German administration could only be maintained in the central organs, whereas in the local administration the use of the maternal language of the people was inevitable.

This dynastic patriarchialism created a new generation of bondsmen whose cultural and economic knowledge grew more intensive, and who began to read books in their mother-tongues, who were administered more frequently by their own co-nationals, and who enjoyed the protection of the imperial power against the abuses of the feudal rule. This process of evolution had inevitably a national reaction. The serfs began to think more critically concerning their own situation. The economic and political pressure of feudal society was felt as a national exploitation. The Czech, the Slovak, the Rumanian, the Ruthenian, and the other masses of bondsmen identified the system of feudal oppression with the national oppression exercised by the German, Hungarian, or Polish upper classes. The rebellions of the serfs very often took on a national hue. On the other hand the fear and hatred of the privileged classes against the revolting serfs assumed the form of national prejudice.

In this way the educational and the cultural policy of enlightened absolutism aroused in all parts of the monarchy a certain amount of national consciousness among the backward peoples who began to awake from their nationless dream. This general awakening of national consciousness became a powerful instrument in the hands of absolutism in counterbalancing with it the influence of the more powerful nations of the monarchy by playing up the national aspirations of the oppressed peoples. There began the conscious policy of a Machiavellistic *divide et impera* based on the national divisions of the country. . . .

The imperial power, however, was soon frightened by the ghost which it awakened because the national movement proved to be a double-edged sword. It was not only an instrument of the *divide et impera* policy, but it became more and more a conscious and irresistible endeavor of all the nations to build up a constitutional type of national government. This tendency could not be reconciled with an absolutist centralized power and that is the reason that, after the short episode of the enlightened absolutism, the system of Metternich and its successors fought national democracy as bitterly as constitutional liberalism. On the other hand, the growing force of dynastical German centralization aroused inevitably a semi-national resistance of those feudal elements which the Habsburg administration menaced in their governmental independence and social privileges.

All these developments, however, were only a prologue in the history of the national consciousness. The movement gets a quicker tempo and a more powerful repercussion only in the period when, in the first half of the nineteenth century, the capitalistic process of production infiltrated more and more into the economic structure of the monarchy. . . .

The new nationally motivated middle class attacked the old institutions and aspired for a nation state, or at least for national local autonomy based on the principles of modern democracy. Parallel to this process the social unrest of the peasantry grew more and more dangerous because a higher type of agriculture and a more developed civic consciousness was entirely incompatible with the old institutions of bondage.

Under such circumstances the position of the former feudal elements became precarious. The peasantry assailed their estates and manorial rights, the new middle class in the towns their political privileges and their apathy concerning the new democratic national interests. Already at the end of the eighteenth century vehement complaints were launched against the anti-national attitude of the Czech nobility. . . .

Another important feature of the new situation was the growth of an industrial proletariat in Austria and its beginning in Hungary too. This new class concentrated in the bigger cities was less dependent in its ideology on the historical traditions of the privileged elements. Its ideology was far more social and revolutionary than national. In spite of this, as a part of the surplus population of the villages, this class, too, had a warm feeling for its native language and customs. In its general radicalism it was inclined to support the claims for a national independence and equality. As a matter of fact the industrial proletariat became a very important element of the national struggle. The concentration in the towns, an unavoidable consequence of the capitalistic system, caused an intense migratory movement in the whole monarchy. Great masses of population, which the feudal agricultural system could not employ, gathered in the manufacturing towns and often altered to a large extent their former ethnic composition. For instance in Austria, some of the former cities of a German character lost their homogeneity and important Slav minorities arose. The same process in Hungary rather favored Magyarization because the Magyars with a greater mental elasticity and more oppressed by the latifundist system, became the chief elements of the industrial migratory movement.

It was everywhere the concomitant phenomenon of capitalism that important ethnographic changes occurred in consequence of the migratory movement of the workers. There arose new, more or less compact, national minorities or many urban agglomerations got a new ethnic majority. As a matter of fact, these new immigrants proposed claims for schools and administration in their own tongues. These quite natural aspirations aroused the uneasiness of the former ruling national groups. This antagonism became an important factor in political struggles. The defense of the old national character on the one hand and the establishment of a new school system and administration fit for the new linguistic needs on the other, determined the very essence of national struggles even in regions where national minorities did not aspire to a constitutional state independence. . . . .

The situation was complicated and envenomed by the fact that not only the non-German nations faced the Germans with hostility but often also acute struggles arose among the so-called oppressed nations. This observation leads us to the darkest point of the national struggles both in Austria and in Hungary. Namely we see that the same nations, which carried on the most exacerbated fights through generations against foreign oppression and the system of a forcible assimilation and which denounced this system as wicked and immoral before the public opinion of the whole world, did not hesitate to apply this same system when the wheel of history turned and they gained the ruling position. The Magyars for instance who struggled for centuries against the Austrian policy of assimilation, when they "got into the saddle" had no scruples against the application of the same methods not only toward the nationalities of the country which they regarded as inferior but also against the Croats, the national distinctness of whom was at least theoretically acknowledged. The Poles who threw the force of their indignation against the cruel system of Russian oppression refused to recognize the national independence of the Ruthenians, and brutally exercised against them Polish supremacy. The Italians, too, who themselves experienced all the sufferings of foreign oppression vindicated on their own account a ruling position over the big majority of the Croats in Dalmatia. The hatred and rivalry between the closely related Croats and Serbs was for a long time an easy means of domination for Magyar absolutism in Croatia-Slavonia.

The political morality of an oppressed nation changes completely when it attains a ruling position. The former claim for national equality easily drops into a claim for national supremacy. At the beginning of the struggle we ordinarily hear the vindication of national autonomy. Later when they become a majority they assert the political unity of the country against the former rulers now in a minority. When they acquire still more power, they begin to lay plans for the reconquest of territories for which they have a so-called historical claim but from which they were ousted by foreign rule. From here it is only a step to a naked imperialism when a victorious nation announces as its cultural and historical mission the occupation of the settlements of weaker foreign nations. . . .

The doctrine (of Magyarization, for example) repeated in various forms found its expression not only in rhetorical formulas but also under the slogan, "the fight against Pan-Slavism." Professors and students with Slav feelings were persecuted. The spirit of an intolerant Magyarization permeated more and more the whole public life. Naïve and adventurous plans were in circulation concerning the rapid and complete Magyarization of the country. Winged words of hatred were used against the nationalities envenoming the social atmosphere. ("Potato is not a food, a Slovak is not a man. . . ." "The stinking Wallachian. . . ." "The German is a rogue. . . .") The use of such and similar invectives, however, was not a specialty of the Magyars.

THE NAZI RACIALIST INTERPRETATION OF HISTORY

The Nazis state their objectives of their rewriting of cultural history in these terms: "Such contemplation of what is specifically ours leads to greater emphasis on the bond of blood which unites us to our kinsmen in neighboring regions and elsewhere abroad. It allows us to hope for increasing recognition in the kindred Germanic countries, that the Nordic peoples must feel themselves a community united by destiny upon the maintenance of which absolutely depends the existence of all higher Nordic civilization."

THE GERMAN MINISTER of the Interior, Dr. Frick, has issued a circular (under official reference number III 3120/22-6) containing "guiding ideas" for historical instruction in all German schools, and has transmitted them to all educational authorities in Germany. These "directive principles" have been issued also to the Union of Schoolbook Publishers, and are to serve as a standard for the educational authorities in forming their opinion of historical text-books submitted to them for adoption. Until the publication of these historical textbooks, which can scarcely be expected before Easter 1935, these "directive principles" are also to be regarded as guiding ideas for historical instruction in all German schools.

From prehistoric times through all subsequent millennia until the present day, the significance of race must receive due attention; for it represents the ground from which all fundamental characters both of individuals and of peoples spring.

A further point of view is the idea of nationality as opposed to the international idea, the creeping poison of which has for the last hundred years been threatening to corrode the German soul itself; for Germans are more prone than any other people to pursue dreams that are not of this world.

With the idea of nationality is intimately connected that of national citizenship. Today a full third of all Germans live outside

---

Excerpts from document on "The Teaching of History and Prehistory in Nazi Germany," in *Nature* (London: Macmillan & Co., Ltd., Feb. 24, 1934), pp. 298-299.

the frontiers of the Reich. Historical study in treating of German history must therefore not be restricted to the area comprised within Germany's frontiers, but must always keep in view the fortunes of our brethren dwelling beyond them.

In opposition to tendencies of a different trend, it is to be required that the description of conditions of life—cultural history—however important it may be for the characterization of great periods of development, shall not be given pre-eminence over the political history which shapes the fate of nations. This means bringing out the forces that make history, so that the pupil shall not be lost in the bewildering multitude of isolated events, but shall grasp the main lines and deeper connections and so be assisted in the formation of his political judgment and will.

The heroic idea in its Germanic expression, associated with the idea of leadership of our own day, that is linked with the earliest models of the Germanic past, must penetrate historical instruction at all stages. The two together with their inherent heart-stirring power arouse the enthusiasm without which the study of history may easily become for the majority of pupils a tedious accumulation of facts. The heroic idea, however, leads on directly to the heroic outlook which specifically befits us as a Germanic people, as no other does, and inspires us with ever-renewed vigor in the struggle for national self-assertion in the midst of a hostile world.

In detail, the following points are still to be noted. The textbooks are to begin with an account of the primeval history of Central Europe (the Ice Age) and show how distinct races (Neanderthal, Aurignac, Cro-Magnon) were the bearers of specific cultures. It can be shown, in primeval history already, that culture is a creation of race. This fact is only obscured, but not cancelled, by the racial mixtures of later times.

From the beginnings of prehistory (post-glacial times) the Nordic and Gaelic races spread over North and Central Europe. The principal areas of their distribution, as well as those of the remaining primary races of Europe, are to be illustrated with simple sketches. The history of Europe is the work of peoples of Nordic race; their cultural level is revealed to us not only by the relics they have left in the way of stone and bronze implements, but also by their achievements in the spiritual domain, that science can infer—not least in the highly developed Nordic (Indo-Germanic) parent tongue which has ousted (save for survivals) the languages of the remaining European races.

We take the path to Hither Asia and North Africa with the first Nordic invasions which must have taken place already in the fifth millennium B.C. This is indicated by finds of Nordic skulls in the earliest Egyptian graves and by the early-attested blonde population of the coastal region of North Africa. The racial origin of the Sumerians is still obscure, but their language permits of hundreds of comparisons with Indo-Germanic roots which could be most readily explained by the assumption of a former upper class of Nordic conquerors. A decisive influence on the history of Hither Asia was first exercised by the Indians, Medes, Persians and Hittites, originally of Nordic stock. . . . The history of the Greeks has again to begin from Central Europe. . . . The Nordic Greeks, as conquerors, formed the aristocracy in the land. Here in the south the struggle of classes was based upon a contrast of races. Both in Athens and in Sparta the full citizens constituted only a minority over against the indigenous population and the slaves; these, at least in Athens, were largely of Asiatic origin. Hence with the breaking down of class barriers by the democracy and with the unrestrained mixture of races that followed, hastened by the growing decline in birthrate the fate of the Nordic race in Greece was sealed, and the decay of Greek culture proceeded with such furious speed that in barely 200 years the Greek people sank into complete insignificance. . . .

The history of the Nordic peoples of Italy must likewise begin in Central Europe, so that here too the racial kinship may be felt. The struggle between patricians and plebeians is to be understood mainly as a racial struggle, hence, too, the particularly fierce resistance to the grant of the right of intermarriage to the plebeians. The Nordic element in the Romans was nearly worn out in unceasing wars. By the time of Tiberius only six of the old patrician families survived! The overwhelming majority of the total population of Italy consisted of the descendants of Oriental slaves. The hopelessness of their plight was the background for the stoic outlook of the Romans. And so by the beginning of our era the denordicising of southern Europe was nearly complete.

The significance of the Germanic folk-migration lies fundamentally in the fact that it brought fresh Nordic blood into the Roman Empire, degenerated as it was through this racial hotch-potch. Hence the new culture of the Middle Ages bloomed only where Germanic peoples settled permanently: in North (but not South) Italy, in Spain, France, England, but not in the Balkans. The racial influence of the Nordic Varangians in Russia was too slight to permeate the enormous region with civilizing force. Only the fact that the Germanic ruling class in Central, West and South Europe was the bearer of medieval culture makes it possible to understand how medieval chivalry at its height exhibits everywhere such a uniform character.

More emphasis than heretofore is to be laid upon the greatest achievement of the German Middle Ages, the recovery of the area east of the Elbe. In this connection, it must again be insisted with reference to conditions before the migration period that this area east of the Elbe right away to beyond the Vistula was once Germanic national soil at a time when the slavonic peoples still dwelt as poor fishermen in the Pripet swamps.

For the rest, however, the insistence on nationality must not lead to an unfair estimate of the Middle Ages. They were a time of very great expansion of German power. The foundation of national States was then achieved in no European country; take, for example, France with its constituent states—Provence, Burgundy, Normandy, Ile-de-France and Lorraine.

Modern history reveals for the first time evolution in the direction of the national State. Yet from the beginning of the modern period, international influences too make themselves gradually more strongly felt. They lead to a lamentable intrusion of alien elements into German blood, German speech, German law, German constitutional theory and finally into the whole outlook on the world. In opposition to them the development of German national consciousness is to be brought out; today it receives new vigor from the more thorough investigation of our own history. Such contemplation of what is specifically ours leads to greater emphasis on the bond of blood which unites us to our kinsmen in neighboring regions and elsewhere abroad. It allows us to hope for increasing recognition in the kindred Germanic countries, that the Nordic peoples must feel themselves a community united by destiny upon the maintenance of which absolutely depends the existence of all higher Nordic civilization.

NATIONAL MINORITIES IN THE SOVIET UNION

The Soviet Union can claim with a high degree of accuracy that it has solved the difficult problem presented by the existence of national minorities within a strongly centralized state. It has found this solution by the novel device of disassociating statehood from both nationality and race. It has put its trust in a genuine equality of citizenship as completely irrespective of race or language, as of color or religion.

THE BOLSHEVIKS believe that they have solved the problem presented by the existence, in the vast territory for which a constitution had to be provided, of a hundred or more distinct nationalities. One of the difficult problems presented to political science by the geographical unity of the Eurasian plain has always been that of the extreme diversity of the population found upon it, in race, religion, language, degrees of civilization and culture, habits of life, historical tradition and what not. The continuity of land surface from the Gulf of Finland to the Pacific Ocean prevented the rest of the world from recognizing in the tsarist regime what was essentially a colonial empire, ruled from St. Petersburg by the upper class of a superior race—not without analogy to the colonial empire of Holland, ruling its East Indian dependencies from the Hague; or indeed to that of the Britain of the eighteenth century, ruling its heterogeneous colonies from Westminster. The systems of the Dutch and the British appealed to the Bolsheviks no more than those of the Spanish and the French. The compulsory "russification" aimed at by the Russian autocracy was not only manifestly impracticable, but also in the highest degree unpopular.

Lenin and his colleagues in the Social Democratic Party of Russia had not failed to notice, from the very beginning of the twentieth

Excerpt from Sidney and Beatrice Webb, *Soviet Communism: A New Civilization?* (New York: Charles Scribner's Sons, 1938), pp. 139-158.

century, how strong and persistent was the popular discontent caused by the tsarist insistence on the "russification" of all the national minorities within the Empire. Already at the London Conference of 1903, Lenin got carried a resolution stating that "The Conference declares that it stands for the complete right of self-determination of all nations"; to which the Second Congress of the Party in August 1903 added the important words "included in any state." The Central Committee of the Party, at the meeting of September 25, 1913, emphasized the necessity of guaranteeing "the right to use freely their native language in social life and in the schools." Ignoring the indications in the Communist Manifesto of 1848, as to proletarian supremacy leading to the passing away of national differences, and resisting the growing feeling through Europe in favor of united nationalist states, Lenin insisted that the Bolsheviks should declare themselves in favor, along with the right of self-determination of even the smallest nationality, also of the concession of "cultural autonomy" to national minorities included within states. This proved to be an important factor, so far as the national minorities of tsarist Russia were concerned, in securing their participation in the revolutions of February and October 1917.

How were the insistent demands of the various nationalities to be met? The Provisional Government had left this problem, along with so many others, to the prospective Constituent Assembly. But in October 1917 Lenin and his colleagues found themselves in power, before anyone had worked out any scheme of organization that would satisfy the national minorities without endangering the strength and unity of the central authority. This did not prevent the new government from issuing a flamboyant proclamation promising autonomy in return for support.

"Mohammedans of Russia," it began, "Tartars of the Volga and Crimea; Kirghiz and Sartes of Siberia and Turkestan; Turks and Tartars of Transcaucasia, your beliefs and customs, your national institutions and culture, are hereafter free and inviolable. You have the right to them. Know that your rights, as well as those of all the peoples of Russia, are under the powerful protection of the Revolution, and of the organs of the soviets for workers, soldiers, and peasants. Lend your support to this revolution, and to its government."

The working out of the problem of national minorities was entrusted to Stalin, who, as a member of one of the innumerable tribes inhabiting the Caucasian mountains, had long had a personal interest in the subject. In 1913, indeed, he had published a pamphlet in which he endeavored to reconcile cultural autonomy with the supremacy of the whole proletarian mass. He was made People's Commissar for Nationalities, with the opportunity of concentrating his whole energy on the task.

The first ethnic group actually to achieve autonomy were the German settlers on the Volga, who, even under the old regime, had had certain privileges. They were organized in 1918 as a so-called "Labour commune," which later became an autonomous republic. The establishment of the Bashkir State followed a year later. This was the first soviet state with an Oriental, that is, Turkish and Moslem, population. Upon soil once ruled by the khans of the Golden Horde the Tartar Republic was proclaimed in 1920. The Volga Tartars are the dominant nationality here, and the ancient city of Kazan is the administrative and cultural center. About the same time the Karelian Republic was formed on the Finnish border, while the territories occupied by the Kalmyks, the Votyaks and the Mari were given the status of autonomous regions. Within the next two years the Crimean Republic came into being, the Komi people of the north was allotted a spacious region of its own, and the Chuvashian territory, now a republic, also became an autonomous region. Thus, by 1922 all the more important ethnic groups in the European part of the Russian federation had become masters of their own houses.

The work done by Stalin, during his four years' tenure of office as People's Commissar for Nationalities, was of great and lasting importance. What he worked out in the vast domain of the RSFSR (Russian Socialist Federation of Soviet Republics) was not federalism (which came only in 1922-1923, when the nationalities outside the RSFSR joined with it in the federal USSR) but the concession of "cultural autonomy," coupled with an actual encouragement of the admission of members of the national minorities to the work of local administration.

It is, we think, owing to the whole-hearted adoption of this policy of cultural autonomy, and even more to its accompaniment of leaving the local administration to be carried on mainly by "natives," that the Soviet Union, alone among the countries of Eastern Europe, can claim, with a high degree of accuracy, that it has solved the difficult problem presented by the existence of national minorities within a strongly centralized state. It has found this solution, not, as France has done, along the road of absorbing the national minorities by the creation of an overpowering unity of civilization from end to end of its territory; nor, as tsarist Russia sought in vain to do, along that of forcibly suppressing all other national peculiarities in favor of those of the dominant race; but by the novel device of dissociating statehood from both nationality and race. . . .

So far the important concession of cultural autonomy had involved little or no difference in political structure between the areas recognized as occupied by distinct nationalities and the other parts of the RSFSR organized in congresses of soviets for provinces (gubernia), counties (uezd) and rural districts (volost). The various minorities were, in fact, induced to adopt, in substance, the same constitutional structure as the rest of the RSFSR. What the concession of cultural autonomy amounted to between 1918 and 1922 was merely that the central authorities of the RSFSR did not, in practice, prevent those of each autonomous republic and autonomous area from adopting its own vernacular as the official language; or from using it in councils and courts of justice, in schools and colleges, and in the intercourse between government departments and the public. The local authorities could give preference to their own nationals as teachers and local officials, and were even encouraged to do so. Their religious services were not interfered with by the Central Government. They could establish theaters, and publish books and newspapers in their own tongues. These were exactly the matters in which local autonomy was most warmly desired. The limits to this "cultural autonomy" should be noted. Apart from the highly important matter of local administration by the natives, it is mainly a matter of permitting the use of the vernacular for all activities that are lawful in the Soviet Union; not a new right to conduct any activities that may be alleged to have been part of the vernacular culture. Thus it must not be assumed that the Ukrainians, the Georgians or the Germans, in the autonomous areas of the USSR, were to be given unlimited freedom to maintain or enter into relations with persons of the same nationality outside the USSR, including émigrés or exiles. In the concession of cultural autonomy within the USSR loyalty to the regime of the country was presupposed. In short, cultural autonomy (as distinguished from native government) was a reversal of the tsarist policy, of "russification," and nothing more. "The Soviet Government," it has been said, "is not Russian, but proletarian: it does not seek to russify the peoples of the Union, but to train them as communists like the Russian people itself, partners in the building up of socialism." . . .

It remains to be said that, during the dozen years since the formation of the Soviet Union in 1923, the position of nearly all these autonomous republics and autonomous areas has been largely transformed. It is not that there has been any important alteration in their political structure, or in their nominal relation to the central authorities of the constituent republics within which they are situated, or to those of the Soviet Union. Their position of cultural autonomy has, indeed, been strengthened, not only by long enjoyment of their privileges, but also by the scrupulous care taken at Moscow always to treat the minority cultures with respect, even on occasions when counter-revolutionary aspirations of a nationalist character have had to be sternly repressed. This policy has not been maintained without an occasional struggle. From time to time it has been complained that the recognition of all these national minorities and their cultures was costly in money and detrimental to educational and administrative efficiency; and worst of all, that it was admittedly made use of occasionally as a cloak for "separatist" machinations.

The number of autonomous republics and autonomous areas has been, in fact, from time to time increased. Even the Jews, who are dispersed all over the Union, have been encouraged and assisted to form locally autonomous groups, especially in Southern Ukraine and the Crimea, and have been formally granted an autonomous oblast (in due course to be promoted to an autonomous republic) at Biri Bidjan in Eastern Siberia. The Soviet Government has even begun to "settle" the gypsies, who swarm restlessly in the USSR as elsewhere. . . .

It would be too much to expect the reader to examine, in detail, the varying developments of the twenty-seven autonomous republics and autonomous areas. Actually the first to be granted cultural autonomy as a region in 1918, and as a republic in 1923, with the right to give preference in filling local offices to its own nationals, was the Autonomous Socialist Soviet Republic of the Volga Germans, a settlement founded as long ago as 1764. . . . No fewer than twelve of the autonomous republics are within the RSFSR; and these autonomous republics alone extend to more than eight million square kilometers out of the total area of that constituent republic of less than twenty million kilometers, though including only sixteen and a half million inhabitants out of more than one hundred million. The one autonomous republic in the Ukraine extends to only a small part of its total area; and those of the Transcaucasian Federation to no great proportion of its total area. White Russia contains no autonomous republics or areas. On the other hand, the three newest constituent republics (Turkmenistan, Uzbekistan and Tadzhikistan) may be considered to be wholly composed of national minorities. . . .

We must content ourselves with a particular account of a single specimen, in its progress perhaps the most remarkable of all: the Tartar Autonomous Republic which the authors had the advantage of visiting in 1932. Twenty years ago its present area was an indistinguishable part of the vast gubernia or province of Kazan, with a poverty-stricken agricultural population almost entirely of Tartar race; 85 per cent illiterate; the women veiled; and the whole people completely debarred from self-government; and indeed, outside the city, left almost without administrative organs of any sort. There were a few dozen small elementary schools of the poorest kind, and only three places of higher education, in which but ten Tartar students, none of them the sons of peasants or wage-earners, were to be found. Today there are over 1700 elementary schools, with more than 99 per cent of all the children of school age on the register, including girls equally with boys. The vernacular colleges and institutes of higher education are numbered by dozens, and filled with Tartar students, the great majority coming from peasant or wage-earning homes, whilst many more are to be found in colleges in other parts of the USSR. All the women are unveiled, and are taking their share in every department of public life. When the authors interviewed the Sovnarkom of People's Commissars (all of Tartar race) we found one of them a woman, who was Minister of Education. The health service for the village is an entirely new creation. Doctors (mostly women) and small hospitals (including lying-in accommodation), now cover the whole rural area, whilst at the capital, the city of Kazan, there are not only specialist central hospitals, but also a completely reorganized medical school, now filled mainly with Tartar students. More than two-thirds of the peasants have joined together in collective farms, which cover three-quarters of the entire cultivated area, and which, alike in 1932, 1933 and 1934, were among the first in the Union to complete their sowing, whilst they harvested more than 100 per cent of the planned yield. Fifteen years ago Tartar industry was practically non-existent; in the years 1931 and 1932 the planned industrial output was respectively 239 and 370 million roubles; and in each of the past three years the plan was more than fulfilled. The Tartar People's Commissar of Health, evidently a competent medical practitioner, explained how the crude death-rate for the republic as a whole had steadily declined year by year, whilst the infantile death-rate had been halved. There are, as we saw, still a few Mohammedan mosques functioning in Kazan, but the great majority of the population appear to have dropped Islam, almost as a spontaneous mass movement. There is a flourishing state publishing house, which pours out a continuous stream of Tartar books and pamphlets, for which there is a large sale. There are Tartar theaters and cinemas, Tartar public libraries, and a well-frequented museum of Tartar antiquities and modern art products. In all sorts of ways the Tartar autonomous republic demonstrates how proud of itself it has become!

We cannot omit to mention one important and peculiar minority, racial and religious rather than national, with which the Soviet Union has had to deal, namely that of the Jews. Under the Tsars their oppression had been severe and unrelenting. . . . The Jewish problem, as it presented itself to the Soviet Government, was twofold. It was important to rescue from misery, and to find occupation for, the families of the ruined traders and shopkeepers of the small towns of White Russia and the Ukraine. To all the aggregations of Jews, although not recognized as a nation, the Soviet Government concedes the same measure and kind of cultural autonomy as it accords to the national minorities properly so called. . . . Wherever there is a group of Jewish families together they have their own local government and their cultural autonomy. They are not prevented from maintaining their racial customs and ceremonies. "The Jewish Soviet Republic," it has been said, "envisaged by the orthodox communist, differs fundamentally from Herzl's polity in Zion, as well as from the Territorialists' Homeland. It is not intended to furnish the Jewish race throughout the world with the political life that it has lacked for so long. Nor is it intended to become the seat of the putative civilisation of the race. . . . For the present, the state extends to the Jewish masses what it offers to the other minorities: government institutions using their own language, and instruction entirely in their own tongue." . . .

Nevertheless, it cannot be denied that all the blessings of security from pogroms and freedom to enter professions that the USSR accords to the Jews involve in practice, their acceptance of the soviet regime; and make, on the whole, for assimilation. The policy of the Soviet Union accordingly meets with persistent opposition, and even denigration, from the world-wide organization of the Zionists, among whom the building up of the "national home" in Palestine brooks no rival.

In spite of the numerical dominance of the Russian race in the USSR, and its undoubted cultural pre-eminence, the idea of there being a Russian state has been definitely abandoned. The very word "Russia" was, in 1922-1923, deliberately removed from the title of the Soviet Union. All sections of the community—apart from those legally deprived of citizenship on grounds unconnected with either race or nationality—enjoy, throughout the USSR, according to law, equal rights and duties, equal privileges and equal opportunities. Nor is this merely a formal equality under the law and the federal constitution. Nowhere in the world do habit and custom and public opinion approach nearer to a like equality in fact. Over the whole area between the Arctic Ocean and the Black Sea and the Central Asian mountains, containing vastly differing races and nationalities, men and women, irrespective of conformation of skull or pigmentation of skin, even including the occasional African Negro admitted from the United States, may associate freely with whom they please; travel in the same public vehicles and frequent the same restaurants and hotels; sit next to each other in the same colleges and places of amusement; marry wherever there is mutual liking; engage on equal terms in any craft or profession for which they are qualified; join the same churches or other societies; pay the same taxes and be elected or appointed to any office or position without exception. Above all, these men and women denizens of the USSR, to whatever race or nationality they belong, can and do participate—it is even said that the smaller nationalities do so in more than their due proportion—in the highest offices of government and in the organized vocation of leadership; alike in the sovnarkoms and central executive committees of the several constituent republics and in those of the USSR, and, most important of all, in the Central Committee of the Communist Party (and its presidium), and even in the all-powerful Politbureau itself. The Bolsheviks have thus some justification for their challenging question: Of what other area containing an analogous diversity of races and nationalities can a similar assertion be made?

The policy of cultural autonomy and native self-government is, indeed, carried very far. It is not confined to the more powerful national minorities, nor even to groups of magnitude. Wherever a sufficient minimum of persons of a particular race or culture are settled together, the local administration allows for their peculiar needs. . . .

Hardly any of the distinct races or cultures, not even the Russians who count so large a majority, are without their local minorities, dwelling amid alien local majorities. On the other hand, some of the races are wholly dispersed, and are to be found everywhere. Hence the autonomy has to be, and is, carried so far as to secure, for even the smallest minority group, its own autonomy, as regards primary school and local officials, even against the dominant minority culture.

Yet the state as a whole maintains its unity unimpaired, and has even, like other federal states, increased its centralization of authority. It is only in the USSR that this centralization involves no lessening of the cultural autonomy of the minorities, and even occurs concomitantly with the strengthening of the various regional cultures. This unbroken unity, and this increasing centralization of authority, is ensured in ways that will become plain as our exposition proceeds. It will suffice for the present to note, first, that, legally and formally, the powers of the superior authorities in disallowance and cancellation, are the same over the autonomous republics and autonomous areas as over other oblasts, rayons, cities and villages; the cultural autonomy, though formally established in principle by general law, being essentially a matter of administrative practice. Next, the great leveling influence of the economic relations exemplified in widespread industrialization and collectivism, which operate irrespective of race or nationality, or any geographical boundaries, constitutes a silent but continuous unifying factor. Finally, the ubiquitous guidance and persuasion of the essentially unitary Communist Party, composed of members of every race and every distinctive culture in the USSR, ensures not only unity but also all the centralization that is necessary.

Alongside this maintenance and strengthening of the minority cultures, there has been an unmistakable rise in the level of civilization. Note first, and perhaps as most important, a marked increase among the national minorities, of their own self-respect. It is, indeed, the many backward populations, which had suffered so much under tsarist repression that they had nothing that could be destroyed, which have gained most from the nationalities policy of the Soviet Government. They have, to a considerable extent, already lost their "inferiority complex," and gained in confidence and courage. The women, in becoming literate, have become effectually free, alike from the veil and from the control of husband or father. The children have been almost universally got to school, and have been provided with technical institutes and colleges of university rank, using the vernacular. The health of the whole people has been improved. With hospitals and medical services, epidemics have been got under, and the death-rate has everywhere been greatly reduced. All this has been carried out by the local administration, largely in the hands of "natives," but with the constant guidance of the various commissariats of health and education, and of the Communist Party, with abundant encouragement and financial assistance from Moscow, always under conditions of "cultural autonomy." Even more influential in change has been the economic development. The nomadic tribes have, to a great extent, become settled agriculturists, grouped in collective farms; the peasants have been helped to new crops; the collective farms have been mechanized; the surplus of labor has been absorbed in extensive industrial enterprises in mining and manufacturing, largely in the various localities themselves; additional railways have been constructed; and dozens

of new cities have sprung up. This has been, in the main, the outcome of the First and Second Five-Year Plans of 1929 and 1933.

Fundamentally what the Bolsheviks have done, and what Stalin
may be thought to have long been looking for, is something which
does not seem to have occurred as a possibility to western statesmen.
In devising the federal organization that we have described, they
threw over, once for all and completely, the conception that statehood
had, or should have, any connection with race or nationality. Political
science had, for the most part, come to see, during the nineteenth
century, that statehood need have nothing to do with the color of the
skin or with the profession of a particular creed. It had even sometimes contemplated the possibility of doing without a dominant national language. But right down to the resettlement of European
boundaries according to the Treaty of Versailles and its fellows in
1919, the political scientists have allowed statesmen to cling to the
value, if not the necessity, of a unity of race as the basis of perfect
statehood. This conception is connected with, if not consciously based
upon, that of an inherent and unalterable superiority of one race—
usually one's own race—over others; and with the belief, for which
neither history nor biological science knows of any foundation, that
what is called "purity of blood" is an attribute of the highest value.
The Bolsheviks put their trust in a genuine equality of citizenship,
as completely irrespective of race or language as of color or religion.
They neither undervalued nor overvalued the national minority cultures. What they have sought to do is to develop everyone of them,
in its own vernacular and with its own peculiarities. They refused
to accept the assumption that there is any necessary or inherent inferiority of one race to another. They declared that scientific anthropology knows of no race, whether white or black, of which the most
promising individuals could not be immeasurably advanced by appropriate education and an improvement in economic and social environment. The Bolsheviks accordingly invented the conception of the
unnational state. They abandoned the word "Russia." They formed
a Union of Socialist Soviet Republics in which all races stood on one
and the same equal footing. And just because it is not a national state,
belonging to a superior race, the Soviet Union has set itself diligently,
not merely to treat the "lesser breeds within the law" with equality,

but, recognizing that their backwardness was due to centuries of poverty, repression and enslavement, has made it a leading feature of its policy to spend out of common funds considerably more per head on its backward races than on the superior ones, in education and social improvements, in industrial investments and agricultural reforms. The record of the USSR in this respect during the past eighteen years stands in marked contrast with the action toward their respective lower races of the governments of Holland or France, and even of that of the United Kingdom, which has been responsible for the government of India, and many of the West Indian islands, and much of Africa, for more than a century.

15

MINORITY ISSUES IN AMERICAN DEMOCRACY

THE UNITED STATES, for all its distinctiveness, is culturally an offshoot of Europe. For a long time, it was in its thinking a cultural province of the homeland of its dominant stocks. That tradition has often blinded America to its own uniqueness and difference, and in no matters more conservatively than in its cultural outlook. In its conception of nationhood the English pattern has been interpreted more strictly even than in English political and legal thought. National unity has been a passionate public interest in America more than it could possibly have been in a country explicitly a United Kingdom, with four different historic ethnic stocks. America has thus always been a multi-national state without much general public recognition of that fact. This illusion has been fostered by the absence of settled historic traditions at the time of its foundation, and has been promoted by the apparent dominance of a single language and cultural tradition.

In addition to its allegiance to the myth of national cultural uniformity, the United States in later stages of its history has been inconsistent in practice with certain precedents of its early settlement, for these early settlements were, for the most part, refugee colonies of oppressed and non-conformist minorities. Only in periods of labor need has the immigration policy of the country been extremely liberal, while at other periods the principle of restriction has been exercised drastically. The tradition of America as the asylum and refuge of the oppressed is not quite borne out by a detailed examination of the immigration laws, restricting both quantitatively and qualitatively, the influx of the foreign-born.

Woofter shows that since 1900 immigration policies have been increasingly restrictive, and have shifted from political to racial and eugenic standards as grounds for exclusion. Medical regulations have reflected an objective and scientific sort of standard which most persons would concede. The racial restriction clauses, relating to Orientals, particularly the Chinese and Japanese, especially since connected with disqualification for citizenship, reflect factors of an indefensible kind. It is claimed that such exclusion is protective, but this is historically fallacious. Restrictive acts against Oriental immigration were preceded by periods when Chinese and Japanese were induced to come to this country to labor in building the Western railroads and for service in the pioneer intensive farming of the hand-cultivated West Coast farms. The stream that was checked was opened up by American initiative and needs, and so far as the experience of the country has gone with Oriental residents, little adequate justification can be given for such restrictive exclusion and civil disability. Most frank observers will admit racial and cultural prejudice as one of the main components in our Oriental exclusion policy.

The quota restrictions of our immigration laws also show cultural bias, in that they are heavily weighted in favor of the older and northern European stocks. The national origins clauses reflect a desire and determination to keep ethnic national character in line with the traditional Anglo-Saxon majority. But historically from time to time, the dominant economic policy of the country has relaxed this cultural policy in favor of any source of needed labor, however ethnically diverse: the presence of thirteen million Negroes of African descent, being a forceful illustration of the operation of this principle of economic advantage—controlling majority practice, whether in or out of line with traditional policy. But when not otherwise countered by economic need, American immigration policy has shown tendencies toward restrictive exclusion and to swinging out of line with democratic and traditional American ideals.

Reinhold, treating the role of refugees in American history, charts the waves of migration fleeing oppression and persecution abroad which have given America her reputation as the haven of the oppressed and persecuted. The mass movements that have contributed the bulk of the population of the country have had by no means so romantic and idealistic a motivation. The refugee, as a symbol of the conditions associated with the earliest American settlement, has come to stand for a rationalized tradition, not always carried out in practice. Group prejudice was never quite absent, even in the early colonies, as shown by the mutual distrust and intolerance of many of the colonies. The great expanse of unsettled country, capable of absorbing any dissident or ostracized group, facilitated physically the problem involved in the treatment of minority and refugee groups. The increased pressure of refugees later, when that elasticity had vanished, has brought reactions of a quite different sort to the traditional American liberality.

Refugee groups and individuals have contributed spectacularly in their land of refuge, and their history has justified the policy of open welcome and ready assimilation. But the very existence of so many quite unabsorbed foreign communities, both in rural settlements and in city slums, tells a general story of majority exclusiveness and cultural intolerance. Certain clannishness on the part of the foreign-born communities, and definite differences in standards and modes of living, have had, of course, their share in this situation. But cultural prejudice has been one of the great deterrents of the assimilative process, and many of these foreign-born communities have passed generations without cultural absorption, even after having assimilated the basic institutional mores of American life.

The United States is, after all, one of the most polyglot and multiracial nations on earth, and has relatively speedier assimilative processes and less historical antipathies than any of the great European nations having heavily mixed populations. As such this country has the unique opportunity of working out the adjustment of many national and racial groups under common institutions and democratic ideals.

In addition to the problem of the cultural absorption of the immigrant, Orientals, the American Indian and the Negro have traditionally been carried in the public mind outside the pale of the majority democratic tradition, although enlightened liberal opinion has repeatedly urged their inclusion. These more acute minority problems of America have been constantly there as obvious exceptions, and also as challenging tests of the American tradition and its professions of equalitarianism. They have passed through several historic crises of reform and reaction, without any basic resolution as yet. The more objectively they are viewed, however, or in longer range historical perspective, the less they seem to be so exceptional. They are in final analysis, important segments of the general minority problem, and are of a piece with the more moderate varieties of majority prejudice and discrimination that often pass almost unnoticed between the majority and less obviously divergent groups. Thus our shortcomings in social democracy are part and parcel of one and the same majority policy and attitude. In the extreme cases of racial prejudice, cultural prejudice only becomes all the more manifest, but a majority bias of the same essential source and character underlies both. Admittedly these racial divides are the more difficult of the social cleavages to bridge but, as with the immigrant and the foreign language minorities, cultural assimilation makes their continuance extremely difficult, if not, in the long run, impossible.

Beliefs in the unassimilability of these groups and of their fundamental cultural difference are, thus, the crux of all our racial minority problems. Majority stereotypes of this character impede even the recognition of the substantial amount of integration that may have taken place. So it is a very significant situation for all minorities, racial as well as cultural, when cultural non-conformity comes to be respected. Eventually this would entail a different standard of group judgment on the part of the majority. No minority group, in fact, can be in a sound position when cultural difference connotes inferiority. Therein lies the profound significance of any change in American attitudes on the question of cultural conformity. This affects all minority groups, and is not a special concession to this one or to that, but involves a fundamental revision of the dominant majority attitude all along the line.

More promising for an improvement of minority status in American democracy than any fluctuating of attitudes toward specific minorities, would be general and fundamental change in the traditional conception of the nature and goal of American culture. The government report on "Cultural Diversity in America," raises just that basic question. It calls attention to the persistence of cultural difference, combined with the increased juxtaposition of these differences with the rapidly increasing urbanization of America. It thus points to new factors that may force a new cosmopolitan character into the typical American community. Cultural change, according to the report, is not ironing out the cultural divergencies of the many national and racial elements in the American population, but is forcing them into new situations of mutual stress and common experiences. It is no longer a diversity of isolation, but a more challenging type of situation involving reaction across lines which have previously divided.

The excerpt from Cayton and Mitchell on Negro and white workers in Birmingham, forced into a non-traditional co-operation against the grain of deep traditional separatism by common interest under new industrial conditions and programs is certainly a case very much in point. No two elements have been pushed further apart than the poorer white Southern laborer and the Negro laboring group. The narrative of mixed unions in a Southern urban center, functioning against the opposition of inveterate caste and racial prejudice, shows the force of common interests and social forces to dissolve crystallized inhibitions and inveterate animosities. A close industrial alignment has dictated comparatively wide-scale and effective ignoring of these differences; with what results of group interaction only actual experience can demonstrate; since the forecast, on the basis of the racial tradition of the two groups, would have insisted on the utter impossibility of what is now actually taking place.

The more disadvantaged minority elements are experiencing more rapid cultural change under American conditions than the older majority stocks. This means for them not only enhanced assimilation, but greater impetus toward original and exceptional adjustments and creativeness. Their unusual stress and strain brings in this way considerable dividends of positive benefit both to themselves and to the general culture. The cultural changes, particularly of the urban community, are leveling off the provincialisms of the native-born population more markedly than they are melting down the cultural distinctiveness of the minorities and the foreign-born. It is that majority provincialism and intolerance which has been the great handicap for the underprivileged groups in their struggle for adjustment and improved condition and status.

Randolph Bourne's article carries this challenge straight to the heart of majority policy. His formula for a sound American culture, and for any democratic society, in fact, is whatever diversity historical circumstances have given it, reconciled by attitudes of cultural reciprocity and tolerance, rather than pressed into any uniformitarian mold or stratified in that unstable dominance and subordination of majority and minority groups. This, he thinks, depends on the enlightened concession of the majority, which it behooves the majority to make unless it would reap a later harvest of minority counterassertion and inner conflict. The American situation permits just this, and in Bourne's opinion, the democratic ideal calls for it. The prime obstacle in the path of the actual realization of cultural democracy is an unfortunate tradition of majority-prescribed and dominated culture. Stripping minorities of their culture not only impoverishes them, but enfeebles them for assimilation and proper functioning in relation to cultural change and progress. Building up a cultural superiority on their disparagement and repression leads to stagnation of the cultural life of the majority culture itself. In intercultural reciprocity, Bourne finds what he regards the only safe way to cultural democracy.

IMMIGRATION ATTITUDES AND POLICIES IN THE UNITED STATES

Important shifts in public attitudes and policies toward immigration and toward the foreign born in the United States have occurred in recent years. These are traced here through an analysis of articles which appeared in current periodicals.

INTEREST IN immigration has fluctuated widely since 1900. The trend was gradually upward, reaching a peak in 1921 as indicated by the number of articles concerning immigration and immigrants in the United States listed in the *Reader's Guide*. The largest number of articles appeared in the years 1907, 1909, 1913, 1916, 1921, 1924, coinciding with agitation upon the subject of immigration in Congress in all but one case. . . .

The discussion from 1900 to 1907 showed that immigration was regarded primarily from the economic and secondarily from the ethnic viewpoint. Restriction was urged to prevent the lowering of wages and of the American standard of living, to prevent pauperism and crime, to prevent bossism in politics and the decay of the American democratic ideal. In this early period, the magazines sampled spoke much of the new type of immigration from Southern Europe, but seldom regarded it as a serious menace, nor did they raise the question of greatly reducing the number of immigrants. They felt that the effort should be to improve the quality of the immigrants through selection, to admit freely the desirable majority and keep out the undesirable minority. Among the qualities to be sought for the following were listed: good character, good health, thrift, honesty, and intelligence. If an immigrant met these conditions he was considered a desirable potential citizen regardless of race. . . .

The period from 1907 to the beginning of the World War in 1914 marked a continued interest in the economic effects of immigration, but the racial and eugenic aspect came to dominate all others. Articles

Excerpts from T. J. Woofter, Jr., *Races and Ethnic Groups in American Life* (New York: McGraw-Hill Book Company, Inc., 1933), pp. 22-25, 28-35, 38-39, 42-45.

began to appear in these magazines warning the readers of the danger that the Anglo-Saxon stock would not survive in the United States if the present type of immigration continued. Heterogeneity of race in itself was commencing to be considered harmful and the lack of assimilability of the South Europeans was often emphasized. Possibly the report of the United States Immigration Commission helped to strengthen this viewpoint. A few magazines were coming to believe not merely in the selection of desirable immigrants but also in restriction which would lower the total number entering this country without regard to fitness. . . .

The period from the beginning of the war to 1919 marked a continuing sentiment for restriction based on political and racial grounds. These magazines for the most part did not favor the method of restriction embodied in the literacy test bill which finally passed over the President's veto in 1917. Little attention was paid to matters of immigration policy which was left to the future, except for speculations concerning the flow of foreigners to this country after the war. Attention was centered on the assimilation of aliens already here.

At the close of the war because of the heightened sense of nationality in this country, immigration was regarded from a political aspect. The danger of the foreigner to us and our institutions was urged in the popular press as a reason for further and more drastic restrictions. The wave of antagonism against the foreigner which swept over the country at this time was not shared by the magazines sampled. Taking a broader view opened up by the World War, several contended that a true internationalism demands free immigration for all. A false and narrow nationalism was decried, and a sounder immigration policy based on economic demand and supply was urged. "The time has come for a scientific regulation of all immigration, free from race discrimination, but admitting only so many of each people annually as our developing experience shows we can truly incorporate into our body politic and into our economic life." The majority of the magazines had now come to believe that some restriction was necessary, the basis for regulation being ease of assimilability to American institutions.

After the passage of the temporary quota bill in 1921 there continued to be considerable agitation concerning the danger of aliens to our institutions, and the Red Peril was widely advertised. The magazines went counter to this campaign; while admitting the undesirability of certain classes of immigrants they did not see a real foreign menace.

Gradually there was a shift of attention from the political to the racial and eugenic aspects of immigration. Interest centered on one policy more than at any other time in the whole period since 1900. The discussion pro and con was very heated. The Nordic cult asserted that the Northern European races formed a group which was biologically superior to all others. It followed that all other races were inferior and should be denied admission to this country since no amount of Americanization could change their germ plasm. Bad heredity presented an insurmountable barrier to their assimilation. Few of the magazines sampled held such an extreme view and several did much to combat it. The idea is set forth that the selection of immigrants should be turned over to an expert commission to draw up rules and regulations. It was asserted that the "character of the immigrant is of more moment than the country of his origin." The practical though crude application of the eugenic principle as expressed in the quota laws was generally disapproved.

With the passage of the Immigration Law of 1924, interest in the subject rapidly subsided as the issue was considered permanently settled. Attention turned to the administration of the law and to the condition of foreigners in the United States while questions of policy were neglected. Application of the national origins quotas brought little new interest. . . .

The discussion of the distribution and protection of immigrants so prominent before 1914 was replaced after the beginning of the European conflict by an interest in the assimilation of aliens already in this country. The flow of new immigrants was almost cut off, but it was feared that those here were a serious danger to American institutions because of the foreigners' alleged proneness to put loyalty to the land of their birth above loyalty to the land of their adoption. To counteract this the Americanization campaign was begun. No other single topic relating to immigration received so much discussion in the magazines as this effort to Americanize foreigners. . . . By 1924, interest in Americanization had almost subsided and the value of the whole movement began to be questioned. A few years later in 1929, Americanization had become adult education and the earlier word had almost disappeared.

Another factor working for assimilation was the emphasis upon the contribution of immigrant groups to American life. Such articles appeared rather regularly throughout the entire period. Life histories of successful immigrants were used to inspire confidence in the opportunity which the United States presents for bringing out the best abilities of the foreign born. They appeared most often in 1916 and in 1918 and helped to counteract the effect of anti-alien propaganda. Little space was given to naturalization or to the foreign language newspapers or organizations.

On the other hand, the factors which tend to prevent the fair treatment of the immigrant and to make his assimilation more difficult claimed the greatest attention in 1906, 1914, and 1920. At first it was not definite anti-alien propaganda that was described, but the hardships which immigrants undergo in coming to this country and fitting themselves into the social and industrial life of American communities. Bad conditions at Ellis Island received discussion with great regularity throughout the entire period. From 1903 to 1908 articles on steamships related to crowded and unhealthy steerage conditions, while in 1922 and 1923 they referred to the evils of racing to beat the quota and the resultant hardship on those debarred.

Anti-alien propaganda began in 1915 and continued until 1924 reaching its peak in 1920. Most of the magazines strongly denounced this mistreatment of foreigners and cited examples of grave injustice. During the same period there appeared numerous articles condemning the deportation of aliens which occurred during the anti-red movement in this country.

Emigration, the effect rather than the cause of poor assimilation, was noted in 1908 following the financial depression and again in 1919 to 1922 owing to the close of the war and the harsh treatment received by aliens here.

Social problems caused by immigration were not discussed by these magazines to any great extent. The largest number of articles were on crime, with dependency, mental disease, and physical disease receiving about the same amount of treatment.

Descriptions of the characteristics of national groups who have settled in the country most frequently relate to Slavs and Italians. In the beginning these were the only two groups described, but interests became broader during the period from 1909 to 1914 and the Belgians, French, Germans, Greeks, Hebrews, Irish, Polish, and Russians also received attention. After the war there was little purely descriptive material relating to national groups.

The flow of immigration has always been a subject of interest to these magazines. In the first period from 1900 to 1907, the change in type of immigration from North to South Europe was commented upon. During the war the change to North Europe is noted with pleasure. After 1921, with the passage of the quota bill, attention shifted to Mexican immigration and in a much lesser degree to Canadian immigration. The Mexicans were felt to be very undesirable and replaced the South Europeans as a "menace." Attempts to restrict Canadian workers are considered inadvisable. . . .

The policy of excluding from entry into the United States aliens subject to physical, mental, moral, and economic defects was established during the last twenty years of the nineteenth century. The legislation of the first twenty years of the twentieth century was concerned with the amendment and extension of these provisions. In 1921, however, a wholly new principle was introduced into immigration legislation. This was the exclusion of all over a certain number from each country in Europe while movement from North American countries was unrestricted.

The following is a brief summary of the restriction before 1920:

1882. Head tax of fifty cents doubled in 1894, 1903, 1907, 1917, now eight dollars per entrant.

1882. Exclusion of defectives, idiots, lunatics, persons likely to become a public charge, convicts (except those convicted for political offenses).

1885. Contract laborers.

1888. Deportation provided.

1891. Paupers, persons suffering from a loathsome or dangerous contagious disease, polygamists, and assisted immigrants.

1903. Insanity clause strengthened, addition of epileptics, professional beggars, anarchists, or persons who believe in the overthrow by force or violence of the government of the United States; prostitutes, persons who have been deported within a year, accompanying aliens added to the excluded classes.

1907. Strengthening of polygamy and prostitution provisions, addition of tubercular persons, feebleminded persons, persons certified to have mental or physical defect which may affect ability to earn a living; unaccompanied children under 16 years of age.

1917. Persons of constitutional psychopathic inferiority, persons with chronic alcoholism, vagrants, and stowaways added to excluded classes.

1917. Asiatic barred zone established excluding inhabitants of India, and islands surrounding Asia, territory not already covered by the Chinese Exclusion Act.

1917. Literacy test, added excluding all aliens over 16 years of age, physically able to read, who cannot read English or some other language or dialect.

Legislation concerned with Orientals has been entirely separate from that relating to European immigration. Early in the development of the Pacific States the Chinese were considered a valued and needed factor in industrial life, but by 1880 they had come to be regarded by many as dangerous rivals in competitive fields. Racial antipathies appeared as natural outgrowths from the strained economic situation and the sharp contrasts of physical characteristics and cultures. At first legislation against the Chinese was purely local, but in 1876, with the appointment of a congressional committee to investigate Chinese immigration, the subject assumed national importance. The outcome of this committee was the treaty of 1880 which was followed in 1882 by the first national restriction law. It provided that all immigration of Chinese laborers, skilled or unskilled, should be suspended for a period of ten years. In 1884 and in 1888 other acts were passed strengthening and more clearly defining the provisions of the first law.

After the law of 1882 Chinese immigration dropped off suddenly and never again reached its former proportions. The resident Chinese population gradually scattered throughout the states of the union thus relieving the pressure along the Pacific Coast. Since 1890, therefore, Chinese immigration has gradually ceased to be of much concern to

the general public, although it has continued to be a serious administrative problem to immigration officers. In 1892 and again in 1902
the existing laws were re-enacted and the time limit extended. The
law of 1904 did away entirely with the time limit. In recent years
the outgoing and incoming movement of Chinese has been small
and compensatory.

At first the Japanese were welcomed as they filled a gap in the labor
market caused by Chinese exclusion, but as soon as the number of
arrivals increased to the point where they entered into competition
with American labor, antagonism developed. As early as 1900 demands
arose for the extension of the exclusion law to the Japanese. The
problem acquired national interest in 1906 when the San Francisco
school board passed a resolution barring Japanese children from white
schools. Although this was rescinded under pressure from Washington,
it was evident that something had to be done to stem the increasing
flow of Japanese immigrants. The result was the gentlemen's agreement of 1907, according to which Japan promised to stop issuing
passports to laborers "skilled or unskilled, except those previously
domiciled in the United States, or wives, or children under 21 years
of age of such persons." By failing to restrict the immigration of women
the gate was left open for an influx of female immigrants to become
wives of Japanese domiciled here. This led to an apparently high birth
rate which was seized upon as an excuse for further restrictions. In
1920 Japan agreed to refuse passports to "picture brides."

The immigration act of 1924 provided that "no alien ineligible to
citizenship shall be admitted to the United States." This, instead of
placing Orientals on the quota, completely excluded Chinese, Japanese, East Indians, and other people not whites or Negroes of African
descent. The most important effect of the act of 1924 on Chinese
immigration was the barring of alien wives of citizens. Japanese immigration was more drastically affected because the provisions of the
gentlemen's agreement had been more liberal than those of the
Chinese Exclusion Law. . . .

The most radical policy of European immigration restriction ever
undertaken by the United States was begun with the passage of the
quota act of 1921. It provided that "the number of aliens of any
nationality who may be admitted under the immigration laws to the

United States in any fiscal year shall be limited to three percent of the number of foreign born persons of such nationality resident in the United States, as determined by the United States Census of 1910." . . .

The most recent phase of immigration restriction is the national origins clause, which, after being postponed in 1927 and in 1928, finally went into effect on the first of July, 1929. As written in the law of 1924 this provision read, "The annual quota of any nationality for the fiscal year beginning July 1, 1927, and for each fiscal year thereafter, shall be a number which bears the same ratio to 150,000 as the number of inhabitants in the Continental United States in 1920, having that national origin, bears to the number of inhabitants in Continental United States in 1920, but the minimum quota of any nationality shall be 100." The national origin was to be ascertained "by determining as nearly as may be in respect of each geographical area . . . the number of inhabitants in the Continental United States in 1920 whose origin by birth or ancestry is attributable to such geographical area. Such determination shall not be made by tracing the ancestors or descendants of particular individuals, but shall be based on statistics of immigration and emigration, together with rates of increase of population as shown by successive decennial United States censuses and such other data as may be found reliable." The effect of this provision was merely to change somewhat the quotas without affecting the general working of the immigration law. The decreases were largely centered in northern Continental Europe and Ireland, and the principal increases were in England. . . .

The principles set up by the act of 1921 and extended by the act of 1924 thus marked an entire change in immigration policy. Previously exclusion laws and treaties, with the exception of those relating to Asiatics, had dealt only with classes of immigrants who for certain definite reasons were considered not desirable as residents of the United States. In each case it was a concrete condition within the immigrant himself which debarred him. Since 1921, volume of immigration alone has been considered harmful. The quota method was used to limit the number of immigrants entering this country, excluding the fit along with the unfit. Although not mentioned specifically, the idea of eugenic differences and racial preference was implied in the new laws. The first real attempt at positive selection is seen in the preference classes within the quotas, but even then there is no general acceptance of the policy of choosing individual immigrants who are the most desirable rather than the exclusion of those least desirable. . . .

Though it was hoped that immigration restriction by quotas would decrease the heterogeneity of the composition of the United States, there have been more or less unforeseen results. The stoppage of European immigration has resulted in a partially compensatory movement from Canada, Mexico, and from our own territories. . . . In the fiscal year ending June 30, 1929, the last period before the present depression was felt, countries outside of North and South America furnished only 52 per cent of all immigrants as against 93 per cent in 1911; Mexico sent 16 per cent as against 3 per cent in 1911; other American countries sent 32 per cent as compared with 3 per cent in 1911.

Net immigration both from Mexico and from other parts of America reached its peak in 1924. European immigration was greatest in 1913 and 1914. Since 1924 the gain by immigration from Canada has shown a steady drop and since 1927 Mexico has followed a like trend, while European immigration was fairly stable from the passage of the 1924 law up to 1931.

Immigration from the dependencies of the United States has markedly increased since the World War. Although in a sense citizens of this country, the residents of our island possessions constitute a real racial problem. The figures available do not differentiate between white Americans and native members of colored races in the movement to and from the territories. Undoubtedly much of it should be attributed to the movement of unskilled colored labor, but the exact amount remains a matter of conjecture. The greatest net gain has been from Porto Rico, with Hawaii second and the Philippine Islands third. Since 1920 the number from Hawaii has more than trebled, the number from Porto Rico doubled, and that from the Philippines increased more than seven times.

The movement to the United States from Hawaii has consisted not so much of natives of those islands as of the Filipinos. Between 1920 and 1925 the larger proportion of the immigrants from the Philippine

Islands came via Hawaii. In recent years, however, more have been coming directly to California. There the Filipino has become a serious problem in the minds of many citizens. The strength of the anti-Filipino sentiment was shown by the race riots in scattered places along the Pacific Coast in 1929 and 1930, occasioned by economic competition with white and Mexican itinerant workers. Bills were introduced into Congress proposing a complete ban on immigration from the Philippine Islands, but so far have failed of passage. The question of granting the Filipinos independence has been linked with the idea of exclusion. . . .

The latter half of the year 1930 and the year 1931 witnessed a drastic reduction in the volume of immigration. The more strict administration of the law applied to Mexico in March, 1929, and to Canada in April, 1930, was made applicable to all countries in September, 1930. The clause relating to the danger of becoming a public charge was interpreted so that the entrance of members of the working class was made almost impossible.

EXILES AND REFUGEES IN AMERICAN HISTORY

Colonial immigrants were political refugees in the cause of religion; post-Revolutionary immigrants, exiles in the cause of political conservatism; nineteenth-century immigrants, exiles in the cause of political liberalism and racial intransigence; while twentieth-century refugees have been exiles in the cause of political reaction, political radicalism, religion, nationality, and race.

COLONIAL IMMIGRANTS were political refugees in the cause of religion; post-Revolutionary immigrants, exiles in the cause of political conservatism; nineteenth-century immigrants, exiles in the causes of political liberalism and racial intransigence; while twentieth-century refugees have been exiles in the causes of political reaction, political radicalism, religion, nationality, and race.

Excerpt from Frances L. Reinhold, "Exiles and Refugees in American History," in *The Annals of the American Academy of Political and Social Science*, Vol. 203 (May 1939), pp. 63-69.

America's exile origins comprise a registry of incomparable experience. Tritely, the stress of Old World persecution projected colonies to the New. Our successes and failures have been largely incidents of immigration—religious, political, economic. It is significant that early independence seekers were not all of the same mind, staking their claims in diverse directions, erecting veritable Chinese walls of prejudice and provincialism within which they breathed the rarefied air of ingrown righteousness. . . . The story of Colonial refugees, moving back and forth as it does from the pole of Massachusetts to the pole of Virginia in rhythmic chronological sequence, admirably reflects political conditions east as well as west of the Atlantic. Individualistic though they were, these tiny centers of intolerant vested interests unwittingly spun the threads of their union by their respective persecutions. Once the expelled of Massachusetts moved downward little by little to meet the creeping upward flow of the expelled from Virginia, and once the line of secondary plantings became contiguous, the independence of the United States was merely a question of time and arbitrary circumstance. Upon a broad historical canvas is painted the exile narrative of French Huguenots, English Puritans, German Protestants, Irish Catholics, Scotch-Irish Protestants, Dutch Walloons, Quakers, Independents, Baptists, and Jews. Interwoven with the greater epics of nationality and creed are the minor epics of individual exiles—Roger Williams, Thomas Hooker, Anne Hutchinson, Anne Austin, Mary Fisher.

While the banishment of thousands from Europe was an important factor in founding the Colonies, and while the banishment of hundreds from the Colonies was an equally consequential factor in the emergence of statehood, the banishment of one hundred thousand Loyalists from the Confederation was an even more momentous factor in the birth of an independent federal United States. Having expurgated our way to an integral freedom, we were then ready to underpin and expand our society with Europe's purged populations. With the tradition of political liberty established and the goal of economic expansion achieved, we are now in a transitional period where political as well as economic immigration is to be reoriented.

Enumeration of refugee groups accommodated in the United States since 1789 reads like a Biblical roster of Old Testament tribal wanderings. Yet the evidence upon which our asylum tradition rests is conclusive proof of a rationalization of motive—a motive that has disguised political expediency and economic advantage under the more palatable cloak of humanitarianism.

Following the French revolution, political *émigrés* sought refuge in our midst from Toussaint L'Ouverture's Santo Domingo rebellion, from the Napoleonic regime, the Bourbon Restoration, the reign of Louis Philippe, the Second Republic, the Third Empire, and the Third Republic. Posterity bows in passing to the exiled shades of Minister Genêt, Moreau de Saint Meury, Talleyrand, the Duc d'Orléans, Pierre Du Pont de Nemours, Joseph Bonaparte, and Pierre Soulé. During the nineteenth century our littoral was inundated with a tidal wave of German refugees as a result of the student society persecutions of 1817-20, the political tyranny of the 1830's, the socialist upheaval of 1848, and Bismarck's socialist purges of the 1880's. Francis Lieber, Carl Schurz, Dr. A. Jacobi, Lorenz Brentano, and Charles Steinmetz, representing their kind, hold places of rank in America's cumulative roll of honor. From the ill-fated Polish revolutions of 1830, 1846, 1848, 1861, and 1862 came a splendid group of educated refugees not the least of whom was the brilliant, romantic John Sobieski.

Again, a transposed Ireland found new green pastures in the westland after the revolutions of 1798, 1800, and 1848. With her Rutledges and Carrolls in our government, her Sullivans and Waynes in our army, her Barrys and McDonoughs in our navy, Erin has prospered in receptive soil. Abortive socialist uprisings in Austria-Hungary in mid-century added Hungarians, Slovaks, and Czechs to our inbound refugee traffic. One need but mention the enthusiasm of Americans for Louis Kossuth and Martin Koszta to remember that the age of humanitarianism was then reaching its peak. In passing, cognizance should be taken of the potato famines in Belgium, the Netherlands, Ireland, and Germany, which resulted in the indistinguishable intermingling of economic immigrants with political refugees from these low-land regions. Moreover, religious restrictions in Portugal, the Netherlands, and the Scandinavian countries added to economic and political migrants many who came for spiritual freedom.

From the close of the Civil War until the problem of Chinese immigration arose in 1882, immigrant sources shifted from North European to South European origins. During this interim period, also, Italians and Austro-Hungarian people sought to escape excessive taxation by emigrating to America in large numbers. Contemporaneously with the Asiatic influx to the west coast at the close of the nineteenth century came the Russian Jewish influx to the east coast. The twentieth century brought Great Russians, Little Russians, and White Russians from premature liberal revolutions. The torrent mounted in 1919, 1920, and 1921 when the Bolshevik Revolution burst like a bombshell upon the western state system. Postwar political refugees were admitted in small proportions from the Near East and from Italy in 1922 and 1923. Since then the bulk of our quota-restricted European immigration has come from Germany—and that largely during the Third Reich.

Swinging the academic searchlight from Europe to the Western Hemisphere, we find that Canada no less than the Old World, supplied us with refugees during our War for Independence from 1776 to 1783, and during her own unsuccessful War for Independence in 1838. From the founding of our government until the War Between the States, we were beset with refugee problems incited by our northern neighbor. From the Civil War to date, however, it has been the Latin American republics to the south that have used our mainland as a depository for political outcasts.

Of all immigrants who have sought a haven in this country for one reason or another, Jews have been most clearly and consistently refugees from political oppression. Indeed, "Jew" and "refugee" have become nearly synonymous. Graphically speaking, there have been four distinct tides of Jewish migration to the United States. The first was the Sephardic movement prior to the eighteenth century, when Jews were dispersed from the Iberian Peninsula by the Spanish Inquisition. It is said that the first to set foot on the Western Hemisphere was one Louis de Torres, Jew, interpreter for Christopher Columbus. Indeed, the historian Lecky goes so far as to say that "Jewish mortar cemented the foundations of American democracy." The second, or Ashkenazic, migration stemmed from Germany during three quarters of the nineteenth century, quadrupling the numbers of that race in

America. But it was with the third exodus in 1871 that the so-called "Jewish problem" began in the United States. Wealthy Spanish Jews and intellectual German Jews were now eclipsed by the poverty-stricken Russian strain that far outnumbered them. Three million Russian Jews were thus added to our census count—the truest of political exiles, a group whose presence here was due to a frenzy of political reaction in Central Europe.

In the 1930's the fourth migration commenced in a new German despotism. Never before were we privileged to receive so large a share of the world's intellectual talent as that which has come to us since Hitler's rise to power. Yet neither in magnitude nor in remorselessness does this last exodus compare with its immediate predecessor. In intensity it may be equal to prior pogroms, but its victims are counted in thousands, while sufferers from [Czarist] Russian persecutions were counted in millions. There are, however, two major dissimilarities in the current phenomenon, namely, the absence of foreign havens and the individual's deprivation of virtually all wealth. For example, Russia's displaced Jews never lacked a foreign asylum. Alien destinations for Germany's dispossessed are few and far between. Furthermore, Russia's Jews left their native land with whatever wealth they could transport. Germany's prey leave without resources if they can leave at all.

Thus we have seen that the heavy hand of oppression in Europe, the Near East, Canada, and Latin America has instigated forced migrations which have terminated in the United States. Only Asia remains unrepresented in this particular kind of population shift. Nevertheless, emigrations from the areas named above were not resultants of identical causes. For illustration, it may be noted that our religious immigrant army drew largely from England, the Netherlands, and Scandinavia; our political immigrant army from Germany, France, Poland, Russia, Ireland, Hungary, Canada, and Cuba; our racial immigrant army from Spain, Poland, Russia, Austria-Hungary, and Germany; our economic immigrant army from Ireland, Italy, and Mexico. Emigration originated in Anglo-Saxon sources in the Colonial period, Latin sources in the post-Revolutionary era, Teutonic in the first quarter of the nineteenth century, Celtic in the middle quarter,

Slavic in the third quarter, Jewish in the fourth quarter, and Hispanic American in the twentieth century.

Within the "asylum of the oppressed" a new England, a new Ireland, and a new Israel were reared on the eastern seaboard. French exiles left their impress in the south. Germans, Polish, Portuguese, Dutch, Magyar, Czech, and Scandinavian refugees perpetuated their cultures in the midwest. Latin American, Russian, and German-Jewish exiles have ultimately found their way to the western Golden Gate; so that no region of the United States now remains uninfluenced by an exile mentality. Ghosts of an ancient "League of Nations" trail benightedly through the domains of New Haven, New Bedford, New Rochelle, New York, New Buda, New Orleans, New Holland, Bellefonte, Moscow, and other transposed communities.

Permeation of exile influences has not been merely geographic in nature. Horizontal spread has been accompanied by a vertical infiltration of America's emerging class pattern. For example, the Puritanism of English exiles has fixed the moral pattern of the Protestant clergy. French royalist *émigrés* have left their mark on our élite with their literature, art, music, and culinary talents. German intelligentsia have disciplined our academic aristocracy. Army circles have reflected the brilliant legacies of Polish military refugees. The Irish proletariat in exile have changed the nature of our political party system. Hungarians, Czechs, and Slavs have been happily received into our peasant and artist groups. Russian exiles seem to have cut class lines from top to bottom, providing at varying periods disillusioned royalty, wealthy nobility, professionals, peasants, and Jewish clothing workers. . . .

Between the brackets of the Declaration of Independence and Lee's surrender at Appomattox, the United States pursued an accoladed role of protector and persecutor of oppressed minorities. While the Civil War marked the end of our era of persecution and launched a new era of protection for Europe's dispossessed, in the secret closet of America's family history rattle the skeletons of those whom we banished for weal or for woe. One hundred thousand "good men and true," Loyalists of the Revolutionary War, were exiled to Canada, Nova Scotia, the West Indies, and England, by Patriots who preferred to found their new government without the brake of the most conservative elements of the day. Following the passage of the Alien and Sedition Acts, residents of French nationality fled in fear of a fate that had met English Loyalists two decades before. Some fifty thousand Free Blacks were "transferred" to Liberia under the auspices of the American Colonization Society between the years 1816 and 1865. Innumerable Indians were exiled to the Siberia beyond the Mississippi—outside the then territorial limits of the country, be it noted. Mormons were literally hounded from state to state at the point of the gun and ultimately banished to Mexican lands beyond the jurisdiction of Federal or state governments. Runaway slaves, though considered only as fugitives from economic servitude by the South, were received as political refugees by the North. Some states, notably Pennsylvania, exiled Quakers during the Rebellion because of their pacifist attitude. After the Civil War, large numbers of Confederate refugees fled to Mexico, Canada, Europe, and South America.

In brief, it should be recorded that while the United States was welcoming French monarchist exiles, German liberal refugees, Polish military *émigrés*, and the like, we were engaged upon our own particular banishments of Loyalists for their conservatism, Quakers for their pacifism, French for their nationality, blacks for their color, red men for their property holdings, Mormons for their religious beliefs, and Confederates for their sectional loyalty. . . .

Not only have we fallen heir to the customary motives of other persecuting governments, and not only have we offered the usual rationalizations of motive, but we have also employed the traditional means of obtaining extermination of undesirable minorities. That is to say, we have used both legal and extra-legal methods in compelling migrations. We have been known to apply "test laws" (during the Rebellion) by which suspected patriots had to prove their loyalty. We have confiscated and converted property (Loyalists' and Confederates'). We have forced treaties from unwilling Indian minorities. We have brought diplomatic pressure to bear on other governments to restrain emigration of marked groups (Mormons). We have devised colonization schemes, offered banishment as an alternative to death or imprisonment (Vallandigham), and finally resorted to the last legal outpost, namely, the declaration of war upon recalcitrant minorities

(Loyalists, Indians, Mormons). Nor has this been all. Extra-legally our history is besprinkled with mob insults, lynchings, refugee man hunts, organized terrorism, fraud, corruption, subtle denial of legal rights, and expulsion from homes and land by social prejudice.

CULTURAL DIVERSITY IN AMERICAN LIFE

A change of attitude toward cultural diversity is supported by the democratic humanitarian impulse to make the ideal of equal opportunity for all a reality, even as affecting the lives of members of minority groups. It clearly follows, as a corollary to this ideal, that cultural diversity shall not prejudice personal or group development.

HISTORICALLY, the cultural diversity in American civilization has arisen as the by-product of movements and policies that were largely controlled by quite different aims or by the blind force of geographic and historic circumstance. The meeting of English, Spanish, and Indian cultures in the Southwest may be spiritually stimulating, but it was not arranged on this account. The Negro may make an important cultural contribution to American life, but he was not brought here for this purpose. The positive encouragement of immigration to the United States, beginning in the sixties—which at first went to the length of legalizing the importation of contract laborers—was primarily motivated by expectation of profits to entrepreneurs and landowners from the influx of laborers. The early modifications of this immigration policy—the repeal of the legislation favoring contract labor and the exclusion of Chinese settlers—were dictated by organized labor groups to protect their own levels of living. It is true that opposition on cultural grounds to mass immigration had already been fostered by the "Know Nothing" faction, or American Party, a secret organization with ideas similar to those of the recent Ku Klux Klan; but the popular line of action found moral sanction in

Excerpt from National Resources Committee, "Cultural Diversity in American Life," in *The Problems of a Changing Population* (Washington: Government Printing Office, 1938), pp. 222-229, 234-239.

the more generous ideal of America, "Asylum for the Oppressed of Every Land."

The same mixture of conflicting economic motives and conflicting cultural interests marked the discussion that preceded the passage of the legislation now in force for the restriction of overseas immigration. By this time a strong reaction had developed against the further introduction of groups with cultures very different from those of the dominant groups in this country. It is significant that the new legislation was based on the "quota principle," explicitly formulated to limit immigration in proportion to the elements of different national origins already established on this soil. In general, however, cultural considerations have as yet played a very minor role in shaping the nation's destiny; and where they have been invoked it has usually been on a rather meager scientific or theoretical basis.

The cultural heritage of most rural groups in the United States involves few sharp breaks with tradition. Most of our cultural institutions have their ultimate roots in rural communities. And in spite of important changes in agricultural methods and increasing contact with city ways, materials, and ideas, social change has been fairly gradual in rural America. This has been true of the main immigrant groups in American villages and on farms as well as of the older native stocks. On the other hand, there has been much regional differentiation of culture in various parts of the country; and contact with the cultural changes of industrial society has varied in different areas from complete identification in some places to the almost absolute isolation of the Kentucky highlander (outside of the mining villages). Cultural isolation almost as complete has also characterized communities in other areas where physical distance has been reinforced by other conditions—by poverty as among poor white and Negro families in the Cotton and Tobacco Belt, or by language barriers as among Swedish, German, and Czech communities in some parts of the Northwest, or by religion as among the Mormons, or by the conditions of migratory labor characteristic of Mexicans in the Southwest. Such isolated rural groups are usually characterized by traditional folk practices, strong family loyalties, and fixed beliefs. The extremely high birth rates of such communities are one expression of cultural persistence. The decline in birth rates recently recorded in most of these same groups is an index of the breaking down of this isolation and the revision of the traditional cultures. According to this index, cultural change is now proceeding rapidly in the Gulf and South Atlantic States, Utah, and the Far West.

The adjustment of immigrant families to established American institutions has usually involved less strain in rural than in urban areas. The earlier immigrants from northwest Europe arrived in time to take part in the frontier process, the Irish being the only large group from northern and western Europe that did not share to any great extent in this movement. They pushed out on the fringe of settlement and took up new lands which they soon made productive. They shared with old American neighbors the all-absorbing tasks of pioneer life. The cultural transition of the newcomers, accordingly, was relatively easy, and their assimilation proceeded as a matter of course.

A comparison of farm operators of immigrant stocks in the Middle and Northwestern States with old Americans in the same region shows that the former own farms equally large and equally fertile, and adopt as good or better farm-management practices. Their incomes from agriculture equal or exceed those of native farmers.

The situation is somewhat different with respect to cultural participation. Certain communities which achieved competence and the respect of their neighbors are still set off by a certain amount of enforced isolation. In all these communities the amount of intermarriage between the immigrant families and the old American families was slight at first, but there is a pronounced tendency toward increase of mixed marriages in the later generations. In social life the chief barriers are those of language, indifference, and prejudice. The amount of social participation, however, is higher than might have been expected. Studies of 70 communities of 21 nationalities showed that they participate quite generally in American institutions, having joined more native organizations than they formed themselves. They secure more recognition in political organizations, however, than in those purely social. In intellectual achievement the children of immigrant farmers stand well. Their children generally make as high scores and reach as high grades as the native children in rural schools.

The pioneer experience of "starting from scratch"—immigrants from Europe and newcomers from the east meeting in the western plains on equal terms, passing from a tense struggle for existence to the mastery of the means of production in a fertile land, from the era of the sod house to the era of the mechanical reaper—led to an emphasis on action, common sense, and constructive enthusiasm. This has found expression in a vigorous literature dealing with the clearing of the wilderness, the struggle of man against nature, the growth of communities, and the whole epic of frontier movements, exploration, and settlements. The treatment varies from the simple, powerful folk realism of O. E. Rölvaag's *Giants in the Earth* to the lyric mysticism of Elizabeth Madox Roberts' *The Great Meadow* and Willa Cather's *O Pioneers!*, *My Ántonia*, and *Death Comes for the Archbishop*.

The experience of the older Spanish-American settlers who became landowners in the Southwest is in many respects similar to that of farmers from northwestern Europe who settled in the Northern and Western States. But that of the agricultural migratory workers from Mexico has been very different.

It is difficult to estimate accurately the number of persons of Spanish-speaking ancestry in the United States, but altogether there are probably about 3,000,000. A majority of them still retain the Spanish language and Spanish traditions. Immigrants from Mexico and their children are the largest group in this total. Before 1900 there was relatively little immigration from Mexico to the United States, but the coming of the railroad and the attendant increased activity in industry and agriculture started a mass movement across the northern border of Mexico. There was pressing need for manual labor on the new railroads, in the mines, and in the extensive cultivation of crops now made profitable by cheap and rapid transportation. The coincidence of civil strife in Mexico with the development of economic opportunity combined to attract large numbers of Mexicans, rich and poor, skilled and unskilled, into the United States. With them they brought the Spanish language and their own customs, manifestations of Indian and Spanish cultures which they had inherited from colonial days and which they had continued to develop in republican Mexico.

Most Mexican immigrants enter into unskilled labor jobs. They serve as day laborers and tenants in the cotton lands of Texas, Arizona, and New Mexico. They are found on the beet farms of Colorado and in the fruit groves and garden fields of California. While they form the section gangs of western railroads, the "muckers" in the mines of the West, and are to be found in large numbers as laborers in the industrial region of Chicago and the Calumet area, the typical Mexican laborer is the migratory worker who follows seasonal farm crops. Chopping and picking cotton, thinning and cutting lettuce, transplanting and pulling onions, cutting and tying spinach and carrots, thinning sugar beets, and picking melons, the Mexican laborer moves over the States of the Southwest with the growing seasons. He stays in one place only as long as there is crop work to be done and a few dollars to be earned. Although many Mexicans have settled permanently in various parts of the country, tens of thousands—men, women, and children—lead nomadic lives. Their situation raises many problems. The task of housing large groups of people who, overnight, have invaded a farming district is in itself a serious matter. Large families are obliged to live in overcrowded quarters in the poorer parts of town. Converted box cars, dilapidated tenements, and makeshift shacks are utilized by this mobile labor supply which, because of its very mobility, cannot afford more suitable housing. The education of the laborers' children is made extremely difficult by the seasonal migrations, by economic and racial prejudice, by inadequate school facilities, and by the system of family contract labor which practically compels all members of a family to labor in the fields.

One of the most interesting large cultural groups in this country is strictly indigenous, stemming in culture as in descent from New England puritanism. Its distinctive institution, the Church of Jesus Christ of Latter-Day Saints, is an expression and development of the millennial zeal of the 1840's. . . . One distinctive adaptation, the location of the agricultural population in villages rather than on isolated farms, simulates, though it is not derived from, a feature of farm life in many parts of Europe, as well as in New England. . . . The great emphasis on religion, moral discipline, and education still gives life in Mormon communities a strong similarity to that in old New England. . . .

In America the problems of urban civilization have been intensified by the fact that rapid city growth has taken place through the attraction of successive waves of immigrants from many different sources.

For most of these immigrants, transition from European provinces to American cities has involved a double shock: Transition to a new national culture, and transition from rural to urban modes of behavior. This rural-urban adjustment is an essential feature of the problem of immigrant assimilation. The high birth rates characteristic of the first generation of the foreign born in this country represent simply the persistence of the same sort of family traditions that are manifest in the high birth rates of typical rural groups in the native population. Similarly, the rapid drop in the fertility of the foreign-born population of the United States during the past 15 years is evidence of the same sort of cultural change that is found among various native rural groups, except that among immigrant families in American cities the tempo of such changes is more rapid, and in the case of the second-generation Americans they frequently involve even greater personal strain and conflict.

From the early years of the nineteenth century, the continuous drift of rural people into urban industrial communities has reflected the transformation of farmers or their children into factory hands. Relying first on a nearby supply, industries have had to seek their workers further and further afield, both in America and overseas. When unsuccessful in attracting the type of labor desired, they have changed their location to tap new areas. The history of the cotton textile industry illustrates this process. The earliest mills relied on the poorer farmers from the hills and stony fields of southern New England. As the industry expanded, this source became insufficient, and mill owners looked for ways to attract workers from more distant and more substantial farms. The famous "boarding-house system" of the New England mills in the 1820's and 1830's, designed to attract farm girls into the mills, drew each year from a wider radius in northern New England. When the westward movement in the 1840's checked the native labor supply at the same time that the mills were expanding, the Irish, first of the peasant immigrants, were brought into the mills to fill the demand. As the industry grew, successive groups of immigrants took their places tending spindles and looms—French Canadians after the Civil War, Italians, Portuguese, Greeks, and others in the early years of the twentieth century. In its latest stage, the textile industry has turned to yet another source or rural labor. The cycle is being repeated in the migration of the industry to the Southeast to tap the reservoir of impoverished tenant farmers and mountain people.

In some industrial areas there has been a succession of different immigrant groups, each starting at the bottom of the industrial scale and occupying residential quarters abandoned by other groups that by this time were enjoying more favorable situations. These successive groups have gone through similar processes of economic and cultural conflict and adjustment.

The majority of our newcomers were at first absorbed into industry as unskilled workers. "America at first has nothing for us but the shovel," is a common saying among immigrant groups. . . .

While it is true that considerable concentration in the unskilled group is still shown for the foreign-born, it is by no means true that they are restricted to the lowest unskilled jobs. They have a considerable representation in each group, although they are not so evenly distributed among the various classes as are the native whites. In most regions the foreign-born have a larger proportion who are unskilled laborers, and a smaller proportion who are clerks, skilled and semiskilled workers than is true of the native whites. Some interesting deviations appear in the regional comparison. In the Southeast and the Southwest, the proportion of foreign-born in the "proprietor" class is almost twice as great as the corresponding proportion among the native whites, and is also very much larger than the percentage of unskilled workers among the foreign-born in these two regions. The number of foreign-born whites in the South is relatively small, but the ones who are living there are professional workers and tradesmen rather than unskilled workers.

Available economic indices seem to point to the fact that, judged by externals, the immigrant is becoming assimilated. This may be due primarily to the fact that enormous numbers of migrants from abroad are no longer being poured at random into the American urban melting-pot. But whatever the reason, the immigrant is no longer restricted to the lowest unskilled jobs, and the conditions under which he lives do not differ greatly from those of the native American.

A recent special study of crime rates among native and foreign-born whites in the United States showed no significant differences between these two groups, when the data were controlled by elimination of differences in age composition and size of community.

Statistics for the United States and Canada on intermarriage among groups of different national origin indicate that in the first generation there is usually a tendency to marry within the group, although this tendency is more pronounced in some groups than in others. Among all the groups, higher rates of intermarriage were found in later generations than in the first, indicating a definite trend toward cultural assimilation and intermingling.

With the virtual ceasing of foreign immigration, our cities are dependent on rural migration for population expansion or even stability. The northward wave of Negro migration in the war and post-war period marked one important phase of this movement. The cultural divergence of the Negro peasant who has turned cityward is obvious; his background of southern rural ways is greatly accented by his physical diversity. Both have operated to accord him a lower economic position involving rougher work, lower wages, and a large measure of exclusion from union organization. Housing is a primary problem for the transplanted Negro worker, as for the newly arrived immigrant. Practically every city has one central district where half or more of its Negro population lives. As the Negro population expands, the structural community meets the line of dwellings held by white laborers, and spatial expansion is blocked. New Negro communities are started but the resulting crowding leaves the Negro with the highest percentage of concentration of any group in our cities. Nevertheless, for one Negro group, those from the Sea Islands off the coast of South Carolina, Kiser has been able to show that they have bettered their economic status, kept something of their group cohesion, lost or partly lost attachment to their families, and found less prejudice and better economic opportunity. Some are found to complain of the tempo of work and the "coldness" of employers and associates.

No studies comparable to those of Negroes have been made of recent white migration, but it is known that there has been a large movement of native whites from the cotton areas and the southern highlands both northward and into the expanding textile towns of the southeast. The difficulties of cultural diversity and conflicting standards created by this situation are especially pertinent to this discussion. Here the problem is particularly clear-cut, in that it is not one of biological heritage, physical diversity, or even language differences. We have here a native colonial stock, whose cultural diversity is based on retarded economic status, health, and educational opportunity. . . . The common attitudes formerly shown the immigrants from southeastern Europe are now turned against the white native-born stock newly arrived in industrial centers.

In the Far West the same problem of native migrants is met in agricultural labor. During the 4 months ending October 5, 1935, more than 30,500 men, women, and children in parties "needing manual employment" entered California in automobiles bearing out-of-State licenses. These "pea pickers" and "fruit tramps" build and live in squalid shanty towns, lacking the elements of sanitation and decent living. In many instances, the immigrants from the southeast are now casual laborers and odd-job men, performing the tasks once done by Mexicans.

The problem of cultural assimilation in urban life is not merely that of immigrant and native. In fact, the primary adjustment necessary is that between fundamental rural patterns of living and contemporary urban ways—except that, where physical racial differences are involved, this process may be complicated by other, more persistent problems of cultural adjustment. . . .

The existence of diverse cultural heritages in American society has often been regarded as an evil, to be overcome as rapidly as possible. Movements initiated for the purpose of promoting harmony have sometimes tended toward enforced assimilation or regimentation. They have tended toward the suppression of initiative, the destruction of traditional moral and artistic values, the fostering of feelings of inferiority and confusion, and toward personal and social conflict. "Assimilation if it takes place at all must be," as Fairchild has observed, "unenforced, primarily the product of natural spontaneous associations with those who embody the assimilating nationality. It was and is a great injustice to the immigrant to assume that he might assimilate himself by an act of the will. The first step in assimilation is the cultivation by native Americans of the greatest possible sympathy toward immigrant life and culture. The first step for the immigrant is that he must have an opportunity to 'live in America.'" Blame of the immigrant for his lack of assimilation, probably the greatest hindrance to the old Americanization movement, completely prevents this sort of sympathy.

Amalgamation and adjustment are beyond the sphere of government; they are the function of society in its unofficial aspect. Cultural assimilation can be affected by education or thwarted by legislative interference; but above all it remains a matter of community process and of participation—economic, political and social. Accordingly, the waning enthusiasm for Americanization programs and the much-advertised failure of the melting-pot are to be accepted not as failure, but as a change in emphasis—a change away from attempts to enforce conformity and toward an understanding of the fundamental conditions and character of cultural processes.

A change of attitude toward cultural diversity is supported by the democratic and humanitarian impulse to make the ideal of equal opportunity for all a reality, even as affecting the lives of members of minority groups. It clearly follows, as a corollary to this ideal, that cultural diversity shall not prejudice personal or group development. In the well-established principle of religious tolerance, great diversity of belief and faith is cherished as a matter of public policy. It has been constitutionally established that race, color, or creed shall form no barrier to political participation. While not established by law, it is a quite definite popular conception that part of the promise of American life is participation in the community and the opportunity to earn and enjoy the "American standard of living." These criteria, if they are interpreted realistically, carry far-reaching implications.

The American community was not really visible to many of the immigrants coming to industrial towns and cities in this country. By its separation of classes and ethnic groups, the American city showed the immigrant its worst aspect, the slums. His acquaintance with older Americans was often limited to the boss, the policeman, and the school teacher. He saw but little of the America described in his textbooks, and he saw only enough evidence of luxury to make him envious. The resulting sense of loneliness and frustration was frequently intense.

Even for the native-born, casual contacts are necessarily restricted in the crowded urban centers; the immigrant, of course, is even more intensely affected in this way. Enforced isolation was not confined to unskilled laborers; it extended to middle-class intellectuals.

In many respects the experience of the second generation—the children of immigrants—has been even more difficult than that of their parents. Failure in their case cannot be accepted with resignation. They lack spiritual solidarity with old world culture; but in many cases they find little opportunity for participation in American culture. Part of the damage worked by the cruder sort of Americanization programs is that they destroy the loyalties and values that might have facilitated the cultural development of young people who otherwise find themselves between two worlds, without being quite a part of either. Many of the newcomers to the United States and many of their children have found opportunity for satisfying activity, and some have become leaders in all sorts of endeavor. But for millions of others, America has not been, in any significant sense, a "land of opportunity." Thus Louis Adamic writes: "The chief and most important fact . . . about the New Americans is that the majority of them are oppressed by feelings of inferiority in relation to their fellow citizens of older stock, to the main stream of American life, and to the problem of life as a whole; which, of course, is bad for them as individuals, but, since there are so many of them and their number is still rapidly increasing, even worse for the country."

Appreciation of the nature of culture and the values of cultural diversity leads to a recognition of the important function of the spontaneous enterprises and institutions of minority groups, such as the foreign-language or race press, religious, artistic, and social organizations, co-operatives as among the Finnish, and other organizations that enlist the loyalty of individuals and minister to their needs. The monumental study of Polish culture in the United States by Thomas and Znaniecki gives a penetrating analysis of the role of such institutions as instruments of cultural adjustment.

It would seem *a priori* and it is generally assumed that the main problems concerning the immigrants can be stated in terms of individual assimilation or non-assimilation. . . . But we find that the problem of individual assimilation is at present an entirely secondary and unimportant issue. . . .

The striking phenomenon . . . [is] the creation of a society which in structure and prevalent attitudes is neither Polish nor American but constitutes a specific, new product whose raw materials have been partly drawn from Polish traditions, partly from the new conditions in which the immigrants live and from American social values as the immigrant sees and interprets them. . . . The only method which can check demoralization, make of the immigrants—and particularly of their descendants— valuable and culturally productive members of the American society and imperceptibly, and without violence lead to their real Americanization, is to supplement the existing Polish-American institutions by others—many others—built on a similar foundation but in closer contact with American society.

The importance of diverse cultural heritages as such is rapidly waning, except where these are tied up with racial distinctions or present economic, religious, or other powerful and persistent interests. There is a natural tendency toward the assimilation of diverse cultures in the same communities. It is quite likely that this process has actually been forced too rapidly in the United States, with results that have often been personally and socially injurious.

But although it may be too late to save much of the vigor and richness of the new cultural resources brought to this country during the past half century by various immigrant groups, there still remains in the United States such a diversity of social values as to make renewed emphasis on tolerance and experimentation in the realm of social relations and ideas a matter of prime importance.

The aborigines in America are the least "Americanized" of all groups, in the sense of assimilation to the dominant civilization in our society. Without daily contact with white culture, and effectively debarred from participation on equal footing in most enterprises, the Indian has remained a problem for political administration and evangelical enterprise. In many instances, tribal cultures have succumbed to the destruction of traditional economy and the impact of other influences. In other situations, indigenous institutions remain intact, or have been progressively developed.

Recent governmental policy in Indian affairs has made a radical departure from earlier practices. This represents the first conscious official attempt to preserve and creatively develop cultural traditions fundamentally divergent from those of the majority. The new respect for the integrity of Indian tribal life may be influenced by the possibility that anxiety concerning Indian raids on white settlements has been supplanted by anxiety concerning the economic costs of supporting a population that older methods have been forcing into chronic dependency. Such an interpretation of official policy would, however, be inadequate, if not wholly unjust. It is much more accurate to conceive of the policy as symbolizing the newer approach to the whole question of cultural diversity.

The present Indian population is composed of more than 330,000 individuals, living in scattered rural communities. In 1935 the full-blooded Indian population increased nearly twice as fast as the general population of the United States. No group in the country has a higher rate of natural increase. The Indians in the United States are only one forty-fifth of all Indians. The fact that in some other countries, particularly Mexico, social experimentation by and through Indians is now under way, gives an enhanced importance to present experiments in this country.

For this minority group, the Federal Government acts as guardian of tribal interests. Two radically different procedures are possible in this situation. One is to conceive as the desirable result the complete absorption of the Indian into the American scene; the other has as its purpose the separate economic and cultural continuance of the group under conditions most favorable to Indian welfare. It is the latter point of view, generally speaking, that has come to prevail, as the Office of Indian Affairs has had to take the role of sociologist, anthropologist, land manager, educator, legal and business adviser. It has made positive attempts to meet the problems raised by the adjustments of a non-European culture within the American pattern.

The two major emphases in recent Indian policy are on the one hand a physical and on the other hand a spiritual reinforcement of Indian life and values. In contrast to the earlier policy of attempting to reconcile the Indian and white civilizations by the breakdown of geographic and cultural boundaries, the present aim is a consolidation of Indian resources and the maintenance of organic and traditional patterns. . . .

The present official policy toward the Indians is to accept permanence of divergent cultures, accompanied by the interaction of these cultures within the American system. This is expressed through a wide range of practical programs. Co-operative association for land management, based on tribal communal organization, and the fostering of self-reliance through improved opportunity and specialized training for individuals are among the goals desired. The organizations fostered may be ancient tribal systems, furnished now with such modern tools as credit and co-operative trade; or they may be wholly modern community organizations of "Americanized" Indians. The stress is upon the small group, and where the group is culturally ancient this stress is in the direction of conservation, even revival of ancient values. For the Indian, this policy means the preservation of cherished traditions, and an increased sense of personal dignity; for the Nation as a whole it means an enlargement of interests and perspective.

NEGRO AND WHITE IN TRADE UNIONS

The immediate object of the mixed union movement is the removal from the minds of both groups, but more particularly of the whites, of the fear of loss of work or of lowering of wages through racial competition.

BIRMINGHAM IS decidedly not of one mind in answering the question: "Does this business of Negroes and whites going into trade unions make for better or for worse feeling between the races?" Nearly all trade unionists thought organization of Negroes a desirable step. Most of the non-union people, and the company union people interviewed were against it, on grounds of race relationships. Persons concerned with management were in the main against it on the same grounds, although there were exceptions. Such news of the mixed union movement as had trickled through to suburban folk had fitted

Excerpts from Horace R. Cayton and George S. Mitchell, *Black Workers and the New Unions* (Durham: The University of North Carolina Press, 1939), pp. 342-343, 352-353, 358, 364-366.

easily into perhaps natural predispositions against it; business Birmingham feared and disliked Negro trade unionism. . . .

Many features of the union movement in the district make for improvement of race relationships. A united movement of the laboring population of the region has as its *sine qua non* intellectual acquaintance of at least a few members of both groups. It is conceivable that the two races could carry forward a joint movement with associations between members of the two races only among a few leaders in each group; those in the district who would prefer separate Negro and white locals are in effect pleading for this policy, that ordinary white and Negro members be spared the unaccustomed (and some think socially dangerous) experience of mixed meetings. But this has not been the course taken by the Birmingham movement. Whether from experience of failures under the separate unionism of the past, or from ideological convictions, or from a sensing of the requirements of the situation by those concerned with it, the new mining and metal unions have in the main adopted the form of interracial association that calls for regular association of the membership from each race with that from the other in trade union meetings. Undoubtedly the basic reason for the adoption of this form of unionism by the whites has been their feeling of the sincerity of the whites by regular attendance at meetings at which the Negroes were present. The link through officers of the separate race locals would be too weak, and would leave the two groups too open to the efforts of their employers to "spread confusion." On the floor of the mixed union meeting the issues that might divide the two groups can be brought up when the chances of explaining or correcting the difficulties are greater than at a later stage. The force depended upon for holding the two races in a common line of behavior on industrial questions is the discussion of matters of common interest by the rank and file of workers of both races, in mixed trade union meetings. . . .

The mere juxtaposition of the two races for purposes of discussing trade matters places at the disposal of the less advantaged race the whole store of tradition, fact, and feeling of the race which in the South has always maintained a monopoly on the most developed culture. Negroes move about from meeting to meeting, "making" all the meetings they can, listening. In more detailed ways, trade unionism calls forth the best effort of many Negro members. Some Negroes are required to keep union records, and carry on the correspondence necessary for the conduct of the local. In the most unexpected plank house on a back street you may come across a Negro whose second bureau drawer contains the books of his local. Negroes serve on shop committees and go up to see their employers as members of bargaining committees, or are elected as delegates to visit or negotiate with other locals. Negro union officers show some tendency to become respected, useful men among their own group. Simple members of unions have a duty to study out the constitutions and by-laws of their societies. In most locals one or another kind of trade journal is circulated. A Negro union man in a pipe shop said "Colored people do more reading. They read these different books as the union gives them." A white officer of a mixed Federal Labor Union stated that the Negroes in his local were reading much more than they used to. . . .

The habit of public discussion is one slowly acquired by the new Negro membership, but many whites testified both to the growth of Negro participation in union meetings and to the ability which occasional Negro speeches revealed. "When you can get the Negroes to talk, they talk, but it is hard to get them to talk," said one official. Said another, "The Negro man is able, after the training of his union experience, to bring his grievance more out in words than before." Many white trade unionists declared that individual Negroes had shown unsuspected power in talking about union affairs. . . .

Any trade union containing two or more quite different groups of people is liable to division by company managements. It is almost universal testimony among white union people that efforts have been made by lower company officials all through the Birmingham district to weaken the mixed union movement by playing upon racial prejudices. From a few sample statements by white workers, not all of them trade unionists, the prevalence and manner of occurrence of this practice can be seen. . . .

"The company threw it at us both white and colored that we was practising social equality. A certain clerk and a yard foreman were company henchmen. They said the Negroes already thought themselves better than the whites and if this kept up the Negroes would soon be riding the street cars and all that the same as whites. The general manager of the factory three months ago told some of the Negroes that the company would not give the men a contract, would not recognize unions, but would let the white men strike and then give their jobs to Negroes and at the same time discover what white men were in the union. The Negroes merely told the union about it. They understood it was just a move to break the union up. Just recently a time-keeper asked a white man who was a simple member of the union how he and his brother Abe (Abe was Negro Vice-President of the local) were getting on. There was quite a bit of words about that and some blows. Talk like that was nasty for a while when the union was first being formed and it like to have broke up the union." (Local union president.)

Companies spread bad feeling, trying to fight the union. A foreman will go to a Negro and say, "Them white fellows ain't after nothing but your money." An assistant superintendent held a meeting of the boiler employes only and said, "Before he would get up in an organization and call a Negro a brother he would get out of the organization." (Group of white strikers) . . .

In the Birmingham district the trade unionism . . . has as its chief drive the belief of the white workers in those industries that their wages are held down by the possibility which the employers have of using Negro labor in their places; it is in an effort to bind the Negro group to act not against the interests of the whites but in concert with those interests that the whites have urged membership in the union upon the Negroes. The Negroes for their part join in the hope that concerted action with the whites will mean a rise in Negro wages as well. A natural process of mutual concession can be seen in operation in the unions, a process which stands both to bring the Negro population more nearly to the economic level of the whites and to prevent white antagonism to such gradual approach to better standards. The whites require the Negroes as union members if they are themselves to make gains. Negroes are paying good money into the unions, and can hardly be expected to keep up their dues unless positive benefits can be shown them. Negroes cherish the ambition of a more equitable distribution of the chance of employment and of promotion, and they do actively register in union loyalty or its opposite the degree of concession which white unionists make to them in the matter of jobs and pay. . . .

The immediate object of the mixed union movement is the removal from the minds of both groups, but more particularly of the whites, of the fear of loss of work or of lowering of wages through racial competition. The crucial question in the mind of the leaders of the mixed union movement is whether or not the Negroes will "stick"; whether they can be depended upon both in day-to-day negotiations with employers and in times of industrial strife to stand with the whites in the effort to procure better conditions. That the Negroes are at present in the mood to stand with the whites was the almost universal belief of the white trade union people seen in the district. That belief in the minds of large numbers of white people in the district would appear to be of importance in the general race relationships of the area. White men relieved of fear of Negro competition, and aware that the continued absence of the threat depends upon reasonable treatment of the Negroes in their unions, have a double reason for a more kindly attitude toward Negroes than has by all accounts commonly characterized the industrial South.

MINORITIES AND AMERICAN DEMOCRACY

If freedom means a democratic co-operation in determining the ideals and purposes and industrial and social institutions of a country, then the immigrant has not been free, and the Anglo-Saxon element is guilty of just what every dominant race is guilty of in every European country: the imposition of its own culture upon the minority peoples.

NO REVERBERATORY effect of the great war has caused American public opinion more solicitude than the failure of the "melting-pot." The discovery of diverse nationalistic feelings among our great alien population has come to most people as an

Extracts from Randolph Bourne: *The History of a Literary Radical* (New York: B. W. Huebsch, Inc., 1920), pp. 266-285, 287-288, 297-298. (By permission of The Viking Press, Inc., New York.)

intense shock. It has brought out the unpleasant inconsistencies of our traditional beliefs. We have had to watch hard-hearted old Brahmins virtuously indignant at the spectacle of the immigrant refusing to be melted, while they jeer at patriots like Mary Antin who write about "our forefathers." We have had to listen to publicists who express themselves as stunned by the evidence of vigorous nationalistic and cultural movements in this country among Germans, Scandinavians, Bohemians, and Poles, while in the same breath they insist that the alien shall be forcibly assimilated to that Anglo-Saxon tradition which they unquestionably label "American."

As the unpleasant truth has come upon us that assimilation in this country was proceeding on lines very different from those we had marked out for it, we found ourselves inclined to blame those who were thwarting our prophecies. The truth became culpable. We blamed the war, we blamed the Germans. And then we discovered with a moral shock that these movements had been making great headway before the war even began. We found that the tendency, reprehensible and paradoxical as it might be, has been for the national clusters of immigrants, as they became more and more firmly established and more and more prosperous, to cultivate more and more assiduously the literatures and cultural traditions of their homelands. Assimilation, in other words, instead of washing out the memories of Europe, made them more and more intensely real. Just as these clusters became more and more objectively American, did they become more and more German or Scandinavian or Bohemian or Polish.

To face the fact that our aliens are already strong enough to take a share in the direction of their own destiny, and that the strong cultural movements represented by the foreign press, schools, and colonies are a challenge to our facile attempts, is not, however, to admit the failure of Americanization. It is not to fear the failure of democracy. It is rather to urge us to an investigation of what Americanism may rightly mean. It is to ask ourselves whether our ideal has been broad or narrow—whether perhaps the time has not come to assert a higher ideal than the "melting-pot." Surely we cannot be certain of our spiritual democracy when, claiming to melt the nations within us to a comprehension of our free and democratic institutions, we fly into panic at the first sign of their own will and tendency. We act as if we wanted Americanization to take place only on our own terms, and not by the consent of the governed. All our elaborate machinery of settlement and school and union, of social and political naturalization, however, will move with friction just in so far as it neglects to take into account this strong and virile insistence that America shall be what the immigrant will have a hand in making it, and not what a ruling class, descendant of those British stocks which were the first permanent immigrants, decide that America shall be made. This is the condition which confronts us, and which demands a clear and general readjustment of our attitude and our ideal.

Mary Antin is right when she looks upon our foreign-born as the people who missed the Mayflower and came over on the first boat they could find. But she forgets that when they did come it was not upon other Mayflowers, but upon a "Maiblume," a "Fleur de Mai," a "Fior di Maggio," a "Majblomst." These people were not mere arrivals from the same family, to be welcomed as understood and long-loved, but strangers to the neighborhood, with whom a long process of settling down had to take place. For they brought with them their national and racial characters, and each new national quota had to wear slowly away the contempt with which its mere alienness got itself greeted. Each had to make its way slowly from the lowest strata of unskilled labor up to a level where it satisfied the accredited norms of social success.

We are all foreign-born or the descendants of foreign-born, and if distinctions are to be made between us they should rightly be on some other ground than indigenousness. The early colonists came over with motives no less colonial than the later. They did not come to be assimilated in an American melting-pot. They did not come to adopt the culture of the American Indian. They had not the smallest intention of "giving themselves without reservation" to the new country. They came to get freedom to live as they wanted to. They came to escape from the stifling air and chaos of the old world; they came to make their fortune in a new land. They invented no new social framework. Rather they brought over bodily the old ways to which they had been accustomed. Tightly concentrated on a hostile frontier, they were conservative beyond belief. Their pioneer daring was reserved for the objective conquest of material resources. In their folkways, in their social and political institutions, they were, like every colonial people, slavishly imitative of the mother-country. So that, in spite of the "Revolution," our whole legal and political system remained more English than the English, petrified and unchanging, while in England itself law developed to meet the needs of the changing times.

It is just this English-American conservatism that has been our chief obstacle to social advance. We have needed the new peoples— the order of the German and Scandinavian, the turbulence of the Slav and Hun—to save us from our own stagnation. I do not mean that the illiterate Slav is now the equal of the New Englander of pure descent. He is raw material to be educated, not into a New Englander, but into a socialized American. . . . I do not believe that this process is to be one of decades of evolution. The spectacle of Japan's sudden jump from medievalism to post-modernism should have destroyed that superstition. We are not dealing with individuals who are to "evolve." We are dealing with their children, who, with that education we are about to have, will start level with all of us. Let us cease to think of ideals like democracy as magical qualities inherent in certain peoples. . . . We are all to educate and to be educated. These peoples in America are in a common enterprise. It is not what we are now that concerns us, but what this plastic next generation may become in the light of a new cosmopolitan ideal.

We are not dealing with static factors, but with fluid and dynamic generations. To contrast the older and the newer immigrants and see the one class as democratically motivated by love of liberty, and the other by mere money-getting, is not to illuminate the future. To think of earlier nationalities as culturally assimilated to America, while we picture the latter as a sodden and resistive mass, makes only for bitterness and misunderstanding. There may be a difference between these earlier and these later stocks, but it lies neither in motive for coming nor in strength of cultural allegiance to the home land. The truth is that no more tenacious cultural allegiance to the mother country has been shown by any alien nation than by the ruling class of Anglo-Saxon descendants in these American States. English snobberies, English religion, English literary styles, English literary reverences and canons, English ethics, English superiorities, have been the cultural food that we have drunk in from our mothers' breasts. The distinctively American spirit—pioneer, as distinguished from the reminiscently English—that appears in Whitman and Emerson and James, has had to exist on sufferance alongside of this other cult, unconsciously belittled by our cultural makers of opinion. No country has perhaps had so great indigenous genius which had so little influence on the country's traditions and expressions. The unpopular and dreaded German-American of the present day is a beginning amateur in comparison with those foolish Anglophiles of Boston and New York and Philadelphia whose reversion to cultural type sees uncritically in England's cause the cause of Civilization, and, under the guise of ethical independence of thought, carries along European traditions which are no more "American" than the German categories themselves. . . .

The non-English American can scarcely be blamed if he sometimes thinks of the Anglo-Saxon predominance in America as little more than a predominance of priority. The Anglo-Saxon was merely the first immigrant, the first to found a colony. He has never really ceased to be the descendant of immigrants, nor has he ever succeeded in transforming that colony into a real nation, with a tenacious, richly woven fabric of native culture. Colonials from the other nations have come and settled down beside him. They found no definite native culture which should startle them out of their colonialism, and consequently they looked back to their mother-country, as the earlier Anglo-Saxon immigrant was looking back to his. What has been offered the newcomer has been the chance to learn English, to become a citizen, to salute the flag. And those elements of our ruling classes who are responsible for the public schools, the settlements, all the organizations for amelioration in the cities, have every reason to be proud of the care and labor which they have devoted to absorbing the immigrant. His opportunities the immigrant has taken to gladly, with almost a pathetic eagerness to make his way in the new land without friction or disturbance. The common language has made not only for the necessary communication, but for all the amenities of life.

If freedom means the right to do pretty much as one pleases, so long as one does not interfere with others, the immigrant has found freedom, and the ruling element has been singularly liberal in its treatment of the invading hordes. But if freedom means a democratic co-operation in determining the ideals and purposes and industrial and social institutions of a country, then the immigrant has not been free, and the Anglo-Saxon element is guilty of just what every dominant race is guilty of in every European country: the imposition of its own culture upon the minority peoples. The fact that this imposition has been so mild and, indeed, semi-conscious does not alter its quality. And the war has brought out just the degree to which that purpose of "Americanizing," that is to say, "Anglo-Saxonizing," the immigrant has failed.

For the Anglo-Saxon now in his bitterness to turn upon the other peoples, talk about their "arrogance," scold them for not being melted in a pot which never existed, is to betray the unconscious purpose which lay at the bottom of his heart. It betrays too the possession of a racial jealousy similar to that of which he is now accusing the so-called "hyphenates." Let the Anglo-Saxon be proud enough of the heroic toil and heroic sacrifices which molded the nation. But let him ask himself, if he had had to depend on the English descendants, where he would have been living today. To those of us who see in the exploitation of unskilled labor the strident red *leit-motif* of our civilization, the settling of the country presents a great social drama as the waves of immigration broke over it.

Let the Anglo-Saxon ask himself where he would have been if these races had not come? Let those who feel the inferiority of the non-Anglo-Saxon immigrant contemplate that region of the States which has remained the most distinctively "American," the South. Let him ask himself whether he would really like to see the foreign hordes Americanized into such an Americanization. Let him ask himself how superior this native civilization is to the great "alien" states of Wisconsin and Minnesota, where Scandinavians, Poles, and Germans have self-consciously labored to preserve their traditional culture, while being outwardly and satisfactorily American. Let him ask himself how much more wisdom, intelligence, industry and social leadership has come out of these alien states than out of all the truly American ones. The South, in fact, while this vast Northern development has gone on, still remains an English colony, stagnant and complacent, having progressed culturally scarcely beyond the early Victorian era. It is culturally sterile because it has had no advantage of cross-fertilization like the Northern states. What has happened in states such as Wisconsin and Minnesota is that strong foreign cultures have struck root in a new and fertile soil. America has meant liberation, and German and Scandinavian political ideas and social energies have expanded to a new potency. The process has not been at all the fancied "assimilation" of the Scandinavian political ideas as social energies have expanded to a new potency. The process has not been at all the fancied "assimilation" of the Scandinavian or Teuton. Rather has it been a process of their assimilation of us—I speak as an Anglo-Saxon. The foreign cultures have not been melted down or run together, made into some homogeneous Americanism, but have remained distinct but co-operating to the greater glory and benefit, not only of themselves but of all the native "Americanism" around them.

What we emphatically do not want is that these distinctive qualities should be washed out into a tasteless, colorless fluid of uniformity. Already we have far too much of this insipidity—masses of people who are cultural half-breeds, neither assimilated Anglo-Saxons nor nationals of another culture. Each national colony in this country seems to retain in its foreign press, its vernacular literature, its schools, its intellectual and patriotic leaders, a central cultural nucleus. From this nucleus the colony extends out by imperceptible gradations to a fringe where national characteristics are all but lost. Our cities are filled with these half-breeds who retain their foreign names but have lost the foreign savor. This does not mean that they have actually been changed into New Englanders or Middle Westerners. It does not mean that they have been really Americanized. It means that, letting slip from them whatever native culture they had, they have substituted for it only the most rudimentary American— the American culture of the cheap newspaper, the "movies," the popular song, the ubiquitous automobile. The unthinking who survey this class call them assimilated, Americanized. The great American public school has done its work. With these people our institutions are safe. We may thrill with dread at the aggressive hyphenate, but this tame flabbiness is accepted as Americanization. The same molders of opinion whose ideal is to melt the different races into Anglo-Saxon gold hail this poor product as the satisfying result of their al-chemy. . . .

The influences at the center of the nuclei [of nationalistic cultures] are centripetal. They make for the intelligence and the social values which mean an enhancement of life. And just because the foreign-born retains this expressiveness he is likely to be a better citizen of the American community. The influences at the fringe, however, are centrifugal, anarchical. They make for detached fragments of peoples. . . . They become the flotsam and jetsam of American life, the downward undertow of our civilization with its leering cheapness and falseness of taste and spiritual outlook, the absence of mind and sincere feeling which we see in our slovenly towns, our vapid moving pictures, our popular novels, and in the vacuous faces of the crowds on the city street. This is the cultural wreckage of our time, and it is from the fringes of the Anglo-Saxon as well as the other stocks that it falls. America has as yet no impelling integrating force. It makes too easily for this detritus of cultures. In our loose, free country, no constraining national purpose, no tenacious folk-tradition and folk-style hold the people to a line.

The war has shown us that not in any magical formula will this purpose be found. No intense nationalism of the European plan can be ours. But do we not begin to see a new and more adventurous ideal? Do we not see how the national colonies in America, deriving power from the deep cultural heart of Europe and yet living here in mutual toleration, freed from the age-long tangles of races, creeds, and dynasties, may work out a federated ideal? America is transplanted Europe, but a Europe that has not been disintegrated and scattered in the transplanting as in some Dispersion. Its colonies live here in-extricably mingled, yet not homogeneous. They merge but they do not fuse.

America is a unique sociological fabric, and it bespeaks poverty of imagination not to be thrilled at the incalculable potentialities of so novel a union of men. To seek no other goal than the weary old nationalism, belligerent, exclusive, inbreeding, the poison of which we are witnessing now in Europe—is to make patriotism a hollow sham, and to declare that, in spite of our boastings, America must ever be a follower and not a leader of nations. . . .

As long as we thought of Americanism in terms of the "melting-pot," our American cultural tradition lay in the past. It was something to which the new Americans were to be molded. In the light of our changing ideal of Americanism, we must perpetrate the paradox that our American cultural tradition lies in the future. It will be what we all together make out of this incomparable 'opportunity of attacking the future with a new key.

Whatever American nationalism turns out to be, it is certain to become something utterly different from the nationalisms of twentieth-century Europe. This wave of reactionary enthusiasm to play the orthodox nationalistic game which is passing over the country is scarcely vital enough to last. We cannot swagger and thrill to the same national self-feeling. We must give new edges to our pride. We must be content to avoid the unnumbered woes that national patriotism has brought in Europe, and that fiercely heightened pride and self-consciousness. Alluring as this is, we must allow our imaginations to transcend this scarcely veiled belligerency. . . .

The failure of the melting-pot, far from closing the great American democratic experiment, means that it has only just begun. Whatever American nationalism turns out to be, we see already that it will have a color richer and more exciting than our ideal has hitherto encompassed. In a world which has dreamed of internationalism, we find that we have all unawares been building up the first international nation. The voices which have cried for a tight and jealous nationalism of the European pattern are failing. From that ideal, however valiantly and disinterestedly it has been set for us, time and tendency have moved us further and further away. What we have achieved has been rather a cosmopolitan federation of national colonies, of foreign cultures, from which the sting of devastating competition has been removed. America is already the world-federation in miniature, the continent where for the first time in history has been achieved that miracle of hope, the peaceful living side by side, with character substantially preserved, of the most heterogeneous peoples under the sun. Here, notwithstanding our tragic failures of adjustment, the outlines are already too clear not to give us a new vision and a new orientation of the American mind in the world.

Against the thinly disguised panic which calls itself "patriotism" and the thinly disguised militarism which calls itself "preparedness" the cosmopolitan ideal is set. This does not mean that those who hold it are for a policy of drift. They, too, long passionately for an integrated and disciplined America. But they do not want one which is integrated only for domestic economic exploitation of the workers or for predatory economic imperialism among the weaker peoples. They do not want one that is integrated by coercion or militarism, or for the truculent assertion of a medieval code of honor and of doubtful rights. They believe that the most effective integration will be one which co-ordinates the diverse elements and turns them consciously toward working out together the place of America in the world-situation. They demand for integration a genuine integrity, a wholeness and soundness of enthusiasm and purpose which can only come when no national colony within our America feels that it is being discriminated against or that its cultural case is being prejudged. This strength of co-operation, this feeling that all who are here may have a hand in the destiny of America, will make for a finer spirit of integration than any narrow "Americanism" or forced chauvinism.

In this effort we may have to accept some form of that dual citizenship which meets with so much articulate horror among us. Dual citizenship we may have to recognize as the rudimentary form of that international citizenship to which, if our words mean anything, we aspire. We have assumed unquestioningly that mere participation in the political life of the United States must cut the new citizen off from all sympathy with his old allegiance. Anything but a bodily transfer of devotion from one sovereignty to another has been viewed as a sort of moral treason against the Republic. We have insisted that the immigrant whom we welcomed escaping from the very exclusive nationalism of his European home shall forthwith adopt a nationalism just as exclusive, just as narrow, and even less legitimate because it is founded on no warm traditions of his own. . . .

We cannot Americanize America worthily by sentimentalizing and moralizing history. When the best schools are expressly renouncing the questionable duty of teaching patriotism by means of history, it is not the time to force shibboleth upon the immigrant. This form of Americanization has been heard because it appealed to the vestiges of our old sentimentalized and moralized patriotism. This has so far held the field as the expression of the new American's new devotion. The inflections of other voices have been drowned. They must be heard. We must see if the lesson of the war has not been for hundreds of these later Americans a vivid realization of their transnationality, a new consciousness of what America means to them as a citizenship in the world. It is the vague historic idealisms which have provided the fuel for the European flame. Our American ideal can make no progress until we do away with this romantic gilding of the past.

WHO'S WHO

The Editors

ALAIN LOCKE is Professor of Philosophy at Howard University, and author of *Race Contacts and Interracial Relations* (1916), *The New Negro* (1925), *The Negro in America* (1933), and various critical studies in the artistic and cultural contribution of the Negro, *The Negro and His Music* (1936), *Negro Art: Past and Present* (1937), and *The Negro in Art* (1941). In 1927, as observer for the Foreign Policy Association, he made a study in Geneva of the work of the League of Nations' Mandates Commission, and in 1934 organized at Howard University the first conference of the Social Science Division on Problems, Programs and Philosophies of Minority Groups. Since 1937 he has been a member of the Commission on Human Relations of the Progressive Education Association.

BERNHARD J. STERN is Lecturer in Sociology at Columbia University and in Anthropology at the New School for Social Research. He was formerly Assistant Professor of Sociology, University of Washington (1927-1930), and Assistant Editor of the Encyclopaedia of the Social Sciences (1930-1934). His work on *The Family: Past and Present* (1938) was prepared for the Commission on Human Relations of the Progressive Education Association, and that on *Society and Medical Progress* (1941) under a grant by the Committee on Research in Medical Economics. He is also the author of *The Lummi Indians of Northwest Washington* (1934), *Lewis Henry Morgan, Social Evolutionist* (1931), and *Social Factors in Medical Progress* (1927); co-author of *Technological Trends and National Policy* (1937); editor of *Young Ward's Diary* (1935), and of the editors of *Science and Society*. He has recently been associated with the Carnegie study of the Negro in America.

The Contributors

HAROLD E. ADAMS is Assistant Professor of Sociology at Western Reserve University.

734

ROMANZO ADAMS, Professor Emeritus of Sociology at the University of Hawaii, is the author of *Interracial Marriage in Hawaii* (1937).

JAMES S. ALLEN is the author of *Reconstruction, the Battle for Democracy* (1937) and *The Negro Question in the United States* (1936).

ELIN L. ANDERSON is a New England social worker who was awarded the John Anisfield Prize for *We Americans* (1937).

JACQUES BARZUN, Assistant Professor of History at Columbia University, is the author of *Of Human Freedom* (1939), *Race: A Study in Superstition* (1937), and *The French Race* (1932).

RUTH BENEDICT is Associate Professor of Anthropology at Columbia University, editor of *The Journal of American Folklore,* and a vice-president of The American Anthropological Association. She has written *Race: Science and Politics* (1940), a two-volume work on *Zuni Mythology* (1935) and *Patterns of Culture* (1934).

FRANZ BOAS, Professor Emeritus of Anthropology at Columbia University, is dean of American anthropologists. He is a member of the National Academy, a Fellow and former President of the American Association for the Advancement of Science, and of the American Anthropological Association. Among his best known works are *Race, Language and Culture* (1940), *The Mind of Primitive Man* (1911; rev. ed. 1939), and *Anthropology and Modern Life* (1927).

RANDOLPH BOURNE was a noted publicist of the pre-war era whose essays were collected after his death in 1918 and edited by Van Wyck Brooks under the title of *The History of a Literary Radical* (1920), and by James Oppenheim under the title of *Untimely Papers* (1919).

STERLING A. BROWN, Associate Professor of English at Howard University and guest lecturer at New York University, is the author of *The Negro in American Fiction* (1937), *Negro Poetry and Drama* (1937), and a volume of poetry entitled *Southern Road* (1932). He was associated with the Carnegie study of the Negro in America.

W. O. BROWN, Assistant Professor of Sociology at Howard University, has written many articles for current sociological journals on race relations, and is a contributor to *Race and Culture Contacts* (1934).

FLORENCE G. CASSIDY has been secretary of the Nationalities Committee of the Council of Social Agencies of Detroit.

HORACE R. CAYTON, a Rosenwald Fellow at the University of Chicago, is now directing, in collaboration with W. Lloyd Warner, a group of studies of the Chicago Negro community, under the auspices of the American Youth Commission. He is co-author of *Black Workers and the New Unions* (1939).

LEWIS C. COPELAND, a Rosenwald Fellow at Duke University, is a contributor to *Race Relations and the Race Problem* (1939).

CHARLES DARWIN at the age of 23 undertook his first scientific observations abroad during a voyage around the world in 1831 on the *Beagle*. *The Voyage of H.M.S. Beagle*, from which the selection is taken, is Darwin's first published work.

C. A. DAWSON is Professor of Sociology at McGill University in Montreal. He is author of *Group Settlement; Ethnic Communities of Canada* (1936) and another volume in the series on *Canadian Frontiers of Settlement* entitled *Settlement of the Peace River Country* (1934).

JOHN DOLLARD is Research Associate in Sociology at Yale University. He is co-author of *Frustration and Aggression* (1939), and author of *Caste and Class in a Southern Town* (1937) and *Criteria for the Life History* (1935).

ALFONS DOPSCH is Professor Emeritus of History at the University of Vienna. He is the author of a number of historical works in German. *The Economic and Social Foundations of European Civilization* (1923) was published in English translation in 1937.

CEDRIC DOVER is a biologist living in England. He has written *Know This of Race* (1939) and *Half-Caste* (1936).

A. P. ELKIN, Professor of Anthropology at the University of Sydney, Australia, is editor of *Oceania*, and the author of *Australian Aborigines, How to Understand Them* (1938).

THOMAS E. ENNIS, Assistant Professor of History at the University of West Virginia, is author of *French Policy and Developments in Indo-China* (1936).

RAYMOND W. FIRTH, Reader in Anthropology in the University of London, is the author of *Primitive Polynesian Economy* (1939), a supplement to his earlier volume on *Primitive Economics of the New Zealand Maori* (1929). He has also written *Human Types* (1938) and *Art and Life in New Guinea* (1936).

GRANT FOREMAN was a member of the Dawes Commission appointed at the opening of the century to investigate Indian Affairs. He remained in Oklahoma and became a student of Indian and Southwestern history. Among the books he has written are: *The Five Civilized Tribes* (1934), *Advancing the Frontier* (1933) and *Indians and Pioneers* (1930).

E. FRANKLIN FRAZIER, Professor of Sociology at Howard University, is the author of *The Negro Family in the United States*, which was awarded the 1939 John Anisfield Prize, and *The Negro Family in Chicago* (1931). He was awarded a Guggenheim Fellowship in 1940 for a study of the family in the West Indies and Brazil.

CARL GEORG E. FRIEDERICI, German anthropologist, is an Honorary Fellow of the Royal Anthropological Institute of Great Britain and Ireland.

BUELL G. GALLAGHER, President of Talladega College, Alabama, is author of *American Caste and the Negro College* (1938).

G. S. GHURYE, Reader in Sociology at the University of Bombay, India, is author of *Caste and Race in India* (1932).

LOUIS GOLDING is a British novelist and poet. His recent works are *Mr. Emanuel* (1939) and *The Jewish Problem* (1938).

MELVILLE J. HERSKOVITS, Professor of Anthropology at Northwestern University, is a member of the Committee for the Study of

Acculturation of the Social Science Research Council. He is author of *The Economic Life of Primitive Peoples* (1940), *Dahomey* (1938), *Acculturation, the Study of Culture Conflict* (1938), *Life in a Haitian Valley* (1937) and *The American Negro* (1928).

ISAAC A. HOURWICH, economist and publicist, was best known for his book, *Immigration and Labor* (1912). He died in 1924.

G. F. HUDSON, a Fellow of All Souls College, Oxford, is author of *The Far East in World Politics* (1939), *An Atlas of Far Eastern Politics* (1938), and *Europe and China* (1931).

MONICA HUNTER has been a research student in anthropology at the University of Cambridge. *Reaction to Conquest* (1936) is her first published work.

W. H. HUTT, Professor of Commerce at the University of Cape Town, South Africa, is the author of *Economists and the Public* (1936), and contributor to *Western Civilization and the Natives of South Africa* (1934).

OSCAR JASZI is Professor of Political Science at Oberlin College. He is author of *The Dissolution of the Hapsburg Monarchy* (1929), and *The Evolution of the Nation States and the Nationality Problem* (in Hungarian) (1912).

CHARLES S. JOHNSON is Director of the Division of Social Science at Fisk University. He is associate editor of the *American Sociological Review* and a former vice-president of the American Sociological Society. Among his best known works are *The Negro College Graduate* (1937), *Shadow of the Plantation* (1934), and *The Negro in American Civilization* (1930).

GUY B. JOHNSON, Research Associate in the Institute for Research in Social Science at the University of North Carolina, is on the staff of the Carnegie study of the Negro in America. His publications include *Folk Culture on St. Helena Island* (1930), and *John Henry: Tracking Down a Negro Legend* (1929).

OTTO KLINEBERG, Assistant Professor of Psychology at Columbia University, is author of *Social Psychology* (1940), *Race Differences* (1935) and *Negro Intelligence and Selective Migration* (1935).

HANS KOHN is Professor of Modern History at Smith College and Lecturer at the New School for Social Research. He is author of *Western Civilization in the Near East* (1936), *Orient and Occident* (1934), and *History of Nationalism in the East* (1929).

RALPH LINTON, Professor of Anthropology at Columbia University, editor of the *American Anthropologist*, and a member of the Committee for the Study of Acculturation of the Social Science Research Council, is author of *The Study of Man, an Introduction* (1936) and *Tanala, a Hill Tribe of Madagascar* (1933). He is also editor of *Acculturation in Seven American Indian Tribes* (1940).

C. A. MACARTNEY has been Secretary of the Minorities Committee of the League of Nations since 1928. He is the author of *National States and National Minorities* (1934) and *The Magyars in the Ninth Century* (1930).

I. D. MacCRONE is Professor of Psychology at the University of Witwatersrand, Johannesburg. He is author of *Race Attitudes in South Africa* (1937), *World Labour Problems* (1935), and *Psychology in Perspective* (1932).

C. A. MACE is Reader in psychology at the University of London, and author of *Sibylla, or the Revival of Prophecy* (1930), and *Principles of Logic* (1933).

LEWIS A. MAVERICK is Associate Professor of Economics at the University of California in Los Angeles.

V. T. McGILLICUDDY, as Assistant Adjutant General on the staff of the Governor of Dakota, represented the Governor in negotiations with Indians, troops and settlers (1888-1892) .

MARGARET MEAD is Assistant Curator of Ethnology in the American Museum of Natural History. Among her works are *Sex and Temperament in Three Primitive Societies* (1935), *The Changing Culture of an Indian Tribe* (1932), *Growing Up in New Guinea* (1930), and *Coming of Age in Samoa* (1928). She is also the editor of *Cooperation and Competition among Primitive Peoples* (1937).

PHILIP AINSWORTH MEANS, formerly associated with the Peabody Museum at Harvard as anthropologist, is the author of *Fall of the Inca Empire* (1932) and *Ancient Civilization of the Andes* (1919).

GEORGE S. MITCHELL, formerly on the faculty of Columbia University, is Assistant Administrator of the Farm Security Administration. He is author of *Textile Unionism in the South* (1931) and co-author, with Broadus Mitchell, of *The Industrial Revolution in the South* (1930), and with Horace R. Cayton, of *Black Workers and the New Unions* (1939).

DONALD PIERSON was formerly Research Associate at Fisk University, and is now Assistant Professor of Sociology at the University of Sao Paulo in Brazil.

GEORGE HENRY LANE-FOX PITT-RIVERS is a British anthropologist best known for his work on *The Clash of Culture and the Contact of Races* (1927). He is the general secretary of the International Union for the Scientific Investigation of Population Problems, and has edited its proceedings under the title *Problems of Population* (1932).

HORTENSE POWDERMAKER, an anthropologist who teaches at Queens College, New York, is author of *After Freedom* (1939) and *Life in Lesu* (1933).

ROBERT REDFIELD, Professor of Anthropology and Dean of the Division of Social Sciences at the University of Chicago, is Chairman of the Committee for the Study of Acculturation of the Social Science Research Council. He is co-author of *Chan Kom, a Maya Village* (1934), and author of *Tepoztlan, a Mexican Village* (1930).

IRA DE AUGUSTINE REID is Professor of Sociology at Atlanta University and managing editor of *Phylon*. He was formerly director of a survey of the Negro in New Jersey. He is the author of *The Negro Immigrant* (1939) and co-author with Arthur Raper, of *Sharecroppers All* (1940).

FRANCES L. REINHOLD, Instructor in Political Science at Swarthmore College, is co-author of *The American Politician* (1938).

STEPHEN H. ROBERTS, Professor of Modern History at the University of Sydney, Australia, is the author of *The House That Hitler Built* (1937) and a *History of French Colonial Policy* (1929).

MICHAEL I. ROSTOVTZEFF is Professor of Ancient History and Archaeology and Director of Archaeological Studies at Yale University. Among his many books are *Dura-Europos and Its Art* (1938), *Caravan Cities* (1932), *Out of the Past of Greece and Rome: a Social and Economic History of the Roman Empire* (1932), and *History of the Ancient World* (1926-27).

EDWARD SAPIR was, until his death in 1939, Professor of Anthropology and Linguistics at Yale University. He was co-author of *Wishram Ethnography* (1930), author of *Language—an Introduction to the Study of Speech* (1921), and a contributor to many publications in ethnology, anthropology, and comparative linguistics.

I. SCHAPERA, Professor of Social Anthropology in the University of Capetown, South Africa, is the author of *Khoisan Peoples* (1930) and editor of *The Bantu-Speaking Tribes of South Africa* (1937), *Western Civilization and the Natives of South Africa* (1934) and *The Early Cape Hottentots* (1933).

FRANCE V. SCHOLES is associated with the Division of Historical Research in the Carnegie Institution of Washington and is author of *Documentos Para La Historia de Yucatan* (1936).

H. L. SHAPIRO lectures in Physical Anthropology at Columbia University and is Associate Curator of the American Museum of Natural History. He is best known for his study of the descendants of the mutineers of the Bounty, *The Heritage of the Bounty* (1936). His volume, *Migration and Environment* (1939) is based on research under the auspices of the University of Hawaii.

KRISHNALAI SHRIDHARANI, who has been an active participant in the Indian Nationalist Movement, is author of *War Without Violence* (1939), which was his doctoral dissertation in Sociology at Columbia University.

CHARLES SINGER is Professor of the History of Medicine in the University of London. DOROTHEA WALEY SINGER has collaborated with him in a number of studies. His best known works are *The Beginnings of Science* (1931), *A Short History of Biology* (1931), and *From Magic to Science* (1928). He is co-editor of the *Legacy of Israel* (1927).

EVERETT V. STONEQUIST, Professor of Sociology at Skidmore College, is author of *Marginal Man* (1937).

FREDERICK J. TEGGART is Professor Emeritus of Social Institutions at the University of California and author of *Prolegomena to History* (1916), *The Processes of History* (1918), *Theory of History* (1925), and *Rome and China* (1939).

ARNOLD J. TOYNBEE is Director of Studies of the Royal Institute of International Affairs and Research Professor of International History in the London School of Economics. He is co-editor of *Survey of International Affairs* (1930-34), and he has recently completed his three-volume work entitled *A Study of History* (1934-39).

STANLEY VESTAL is the *nom de plume* of W. S. Campbell, Professor of English in the University of Oklahoma, and author of *New Sources of Indian History* (1934), *Sitting Bull, Champion of the Sioux* (1932) and other works on Indian life.

CAROLINE F. WARE is Chairman of the Committee on Social Studies of the American Association of University Women, author of *Modern Economy in Action* (1936), and *Greenwich Village* (1935), and editor of *The Cultural Approach to History* (1941).

T. T. WATERMAN, while an anthropologist at the University of California, collaborated with A. L. Kroeber on the *Source Book in Anthropology* (1931). He died in 1936.

SIDNEY and BEATRICE WEBB, noted British economists, are co-authors of *Soviet Communism—a New Civilization* (1938), *The Decay of Capitalist Civilization* (1923), *The History of Trade Unionism* (Revised, 1920), *English Local Government* (1906-08), and other works.

DIEDRICH WESTERMANN is Director of the International Institute of African Languages and Cultures in London. His most recent books are entitled *Africa and Christianity* (1937) and *The African Today* (1934).

LOUIS WIRTH is Professor of Sociology in the University of Chicago. He is associate editor of the *American Journal of Sociology,* author of *The Ghetto* (1928), co-author of *The City* (1925), and collaborator on *Our Cities* (1937).

CLARK WISSLER is Curator-in-Chief of the Department of Anthropology of the American Museum of Natural History, New York, and Professor of Anthropology in the Institute of Human Relations of Yale University. He is author among other works of *Indians of the United States* (1940), *Social Anthropology* (1929), *Man and Culture* (1923), and *The American Indian* (1917).

T. J. WOOFTER JR. is Research Professor at the Institute for Research in Social Science at the University of North Carolina and Economic Adviser to the Administrator of Farm Security Administration. He is author of *Seven Lean Years* (1939), *Landlord and Tenant on the Cotton Plantation* (1936), and *Black Yeomanry* (1930).

LEONARD S. WOOLF, British publicist, is co-editor of the *Political Quarterly Review.* Among his recent works are *Barbarians Within and Without* (1939) and *After the Deluge* (1931-39).

DONALD YOUNG is Professor of Sociology at the University of Pennsylvania, a member of the staff of the Social Science Research Council, and associate editor of *The Annals* of the American Academy of Political and Social Science. He is author of *Minority Peoples and the Depression* (1937) and *American Minority Peoples* (1932).

GEORGE YOUNG, British historian, formerly professor in the University of London, is the author of *New Spain* (1933), *Tales of Trespass* (1932), and *The Pendulum of Politics* (1930).

AUTHORS' INDEX

GENERAL INDEX

Abd-el-Kader, 191
Abd-el-Krim, 191
Abolition movement, 341, 506
Aborigines, 104
Abyssinia, Abyssinians, 28, 58-59
Acculturation, 108, 192, 240, 386, 500, 529, 546, 558, 565, 583, 605
Action, Français, 215
Adamic, Louis, 716
Adams, Abigail, 284
Adams, Harold E., 304, 349
Adams, John, 284
Adams, Romanzo, 255
Africa, 35, 36, 39, 44, 51, 70-74, 74-81, 102, 105, 111, 127, 185, 190, 200, 201, 205, 219-224, 237, 270, 392, 521, 611-613, 634
African colonies, 35, 37, 78, 91, 176-179, 185, 187, 223, 386, 406, 525, 588, 590, 607, 631, 634, 635
African cultures, Africanisms, 36, 37, 78, 79, 80, 71, 86, 74-81, 495, 525, 588
African National Congress, 200
Afrikaans, 377
Aggression, 536, 539, 540-543
Agriculture, 96, 172
Ainu, 430, 443
Akers, Arthur E., 337
Albanians, 657
Alessandro, 219
Alexander VI, Pope, 149
Alexandrine culture, 32
Allen, Fred, 351
Allen, Ira, 293
Allen, James S., 471, 500
Alien and Sedition Acts, 705
Aliens, 215, 376, 691
Alsace, 140, 476, 478
America, 37, 81, 101, 172, 190, 195, 210, 220, 408, 423, 425, 431, 437, 446, 458, 466, 468, 548, 549, 611
America, Central, 112-119, 179-183
American colonies (see also Colonial), 38, 98, 81-89, 195-197, 220, 284, 475, 483, 684
American Legion, 226
American social problems, 220-231, 284-292, 684-687, 723-733
Americanism, 27, 729, 730
Americanization, 226, 724, 728, 732
Americans, Old, 187, 287, 290, 292, 402
Ancestor cult, 202
Anderson, Sherwood, 347

Anglo-Indian, 39, 398
Anglo-Saxon (see also Nordicism), 6, 8, 15, 89, 187, 190, 287, 316, 328, 338, 378, 429, 439, 478, 685, 691, 723-730
Anthropology, 4, 12, 16, 17, 30, 89, 90, 91, 108
Anti-imperialism, 629
Antin, Mary, 724
Antipodes, 98
Anti-Semitism, 234-238, 260-263, 356, 359, 368, 411, 426, 436, 469, 493, 530
Arabia-Arabic culture, 28-35, 39, 41-43, 58-60, 68-74, 95, 219, 257, 259, 262, 439, 632, 660
Arapho, 562
Armenia, Armenians, 49, 134, 144, 263, 436, 479, 483
Aryan, Aryanism, 6, 8, 54, 366-369, 371, 422, 433
Asia-Asiatic cultures, 21, 29, 31, 48, 50, 60, 82, 86, 96-100, 127, 141, 185-190, 264, 605, 612, 613, 697
Asia Minor, 27, 29, 36, 40, 41, 44, 75
Assimilation, cultural (see also Cultural diffusion), 24, 35, 71, 104, 105, 115, 125, 130-138, 142, 152, 205, 239-243, 258, 325, 385-393, 405, 418-425, 432, 468-477, 482, 488-500, 567, 583, 605, 613, 628-632, 662, 666, 679, 687, 692, 693
Assyria, 26, 42, 43
Atahualpa, 148-149, 150
Athenian, 32
Attitudes (see Social attitudes)
Australia, 104, 105, 184, 185, 443, 528, 555, 628, 610
Austria, Austrian, 478, 650, 666
Authority, 123, 133, 134
Autonomy, 141
Avoidance reactions, 245, 279
Aylmer, Bishop, 281
Aztec, 62, 117, 141

Babbittry, 345
Babylon, Babylonian, 26, 32, 39, 40, 42, 75, 314
Backward peoples, 629
Bacon, Roger, 63
Balkans, 134, 141, 143, 427, 650, 652
Baltic, 142, 143
Bantu, Peoples, culture, 13, 91, 105, 203, 221, 376, 386-395, 472, 473, 516-521, 568, 573, 575, 638-648
Baptism, 267, 271, 276, 277